Aviation *in* Canada

Evolution of an Air Force

The Armstrong Siddeley Atlas and Siskin were the RCAF's first offensive combat planes. Serving from 1927 into 1941, the Atlas carried machine guns and light bombs, and could fly a host of missions (its modern-day equivalent is the CF-18 Hornet). Atlas 401 is seen at Camp Petawawa in August 1939. Amazingly, this is the type in which 2 Squadron went to war from Halifax a few weeks later. (LAC C89318)

JOHN
HOPKINSON
& ASSOCIATES LTD.

HEAD OFFICE:
P.O. Box 309
Water Valley, Alberta
Canada T0M 2E0
Tel: (403) 637-2250
Fax: (403) 637-2153
E-mail: sales@hopkinsonassociates.com

November 2010

Dear **Friends and Clients**:

It is our great pleasure to present you with Volume III of Aviation in Canada: Evolution of an Air Force as a token of our sincere appreciation for your business. It is the third of a four volume series currently being written by a great Canadian aviation historian, Larry Milberry.

Rather than make this a holiday gift, we are passing this volume on as it is received.

We hope you and your family will enjoy this book.

We would like to thank you for our relationship and wish you every opportunity for continued success.

Best Regards,

JOHN HOPKINSON & ASSOCIATES LTD.

John Hopkinson

President

:clh
Enclosure

Aviation *in* Canada

Evolution of an Air Force

JOHN HOPKINSON
AND
ASSOCIATES LTD.

all the best!
Larry Milberry

Larry Milberry

Library and Archives Canada Cataloguing in Publication

Milberry, Larry, 1943-
    Aviation in Canada : evolution of an air force / Larry Milberry.

Includes bibliographical references and index.
ISBN 978-0-921022-23-7

1. Aeronautics, Military–Canada–History.
2. Canada. Royal Canadian Air Force–History.
3. World War, 1939-1945–Canada. I. Title.

UG635.C2M532 2010   358.400971   C2010-902933-X

Design: James W. Jones, Iroquois, Ontario
Proofreading: Lambert Huneault, Windsor, Ontario; Ron Pickler, Montreal; William J. Wheeler, Markham, Ontario
Printed and bound in Canada by Friesen Printers Ltd., Altona, Manitoba

Published by
CANAV Books
Larry Milberry, publisher
51 Balsam Avenue
Toronto, Ontario M4E 3B6
Canada

(Title page) One of the RCAF's indispensible coastal defence aircraft of WWII was the Consolidated PBY-5, dubbed variously Catalina, Canso and Canso "A". Shown is a gaggle of PBY-5s at Patricia Bay early in 1945. (LAC PA136642)

(Above) The RCAF's most common trainer during BCATP days was the Avro Anson, some 4400 of which were on wartime strength. This Anson II served with Test and Development Flight in Ottawa. (DND PL9662)

(Front Endpapers) Established in 1920, the Canadian Air Force depended largely on flying boats, including the war surplus Curtiss HS-2L. Here is G-CYGR under way at Jericho Beach, the RCAF's premier West Coast flying station. Then an HS-2L is seen undergoing an engine change. (LAC PA112057, William J. Wheeler Col.)

The engine shop at Camp Borden in 1920, with mechanics working on 130-hp Clerget engines, as used in the CAF's Avro 504K trainer. (K.M. Molson Col.)

The RCAF was daring with its 1927 purchase of new Fairchild FC-2 utility planes. G-CYYT remained on strength late into 1941. (LAC C71168)

One of the RCAF's "modern" types at the outbreak of WWII was the Fairey Battle. Here P2155 sits at Camp Borden after being assembled. Re-numbered 1301, this was the first Battle on RCAF strength (August 21, 1939). It served initially as a fighter with Montreal-based 115 Squadron. (Jack McNulty)

Kittyhawks and Hurricanes were the fighter mainstays on the home front. Kittyhawk 729 of 132 Squadron is seen at Patricia Bay, near Victoria, BC. (LAC PA197485)

The Consolidated Liberator had three roles on the RCAF home front: anti-submarine operations, long-range transport flying, and crew training. Leslie Corness photographed this example at Edmonton.

(Back Endpapers) The Tiger Moth was the RCAF's premier elementary trainer before and during the war – some 11546 were on strength, all (but one) manufactured in North Toronto by de Havilland Canada 1938-41. This example is seen at Camp Borden. (Jack McNulty Col.)

One of the finer Anson photos: 6180 flying low over downtown Winnipeg. This Anson earned its keep, logging nearly 4100 flying hours through the war. (Manitoba Archives, Gingras Col.)

Anson 6531 of 1 AOS, Malton, following a forced landing near Orillia, Ontario on December 12, 1942. Damage was sufficient that 6531 was scrapped. (Jack McNulty Col.)

From the first BCATP wings parade at Camp Borden in 1940, more than 130,000 airmen graduated from the BCATP. Here the inspecting officer takes the salute from a typical graduating class. (Leslie Corness Col.)

Contents

Airmen pose for a candid photo at one of the RCAF Kittyhawk squadrons. (George J. McDowell Col. via Henry Tenby)

Preface		7
Chapter One	Air Force Possibilities	11
Chapter Two	An Air Force Takes Shape	21
Chapter Three	Valleys and Peaks	49
Chapter Four	The British Commonwealth Air Training Plan	107
Chapter Five	Home War Establishment	183
Glossary		322
Bibliography		324
Index		326

Another of the "modern" types with which the RCAF was re-equipping in the late 1930s was the Westland Lysander. This example was licence-built by National Steel Car at Malton, near Toronto. (Lialla Raymes Col.)

A grand overview of Trenton in 1939, when this was the RCAF's showcase flying station. The view is south towards Prince Edward County. The general scene remains roughly similar in 2010. Today, however, C-130s, A-310s and C-17s would be in view, not Battles and Oxfords. (DND PL1222)

Aviation in Canada: Evolution of an Air Force is the third title in CANAV's new series. Having covered the pioneer decades to the end of WWI (Vol. 1), then the formative years in commercial aviation (Vol. 2), *ACEAF* starts with the Canadian Air Force in early post-WWI times. Following the debate about Canada so much as even having a home-based, peace time air force, the CAF takes wing in 1920. Equipped with a variety of war surplus aircraft, in 1924 it evolves into the Royal Canadian Air Force.

Initially, the RCAF is the servant of civil government departments. Through the 1920s it has few military functions, but keeps busy doing aerial photography, forestry patrols, fisheries and customs missions, mercy flights and the occasional air display. Camp Borden is the center of training, and seaplane bases develop from coast to coast. In 1922 the first CAF airman visits the Arctic to scout sites for future air operations. In 1926-28 the RCAF participates in the landmark Hudson Strait Expedition, and acquires its first modern combat planes – a pair of Siskin fighters.

Through the 1930s the great world powers re-arm and Canada, naturally, goes along on Great Britain's coat tails. The RCAF gradually adopts a military stance and, with the formation of the Department of Transport in 1936, sheds the last of its civil government functions. *ACEAF* then focuses on the RCAF getting ready for war. However, most of its new equipment is, by the standards of the day, obsolete on delivery.

On the eve of war the RCAF can mobilize a mere eight regular squadrons, and its entire complement is but 4153 officers and men. It has 270 aircraft but, to oppose the enemy, can muster only 53 in the service category (the most modern of these are 19 Hurricanes). *ACEAF* describes this pitiful situation, then shows how the RCAF resolves this crisis. By energetic recruiting, training and re-equipping, almost overnight it emerges as a potent home defence force. The British Commonwealth Air Training Plan is covered thoroughly, as are Eastern Air Command, Western Air Command and the RCAF's domestic and trans-Atlantic air transport operations. In the well-known CANAV style, the text through-out *ACEAF* includes many previously unknown case studies, whether of young men passing through the training system, flying fighters in Alaska or tracking down U-boats off Eastern Canada. No Canadian aviation book has ever shown such lavish photographic coverage of these topics.

Many important sources have been tapped in completing this project. James W. Jones did a wonderful job of designing the page spreads that you see before you. Research-wise, Hugh A. Halliday sourced much relevant material for me at Library and Archives Canada, the Directorate of History and from his own bulging files. Ellis Culliton opened many doors with his father's (J.P. Culliton) photo albums and personal memoir and, through the auspices of Stephen McDonough came more fresh history out of his father's (W.J. McDonough) old boxes of aviation treasures. My own files, begun more than 50 years ago, also proved their worth, and the genesis for this new series – *Aviation in Canada* (1979) – was a font of ideas. Janet Lacroix of the Canadian Forces Joint Imagery Centre in Ottawa helped locate photos and caption information. Lambert "Bert" Huneault, Ron Pickler and W.J. "Bill" Wheeler were my stalwart proof readers.

The many others who have assisted include (some have by now passed on): C.L. Annis, Bagotville Air Defence Museum, Shirley and Keith Barlow, Hugh Bartley, A.W. "Alf" Barton, Eric Billingham, Bruce Best, Dr. John Blatherwick, Peter M. Bowers, Robert

The Link Trainer was essential to the overall success of the BCATP. The first "electronic" flight simulator in RCAF use, it trained thousands of young pilots. This example is shown in 1942 at RCAF Station Alliford Bay, BC. (LAC PA136268)

Brachen, Robin Brass, Brazilian Air Force Museum, John Buzza, Canada Aviation Museum, Canadian Aviation Historical Society, *Canadian Aviation* magazine, LGen William K. Carr, Murray Castator, Tony Cassanova, Larry Chezzie, Anthony Cinquina, Colin Clark, Ralph Clint, Leslie Corness, Norman Corness, Brian Darling, G.R. "Joe" Davis, Ralph Davis, Gordon Diller, W.P. Dunphy, W/C (Ret'd) J.F.D. "Tim" Elkington, Frank H. Ellis, John and Joyce Ellis, Norman Etheridge, Romulo Figueiredo, Robert Finlayson, Arthur Fleming, Bill Ford, Bertram Frandsen, George A. Fuller, Pierre Gillard, Richard Girouard, Glenbow Museum, *Globe and Mail* "Canada's Heritage from 1944", David Godfrey, John Habasinski, Robert

The RCAF had a small but highly professional force of women, who constituted the Women's Division. Members trained at such tasks as clerks, drivers, mechanics, photographers and meteorologists. These WDs worked in the stores section at 3 SFTS, Calgary. (DND PL11315)

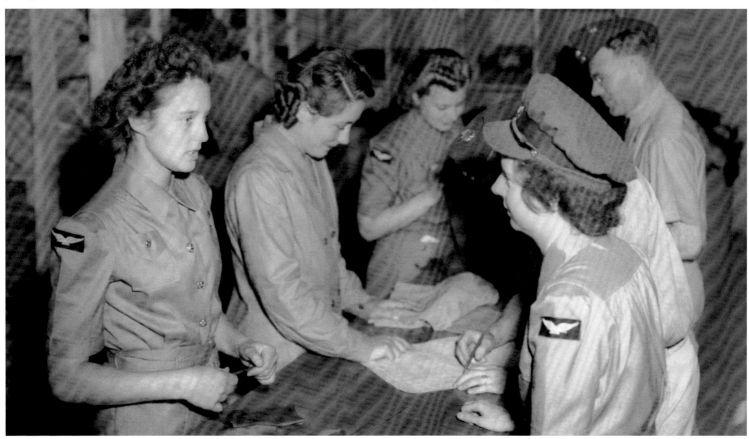

These proud new pilots – Course 52 at 15 SFTS, Claresholm, Alberta – graduated in September 1941. (J. Ashworth Col.)

G. Halford, Chas. Hayes, Fred Hotson, J.D. "Jack" Hunter, G.R. Hutt, Imperial War Museum, A.T. "Tony" Jarvis, Joseph P. Juptner, George F. Kimball, C. Don Long, Neil A. MacDougall, Richard K. Malott, Maritime Museum of the Atlantic, Stafford Marlatt, Al Martin, Donald J. McClintock, John McClure, John T. McCreight, Steve McDowell, T.M. McGrath, James G. McGuffin, W.H. "Wess" McIntosh, Ross McKenzie, Alistair Donald McLaren, M.L. "Mac" McIntyre, Gordon McNulty, Jack McNulty, James M. McRae, W.R. "Bill" McRae, W.H.D. Meaden, Simon Milberry, A.J. Milne, Paul Minert, Harry Mochulsky, Kenneth M. Molson, Steve Mouncey, Museum of Science and Technology, National Museum of the United States Air Force, National Naval Aviation Museum (Pensacola), George Neal, Ontario Ministry of Natural Resources, Harry Pattinson, Provincial Archives of Alberta, Provincial Archives of Manitoba, Rick Radell, Lialla and Danny Raymes, Walt Redmond, Rae Reid, Royal Military College, Rob Schweyer, Glenn Scott, J.F. Sears, A.B. Shearer, Eric G. Smith, Ken Smith, St. Paul's Anglican Church (Newmarket, Ontario), Janet Stubbs, Kenneth I. Swartz, Henry Tenby, David J. Thompson, Toronto Public Library, Toronto Star "Pages of the Past", USAF Air University (Maxwell AFB), Basil Van Sickle, Vancouver Public Library, Ventura Memorial Flight Association, J.E. "Jerry" Vernon, Art Walker, George Webster, Ernie Weeks, Gordon S. Williams, Lou Wise.

As most CANAV readers realize, Imperial measures remain in use here, since Imperial was the system of the day and is still widely used in aviation. In order to maintain a fine-looking page, you will not be bothered by unsightly Imperial-metric conversions. You can quickly work these out if desired. Also, the taxpayer's pocket has not been picked in producing this book. CANAV Books, being a serious publisher, has not so much as applied for a government grant since 1981.

LARRY MILBERRY

LAC K.C. "Ken" Lett receives his wings from Prime Minister King in Ottawa on October 24, 1942. Lett went on to a lifelong RCAF career, including command of 416 Squadron (Sabres) in 1954-56. (DND PL11826)

This Curtiss H-16 "Large America", part of the Imperial Gift to Canada after WWI, began as RNAS N4905, then ended in the Canadian Air Force as G-CYEP, taken on strength on February 2, 1922. Derived from the original 1914 Curtiss America, the H-16 first flew in America in 1917 and in the UK (as the Felixstowe F.3) in March 1918. The H-16 had a massive 98' 8½" wing span, was 46' 6" long and 16' 6" high. Empty weight on paper was 7293 lb, all-up weight 10,650 lb, top speed 93 mph and endurance as long as 6 hours (such details vary from source to source). Engines were the 400-hp Liberty for H-16s, or 345-hp Rolls-Royce Eagle for F.3s. The H-16 was developed for the U-boat war and, as such, flew with 4 x 100- or 2 x 230-lb bombs and 4 independent .303 machine guns. Although excellent in its war role, it was not favoured by the Canadian Air Board. It quickly was struck off strength, the last example leaving service September 1923. (CANAV Col)

Air Force Possibilities

With so many Canadians having served in RFC, RNAS and RAF squadrons (some 20,000 by war's end), the idea of distinct Canadian fighting units within the British air arms was considered. In the summer of 1918 there was a plan to establish eight such squadrons financed by Canada. However, due in part to Britain favouring the Commonwealth atmosphere prevailing in the RAF, this idea did not get off the table. On the common sense side, Ottawa was leery about financing eight squadrons, and also realized that it could not technically support such a large force.

In August 1918 Britain's Air Ministry proposed a modest plan for an organization designated No.1 Wing to comprise two Canadian squadrons – one with fighters, one with bombers. On September 19 Ottawa approved this and the Canadian Air Force (England) was born. On November 20 Nos. 1 and 2 squadrons came into existence at Upper Heyford. In command was LCol W.A. Bishop, but the war was over, so the Canadian wing faced a cloudy future.

The pilots of No.1 Wing mainly were combat-experienced Canadians, many wearing gallantry ribbons. Dolphins,

A No.1 Squadron S.E.5a of the Canadian Air Force (England). Walter R. Kenny, DFC, of Ottawa, previously on RNAS operations, is in the cockpit. While piloting an H-16 on June 3, 1918, Kenny bombed a submerging U-boat, but no results were evident. On a July sortie in a Short 184, he unsuccessfully bombed a U-boat about to attack a steamer. He later served in the postwar RCAF, rising to be A/V/M Kenny during WWII, but dying in 1944. (CANAV Col.)

S.E.5s, Snipes, Fokker D.VIIs and D.H.9s were provided by the RAF. In December, Col R.H. Mulock replaced LCol Bishop, then the organization relocated to Shoreham-by-Sea. However,

LCol W.A. Bishop, VC, MC, DSO and Bar, DFC, who was the first to command the Canadian Air Force in England, September to December 1918. (LAC PA1990)

other than training, the CAF (England) had little purpose. Morale was not sky high, since most members were anxious to get home to their families in Canada. There was some talk that No.1 Wing might return to Canada as a functioning establishment, and newspapers at home carried many opinions about the subject. The feeling was that the nation's large pool of trained aviators and aviation tradesmen, once home, ought to be tapped for some national purpose. But Ottawa had no wish for an expensive, home-based, fighting force; and what direction any peacetime air force or aircraft industry might take was still being discussed. In such an atmosphere No.1 Wing disbanded on February 5, 1920. The Canadian Air Force (England) disbanded as an entity on August 9. Even shorter-lived was the Royal Canadian Naval Air Service. Formed to blunt the efforts of German submarines off Canada's east coast, the RCNAS endured from September to December 1918.

Canadian Air Force at Home

There was a cadre of returned Canadian air war veterans who knew what they wanted. They had flying in their bones, so got straight back into aviation, scarce though opportunities were. The recipe was simple – get hold of a war surplus JN-4 and start hustling. From Charlottetown to Montreal, Toronto, Winnipeg and across the prairies and mountains to Vancouver and Victoria, these characters – the barnstormers – had their day. Theirs was a chancy game, but more promising opportunities awaited. The barnstormers who persevered soon were exploring the potential of airplanes in such areas as forestry and mining. Ottawa, at the same time, was keeping a close eye on events and assigning committees to formulate Canada's first aeronautical policies and regulations.

By mid-1919 the great RAF (Canada) organization had disappeared;

Camp Borden during RFC (Canada) times, when 18 full-size hangars comprised the main operation, but notice the many other facilities. A few of these hangars still remained in 2010. The small pads in front of the hangars, previously thought to have been of concrete, were simple canvas sheets laid down as parking spots for the JN-4s, when mud took over the flightline. Mothballed after November 11, 1918, in early 1920 Camp Borden was reactivated as the Canadian Air Force's main training centre. (DND RE19070-13)

vast amounts of its materiel and real estate had been sold. In light of this, on June 26, 1919 the Toronto *Daily Star* urged Ottawa to retain Camp Borden, where so much had been invested to create an impressive air station (the base remained intact, but in mothballs). This column made other thoughtful points: "The country got a good start in the aeroplane industry during the war and should turn it to some account. We should not be content meekly to fall into a back position as a country that exports aeroplane timber and skilled mechanics to foreign factories... The starting of a vigorous Canadian Air Force ... would ensure the closest touch being kept with every advance ... in aviation."

In 1919 there still was a bit of flying at Camp Borden, from where dozens of surplus JN-4 training planes were gradually being sold. One of these got into the news on April 4, when Lt C.A. Schiller got lost while flying from Camp Borden to Toronto. He landed in a field east of Toronto, overnighted, then continued to Camp Leaside. Schiller may have been ferrying a JN-4 on behalf of war surplus tycoon F.G. Ericson, who had taken over Camp Leaside. Another item in the press that week reported how Lt H. Meicenheimer, formerly a Camp Borden instructor, had flown a JN-4 from Toronto to Milwaukee, apparently in one day. Meicenheimer's home was in Milwaukee, so it is possible that he had bought a surplus JN-4 for his own use.

There still was some surplus business taking place, for that same week there were Imperial Munitions Board newspaper advertisements offering excess coal. One such read: "Soft Coal at Camp Borden. Approximately 3,800 tons Soft Coal, being a mixture of three-quarters lump with small portion run of mine, lying in Aviation Camp Borden. About one-third alongside tracks and two-thirds five minutes' haul from tracks, with C.P.R. or G.T.R. Will be sold in one lot as it lies in the pile. Complete delivery is to be taken not later than May 31st."

The mood may still have been on downsizing, but behind the scenes Ottawa was setting its course for peacetime aviation. Prime Minister Borden had sent Col O.M. Biggar and Arthur Sifton as Canada's emissaries to the International Commission on Aerial Navigation, convened in Paris under the 1919 Paris Peace Conference. Other capable civil servants were busy planning, two key personalities being James A. Wilson and C.C. MacLaurin. They proposed that postwar Canada should stress civil flying. From this, they surmised, would develop aircraft design, manufacture, sales and a cadre of pilots, engineers, tradesmen, administrators, etc. Any future air force would benefit from such a foundation. The efforts of Wilson and MacLaurin resulted in Parliament passing the Air Board Act in June 1919. The Canadian Air Board comprised a Civil Aviation Branch with licencing and regulating powers; a Civil Operations Branch doing government-mandated, non-military flying; and a Canadian Air Force training pilots and tradesmen for non-military duties. For its first fiscal year (1920 - 21) the Air Board received $1,900,000 of which $1,100,000 was for civil aviation.

Air Board Duties

Air Board's activities encompassed everything from registering and certifying airplanes, licencing pilots, recommending aviation safety measures, investigating accidents and doing aeronautical research and development. In charge of the latter (the Technical Services Branch) was LCol E.W. Stedman, a wartime veteran of Handley Page bomber operations. The TSB was interested in everything from studying the strength and life of materials used in aircraft construction, to

the difficulties of cold weather operations, to developing aeronautical theory using the wind tunnel at the University of Toronto.

Typical of aircraft registrations was the case of JN-4 ex-RFC (Canada) C-144. On May 21, 1920 the McCall Aero Corporation, based in the Union Bank Building in Calgary, filled out its "Application for the Registration of an Aircraft" form. President Jack McCoubrey, manager Fred R. McCall and director Samuel G. Steward were listed as company principals. The application, for which the fee was $5.00, specified that McCall Aero would be carrying freight and passengers. Its plane's empty weight was given as 1580 lb, its wing span – 47' 7½", length – 27' 4", height – 9' 10½". "Maximum safe load in pounds" was 550 lb, speed 75 mph. The instruments were listed as an altimeter, "rev counter", oil gauge and fuel gauges. Basil D. Hobbs of the Air Board inspected the plane on July 13, approved it, and the registration G-CABO was assigned. In another case, on May 29, 1920 Irwin Proctor of Hamilton filled out his paperwork to register a JN-4. It became G-CABL of the Canadian Aero Film Co. Early Air Board accident investigations included the August 18, 1920 crash into English Bay, Vancouver of a Boeing BB-1 flying boat. The pilot, H.B. Brenton, had departed the dock of a company called Aircraft Manufacturers Ltd. What happened next is shockingly described in the Air Board report:

The pilot was making a test flight for his Commercial Air Pilot's Certificate. He made one alighting and took off again. At a height of about one thousand feet the machine appeared to be out of control and at the same time the pilot fell out. The machine then glided slowly on her back and crashed into the water.

The Air Board stated that the Boeing was certified and airworthy that day. Brenton was an experienced wartime pilot, having flown 444:20 hours on many types. Even so early in Air Board operations, the wreck of the Boeing was closely examined and all controls found in good order. However, one of Brenton's gloves was mangled. The Air Board mused that this glove might have "jammed the pulley between the passenger seat which carries the elevator control wires [and] caused the machine to get out of hand".

Air Board Accident Statistics (Civil Aviation) 1920

Total accidents	34
Accidents involving injuries	4
Accidents involving death	5
Pilots killed/injured	9
Passengers killed/injured	5
Aircraft miles per accident	30,176
Aircraft flights per accident	1334
Aircraft hours per accident	465
Pilots killed per 1000 flights	.054
Pilots killed per hours flown	.154

Air Board Miscellaneous Statistics (Civil Aviation) 1920

Aircraft manufacturing companies in Canada	1*
Companies operating aircraft in Canada	30
Flights made	18,671
Hours flown	6505
Miles flown	422,462
Duration (minutes) of average flight	21
Passengers carried	15,265
Freight carried (pounds)	6740
Public aerodromes	7
Private aerodromes	23
Private seaplane bases	6
Air harbours with customs facilities	4
Licenced commercial landplanes	58
Licenced commercial seaplanes	4
Licenced flying boats	8
Single-engine commercial aircraft	70
Licenced commercial pilots	71
Licenced commercial air engineers	60

*F.G. Ericson's Toronto company, which was manufacturing a few JN-4s mainly using war surplus components,

The CAF and the Imperial Gift

Under the Air Board Act, the Canadian Air Force was authorized on February 18, 1920, Col R.F. Redpath in command (soon succeeded by Col Douglas Joy). The first year's funding from Ottawa was $800,000 and an establishment of 5245 officers and men was allowed. On April 23 the first "non-permanent" CAF personnel were authorized. Since it had all the necessary infrastructure, the Air Board base at Camp Borden became home to the air force. Through early 1920 the place was re-activated, a hint of coming activity there being help-wanted notices in newspapers for miles around, one such reading: "STORES CLERK: Temporary civil servant, returned soldier only, salary $950 per annum and bonus. Must have good education. Give qualifications and write only to Officer-in-Charge, Stores Depot, Camp Borden, Ont."

Just as the Air Board was coming about, Great Britain was making an aviation future easier for its Dominions by providing hundreds of surplus airplanes to its Dominions through the "Imperial Gift", or for some nominal charges to such other friends as Chile and Portugal. Details of this 1919-20 scheme are included in such

Detail views of Imperial Gift Felixstowe F.3 G-CYDH, which served the CAF briefly from Victoria Beach, Manitoba in 1921-22. The F.3 was much disliked by the CAF, one comment of the times noting that it had "always been difficult to operate". A lack of calm anchorages for refuelling was one of many disadvantages. Featured in these views are the F.3's Rolls-Royce Eagle engines, each of 345 hp. The massive propellers were of wood with protective brass plate on the leading edges. Basic specs for the F.3 included wing span – 102', length – 49' 2", height – 18' 8", all-up weight – 12,235 lb, max speed – 91 mph, endurance – 6 hours. About 100 F.3s had been built by war's end. (G.R. Hutt, CAF)

publications as John Griffin's 1969 *Canadian Military Aircraft Serials and Photographs*, F.H. Hitchins' *Air Board, Canadian Air Force and Royal Canadian Air Force* and Hugh A. Halliday's paper in Vol.47 No.1 of the Canadian Aviation Historical Society *Journal*. The Imperial Gift served three chief goals: it helped the

One of the 62 Avro 504Ks received by the Air Board in the Imperial Gift beginning in early 1920. Assigned to Camp Borden, these trained the first CAF pilots, all of whom had been wartime fliers. Soon, however, the CAF began training *ab initio* pilots, and doing other work. G-CYBK was struck off strength in January 1925, likely due to some accident. The last 504 left RCAF service in 1928. This photo shows the markings decreed in 1920 by the Air Board for its aircraft. "G" on the tail identified the plane as Canadian. "CY" indicated the Air Board, and "BK" the particular plane. The registration also was carried in large letters on top and bottom wings. In 1928 the RCAF adopted a numerical identification system, so the "G-CY" series disappeared, e.g. Avro 504 G-CYAX became RCAF No.14. (CAF RC543)

Motherland dispose of 20,000 surplus airplanes, that otherwise would have to be stored and scrapped; it enabled Dominions to establish government flying services that would contribute to a hoped-for Imperial air defence network; and it laid the groundwork for sales of spare parts and engines, and of future aircraft designs.

Assisted by a competent staff, Canadian Air Board Director of Flying Operations, LCol Robert Leckie, DSO, DSC, DFC, studied the aircraft types on offer. Knowing how his political bosses had no interest in combat aircraft, Leckie chose accordingly. His final selection included: Avro 504 – 62, de Havilland D.H.4 and D.H.9 – 23, SE.5a – 12, Felixstowe F.3 – 8, Curtiss H.16 – 2, Bristol F.2b – 2, Sopwith Snipe – 2, Fairey C.3 – 1. Although some of these had been fighting machines, in Canada they would find only peaceful work. The gift included engines, seaplane beaching gear, cameras, tons of spare parts and prefabricated Bessoneau hangars. Support equipment included some 300 vehicles, e.g. in a February 1920 shipment of motor transport were 43 Crossley cars and light tenders, 65 Leyland heavy tenders, 10 wireless trailers, 13 photographic trailers, 15 ambulances and 43 motorcycles. Most such equipment was organized and packed at Shoreham-by-Sea, then moved to seaports. Until November 1919 this work was overseen by Maj Donald MacLaren, DSO, MC, DFC, later by Maj J.A. Glen, DSC. Shipping was mainly done in the spring of 1920, so as to avoid damage to deck cargo in Atlantic winter storms.

The Canadian Air Board also requested some lighter-than-air equipment, including 12 twin-motor airships and six kite balloons. There was great enthusiasm as to how these might be evaluated on such tasks as topographic surveying and patrolling the forests. The Air Board envisioned having one airship base each in eastern and western Canada. As far as Halliday could determine, four 100,000 cu.ft. and five 71,000 cu.ft. airships were shipped late in 1920, along with 30 kite balloons and tons of support equipment – everything from 18 75-hp Rolls-Royce Hawk engines, to special lorries, winches and sheds, gondola cars, parachutes and hydrogen gas-making equipment. All this was delivered to Camp Borden, where Capt George O. Johnson, MC, was in charge of aircraft assembly and test flying. A Toronto *Daily Star* report of June 4, 1920 claimed that equipment valued at $4 million already was at Camp Borden with much more en route. The reporter then got specific about what he had been shown:

In the big packing cases which almost fill the ... aeroplane hangars ... are the parts of several types of fighting and service planes. There are a dozen of the big SE5 type in which Colonel Bishop accomplished his most spectacular and daring fighting ... They have all 200 horsepower, eight cylinder engines and are single seaters. Another dozen of the machines are known as the D.H.9A type, capable of carrying 425 pounds of bombs ... there are sixty machines of the "Avroe" type, generally used as a standard British training machine.

According to the same press item, Canada at last would be able "to create ... a distinctly Canadian Air Force, free from entangling alliances with even the Royal Air Force." Then Air Commodore A.K. Tylee, AOC of the Canadian Air Force, was quoted: "By acting now and in view of the gift from Great Britain, we have the entire Air Force within our hands. The only cost to be borne by the country will be its maintenance." Detailed 1920 dollar values of Canada's gift aircraft included: (Imperial Gift) $800,000 for 62 Avros, $225,000 for 12 D.H.9s, $150,000 for 12 S.E.5s; (leftover from RAF Canada) $10,000 for 10 JN-4s; and (leftover from US Navy base at Dartmouth) $175,000 for 12 HS-2Ls. The eight F.3s apparently were provided in gratitude for the many aircraft donated by Canadian citizens to Great Britain during the war. The F.3s were valued by Canada at $500,000.

Under LCol J. Scott Williams, flying commenced at Camp Borden in July 1920 at newly-formed 1 Wing (CAF) of which the active unit was the School of Special Flying. The object was to offer refresher courses to veterans, in order to provide an initial cadre of CAF pilots and tradesmen. A press report of August 21, 1920 stated that some 5000 were expected to train at Camp Borden in the first two years of the plan. An Air Board report describes how the Imperial Gift aircraft became available, so that training might begin:

Each aeroplane was more or less damaged in transit. Registration of each machine was arranged and markings

A typical flightline scene at Camp Borden in the summer of 1920. Avro 504 G-CYCB is taxiing by S.E.5a G-CYCV. Avro 504 'BZ is beyond. 'CB was wrecked at Camp Borden on December 9, 1921. (K.M. Molson Col.)

In spite its rigours, some winter flying was done at postwar Camp Borden, open cockpits notwithstanding. Here, a crewman there is ready to "prop" a ski-equipped Avro 504. (K.M. Molson Col.)

Meanwhile, the Fairey C.3 and at least one F.3 were assembled by Canadian Vickers in Montreal. Two other F.3s were shipped directly to Vancouver by rail, others went to Victoria Beach north of Winnipeg and to Dartmouth near Halifax. In the end, not all gift aircraft would see service – four F.3s, four Avro 504s, an H.16, a Snipe and a D.H.9 were never registered, but may have been used for spares or as technical training aids.

One of the CAF's JN-4s struggles in Camp Borden's snow after damaging the undercarriage. (CANAV Col.)

painted on the machine while under erection. Each engine was carefully examined and all rubber connections replaced before installed in a machine. After a machine was completely erected, it was tested by at least one hour's flying, then checked over and any necessary minor adjustments made. The machine was then either turned over to the Canadian Air Force ... in flying condition or dismantled ... and shipped to other Operations Stations... The work has now settled down to regular routine of erecting, testing and repairing aeroplanes, and at the same time training mechanics for work at the other stations.

This ex-RAF (Canada) Curtiss JN-4 was one of 11 acquired by the Air Board from the final 53 stored postwar at Camp Borden. The remaining 42 JN-4s were sold to Bishop-Barker Aeroplanes of Toronto, from where they trickled onto the civil market across Canada and the US. Since the Air Board also had a large number of 130-hp Avro 504s, its 90-hp JN-4s were not much used in pilot training; the last was struck off strength in January 1923. (CAF RC663)

False Start

In the end, no lighter-than-air flying seems to have taken place under the Air Board, which quickly adopted airplanes for the jobs previously envisioned for airships and balloons. Rather than immediately scrapping those, however, the Air Board proposed lending them to commercial forestry companies to develop aerial applications. In the Toronto *Daily Star* of July 6, 1921 a story datelined Camp Borden appeared under the headline "Airships Go North To Patrol Forests". So far as is known, only Keewatin Lumber took part in this plan, but there is no evidence that any flying was done:

Two airships of the "blimp" type were shipped from here yesterday to be used by the Keewatin Lumber Company in the Lake of the Woods district. Under the direction of Lieut-Col Redford Mulock, D.S.O., formerly of the Naval Air Service, they will be used for forest patrol work, as well as aerial photography. They are being loaned by the Air Board so that reports on their capabilities may be made by the lumber company.

Nothing further was heard of this project, however, the Air Board's May 1921 "Progress Report" included a reference to surplus Fiat and Berliet airship engines being donated to universities and technical schools as training aids. What remained of some 250 tons of lighter-than-air materiel languished at Camp Borden, the last being disposed of in 1925. After removing useful components, salvaging great lengths of rope and rubberized airship fabric, etc., everything else was scrapped or burned (the airship fabric material sometimes was used at Camp Borden to patch roofs).

Putting the Planes to Use

The Imperial Gift aircraft soon were proving useful. In 1920 the Fairey, an F.3 and some D.H.9s took part in the first trans-Canada flight, an event documented in many books and journals. LCol A.K. Tylee, AOC of the Canadian Air Forces summarized the great success of this enterprise:

The flight has thoroughly convinced me that trans-continental flying can

February 5, 1927 views at Camp Borden of de Havilland D.H.9A G-CYBF. Formerly RAF E995, 'BF was taken on CAF strength in January 1920. Its skis likely were made in the station carpentry shop. From October 13-17 'BF flew in the 3265-mile trans-Canada flight, covering the final stretch from Calgary to Vancouver via Field, Golden, Revelstoke, Merritt and Agassiz. First flown in early 1918, the D.H.9A, of which Canada received 12 via the Imperial Gift, gained RAF fame as a day bomber. Some 2140 were delivered, the final batch in 1927. Gross weight was 4645 lb, top speed 114 mph and endurance about 5 hours. CAF D.H.9As were powered by the 400-hp Liberty. The fleet served well on photographic and forestry duties. The last RCAF examples were struck off strength on February 18, 1929, although the type remained in RAF service into 1931. Unfortunately, no one thought to preserve one of the CAF's D.H.9As – they all went for scrap. (CAF RC597, '596)

be successfully undertaken. At the same time the following ground organization will be necessary:
(i) Well marked aerodrome every 50 miles.
(ii) Wireless communications on the machine.
(iii) Wireless directional apparatus on the ground to guide the machines as they are flying.

Tylee also urged that there be weather stations at each aerodrome, receiving forecasts by wireless from stations up and down the line, so that a pilot always knew what conditions lay before him. The Air Board finished its report by concluding that, "... even in unfavourable circumstances, long-distance flying by night and day [is] quite feasible in Canada." Through FY1920 the Air Board Civil Operations

Branch, staffed with about 110 people (32 pilots included) employed 18 HS-2Ls, 4 F.3s, 11 D.H.4s and 3 Avro seaplanes on a host of duties on behalf of nine federal bureaus. Some 2200 hours were flown on such duties as forestry, customs and immigration patrols, treaty flights, and general liaison and transport. The Avros and S.E.5s served well in pilot training at Camp Borden and a Bristol Fighter and an Avro did experimental photographic work. As the 1920s proceeded, Avros and de Havillands also served during summer training at militia camps, taking up Army personnel for reconnaissance and artillery spotting. In one case, following an exercise of August 14, 1923 at High River, where S/L G.M. Croil and F/L A.A. Leitch had co-operated with the Royal Canadian Horse Artillery, Maj J. Crossley Stewart wrote to Croil:

Canada's share of the Imperial Gift also included 12 de Havilland D.H.4s. First flown in August 1916, this versatile RAF day bomber first fought in March 1917. In spite of many flaws, it persevered to war's end, while being gradually replaced by more modern D.H.9As. Some 1449 D.H.4s were built in the UK, a further 4846 in the US. Powered by a 375-hp Rolls-Royce Eagle or 400-hp Liberty, the D.H.4 (depending on the version) had a gross weight of 3500 to 4300 lb, top speed of 106 to 143 mph and an endurance of 3 to 4½ hours. The CAF employed its D.H.4s mainly in photography and forest fire patrols from High River. G-CYDK was taken on CAF strength. On April 24, 1922 it crashed while on a photo assignment from Camp Borden. Pilot, S/L Hubert L. Holland, MC, was killed, while photographer E.R. Owen was injured. (George F. Kimball/CANAV Col.)

On October 11, 1920 LCol Arthur Tylee (CAF commander) and Capt J.B. Home-Hay departed Winnipeg in D.H.9A G-CYAN. They were on the continuation of the inaugural trans-Canada flight, but had engine trouble near Regina. They force-landed and 'AN was out of the running, replaced by G-CYBF. Such accidents were common, but were readily repairable. Spare propellers were usually available, since several normally were smashed in any month of operations. CAF carpenters, engine mechanics and airframe fitters soon would have had 'AN airworthy, although extra time would have been needed in dismantling and transporting it – probably back to Camp Borden. G-CYAN remained on RCAF strength into September 1927. (CAF)

Jericho Beach Opens

At Jericho Beach (Vancouver) in 1920 the first task of Maj C.C. MacLaurin, DSC, was to get his station operational and his aircraft into the waters of English Bay. The talented MacLaurin came to his posting following a prominent wartime career. Having graduated from the Curtiss school in Toronto, in July 1915 he was one of the first WWI Canadian airmen to sail overseas. He excelled in combat as an RNAS flying boat pilot, then was instrumental in 1918 in establishing the Royal Canadian Naval Air Service. Trades represented on his small staff of about 30 men included: pilot, photographer, storekeeper, carpenter, engine fitter, machinist, aircraft hand, clerk, boat builder, driver and labourer. A Canadian Press report of August 18, 1920 hinted at important things to come for MacLaurin's command: "Arrangements have been made with Major MacLaurin, commandant of the Jericho Beach seaplane station ... for the use of one or two of the big flying boats for coast fisheries patrol purposes. This will probably constitute the first aerial fisheries patrol in history." The beginnings at Jericho Beach are described further by W/C F.H. Hitchins in his *Canadian War Museum Paper No.2* from the 1972 "Mercury" series:

It was certainly a most interesting and instructive shoot and I think, taking everything in consideration, such as the error of the gun and the rustiness of both the pilot and myself in this type of work, also the limited amount of ammunition available, that it was a most successful shoot and that the number of effectives obtained were above that as laid down in the probability table of the gun.

Not all was satisfactory with the Imperial Gift. The F.3 was a disappoint-ment – it had poor performance, so could not safely be used on small lakes (where the HS-2L shone). S/L A.B. Shearer pointed out that an F.3 needed 56 in. of water for safe launching, compared to 34 in. for an HS-2L. The F.3 also was hard on fuel and, for all its impressive size, carried a small payload. In September 1922, Victoria Beach Air Station in Manitoba was advised to scrap its F.3s, and send any useful components to Vancouver and Ottawa. The last CAF/CGAO F.3 was struck off strength on September 12, 1923.

The province provided the site free of charge and agreed also to defray a substantial part of the cost of operations which were to include forestry protection and survey, transportation to inaccessible districts, photographic survey, and fishery patrol on behalf of both the federal and provincial governments. Temporary Bessoneau hangars were erected ... and the groundwork was sufficiently advanced by the end of August to permit erection of the first HS-2L.

Major MacLaurin made the first test flight on 24 September ...

Air Board Flying Stations 1920

Dartmouth, Nova Scotia
Roberval, Quebec
Ottawa, Ontario
Camp Borden, Ontario
Victoria Beach, Manitoba
Morley, Alberta
Vancouver, British Columbia

A grand bird's eye view in the early days of Jericho Beach. Two large Bessoneau hangars housed the equipment. The long narrow building probably was station HQ. HS-2Ls G-CYEA, 'DX and a third one (unknown), and F.3 'DI are sitting in the sun. Notice how much bigger the F.3 was. (CANAV Col.)

One of the great photographs from CAF 1921 "fisheries preventative" days: HS-2L G-CYDX is seen pretty well surrounded while inspecting the salmon fishery in the lower Fraser River. 'DX (formerly US Navy A1993) was one of the H-boats acquired soon after the US Navy closed its convoy patrol base at Dartmouth early in 1919. It served into late 1923, then was scrapped. (CANAV Col.)

From 1920-22 the Canadian Air Force trained only experienced pilots on refresher courses. Beginning in 1923, however, it began the "Provisional Pilot Officer" *ab initio* (beginners) scheme. Here are six of the 1929 P/P/O graduates from Camp Borden: George Jacobi, P.B. "Phil" Cox, George Kimball, R.C. "Bob" Mair, Bill Pinkerton and Claude W. Morrison. (RCAF RC2160)

Camp Borden on the Go

At Camp Borden airmen polished flying skills they had learned when they first had trained at schools from Dayton to Long Branch, Leaside and Camp Borden itself. For CAF purposes the well-proven RAF "Gosport" pilot training syllabus was adopted and implemented over a 28-day schedule. Instructors and students both were experienced wartime men, including many who later would excel in the RCAF or commercial aviation. One was S/L R.A. Logan, who organized Camp Borden's ground school. Subject matter included airframe and aero engines, navigation, artillery observation, aerial photography and wireless (radio). Most flying was on Avro 504s. Although a few JN-4s still were kept serviceable, these were shunned, due to their limited performance compared to the "504s". Advanced training was on D.H.4s and S.E.5s; a few of the latter had been converted to dual controls. Qualifying pilots were assessed on aircraft handling, formation flying and landings, overall judgment, and how they might fare as instructors. In this period the staff at Camp Borden rarely exceeded 100. A Toronto *Daily Star* editorial of June 30, 1921 praised what was happening at the revitalized base, noting of the airmen on course:

Most of them are in business and put in their vacation of two weeks in taking

About a hundred Provisional Pilot Officers on parade at Camp Borden *circa* 1928. These men were at various stages of training, some with wings, some not. The "parade square" looks a bit rustic. (George F. Kimball/CANAV Col)

The original P/P/O class at Camp Borden on August 17 1923: C.M. Anderson, E.J. Durnin, H.M. Durnin, B.C.C. Glynn, R.E. Knowles, C.R. Slemon, W.O. Stevens and W.C. Weaver. However, which man is which was not learned in time for this caption to be made complete. (DND PL117004)

this special flying course ... and learning of the latest developments in aviation ... There is flying in the forenoon and lectures, and the afternoons are given over to athletics. Expert mechanics, who are also taking refresher courses, keep *the machines tuned to the finest pitch... Everyone there believes in flying [and] feels so confident of its future ...*

Over the 1920 training season 86 officers and 111 airmen completed

Imperial Gift Avro 504K trainers at Camp Borden in the mid-1920s. First flown in 1913, the 504K became the standard British WWI trainer, and even saw some early combat. Powered by a 130-hp Clerget rotary engine, it had a top speed of 85 mph. These 504Ks had solid careers, G-CYAT lasting into 1930, 'EE into 1928. (George F. Kimball/CANAV Col)

SUBJECT	ANNIXTON W.T.	FERGUSON J.H.	MORRISON G.M.	JACOBI G.M.	KIMBALL G.F.	HAWTROW R.C.	COOK L.C.	COX R.D.	MAIR R.C.	GORDEL J.A.	TOTAL MARKS POSSIBLE
WORKSHOPS & ENGINES	132	114	129	126	135	133	138	133	123	133	150
do do	108	106	112	119	125	122	119	119	99	126	150
CARPENTRY & RIGGING	87	72	88	72	85	80	84	73	72	90	100
do do	96	100	92	88	98	91	97	94	76	90	100
PHOTOGRAPHY	85	80	68	75	91	95	85	77	82	77	100
LAW & ADMINISTRATION	89	76	88	73	77	78	71	71	86		100
ARMAMENT	78	72	83	77	90	67	82	78	85	87	100
SIGNALLING	98	93	99	98	92	99	100	99	98	99	100
AIR PILOTAGE	134	141	123	167	173	159	181	167	120	145	200
DRILL & GEN EFFICIENCY	178	170	172	168	162	182	170	164	176	170	200
PRACTICAL FLYING	480		450	480	582		510	450	510		600
do do	95	117	125	90	105	106	98	90	98	113	150
TOTAL MARKS OBTAINED	1660	1444	1639	1633	1885	1272	1765	1615	1625	1128	2050
PERCENTAGE & AGGREGATE	81	70.5	79.5	79.7	88.5		83.2	79	79.2		
ORDER & MERIT	3	8	5	4	1		2	7	6		

AB INITIO FLYING TRAINING COURSE 1929 3RD TSPM

Students learn the basics of airframe rigging, repair and maintenance at Camp Borden. Then, P/P/O academic results over the 1929 *ab initio* season. It is signed by the OC of the Ground Instruction School, F/L George E. Wait, a member of the RCAF since its birthday, April 1, 1924. (Below) P/P/Os in one of the GIS lecture rooms. Note the coal-burning potbelly stove – the latest in "heating technology" at Camp Borden. Finally, a standard WWI-era oblique aerial photo used by the GIS in teaching artillery reconnaissance theory. (LAC PA62793, next two George F. Kimball/CANAV Col, RCAF RC882)

courses, and 934 hours were flown. A press release of November 9 noted that six airmen had recently received commercial pilot licences following refresher training. In typical newspaper style, nearly every name was misspelled, but here they are correctly spelled: Frank M. Bradfield (Toronto), William H. Brown (Victoria), Albert A.L. Cuffe (Winnipeg), John G. Hamilton (Winnipeg), Robert C. Love (Toronto) and Keith Tailyour (Edmonton). The following year, 375 officers and 835 airmen took various courses.

To this time only wartime veterans were included in CAF training, so the system, ironically, was self-defeating. The tendency was for summer course men to drift back to civilian life after a season or two at Camp Borden. Realizing this, the CAF terminated veterans-only refresher training at the end of 1922. By this time 550 officers and 1271 airmen had completed courses. For 1923 recruitment centred on the universities with a new scheme to train Provisional Pilot Officers for longer term service at better pay. That summer nine students commenced training, four of whom persevered and the following summer earned their wings and commissions: P/P/Os C.M. Anderson, E.J. Durnin, W.C. Weaver and C.R. Slemon.

Camp Borden In the News

Most days found some newspaper tidbits about Camp Borden. The Toronto *Daily Star* reported on February 11, 1919 that Lt Kenneth B. Watson of Malton, near Toronto, had been awarded a DFC. Watson had trained at Camp Borden, went overseas in April 1917, shot down several enemy aircraft and, in one engagement, was one of six RFC aircraft in a scrap with 22 Fokkers. The same item announced that veteran B.E.2 and D.H.9 pilot, Maj Bert S. Wemp, DFC, now a reporter with the Toronto *Evening Telegram*, had been awarded the Belgian Order of Leopold. A vocal supporter of peacetime efforts at Camp Borden, Wemp later was a Toronto city councillor, then mayor. He eventually campaigned to draw flight training away from Camp Borden to a new airport planned for Toronto.

The Accident Scene

There sometimes were sad reminders in the press of earlier times at Camp Borden. In one case, this memorial, placed by "Sister, Anna Belle", appeared in the Toronto papers of June 17, 1920:

SAUNDERS – Pilot J.F. Saunders. 153270, who was killed at Camp Borden, June 17th, 1918.
'Tis with sad hearts we
commemorate the day,
When from our midst a dear one
passed away.
His place left so empty,
his loved voice killed,
We strive to be comforted,
it was as God willed.

Cadet Saunders' wartime service had begun with a tour on east coast naval duties, then he remustered to the RFC in November 1917. He was due to begin the final phase of flight training at Camp Leaside, when he died in a Camp Borden prang. Postwar, it was a matter of when (not if) Camp Borden suffered its first accidents. Naturally, it was expected that minor "prangs" – breaking landing skids or wooden propellers – were unavoidable. But worse things were around the corner. On March 23, 1921 P/O D. Wilkinson escaped serious consequences when he landed an Avro 504 that had caught fire at 2000 feet. Capt Murray B. Galbraith, DSC and Bar, Croix de Guerre (France), of Carleton Place, Ontario, died when his car flipped on the station on March 29.

Then, Capt Joseph A. Le Royer, MC, lost his life. Age 21 and from Quebec City, he had served initially in the Canadian Army, then remustered to the RFC. His profile was fairly typical for a CAF recruit. He flew the Nieuport 17 on 11 Squadron in France, switched to the F.E.2, and had several enemy aircraft to his credit. A recommendation submitted to RFC HQ noted of his good efforts: "His accurate and quick shooting was responsible to a large degree for these successes and he has shown, on numerous occasions, coolness and skill in engaging hostile aeroplanes." Postwar, something drew Le Royer back into aviation and 1921 found him at Camp Borden. On April 1, having taken some instruction from F/L Cuffe, he went solo in Avro G-CYBD. A witness reported seeing the plane in a spin at low altitude.

A typical flightline scene at Camp Borden. The aircraft are Avro 504Ns, the Armstrong Siddeley 180-hp Lynx-powered version of the 504K. The RCAF purchased two 504Ns from Avro in 1924, then had Canadian Vickers of Montreal convert 21 "K"s to "N"s. UK 504N production continued into 1933 and totalled 590. (George F. Kimball/CANAV Col)

P/P/O Phil Cox flying 504N G-CYBM in a rare air-to-air scene near Camp Borden *circa* 1928. (George F. Kimball/CANAV Col)

It crashed, gravely injuring Le Royer, who died four days later.

On April 6 the Toronto *Globe* commented that, "There are too many people being killed at Camp Borden. Ottawa should look into conditions there." This raised the ire of E. Graham Joy of the Ontario branch of the Canadian Air Force Association. He pointed out that, for all the flying at Camp Borden, serious mishaps were few. In fact, there had been numerous serious "Category A" accidents at Camp Borden, i.e. ones that resulted in complete loss of the airplane. But unless involving injury or death, accidents rarely were reported in the press. The following "Cat A" accidents occurred over a mere four months at Camp Borden:

Avro 504K G-CYCX in a Camp Borden scene to make the engineering officer wring his hands. Rare was the week that one of the station's aircraft wasn't damaged. Being a dicey machine to land, especially in a breeze, the 504K often broke its undercarriage and/or propeller. 'CX likely had many such prangs, yet survived on strength into 1934, by which time it likely was a training aid. (RCAF RC541)

Avro 504K 'FN in another of Camp Borden's all-too-common airfield mishaps. (RCAF RC1143)

Date	Aircraft
Jan. 3, 1921	Avro 504K G-CYCL
Jan. 26, 1921	Curtiss JN-4C G-CYCP
Feb. 15, 1921	Avro 504K G-CYCS
Mar. 22, 1921	Avro 504K G-CYCH
Apr. 5, 1921	Avro 504K G-CYBS
Apr. 10, 1921	Avro 504K G-CYCJ
Apr. 11, 1921	Avro 504K G-CYCY

April 11, 1921 was a dark day for Camp Borden, with instructor S/L Keith Tailyour being killed. Other prangs followed, including one of April 24, 1922 that killed S/L Hubert L. Holland, MC, and injured his photographer, E.R. Owen. They had been en route from Camp Borden to do photography over London in D.H.4 G-CYDK. When their water pump failed, they forced landed near Grand Valley, made repairs, but crashed on takeoff. Holland had specialized in aerial reconnaissance during the Italian campaign, flying the R.E.8 and Bristol Fighter on 34 Squadron, and later flew the D.H.9 with the Canadian Air Force

(England). The citation to his Military Cross reads: "For conspicuous gallantry and devotion to duty when working with artillery in carrying out six successful shoots whereby many enemy guns pits were destroyed and explosions caused... He carried out a good low reconnaissance of two suspected hostile batteries and also obtained other very useful information."

On February 24, 1925 F/L Joseph White, MC and Bar, DFC, Croix de Guerre (France), and his student, Lt Ronald H. Cross, died at Camp Borden, when their Avro 504K, G-CYAM, collided with another, G-CYAU, flown by F/O A.L. Morfee (who was able to land). Postwar, White had attended Dalhousie University in Halifax and worked at the local *Morning Chronicle*. He had some 13 confirmed wartime victories. Cross recently had begun refresher flying. White and Cross were the RCAF's first casualties.

On October 22, 1925 P/O T.G.C. Matthews died in the crash of Avro 504 G-CYBH at Camp Borden. From Macleod, Alberta, he was 24 and a 1924 RMC graduate. Another of Camp Borden's growing list of prangs occurred on July 27, 1926. That day P/O A.W.B. Stevenson, a P/P/O who had begun in the RCAF in 1923, was piloting Avro 504K G-CYFK to Toronto when he collided fatally with a 45-foot windmill on the farm of George Harding near Richmond Hill. In one of the RCAF's last serious Avro 504 accidents, on August 16, 1929 F/O G.R. Stafford died and AC G.A. Hanson was injured when 504N No.38 crashed into a residence at Camp Borden. An Irishman and RAF veteran, Stafford had emigrated to Canada in 1927.

The awful scene following P/O T.G.C. Matthews' October 22, 1925 crash in Avro 504K G-CYBH. The Toronto *Globe* noted that Matthews "was trying a landing test ... when approaching the ground the machine appeared to lose flying speed, stalled and fell." Then F/O Stafford's funeral cortege at Camp Borden. (George F. Kimball/CANAV Col, RCAF RC2148)

Total destruction reigned once the Camp Borden fire of August 1923 took hold. (CAF RC868)

Other Camp Borden Developments

To the local press, Camp Borden was always a locus for interesting material. Sometimes reports could verge on the humorous. One such concerned a Lt Hamilton who, as a report of January 21, 1921 suggested, had been caught flying off in a JN-4 to Tennessee with a woman. They were detained in Buffalo upon landing, the plane was seized, but Camp Borden denied any knowledge of Hamilton or the plane. Details later surfaced: the plane was not from Camp Borden, but the pilot, Capt J.G. Hamilton of Winnipeg, had been on his 28-day course there. On the side, he had a contract with F.G. Ericson of Toronto to deliver a surplus JN-4 to Oberlin, Ohio, but somehow ran afoul of officials in Buffalo. His passenger was his wife. On a somber note, on February 22, 1921 Camp Borden sent two aircraft to fly a salute over the funeral at Woodbridge, Ontario, of Member of Parliament Tom Wallace. In the third week of August 1923 the first RCAF Vickers Viking set off from Camp Borden on a long cross-country flight. Crewed by pilot F/O G.R. Howsam and fitter FSgt S. McConnell, the Viking stopped first at Sault Ste. Marie, then made the long flight next day (August 20) to Fort William in 4:15 Hours.

A fire at Camp Borden on August 29, 1923 at first was reported as an inferno of mysterious origin causing $500,000 in damage. Hangars, three S.E.5s and other airplanes, Rolls-Royce and Liberty engines, and much other equipment were destroyed. The press reported how station commander Col W.G. Barker, VC, "is keeping newspapermen and others out of the area ... and all information regarding the fire is to come through him". A week later, the spin doctors of the day had cast a new light on the losses, which the press was happy to regurgitate. The dollar figure had been adjusted to $35,000 and the *Daily Star* of September 8 reported that much of the loss was "old equipment and of little value ... and no mystery enshrouds the facts concerning the blaze."

Camp Borden's athletic teams frequently appeared in the sports pages. Its 1924-25 football squads showed well in practice games with the Toronto Argonauts, and shone in their own ORFU senior league, including against such fierce Toronto competition as Balmy Beach and Varsity. Team members included rising-star pilots N.R. Anderson, B.G. Carr-Harris, Dave Harding (captain), George K. Trim, W.D. Van Vliet and George E. Wait. An October 19, 1925 *Daily Star* report by Lou Marsh, himself a veteran, athlete and aviation fan, described some of the action in a Camp Borden win over Varsity: "Camp Borden won because they were steadiest everywhere. Harding and Carr-Harris caught almost faultlessly behind the line and both ran and dodged well... Good hard running and hard tackling by Van Vliet, Haynes, Cameron and Gibbs backed up Harding's punting ..." Marsh had fun tossing out nicknames for the airmen – the "Air Vaqueros", "Borden Burlies", "Boys from the Plains of Angus", "Bordonites", "Cloud Chasers" and "Sky Pilots", so who knows what the team's name was.

Eventually, there were rumours that Camp Borden might be phased out, due mainly to its remote location. To break the sense of isolation, station commanders would bring in guest speakers. In one case, Mr. H. Lawrence of Traveler's Insurance was flown from Camp Leaside to speak on March 19, 1921. Next day he reported: "... the men are hungry for visits from the city. Someone to talk to and listen to ... on subjects apart from their everyday occupations is a boon which they eagerly appreciate."

Besides isolation, nearly all Camp Borden's infrastructure was WWI era, and there were few amenities for families posted there. So, when news was heard that the Department of Militia and Defence was looking at property in Long Branch on the Lake Ontario shore, the press assumed that the Toronto suburb would replace Camp Borden. Meanwhile, Toronto's city fathers were agitating for a new airport. If built, they wanted the RCAF to consider relocating from Camp Borden. Nearby Whitby and Oshawa also were anxious to woo the RCAF, once they heard the rumours. (Begun in 1917, Camp Borden would endure. In 2010 it still was a key Canadian Forces training base.)

Camp Borden Album

The Avro 504K was the airplane that put postwar Camp Borden on the map. Here is a fine side view of C-CYFF, which served Camp Borden 1924-29. (RCAF RC1556)

Avro 504K G-CYFN was on RCAF strength from June 1924 to January 1931. (George F. Kimball/CANAV Col)

Avro 504s tucked away in one of Camp Borden's spacious WWI hangars. (RCAF RC544)

S/L Clifford M. McEwen, MC, DFC and Bar, gets ready for some winter flying on January 25, 1926. Uncomfortable would be the word to describe how he would be feeling for the next hour or so in the cold. McEwen typified officers in Canada's postwar years. Born in Griswold, Manitoba in 1897, he fought on the ground early in the war, then transferred to the RFC in April 1917. He then served on 28 Squadron, flying Camels over the Italian Front, where he scored 22 times. The citation to his DFC notes: "A skilful and fearless officer who in three weeks destroyed five enemy aeroplanes." He had a splendid interwar career, then (1944-45) commanded 6 Group (RCAF), RAF Bomber Command as A/V/M McEwen. (RCAF RC1418)

N7367 was one of 10 Sopwith Camels taken on RCAF strength in 1924-25. Based at Camp Borden, they were used by capable WWI veterans and advanced students to train in fighter tactics. The last RCAF Camel was SOS in July 1929 and all went for scrap. (George F. Kimball/CANAV Col.)

Students take turns during a class at Camp Borden teaching the dos and don'ts of swinging a propeller to start the engine. The aircraft is Avro 504K G-CYHC, which served at Camp Borden 1926-30. (RCAF RC1613)

P/P/O George Kimball of Winnipeg receives the Sword of Honour at the 1929 Wings Parade. At the same event he is seen with the brass: W/C Croil, AFC, (station commander), Kimball, S/L Brookes, S/L McEwen and F/O O'Brien-Saint. A WWI pilot who served in Mesopotamia, Croil was Chief of the Air Staff 1938-40, Brookes commanded No.6 Group (RCAF) RAF Bomber Command 1942-44, but O'Brien-Saint died early in a Toronto Flying Club accident. (George F. Kimball/CANAV Col, RC2159)

"Hungry Lizzie" is what the men at Camp Borden sometimes called their station ambulance. (All, George F. Kimball/CANAV Col.)

This ambulance snowmobile was a unique Camp Borden creation based on the gondola of a redundant Imperial Gift airship. Other photos show this machine on wheels.

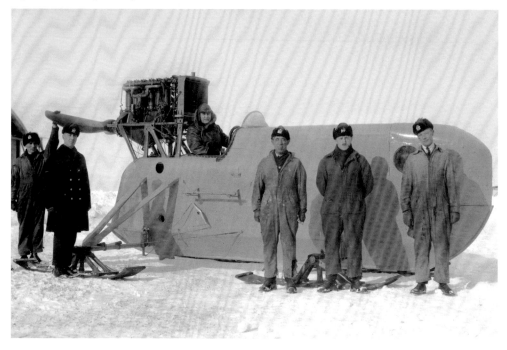

Camp Borden instructor *circa* 1927: F/O Pudney with a Lynx-powered Avro 504N.

Some of the airmen concocted this crazy "Spirit of Camp Borden" float for the annual Sports Day parade. They also came up with the skeleton-in-a-rickshaw skit. Maybe being so isolated at Camp Borden brought out the zany and macabre in a fellow.

Until post-WWII days, people travelled mainly by rail in commuting to or from Camp Borden. The busiest train station serving the base was Angus about 5 miles north. Essa, shown *circa* 1925, was about 12 miles east. Spur lines branched into Camp Borden from such centres, and there were road connections. "Essa" was emblazoned on the roof of the station to assist pilots needing help finding their way. (RCAF)

Being in a snow belt, Camp Borden struggled with winter operations (unprepared to handle this, the RFC Canada had packed up the whole operation and moved to Texas over the winter of 1917-18). This scene from the mid-1920s shows a usual setting, with the planes on skis. Then, a January 1926 scene with workers battling the effects of a blizzard. (RCAF RC546, RC1425)

For several years after WWI anyone wandering through the hangars at Camp Borden would come across some impressive planes. Several war prize Fokker D.VIIs were resident, before being piled up and burned – the station commander was fearful his pilots might try flying these, hurting themselves in the process. (CAF RC1277)

One of Camp Borden's S.E.5a fighters converted to a 2-seater. Oddball that it was, it survived on RCAF strength into 1926. (CF RE15534)

This nifty Thomas Morse Scout was purchased in some 1923 war surplus deal by C.S. Caldwell of Laurentide Air Service. A Hamilton resident, Robert Dodds, MC, later owned 'EH, but his friend P/O D.A. Harding, AFC, of Camp Borden, wrecked it at Beachville, Ontario on July 27, 1927. (George F. Kimball/ CANAV Col.)

The only Bristol Fighter in Canada's Imperial Gift became G-CYBC. Usually flying from Ottawa and Camp Borden, 'BC had a brief career. A fine machine in combat, it was unsuitable for civil duties, being almost impossible to fly in a smooth, straight line for the long missions required in Canada. It was SOS in February 1922. There had been a plan to mount 'BC on floats, but this idea was scrubbed. (CF RE13848)

Camp Borden had other roles besides training, e.g. airplanes imported to Canada might pass through to have customs paperwork finalized. This gave Camp Borden a chance to see some of the latest aviation products. Some R&D also took place, as with the eclipse of 1925, and development of the Turnbull controllable pitch propeller. Wallace R. Turnbull had been doing aeronautical research since 1902. In a small wind tunnel at his Rothesay, New Brunswick base he tested a multitude of airfoil shapes. In 1906 he brought the first purpose-built aero engine to Canada, using it to test propeller thrust and pitch. From 1916 he was developing the controllable pitch propeller. This was ground-tested on an Avro 504 at Camp Borden in 1923, then flown from there on June 6, 1927 by F/L G.E. Brookes. This view shows the pitch control apparatus. A small electric motor in the propeller hub powered the equipment. (George F. Kimball/CANAV Col)

Some of the great men of Camp Borden: G/C James S. Scott, MC, AFC, was a militiaman in Quebec in 1914 and went overseas with the artillery. He transferred to the RFC, serving in France with Nos.5 and 6 squadrons. Injured in an August 1916 crash, he was more than a year recovering, then got home. By war's end he commanded the training wing at Camp Borden. Postwar, he became Canada's first Controller of Civil Aviation, then commanded Camp Borden from July to September 1922. His career continued through WWII, when he rose to be an Air Commodore. Then, S/L Albert Earl Godfrey, MC, AFC, of Vancouver. Godfrey began in the Army, but transferred to the RFC in 1916. Trained as an observer, he served on Nos.10 and 25 squadrons, then flew Nieuports on 40 Squadron, finishing with 13 confirmed victories, then serving in the CAF (England). In the 1920s he made two landmark trans-Canada flights, including the famous 1926 flight with J. Dalzell McKee (the first across Canada using the same airplane). Godfrey commanded Camp Borden in May-June 1922. He served in WWII, rising to be an Air Vice Marshal. Third is A/V/M George M. Croil, pictured during WWII days. He had commanded Camp Borden from December 1927 to December 1932. (LAC PA64569, CF PL117416, CF RE13434)

Capt Roy S. Grandy and Maj R.A. Logan modelling the CAF uniform in 1920. Having flown Camels on 43 Squadron, Grandy became a renowned postwar instructor at Camp Borden, then left to become a bush pilot. He joined the RCAF in 1925, serving into WWII, including as station commander of Camp Borden. In 1920 Logan set up the Ground Instruction School at Camp Borden. In 1922 he accompanied a seaborne expedition to the Arctic, becoming the first Canadian air force representative in that region. His tasks there included weather observation and surveying for potential landing strips.(CF RE 13434)

Eclipse Excitement

January 24, 1925 was the date over Southern Ontario for a total solar eclipse. In preparation, the Toronto *Daily Star* requested RCAF support to observe and photograph the event. Ottawa and Camp Borden agreed and two Avro 504s were assigned. Crewing one were pilots F/L George E. Brooks and F/O A.M. Morfee (doubling as photographer). In the other were F/L R.S. Grandy and *Daily Star* photographer Fred G. Griffin. At 0800 W/C Lloyd Breadner, Camp Borden station commander, sent the planes off.

In his column, published later that day, Griffin wrote: "It was a cold, dreary and utterly depressing landscape from the air." The towns of Alliston and Cookstown passed below as Grandy bucked a 40-mph headwind. With their 180-hp Lynx engine, Brooks and Morfee easily passed Grandy and Griffin with their 130-hp Clerget. They surged ahead, then climbed into a wall of cloud, hoping to break out in time for some photography. Then, Grandy's engine began missing. Wrote Griffin in his later column, "After half an hour's flying we had the worst kind of engine trouble and were forced down in a small farm field near Newmarket. The connecting rod broke and smashed right through number seven cylinder, putting the engine clean out of commission in the air, and sending us down with a jagged tear in the steel cylinder." So it happened that it was from Edward Goodwin's farm that Grandy and Griffin would catch a bare a glimpse of the eclipse: "At last the eclipse, such as it came, a mere flash of darkness, quickly passed, for we were not even in the totality belt."

Later that morning F/O Dave Harding landed to pick up Griffin to get him back to Toronto. But the excitement was not yet over. Minutes after rising from the Goodwin farm, Harding's engine pooped out, and they were down again, this time on A.B. Morning's farm. Morfee, however, had been able to take a few photographs as the eclipse waned, shooting these after Brooks had battled to about 9000 feet, nearly all in cloud. Brooks then sped down for a landing on Toronto Bay, where the film was rushed to the *Daily Star*. Griffin finally appeared back at his desk to file his story, on which his editor spared no ink that afternoon.

Air Board HS-2L G-CYAH in an idyllic summer setting. This flying boat was the backbone of early Air Board operations, serving from Atlantic to Pacific, 'AH from 1920-24. One of the fellows on the left has his bellows camera ready for action. Wherever an HS-2L turned up, someone usually was around to photograph it, much as camera phones cover today's candid scene. (CANAV Col.)

Far Flung Operations

An important step that strengthened aviation in Canada occurred on June 28, 1922 when the National Defence Act was passed by Parliament. This amalgamated the Department of Naval Service, the Department of Militia and Defence and the Air Board. At year's end the Air Board flying stations were handed over to the CAF. A new type of operation that year was a series of 21 flights in Northern Manitoba on behalf of the Department of Indian Affairs. CAF crews using HS-2Ls transported an Indian agent, whose job was to distribute annual treaty money to remote settlements. On some missions a doctor also was along. Assisted by the plane's crew, his job was to deliver some basic health care mainly in the form of vaccinations. Treaty flights now replaced the usual annual visitations whereby agents and doctors had spent months travelling by canoe to northern settlements. These airborne trips introduced the native people to the airplane and were much anticipated each year. CAF crews were warmly welcomed and sometimes received honourary titles. One pilot, A.D. Ross, received from one native band the title "Chief of the Flying Gasoline Canoe".

Another lovely aviation scene, this one featuring HS-2L G-CYDS in a secluded spot among the lily pads. This fine-looking machine had a short Air Board career. Taken on strength on July 18, 1921, it burned on August 8. (CANAV Col.)

Aerial Photography

One function especially promoted by the Canadian Air Board was aerial photography. The technology was available – WWI combat planes and cameras adapted for peacetime use. Previously used to photograph enemy trenches, artillery, troop concentrations, supply depots, canals, harbours, etc., now they could be used on such projects as map-making and watershed surveys. To facilitate this, Ottawa established the Aerial Surveys Division of the Department of the Interior. By 1920 wartime veterans on refresher courses at Camp Borden were brushing up on their aerial photography techniques, and the Air Board was experimenting from Atlantic to Pacific. On one project, a plane assisted the Geological Survey of Canada by taking photos along a disputed section of the Canada - US boundary between New Brunswick and Maine. That year some 91.5 hours were flown on photographic trials and 1233 aerial photos were catalogued; and newly available cameras and lenses were evaluated. One of the chief conclusions from the 1920 season was that vast areas could be surveyed by air in hours, compared to weeks or months by land and water.

That season the five HS-2L and F.3 flying boats at Jericho Beach, near Vancouver, alone made 176 flights on various duties, logging 304 flying hours, much on it doing photography. Other photo planes were the Avro 504, Bristol Fighter and D.H.4, although none was ideal. For flying boats, the camera

Air Board Vickers Viking G-CYET at Victoria Beach air station on Lake Winnipeg in 1924. Photographic officer P/O J.R. Cairns is in the nose chatting with pilot F/O L.R. Charron. This year RCAF Station Winnipeg, with bases at Victoria Beach and Norway House, was Canada's largest civil government operations base. Commanded by S/L Basil D. Hobbs, staff included 6 pilots, a photographic and an equipment officer and 47 airmen. The base was assigned 6 of the RCAF's 8 Vikings. The flying season (June 3 to October 10) entailed 1183 flying hours, 85% being on forestry duties. (A.J. Milne Col.)

operator occupied the nose cockpit, exposed to the miseries of cold and rain. The Avro 504 had a low service ceiling, while the Bristol Fighter was so sensitive on the controls, that a pilot had trouble keeping it straight and level. In no type was voice communications practical between camera operator and pilot.

CAF photo missions included ones over the mountains of BC and Alberta. This highly-detailed view is labelled "Kananaskis Ranges". (CANAV Col.)

A standard RCAF oblique photo showing the RCAF sub-base on Forestry Island at Norway House. A Viking and an Avro are at their buoys. Then, Forestry Island in a 2010 view. (CANAV Col., Dr. Shirley Hiebert)

Jericho Beach CGAO aircraft in 1928. First is HS-2L G-CYGA (on strength from October 1924 to July 1928). Then, a pair of Avro 504N floatplanes. Both served on forestry and fisheries duties, but could do customs missions, photography and general transportation. HS-2Ls also were much used here to train flying boat pilots. (LAC PA133584, PA112047)

Airman Eric Fry assures that the big Fairchild K-3 camera on a Victoria Beach Viking is ready for service. Then, a head-on view of a Fairchild mounted on an HS-2L. (A.J. Milne Col., LAC PA62897)

Over 1921-22 the Air Board initiated many projects, from relocating its aerodrome at Morley to High River, Alberta, to opening a new station at Victoria Beach on lower Lake Winnipeg and one at Sioux Lookout. A 1921 survey of London, Ontario covered 42 sq.mi. and used 25 rolls of 100-foot film. Combined with the work of ground survey parties, the aerial photos eventually resulted in a detailed urban land use map of the city. In July and August some 36 flying hours were logged doing photography along the Lake Ontario-St. Lawrence River waterway between Kingston and Montreal. The Ottawa-based crew of Capt H.L. Holland and E.R. Owen conducted this operation, using a D.H.4 and HS-2L. The results greatly impressed members of the International Joint Commission, studying the potential of opening the Great Lakes to deep sea shipping. (On April 23, 1922 Holland died and photographer Owen was injured, while en route to take photos

One of the Imperial Gift Bessoneau hangars used at such stations as Victoria Beach, Morley and Jericho Beach. These buildings comprised sturdy wooden frames clad in heavy canvas, but they proved unsuitable in Canadian conditions. Notice the mobile workshop and crawler tractor in this view at Victoria Beach from September 1921. (CANAV Col.)

High River air station with its Bessoneau hangars. Then, four High River types getting ready to "crack the whip" to get an Avro 552A "Viper" started. (Glenbow Museum 1170-3, 2097-17)

A High River Avro 552A with salvage team, perhaps after a forced landing away from base. (Glenbow Museum 2097-23)

Unloading a Roberval-based HS-2L in northern Quebec. (CF RE19518)

over London, in order to fill in a few gaps from the previous year's work.)

HS-2L forest survey flying from Roberval in Northern Quebec brought only marginal results in 1921, due to poor weather and persistent forest fire smoke. Better results were obtained by a Sioux Lookout detachment. In both cases, the respective provincial governments helped finance the operations. Sioux Lookout was able to process film in a railway boxcar converted as a photo lab. The F.3s and HS-2Ls at Victoria Beach spent 1921 doing experimental forest fire spotting and suppression flights. However, on one mission Maj B.D. Hobbs took along on a patrol a Manitoba natural resources officer, who later concluded: "I have had considerable experience in mapping territory from the canoe and feel satisfied and more than ever impressed ... that the only way in which northern territory can

be mapped is by the camera from the air." Overall that year, Victoria beach made 103 flights and logged 184 flying hours.

High River also was mainly concerned with forest fires. Two patrols were flown daily and, in one case, radio-equipped D.H.4s were able to help in controlling a major outbreak by regularly radioing information about the fire. This is thought to be a "first" in forest fire control. Photographic flights were made over the Jasper area, where a national park was being developed. Those photos assisted the project, e.g. in planning trails.

Jericho Beach at Vancouver was the Air Board's busiest station in 1921, with duties undertaken on behalf of several Ottawa bureaus. During fisheries, immigration and anti-smuggling flights, suspicious vessels were photographed and sometimes inspected, for the

patrolling aircraft often could land at the scene. Another BC contract involved photographing mosquito breeding areas in interior BC, in an effort by the Department of the Interior to control infestations. Photography over BC that year greatly aided ground teams from the Geodetic Survey Branch of the same department. By season's end it was clear that aerial photography had a vital role to play in the postwar development of Canada.

Air operations continued routinely in subsequent years. In 1922, for example, Jericho Beach with its barebones 20 personnel successfully completed many tasks. Its five flying boats made 176 flights, logging 304 hours. Prominent were forestry patrols and missions supporting forest fire suppression teams. RCAF historian W/C Hitchins outlined some of the other 1922 activity from this base:

Preventive patrols for the suppression of smuggling were continued, 27 flights being made ... and about the same amount of flying was done for the Department of Agriculture in an investigation if white pine blister rust ... The Air Board was asked to assist in the work and E.L. MacLeod and A.T.N. Cowley, two of the station's pilots, made reconnaissance flights totalling 61 hours, to carry members of the field party and three American scientists to infected areas ...

The use of aircraft in the Geodetic Survey's triangulation work, which had started at Vancouver the previous year, was continued in 1922. Eight flights (21 hours) were made between 7 June and 8 July to transport a party engaged in the preparation of primary geodetic stations along the Fraser River valley... Extremely poor flying weather and the limited visibility due to smoke from forest fires greatly restricted photographic work until late in August.

Tragedy struck at Jericho Beach on September 11, 1922, when Maj MacLaurin lost his life in a crash. A Canadian Press dispatch describes what happened:

Major C. MacLaurin, officer in charge of the Dominion Government air station here, was drowned today when a seaplane which he was piloting plunged into shallow water on the Point Grey

Air Board Bases and Results for 1921

Base	Commander	Aircraft	Flights	Hrs Flown
Dartmouth	S/L A.B. Shearer	HS-2L	25	41
Roberval	F/L W.R. Kenny	HS-2L	102	178
Rockcliffe	Maj H.L. Holland	HS-2L	145	270
		D.H.4		
		Bristol Fighter		
Sioux Lookout*	F/L A.W. Carter	HS-2L	188	329
Victoria Beach	Maj B.D. Hobbs	HS-2L	103	184
		F.3		
High River	Maj G.M. Croil	D.H.4	284	710
Jericho Beach	Maj C.C. MacLaurin	HS-2L	362	488
		F.3		

* Ontario detachments at Haileybury, Whitney House, Parry Sound

Avro 504K G-CYDA and HS-2L G-CYDT of the 1922 Northern Ontario detachment. Then, detachment commander C.M. McEwen (right) having a break with a survey crew. It seems that ties were de rigueur in the bush. This season McEwen's 4-plane detachment made 299 flights for 616 hours, mainly patrolling for fires in Algonquin Park (84 were spotted). At season's end, McEwen became superintendent at Rockcliffe air station (Ottawa), replacing H.L. Holland, killed in a D.H.4 crash. (1st two G.R. Hutt, CF RE15414)

shore of English Bay this afternoon. John R. Duncan of the Duncan Iron Works here, a passenger, suffered a broken leg ... while A.L. Hartridge, mechanician, was injured about the back... The plane had left the Jericho station bound for Sumas, where Mr. Duncan intended to inspect the progress being made in the reclamation work there... The craft ran into the beach, where there was about four feet of water, and turned over.

Activity in Ontario between May and October 1922 involved forestry patrols contracted by the Ontario government. Two HS-2Ls and two Avro 504s on floats were used. Based at Whitney House and Parry Sound, these were under the command of F/L C.M. McEwen, MC, DFC. The detachment enjoyed 127 good weather days, logging 299 flights for 616 hours; 84 forest fires were reported. Meanwhile, Roberval was busy on a Quebec government forest survey centred 100 miles to the north. Three HS-2Ls were used, one being dedicated to hauling supplies and fuel to the northern base camp. Quebec foresters rode along on many flights, sketching stands of trees for later mapping purposes. As well, some 2300 aerial photos were taken. Roberval also provide an HS-2L in August for forest surveying in the Quebec North Shore region as far downriver as Natashquan. On September 21 this aircraft sank while attempting to take off to return to home base. Happily, the crew escaped.

The Arctic: S/L Logan's Report

In 1922 Ottawa sent an expedition into the distant north aboard the vessel *Arctic*. Included among the crew was S/L A. Logan, whose task was to report on the Arctic's aviation potential. Returned to his desk at RCAF HQ, he produced a summary of what he had learned and what he envisioned for the airplane in this seemingly forbidding land. Logan's report – "Aviation in the Arctic Archipelago" – focused mainly upon natural resources and sovereignty, and foresaw the airplane being pivotal in developing both:

In such a widespread territory it is possible that untold wealth may be lying dormant, awaiting only discovery and development to make this one of the most prosperous countries in the world, but before we have development we must first find out what we have to develop.

Logan recommended that the "development and conservation" of the Arctic's natural resources be hastened by pairing the airplane and wireless radio. He also envisioned a time when Russia might be Canada's enemy, so urged some prudence – Canada should consider developing Arctic air defences lest Russia ever attack from the air over the pole. Being practical, however, Logan realized that Canada would not soon be investing in Arctic aerial defence, but urged that the first steps be taken to get to know the Arctic flying environment and that Ottawa at least should support civil government air operations in the region (Logan's "wild conjecture" about Russia would come to be a generation later as the Cold War).

Logan described Canada's Arctic Archipelago vaguely – he had few precise facts. He estimated that the region totalled about one fifth of the Canadian landmass – some 600,000 sq.mi. all ceded by Great Britain to Canada in 1880. From 1903-1911 Ottawa had sent four sovereignty expeditions into parts of the region to over-winter and (as Logan wrote) "take formal possession by raising the British and Canadian flags and by depositing copies of the proclamation in cairns erected at various points."

In preparation for his voyage aboard the *Arctic*, Logan had studied existing Arctic literature. He probably had a copy

Summer tents at Pond Inlet during the 1903-04 Canadian government Arctic expedition aboard the vessel *Neptune*. ("Cruise of the Neptune")

of the Canadian Government Printing Bureau's 1906 *Report on the Dominion Government Expedition to Hudson Bay and the Arctic Islands on Board the D.G.S. Neptune 1903-1904.* Other reliable publications existed, including by the Norwegian, Otto Sverdrup, who recently had spent four seasons exploring Ellesmere Island. There also was Knud Rasmussen's 1921 *Greenland by the Polar Sea: The Story of the Thule Expedition from Melville Bay to Cape Morris Jesup.*

The chief goal in 1922 was to establish far northern RCMP posts. These would confirm possession "by occupation of several of the islands in the eastern frontier of the Archipelago". For his part S/L Logan, representing the Air Board, would make general aviation observations and recommend sites for air operations. Even in 1922 something as

basic as the extent of Baffin Island was controversial. Logan knew only that it was roughly 1000 miles by 500 miles, and that its highest point was about 5000 feet. He reported that: "The charts have been generally compiled from notes and records of explorers who were endeavouring to find a passage to Asia, and who had no interest whatever in the interior of the country... Only the high hills of the interior have been observed and the interior of the islands may be entirely different from ... the seacoast."

The coast-dwelling Eskimos and traders (Hudson's Bay Co. and Sabellum Trading Co. operating from Pond Inlet to the south shore of Baffin Island) were unfamiliar with the interior. Recent expeditions had added little to mapping, soundings or a knowledge of geography, geology, or flora and fauna since expeditions were so hard-pressed by the

The coastline seen from a First Air HS748 nearing Pond Inlet on August 1, 1992. The government steamer *Arctic* would have sailed by this very stretch. No doubt S/L R.A. Logan was observing from the rail. (Larry Milberry)

brief sailing season. Always worried about freeze-up, ship masters were loath to dillydally on behalf of science people who might be aboard. Often, scientists could do little more than observe using binoculars, or quickly gather reports from local people. In one case, Logan heard of two large lakes in southwestern Baffin Island which he recorded as "Nettilling and Amadjuak".

The presence of coal and oil shale in the Canadian archipelago interested S/L Logan. He noted that some coal was of decent quality and that oil shale deposits had been noted as containing as much as 140 gallons to the ton: "This might sometime be developed and in time would supply all the fuel required for aircraft and motor transport in the North ..." He alluded to indications for copper and gold, and looked forward to the day when airplanes might carry prospectors throughout the region – Logan certainly was on the ball. Other commentary was wide-ranging:

Topographical and Geological surveyors may be transported to other-wise inaccessible places ... where their season of operations may be greatly extended by the reduction of time required for travelling ... The extent of grazing grounds capable of supporting animal life, such as musk-oxen, caribou and reindeer, may be found ... When the reindeer or musk-ox industry is in operation, it is probable that the greater part of the herding and range patrols will be done by aeroplanes ... It is certain that aircraft can be of great assistance in

connection with Mounted Police work ... it would be advisable to make a reconnaissance to locate the best place possible for a combined headquarters for Mounted Police and Air Force and a base of operations for Topographical and Geological surveyors...

Logan suggested that aircraft in the Arctic would deter crime as well as foreign interlopers. Survey parties could be transported and supplied and aerial photography would assist in compiling local maps and "in obtaining a practical knowledge of the ice movements upon which navigation depends so much ..." and added:

When regular navigation is established through the Hudson Strait, it will be necessary to have one or more detachments of aircraft to watch the ice and report positions to the ships ... Ships will not require to waste time trying to get into harbours which are not clear of ice, and advantage will be taken to call at open ports first, while through traffic will be able to follow the open water. Once the relation between weather conditions, tide and general ice move-ments is determined, and forecasts completed by utilizing aircraft and wireless, navigation through the Hudson Strait will lose much of its hardship and danger.

Logan thought that ski planes could operate safely along coastal Baffin Island between freeze-up in September and break-up in July. He found that some

areas were excellent well into summer, as on the Ellesmere Island ice cap at 3000 feet: "The surface was swept smooth by the wind and covered with a fairly heavy crust in most places..." He reported that there were beaches on the east coast suitable for wheel planes, but warned that sea ice often was rough due to tidal action.

Naturally, Logan also had airship operations in mind, this being the era of these long-range, heavy-lifting vessels. "In many ways," he wrote, "the Arctic is an ideal country for lighter-than-air craft," especially since there was a narrow range of diurnal temperature and round-the-clock daylight for extended operations. Logan discussed the likelihood in the coming years of globe-encircling commercial airship routes (these were a reality a decade later). He was aware that, by following the great circle route across the Arctic, 3000 miles could be saved between Europe and Japan. Airship service centres in Canada's Arctic seemed almost inevitable to Logan. However, winter possibilities for any kind of flying worried Logan, e.g., he noted that at Pond Inlet total darkness existed from November 9 to February 3.

In discussing potential airfields, Logan, having learned about the frequency of coastal fogs, recommended no strip being built nearer than 15 miles from the coast. The head of a long inlet was his preferred site, as such locations usually were fog free and had a wide, open natural area. He recommended using aircraft easily convertible between

Today's airport at Pond Inlet sits about where S/L Logan envisioned it in 1922. Suitable land was at a premium and he selected the best likely spot. Pond Inlet is a busy airport. Here a Summit Air Skyvan is readied for a supply flight to Mary River Mine, while a First Air ATR-42 awaits departure. (Larry Milberry)

S/L Logan had little idea about what lay south of Pond Inlet. Just a few miles inland, this is the scene – wild country criss-crossed by massive glaciers. (Larry Milberry)

wheels and skis. Flying boats would not do on account of the brief open water season, and a flying boat's susceptibility to damage by ice. For flights more than 20 miles, Logan insisted that two aircraft be used, lest one encounter trouble. He listed the essentials in the survival kit to be carried by each plane: sleeping bags, a week's rations, small silk tent, gas cooking stove, rifle with 300 rounds, snow knives, ice chisel, snow goggles and ice anchors, then added: "One Eskimo should always be carried ... [he] can find food and direction where a white man would be lost, starved or frozen to death."

Logan suggested using a radial-engine plane having a 1000-lb payload, but preferred a twin-engine type, specifying the Vickers Vimy. Such a plane would allow photography straight ahead from the nose cockpit. Quite naively, however, he thought that a Vimy down on the ice could taxi a great distance to safety. As to a single-engine plane, Logan preferred a tractor-type, but was not averse to such a pusher as the F.E.2D, which he envisioned for photographic work. He assumed that this type was readily available in the UK (nearly all had been scrapped by this time). He also wrongly

assumed that re-engining something like an F.E.2D, and adapting it to skis, would pose no problems ("a proper engine could probably be installed with a few alterations"). Logan discussed the pros and cons of water-cooled and air-cooled engines and recommended the Mercedes aero engine series, but also suggested that several engines might be ground-tested in the Arctic to study their characteristics.

Logan covered the important topic of aircraft hangars, urging special design features. Quarters, workshops and sheds should be prefabricated in the south using of the best materials. They should have double or triple walls for insulation, anterooms at entrances, etc. Such buildings ought not require special skill in assembly. Supplies should be stored in widely separated tents and buildings, to guard against fire. Fuel should be kept away from structures. He understood the logistics of aviation fuel, especially should twin-engine planes be used. He wrongly assumed that local coal would be available for heating (on Baffin Island the only mineable coal was near Pond Inlet). For motor transport, Logan recommended ski-equipped Ford auto- mobiles and caterpillar tractors. He suggested that information be obtained

about such equipment as used in Alaska and in the recent North Russia campaign. In all his analysis, Logan often repeated how only first-hand experience would answer the mysteries about Arctic air operations.

The *Arctic* met its expectations during the 1922 expedition. S/L Logan, however, described it as too small and slow between Quebec and Pond Inlet if it were to supply air stations along with its regular work. He was thinking ahead when recommending that Ottawa some day acquire a ship especially to support Arctic aviation. This vessel would carry a small floatplane "for scouting purposes", or perhaps use a manned, tethered balloon for making ice, navigation and weather observations. He recommended Dundas Harbour on the south coast of Devon Island as a sea-supply base.

S/L Logan also dealt in his report with the manpower issue, noting: "The success or failure depends on the type of individual, and the greatest care must be taken in choosing men of the proper character, as well as those having the proper technical qualifications ... physically, mentally and temperamen- tally... Pilots and mechanics should ... have as many other technical qualifications as possible in order that the number of persons actually require ... will be as low as possible." Men selected should have no aversion to heavy manual labor, coal mining included. A candidate should be ready to spend a 2-year tour in the Arctic, and Logan recommended that a pay rate regardless of rank should be $6 daily per man.

Any Arctic RCAF base, proposed Logan, should have four aircraft – two in constant readiness, two in reserve. Each base should have three pilots and have two mechanics per plane. Other requirements were having two photographers, two wireless operators and a doctor. Photographers should have a well-equipped lab. Vertical and still photography and movie making should be done. Wireless equipment would connect stations with points to the south, with other Arctic bases, and with aircraft on patrol. A well-equipped weather station was essential, Logan especially touting the need to understand upper level winds ("It is often possible to gain much time by taking advantage of ... winds at various heights, as a round trip journey between two points may sometimes be made with a favourable wind in both directions by flying at two different heights."). Logan warned that the magnetic compass would be useless in the Arctic. Celestial navigation, he urged, should be used, along with the latest in navigation instruments, including the gyroscopic compass and artificial horizon: "It will also be necessary ... to land fairly frequently and take astronomical observations for the accurate determination of positions of prominent objects on the earth's surface. Many observations will have to be taken to determine the magnetic variation throughout the whole territory ... All existing charts will have to be revised as far as magnetic variation is concerned." Logan proposed using oblique photography to gradually build up detailed topographic maps.

Logan urged that great care be taken in supplying the proper diet and clothing. He foresaw a bountiful supply of local foods: fish, caribou, seal, fish, then noted: "The clothing worn by all aircraft personnel should be as much as possible similar in every way to that worn by the natives of the islands ... The usual clothing worn ... consists of two suits of fur garments, the inner one worn with the fur inside and the outer one worn with the fur outside ... seal skin boots are absolutely necessary... It will be necessary to employ at least one Eskimo woman at each base for ... looking after the repairs of boots and other garments. For recreation, Logan suggested that each base have a small library, games, gramaphone, musical instruments, writing supplies, etc.

Logan had much to say about the native people of Baffin Island, then generally called Eskimos. He recommended that their language be standardized by using the Greenlandic model of written syllabics. This, as per the Denmark-Greenland system, should be supervised by Ottawa, as should education and family resettlement. However, Logan recommended that the imposition of the Whiteman's ways be avoided and that trading posts be strictly managed to avoid corrupting native culture.

S/L Logan surveyed Craig Harbour, site the new RCMP station on the southeast shore of Ellesmere Island, for its airstrip possibilities. These were found to be marginal. The shallow depth of the fjord combined with a tide estimated at 9.5 feet would make for rough winter ice; while the best clearing near the shore was found to be 600 x 200 yards, but not ideal for air operations. Compared to Craig Harbour, Logan found Dundas Harbour on the south coast of Devon Island a better aviation prospect. The water was deep and there was a flat area at the head of the bay where landplanes could operate. The likelihood of fog from adjacent Lancaster Sound might limit operations. S/L Logan made a detailed study of the area then known as Pond's Inlet at the top of Baffin Island. Here he found a small Eskimo settlement, an HBC post and a trading post operated by the Arctic Gold Exploration Co. He carefully studied the area, finding part of it suitable for landplanes, so posted the following notice on a stake:

Modern day Lake Harbour, one of the sites recommended by S/L Logan for a potential RCAF base. Then, a Twin Otter on one of the daily sked flights to Lake Harbour (since renamed Kimmurut). The gravel runway here (R17-35) is 1900' x 75'. A 2010 Transport Canada advisory was that this airport should be used only by experienced

From the line bearing 340° true from this point to the intersection of the shore, thence easterly along the shore thirty chains, or 1980 feet, the land inland to a depth of one mile is liable for reservation for military and aviation purposes.

A similar notice was staked at a point considered the back line of the HBC and RCMP lots:

All the land for a distance of 1320 feet westerly along the shore from the line with a true bearing of 105°, from and passing through this point, and inland to a distance of one-half mile, is liable to reservation for military and aviation purposes... While no instructions from Ottawa had been given for any such monuments to be placed here, they were placed by a duly qualified Dominion Land Surveyor, and if it is desired to use them to designate the boundaries of the Government Reserve, such can be done without irregularity.

In his summary S/L Logan recommended that a future RCAF Arctic air establishment include 4 single-engine, 4 twin-engine and 2 small scout planes with the supplies and support equipment that he earlier had described. He estimated an annual cost per air station of $200,000 to be borne by the RCAF, but offset by contributions from other departments involved. He suggested that a year be dedicated to selecting the best sites, with qualified officers sent to reside with the RCMP or HBC at Pond's Inlet, South Ellesmere Island and Lake Harbour. He discussed the cost of such work (about $60,000 for one year), adding: "A few thousand dollars spent in preliminary work might result in the saving of many thousands of dollars, when regular air operations are inaugurated ..." He was much in favour of sending an RCAF air detachment to Pond's Inlet to evaluate flying, photographic, wireless and meteorological operations the following summer. adding: "It will be imperative ... to communicate with the natives of the country ... and during one year's sojourn amongst the Eskimos a sufficient knowledge should be gained to be of great assistance to those ... who come after." Initially, Logan thought that a small plane would be best to begin evaluation. In summary, he was enthus-

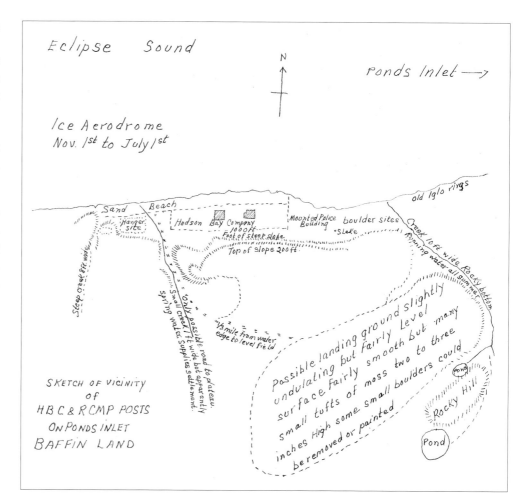

The rough map made by S/L Logan showing the "lay of the land" at Pond's Inlet and one potential landing field. Logan noted that "The length of runway on this level area would be probably three hundred yards in most directions, with very good approaches." (Logan Col.)

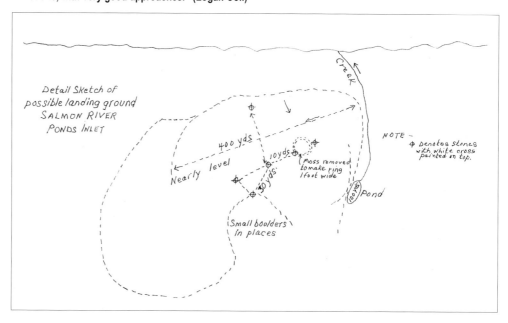

iastic about a 1923 mission to Pond's Inlet, even if no urgent need arose for Arctic air operations for another 20 years. To him the experience would be invaluable:

If there were a sudden emergency requiring aircraft to be operated on a fairly large scale, such as certainly would arise in the event of a big mineral or oil strike, and there had been no such preliminary investigation of actual flying

conditions, much time and money would in all probability be lost in trying to carry on service operations under practically unknown conditions..."

In summarizing the 1922 expedition, the Air Board concluded that there was no reason to doubt that "when the need arises, with special machines and precautions, aircraft cannot be operated to advantage in the Arctic".

Birth of the RCAF

On February 15, 1923 King George V approved the creation of the Royal Canadian Air Force, the official birthday of which was delayed by administrative requirements until April 1, 1924. In early 1923 S/L Croil of High River was petitioning Ottawa regarding some fundamental issues – living conditions and the need for some basic airfield maintenance:

Rentals, in this town, for houses of any description at all, range from $20.00 to $35.00 per month for married personnel. Board and rooms range from $40.00 per month and up for single personnel. When fuel and light are added, in the case of married personnel ... it is estimated that to married men the loss due to inadequate recompense in lieu of accommodation to which they are entitled is equivalent to approximately $50.00 per month; and in the case of single men to approximately $15.00 per month... Authority requested to expend $90 for purpose of sowing 40 acres land sub station Pincher Creek with timothy seed. At present stubble only on land. Urgently required for proper landing surface and to keep down weeds. Also authority to expend $10 for removal of weeds High River aerodrome accordance with lease.

The RCAF now had control over civil government flying. A notable 1924 CGAO task was a survey using one of the RCAF's new Vickers Vikings. The plan was to conduct a photo survey of 15,000 sq.mi of the Reindeer Lake - Churchill River area. The expedition had been planned through the previous year, including the caching of fuel, freighted north by canoe in 4-gallon cans. A new Fairchild aerial camera, equipped with a film advance mechanism, was purchased, along with film magazines and 25 rolls of film each 100 feet long.

To carry its crew and payload, the Viking was stripped of excess weight, especially its 200-lb undercarriage. The weight and balance inventory included: crew – 720 lb, survival gear – 212 lb, fuel – 840 lb. In all, 2063 lb was loaded into the plane, for an all-up weight of 5863 lb. Such care to detail was necessary as the Viking had long distances to fly and was a marginal performer at best. Takeoff

These two well-used photos are mandatory in any history of the 1924 Reindeer Lake expedition. First, the crew with all the kit they squeezed into their shiny new Vickers Viking: F/O J.R. "Jimmy" Cairns, Mr. R.D. Davidson (DLS), S/L Basil D. Hobbs and Cpl A.J. "Alex" Milne. Then, the fellows in a fine set-up shot: Milne, Hobbs, Davidson, Cairns. (A.J. Milne Col., LAC PA53239)

alone could use up 3 or 4 miles of water, while the climb to the ideal photo altitude of 5000 feet took an hour.

On July 18, 1924 the Viking departed Victoria Beach on its summer assignment. It reached The Pas later that day, having covered 325 miles in about 4 hours. Photography began next day and over the next two weeks 2000 line miles were flown over 49 flying hours. The cameraman, F/O J.R. "Jimmy" Cairns, rode in the nose cockpit, lashed in lest a sudden bump toss him overboard. Cairns changed his film magazines on the fly,

doing this inside an eiderdown that doubled at night as a sleeping bag. He and mechanic Alex Milne maintained the camera, even doing detailed teardowns.

Cairns would make some 1800 exposures during this operation. The expedition returned to base after 25 days. The film was shipped to Ottawa for processing and became the basis for turning out the first detailed map of this vast area. Detachment commander S/L Basil D. Hobbs, DSO, DSC and Bar, reported on the season's work, noting such daily challenges as operating in

A classic "bushing flying" scene with Hobb's Viking 'ET on a July 1924 stop at Rabbit River, Saskatchewan. The crew are transferring gas from a 45-gallon drum into manageable 5-gallon cans, so that they can refuel. On July 11, 1927 'ET disintegrated in flight near Hilbre, Manitoba, with the loss of P/O W.C. Weaver, AC1 J.T. Eardley and Mr. F.H. Wrong (DLS). W/C E.W. Stedman conducted an investigation which uncovered a grave Viking weakness. This was rectified by adding strengthening planks, but too late for 'ET. (LAC PA53286)

unfamiliar waters, getting to cruise height as quickly and early in the day as possible, keeping the sun at their backs, and making the most of cloudless conditions. After listing the chief difficulties of the trip he concluded:

"That these and many other adverse conditions were overcome ... gives assurance that even longer journeys can be planned with every prospect of success."

In 1924 another stellar performance was delivered by Jericho Beach, now commanded by S/L A.E. Godfrey, MC, AFC. From Vancouver, Godfrey had served in the army early in WWI, but transferred to the RFC in August 1916.

RCAF pigeoneers load a pigeon for a September 1931 mission from Rockcliffe. Pigeons long since had proven their worth as life savers, as in the case of Robert Leckie and crew lost at sea in September 1917 (see *Aviation in Canada: The Pioneer Decades*). Then, a typical message delivered by pigeon courier, this being from P/O D.F. MacDonald. (LAC PA62838, PA204856)

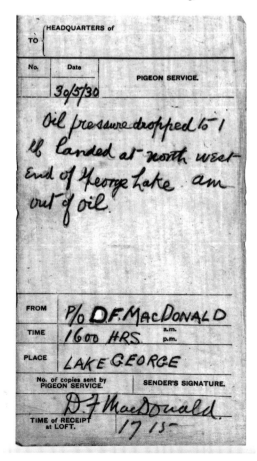

HEADQUARTERS of
TO

PIGEON SERVICE.

30/5/30

Oil pressure dropped to 1 lb landed at north west end of George Lake am out of oil.

FROM P/O D.F. MacDonald
TIME 1600 HRS a.m. / p.m.
PLACE LAKE GEORGE

No. of copies sent by PIGEON SERVICE. SENDER'S SIGNATURE.

D.F. MacDonald

TIME of RECEIPT at LOFT. 17 15

He flew as an observer, then a pilot on Nieuports and Camels. He later served in the RAF (Canada) and flew the D.H.9 on 2 Squadron, CAF (England). Under Godfrey were two other pilots, a photographic officer, an equipment officer and 21 airmen. Godfrey's aircraft were one of the new Vikings and two veteran HS-2Ls (he also had a loft with 36 pigeons). The chief duties this year were fisheries patrols, for which the radio-equipped HS-2Ls were based at Prince Rupert. Most patrols were flown on weekends, when the fisheries were closed. Meanwhile, Dartmouth, a small base at the other end of the country, concentrated on photography. Using its lone HS-2L, Dartmouth, commanded by S/L J.H. Tudhope, flew 61 hours photographing over Nova Scotia. At season's end, the station was mothballed until the following spring.

For its fiscal year 1925 the RCAF logged 5111 hours about equally split between civil and military duties, forestry patrols, aerial surveying, treaty and mercy flights, and army co-operation being flown. In Alberta alone some 86,000 sq.mi. of mostly remote country were photographed by the High River D.H.4s, the largest area being 4350 sq.mi. around Edmonton that was photographed vertically from 12,000 ft. Writing of the efforts of the Victoria Beach base for 1925, W/C F.H. Hitchins wrote:

The value of aerial photography for the revision of maps was strikingly demonstrated when a new complete map was published of the mineral area lying on either side of the Manitoba - Ontario boundary. Previous maps of the area were largely blank and marked "unexplored". Following publication of the new map, prospectors were able to travel with certainty through the district, and important mineral discoveries were made at Red Lake and other points. Timber types were marked on the map which was of great value to foresters also.

Special Victoria Beach duties in 1925 included transporting a provincial health official to inspect sanitary conditions in some remote Manitoba mining camps; and several medical air evacuations of injured workers. A gravely ill woman was flown from Island Lake to Winnipeg for hospital care. The first Canadian Vickers Vedette flying boat was taken on strength this year, and the twin-engine Canadian Vickers Varuna was being evaluated. By this time each air station had a forestry patrol plane (usually an Avro Viper on floats) and an HS-2L fire suppression plane to transport rangers and gear – pumps, hose, shovels, axes, grub, collapsible canoes, etc. Experimental work also was on people's minds: On August 31, 1925 S/L A.A.L. Cuffe wrote to W/C J.S. Scott about plans to conduct some cold weather trials:

Regarding winter flying experiments, I do not consider that High River is the most suitable place for this, in view of the fact that weather conditions here are most erratic; we may have snow for a few days which will be removed suddenly by a chinook wind, and there may be no snow again for ... weeks. The same is applicable to erratic temperature conditions. I personally think that Camp Borden, Winnipeg or Ottawa weather would be more suitable for experimentation along the lines proposed, as weather conditions at these points are not so variable as they are

High River-based **D.H.4s** *circa* 1922. 'DM had a lengthy Canadian career – 1921-28. This type proved suitable in foothills country, being able to climb to 10,000 feet. (Eric Billingham Col.)

Varuna G-CYZR and Viking 'EX at Cormorant Lake over the 1927 summer season. These were Manitoba's chief forestry types in this period. Then, an RCAF Avro 552A forestry patrol plane, 14 of which were acquired beginning in 1924. With a 200-hp Wolseley Viper, a 552A was powerful enough for High River operations, and also had good performance on the water. Here, G-CYGC is being readied for operations. Once fuelled it carried 25 gallons in each of two underwing tanks. The last RCAF "552" retired in September 1929. (RCAF TS11197, CF PMR72-443)

This also was the year the RCAF began training pilots in parachuting, F/O Albert Carter, MM, and Cpl A. Anderson, having taken a parachute course with the US Army, taught practical courses at Jericho Beach, High River and Camp Borden, qualifying 16 air and ground crew. According to a memo from G/C J.S. Scott in Ottawa, the purpose of these courses was to qualify at least one man at each air station "who is capable of supervising minor repairs to parachutes and to carry out the monthly inspection, folding and re-packing." From April 1925 it was mandatory that RCAF aircraft carry parachutes. A handful of RCAF officers was abroad in the UK this year attending RAF Staff College, the RAF armament school at Eastchurch, and on liaison duties with the Air Ministry. At year's end the RCAF roster included 75 officers and 343 airmen.

here. Again, the overhaul season of this unit is very short, and a great deal of reconstruction work will be necessary this *winter in view of the shrinkage which has occurred in Avro spars and the deterioration in longerons through oil soakage.*

From 1925 onward RCAF aircrew needed practical knowledge in the care and use of parachutes. Practice jumps were in the training syllabus. Here, Cpl Cameron descends at Camp Borden. Then, parachute training from Jericho Beach, where HS-2L G-CYDU was used. (RCAF, CANAV Col.)

With a jumper aboard, Avro 504K G-CYAR sets out at Camp Borden on a parachute exercise. This 504 is in interim markings. While displaying the old-time Air Board letters, the "G" on the tail has given way to the RCAF tricolours. (CF RE18663S)

P/P/O "Mattie" Mathewson modelling 1920s RCAF kit – main 'chute on his back, auxiliary 'chute on his chest. (George F. Kimball/CANAV Col)

P/P/Os on a parachute course at Camp Borden circa 1928: George Jacobi, R. Court Hawtrey, J.H. "Jack" Ferguson, Claude "Morrie" Morrison, "Bobby" Mair, "Phil" Cox, Bill "Pink" Pinkerton, "Kimmie" Kimball and "Bud" Cook. (George F. Kimball/CANAV Col)

Personnel in a parachute rigging class at Camp Borden: Cpl Cameron (left), S/L Leach (with the cane), Cpl Anderson (on Leach's left) and Cpl Archdeacon (far right). The corporals were instructors. (George F. Kimball/ CANAV Col)

Sgt Arthur Fleming and F/O A. Carter from Camp Borden are up on the wing for a parachute sortie while on course with the US Army at Chanute Field, Illinois. A third jumper is in the rear cockpit for this seemingly wild and crazy training session. (Arthur Fleming Col.)

Taken in 1925, this south-looking RCAF oblique aerial view shows Cormorant Lake Air Station found on the east side of the lake (54º 12' N Lat., 100º 32' W Long.). The Hudson Bay Railway is prominent, this stretch leading to The Pas about 25 miles down the line. A Vedette and a Viking are on shore while two Varunas and two Vedettes are at anchor. In 1925 Cormorant Lake flew a host of missions, including 254 hours on forestry duties. (CANAV Col.)

Valleys and Peaks

Highlighting 1926 in the RCAF's annals was the famous McKee-Godfrey trans-Canada flight. This marked the first time that Canada was traversed by a single airplane. But 1926 also was a year of RCAF budget cuts that saw Dartmouth air station mothballed and Vancouver having to reduce fisheries patrols due to the poor condition of its two HS-2Ls. On the bright side, new Vedettes and Varunas were on order, and two Siskin fighters were on loan from the RAF for winter trials at High River (these were Canada's first modern combat aircraft).

In other important activity, from September 17 and October 5 a Viking surveyed the proposed route across northern Manitoba of the Hudson Bay Railway. Based at Cormorant Lake, then Norway House, it covered some 24,000 sq.mi. For 1926 Victoria Beach and its satellites at Norway House and Cormorant Lake flew 1652 hours, 1417 on civil operations. Forestry involved 886 hours, which covered 53,000,000 acres; 256 fires were reported. Flying ceased on October 27, then the winter months were spent overhauling aircraft, engines and instruments. Sad to say, on August 19, 1926 P/O Redford McLeod Carr-Harris had died in the crash of Avro 552A seaplane G-CYGF at Mile 185 of Hudson Bay Railway.

Over the winter of 1926-27 Ottawa, itself short of airplanes, chartered Fokker Universals and Fairchild FC-2s from newly-formed Western Canada Airways. These supported the seaport project at Fort Churchill, the Hudson Bay Railway's eventual head-of-rail.

Vedette Mk.II G-CYYF overflying Orient Bay, a seaplane base at the southeast corner of Lake Nipigon. Built in March 1928, 'YF was lost in a crash on July 17, 1930. Proving its durability, the Vedette served the RCAF into the early days of WWII. (LAC C10450)

New Vedettes were being delivered to the RCAF as late as May 1930. This old Canadian Vickers photo, showing RCAF examples being finished, is labelled "Mk V-A Vedettes February 1930". Materials used in building the all-wood Vedette included choice cedar, rock elm and spruce. (CANAV Col.)

One of the Fokker Universals chartered by Ottawa late in 1926 to support development of the seaport at Fort Churchill. Designed by Robert Noorduyn at Fokker's American subsidiary, Atlantic Aircraft of New Jersey, the Universal was one of the great commercial transports of the post-WWI era. In 1926 the RCAF still had no such modern planes. Often it was commercial aviation that led the way, with the RCAF following. (Provincial Archives of Manitoba)

The sole Canadian Vickers Vanessa (G-CYZJ) in a photo dated September 2, 1927. Seven days later 'ZJ attempted the inaugural Rimouski-Montreal seaplane mail flight, but ended up wrecked. Pilots had reported that the Vanessa, one of the first enclosed cabin biplanes, flew well. Unfortunately, the project was abandonned, just as customers were demanding enclosed cabins. Companies such as Buhl, Stinson and Waco in the United States quickly cleaned up in this market. (Canadian Vickers 1342 via David Godfrey)

Ahead of its time in design, the Vanessa inexplicably was dropped by Canadian Vickers. Canada might have led nationally in the cabin biplane market. Instead, Canadian operators began equipping with such new American designs as the Buhl CA-6. C. Don Long photographed this CA-6 at Leaside near Toronto.

In these years there often was lively discourse in Parliament over defence. In the 1926-27 session, for example, the pacifist-socialist Winnipeg member, J.S. Woodsworth, harangued the Mackenzie King government for supporting Britain's plans for a global airship route. Woodsworth feared that this would commit Canada militarily to Britain. In the same session, the powerful Quebec member, Henri Bourassa, complained that the RCAF was "nothing but a training body for the preparation of a military air force", and that Canada was on a nasty path to military co-operation with Great Britain. Other members proposed separating civil and military air operations, both of which were under the Minister of National Defence.

For Fiscal Year 1927 Ottawa's budget for aviation was nearly $3.9 million, much of it for new equipment. In addition, the Department of Railways and Canals received $850,000 to undertake an aerial expedition to the Hudson Strait region. Politically, civil and military aviation finally were

separated, the RCAF coming under a director answering to the Chief of the General Staff. All other aviation functions were headed by the Deputy Minister of National Defence: civil government air operations, aeronautical engineering, and control of civil aviation. However, civil functions remained

The first NCO pilots course at Camp Borden started with six students on February 1, 1927. Four earned their wings: Sgts A. Anderson, A.J. Horner, R. Marshall and E.C. Tennant. Here Cpl R. Marshall (he soon put up his sergeant stripes) receives his wings from station commander W/C N.R. Anderson after completing his course. F/L Albert W. Carter, MM, looks on. (RCAF RC1627)

staffed chiefly by RCAF personnel, so this "new look" was more of a compromise to appease people ranting about militarism. The main figures in the new organization were G/C Stanley Scott (Director of the RCAF), W/C Lindsay Gordon (Director of Civil Government Air Operations), W/C E.W. Stedman (Chief Aeronautical Engineer) and J.A. Wilson (Controller of Civil Aviation). The main role of the RCAF still was to train pilots and tradesmen for the civil air stations. Primary training continued at Camp Borden, while Vancouver trained Camp Borden graduates on seaplanes. The RCAF began training its first sergeant pilots in 1927, and the formal system of exchange postings began between the RCAF and RAF. By March 31, 1928 (the end of Fiscal Year 1927) RCAF strength was 117 officers and 454 airmen.

In April 1927 the first Universal transport plane for the expedition to Hudson Strait arrived at Camp Borden from Fokker in New Jersey. On April 28 F/L T.A. Lawrence delivered it to

Ottawa, averaging about 90 mph en route. The RCAF also undertook some experimental aerial dusting and air mail flying this year. In one case, on September ninth, sacks of mail were transferred at Father Point from the inbound trans-Atlantic liner *Empress of France* to an RCAF Vanessa. Assisted by Sgt G.L. "Gerry" Le Grave, Maj J.H. Tudhope was to fly the mail to Montreal and Toronto, but a float collapsed on takeoff. The crew was safe and the rescued mail continued by train. Mail flying totalled 59 hours in 1927, after which one conclusion was that there were too few safe anchorages along the St. Lawrence for seaplanes. The last two flights of the season used Fairchild landplanes

One accident investigated by the RCAF in 1927 involved JN-4 G-CABE at Niagara Falls, in which passenger Stanley Bryusziewicz died and pilot Fred Hartwick was injured. The Air Board convened a board of enquiry in Niagara Falls, F/L George R. Howsam presiding. Witnesses interviewed included pilot L.J. "Len" Tripp, and Bryusziewicz's widow (honeymooning from Philadelphia). The airfield was found suitable for a JN-4 and the plane had been airworthy. What concerned the enquiry was that Hartwick had been stunting while carrying a passenger, an infraction of air regulations.

The steady growth of RCAF activity is reflected by the size in 1927 of the Manitoba fleet: 5 Varunas, 6 Vedettes, 5 Vikings, 5 Avro 552As and 1 Keystone Puffer duster. There were four forestry bases each with an Avro, Varuna and Vedette; and two photo bases each with 2 Vikings. 2028 hours were flown, of which 1377 were on forestry, 600 on photography, 58 on dusting and 26 on transportation and miscellaneous duties.

Newly-delivered Fokker Universals G-CAHI "Alberta" and 'HJ "Quebec" at Camp Borden in July 1927. First flown in 1925 at Teterboro, New Jersey, the Universal received United States Type Certificate ATC#9 in June 1927 and 23 examples were built that year. The Department of Marine and Fisheries ordered six Universals to support the Hudson Strait Expedition (Fokker's advertised price per aircraft on wheels was $14,200). Note the pilot's position in the open air. The cabin accommodated as many as six passengers. (C. Don Long)

Hudson Strait Expedition

The waters and shores of Hudson Strait and Hudson Bay had been sailed over the centuries by the likes of William Baffin, Henry Hudson, and Radisson and Grosseilliers, but there was only vague knowledge as to tides, currents, soundings, ice, fog, winds, etc. Now, however, navigation to and from the new port at Fort Churchill would have to be guaranteed safe. To gather the data, in 1926 Ottawa planned a full-scale science expedition to Hudson Strait – the waters between Baffin Island and Ungava that connect the Atlantic Ocean and Hudson Bay. At a reception of July 5, 1927 Charles A. Dunning, Minister of Railways and Canals (senior bureaucrat in charge of the expedition) addressed the expedition's RCAF contingent:

You men all know something about Hudson Bay and Strait and the part they have played in the history of the country. We say in the West that Hudson Bay was

Pilots of the Hudson Strait Expedition: In their best "civvies" are F/L Alfred A. "Ack Ack" Leitch, MC, DFC, F/O A.J. Ashton, F/L F.S. Coghill, S/L T.A. "Tommy" Lawrence, F/O Brian G. Carr-Harris and F/O A. Lewis. All these were experienced men who would rise in the RCAF ranks. In WWI Leitch had flown Camels on 43 and 65 squadrons. Ashton was destined to command 4 (GR) Squadron in 1939. Coghill had attended the RAF army co-operation course at England in 1926. Lawrence would become an Air Vice Marshall with such WWII commands as North West Air Command. Carr-Harris commanded 1 Squadron (Siskins) in 1937-38. As W/C Carr-Harris he died at age 39 on July 5, 1942. Then with RAF Ferry Command HQ at Dorval, he was flying Hudson FH395 when it crashed into Lake St. Louis, near Dorval. Lewis commanded 11 (BR) Squadron in 1939-41. (CF PMR75-588)

the first front door of Western Canada. As an entry port for settlement, it was ... more or less abandoned when the trans-continental railways ... were built... Hudson Bay is a great inland sea, probably the largest inland sea not yet exploited in the whole world ... The Government intends to construct a railway to the Bay. That railway is well on the way to completion now. It is the intention of the Government also to develop a port there ... to develop to the fullest possible limit Hudson Bay and Strait as a transatlantic outlet for the products of the West...

Your part has to do with determining what aids to navigation can be devised, as the result of your observation of conditions there, to lengthen to the uttermost limit the period of navigation through the Strait... We are trying something new in the field of exploratory work ... in bringing to bear in this large way the courage and the skill of flying men, equipped with the most modern facilities and support by the best and most complete appliances which this marvellous age has made possible. It is an opportunity which should enable you to demonstrate the value of your craft in work of this nature ... You know there is an element of risk about your job ... we are glad that you have volunteered with your eyes open to assume those risks, whatever they may be. It speaks well for the Royal Canadian Air Force that Group Captain Scott was simply overwhelmed with applications to accompany the expedition.

The expedition, under N.B. McLean of the Department of Marine and Fisheries, began assembling at Halifax in

the spring of 1927. Some 5000 tons of materiel were gathered at dockside – prefabricated buildings, tracked vehicles, small boats, six Fokker Universals, a D.H.60 Moth, lumber, sand, cement, coal, heating oil, aviation fuel, rations, radio equipment and all else needed to sustain a 44-man party for 16 months (it is likely that the mission planners had made good use of S/L R.A. Logan's 1922 report). The lead ship was the Coast Guard icebreaker *Stanley*, supported by the smaller *Larch*. Key to the operation would be communications – three radio stations linked with others from Greenland to Ottawa were to be established along Hudson Strait. The Fokkers used the 200-hp Wright J-4B, then considered a powerful aero engine. The aircraft had been test flown at Camp Borden before being crated and delivered to Halifax.

A 1903 view of Port Burwell at the eastern entrance to Hudson Strait. ("The Cruise of the Neptun")

The expedition set sail on July 17 and in less than two weeks reached Port Burwell, site of a Moravian mission post on the northeast tip of Ungava Peninsula. Here a "winter proof" base camp was established, then the ships sailed west, depositing men, supplies and everything needed for similar camps at Wakeham Bay and Nottingham Island. The tiny Moth was used successfully in siting camps and anchorages. The three camps were in operation by early September. Each had its own doctor, RCMP officer and Eskimo support staff.

Fokker operations commenced using floats then, by early November, skis were used. Rough runways were ploughed on the sea ice, but these were susceptible to tides, so often had to be rebuilt. One object was to determine the value of aircraft assisting ships in navigating Hudson Strait. Each plane had a radio transmitter, but not a receiver. On any sortie a pilot was obliged to radio base every few minutes, thus keeping safely in contact. The only navigation aids at first were Admiralty sea charts made a century earlier, so there was plenty of "seat-of-the-pants" flying. Maps gradually were improvised using day-to-day observations, photographs and sketches.

Film from the expedition shows problems encountered when recovering float-equipped Fokkers, which lacked water rudders. Also shown is the fun instigated by expedition members. There was baseball in the snow and, on Dominion Day, races and even a game of find-your-shoes-in-the-pile. There also were some dicey times, as when the Moth sank in a storm of August 26, 1927 and, when F/L Leitch became lost on December 15, 1927. Returning to Nottingham Island after a mission to Eric Cove, he had to land on a thin ice floe to wait out some weather. He and his mechanic and Eskimo helper had to overnight in the plane, after draining the engine oil to keep it warm overnight. Come morning, Leitch determined his position, they poured the oil back into the engine, then returned to base.

Leitch was typical of the qualified Hudson Strait aircrew. During the war he had fought in Camels on 43 and 65 squadrons. He received the Military Cross, and DFC, the citation for which notes: "During the recent operations he heavily bombed an enemy dump,

The "Wakeham Bay" (Base "C") "orchestra" in rehearsal: F/O Carr-Harris (pilot), Romeo Lemieux (storekeeper), A.E. Axcell (wireless operator), S/L Tommy Lawrence (pilot) and Dr. W.J.K. Clouthier (physician). (LAC PA55643)

causing several fires; he then attacked hostile troops in the vicinity. Frequently he has returned to our lines with his machine riddled with bullets." Postwar, Leitch conducted experimental take-offs from HMS *Argus*, and served in the RAF during the North Russia campaign.

After being forced down by a blizzard on January 8, 1928 S/L T.A. "Tommy" Lawrence also had to set down. Next day he made some progress towards Wakeham Bay, but again was beaten by the weather. Nine days of storms now pounded the area and almost buried the plane. Finally, on January 16 F/O Brian Gethyn Carr-Harris and crew located Lawrence and landed. By day's end both planes had returned to base. F/O A.A. "Jaggs" Lewis would not have it so easy when he became lost.

On February 17 F/O Lewis accompanied by FSgt N.C. Terry and Bobby Anakatok had engine trouble on a flight from Port Burwell in Fokker G-CAHG. In dealing with this he became disoriented in snow and fog. According to one report, his last radio message said. "4:25 p.m. Weather bad. Landing on ice. Out of sight of land. Short of gasoline. Position unknown." While landing, Lewis damaged 'AHG. The trio then set out on foot pulling a raft and survival kit (their plane was never seen again).

Search efforts commenced when F/O Carr-Harris patrolled from Wakeham Bay to Cape Hope's Advance, but the weather beat him back. On the 19th, Leitch and Lawrence flew two Fokkers from Wakeham Bay to Port Burwell, searching for 3:40 hours and covering a

Using an old Admiralty chart, S/L Tommy Lawrence does some planning for a Hudson Strait patrol. Lawrence's RCAF career was exemplary, then a son and grandson followed him into the air force – both also excelled, son Bud commanding 444 Squadron on Sabres and grandson Brooke flying with the Snowbirds. (CF RE12407-12)

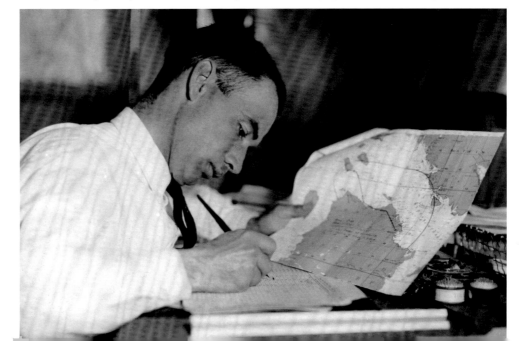

Preparing for a mission during the search for the Lewis crew. Looking over their survival kit are F/O Carr-Harris, F/L Leitch, S/L Lawrence and base photographer G. Valiquette. (LAC PA202545)

25-mile wide swathe. An early media report (Toronto *Daily Star* of March 7, 1928) ridiculously portrayed the situation: "In the skies of sudden storms and baffling fog the gray-winged giant gull of the Royal Canadian Air Force lost itself on February 17 when the land was blotted out and the fierce cross winds made dead reckoning navigation an impossibility." The horrid writing worsened with the reporter's comment that the Eskimo crewman had the "unpronounceable name" Bobby Anakatok.

The lost men struggled east for two days, then turned towards what appeared to be land to the west. They abandonned their raft, resorting to ice pans to bridge open water. Lewis later described their predicament by Day 3:

We breakfasted on frozen walrus squares, biscuit, chocolate and tea. Feeling like normal men again, we set out on our way. Though this day passed uneventfully enough, the one that ensued did not. We had been walking for about two hours when, sure enough, we came to a lead. It was impossible to determine how far it stretched in either direction but, since we now had no raft, there was nothing for it but to walk north in the direction of the drift.

After walking for about an hour, we decided to pry loose a pan of ice ... after we had separated a fairly large pan from the main pack, Bobby took a flying leap onto the centre of it and kept it level while we, in turn, jumped on. The pan,

under our combined weights, sank into the water at least three inches, and our feet ... rapidly became numb. We crouched down as low as we could to prevent the pan from capsizing, and quickly paddled our way across the few feet that barred our way to deliverance. When we hit the shore, Terry, in a hurry to get off, slipped and fell into the water. His immersion gave us some concern, but the water had not penetrated sufficiently to cause him any great discomfort. We bivouacked in the lee of an ice ridge and there we remained until dawn, drinking tea and sipping brandy.

On March 1 (13 days into their adventure) the trio suddenly turned up about midnight at Port Burwell, accompanied by some Eskimos whom they had met. On March 2 the *Daily Star* ran a banner headline: "Missing Aviators Battle Way to Burwell". The paper reported that "Mrs. Lewis, who resides in Winnipeg, was notified at once and Terry's relatives in England were cabled." It soon was known that on the ninth day the men had reached land and realized that they had not been on Ungava Bay, but the frozen Atlantic to the east. F/L Tommy Lawrence later radioed a message from Port Burwell, which was fine fodder for the daily press from coast to coast:

From 19th to 23rd conditions entirely unfit for flying. After careful study of Lewis' wireless report, unanimous decision was that missing machine was

down in Ungava bay and on the 23rd two machines proceeded southeast and, after three hours and forty-five minutes' flying, were force to land at the base on account of bad visibility ... From 24th to 29th inclusive, weather conditions ... impossible ... March 1 two machines again proceeded southeast down Ungava bay and, after four hours and 29 minutes' flying, returned to base, having met unsuitable weather ... On every occasion when flights were carried out, the visibility to the east over the Atlantic was very bad ... On night immediately following date on which machine went missing, bonfires were kept going and flares and distress signals fired at intervals ... This was discontinued due to the shortage of fuel and flares.

On Feb. 18 ... natives and komatiks with dog teams were despatched ... one team down Labrador coast with instructions to proceed as far as Hebron ...one team down east coast Ungava bay to George's river ... to relay news to posts around Ungava bay; one native to inform native hunters already at Cape Chidley to keep lookout.

Since return of F.O. Lewis it has been established beyond doubt that his course from Resolution Island carried him down the east side of Ungava to somewhere in vicinity of Omanek ... Flying as he was with a failing engine the pilot did not dare to lose his altitude by coming down to establish accurately his position ... It is considered that the engine trouble experienced was due to freezing up of carburetor jets.

At its conclusion, the Hudson Strait expedition had flown 227 sorties. Information gathered permitted the updating of maps and charts, and there now was a better understanding of spring break-up in the region. All this helped ensure that future shipping could operate safely and three radio navigation stations eventually were set up to aid vessels. Valuable experience in Arctic air operations also was gained, although any thought that aircraft might be used to assist shipping directly seems to have been abandonned. On November 18 most of the expedition arrived in Quebec City aboard CCGS *Montcalm*. It had been hoped to fly the Fokkers south, but their float fittings were found to be corroded – the five planes went home as crated deck cargo. They were stored at the old wartime base at North Sydney on Cape Breton, but soon were purchased by a local aviation pioneer and businessman, J.R. McCowan. Three were written off as being non-repairable, the other two eventually ended in Western Canada, surviving for several years hauling freight, furs and fish.

Department of Marine and Fisheries: Aircraft of the Hudson Strait Expedition

Registration	Type	Final Owner/Fate
G-CAHE	Fokker Universal	Peace River Airways, certificate lapsed July 1940
G-CAHF	Fokker Universal	J.R. McCowan, Sydney, NS, certificate lapsed August 1930
G-CAHG	Fokker Universal	abandonned on the ice off Labrador February 17, 1928
G-CAHH	Fokker Universal	J.R. McCowan, Sydney, NS, certificate lapsed August 1930
G-CAIII	Fokker Universal	J.R. McCowan, Sydney, NS, certificate lapsed August 1930
G-CAHJ	Fokker Universal	Peace River Airways, certificate lapsed January 1939
G-CAHK	de Havilland Moth	lost while moored at Wakeham Bay, August 26, 1927

A moralistic item in the Toronto *Globe* of March 10, 1928 praised the good work of Bobby Anakatok. Apparently it was suggested in Parliament that he be rewarded for, "Had it not been for the Eskimo there seems little doubt that the two aviators would have perished ... Bobby has shown real grit, fidelity and endurance ... the qualities that go to make a hero are not the prerogative of any one race, but are to be found among all peoples."

Ground crew assist as G-CAHJ manoeuvres for takeoff. Although the surface shown looks hummocky, the "runway" would have been adequately groomed. A forced-landing on an unprepared snow surface would have been rough on both plane and crew. (CF RE2698-4)

Sgt Craggie of the Hudson Strait Expedition spent his spare time usefully – building a detailed model of Universal "Alberta". (LAC PA202544)

Fokker Statistics: Hudson Strait Expedition

Base	Patrols	Hrs. Flown	Photos
"A" Port Burwell	47	83:46	227
"B" Nottingham Island	82	134:10	756
"C" Wakeham Bay	98	151:48	1302

"British Columbia" swings on the hoist during some stage of servicing. Then "Ontario" is readied for its last ski flight of the season at Wakeham Bay, June 1928. The buildings seen had been brought north by ship in pieces. (LAC PA55481, PA123498)

For safety, patrols usually included two Universals. Here 'HJ and 'HI are ready to go flying. Each had a radio transmitter, although no receiver. Regular Morse signals were sent by the pilot to home base – a challenge while flying in the open in sub-zero weather. (LAC PA202546)

Changing HI's Wright J-4B engine on a warm, sunny day on Hudson Strait. Although rated at only 200 hp, the J-4B somehow was sufficient for the 4000-lb Universal. (LAC PA202543).

Having flown on skis through the winter, Fokker 'HE "Ontario" has been changed over to Hamilton floats and is being launched at Wakeham Island in June 1928 for its first flight of the season. As a landplane the Universal had an empty weight of 2192 lb, on floats 2653, making for a loss in useful load on floats of 461 lb. (LAC PA123505)

This scene may show Universals being readied for shipment south following completion of their mission. The coastal fog enshrouding the hills often had curtailed flying operations. (CF RE13778)

Last of the Imperial Gift Planes

Some Imperial Gift aircraft served well into the 1920s, when the RCAF was acquiring such modern types as the D.H.60 Moth trainer, and Bellanca and Fairchild utility planes. In February 1929 G-CYBF, last of the wartime de Havillands, retired. But disposal caused a dilemma: Might such aircraft be scrapped, or sold for civil use? In June 1928 W/C E.W. Stedman, heading RCAF technical affairs, commented about the re-sale of D.H.4 G-CYDL:

Although one argument may be that we assist civilian aviation by the disposal at a low price of flying equipment no longer required in the Service, I am of the opinion that in the end we only retard progress by encouraging the use of equipment which is already obsolete...

The D.H.4 aeroplane required a thorough overhaul, and would cost several thousand dollars to be put into good shape. It is very doubtful whether a man who purchased an aircraft through a junk dealer would be prepared to put up the necessary funds to make a thoroughly sound job of this aircraft. The D.H.4 is a high powered machine, and, if not in good condition, is liable to be exceedingly dangerous. Under these circumstances I think that the D.H.4 aircraft should be destroyed rather than sold. (it was sold to a buyer who agreed not to fly it.)

G-CYFN, the RCAF's last serviceable Avro 504N was struck off strength on January 8, 1931 and sent to Toronto Technical School as a training aid. The last of the original Imperial Gift planes – Avro 504K G-CYCX – was written off in November 1934 after spending six years as an instructional airframe at Camp Borden. Unfortunately, not one of the 114 aircraft was preserved. Meanwhile, several Canadian Vickers Vedettes were taken on strength in 1926, but when RCAF personnel inspected a Fokker Universal passing through Camp Borden and a Fairchild FC-2 passing through Ottawa to Red Lake (both for Western Canada Airways), they were envious. Soon the RCAF's first Fairchilds were on order.

Relief from the tired old Avro 504K finally came in the form of the de Havilland D.H.60 Moth. Introduced at Camp Borden in January 1929, the Moth would fly to the brink of WWII. These factory-fresh Moths were photographed at de Havilland of Canada in North Toronto in September 1930. Then, Moth 68 on a formation exercise near Camp Borden. Note the friction-type airspeed indicator. (Fred Hotson Co., LAC PA120747)

Air Force Modernization

The revolutionary line of Fairchild utility planes gave the RCAF hope of brighter days ahead. Here is FC-2 No.31 in the snow at Camp Borden *circa* 1931. Powered by a 220-hp Wright J-5, several RCAF FC-2s later became Fairchild 51s (300-hp Wright or Pratt & Whitney). In flight near Lake of Two Mountains, Quebec is G-CYXP, an FC-2W with a 400-hp P&W Wasp. On wheels at Vancouver in 1938 is 621, a "51" that previously had been FC-2 No.29. (CANAV Col., RCAF A522-87, Gordon S. Williams)

Modernization was a slow but sure process for the interwar RCAF. Even though money for new equipment usually was tight, RCAF HQ followed all aircraft and equipment developments. Technical personnel from W/C Stedman's bureau toured aircraft factories in the US, UK and Europe and attended trade events and airshows to keep current. A close relationship arose between AFHQ and Canada's industry and, as opportunities arose, orders were placed. Here is the modern factory built by Fairchild in Longueuil, Quebec in 1929 – company expectations included doing good, long-term business with the RCAF. The RCAF already had been ordering Fairchild's classy products, its first FC-2 (G-CYYV) having been delivered in October 1927. Included in this view is Fairchild 71B G-CYVX. Built by Fairchild on Long Island, it served the RCAF 1930 to 1941. (CANAV Col.)

The Canadian Vickers Varuna was warmly greeted by the RCAF for forestry/photography duties. Introduced in 1926 and powered by two 180-hp Armstrong Siddeley engines, it promised high performance. But, according to K.M. Molson in *Canadian Aircraft since 1909*, the Varuna was a poor performer and the fleet was retired at the end of 1930. (RCAF HC844)

The RCAF was delighted to add both the Moth and FC-2. Sturdy, reliable and economic, they served on a host of duties. Here, a Moth and FC-2 'XT warm up at Cormorant Lake for a spring forestry mission. Then, High River forestry Moths 'YK and 'YJ at Grande Prairie, Alberta, *circa* 1929. As a rule all such RCAF planes had a yellow-overall paint job. Note the narrow hangar doors, but they were suitable for planes such as the Moth or FC-2 which had folding wings. (Arthur Fleming Col., CANAV Col.)

In 1929-30 the RCAF added eight Curtiss-Reid Ramblers. Built at Cartierville, the Rambler was a decent trainer, but there were no further RCAF orders. Here sits Rambler 145 at Camp Borden. SOS in October 1933, it became CF-CDZ with the Border Cities Aero Club in Walkerville, Ontario. It crashed near Kitchener on July 7, 1934. (RCAF RC2439)

More successful in the RCAF than the Rambler was the Fleet 7 Fawn, 51 of which were delivered 1931-36. Canada's great aviation photographer, J.F. "Jack" McNulty, photographed this example at Camp Borden. No.198 was on strength from 1931 into 1944.

An RCAF Keystone Puffer dusts crops near Morden in southern Manitoba. Such work was done in conjunction with federal agriculture, forestry and entomology experts. (LAC PA41286)

(Facing page) Entering RCAF service in May 1929 was the Bellanca CH-300 Pacemaker. By May 1931 thirteen of these speedy (140 mph) utility planes had been delivered. Here G-CYVG sits alongside Vedette 'WS on August 16, 1931 at the RCAF's Aylmer Lake, NWT gas cache. Powered by a 300-hp Wright J-6 Whirlwind, the Bellanca had an all-up weight of 4610 lb on floats. "Fly-away" price at Bellanca in Newcastle, Delaware was $14,950 on wheels, $17,400 on floats. 'VG served into 1937, then was sold to Quebec Airways, where it flew as CF-BFA until wrecked at Baie Comeau in December 1942. 'WS served from 1929-35, then went for scrap. Then a standard 3/4 front set-up shot of Bellanca 609. Formerly G-CYVH it flew into early wartime days, then became a ground school training aid, surviving on RCAF strength to February 1944. (RCAF, Bruce Best Col.)

Following good results with its Keystone Puffers, in May 1929 the RCAF acquired Ford Trimotor G-CYWZ to continue aerial dusting trials. 'WZ would serve many other good uses until sold in 1937. It often appeared at airshows and was the chief support plane for the Siskin team in the early 1930s. Here 'WZ sits on floats in Toronto Bay over the summer of 1929, on skis at Rockcliffe on January 17, 1931 and on wheels at Trenton in June 1934. (C. Don Long, LAC PA62755, Jack McNulty)

RCAF Modernization 1923-1930*

Type	Initially TOS	Eventual Total
Vickers Viking	June 1923	8
Sopwith Camel	October 1924	10
Canadian Vickers Vedette	July 1925	44
Armstrong Whitworth Siskin	January 1926	12
Canadian Vickers Varuna	June 1926	8
Armstrong Whitworth Atlas	December 1927	16
Keystone Puffer	June 1927	2
Fairchild FC-2	October 1927	15
Ford Trimotor	June 1929	1
de Havilland D.H.60 Moth	January 1928	91
Consolidated Courier	February 1928	3
Fairchild FC-2-W	May 1928	6
Fairchild 71	April 1929	11
Canadian Vickers Vancouver	August 1929	6
Bellanca CH-300 Pacemaker	October 1929	13
Curtiss Rambler	October 1929	9
Fairchild 71B	May 1930	12
Hawker Tomtit	May 1930	2

*Excludes most one-off types

1929 brought also its share of grief to the RCAF. In one case, F/O Paul G. Stanley (pilot, age 23) of Toronto and John McLaughlin (aeronautical inspector, age 35) of Montreal died when Vedette 'WR crashed on Boul. Pie IX in Montreal. They had been testing 'WR, which only recently had been completed. McLaughlin had been a CAF "original" and on the support team for the 1920 trans-Canada flight. (CANAV Col.)

For 1928 Camp Borden trained 62 P/P/Os from RMC and other universities, 43 being on that year's intake (21 eventually earned wings). Other courses included 19 personnel on parachute training, 35 on pilot refresher courses and 15 RCAF pilots and 32 civilians on instructor courses. Vancouver trained 66 pilots. 1928 casualties included P/P/O R.B. Brown, killed at Wasaga Beach on July 26 in an Avro 504N, and F/O A.E. Reynolds, who crashed a new Moth trainer on November 1. At year's end RCAF stations were manned as such: Vancouver – 22, High River – 26, Winnipeg 113, Camp Borden – 261, Ottawa – 297, Montreal – 2. Aircraft in

the civil government fleet included: D.H.60 Moth – 16, Douglas MO-2B – 1, Fairchild – 17, Puffer – 1, Varuna – 5, Vedette – 15, Viking – 4, Vista – 1.

The Puffer was used to dust wheat in Manitoba and forests in Northern Ontario, but pilots complained about the danger of this low-level work. They recommended a multi-engine plane with greater payload. At High River the wartime D.H.4s finally were replaced by Moths, which logged 700 hours and reported eight fires. Winnipeg added two Fairchilds at the head

of rail (Mile 437) of the Hudson Bay Railway from where flights operated to Fort Churchill, and ice patrols were flown along Hudson Bay's west coast.

A 1928 highlight for the RCAF was a flight by S/L A.E. Godfrey and Cpl Martin Graham to evaluate a trans-Canada, floatplane mail service. Leaving Ottawa on September 5 in a US-registered FC-2W, they flew 1100 miles to Lac du Bonnet. Next day they made Edmonton via Ladder Lake in northern Saskatchewan (775 miles) and on the 8th flew to Vancouver (790 miles). On September 10, they departed for Prince Rupert, this time with W/C Breadner and W/C Gordon aboard. They finished the day at Fraser Lake, BC, then proceeded on the 14th to Peace River, Alberta, thence next day to Fort Smith, NWT. But smoke from forest fires blocked the way, so Godfrey opted to land. In the process he wrecked the Fairchild. After several days out of touch

Two of the RCAF's many top people of the 1920s-30s: Frederick Joseph Mawdesley was known as a competent and loyal airman, but also as one of the RCAF's renowned pranksters. He flew all RCAF types in these years and also qualified on the RAF flying boat course at Calshot in 1927. In the spring of 1929, when the lakes still were frozen, Mawdesley completed many Fairchild flights from Cormorant Lake, assisting in a series of raging forest fires. Here Mawdesley is shown in his CAF uniform with his observer's wing. (CF RE12809)

N.R. Anderson was present at Camp Borden when it re-opened in 1920. Initially a flying instructor, by 1923 he commanded Eastern Air Command. He attended RAF Staff College in 1927, commanded RCAF Station Winnipeg in 1931 and, as G/C Anderson, commanded Eastern Air Command in 1938-42. (Arthur Fleming Col.)

Cold weather efforts at Rockcliffe over the winter of 1928-29 included practicing engine pre-heating. Here an airman organizes a nose tent around the nose of an FC-2. With the tent secured, he would get inside, fire up his simple little plumber's blow pot (visible on the ground) and wait until his Wright engine was warm enough to start. (RCAF HC1925)

with the world, the party was located. Breadner and Gordon were flown south by F/L Mawdesley, while Godfrey and Graham remained to salvage their engine.

FY1929 saw the RCAF log 10,537 hours, a record high. Of this, 9630 were on training, mostly at Camp Borden. Of 10 students taking their third season's training there, nine earned their wings, P/P/O George F. Kimball taking the coveted Sword of Honour as top graduate. Discussion was still hot as to what to do about this station, which was

One of the RCAF's new Canadian Vickers Vancouver flying boats. Six of these useful transports were taken on strength in 1929-30. The Vancouver would serve for more than a decade, mainly in forestry. (DND RE69-2965)

wearing down and still considered isolated. RCAF HQ was considering a new station for land and seaplane training. Located on the Bay of Quinte, Trenton was thought ideal, but the matter was set aside by the government.

Few years passed without the RCAF flying some air ambulance trips. One 1929 case involved a gravely ill missionary in York Factory on the Hudson Bay shore. On May 2 F/L Mawdesley flew a doctor and two nurses there from Cormorant Lake, Manitoba in a Fairchild. He arrived in blizzard conditions, the patient was treated, but it was days before Mawdesley could depart, due to weather. In these years the RCAF was doing little operational winter flying, and most "mercy flights" were flown by commercial operators, who had Canada's most experienced northern pilots and, quite often, better equipment than the RCAF had. In a typical case, Roy Maxwell of the Ontario Provincial Air Service rescued Rev. Morrow, an injured missionary. On March 9, 1929 Maxwell took off from Toronto for Camp Borden, where his Moth was fitted with skis, likely borrowed from the RCAF. He pressed on to Sudbury and Cochrane from where, on the 10th, he departed with a doctor to Moosonee, then crossed to Rupert House, Quebec. After being treated, Morrow was flown by Maxwell to Cochrane, then sent by train to Toronto for further care. The press always covered such stories enthusiastically, keeping the spotlight on aviation around the country.

Gradually, the RCAF edged into cold weather operations. Over the winters of 1928-29 and 1929-30 S/L R.S. Grandy of Ottawa air station flew a Wright-powered FC-2, then a P&W-powered FC-2W on trial geodetic survey work in northern Quebec. Much was learned about winter flying, e.g. about engine pre-heating,

skis, lubricants, outdoor maintenance tents, winter clothing. Trials continued in the coming years at the Aeronautical Engineering Division under W/C Stedman and in co-operation with the National Research Council, where Dr. J.J. Green was running a wide-ranging ski research project. Green's treatise "Aerodynamic Improvement in Aircraft Ski Design" appeared in the April 1936 edition of *Canadian Aviation* magazine.

Ottawa's annual aviation appropriation reached a postwar peak in FY1930 with $7,475,700 allotted ($2,510,00 for the RCAF). Service flying and training soared, but only in time for the RCAF to meet head on with the Depression – things would be largely downhill in the coming years. The third year 1930 P/P/O class graduated 19 of its 20 members (P/P/O G.D. Pooler had been severely injured in a flying accident, so could not graduate). Members of this class all went on to noteworthy RCAF careers, e.g. Hugh L. Campbell, who became Chief of the Air Staff 1957-62.

In 1930 the RCAF added instrument training to the syllabus at Camp Borden. Several experienced pilots were on the

inaugural course. Meanwhile, research was done into aircraft instrumentation regarding what was referred to as "blind flying", and into what the RAF was doing in the field. (The first practical course was introduced in the spring of 1932, with air mail pilots on the Montreal - Rimouski air mail service, and some RCAF instructors and CCA inspectors among the first graduates. Progress was steady and by late 1934 *ab initio* pupils at Camp Borden were receiving instrument flying instruction. Cold weather trials over the winter of 1930-31 involved Westland Wapiti Mk.II J9237. The unexplained crash on April 22, 1930 of FC-2 G-CYXX in Regina killed two experienced men: F/O H.W. Carew of Vernon, BC and Sgt A. Richards of Winnipeg. From 2 Photographic Detachment in Winnipeg, they had been positioning on a photo assignment to the Dundurn Forest Reserve south of Saskatoon. Heavily loaded, they crashed moments after takeoff, one report claiming that their engine had quit. By the end of FY1930, RCAF strength totalled 177 officers and 729 airmen.

The horrendous scene after Fairchild 'XX crashed at Winnipeg on April 22, 1930. (CANAV Col.)

Military Prospects: Siskin and Atlas

Late in 1926 the RCAF had acquired on loan from the Air Ministry its first modern, post-WWI combat aircraft – two Armstrong Whitworth Siskin IIIs. These were test flown, reported upon and one crashed fatally, but little further transpired until December 1927, when eight of the advanced Siskin IIIa were purchased. At the same time, five Armstrong Whitworth Atlas army co-operation planes were added (11 further examples in 1929-34). These types were stationed at Camp Borden to train pilots in some long-lost skills and participate in army summer manoeuvres. While the RCAF had no doctrine to justify such equipment, pacifist parliamentarians in Ottawa were able to take advantage of their presence to rail against imperialism, Canada becoming a war monger, etc. The Siskin and Atlas,

Siskin IIIa Specifications

First flight	October 1925
In RAF service	111 Sqn, Sept. 1927
Production	400 by 1931
Retired from RAF	1931
Length	25' 4"
Wing span	33' 2"
Gross weight	3012 lb
Engine	420 hp Jaguar IV
Armament	2x fixed forward firing .303 Vickers m/g, 4x20-lb bombs
Top speed	156 mph

however, did represent baby steps in breaking away from the RCAF's bush flying reputation. They would serve long, a few even into early WWII, then they were scrapped or relegated as ground training aids.

Canada's first modern post-WWI fighter was the Armstrong Whitworth Siskin, two of which (J7758 and '59) were acquired in 1926. Here they are (above) on skis at a public affair at Edmonton's Blatchford Field over the winter of 1926-27. Then, J7759 refuelling at Camp Borden. Finally (below), J7758 connected to a Huck's Starter at Camp Borden. J7758 crashed at High River on June 28, 1927, killing P/O C.M. Anderson, a graduate of the original 1923 P/P/O course. J7759 later was No.10 and 301. It served as a trainer at Camp Borden into 1935, then went for scrap. (First two Glenbow Museum, second two J.F. "Jack" McNulty Col.)

Siskin 302 being fuelled at Camp Borden in 1938. Then Siskin 20, on RCAF strength from December 1927 to September 1946, likely ended its days as a ground training aid. Right, an air-to-air of Siskin 60 on a winter sortie. The highest Siskin tail number was 309, this being followed by 310 – the first RCAF Hurricane. Postwar, at least two Siskins ended with Air Cadet squadrons: 303 with 58 Squadron in Kingston, Ontario, 304 with 92 Squadron. 303 was not SOS until August 1947. (LAC PA92504, RCAF HC2093, Jack McNulty Col.)

Siskin 23 after P/P/O McGowan, who had earned his wings in 1928, landed heavily at Camp Borden. The engineering officer quickly had his men on the wreck, getting No.23 back in the air as soon as possible. (CANAV Books/ George F. Kimball Col.)

On July 23, 1928 the Toronto *Globe* reported on F/L Hubert W. Heslop's accident of the previous day.

This local newspaper advertisement announced the Toronto airshow of September 7, 1931, Siskins included.

Atlas I Specifications

First flight	May 1925
In RAF service	26 Sqn, Oct. 1927
Production	449 by 1933
Retired from RAF	1935
Length	28' 6½"
Wing span	39' 6½"
Gross weight	4020 lb
Engine	450 hp Jaguar IV
Armament	2x fixed forward firing
	.303 Vickers m/g,
	1 flexible .303 m/g
	in rear cockpit,
	4x112-lb bombs
Top speed	142 mph

First flown in May 1925, the Armstrong Whitworth Atlas army co-operation plane was developed to replace the RAF's weary Bristol Fighter. In service in October 1927, it proved rugged and reliable, serving to 1935. Mainly due to budget restraints, the RCAF had to keep its Atlases flying into 1940. Shown is No.408 being assembled at Ottawa Car in 1934 (it was taken on strength at Camp Borden that November). 118 Squadron of Saint John, New Brunswick flew this ancient type into June 1940. Then, the same Atlas after a brutal landing. (CANAV Col., RCAF HC8414)

Atlas G-CYZA at Camp Borden *circa* 1928. Note the Vickers machine gun on the lower starboard wing and underwing bomb shackles. This Atlas later was No.17 and remained on strength into 1942. (RCAF RC1786)

The versatile Atlas was the pre-WWII CF-18 of its day. It could bomb, strafe, do photo recce, artillery spotting and (something a CF-18 never tried) airborne message pick-up. The latter task certainly qualified as (to use today's parlance) "real time" communications. Here No.19 practices a message pick-up and what a barebones operation it seems to have been! A wire is strung between two rifles and the Atlas is dragging its pick-up hook. If the pilot was lined up accurately, the hook snagged the line, to which the message was attached. Note the crewman leaning over to check for results. (CANAV Books/George F. Kimball Col.)

These 2 (AC) Squadron Atlases were taking part in army co-operation manoeuvres from Silver Dart Aerodrome at Camp Petawawa on June 17, 1936. Following a serious prang at Ottawa in November 1938, Atlas 409 was permanently grounded. (RCAF HC7561)

Atlas 19 (later 404) was tested as a seaplane at Trenton. It later became training aid "A60", likely following a prang at Camp Petawawa in July 1938. It remained on RCAF strength until August 1941. (RCAF)

A vic of Atlases 16, 17 and 19 during Air Force Day at RCAF Station Rockcliffe, July 14, 1934. One trails its message pick-up gear. A reputed 15,000 citizens turned out on this fine summer's day. (RCAF HC7020)

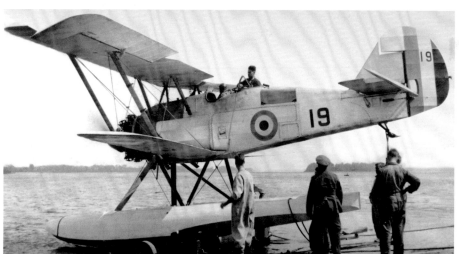

Atlas No.16 (later 401) running up at Camp Borden. This example actually went to war, being with 118 Squadron at Saint John through 1940. It was SOS in January 1941. (CANAV Books/George F. Kimball Col.)

Siskin Flight Demo Team

Where the Siskins really shone was in flight demonstration. This came about after F/L Dave Harding devised a 3-Siskin right-hand spin. E.A. McNab later recalled how in 1929 Harding had cooked up the idea of a Siskin demo team, when he heard that a squadron of US Army Curtiss Hawk fighters was to visit Toronto. That summer the Siskins amazed the crowds at the Canadian National Exhibition. This likely was the first such demonstration since W.G. Barker led a formation of Fokker D.VIIs at the 1919 CNE. In 1929 the Siskins also visited Cleveland, Ohio, for the US National Air Races. About this the Toronto *Globe* of August 30 report under the heading "Arriving Fliers Stunt":

Three daring members of the Royal Canadian Air Force put on a thrilling exhibition of aerial acrobatics. It was the first time a Canadian air unit ever visited the United States. The three Canadian pilots were Flight Lieutenants F.V. Beamish, D.A. Harding and G.R. Howsam from Camp Borden, Ont. They were in their regular army pursuit planes, single seaters specially built for the Royal Air Corps. Their exhibition

Siskin 23 at Leaside during the 1929 CNE airshow. On July 26, 1932 it was lost at Trenton. That morning, as the 5-plane Siskin aerobatic team was practicing, F/L Henry W. Hewson and F/O Fowler M. Gobeil collided over the station, Gobeil's Siskin striking Hewson's from the rear and taking off its tail. Gobeil parachuted to safety, but Hewson crashed fatally. (C. Don Long)

included a variety of stunt flying, combat manoeuvres and formation flying ...

On September 5 all eyes were on the sky over the CNE as the Siskins repeated their spectacular show. This time the sky also was busy with 19 US Army fighters from the Selfridge, Michigan. The OPAS, Firestone Tire's Ford Trimotor, the Canadian Flying Clubs Association and the Goodyear blimps *Defender* and *Vigilant* were some of the other participants at this grand event.

From July 1 to September 12, 1931 the Siskins toured Canada with the Trans-Canada Air Pageant, winning acclaim across the land. Heading the team was F/L H.W. Hewson. His 2 i/c was F/L W.I. Riddell, the other pilots being F/Os Gobeil, Hawtrey and McNab. In *Canadian Aviation* of July 1935, Sandy MacDonald described Riddell and the team:

Iron-willed, Riddell possesses all the attributes of a forceful personality, whether expressed in a blunt refusal to take a drink, or the masterful handling

it takes to hurl a plane through a violent manoeuvre in the sky... Riddell is an inexorable taskmaster. In close form-ation, only a few yards separate the machines. Let a pilot lag or overshoot that spacing by so much as even a hairsbreath and Bill's withering look will make him feel that he's allowed the whole expanse of the wide Atlantic to separate him from the Flight. The Siskins normally cruise at 100. Loops in V-formation are commenced at no less than 150. In some of the more violent evolutions they attain a speed of 230 ... torrid midsummer weather [makes] tight formation flying a ticklish business fraught with plenty of suspense, particularly at low altitudes where air disturbances are most violent. Canadian pilots have often been criticized for flying as low as they do, to which Riddell replies that low stunting ... is perfectly safe if executed with a good margin of surplus speed...

The decision having been reached ... that Air Force pilots would give the citizens of the Dominion a "show", the personnel selected to take part unanimously agreed that it must be as

good, if not a better show, than British Fury or American Hawk were capable of achieving. The Siskins were obsolete old "crocks" when purchased back in 1927... To be effective, the show must have punch and pep, uninterrupted action from the moment the planes were off the ground. A 30-minute programme was drawn up ... Into that 30 minutes were crowded as much action, as many thrills as the tough fiber of Canadian youth was capable of uncorking. During the tour Riddell did 28 solo programmes of 10 minutes duration...

Boeing P-12s from the Selfridge invasion. The P-12 and P-6 also were about comparable to the RCAF's Siskin. Powered by a 500-hp P&W R-1340, the P-12, first flown in 1928, had a top speed of 189 mph and a gross weight of 2690 lb. Comparable Siskin figures were 156 mph and 3012 lb. Even though the Siskin was slower than its US Army contemporaries, considering the calibre of RCAF fighter pilots, it likely would have fared well in a dogfight with either. (C. Don Long)

This Curtiss A-3 Falcon also came in from Selfridge for Toronto's 1929 show. Such events spot-lighted general aviation, military advances and Canada-US co-operation. The A-3 was the attack version of the O-1 observation plane, introduced in 1925 to replace the US Army's D.H.4. The Falcon was comparable to the Atlas, e.g. 435 hp Curtiss V-1150, gross weight 4476 lb, top speed 139 mph. During airshow week the Siskin team would have been carefully inspecting the US Army planes at Leaside, while their visitors from Selfridge would have been making their own notes. (C. Don Long)

Views of the US Army Curtiss P-6 Hawks at Leaside for the 1929 CNE airshow. In the first photo Toronto Flying Club D.H.60 Moth G-CAJU "Sir Charles Wakefield" is part of the scene. Powered by a 600-hp Curtiss V-1570 engine, the P-6 had a top speed of 198 mph. (A.W. "Alf" Barton, C. Don Long)

Gradual Improvements

As the 1930s progressed, the RCAF became polished at its many tasks. Forest and fishery preservation and development, aerial photography and mapping, and customs and immigration enforcement all continued, but a plan slowly was emerging to withdraw from most of these missions and concentrate on building a fighting force. The economic hard times of the Depression, however, frustrated AFHQ – without the money, little progress could be made. Equipment-wise, the Vedette and Varuna were proven workhorses by 1930 and the large, metal-hull Vancouver flying boat was broadening the scope of maritime operations.

RCAF Bellanca 'VJ at Charlottetown's Upton Airport some time in 1932. Then, 'UZ looking like new on the Ottawa River. Little has been published as to the colour schemes used by the RCAF in this period. The best current source remains *Sixty Years: The Royal Canadian Air Force* and *CF Air Command 1924-1984*, which includes many carefully researched colour profiles. Those of the Bellanca and Fairchild show them to have been yellow overall with black lettering, and with red, white and blue rudders. (CANAV Col., HC4822)

The 1930s RCAF is best recalled for its splendid forestry and photographic accomplishments. Here are Winnipeg-based Bellancas and a Fairchild 71B of 9 Photo Detachment at Fort Fitzgerald, NWT. Commanded by F/L C.R. Slemon, it was one of eleven 1930 detachments, its task being to support two NWT photo detachments with such essentials as fuel, food, film and spare parts. Slemon's detachment operated July 4 to October 6. But he miscalculated the onset of winter – his three planes did not get home that year. With the sudden arrival of Jack Frost they were stranded at Cormorant Lake until spring break-up. For 1930 the RCAF logged almost 14,000 flying hours on CGAO duties – 5500 on forestry, 3500 on photography. (LAC C27035)

A January 30, 1931 news item in the Toronto *Globe* announced a $200,000 order for six Bellanca CH-300s needed for aerial survey. Bellancas were known for ruggedness and reliability, and even had flown the Atlantic. In this deal Bellanca shipped fuselage frames to Canadian Vickers in Montreal, which then manufactured the wooden wings, etc., and did final assembly. Canadian Wright, also of Montreal, imported 300-hp J-6 engines

from its US parent, then prepared them for installation, so there was solid Canadian content in this contract. This "branch plant" or "industrial benefit" arrangement soon became the norm for foreign aircraft supplied to the RCAF. W/C E. W. Stedman commented in his memoir in this regard, "... every new type of aeroplane introduced from Britain or the United States necessitated considerable conversion work to make it

A fine Basil Van Sickle photo showing Bellanca 602 (formerly 'YU) sitting at Camp Borden in 1938.

A detail view showing the port oblique camera and rear-facing belly-mounted camera in a Bellanca. Then, the cabin set up with all three cameras. (LAC PA63076, PA63078)

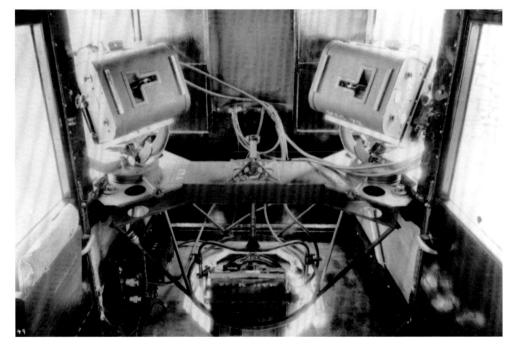

suitable for floats and/or for winter flying". Such work was costly, but helped lay the groundwork for Canada's aircraft industry.

For 1931 aviation appropriations dipped to $5,142,000. Included were funds for 20 Kinner-powered Fleet 7B Fawn trainers, the Bellancas and some early development at Trenton. The usual CGAO duties – forestry patrols, fire suppression, aerial photography, fisheries patrols, etc., continued, but were reduced. It was fortunate for Ottawa that Manitoba

and Saskatchewan recently had decided to establish provincial air services (Ottawa provided each with several aged Vedettes). By year's end the aviation appropriation amounted, in reality, to but $4,129,790. Of this historian W/C Hitchins wrote, "The lean years were beginning for the RCAF." At the end of FY1931 RCAF strength was 178 officers and 700 airmen.

RCAF Station Trenton opened on a small scale in September 1931, the chief event being the arrival of the Atlas and

Siskin flights from Camp Borden. Vancouver continued with flying boat training, but had such other assignments as co-operating with the RCN in protecting seals from illegal hunting. Due to budget austerity not all of this year's 23 Camp Borden graduates were taken on RCAF strength. Also in 1931, the 3-term P/P/O course begun in 1923 for university students ended (97 pilots had graduated). Flying for 1931 totalled: RCAF 19,172 and CGAO 11,185.

If 1931 was lean, 1932 was disastrous with Ottawa offering a mere $1,750,000 for all air services. Of this the RCAF received $1,555,000, then had to release 78 officers (65 pilots), 100 airmen and 110 civil employees. Activities from training and refresher flying to CGAO projects, airport improvements, construction at Trenton, air mail, etc, all were cut. In a reorganization CGAO bases became RCAF air stations:

No.1 RCAF Depot, Ottawa: RCAF Photographic Section, and RCAF Station Ottawa comprising test and development and general purpose flights, plus 7 detachments. CO W/C A.E. Godfrey.

RCAF Station Trenton: army co-operation (Atlas) and fighter (Siskin) flights. CO W/C L.S. Breadner.

RCAF Station Camp Borden: flying, air armament, bombing and technical training. CO W/C A.A.L. Cuffe.

RCAF Station Winnipeg: 3 general purpose flights, sub-bases at Lac du Bonnet and Cormorant Lake. Sub-bases at Ladder Lake and Fort Fitzgerald were in mothballs. CO S/L E.L. MacLeod.

RCAF Station Vancouver: 4 (Flying Boat) Squadron and 2 detachments. CO S/L A.B. Shearer.

RCAF Station Dartmouth and RCAF Station High River: in mothballs.

RCAF No.1 Depot hangar at Victoria Island (Ottawa) in July 1928. Then, a low-tide view of Fairchild 71B G-CYWD at the Shediac, N.B. wharf cluttered with lobster traps during 1932 preventative duties. (LAC PA132381)

NPAAF, Rum Runners and Air Mail

An important development in FY1932 was the formation of three Non-Permanent Active Air Force squadrons: No.10 at Toronto, No.11 at Vancouver and No.12 at Winnipeg. However, these were slow to come to life and it was 1934 before flying commenced. Some 1697 hours were flown by the RCAF in 1932 supporting RCMP preventative (rum-running) patrols, mainly over the Lower St. Lawrence, Bay of Fundy and Atlantic coastal waters. Vancouvers and Fairchild 71s were operated from Rimouski, Gaspé, Shediac, Dartmouth and Sydney. By combining air and sea resources, life became more challenging for the smugglers. RCMP agents in St. Pierre and Miquelon could radio the sailing times of rum runners heading for the rendezvous, then an RCMP vessel or RCAF plane could attempt an intercept. In one case Sgt J.D. Hunter, flying a Fairchild 71, on spotting a rum runner called in the RCMP's *Alachasse*. The smuggler outran the police, who then launched a speedier motor boat. This fired on the rum runner, forcing it to stop. Meanwhile, Hunter had observed the fugitives hurriedly dumping contraband overboard.

Another 1932 operation was a trial air mail service. RCAF planes took on the trans-Atlantic mail from ocean liners in the Strait of Belle Isle, then hurried it to Ottawa, where the Imperial Conference

Canadian Vickers Vancouvers at Gaspé during the 1932 Imperial Conference. Built in 1930, they served long beyond any reasonable "expiry date". Some of the first RCAF West Coast wartime patrols were flown by Vancouvers jerry-rigged with armament. (LAC PA132377)

was underway. A Bellanca seaplane from Red Bay, Labrador first carried the mail to Rimouski. A Vancouver continued with it to Montreal, from where a Fairchild seaplane covered the final leg to Ottawa. On the first mission, 1100 miles were covered in 11:05 flying hours over an elapsed time of 14:38 hours. The operation, which totalled eight missions, saw the mail reaching Ottawa in under 100 hours since leaving the UK.

On an Imperial Conference flight of July 24 the crew of Vancouver "VU" (F/L de Niverville and Sgt Hunter) had to land on the Gulf of St. Lawrence with engine trouble. As they discussed their situation, a pressure relief valve was dropped overboard. There was no replacement, so Hunter began filing a ¼-inch aircraft bolt.

After several hours he created a facsimile which fit and they got away. The failed Wright J-6 later went for overhaul. When it was shipped back to Ottawa air station, Hunter found that his improvised valve still was in place, apparently having passed inspection at Canadian Wright. F/L Mawdesley also had problems on an Imperial Conference flight. Forced down onto the St. Lawrence, he hailed a passing rum runner, who delivered the mail sacks to the dock in Rimouski. At year end FY1932 all CGAO services were taken over by the RCAF, so this phase of reorganization was complete. Flying totalled 10,425 hours including: training – 3963, refresher flying – 760, exhibition flying – 198, CCA (mainly transportation) - 665, CGAO - 3521.

A Vancouver sets off from Havre-Saint-Pierre on Imperial Conference duties. (J.D. Hunter Col.)

Trans-Canada Airway

A trans-Canada airway had been under discussion for years. The cross-Canada flight of 1920 anticipated this and the Air Board, RCAF, Aerial League of Canada and commercial operators all anticipated the day when it became reality. Yet, Canada still had few airports and the only navigation aids were those on a few air mail routes. MGen A.G.L. McNaughton (Chief of the General Staff 1929-35) commented on behalf of the RCAF that "the Airways would give us a great military advantage ... the ability to rapidly reinforce by air our Pacific coast if that were required". Presently, McNaughton explained, that was impossible, transporting aircraft by rail from eastern Canada being the only option.

Following the 1920 trans-Canada flight and that in 1926 by S/L A.E. Godfrey, the next step toward a national airway was a 1927 experimental RCAF

"Royal Twenty-Centers" clearing ground at a trans-Canada airway site near Megantic, Quebec. (LAC PA34544)

Winter operations at "Relief Project 12" (Nakina airport) in remote northern Ontario in April 1933. Then, a road gang slogs away in 1934 at "RP28" – laying pipe at RCAF Station Trenton. (LAC PA34746, CF RP28-197)

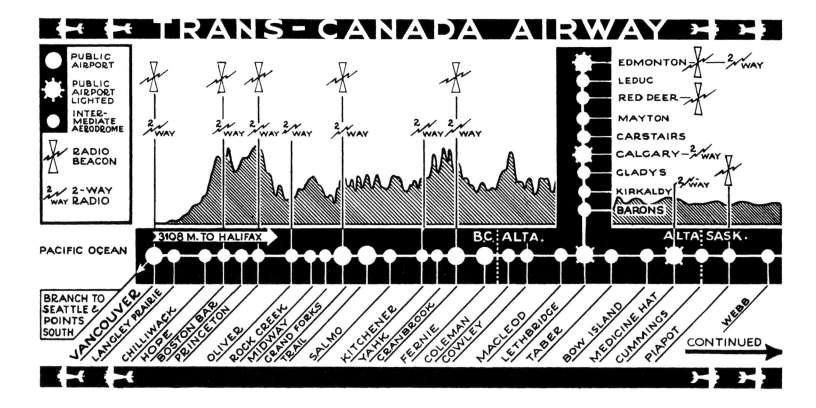

mail service between Montreal and Rimouski (59 flying hours logged by Ottawa air station during 10 flights). Air mail flown by commercial carriers then became an impetus for many Quebec and Ontario centres to construct airports, some of which were relatively modern, though not comparable to those in Europe or America. The opening of the prairie air mail in 1928-29 had the same result, as cities from Winnipeg to Brandon, Regina, Moose Jaw, Lethbridge, Calgary and Edmonton

funded airports. In British Columbia, Vancouver and Victoria, enthusiastic aviation centres since Early Bird days, also maintained serviceable flying fields. The same was true for Atlantic Canada, and the founding of the Canadian Flying Clubs Association in 1928 spurred smaller communities such as Sydney and St. Catharines to build airports. What was missing, however, was a means to connect these widely spread regions. Only the federal government could resolve such an issue.

Ironically, it was the Depression which brought something concrete to the dream of trans-Canada flight. On October 8, 1932 MGen McNaughton encouraged by J.A. Wilson (Controller of Civil Aviation) submitted a proposal to Prime Minister Bennett to create work for Canada's unemployed. McNaughton's idea was to employ 2000 single, homeless men on a series of relief projects that included roughing out a 3108-mile cross-Canada airway. Bennett accepted this plan, known henceforth as the "National Defence

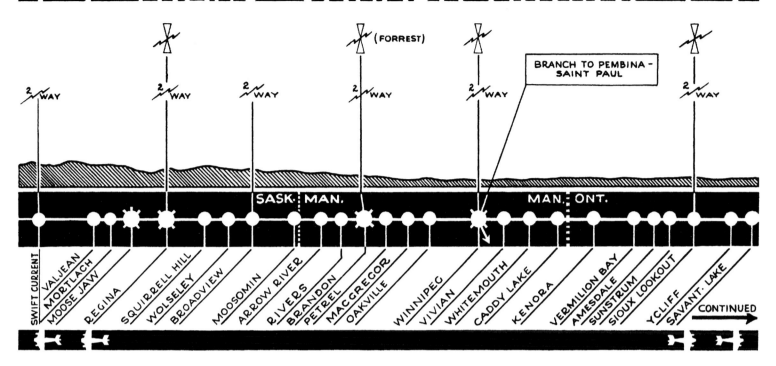

Unemployment Relief Camp". To begin, some 114 new sites were pinpointed by aerial survey, then engineers walked the land site by site and made their recommendations. Where land was privately owned, or timber or mineral rights held, negotiations were begun with those involved.

On average there would be a landing field every 25 miles coast to coast. Soon camps were booming from the Maritimes, across Quebec, Ontario and the Prairies to British Columbia. The project was designed to create as much work as possible, so old-fashioned elbow grease was the order of the day. Workers were paid 20 cents a day, giving rise to their ironic title – "the Royal Twenty Centers". Clearing, draining and grading sites was followed by runway construction, there usually being two strips each 3000 by 600 feet. Key sites would have a hangar, radio station, lighting, and refuelling and weather reporting facilities. Lighting could include a rotating beacon (perhaps with an electricity generator), obstruction lights, ground approach lights, and white boundary lights. Secondary strips would have a resident caretaker, but only barebones equipment. Most of the 114 sites would be emergency fields, i.e. supplementary to existing municipal airports. Meanwhile, other projects were completed under McNaughton's scheme, e.g. Trenton and Dartmouth were improved using relief workers.

TRANS-CANADA AIRWAY

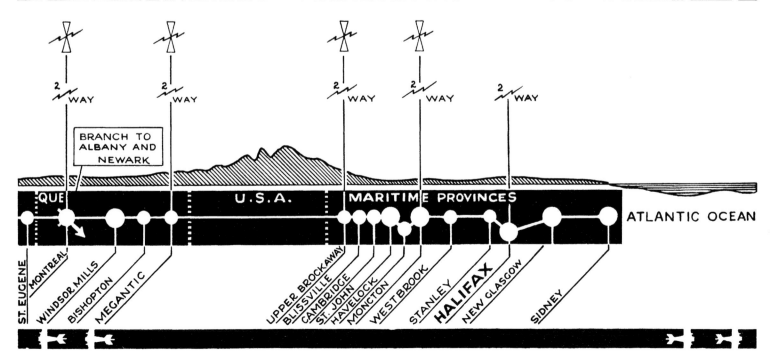

Ottawa's aviation budget for FY1933 was smaller than ever. All flying was restricted, whether training, service flying or civil government duties. Only 3491 hours were flown on the latter, 2094 being on RCMP preventative duties. Total flying was 10,763 hours. Winter trials were conducted with a Hawker Audax on behalf of the UK Air Ministry. Tested were new high-speed National Research Council skis developed with the help of wind tunnel experiments. Meanwhile, further winter trials at Camp Borden looked into ways of improving cockpit comfort, such flying gear as goggles and gauntlets, etc. At year's end the RCAF had 184 aircraft, mainly obsolete:

Armstrong Whitworth Atlas	5
Armstrong Whitworth Siskin	9
Avro Tutor	6
Bellanca CH-300	12
Canadian Vickers Vancouver	5
Canadian Vickers Vedette	17
Consolidated Courier	1
D.H.60 Moth	56
D.H.75 Hawk Moth	2
D.H.80 Puss Moth	15
Fairchilds	35
Fleet 7	17
Ford Trimotor	1
Hawker Tomtit	2
Keystone Puffer	1

R&D: The RCAF normally had a small budget to evaluate aircraft and equipment. This Fairey IIIF was sent out to "the colonies" in October 1929 for trials through the 1930 float season at Victoria Beach, Manitoba. First flown in 1926, the IIIF descended from a 1917 design and served the RAF into 1935. Powered by a 570-hp Rolls-Royce Napier Lion, the IIIF had a top speed of 120 mph. (CANAV Col.)

The RCAF conducted much ski R&D. So experienced did it become that during WWII even such types as the Harvard, Hurricane and Ventura flew on skis. Here is Siskin 22 ready for a January 1929 sortie at Camp Borden. (RCAF RC1954)

Hawker Audax K3100 was used 1933-35 to test skis developed by the NRC in Ottawa. Such other cold weather issues as engine performance likely also were investigated. First flown in 1931 the Audax was the army co-operation edition of the Hart, the RAF's standard light bomber of the day. Powered by a 530-hp Rolls-Royce Kestrel, the Audax could top 170 mph. (RCAF)

NPAAF Progress

Canada's Non-Permanent Active Air Force (i.e. reserve or auxiliary units) began as "paper squadrons" having token funding. These units did evolve, however, recruiting, parading and running classroom courses until a few aircraft finally were provided. Typical was 12 (Army Co-Operation) Squadron of Winnipeg. Authorized in October 1932, the squadron commenced flying in 1934 under S/L J.A. Sully, who was a typical CO of the period. He had fought in the CEF during WWI, then joined the RFC. Later, he was attached to a British mission in the US, assisting the American air service with its training syllabus. For this he received an AFC, plus the Aero Club of America Aviation Medal of Merit.

Postwar, S/L Sully contributed towards the formation in 1928 of the Aviation League of Canada and helped found the Winnipeg Flying Club and Canadian Flying Clubs Association. His "right hand men" at 12 Squadron were F/L H.P. Crabb ("A" Flight commander), F/L J.C. Huggard ("B" Flight), F/L R.H. Little ("C" Flight) and F/O W.F. Hanna (Photographic Officer). All were wartime veterans. Crabb had been an RFC instructor in the UK and Handley Page bomber pilot, Huggard had flown Camels and been a POW, while Little and Hanna had served on Bristol Fighters. At this time 12 Squadron's PAAF (Permanent Active Air Force) officers were Siskin pilots F/O E.A. "Ernie" McNab and F/O Fowler M. Gobeil. There also were seven PAAF airmen on such duties as engine maintenance and parachute rigging.

No.12 Squadron's first realistic flying training took place from June 28 to July 7, 1935 at Camp Shilo, Manitoba, where 11 officers and 33 airmen participated in Army exercises. Using four Moths, artillery spotting sorties were flown with some 125:25 hours logged, including 36 on a single day. During this camp several officers attained new qualifications, the squadron's signals personnel upgraded their semaphore, heliograph (flashing mirrors) and Lucas signalling lamp skills, and the fitters and riggers gained experience keeping their Moths in trim. This was the first time that a Non-Permanent RCAF squadron had attended summer camp to train with the Permanent Force.

On August 9, 1935 F/O Gobeil led 12 Squadron on its first cross-country trip: four Moths flew 340 miles from Winnipeg to Regina (with intermediate stops). Six pilots and two airmen comprised the crew, so every cockpit was occupied, thus maximizing training value. The visit to Regina coincided with that year's John C. Webster Memorial Trophy competition being held there. The trophy was won by Gordon R. McGregor of Montreal (soon to be well-known in the Montreal NPAAF). The squadron flew home on August 11 with stops at Portage la Prairie, Carberry, Brandon and Virden.

Meanwhile, 10 Squadron was forming in Toronto and in the summer of 1934 found a place to fly – businessman Frank Trethewey's old de Lesseps Field, where a famous 1910 air meet had been held. A news item in *Canadian Aviation* (June 1935) covered NPAAF affairs at 11 Squadron: "The Vancouver squadron, which is under the capable direction of Squadron Leader A.D. Bell-Irving, MC, is virtually an outgrowth of the Aero Club of B.C. from which organization possibly the earliest request was made to the Department of National Defence for establishment of Non-Permanent Squadrons in Canada ..." The squadron of 13 officers and 74 airmen was flying from Sea Island airport and parading at the Horse Show Building on Georgia Street. As did each NPAAF squadron, 11 had its PAAF liaison personnel, but also an Honourary Wing Commander.

The heart of the early NPAAF was the D.H.60 Moth, although squadrons had to suffer 2 or 3 years *sans ailes*. Eventually, Camp Borden could spare a few Moths, so No.155 went to Vancouver-based 111 (AC) Squadron in 1934. It was shot by a young aviation enthusiast from Seattle, Gordon S. Williams, who often got up to Vancouver to cover the local aviation scene. Gordon went on to a dream career at Boeing in photography and PR.

The Westland Wapiti evolved from a 1927 RAF requirement – a replacement for the ancient D.H.9A. Contenders were obliged to recycle D.H.9A components in their designs. Several manufacturers participated, e.g. Armstrong Whitworth offered a beefed-up Atlas, Bristol the Type 93A Beaver. In the end Westland, which had developed the original D.H.9A, prevailed with the Wapiti. First flown in March 1927, it entered service in 1928 and eventually saw combat in Mesopotamia and Afghanistan. Much R&D ensued, e.g. in 1930 J9237 came to Canada on cold weather trials. In 1935 Canada ordered six Wapiti Mk.IIAs – the RCAF's first bombers. Here sit three Wapitis at some air event, perhaps at Camp Borden, but maybe Leaside. (C. Don Long Col.)

Modernization Inches Along

The mid-1930s brought the RCAF further modernization and a stepped-up sense of military purpose. In 1936 it added two Fairchild Super 71Ps. Unfortunately, these were fraught with technical snags and one crashed in northern Manitoba. Here, "71P" 665 is on wheels, but its work-a-day configuration on detachment was on floats. The only other Super 71 was a civilian version with the pilot's cockpit near the tail. Happily, this machine (CF-AUJ) survives with the Western Canada Aviation Museum. (William J. Wheeler Col.)

Wapiti 509 with a Canadian cockpit hood mod. Basic specs were: crew 2, engine 460-hp Bristol Jupiter VI, wing span 46' 5", length 31' 8", all-up weight 5400 lb, max speed 135 mph, armament: 1 fixed Vickers gun, 1 flexible Lewis gun, bombs 580 lb. The Wapiti finished with a solid RCAF record: the only "Cat. A" accidents involved 530 at Calgary in July 1939, and 533 at Trenton in February 1939. (CF RE64967)

Wapiti 528 after a bruising nose-over, location unknown. Hefty, complex machines, RCAF Wapitis later found useful work as instructional airframes. (CANAV Col.)

Wapiti 512 at Rockcliffe in October 1939. Canada's Wapitis began with 3 (B) Squadron at Rockcliffe in June 1937. The squadron moved to Calgary in 1938, then was pushed to Halifax in September 1939. Wapitis also equipped 10 (BR) Squadron at Halifax from September 1939 to June 1940. One example was loaned to Fleet Aircraft in Fort Erie in 1941, likely for some development project. (Jack McNulty)

Unlike the Wapiti the Northrop Delta was a sleek, modern design first flown in 1933. US historian Joseph P. Juptner describes it as having "racing-plane performance" (top speed 205 mph). In 1935 the RCAF ordered three Deltas for aerial photography. The contract went to Canadian Vickers of Montréal, which flew its first Delta on August 21, 1936. Twenty aircraft eventually were delivered, the last in 1940. Being so much faster than the old Bellancas, Fairchilds, etc., the Delta revolutionized RCAF photography. Here, Nos.669 and 667 near completion in the factory in September 1936. Two Bellancas in for overhaul complete the scene. (CANAV Col.)

A float-equipped Delta at Jericho Beach in June 1938. Note the large cargo door that handily accommodated large Fairchild cameras and other bulky equipment needed by remote detachments. (LAC PA501524)

Gordon S. Williams photographed Delta 669 at Vancouver, perhaps while it was with 6 (GP) Detachment over the summer of 1937. The tail logo reads "Northrop Delta M-1A built by Canadian Vickers Limited".

Aviation funding continued to increase, that for 1935 being $4,302,900, most for the RCAF. Manpower increased and new aircraft were ordered, including the Blackburn Shark, Fairchild Super 71P, Northrop Delta and Westland Wapiti. F/L C.R. Dunlop, on exchange at the RAF Armament School in 1935, was candid when describing the Wapiti to W/C L.S. Breadner, attending the Imperial Defence College the same year: "The Wapiti is without doubt the worst apology for an aircraft that it has ever been my misfortune to fly." W/C Breadner disagreed, chastising Dunlap for his openness. Dunlap later heard that Breadner had been the one responsible for selecting the Wapiti for the RCAF, doing so mainly because of the bargain-basement price tag Britain had placed on its surplus Wapitis.

Camp Borden had 39 student pilots on course (24 received wings in May 1936). Meanwhile, the RCAF Technical Training School at Camp Borden turned out 29 fitters, 28 wireless operators, 13 armament artificers, 8 motor mechanics, 7 fabric workers, 7 motor boat crew, 5 instrument makers, 2 coppersmiths and 2 machinists. Aeronautical Engineering Division projects included converting two Vancouvers to the Armstrong Siddeley Serval engine and converting a Fleet Fawn to a Civet engine (10 such were ordered). By year's end manning was 142 officers and 884 airmen – an all-time high. Flying exceeded 16,000 hours.

For 1935 the NPAAF squadrons flew 2171 hours and new auxiliary squadrons were in the making. Included was 119 (Bomber) Squadron, which was authorized in May 1935 under S/L D.U. McGregor, MC. Initially without airplanes, 119 paraded, held lectures, etc. in the James Street Armoury. The first RCAF awards for chivalry were made in 1935: OBEs for S/L R.S. Grandy and S/L G.E. Brookes; an MBE for WO1 A.A. Rabnett. Also formed in 1935 was 120 (Bomber) Squadron at Regina under S/L Roger A. Delahaye, DFC. Having studied law before the war, he had trained with the RFC (Canada), then fought overseas on the B.E.2 and SPAD, attaining several victories. By year's end 1936, 120 Squadron had recruited about 50 airmen.

RCAF Station Ottawa officers during a lecture in map studies. Such courses usually occurred in winter, when the detachments had finished their season in the field and the planes were down for overhaul. (LAC PA63658)

Map Making

The important role of the RCAF in aerial photography and map-making was summarized in an April 1935 article in *Canadian Aviation*. The author, F.H. Peters, Surveyor General in the Department of the Interior, noted how 567,000 of Canada's 3,690,643 sq.mi. had been photographed specifically for map-making purposes. About 750,000 aerial photos were on file and some 1000 map sheets had been published since the program began in 1922. Included were 240 topographic map sheets useful for pilots, and the first few specific air navigation sheets:

A flying detachment usually consists of two camera-equipped aircraft and, in northern work, where no flying fields exist, the seaplane type is used. Invariably, for oblique photography, three cameras are mounted as a unit in the aircraft. These cameras are so arranged as to produce a resulting fan of pictures, the side ones overlapping the centre one so that the side pictures each have a portion of terrain exhibited that is common to the central picture. The cameras are electrically interconnected and the three simultaneous exposures are operated by an automatic intervalometer, in other words a clock that can be set to make contact at any desired number of seconds interval between exposures of successive fans.

In oblique photography the parallel flight lines are spaced about eight miles apart and the fan exposure is made every one and three-quarter miles along the line of flight. One fan exposure covers about 15 square miles of terrain, with

sufficient clarity for accurate mapping. The essential feature of oblique photography is the exhibition of the horizon line of the photographs.

The altitude at which obliques are taken may vary from 5,000 to 10,000 feet above the ground, according to the height at which clouds, that would prevent a camera view of the horizon, may be lying. In vertical photography the parallel flight lines are spaced about one mile apart. The exposures are made at an altitude of about 10,000 feet. One photograph at this altitude covers about three and three-quarter square miles. The exposures are made at suitable intervals to ensure their having an overlap exceeding fifty per cent. This overlap is necessary for plotting and the stereoscopic examination of the prints. Ground survey control and astronomic observations for latitude and longitude are carried out in conjunction with the air work, in order to control the scale and positions of the plots of the photographs.

By this time it was clear where the international situation was heading. Germany was expanding it military might and promising revenge on its neighbours who had taken part in the 1919 Peace of Paris. Nazis policies were making life very difficult on minorities, so many were attempting to emigrate. Italy was allied with Germany and rampaging in Ethiopia, while Japan, which had invaded Manchuria in 1931, also was building a fearsome military and committing atrocities throughout its sphere of influence. Not even blissful Canada could watch as such forces prepared to pounce. Its defence budget

slowly came into line. For 1936 the RCAF received $4,685,028. Three Northrop Deltas, the RCAF's first all-metal airplanes, were delivered in September 1936 at a cost of $60,000 each. Although for civil photography, the Deltas could be converted for military use.

With the creation in 1936 of the Department of Transport (by amalgamating the Department of Railways and Canals and the Department of Marine), the RCAF passed its civil responsibilities to the DOT (civil aircraft certification, accident investigation, licencing of civil pilots, etc.). Administrative steps were taken to turn the Siskin flight of 2 (Army Co-Operation) Squadron into 1 (Fighter) Squadron. No.6 Squadron finally received its first Shark torpedo bombers and the air force logged nearly 17,000 flying hours.

On May 23, 1936 two Fairchilds were assigned to a medical evacuation from Sable Island, more than 100 miles east of Nova Scotia. Piloted by FSgt Gibb and Sgt O'Connor, the aircraft left Dartmouth at 1525, reaching Sable Island about two hours later. The patient was loaded and the Fairchilds returned to base at 1950. On November 16, 5 Squadron at Dartmouth sent three Fairchild 71s to Longueuil for overhaul by Fairchild of Canada. They only got as far as Saint John, New Brunswick, where weather forced them down. When they tried again on the 21st, there was more bad weather, so they headed to Dartmouth, but could only make Shediac. There they were dismantled for shipment by rail to Longueuil.

The Blackburn Shark boosted RCAF modernization in 1935. Four were ordered from the UK, others were built later by Boeing in Vancouver. 26 finally were on RCAF strength: 7 Mk.IIs, 19 Mk.IIIs. In WWII these did stop-gap service on the West Coast, until relieved by the Bolingbroke, Catalina, etc. (Gordon S. Williams)

With the Shark the RCAF had a fairly modern airplane. First flown in 1934, it entered service with the RN Fleet Air Arm in May 1935. Basic Mk.III specs were: crew 2-3, engine 800-hp Bristol Pegasus, wing span 46', length 35' 3", all-up weight (seaplane) 8610 lb, max speed (seaplane) 139 mph, armament: 1 fixed Vickers gun, 1 flexible Lewis gun, bombs 1500 lb. Here target tug Shark 502 sits at Patricia Bay in December 1941. Its paint job was yellow with black stripes on fuselage and wings. (Robert Finlayson Col.)

Shark 502 in a wintery February 1940 scene. The full story of this type in RCAF service is found in Carl Vincent's definitive 1974 book *The Blackburn Shark*. (RCAF WRF-118)

More of the Great Fairchilds

No service type from interwar years was more important to the RCAF than its Fairchilds. Of all models there were 61 on strength, although some of those had been reconstructed from early models. The Fairchild 51s, for example, were rebuilt from earlier FC-2s. Here is 628 on skis at Camp Borden. Originally a 1928 FC-2, it was converted to "51" standards in 1931 and served into wartime years. (CANAV Col.)

Fairchild 71B 'VE (later 630) over Hudson Bay ice floes between Fort Severn and Weenusk on August 13, 1932. (LAC PA95003)

RCAF No.636, location unknown. Having joined the RCAF in May 1930, this "71B" worked solidly until wrecked in a gale on September 17, 1939. (A.B. Shearer Col.)

Fairchilds undertook tasks from photography to forest fire and fisheries patrols, mercy missions, army co-operation, general transportation and anti-smuggling and immigration patrols. FC-2W G-CYXO joined the RCAF in June 1928. It served until damaged in an accident on March 3, 1936. (CANAV Col.)

Fairchilds 'VO and 'WA at the Shediac wharf during high tide (see low tide on page 75) perhaps on preventative duties. Then, 'VO hangared somewhere for servicing. (A.B. Shearer Col.)

More from the Shearer Collection: Fairchild 71 'WE on the slipway, location unknown. It served into 1941, when the RCAF was equipping with new Norsemans. As CF-BVI it then served Wings Ltd. of Winnipeg, CPA and, finally, Austin Airways, which bought it for $7660. Austin pilot George Charity checked out on 'BVI at Sudbury in March 1946: "I had never flown the 71 before," he later wrote. "I started the engine, warmed it up and took off. I soon discovered what a delight the Fairchild was. From then on, I enjoyed every trip ... It handled like a Cub."

CF-BVI in Austin Airways times. In July 1949 Chuck Austin wrecked 'BVI near Timmins. In 1962 bushplane restoration aficionado, Gord Hughes, recovered the wreck, which he still had at his base in Ignace, Ontario in 2010. (CANAV Col.)

The presence of FC-2W 'YU is no surprise in this British Columbia scene *circa* 1935-36, but Royal Navy Fairey III S1858 beyond is a surprising sight. (A.B. Shearer Col.)

Fairchild 71 No.114 came to a sad end about 10:30 A.M. on Saturday, October 24, 1931. On a cross-country exercise from Camp Borden, F/L Gordon Apps, DFC, was landing at Peterborough where, coincidentally, an air display was scheduled. The weather was iffy, although F/L Mawdesley had just landed ahead of Apps. It seems that Apps decided to go around, but struck a tree and crashed. All aboard were injured: F/L Apps and Sgts George Gillespie, John Hand, Claude Keating and Humphrey Madden. At first it was reported that all would survive, but by Monday F/L Apps and Sgt Hand had died. On October 26 the Toronto *Globe* reported that, once the engine and other useful parts were removed, 114 was burned. (CANAV Books/George F. Kimball Col.)

An idyllic 1933 scene as S/L E.L. MacLeod and his crewman refuel their Fairchild at the RCAF's Slemon Lake, NWT fuel cache. Facing the camera is RCMP Commissioner James H. MacBrien, who was on a tour of RCMP posts. (RCMP Archives)

Aerial photography and forestry duties continued to occupy the RCAF through 1936. Especially involved was 8 (GP) Squadron in Winnipeg, at this time organized with a communications and a general purpose flight at Lac du Bonnet, plus six roving detachments on summer duties anywhere from Northwest Ontario to Alberta and the NWT. These were real bush operations, e.g. No.4 Forestry Detachment, which W/C Hitchins describes in an unpublished document, following which he summarized the dismantling of RCAF operations in this region as the RCAF adopted a more military stance:

No.4 Forestry Detachment, in charge of FS J.M. Ready, carried out patrols over Riding Mountain National Park from a base (Wasagaming) on Clear Lake near the south-east corner of the park. The personnel, two NCO pilots who were also fitters A.E., and a carpenter, were quartered in a log building and got their meals at local tea rooms. A Moth landplane was used for a few days early in the season until water conditions after the spring break-up permitted the use of a Vedette flying-boat. Operations began on 11 May ... and finally terminated on 13 October. The detachment flew 91:45 hours ... and detected 19 fires...

At the end of the year (1936) Lac du Bonnet was closed down. Forestry patrol operations by the R.C.A.F. ceased, and the personnel of the two photographic detachments were transferred to Ottawa. Three of the squadron's Vedettes were flown east to Trenton on 16 September, and five Bellancas and two Fairchilds to Ottawa and Montreal a month later. The radio station at Cormorant Lake was dismantled and the equipment shipped to Winnipeg for storage. On 1 February the squadron was officially transferred to R.C.A.F. Station Ottawa and re-organized by amalgamating the two photographic detachments and some of the personnel of the general purpose flight at Lac du Bonnet with the photographic detachments of No.7 Squadron ... The re-organized No.8 (G.P.) Squadron was now charged with the service's photographic commitments...

In this period the RCAF was frustrated by Bellanca problems. Summarizing 1936 operations some years later, W/C Fred Hitchins wrote:

The year's operations demonstrated once again that the Bellanca was not a suitable aircraft for photographic operations in northern areas. Nor was the performance of the Wright J-6E engine satisfactory, four engine replacements being required for the five aircraft. On 2 August, Bellanca 610 (FS Horner) force landed 120 miles N.E. of the Aylmer base [Aylmer Lake, NWT]. Three days later Bellanca 604 came down in the same area. In both cases the engine failure was believed to be broken connecting rods ... Replacement engines were flown in to the disabled aircraft...

A major aerial search sapped RCAF northern resources from August 17 to September 16, 1936. After delivering a spare engine to one of the stranded Bellancas, F/L Sheldon W. Coleman and LAC J. Fortey went missing in their Fairchild north of Great Slave Lake. Vast efforts came up dry until bush pilots Matt Berry and Marlowe Kennedy spotted a tent and rescued the airmen.

RCAF manning at the end of FY 1936 totalled 148 officers and 959 airmen. At the end of FY1936 the RCAF had 127 aircraft with such types on order as the Supermarine Stranraer and de Havilland D.H.82 Tiger Moth. By this time aircraft ordered in the 1920s as Imperial Gift replacements themselves were retiring, Varunas and Vedettes included. However, the Vancouver soldiered on with 4 (FB)

Squadron at Jericho Beach. In March 1937 the famous RCAF Ford Trimotor G-CYWZ was sold to Grant McConachie's Yukon Southern Air Transport, becoming CF-BEP.

For FY1937 the RCAF received $11,752,650. An increase of 588 personnel was approved, giving a total by year end of 195 officers and 1498 airmen. Of the year's many operations, two Ottawa-based 6 (GP) Squadron Deltas under F/O Carscallen undertook West Coast photography between April and November (the RCAF's first operational use of the Delta). Through August, three Vancouvers were assigned to a meteorological project at Bella Bella. In this period 4 (FB) Squadron had two RAF pilots on exchange: F/Ls J.W.G. Weston and W.P.G. Pretty. The RCAF placed its two new Fairchild Super 71Ps into service this year, but these caused many technical headaches, then tragedy struck on August 9. That morning F/O C.H. Porter and LAC E.G. Doran set out from Edmonton to ferry Super 71P No.666 to Sioux Lookout. They refuelled at Prince Albert and Cormorant Lake, but late the same day crashed fatally into the bush near Grand Rapids, Manitoba.

Formed in 1936, 6 (Torpedo Bomber) Squadron at Trenton commenced flying Blackburn Sharks in the spring of 1937. In charge was F/L C.L. Trecarten, who by May had three pilots. One of these,

LAC Fortey and F/L Coleman at their tundra bivouac with rescuer Marlowe Kennedy. (NWT Archives N79-003:0298)

Moths of 111 Squadron (Aux) over Vancouver airport in 1935. (Gordon S. Williams)

F/L L.F.J. Taylor (on exchange from the RAF) was killed in a Fleet crash on November 20). Over the winter of 1936-37 Hawker Hart cold weather trials were conducted at Rockcliffe by 7 (GP) Squadron. As the *de facto* RCAF experimental unit, in 1937 the squadron also tested skis for the Delta, a cockpit hood for the Wapiti, and brakes and cockpit heater for the Fleet Fawn. The Fleet 21 was evaluated but not recommended for RCAF use.

Through 1937 the NPAAF doubled to about 1000 members. In the case of Hamilton's 119 Squadron, it received its first airplane (a Moth) in May. It completed its first field training at Camp Borden in May and June, 8 officers and 63 airmen attending. A second Moth was delivered in September, a third early in 1938 (flying was from Hamilton airport where a hangar was shared with the local flying club). 120 Squadron did not receive its first aircraft

until April 1937 – four old Moths. Its first cross-country effort (June 23) turned out to be a mess. Led by F/L Johnny Plant, a Permanent Force pilot, 120's four Moths tangled with a prairie dust storm. Each pilot found his own safe haven in the farmland between Regina and Saskatoon. In one case, F/L Macpherson waited overnight, then set off for Saskatoon. In the process he bent his propeller. A local garageman hammered the prop straight and Macpherson made Saskatoon and was back in Regina by day's end.

Through 1937 orders for more new aircraft were approved and the outmoded Wapits finally were delivered. This prompted one naive parliamentarian from the CCF party (who apparently had not been reading the papers) to complain (about the Wapiti), "The bomber is an offensive weapon: against whom are we arming; whom are we preparing to attack?"

Aircraft on Strength, March 1937

Armstrong Whitworth Atlas	1
Armstrong Whitworth Siskin	8
Avro Tutor	6
Bellanca CH-300	8
Blackburn Shark	4
Canadian Vickers Vancouver	4
Canadian Vickers Vedette	11
Consolidated Courier	1
Fairchild 51	9
Fairchild 71	18
Fairchild Super 71	2
Fleet Fawn	37
Hawker Tomtit	2
Northrop Delta	3

To make more room at Trenton for units relocating from Camp Borden in June 1937, Nos. 2 and 3 squadrons moved to Ottawa. The NPAAF now

Accidents were a reality in the interwar RCAF. Few involved death or injury, so usually did not make the press. Others hit the front page, as did the crash of Fairchild KR-34 CF-AKR at Rockcliffe on March 12, 1930. That day W.G. Barker, VC, (president of Fairchild of Canada) was putting 'AKR through its paces. Inexplicably, the great ace suddenly ended in this jumble on the ground. 'AKR had been registered a few days earlier and Fairchild (US) pilot D. Campbell Shaw had brought it to Rockcliffe for a demonstration. Thousands attended Barker's Toronto funeral two days later, including at least six Victoria Cross holders and such prominent figures as Chief of the General Staff MGen A.G.L. McNaughton, W/C L.S. Breadner, W/C G.M. Croil and W/C A.E. Godfrey. (J.D. Hunter Col.)

totalled seven active squadrons, with two others forming. Lots of money was being spent to improving air stations, while plans were being made for new bases from Prince Rupert to Yarmouth. Service types on order by the end of FY1937 included: 12 twin-engine Bolingbrokes to be built by Fairchild Aircraft of Longueuil, 12 Lysanders (National Steel Car of Hamilton), 13 more Sharks (Boeing of Vancouver) and 17 Deltas and 7 Stranraers (Canadian Vickers of Montreal). These projects gave a boost to Canada's nascent industry. Having been manufacturing planes with wood- or metal-frame fuselages and wooden wings, its factories began modernizing. In the case of the Shark being built by Boeing of Canada in Vancouver, its fuselage and wings both were metal-framed. Great Britain was eager to see such progress for, sooner or later, it would need Canada's industrial support.

Meanwhile, RCAF training continued at a high pitch, some 46 new pilots earning their wings in 1937-38 (many quickly joined the RAF, which was rapidly building squadrons, trying to keep pace with Germany). RCAF technical training also was booming, including with RAF exchange postings and courses. RCAF personnel were on RAF courses: instruments at Cranwell, armament at RAF Eastchurch, engineering at Henley, photographic at RAF Farnborough, torpedoes at Gosport and Portsmouth, etc. Men also were sent on technical duties to such manufacturers as Armstrong Siddeley, Ford Motor Co. and Pratt & Whitney. Losses in 1937 included F/O J.L. Henning. While taking the flying boat course at Trenton, his Vedette (811) crashed into the water on August 4. Cpl Collins, the crewman, survived.

Canada's Aviation Industry in 1937

Armstrong Siddeley Motors (Ottawa)
Boeing of Canada (Vancouver)
Canadian Pratt & Whitney
   Aircraft Co. (Longueuil)
Canadian Vickers Ltd. (Montreal)
Canadian Wright (Montreal)
Cub Aircraft Ltd. (Hamilton)
De Havilland of Canada (Toronto)
Fairchild Aircraft Ltd. (Longueuil)
Fleet Aircraft Ltd. (Fort Erie)
MacDonald Brothers Aircraft Ltd.
   (Winnipeg)
National Steel Car (Hamilton)
Noorduyn Aircraft Ltd. (Montreal)
Ottawa Car (Ottawa)
Standard Machine Works (Winnipeg)
Starratt Brothers (Sioux Lookout)

Vedette 115 from Jericho Beach was a total loss after the engine quit near Blind Bay, BC. Sgt Arthur Fleming alighted, but his plane flipped in swells. He and crewman Cpl L.S. Thompson were rescued. (Arthur Fleming Col.)

Minor accidents were commonplace. P/P/O George Kimball was responsible for this 1930 nose-over of Avian 127 at a farm he called "Cochran's Field" near Camp Borden. (RCAF RC2346)

RCAF Aircraft on Strength, Year End March 31, 1937

Avro 621	7
Avro 626	3
Atlas	14
Bellanca	8
Delta	7
Fairchild 51	7
Fairchild 71	16
Fairchild Super 71P	1
Fawn	32
Moth	25
Shark	7
Siskin	6
Tiger Moth	21
Tomtit	2
Vancouver	4
Vedette	9
Wapiti	24

RCAF Permanent Squadrons with Types, Year End March 31, 1937

1 (Fighter) Squadron at Trenton (Siskin)
2 (Army Co-operation) Squadron at Trenton (Atlas)
3 (Bomber) Squadron at Trenton (Wapiti)
4 (Flying Boat) Squadron at Jericho Beach (Fairchild 71, Vancouver, Vedette)
5 (Flying Boat) Squadron at Dartmouth (Fairchild 71)
6 (Torpedo Bomber) Squadron at Trenton (Shark)
7 (General Purpose) Squadron at Rockcliffe (Bellanca CH-300, Fairchild 71)
8 (General Purpose) Squadron at Rockcliffe (Bellanca CH-300, Fairchild 71, Northrop Delta, Vedette)

The RCAF remained responsible for aerial photography across Canada. Through 1937 some 74,959 sq.mi. were photographed for various government bureaus, this requiring 448 rolls of 100-frame film. Assignments included photographing western portions of the trans-Canada airway, areas of prairie drought and sites for potential West Coast military bases. Preventative patrols now were being flown by the RCMP, which had formed an air division using the D.H.90 Dragonfly. By year's end new aircraft added to RCAF inventory included: Delta – 7, Shark – 7, Tiger Moth – 21. A Link trainer was delivered to the RCAF at Trenton, F/L Frank R. Miller being the first trained on the new system. But the initial course would not run until late 1938 (the RCAF was not immediately sold on training pilots in a simulator).

RCAF Aircraft on Order, Year End March 31, 1937

Avro 626	9
Bolingbroke	18
Delta	13
Fawn	11
Goose	1
Lysander	12
Norseman	4
Shark	19
Stranraer	10
Tiger Moth	9

The RCMP's fleet of D.H.90 Dragonflys on their acceptance at DHC in Toronto on May 5, 1937. These aircraft were dedicated to national policing duties – customs, immigration, etc. (C. Don Long)

Civil Aviation Developments

Year by year since there was talk of a trans-Canada airway, the RCAF closely watched developments. RCAF HQ followed how James A. Richardson of Canadian Airways planned to launch a 3445-mile trans-continental air service as soon as the airway was ready. His fleet would include a dozen speedy Lockheed 10 airliners, more modern than anything in RCAF service. Beginning in 1936, Canadian Airways was hiring staff and training pilots in the latest instrument flying techniques (many of these men had trained as RCAF P/P/Os or as commercial pilots at Camp Borden).

By early 1937, however, it was clear that Ottawa wanted control of the new airway. Instead of Canadian Airways inaugurating transcontinental service, as anticipated, on April 10 Ottawa established Trans-Canada Air Lines. A great moment for the airway occurred on July 30 when a DOT Lockheed 12 took off from St. Hubert on the first Canadian dawn-to-dusk flight. Crewed by ex-RCAF pilots J.H. Tudhope and J.D. Hunter, the plane headed west for Vancouver carrying Minister of

On July 30, 1937 DOT Lockheed 12 CF-CCT completed the first dawn-to-dusk flight across Canada. 'CCT served from 1937 to 1963. When it retired, K.M. Molson procured it for Canada's National Aeronautical Collection. (J.F. Sears Col.)

Transport C.D. Howe and other VIPs. With intermediate stops at Gillies, Sioux Lookout, Winnipeg, Regina and Lethbridge, the flight entailed 14:20 flying hours with a lapsed time from St. Hubert of 17:10, so all stops had been brief. Soon, Canadian Airways returned to its regional bush operations. TCA Lockheed 10s began testing the airway, although cautiously at first – it would be 1941 before Halifax was connected to the system. Meanwhile, the RCAF remained modest in size, though well-organized. It had few service aircraft and remained stymied with an inventory of obsolete types. Even commercial operators had speedier, more up-to-date equipment, e.g. Canadian Airways of Winnipeg had a Lockheed 10 as early as August 1936, Starratt Airways of Hudson introduced the Beech 18 into Canada in December 1937, and Mackenzie Air Service of Edmonton had a Norseman earlier than did the RCAF.

At St. Hubert as CF-CCT sat ready for the dawn-to-dusk flight: Donald W. Saunders (DOT), Lew Parmenter (engineer), F.I. Banghart (airport manager St. Hubert), W.H. Hobbs (TCA), H.J. Symington (CNR, president of TCA, passenger), Hon. C.D. Howe (Minister of Transport, passenger), S/L John H. Tudhope (pilot), CMDR C.P. Edwards (DOT, Chief of Air Services, passenger), John D. Hunter (DOT, pilot), J.A. Wilson (Controller of Civil Aviation), George Wakeman (DOT), Donald R. MacLaren (TCA) (LAC C63377).

Between the wars, commercial aviation led the RCAF in modernization. Foremost was Canadian Airways. An example of its visionary planning came in 1931, when it added Ju.52 CF-ARM. At this time the RCAF had no comparable transport plane. (A.B. Shearer Col.)

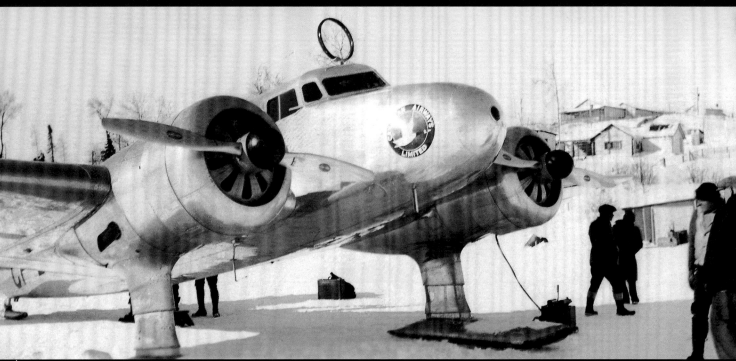

While the RCAF was operating aged Bellancas and Fairchilds, Canada's airlines introduced three high-speed, all-metal types. First came the Lockheed 10, the first (CF-BAF) being registered to Canadian Airways in August 1936. 'BAF quickly was joined by 'AZY. Here is one of them on skis at Red Lake. In May 1937 the DOT acquired CF-CCT. Then, in December, Starratt Airways of Hudson, Ontario introduced Canada's first Beech 18, CF-BGY, shown here at home base. A similar modern design, the Barkley-Grow T8P-1, appeared in the summer of 1939: CF-BMW is seen during its CPA era1943-49. (CANAV Col.)

Even the Norseman took years to reach RCAF service, the first being accepted in January 1940. Here, CF-BAM of Mackenzie Air Service awaits delivery at Cartierville in 1936. In February 1940 'BAM itself got into RCAF colours after being impressed under war measures legislation. (R.F. Halford Col.)

The Final Stretch to War

Seventy-five new aircraft were funded out of Parliament's FY1938 $11,686,517 aviation budget. Much photographic work was done this year (3907 flying hours). Detachments found that the speedy new Deltas, along with some improved film processing technology, allowed their work to be completed two months earlier than usual. At 4 (FB) Squadron bomb shackles were developed for the Vancouver flying boat, ancient though this type was.

A major reorganization occurred on November 19, 1938 when the RCAF ceased being answerable to the Chief of the General Staff and, henceforth, reported only to its Senior Air Officer who, in turn, reported to the Minister of National Defence. At this time, the Senior Air Officer – A/V/M G.M. Croil – became the Chief of the Air Staff. Accompanying these changes, the RCAF also established Air Training Command on October 1, and Eastern Air Command on December 17. Other innovations included: Dartmouth formally became an RCAF station on April 1, 1938; and Test and Development Flight at Rockcliffe, whose functions previously had been conducted by 7 (GP) Squadron, formed on December 1.

Several squadrons relocated in 1938, including 3 (Bomber) Squadron, which flew its eight Wapitis along the trans-Canada airway from Ottawa to Calgary

between October 18-21, 1938, demonstrating that the air force had mobility over long distances. In another such demonstration, 2 (Army Co-Operation) Squadron flew its Atlases from Ottawa to Halifax to train with

coastal batteries, then returned. Also on the move (November 1 to 5) was 6 (TB) Squadron, but its transfer from Trenton to Jericho Beach (3 officers, 2 NCO Pilots, 51 airmen and 5 Sharks included) was effected by rail.

An 8 (GP) Squadron Delta on detachment in the NWT. Then, a view of the 1938 (GP) Detachment at Latham Island, NWT with one Delta visible down on the shore. (Robert Finlayson Col., Ralph Davis)

First flown in 1930, the Avro 621 Tutor replaced the RAF's stalwart Avro 504. In 1931 the RCAF acquired seven Tutors. Following service at Camp Borden, these joined the NPAAF. In 1937 and 1942 twelve similar Avro 626s were acquired for NPAAF and Air Cadet squadrons. The Avros trained pilots, but also flew gunnery and message pick-up exercises. Here No.185 of 11 (AC) Squadron sits at Vancouver. Then, F/O E.A. Nanton of 112 (AC) Squadron in Winnipeg occupies the rear cockpit of an Avro during gunnery training. (Gordon S. Williams, CF RE10040-2)

The auxiliary squadrons now numbered seven and all were active, e.g. at 119 Squadron, Tiger Moths and Fleet Fawns replaced the old Moths in 1938-39. The squadron carried out its first winter exercises at Camp Borden, 10 officers and 72 airmen taking part. As war clouds gathered photographic and armament courses were added to the NPAAF syllabus. A November 1938 news item in *Canadian Aviation* magazine covered 112 Squadron (Aux) of Winnipeg (previously 12 Squadron), reporting that it comprised 17 officers and 110 airmen. The officers were parading thrice weekly at Stevenson Field, while the men paraded once weekly at Minto Street Armouries: "Flying equipment includes one Tiger Moth, two Avro Tutor 621s and one Avro Tutor 626... the squadron features training in the various phases of army co-operation – engine and aircraft repair, signalling, reconnaissance, machine-gunning, aerial photography, etc." The first air cadet units were recognized in

1938, these having formerly been army units. The first such was 162 Squadron at Ridley College in St. Catharines, which affiliated in May with 119 (Bomber) Squadron at Hamilton.

Test and development flying at 7 (GP) Squadron in 1938 involved ski trials with the Avro 626 trainer, the Delta, Hart and Shark. General flight testing was done on the Atlas, the remaining Super

NPAAF personnel during airframe rigging instruction at 111 Squadron (Aux) in Vancouver in January 1938. The aircraft is an old Moth, likely by this time relegated to groundschool. (LAC PA133590)

71P and the Norseman and Stranraer. While the squadron still had a Vedette on strength, in July it added the RCAF's first Grumman Goose. This modern amphibian soon was being widely used on VIP duties.

At the end of FY1938 the RCAF totalled 210 aircraft, but also had 166 on order. A highlight was the delivery from the UK of the first Hawker Hurricanes from an order of 50. These replaced the ancient Siskins of 1 Squadron. For FY1939 the RCAF was expecting a budget of $30,000,000, almost 50% of all defence monies for the year. With war expected at any time, the RCAF stepped up all activities. In the case of 4 (FB) Squadron and 6 (TB) Squadron there was a special event on May 29, 1939 when King George VI and Queen Elizabeth travelled by sea from Vancouver to Victoria. For this occasion (and their return to Vancouver two days later) 3 Vancouvers and 6 Sharks were on Royal Tour escort duties. In May 1939, 6 (TB) Squadron finally fitted torpedo-carrying equipment to its Sharks and began practicing torpedo-dropping tactics. On July 16, 4 (FB) Squadron accepted its first Stranraer. On the East Coast the first Stranraer reached 5 (FB) Squadron at Dartmouth on November 14, 1938. On April 29 it flew

to Miscou Island, New Brunswick to assist two Russian fliers stranded following a crash landing during their record-breaking attempt to reach New York non-stop from Russia. By August 1939 5 (FB) Squadron had five "Strannies" and four Fairchild 71s. By this time it was practicing aerial firing and anti-submarine tactics.

Pilot Profile: A.W. Carter, MM

A typical member of the interwar RCAF was Albert W. Carter. Born in Leeds, England in 1895, Carter emigrated to Canada in 1912. Initially, he seems to have earned his living at manual labour. He enlisted in the Army in November 1914 and was in France in the following September. As a result of action at Courcelette on September 15, 1916, Carter was awarded the Military Medal. He joined the RFC in May 1917, beginning in the UK, where one posting was as a balloon pilot. Later he was in France flying the S.E.5 on 60 and 94 squadrons.

Carter joined the Canadian Air Force at Camp Borden in February 1920 and was posted to Morley under S/L G.M. Croil. On August 8 he air tested the station's first aircraft, a D.H.9. The following season Morley air station

relocated to High River. There on May 21 Carter and WO Beattie were badly injured in the crash of D.H.4 G-CYBW. Of this Carter's CO, S/L Croil, reported: "He flew later on in the season ... but his flying was not entirely satisfactory ... It is thought, however, that with a small amount of dual instruction, this self confidence can be regained and Mr. Carter will make a satisfactory pilot." Croil later modified his view, concluding that Carter was his poorest pilot and should be re-tested. If he did not score well, Croil recommended that he not be granted his permanent commission in the RCAF.

In June 1921 Carter was assigned to Sioux Lookout in charge of the Northern Ontario Mobile Unit, using HS-2Ls. Here, he replaced Capt H.S. Quigley, who had been released from the CAF to join Price Bros. in Chicoutimi. In March 1923 Carter was at Camp Borden on a refresher course. Following some instruction from F/L George E. Brookes and being tested by F/L R.S. Grandy he was written up by F/L Keith Tailyour as: "Good pilot; very keen, lots of confidence. Good type of officer." Before returning to High River, Carter got some time on the S.E.5 and took F/L R.A. Logan's course covering such topics as armament, artillery observation, engines and airframes, navigation and wireless. Flying time on course was 8:30 hours.

According to a note in Carter's personnel file of April 1924, he "Qualified as Certificate Examiner and [is] authorized to carry out inspections and examinations of Air Harbours, Aircraft, Air Engineers and Private and Commercial Air Pilots". Putting these qualifications to use, on May 5, 1925 he inspected the landing ground at Cochrane, Alberta. On May 23 he inspected JN-4 G-CAAA at Shaunavon, Saskatchewan, then was back there in July 1926 to investigate the crash of this same airplane after the pilot, R.A. Hawman, fell to his death while inverted.

Carter received his commission in the RCAF on April 1, 1924 and was promoted to flight lieutenant in October 1925. From November until March 1925 he attended a US Army parachute course at Chanute Field, Illinois. There his assessor wrote of him: "An efficient and reliable parachute rigger. Capable of responsibility. Three successful jumps accomplished ... " Carter then was named parachute training officer

at Camp Borden. A 1928 assessment noted: "He has been rated as above the average in flying ability. He takes a keen interest in parachute work and is always eager to give demonstration jumps. He is a keen sport and takes active part in the boxing and association football carried out on the station." However, there were later complaints that he was not showing his old enthusiasm for flying, so in 1931 his superior sent him into the field with a detachment. Here, he flew some 140 hours and his next assessment was especially positive: "This officer's flying has improved considerably during the last season largely due to the experience gained on the Indian Treaty Flight. He is exceptionally keen on his duties of Parachute Officer and owing to this attribute he is an asset on the station. He is a very reliable type of officer, smart in appearance and takes a keen interest in the station work generally."

In 1934 F/L Carter was on staff at the School of Army Co-Operation at Trenton. There, his fortunes again dipped. He did his job well enough, but seemed to be

waning and often was ill. In 1936 G/C Croil, who 15 years earlier had criticised Carter, personally blocked his promotion to squadron leader, recommending that he be pensioned off. In 1938 S/L Van Vliet suggested in a memo: "Considering this officer's experience it is felt that he could be more useful employed elsewhere than in his present capacity as Officer Commanding, the School of Army Co-operation Flight, which is a job that could be handled equally well by a more junior officer." In December, Carter was transferred to RCAF HQ in Ottawa, but in January 1939 finally was promoted. In 1941-42 he was chief ground instructor at 15 SFTS, RCAF Station Claresholm, Alberta, during which time he became W/C Carter. Having heard that Canada might begin training paratroops, he offered his services, but was not accepted. Due to chronic illness, he was posted on administrative duties to Patricia Bay in 1943. He did not adapt to this position, so retired from the RCAF in 1943. W/C Carter passed away in Vancouver on November 9, 1958.

With world war on the horizon, the RCAF at long last was focused on military purposes. Although still doing aerial photography for civil ministries, by the late 1930s it was training for a host of combat scenarios, and adding some more modern types. Seen over Vancouver in April 1939 is one of No.1 Squadron's Hawker Hurricanes. (LAC PA501526)

Other signs of RCAF pre-war modernization were the Supermarine Stranraer (912 TOS July 1939) and North American Harvard I (1325 TOS August 1939). Both soon would prove indispensible in the RCAF Home War Establishment and BCATP. (RCAF, LAC PA63552)

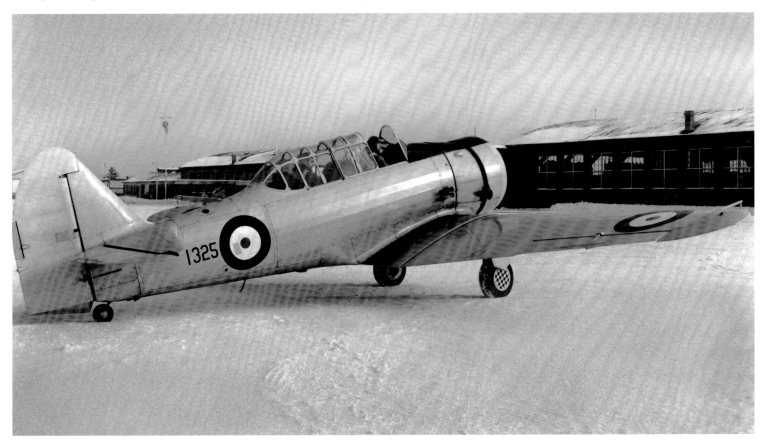

This well-known photo represents the multi-national face of the British Commonwealth Air Training Plan. Posed for the RCAF PR photographer's camera one day in March 1942 were LACs R.W.N. Bennetts of Australia, T.S. Knapman of New Zealand, C. Jackson of Great Britain, Sgt L.R. Young of Newfoundland, Sgt W. McElwee, Jr. of Philadelphia, Pennsylvania and Sgt W.J. D. MacLaren of Ottawa. By war's end the system had graduated: Canada – 72,835 students, UK – 42,110, Australia – 9606, New Zealand – 7002. Many of those who wore the RAF shoulder flash were from such occupied nations as Belgium, Czechoslovakia, France, Norway and Poland. (DND PL8155)

British Commonwealth Air Training Plan

Five new RCAF D.H.82C Tiger Moths await delivery in April 1940 at the de Havilland factory in North Toronto. Although there were other important types in use, the Tiger Moth would be the trademark of BCATP elementary pilot training. The two nearest aircraft both were lost by the summer of 1943. 4004 crashed at 2 EFTS, Fort William on September 15, 1940. (C. Don Long Col.)

On the eve of war in September 1939 the Mackenzie King government was in the midst of a years-long discussion with Great Britain about how (or whether) Canada might supply Canadian pilots to the RAF, and/or train British pilots in Canada. By this time the UK needed a flood of aircrew to man new squadrons being formed to help counter rising German might. In 1936 G/C Robert Leckie, Canada's WWI flying boat hero (then working under Air Commodore A.W. Tedder, head of RAF training) was proposing that a UK-funded air training operation be set up in Canada. Though modest in scale, this was likened to the 1917-18 RFC (Canada) plan, whereby some 20,000 air and ground crew were trained for the British air services. Tedder and Leckie appreciated how this had succeeded so well: Canada had the natural resources, manpower and industrial base, unlimited airspace, suitable climate, and immunity from enemy attack. Admitting to Canada's harsh winters, Leckie explained: "None of these conditions are comparable to the adverse flying weather experienced in England, and the flying can be continued with very few interruptions throughout the year..."

The 1917-18 scheme had been largely British – established and run by the Royal Flying Corps, Imperial Munitions Board, etc. Ottawa acquiesced at every step. Between the wars, however, things changed. Under the Liberal governments of Mackenzie King, Ottawa was little interested in an Imperial defence pact. It agreed, however, that Canadians might volunteer for RAF service and by 1939 some 400 held aircrew positions in the RAF. Some of these men had begun in Canada's flying clubs, others had earned their wings as RCAF P/P/Os or sergeant pilots. Such recruits paid their way to the UK, sometimes with no assurance of acceptance by the RAF. Meanwhile, the RCAF, facing its own manpower shortage, had signed up a few dozen ex-RAF pilots, mainly to instruct at Camp Borden. The declaration of war by the UK and France on September 3, 1939 ended this state of affairs. Great Britain made an immediate plea to the Commonwealth for help, especially in aircrew training. Ottawa, which declared war on September 10, concurred. Great Britain agreed that Canada would oversee whatever organization might result and, in due course, be rewarded by having its own squadrons overseas.

On September 16 a proposal was made at a high commissioners' conference in London that the UK, Canada, Australia and New Zealand establish an air training scheme in Canada. Ottawa liked this, since it would afford a prominent role in the air war with a prospect of reduced casualties. Being so political, however, Mackenzie King wanted it clear that the plan was British in origin. He later obliged the UK to state publicly that Canada could participate in no greater way than by being the centre of Commonwealth aircrew training.

In October 1939 the UK sent a mission to Canada headed by Lord Riverdale, who carried a proposal that Canada prepare to train nearly 10,000 pilots and 15,000 other aircrew annually, almost a half of Great Britain's anticipated needs. As originally drafted, the plan called for 72 Canadian flying schools at a cost over three years of $900 million, about one third to be paid by Canada (as early as October 20, 1939 a headline in the Canadian press announced "Training Plan Will Call for 100 Air Fields").

Lord Riverdale did not endear himself to Ottawa by commenting about Canada probably lacking the ability to run such a plan. This annoyed King, who noted in his diary for October 17: "It is amazing how these people have come out from the Old Country and seem to think that all they have to do is tell us what is to be done." In spite of such ill feelings, negotiations proceeded and terms slowly were hammered out, e.g. that Canada fund almost 81% of the plan, Australia and New Zealand in accordance with their participation. Following a gruelling

The "founding fathers" of the BCATP in a famous photo taken in Ottawa. In front are A/C/M Sir Robert Brooke-Popham (UK, BCATP adviser in Canada), Hon. J.L. Ralston (Canada, Minister of Finance), G/C Hugh W.L. Saunders (New Zealand, Chief of the Air Staff), Senator R. Dandurand (Canada), Lord Riverdale (chief UK BCATP negotiator), William Lyon Mackenzie King (Canada, Prime Minister), J.V. Fairburn (Australia, Minister for Civil Aviation), Ernest Lapointe (Canada, Minister of Justice), Capt H.H. Balfour, (UK, Under Secretary of State for Air), Norman M. Rogers (Canada, Minister of National Defence), A/M Sir Christopher Courtney, CBE, DSO (UK, Empire Air Training Plan). In the middle are J.B. Abraham (UK), Dr. O.D. Skelton (Canada, Dept. of External Affairs), T.A. Barrow (New Zealand, Air Secretary), Sir Gerald Campbell (UK, High Commissioner), Hon. I. Mackenzie (Canada, Dept. of Pensions and National Health), W/C George Jones (Australia), Hon. C.D. Howe (Canada, Minister of Transport), Dr. W.C. Clark (Canada, Dept. of Finance), A/V/M G.M. Croil (Canada, Chief of the Air Staff). Behind are J.R. Smyth (UK), F.R. Howard (UK), C.V. Kellway (Australia), A/C Ernest W. Stedman (RCAF), G/C A. Gray (UK), LCol K.S. McLachlan (Canada, Deputy Minister of National Defence), G/C J.M. Robb (UK), A.D.P. Heeney (Canada, Secretary to Mackenzie King), G/C L.N. Hollinghurst (UK), R.E. Elford (Australia), W.L. Middlemass (New Zealand). (DND PMR81-152)

session, after midnight on December 17, 1939 the participants signed the document bringing into formal existence the Empire Air Training Plan (later re-named "British Commonwealth Air Training Plan"). This would be separate from the RCAF's Home War Establishment.

Prime Minister King made it clear that the agreement was the result of years of tough negotiating, but made no reference to how he had been an obstructionist all along the way. Within hours of the signing, he approved a press release, explaining (falsely) how all had gone smoothly in the previous weeks. Riverdale was quoted: "We have had wonderful co-operation from your government ... all the parties are completely satisfied ..." The official communiqué gave some details: "Primary training in Canada [will] be done on De Havilland Moths and Fleet

trainers, with advanced instruction on North American Harvards." Advanced training Fairey Battles and Avro Ansons would be shipped from the UK. Great Britain would cover the purchasing of all these planes. About 80% of students would be Canadian. Great Britain, Australia and New Zealand would do their primary training at home, then send elementary graduates to Canada for advanced courses. To begin, existing flying club airfields and municipal airports would be used, but dozens of new facilities would have to be constructed from scratch. Some 40,000 military and civilian personnel would staff these and the Prime Minister cautioned that all dollar estimates "were subject to a wide margin of error". The plan would turn out a pilot over a 26-week period, an observer in 22 and an air gunner or wireless operator in 20. The press release of December 18 also

explained that "the go-ahead signal ... means much for the Canadian construction industry and for scores of other ... industries" and that orders for materiel already were being processed. In *Aerodrome of Democracy* Fred J. Hatch explains how the plan would be administered:

Political realities dictated, and King would have it no other way, that overall administration must remain with the Canadian government and military command with the RCAF. The interests of Great Britain, Australia and New Zealand were safeguarded by a supervisory board on which each of the four countries had a voice. It was to meet monthly under the chairmanship of the Canadian Minister of National Defence ... and was empowered to make recommendations directly to the Chief of the Air Staff. In addition, through their air liaison officers in Ottawa the other three partners could make representation to the RCAF on matters pertaining to their own personnel. While serving in Canada, trainees from outside the country were to be "attached" to the RCAF, meaning that they were subject to its jurisdiction and would receive Canadian rates of pay.

A start-up date for training was given as April 29, 1940, when No.1 Initial Training School would open in Toronto. The scheme was to be fully operational two years later, when it would be turning out some 1500 aircrew every four weeks. At first the RCAF recruiting system was overwhelmed, but creases were ironed out and the system began functioning more or less effectively. Meanwhile, the Air Ministry sent Air Commodore Robert Leckie to Ottawa as Director of Air Training. Leckie, who would work under A/V/M George M. Croil, Chief of the Air Staff, proved to be ideal for this job. To rectify the conundrum of being RAF, he transferred to the RCAF in 1942. Ultimately, the BCATP was one of the Allies' most vital organizations. It continued to March 31, 1945 by which time the statistics[†] showed the following numbers of air trades graduated[*] (number of personnel for the RCAF shown in brackets):

Pilot	49,808	(25,747)
Navigator	29,963	(12,855)
Air Bomber	15,673	(6659)
Wireless Operator/		
Air Gunner	18,496	(12,744)
Air Gunner	14,996	(12,917)
Naval Air Gunner	704	
Flight Engineer	1913	(1913)
Total	131,553	(72,835)

[*] 5296 additional RAF and Fleet Air Arm air trades were trained in Canada under separate arrangements, mainly by RAF schools transferred from the UK to Canada.
[†] As per *The Aerodrome of Democracy*

Aircraft of the BCATP

With war clouds swirling, the RCAF already was taking preliminary steps to modernize equipment and step up training. In January 1938, for example, it ordered 26 de Havilland Tiger Moths; in October 1939, 27 Fleet Finches. These were for elementary training and urgently were required to replace 1920s vintage Moths and Fleets. Then, in July 1939, the RCAF ordered 30 North American Harvard Mk.Is, the most modern advanced trainers on the market. With war declared, other orders were rushed for Ansons, Battles, Cranes, etc., but quantities suddenly totalled in the thousands.

The Fairey Battle served in the RCAF first as a fighter with 115 Squadron at St. Hubert, but quickly was relegated to bombing and gunnery training. From the gunner's position of the Battle, students practiced air-to-air gunnery with a cine-camera or fired live rounds at drogue targets towed by Lysanders and other types. They also dropped small practice bombs on ground targets. Shown is Battle 1639 in the standard yellow and black paint of a bombing and gunnery school plane. TOS in April 1940, 1639 served through the war until sold for scrap in 1946. (RCAF)

RCAF/BCATP Basic Trainers 1939-45*

Bolingbroke 10214 was one of 626 of its type on RCAF strength. Canadian-built by Fairchild of Longueuil, Quebec, the "Boly" derived from the Bristol Blenheim, a mid-1930s RAF bomber from which the Beaufighter also evolved. It played various roles, primarily in bombing and gunnery. However, at Annette Island, Alaska, it was a long-range fighter with 115 Squadron, and served on both coasts as a patrol bomber until replaced by such types as the Catalina and Ventura. (John Caron Col.)

Single Engine	Total on Strength
D.H.82 Menasco/Tiger Moth	1546
Fairchild Cornell	1555
Fairey Battle	740
Fairey Swordfish	105
Fleet 16 Finch	431
Fleet Fort	101
Noorduyn Norseman Mk.VIW	30
North American Harvard	1887
North American Yale	119
Northrop Nomad	32
Stearman Model 75	301
Westland Lysander Mk.III	253

Twin Engine	Total on Strength
Airspeed Oxford	819
Avro Anson	4413
Bristol Bolingbroke Mk.IVW/Mk.IVT	422
Cessna T-50 Crane	826

* Figures as per *Canadian Military Aircraft: Serials and Photographs*. Some of these aircraft also served in Home War Establishment units; precise quantities for the BCATP are difficult to determine.

The chief RCAF elementary trainers in September 1939 were the Fleet Fawn and Finch, and the Tiger Moth. The first of 431 Finches was taken on strength in October 1939. Nos.4471 and '72 of 22 EFTS are seen at Ancienne Lorette, Quebec. (LGen W.K. Carr)

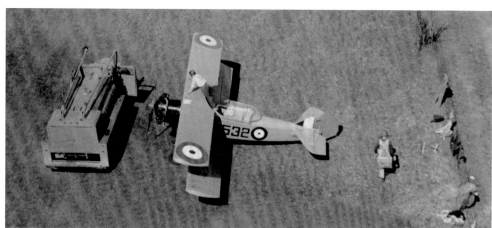

Finch 4532 "gassing up" at 12 EFTS, Goderich. Then, Finches on the flightline, same school. Aviation enthusiast Bruce Best, then a mechanic at Goderich, took these photos *circa* 1941. Bruce later was a prominent Canadian helicopter pilot.

Tiger Moth 4197 of 15 EFTS, Regina, and 4194 on skis. (DND PL6112, Bruce Best Col.)

Some of the RCAF's pre-war "Tigers" still were in use early in the war – here is one at the factory in Toronto. With the flood of new aircraft, aircraft 240 was SOS in August 1940. (W.J. McDonough Col.)

The Fairchild Cornell was chosen to replace the Tiger Moth and Finch. Shown are three in echelon right formation – the pilots were instructors based at Trenton with 1 FIS, so a well-conducted formation was expected. (DND PL11632)

Foreseeing the inevitable – world war – in 1939 the RCAF ordered 30 North American NA-61 trainers. This type dated to the 1934 NA-16, North American's original such design. The RCAF's NA-61s were christened "Harvard I". Here is No.1323 awaiting delivery at North American in Inglewood, California in July 1939. The Harvard became the backbone of advanced single-engine training in the BCATP. Some 1887 were in service, all but 34 being Harvard IIs. Harvard 1323

logged many hours from Camp Borden and Trenton until crashing near Stirling, Ontario on September 12, 1941. That day F/O Lloyd S. Percival (age 21 from Oakland, California) and P/O Joseph F. Laycock (age 25 from Calgary) were flying from Trenton when something went awry. Farmer John Holden, on whose farm the plane came down, reported that, from what he saw, the crew was attempting a forced-landing. Percival and Laycock both were killed. (Jack McNulty Col.)

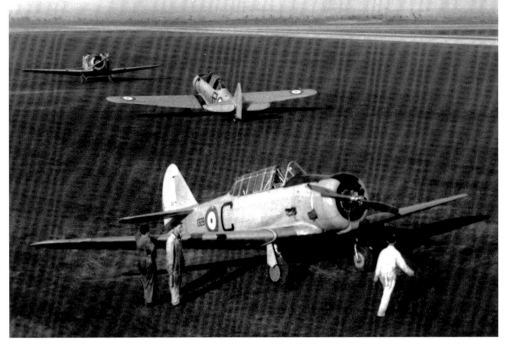

A trio of Harvard Is in a typical Camp Borden setting early in WWII. Nearest is 1328, which survived all of its BCATP wear and tear to be SOS in February 1945. (Jack McNulty Col.)

Camp Borden winter work horses: Harvard Is 1342 and 1345 and Oxford I 1521. (Jack McNulty Col.)

France's capitulation in May 1940 turned out to have beneficial side effect on the RCAF/BCATP: 119 North American NA-64 fixed-undercarriage trainers awaiting delivery to France were turned over to the RCAF. Known as Yales in Canada, they were taken on strength on August 23. The Yales immediately were employed at Camp Borden and Trenton, then at such other advanced schools as Aylmer. Powered by a 420-hp Wright R-975E-3, compared to the more modern Harvard II's 600-hp Pratt & Whitney R-1340, the Yale proved very serviceable. It soldiered on to war's end, by then mainly as a wireless trainer. Here is wireless trainer 3381 in a well-composed view. Then, Yale 3440 awaits takeoff clearance. (Jack McNulty Col.)

Yales on the flightline at 14 SFTS, Aylmer. Then, 3372 restored in the 1980s after being rescued in 1970 from its state of limbo on the late Ernie Simmons' farm in Tillsonburg, Ontario. It's seen during a photo shoot near Peterborough, Ontario on July 20, 1991. (Jack McNulty Col., Larry Milberry)

One of Alf Barton's many excellent Harvard photos – a take-off scene at 14 SFTS, Aylmer, where Alf instructed so diligently that he earned himself an Air Force Cross. (Jack McNulty Col.)

A pair of Ottawa-based 2 SFTS Harvard IIs. The Harvard trained thousands of pilots for operational roles overseas and on the home front. Both of these Harvards made it through the war. 2597 was SOS in 1947. It's fate is not known, but it may have been one of hundreds of Harvards sold postwar by War Assets Disposal Corporation to customers from Sweden to China. 3091 was donated to Italy in 1957 under a NATO give-away scheme. (Jack McNulty Col.)

Another excellent Harvard II formation, this time at 9 SFTS, Summerside in the summer of 1943. Flying 2942 was instructor Keith Barlow. Some teasing critic at the time wrote on the back of this old print, "Come on Barlow, move up in there". 2942 remained on RCAF strength until the end of 1960. (CANAV Col.)

The Fleet 60K Fort was the only Canadian-designed plane of WWII to enter production. Note how the rear cockpit was slightly elevated, and how the front canopy slides forward. Fleet had high hopes for the Fort, which flew initially at Fort Erie in March 1940. But the RCAF was sold on the Harvard for all the right reasons, especially power. With its 330-hp Jacobs engine, the Fort was not a practical stepping stone to something like an 1030-hp Hurricane. Most of Canada's 101 Forts served as wireless trainers at 2 WS, Calgary. This example of the Fort may be seen at the Canadian Warplane Heritage in Hamilton, Ontario. (Rick Radell)

Fleet Forts 3622 and 3626 from 2 Wireless School on a training exercise over southern Alberta. (CANAV Col.)

115

While Canadian factories in 1939 were ramping up production of small training planes, Great Britain was shipping such advanced training types to Canada as the Battle, Anson and Oxford. Shown is a typical bombing and gunnery school Battle at Edmonton. It likely was in for maintenance at Aircraft Repair Ltd., a company founded by Leigh Brintnell after he sold Mackenzie Air Service to CPA in 1940. (Leslie Corness).

Flying alongside the Battle and Bolingbroke at bombing and gunnery schools was the stalwart Westland Lysander – the "Lizzie". First flown in the UK in 1936, it was manufactured under licence at Malton by National Steel Car and flown initially there in August 1939. A further 224 were completed, most for the BCATP. Lysander 2452 is seen in a beautifully composed photo. Unfortunately, it was lost in a crash of September 7, 1944 while at 3 (B&G) School, MacDonald, Manitoba. 2426 towed target drogues at 4 (B&G) School at Fingal, Ontario. By war's end it had logged a mere 627:30 flying hours. (Colin Clark Col., RCAF)

In the summer of 1940 the RCAF acquired 32 Northrop A-17 Nomads (as with the Yales, these had been intended for France). Stationed initially at Camp Borden, the RCAF Nomads were advanced trainers, but later sent down to tow targets. Simultaneously, the Royal Norwegian Air Force (in exile) was doing advanced pilot training in Canada using similar Northrops. Shown is an RNoAF Northrop at Toronto Island Airport. The air terminal beyond remained in use in 2010. (Bruce Best Col.)

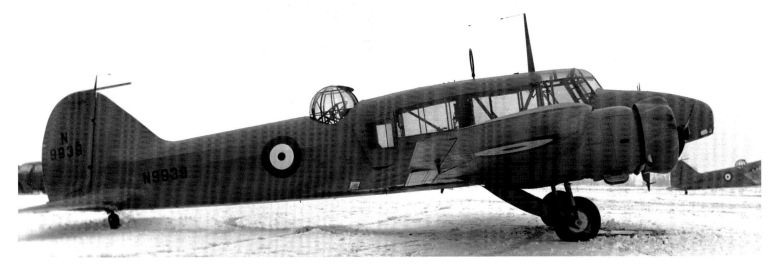

The RCAF's most common wartime twin-engine trainer was the Avro Anson. First flown in the UK in 1935, the Anson was on operations in 1939-40, but quickly was relegated to training and transport. By early 1940 Ansons were being sent to Canada on ships braving the U-boat infested North Atlantic. Anson N9939 (later RCAF 6007) is seen at de Havilland in Toronto, where the first RAF example had flown in February 1940. (C. Don Long)

These fellows labouring over Anson I 6747 at 33 ANS, Mount Hope might have been AC2s on "useless duties" while awaiting course assignments. Although the first RCAF/BCATP Ansons were UK built, most others were manufactured by members of a Canadian consortium under the Federal Aircraft banner. (Jack McNulty Col.)

The handsome Anson Mk.V was a cleaned up Canadian design. Its molded plywood construction was ideal for Canada, a nation rich in forest resources; and its reliable 450-hp P&W R-985 engines were welcomed by anyone familiar with the Cheetahs and Jacobs used in earlier Ansons. (George Neal Col.)

Having entered RAF service in 1937, the Airspeed Oxford was the RAF's first dedicated twin-engine trainer. Powered by 370-hp Cheetah engines, it had a top speed of about 185 mph. Of the 8751 Oxfords built, 1555 went to the RCAF. Shown is an RAF example – L4580 was lost in a September 13, 1938 accident while at 3 FTS. The Oxford left RCAF service at war's end, but continued in the RAF into 1954. (via Gordon Diller)

Oxford 1520 at Trenton early in the war. Although it suffered a Category "B" (severe) accident at Picton on October 28, 1941, it still was in use at war's end. Although all these BCATP photos are black and white, one can mentally colourize them – brilliant yellow airplanes on grass or snow with stunning Canadian skies. (DND PL8523)

The Cessna T-50 Bobcat, dubbed "Crane" in the RCAF, first flew in Wichita in September 1939 powered by two 225-hp Jacobs L-4MB engines. Cessna was aiming the T-50 at the commercial market, but had no funding to proceed. Then came manna from heaven – an order from Ottawa for 644 T-50s needed by the BCATP for multi-engine training. US military orders followed and Cessna never looked back. The Crane entered RCAF service in January 1941 and 826 had been delivered by the summer of 1942. Total production exceeded 5400. Crane 7892 was delivered in August 1941, but was lost in a crash at 3 SFTS, Calgary, on March 6, 1944. Then, a famous view of 7668 of 4 SFTS, Saskatoon. (RCAF, Jack McNulty Col.)

The "front offices" of the three standard BCATP twins: civilian staff pilot George Neal flies a 10 AOS Anson; a typical Oxford cockpit; then an unidentified American student pilot aloft in a 10 SFTS Crane – notice his "USA" shoulder flash. (George Neal, CANAV, W.H.D. Meaden Cols.)

BCATP OTU Types

Beech 18, Bristol Beaufort, Bristol Bolingbroke, Consolidated Liberator, Douglas Dakota, Handley Page Hampden, Hawker Hurricane, Lockheed Hudson, Lockheed Ventura, North American Mitchell

No.1 OTU in Bagotville where pilots made the jump from SFTS to the modern fighter, was the only such RCAF OTU. Here, OTU Hurricane "Nose 58" taxies for an exercise. Often such photos are not "sharp as a dime". After all, they were usually snapped while the photographer was involved in his own issues of the moment. His equipment was far from today's miraculous point-and-shoot digital gizmo. He had to set up his camera: check his shutter speed and f-stop, cock the firing mechanism, frame his shot in the second or two he had to spare, shoot, put the camera away and continue with his flying duties. Thus did he give new meaning to the term "multi-tasking". Meanwhile, he had no business even doing all this, since such photography was strictly forbidden during the war. (George Webster Col.)

Many types served on the OTU side of the BCATP, the stage at which aircrew converted to operational aircraft. Typical was the Mosquito which equipped 36 OTU at Greenwood, Nova Scotia. Nearest in this view is Canadian-built Mosquito B.20 KB179/Y, with KB105/A1 beyond. Then, Hampden A386 (ex-RAF P5435) of 32 OTU, Patricia Bay, where Coastal Command crews trained. (DND 24151, Jack McNulty Col.)

To get the aircrew training job done, Central Flying School and 1 Flying Instructors School at Trenton always had a wide range of aircraft. In this view early in the war the training types seen are the Fawn, Harvard I, Anson, Oxford and Battle along with two Lockheed transports. (DND PL293)

CFS/1FIS two years later. The Fawns have been replaced by Cornells, the Harvard Is by IIs, the Anson Is by Cranes. Also seen are a Stearman and a Finch. (DND PL11645)

The "silent partner" in the grand BCATP scheme of things was the humble Link Trainer. The Link was the world's first practical flight simulator. It was cheap and performed all the basic aircraft manoeuvres. The RCAF gave Ed Link his first large-scale order and a factory was established in Ontario for licenced production. Every RCAF station was equipped with Link Trainers, which remained in service into the postwar years. Here is the Link training room at 19 EFTS, Virden in October 1944. (Right) Some Links even had make-believe wings! Maybe this was a left-over idea from Ed Link's days as a carnival operator. (LAC PA140658, DND PL1050)

Most BCATP types evolved at least in small ways through the war. In co-operation with the RCAF engineering branch, some radical mods were tried. To allay fears of a shortage of Ranger engines, for example, Central Aircraft in London, Ontario modified Cornell 10502 with a 190-hp Lycoming O-435. 10502 first flew in March 1943, but was a one-off airplane, as the supply of Rangers held. (W.J. McDonough Col.)

Oddball Types

Anxious to get involved in what was a training plane bonanza, manufacturers' sales representatives began knocking on doors in Ottawa, showing their brochures, and wining and dining officials. They knew what potentially fruitful sales territory they were cultivating, but few would succeed. The RCAF studied each proposal, but already had a solid plan regarding equipment. In Canada's national archives Vol. RG24 Vol.5137 in Record Group 24 tells the story of the proposed trainers. Included are the original letters that went back and forth, along with manufacturers' brochures, photos, etc. A typical sales pitch was made in January 1940 when the Howard Aircraft Corp of Chicago contacted the Department of Munitions and Supply about its new trainer, the low-wing DGA-165 powered by a 160-hp Kinner. The RCAF viewed the plane as underpowered and was unimpressed that it had no flaps, no coupe top for winter flying, and had too simplistic an instrument panel. Although well reviewed by US operators, this DGA was not widely adapted and production ceased at about 60 aircraft.

On August 8, 1940, the company making the tiny Ercoupe Safety Plane (Engineering and Research Corporation in Riverside, Maryland) wrote to Air Marshal W.A. Bishop in RCAF HQ. ERCO's agent in New York City, W.J. Kearney, claimed how the Ercoupe "will reduce by 50% the time required to teach students to actually fly." He quoted a price of $2890 per aircraft and ended, "I would appreciate hearing from you as promptly as possible regarding this matter, as I feel it is one of vital interest to the Empire." Bishop passed the letter to one of his competent HQ men, W/C R.E. McBurney, who reviewed the ERCO specs, likely asked around for opinions, then wrote an assessment that said it all in two words – "insufficient performance". This decision likely also was influenced by the ERCO's tricycle undercarriage, a feature which caused many pilots in RCAF HQ to recoil; and by the fact that the ERCO was spin-proof, but student pilots needed to learn how to spin. Used in small numbers to train wartime pilots in the US, the Ercoupe went on to great postwar success as a sport and club plane. An

One contender in the BCATP training plane sweepstakes was the aesthetic-looking Ryan PT-22 "Recruit", powered by a 160-hp Kinner. Some 1000 PT-22s were built by Ryan in San Diego. Delivered to US Army civilian flying schools, they trained some 14,000 pilots by war's end. The RCAF, however, passed on the PT-22. Seen is prototype NX18925 while being demonstrated at Rockcliffe over the winter of 1940-41. (RCAF HC11027)

Ercoupe today is a desirable collector's item.

On October 31, 1940 J.A. Burgess of Montreal wrote to Ralph Bell, Director General of Aircraft Production in the Department of Munitions and Supply: "I am instructed to offer you 1,500 Dart Training Planes that can be made over the next twelve months, delivery to start in sixty days from the time of order. These planes make 205 miles per hour and have [Kinner] motors of 175 h.p. The price of these is very low, somewhere in the neighbourhood of $10,000 per plane." The letter ended on the desk of the RCAF's senior engineering officer, G/C Ferrier. Replying to Bell on November 21, Ferrier turned down the Dart because of its side-by-side seating, explaining how this "has definitely been rejected by the training experts".

General Aeronautics Corp of Detroit also threw its hat into the training plane ring, offering the Warner-powered Myers

biplane at $7500. GAC's approach was via mail on December 6, 1940 to Col Douglas G. Joy of the DOT. Joy forwarded the letter to G/C Ferrier. No action was taken on the Myers. In another case, Wendell F. Fletcher of Fletcher Aircraft in Los Angeles offered the FBT-2 trainer at $4500. His representative, F.J. Rutland of Ottawa Car, wrote enthusiastically to A/V/M Stedman on April 24, 1941: "We can supply advanced trainers … and in no time millions can be saved in the training programme.". W/C D. Edwards flew the FBT-2, but found that it exhibited poor stall tendencies. His comment about how "a quick stall is considered a dangerous characteristic for elementary training," would have squelched any hope for Fletcher. On May 15, 1941 A/V/M Stedman wrote to Ralph Bell, "we do not want this plane". In the end the RCAF stayed with the tried and true – Tiger Moths and Finches supplemented with Cornells and Stearmans.

The first Engineering and Research Corporation 2-seater "Ercoupe" flew at College Park, Maryland in 1937. It had no luck in the BCATP sweepstakes, although a few hundred were employed at civil-operated flying schools in the US. Postwar, the Ercoupe became a popular personal plane. The price was right at about $2600, so sales in the US and Canada were brisk. Production continued under various banners into 1970. Here is CF-IQA (Erco 415C c/n 2850) landing at Markham, Ontario on May 11, 1975. (Larry Milberry)

Aircrew Training Begins

The BCATP in Canada was a complex institution. Organization and administration started "at the top" in the Air Ministry (UK) and Canadian ministerial and RCAF HQ levels, then filtered down. The first day to day layer comprised four Training Command HQs: No.1 Toronto, No.2 Winnipeg, No.3 Montreal and No.4 Regina (later in Calgary). Each had a manning depot, initial training schools, flying and trades schools, then such support organizations as equipment and repair depots. An embarkation centre known as "Y" Depot in Halifax facilitated transportation for overseas personnel. Each training station had a commanding officer and staff essential to its workings, whether flying or ground school instructors, maintenance and repair experts, administrators and others in such fields as medical and dental, transport-

From Day 1 of the war, young Canadians poured into the recruiting offices to enlist. The RCAF was unprepared for such enthusiasm, so few recruits were immediately accepted. It took several months before the system began moving freely and for the recruiting personnel to track down and enlist the original wave of men. In this PR photo, eager young fellows, each likely imagining himself in the cockpit of a Spitfire, are briefed at the recruiting centre in downtown Ottawa on September 3, 1943. Those selected for service soon would be learning the basics of airforce life at one of the BCATP manning depots. (DND PL20724)

Three fresh recruits strolling in downtown Edmonton, feeling on top of the world after collecting their RCAF uniforms at the tailor's: W.H.D. "Bill" Meaden, Louis Simpson and Gordon Smith. On the back on this old print Bill wrote: "Gordon and Louis – two of the nicest fellows I met since I joined up. I wonder if we'll ever see each other again? Perhaps we'll run into each other in the old country. Who knows." (CANAV Col.)

ation and logistics, flying control, meteorology, aircraft test and ferry, discipline and law, physical education and entertainment, and construction and site maintenance. This vast organization had one goal – to produce aircrew, so the focus of everything was on flying instructors and trainees.

The BCATP had decided early that elementary pilot and air observer training would be handled at civil-operated schools. The first four elementary schools opened on June 24, 1940, so *ad hoc* training centres, e.g. Patterson and Hill in Toronto, were phased out. The original BCATP flight schools were: 1 Elementary Flying Training School (Malton, operated by the Toronto Flying Club)), 2 EFTS (Thunder Bay, Thunder Bay Flying Club), 3 EFTS (London, London Flying Club) and 4 EFTS (Windsor Mills, Montreal Flying Club). By January 1944, 36 such schools had opened. The first Air Observer School was 1 AOS, opened at Malton on May 27, 1940 and operated by Dominion Skyways, a progressive bush flying company. No.2 AOS opened on August 5 (Edmonton, Canadian Airways) followed by eight other such schools.

Calling on Experience

To establish Canada's home air defence, get the BCATP up and running, and prepare for overseas operations, everyone in the RCAF from the "brass hats" in headquarters to the LACs on the flightline had to chip in. The task seemed impossible, but the RCAF was confident. Small as it was, it could count on its solid experience, organization and determination. The case of Francis Henry Pearce illustrates the high individual standards that existed throughout the RCAF.

Born in Ottawa in 1914, Pearce knocked around as a store clerk and auto mechanic until joining the RCAF in

August 1934. He trained in the technical trades, moved ahead, then was accepted for pilot training. At this he excelled, placing first in a flight training class of 12 and second in a ground school class of 26. One assessment in this period noted: "This LAC flies on instruments with accuracy and confidence... He is considered above average." Pearce earned his wings and sergeant stripes in May 1938. Later that year he was a Wapiti pilot with 3 Squadron in Calgary, where his CO, S/L A. Lewis, wrote of him that December: "A most conscientious and efficient Non-Commissioned Officer. Can be trusted to carry out any work entrusted to him ..."

In June 1939 Sgt Pearce was on the instructor's course at Trenton, where he soloed on such types as the Bellanca and Oxford. With the outbreak of war, by which time he had some 500 flying hours, he was commissioned and assigned at Trenton to teach airforce ways to classes of civilian pilots. In April 1940 he took a Link Trainer course at Malton, so was keeping current with the technology and the philosophy of pilot training. That winter he was posted to 7 SFTS at Macleod, Alberta with such duties as taking student pilots on their crucial wings tests.

In March 1941 F/O Pearce was promoted to flight lieutenant. The following month he was awarded his A-2 instructor's category by S/L Paul Y. Davoud. He was posted to Mountain View in April 1942, thence to 2 Flying Instructor School at Vulcan, Alberta in

August. At Vulcan his duties included improving training procedures and grading students. Pearce was promoted to squadron leader in September 1942 and posted to 4 Training Command HQ in Winnipeg. There he helped manage EFTS and SFTS student loads at various stations, worked in course records and liaised with training units.

In December 1943 S/L Pearce was overseas, attached for about six months to the Empire Central Flying School. There he flew everything from the tiny Magister to the Hurricane, Wellington and Lancaster. He did well, but his RAF superiors were not so lavish in their praise as had been those at home. W/C A.C. Kermode, for example, observed: "This officer has not exceptional ability but he has shown interest and keenness in the ground side of the course.". The CFI, W/C A.J. Shelfoon, noted: "This officer ... has made a fair contribution to the course. He is not over-progressive in outlook." Home in Canada, S/L Pearce took the Mosquito course at 36 OTU in Greenwood. Near war's end he was stationed at 12 SFTS Brandon then, from April 2 to June 19, 1945 completed the course at 6 OTU in Comox on the Beech 18 and Dakota. S/L Pearce's flying time on course (day and night) totalled 54:20 and 50:25 hours. At flying he was graded as: General Flying (340/400), Applied Flying (170/200), Instrument Flying (230/250), Night Flying (90/100) and Link (37/50). Ground school courses, in which Pearce also did well, were: Airmanship, Engines, Aircraft and Ship Recognition, Meteorology, Navigation, and Signals. W/C R.M. Cox assessed Pearce at course end as: "An experienced captain who will prove a capable transport pilot." Overseas once more, Pearce joined 436 Squadron, then supporting the Allied occupation forces in Europe. There he upgraded squadron standards, vital work for which he later received the Air Force Cross, the recommendation for which notes:

Confronted with the task of planning and organizing the training of 48 crews for airline transport flying, he has overcome every obstacle and has worked unceasingly to achieve a very high standard. He has invariably been on hand throughout night flying training, personally giving dual instruction. Also, he has conscientiously attended the

briefing of his crews before all early morning take offs. His thorough understanding of flying training earned for him the Empire Central Flying School course on which he distinguished himself, and later the RCAF War Staff College course. His contribution to the Joint Air Training Plan is worthy of the highest commendation.

A popular RCAF recruiting poster of WWII. (CANAV Col.)

Pearce remained in the postwar RCAF, first as station commander at RCAF Station Suffield, where experimental work in chemical warfare was underway. His superior at Northwest Air Command HQ in Edmonton recommended him for promotion – he became a wing commander in January 1949. In 1954 W/C Pearce was in RCAF

HQ where his annual assessment was done by one of his wartime superiors, the great Nels Timmerman. G/C Timmerman noted how he had not changed his opinion of Pearce. He pointed out such shortcomings as Pearce's "low boiling point and caustic tongue", but how he had improved and "he now appears to be able to suffer fools, if not gladly, at least with kindly tolerance". Timmerman recommended that Pearce be promoted and that he was ideal station commander material. This promotion, however, did not go through. W/C Pearce retired in 1963 and died in Ottawa in 1988.

Civil Pilots Answer the Call

In 1939 the RCAF had few qualified instructors, so was in no shape to launch a massive training scheme. As a stop-gap measure, the call went out to civilian pilots to volunteer as instructors and staff pilots. Included among applicants were flying club personnel, bush pilots, young fellows working their way up in civil aviation, even a few WWI pilots. Once word got out, Americans also began showing up, eager for BCATP flying jobs. Enough men came forward to allow some training to get going at local civilian schools. Few of those selected had any knowledge of air force life, many had nothing but "the basics" of flying to their credit, but all were enthusiastic.

The first of these hopefuls arrived in the fall of 1939 at Camp Borden and Trenton to take crash courses getting familiar with RCAF training methods, and to put in a few hours on the Finch and Tiger Moth. Later in 1940, however,

Civilian pilots on their preliminary course at the flying instructor school at Trenton in 1940. Some of the fellows sport their flying club wings. Then, an unknown 12 EFTS civilian instructor with his BCATP student at Goderich early in the war. (Ernie Weeks, CANAV Cols.)

pilots were being absorbed directly into BCATP schools. One of the first of the "green" pilots at Camp Borden was Wesley H. McIntosh. "Wess" had earned his pilot's licence with Northwest Aeromarine in his home town of Winnipeg in 1934. Through the 1930s he served in the RCN reserve as a telegraphist, but as soon as the war started, he left the navy for the RCAF. Having about 400 civilian flying hours, he was posted straight to Camp Borden as the first direct-entry sergeant pilot in the RCAF. It quickly became clear, however, that McIntosh was ill prepared, as he explains in his 2006 memoir, *Permission Granted*:

I took my flight test at Borden with F/O Ab Hiltz in a Civet Fleet aircraft on 19 October and it turned out to be an exercise in frustration for both of us. When F/O Hiltz asked me to do a few loops, I had to admit that I didn't know how. My second flight on 27 October with an F/O Martin ... revealed other large gaps in my knowledge, including instrument flying, aerobatics, formation flying and emergency landing. These two men ... were very kind, letting me down gently by telling me that most commercial pilots with many hundreds of hours of flying experience lacked the main essentials of service flying. They recommended ... that I be given as much catch-up training as possible, suggesting that I would require at least 50 hours dual and solo flying time before I could be considered equal to intermediate standards.

Fleet 2 CF-AOF served the Kitchener-Waterloo Flying Club 1931-36, then a series of individual owners, until fading from the scene *circa* 1960. It was on such club aircraft that so many young Canadians learned to fly in pre-WWII days. When war came, these fellows were anxious to get into the BCATP as flying instructors. (Alf Barton Col.)

Over the next year, Camp Borden groomed McIntosh well, providing him with 138 flying hours. He began his own instructional career on October 24, 1940. So it went with the civilian volunteers – most made the grade and went on to stellar careers. McIntosh became one of the top instructors at Camp Borden, Virden and Trenton; by the time he moved to Ferry Command in November 1942, his log book showed 2422 hours. He became one of the kings of RCAF long-range transport flying, completing 37 trans-Atlantic crossings. The citation for his Commended for Valuable Services in the Air (which originated from 168 Squadron) notes: "This officer has played an important part in the training of transport fliers ... As a captain and later as a flight commander he has at all times displayed exceptional ability and determination. His devotion to duty has set a high example to all."

Another of the early "civvie" pilots joining the BCATP was Kris H. Moon. Born in Toronto in 1914, he was raised in Edmonton, where he took his secondary schooling at Edmonton Technical Institute. Amateur radio and model aircraft were Moon's hobbies. As a young fellow he worked in the Alberta government telegraph service, getting experience as a messenger boy, clerk and linesman. Having learned to fly at the Edmonton Aero Club, he found work as a mechanic/helper at Mackenzie Air Service. Here, his duties were those of any junior employee – getting his plane ready for daily operations, loading and unloading it, "putting it to bed" at day's end and doing whatever else the pilot requested. A pilot might or might not let

Besides civilians joining the RCAF from the flying clubs and commercial operators in southern Canada, others enlisted from the bush. By the time Kris Moon enlisted in late 1940 he had some solid experience as a mechanic and junior pilot with Mackenzie Air Service of Edmonton. He likely crewed on this 1936 Norseman, his company's first and one of many civil aircraft later impressed into RCAF service. (Robert Halford Col.)

a sprog such as Moon do a bit of flying.

In applying to join the RCAF in November 1939, Moon made the most of his limited experience, writing: "Have flown as co-pilot on all aircraft of the Mackenzie Air Service for the last two years and have covered all of the NWT ... north to the Arctic coast. Have completed primary training with Edmonton Aero Club." He added something that the recruiting officer might have found more interesting – he had five hours of instrument flying training. Moon's references also were noteworthy, including the top man at Mackenzie Air Service – Leigh Brintnell.

Like most civilian pilot recruits, Moon commenced training at Camp Borden, then progressed to Central Flying School at Trenton, where he topped his class. He was commissioned in October 1940 and in December was assessed as, "Very pleasing disposition with excellent deportment. Should make a very capable officer." In June 1941 F/O

Moon was posted to 15 SFTS at Claresholm, Alberta, where he was flight commander in 2 Squadron. Here he also did well, although W/C W.E. Kennedy criticized him in December 1941 as "lacking service experience in many ways". This may have been a fair comment, since not all former civilian pilots readily adapted to military ways.

In April 1942 F/L Moon, then age 28, was overseas on the advanced instructor's course at the Empire Central Flying School. While doing night circuits on June 8, he and F/L Frederick G. Pafford (age 29 from St. Thomas, Ontario) died when their Miles Master inexplicably crashed. By this time Moon had logged more than 3500 flying hours.

Fred Hotson earned his pilot's licence in the mid-1930s. To learn all he could about aeronautics (and be able to fly affordably) he constructed a popular homebuilt of the day – a Heath Parasol. Here is the dandy little plane, then Fred proudly wearing his newly-tailored Empire Air Training Plan blazer. His job at 1 AOS at Malton near Toronto, then at 10 AOS in St. Jean, Quebec, opened the door for Fred and others to life-long careers in aviation. (Fred Hotson Col.)

Many American fliers gave their lives serving for Canada. In 1919 Richard R. Blythe, a Texan, co-founded the Quiet Birdmen, a secret fraternity of prominent aviators that included such men as Richard DePew (later of Fairchild) and Robert Noorduyn (later influential in the design of the Fokker Universal and Norseman). In business, Blythe was a public relations man whose clients included Adm. Richard E. Byrd, Dr. Hugo Eckner and Charles Lindbergh. With the war, Blythe came to Canada "to do his bit". On May 2, 1941 he was on a training exercise from 13 EFTS at St. Eugene to Rockcliffe with his student, LAC A. B. Thomson of Three Rivers, Quebec. Something went wrong and they crashed in Finch 4664. Both were gravely injured; Blythe died next day in an Ottawa hospital. (LAC PA63938)

Also keen to get involved in the training program as soon as it was announced was Fred W. Hotson of Fergus, Ontario. Having earned his pilot's licence at the Toronto Flying Club in July 1938, in 1940 he was assembling Tiger Moths and Ansons at de Havilland of Canada. Along with two DHC cohorts, Don Murray and George Neal, he applied to the BCATP. By this time his log book showed a mere 80 flying hours so, to improve his chances of getting hired, in April 1941 he paid for a few hours of Link Trainer instruction at the University of Toronto. To his delight, he was accepted into the BCATP and made his first flight as a staff pilot at 1 AOS at Malton, Ontario on April 28. That day he and Don Murray (hired earlier) took Anson 6031 on a 4-hour cross-country familiarization flight. Even though this was Hotson's first flight in a twin engine aircraft, he soon was a competent Anson pilot.

The BCATP weathered the bumps in the road as it took shape. Pilots such as Hotson, Murray and Neal became solid figures on the AOS scene, taking thousands of student air observers on countless air exercises. Hotson last flew in the BCATP on February 19, 1944, by which time his log book showed 1447:55 hours. He and Don Murray then moved to Ferry Command.

"Canada's Yanks"

Without help from its American cousins, Canada would have had a much tougher road getting on with the BCATP. From earliest days these men trickled into Canada, keen for adventure and a solid

job. Many had been recruited by a clandestine British organization known as the Clayton Knight Committee, with offices across the United States surreptitiously getting the word out that the RCAF was welcoming American recruits.

By Pearl Harbor Day on December 7, 1941 some 6000 Americans were in the RCAF. They served in the BCATP, Ferry Command and on RCAF operations. One was John G. Wilcox, an early instructor at 19 EFTS Virden, Manitoba. Opened on May 16, 1941, Virden was managed by the Brandon-Virden Flying Club. Wherever Wilcox was from, he heard of the BCATP's urgent appeal, applied and made the grade. One of his first students was LAC W.H.D. "Bill" Meaden of Edmonton.

John G. Wilcox, an American civilian instructing at 19 EFTS, Virden, Manitoba. (CANAV Col.)

On December 29, 1941 Wilcox took Meaden up initially in Tiger Moth 4961, then sent him solo on his 11th flight on January 9, 1942. In all, Wilcox and Meaden would fly together 29 times. Meaden last flew at EFTS on February 26, by when he had been up 56 times for 80:00 flying hours. He then advanced to 10 SFTS at Dauphin. Meanwhile, America had joined the shooting war, so John Wilcox returned home (one of some 1500 who did so), entered the US Army Air Corps and became an instructor at Randolph Field, Texas. On June 24, 1942 he wrote to his former student:

I sure wish I were back in Canada again. For one thing it is too darn hot in this part of the world… we are flying the BT-14 … just about the same as a Harvard. When I came down here they told me I could get in active service, but I am instructing again, damn it.

The big thing that is wrong with this plan is the fact that it is too damn big. We have about 300 aircraft in the air at one time. One has to be really on the ball to stay alive for long. I have been here about three weeks and at least four men have been killed… Write again soon and let me know what they do with you. I'll bet they make an instructor out of you. Lt Johnny Wilcox

Tale of a Civilian Instructor

The close examination of the pre-war flying aspirations of Ernie Weeks explains much about the civilian aviators who sought to make their mark in the BCATP. Weeks' enthusiasm and determination to build flying hours and hone his skills as a junior pilot suggest why such fellows were likely to succeed. Born in Bouctouche, New Brunswick on April 5, 1911, Weeks was the son of a flour miller. The family moved to Beechville, Ontario, where father owned a feed mill, had a hardware store in Oakville, west of Toronto, then one in Waterdown, near Hamilton. Following high school, Ernie studied at the University of Toronto, but left those endeavours to take flying lessons at Cub Aircraft in Hamilton. He flew first in Cub CF-AZK on April 25, 1937, then took lessons along the way (as pocket money allowed) with such local instructors as Ed Hale (later an RCAF Air Commodore) and Ernie Taylor (later chief pilot at Victory Aircraft). Weeks eagerly

Ernie Weeks in Hamilton with a Cub in pre-war times. Then, the famous Puss Moth in which he gained valuable experience. (All, Ernie Weeks Col.)

added new types to his log book, including Aeronca K CF-BJK, Rearwin CF-BEY and Tiger Moth CF-CBT, all of the Hamilton Aero Club.

In May 1938 Weeks and his buddies, J.F. "Frank" Copeland and L.S. Adams, bought Puss Moth CF-AGV from Ed Hale for $900. The trio soon was swanning around, doing impromptu joyriding wherever the sun shone and there was hope of a crowd. In August 1938 they flew on a challenging escapade, first to Montreal on the 12th, thence to Saint John, Moncton, Bouctouche, New Glasgow and Charlottetown, before turning for home on the 16th. Routing via Bangor, Boston and Troy, NY, they pushed on to Syracuse, Rochester and Buffalo, and were home on the 17th. The fellows certainly were no pansies when it came to cross-country flying.

In October 1938 Weeks had CF-AGV in Barrie, Ontario to see what dollars could be scrounged at a ploughing match there. From December 27 to January 2 he, Ted Hall and Harry Pattinson flew to New York City to visit Harry's sister. This entailed about 12 flying hours and took CF-AGV to such stops as Buffalo, Utica and Albany. Along the way they encountered some of New York's worst winter weather and, at one point, had to set down in a field to await better conditions. In February 1929 Copeland put skis on the Puss Moth, but wrecked it on the ice of Hamilton Bay.

For $1000 Ernie Weeks bought Cub CF-BEE in May 1939 from Leavens Brothers Air Services. He continued to upgrade his qualifications, taking lessons from Walt Leavens and Len Tripp (who had learned to fly with the Wright brothers). In 1939 he went north to Sudbury, where he found enough students to keep busy instructing. This

was a ski operation off frozen Ramsay Lake using Taylor Cub CF-BBZ and Taylorcraft BC CF-BLZ, owned by a local, H.F. Milligan. They had no licence to do so, but they took any charter that came along, even though the wee Taylors had the smallest of payloads. Spring came, so there was plenty of joyriding – on a single day Weeks carried 30 passengers. In August, Charlie Robson (later an instructor at 20 EFTS) checked him out on CF-AEC – a big Bellanca Pacemaker.

By this time Ernie Weeks had more than 600 flying hours, so decided to try his luck with the BCATP. Accepted, he went on an initial course to the Central Flying School in Trenton. He flew first in a Fleet on September 10, 1940, finished on October 1 after about 50 hours of flying, and left with the CFI's comment in his log book: "Should be a good instructor." Weeks now joined the staff at 10 EFTS at Mount Hope, where Bill Sumner was CFI with Don Rogers (later chief pilot at Avro Canada) as his assistant. Weeks had digs with relatives in Hamilton and commuted by car to work. Although considered administratively to be in the RCAF as a "sergeant on leave", he wore the civilian uniform of the Hamilton Aero Club, which managed 10 EFTS.

Weeks flew first at 10 EFTS with Ed Hale in Moth CF-CFY on October 14, 1940 – the day the school opened. He set to work next day, taking up a student in RCAF Fleet Finch 4597. Now began the busy routine of turning out pilots who would be ready in a few weeks to advance to Harvards, Ansons, etc. His log book illustrates the EFTS pace in those start-up days – 5, 6 or 7 student

The cover and a typical spread from a young pilot's pre-WWII log book. In 1936 Ernie Weeks and his pals were having great fun swanning around in their Puss Moth.

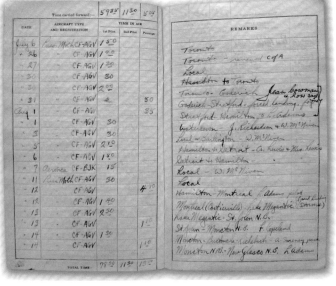

YEAR 1942		AIRCRAFT		PILOT, OR 1ST PILOT	2ND PILOT, PUPIL, OR PASSENGER	DUTY (INCLUDING RESULTS AND REMARKS)
MONTH	DATE	Type	No.			TOTALS BROUGHT FORWARD
JULY	12	TIGER MOTH	4396	SELF	REDFERN	1A·3·6·7·9·16
"	12	"	5880	"	McBRIEN	19
"	12	"	5880	"	FOX	19
"	13	"	5910	"	KENYON	19 WEATHER FLIGHT
"	14	"	8886	"	—	WEATHER FLIGHT
"	14	"	5910	"	—	TEST A/C
"	14	"	5169	"	—	TEST A/C
"	14	"	1222	"	HANNA	1A·3·6·7·9·16
"	14	"	5891	"	McBRIEN	60 HOUR TEST
"	15	"	5880	"	—	FERRY FROM F.K. FIELD
"	15	"	5511	"	BATES	60 HOUR + INST. TEST
"	15	"	5892	"	GILLESPIE	19 + TEST FOR N.F.
"	16	"	8888	"	—	WEATHER FLIGHT
"	16	"	5890	"	HALNAN	1A·3·6·7·9·16
"	16	"	8888	"	PORTEOUS	1A·3·6·7·9·16
"	16	"	1116	"	SAWYER	20 HOUR CHECK
"	16	"	1116	"	STILES	20 HOUR CHECK
"	16	"	1116	"	CAMERON	60 HOUR + INST.
"	17	"	4396	"	W. BAGGS	WEATHER FLIGHT
"	17	"	5881	"	HOLDEN	20 HR. CHECK
"	17	"	5898	"	HOLDEN	20 HR. CHECK COMPLETED
"	18	"	5910	"	—	WEATHER FLIGHT
"	18	"	1116	"	HALL	20 HR. CHECK

GRAND TOTAL [Cols. (1) to (10)]
1848 Hrs. 40 Mins. — TOTALS CARRIED FORWARD
1849 40

trips on a typical day. In November he logged 84:15 hours, in December 75:50. April 1941 shot up to 116:30. In 2009 Ernie Weeks recalled a landmark day: "Due to bad weather and a few extra students early in 1942, we were a bit behind ... On March 26 I put in 10 hours instructing – 7:15 day flying and 2:45 night flying. I was informed not to try that again." In November 1941 Mount Hope exchanged its Finches for Tiger Moths. Ernie Weeks had enjoyed the Finch, noting in 2009 that it was "as easy as a Cub to fly". But he considered the Tiger Moth better for teaching, as it was a bit more demanding, e.g. due to having a narrower undercarriage.

On February 9, 1943 Ernie Weeks began a Harvard course with 6 SFTS at nearby Dunnville (one of his instructors was a former student from Mount Hope, F/O Jewitt). This ended on April 22, then he was posted to fly the Swordfish at No.1 Naval Air Gunners School at Yarmouth, Nova Scotia. He began there on May 5, but a few days later was summoned to Ottawa, interviewed by W/C Z.L Leigh and attached to a hush-hush unit known as the Eastern Arctic Survey Detachment tasked to do the first RCAF exploratory flying in the high Arctic since the Hudson Strait Expedition of 1927.

This page from Ernie Weeks' log book in July 1942 shows typically busy times for an instructor at 10 EFTS. Each of those who flew with Ernie eventually would have his own story. A July 17 entry lists W. "Bill" Baggs of Hamilton who was not yet in the RCAF, but had a job as a time keeper at 10 EFTS. Baggs had never flown, so Ernie decided to give him something to crow about. Baggs went on to terrify the Wehrmacht as a Typhoon pilot with 164 Squadron.

The type of wing worn by civilian instructors at 10 EFTS. Then, one of the school's Tiger Moths on winter gear. (Ernie Weeks, Jack McNulty Cols.)

Link Trainer

E.A. "Ed" Link grew up in Binghampton, NY, where his father repaired church organs. The son, naturally gifted with mechanical things, invented a small flight simulator driven by air forced through bellows, similar to the mechanism of a simple organ. In 1931 he received a patent for this invention, which became a popular "ride" at a Long Island fair ground. Link strove to modify his invention as a flight simulator, but found little encouragement in the marketplace. Finally, the US Army purchased a few "Link Trainers". The Japanese military realized what a good idea Link had and also placed an order.

In the mid-1930s the RCAF evaluated the Link concept. In a letter *circa* 1980 to J.C. "Jack" Charleson of Ottawa, Ed Link credited the RCAF with helping to get his product rolling and especially mentioned A/V/M Robert Leckie for opening the door for him. Charleson later wrote: "Leckie made the decision to buy 200 trainers, an unheard-of order at the time. The first 50 were to be made in the US and the subsequent ones … at a factory to be established near Gananoque in Ontario. Leckie … gave the RCAF and RAF an important training tool, and greatly assisted those services with their part in winning the war." In an item of November 4, 1937 the Toronto *Globe and Mail* reported on a Link milestone:

The first "trainer" for blind flying instruction ever built in Canada was shipped from the Gananoque plant yesterday to the British Air Ministry. It is the first of a large order. The machine … banks, dives and turns and goes through all the normal movements of a regular plane – except actual flying… Standard instrument dials are used and they are registered so that a given movement at the controls brings about the corresponding change in instrument readings that would occur in actual flight… equipment includes a device known as the automatic course recorder, which moves along the instructor's desk and records on a map or chart the actual course flown by the pilot in his trainer.

One of the many pilots who instructed diligently on the Link Trainer was P/O Edward M. Stubbs. Born in 1907 and

F/O Edward M. Stubbs and his wife Ida on their wedding day. (via Janet Stubbs)

A typical page from F/O Stubb's log book while he was instructing at 16 SFTS. (via Janet Stubbs)

raised in Caledonia, Ontario, he graduated from the University of Western Ontario, then obtained a high school teaching certificate. Having begun teaching in Grimsby, Stubbs next was on the staff at Western Technical School in Toronto. In 1941 he joined the RCAF, beginning at 1 Manning Depot on July 11. Finished with those preliminaries, he was posted to train on the Link Trainer at 1 ITS, located at Toronto's historic Hunt Club on Avenue Road. There he first "flew" a Link during a familiarization session under F/L Ayres. This was a busy course that included 2 or 3 daily sessions covering, in lock-step process, some 20 different exercises. The week of August 18-23, for example, Stubbs was on 15 "flights", logging 2:45 hours being instructed on the Link, then "flying" it for 4:15 hours. The course ended on August 27 with P/O Stubbs a qualified Link instructor.

With 31:00 hours "on type", Stubbs was posted to 16 SFTS at Hagersville. In his first week he logged 13 sessions for 11:05 hours instructing students Day, Duncan, Friberg, Ledbetter, Redding, Shepherd, Twillinger, Winn and Young. Most sessions were logged as 1:00 hour, during all of which Stubbs was at the Link table, watching the progress of each

20 EFTS at Oshawa, where F/O Stubbs instructed, graduated hundreds of young pilots, who then advanced to service flying training. In this scene from September 26, 1941, students congratulate a buddy who has just soloed – into the pool he goes! Beyond is one of the school's double-wide hangars. By 2010 Oshawa airport was fully modernized, but a few wartime buildings still were standing, one old hangar included. (DND PL5354)

EFTS Notes and Doodles by Keith Barlow

Born in 1923, Keith Barlow spent his boyhood in Gravenhurst, Ontario. He enlisted in the RCAF in Toronto on June 3, 1941. In a letter of February 16, 1993 to a school friend, Keith explained how his RCAF career had gotten started:

I started out at St. Hubert manning depot south of Montreal, then went further east to Moncton for "tarmac duty" – servicing aircraft and sweeping endless acres of hangar floors. This was followed by classroom work at initial training school in Victoriaville, Quebec. Finally, things became more interesting toward the end of the year when I reported to Stanley, Nova Scotia for elementary flying training. The next step was back to Moncton for service flying training, where the Harvard trainers looked a bit daunting after the little Fleet Finch biplanes. I graduated as a sergeant pilot at a wings parade on 19 June 1942 with two of my aunts looking on.

All along in his training, Keith indulged his passion for everything to do with aviation, and showed his academic and artistic talents by careful note-taking and doodling. These illustrations from his RCAF notebooks show what an enthusiastic young fellow this was. Keith went on to do everything from towing targets in the Fairey Battle, to a tour on Spitfires with 72 Squadron in Italy and France. Postwar, he and his wife Shirley settled in Gravenhurst. A skilled draftsman, Keith earned his living in cartography. He was a master model-builder, whether putting together a plastic kit, or creating "out of thin air" a radio-controlled airplane worthy of any award. As a dedicated bibliophile, Keith created a magnificent personal aviation library. He passed away in 2005.

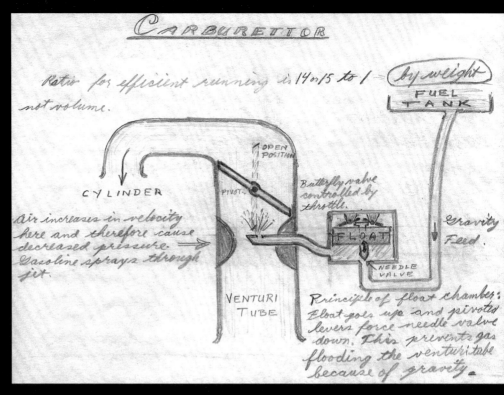

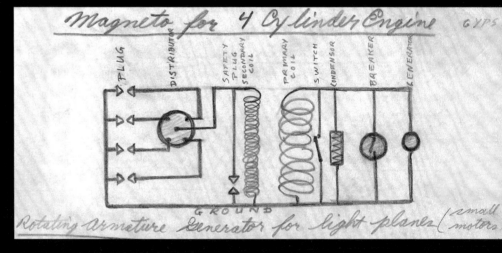

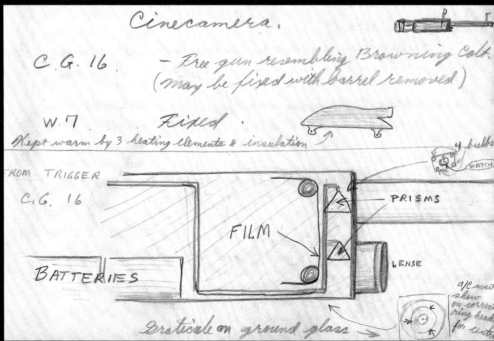

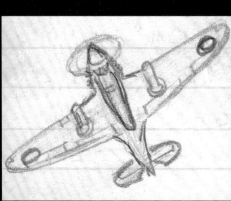

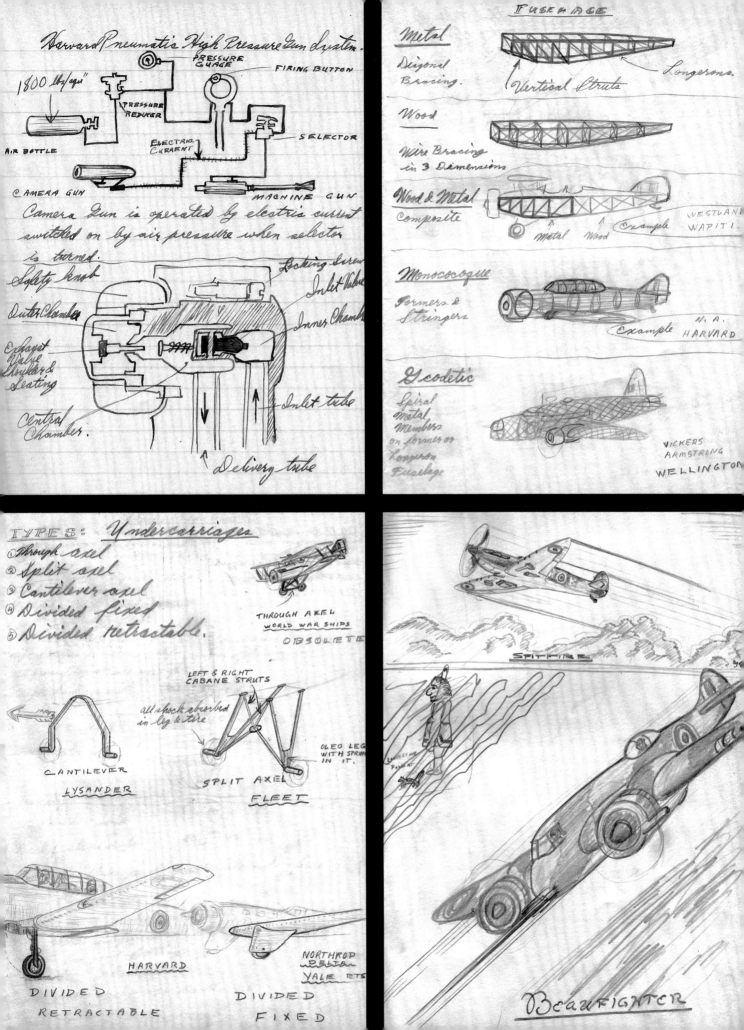

Harvard Pneumatic High Pressure Gun System.

PRESSURE GUAGE

FIRING BUTTON

1800 lbs/sq"

PRESSURE REDUCER

AIR BOTTLE

ELECTRIC CURRENT

SELECTOR

CAMERA GUN

MACHINE GUN

Camera Gun is operated by electric current switched on by air pressure when selector is turned.

Safety knob
Outer Chamber
Exhaust Valve Shoulder & Seating
Central Chamber.

Locking Screw
Inlet Valves
Inner Chamber
Inlet tube

Delivery tube

FUSELAGE

Metal

Diagonal Bracing.

Vertical Struts

Longerons.

Wood

Wire Bracing in 3 Dimensions

Wood & Metal
Composite

metal   wood   Example   WESTLAND WAPITI.

Monococque

Formers & Stringers

Example   N. A. HARVARD

Geodetic

Spiral metal Members on formers or Longeron Fuselage

VICKERS ARMSTRONG WELLINGTON

TYPES: Undercarriages

1. Through axel
2. Split axel
3. Cantilever axel
4. Divided fixed
5. Divided retractable.

THROUGH AXEL
WORLD WAR SHIPS

OBSOLETE

LEFT & RIGHT CABANE STRUTS

all shock absorbed in leg & tire

OLEO LEG WITH SPRING IN IT.

CANTILEVER
LYSANDER

SPLIT AXEL
FLEET

HARVARD

DIVIDED
RETRACTABLE

NORTHROP DELTA
YALE etc

DIVIDED
FIXED

SPITFIRE

BEAUFIGHTER

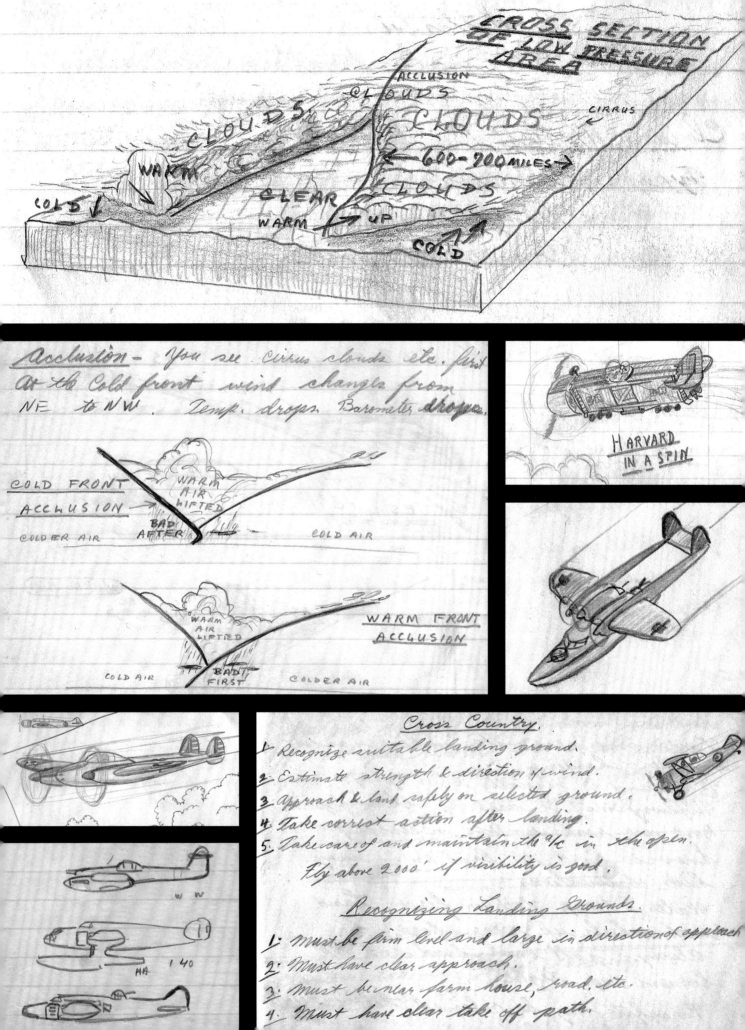

CROSS SECTION OF LOW PRESSURE AREA

CLOUDS
ACCLUSION CLOUDS
CLOUDS
CIRRUS
← 600-900 MILES →
CLEAR CLOUDS
WARM → UP
WARM
COLD ✓
COLD

Acclusion - You see cirrus clouds etc. first
At the Cold front wind changes from
NE to NW. Temp. drops. Barometer drops.

COLD FRONT
ACCLUSION
COLDER AIR
WARM AIR LIFTED
BAD AFTER
COLD AIR

WARM FRONT
ACCLUSION
WARM AIR LIFTED
COLD AIR
BAD FIRST
COLDER AIR

HARVARD IN A SPIN

Cross Country.

1. Recognize suitable landing ground.
2. Estimate strength & direction of wind.
3. Approach & land safely on selected ground.
4. Take correct action after landing.
5. Take care of and maintain the A/c in the open.
   Fly above 2000' if visibility is good.

Recognizing Landing Grounds.

1. Must be firm level and large in direction of approach
2. Must have clear approach.
3. Must be near farm house, road, etc.
4. Must have clear take off path.

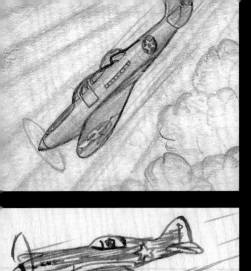

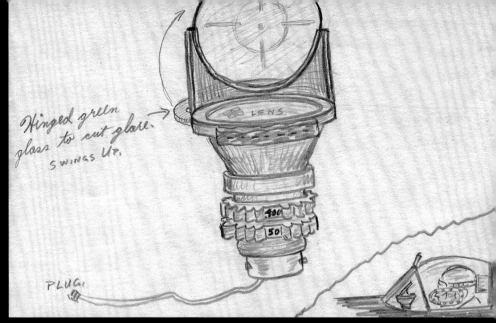

Winged green glass to cut glare. SWINGS UP.

LENS

400
50

PLUG

MIG-3.

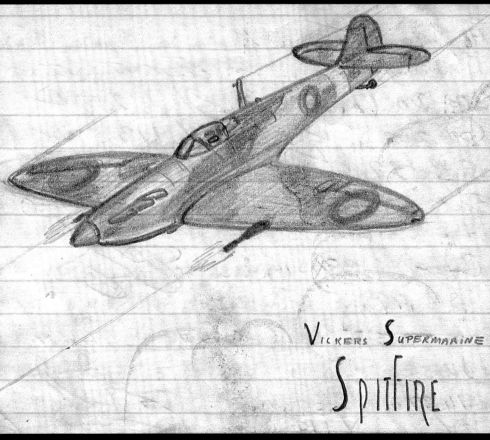

VICKERS SUPERMARINE

SpitFire

Sgt Keith Barlow soon after earning his wings, ther on operations in Italy with 72 Squadron (Shirle Barlow Col.)

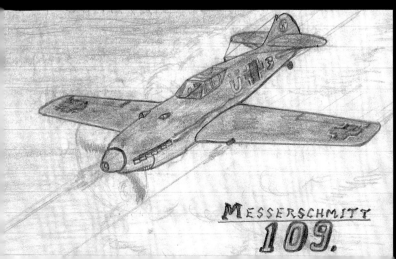

MESSERSCHMITT
109.

"flight". His teaching time was logged (in a regular RCAF log book) under the heading "At Desk" (only occasionally did an instructor log any "In Link" time).

P/O Stubbs completed his first tour with a February 9, 1942 exercise with student Hetherington. F/L A. Patterson, "OC Link Section" signed off his log book which showed 569:50 hours since his course at ITS. March 6 to March 30 he spent back at 1 ITS on a Link refresher course under F/O MacCallum. He then instructed at 1 ITS until February 1943, piling up a further 576 hours (desk) and 17:10 (Link). On February 9, 1943 he was assessed by F/L R. Balfour of 1 Visiting Flight Trenton as "A2 Link ... A keen, enthusiastic and capable instructor."

June to November 1943 P/O Stubbs was instructing at 1 Instrument Flying School at Deseronto, where his pupils,

on June 30, 1945 he logged his final hour in the Link Trainer and entered his total time: 2865:00 hours.

Through Link Trainer days, P/O Stubbs sometimes got to fly, but never as a pilot. He had taken some lessons on the Harvard in 1942 and in 1944 at 14 SFTS, on the Cornell in 1943 at 1 IFS, and on the Tiger Moth in 1944 at 20 EFTS, but never soloed. He taught hundreds at the elementary and service flying levels, most of whom later served in the war effort. Inevitably, some of these young men were lost. In likely the first such case affecting him, Stubbs would have been shaken to hear of the death of his student LAC John N. Forst. Age 19 from Farmingdale, New York, Forst earned his wings at Hagersville and still was there as a sergeant when he took Anson 7186 flying on March 22, 1942. The exercise was to practice formation flying, but the

he would send his protégé solo. This could happen after as few as 5 or 6 dual flights. One of the thousands of EFTS students sent solo one day was AC1 Donald J. McClintock. Born in Ormstown, Quebec in 1921, he had grown up on the farm. After graduating from high school in 1937, he taught elementary school before enlisting in 1940. Air force life began for him at No.1 Manning Depot in Toronto, then he made his way through the various stages until selected for flight training and posted to 13 EFTS at St. Eugene in eastern Ontario. On January 31, 1941 LAC McClintock took his first flight, going up on a familiarization ride with Mr. McGuire in Finch 4732 (McGuire was one of the many "neutral" Americans who had come north to instruct). On February 16, McClintock soloed, an experience he describes in his memoir:

Finch training underway in ideal conditions at 4 EFTS, Windsor Mills, Quebec, a school operated by the Montreal Flying Club. Perhaps the fellow getting airborne was on his first solo. Finch 4492 (nearest) was lost on a flight from here on May 22, 1941. (DND PL2050)

instead of being EFTS sprogs, were senior pilots getting advanced ratings. To deserve such a responsible position, Stubbs clearly was considered to be tops. He left Deseronto with 2320:40 hours (desk) and 84:35 (Link) in his log, then joined 20 EFTS at Oshawa, a school operated by the Ontario County Flying Training School. His first session here was 35 minutes with AC1 Wilson on November 16. All the routines continued until February 1944, when P/O Stubbs joined 12 EFTS – a Goderich school run by the Kitchener-Waterloo Flying Club. In May 1944 he transferred to 14 SFTS in Aylmer, then was at 31 SFTS in Kingston, teaching British students. On January 29, 1945 he was assessed by W/C K.G. Southam, of the prestigious Central Flying School in Trenton, as "An exceptional instructor". In this period he returned to 16 EFTS at Hagersville. Here

Ansons ran into a snow storm. At that point, all his instrument practice in the Link Trainer and his experience aloft somehow failed Sgt Forst. He crashed fatally near Selkirk, a village on the Lake Erie shore. Postwar, P/O Stubbs continued in education, finishing as principal of Bloor Collegiate Institute in Toronto. He passed away in 1985.

EFTS: First Solo

A student's highlight at EFTS was his initial solo flight. Each man faced this event differently, some with elation, others with trepidation, with plenty of room for a range of emotions in between. Soloing normally followed a few "dual" exercises in a Finch or Tiger Moth. As soon as the instructor felt that his student had grasped the basics of "stick and rudder" and was not a danger to himself,

The weather was beautiful. I had done a couple of circuits with my instructor before he stepped out and sent me on my own. I taxied carefully to the other end of the field, did the required pre-takeoff check, turned the Fleet into wind and opened the throttle. Without the second man on board, the plane leaped into the air in a hurry and there I was – all alone.

It is hard to describe the thrill of that moment. I imagine it is the same today, even though airplanes have become so commonplace. I sure felt I had the world by the tail. Now you concentrated like mad to fly a proper circuit – climb to a thousand feet straight ahead, turn left and fly for a couple of minutes, left again for a down-wind leg parallel to the direction of landing, left again for the base leg and start descending for the final turn into wind for landing, then, carefully judging the descent so you came over the boundary at the right height and speed, landing without bouncing too much. I did it! The taxi up to the flight office and a congratulatory handshake by your relieved instructor rounded off the great moment. You felt you were now a pilot. Just as well you didn't realize how little you really knew at this point.

Career Profile: EFTS to PRU

Aircrew profiles throughout this book often include background about the BCATP. Each story begins in about the same way. Once enlisted in the RCAF and accepted as potential aircrew, a recruit took his 4-6 weeks at one of the RCAF manning depots: 1 MD (Toronto), 2 MD (Brandon, Manitoba), 3 MD (Edmonton), 4 MD (Quebec) or 5 MD (Lachine, near Montreal). At manning depot each man underwent medical and dental examinations, was issued a uniform, was assessed academically, learned the fundamentals from drill to deportment and, eventually, was selected for an aircrew trade or sent for further assessment. Next came a month-long course at one of the initial training schools, where more studies, aptitude tests, drill, etc., awaited. For those selected for pilot training, these schools were: 1 ITS (Toronto), 2 ITS (Regina), 3 ITS (Victoriaville, Quebec), 4 ITS Edmonton, 5 ITS (Belleville, Ontario), 6 ITS (Toronto) and 7 ITS (Saskatoon).

Daniel Murray McKenzie of Stellarton, Nova Scotia had enlisted in Halifax in January 1941, starting with the lowliest RCAF rank – Aircraftman Second Class, or AC2 ("Acie Ducie" in the slang of the time). Following manning depot, McKenzie went on course to 3 ITS beginning May 28, ending July 3, 1941. Normally, students travelled to and from such assignments by train, travel arrangements being made by the air force. McKenzie fared well at ITS, his final marks including: Mathematics (100%), Armament (86%), Signals (86%), Hygiene and Sanitation (39/40), Drill (76%) and Law and Discipline (58/60). Finishing 6th in a class of 238, he was assessed in the end as "Keen. Alert and energetic. Good appearance – neat. Has good family background. Sensible and dependable. Trustworthy." Even at this early stage, his chief instructor added, "Recommended for commission."

From ITS, McKenzie was posted to 17 EFTS in Stanley, Nova Scotia for elementary flying training. This busied him from July 3 to August 20. Again, he excelled, placing second in a class of 32. His flying hours on the Fleet Finch totalled 26:55 hours of dual instruction, 24:35 solo, plus 10:00 hours in the Link. His ground school results again showed that he was gifted: Airmanship (186/200), Airframes (91%), Aero Engines (86%), Signals, Practical (92%), Theory of Flight (87%), Air Navigation (176/200), Armament, oral (180/200). He was assessed in Character/Leadership at 150/200, with these notes in his personnel file: "Very good student. Highly intelligent. Keen, alert, energetic, shows great initiative and can be depended on."

LAC McKenzie now advanced to service flying training at 8 SFTS in Moncton, the course beginning August 20 and ending November 7, 1941. Here he flew the Anson for 45:45 hours (dual, day), 42:25 (solo, day), 2:00 (dual, night) and 8:05 (solo, night). He also spent 20 hours in the Link and finished sixth in a class of 53. Naturally, McKenzie would not have known about any confidential comments in his file, including this one from his CFI at 8 SFTS: "General knowledge of flying very good. An above average pilot. No outstanding faults." McKenzie's SFTS ground school courses and marks also were tops: Airmanship and Maintenance (155/200), Armament Written (63%), Armament Practical (70%), Navigation (141/150), Meteorology (40/50), Signals W (38.5/50), Signals P (97%). His chief ground instructor wrote: "Quiet and dependable. Above average ability and above average results on course." Dan McKenzie was proudly on his way.

During these difficult times for the RAF, most RCAF aircrew graduates were rushed overseas. This happened to P/O McKenzie. He reported initially in at 3 (RCAF) Personnel Reception Centre in Bournemouth on January 27, 1942, from where he was posted to one of the RAF reconnaissance schools, completed a Spitfire OTU, then joined No.1 Photo Reconnaissance Unit at RAF Benson. Later, he was on operations with 682 Squadron in North Africa. Records show that to March 1943 P/O McKenzie had logged 413 hours, 140 in the previous six months. Flying from Maison Blanche near Algiers, he completed at least 40 long-range PR sorties. On one of these (February 14, 1943) he ended in a mishap, crashing Spitfire V AB426 at Youk-les-Bains in eastern Algeria.

Of a 3:40-hour high level sortie McKenzie reported: "At 27,000 feet, radiator temperature 140 degrees. Shutter of radiator was opened without effect. After one minute white fumes ... filled cockpit. Started gliding with open hood. Oil temperature above 140 degrees and pressure dropping rapidly. Throttles and pitch control were pulled back and a glide landing made." As far as G/C V.S. Bowling of 323 Wing was concerned, this constituted a good show: "The pilot is to be congratulated on making a successful forced landing." In this period his commanding officer praised McKenzie: "He has always shown great keenness to fly on operations and by his excellent example did much to uphold the high morale of the pilots in his flight during a very trying period." On March 29, 1943 F/L McKenzie was on a sortie to photograph an enemy installation on the Sardinian coast. But the flak gunners got his Spitfire (EN347) in their sites and McKenzie was shot down into the sea (his body was recovered on April 14). A day earlier his DFC had been gazetted, the citation noting:

This officer has taken part in a large number of operational sorties against targets which include Marseilles, Toulon, Genoa, Spezia, Leghorn and Cagliari as well as many airfields and defence lines in Tunisia. He has always shown great keenness to fly on operations and by his excellent example did much to uphold the high morale of the pilots in his flight during a very trying period.

F/L McKenzie also was honoured post-humously (May 31, 1943) with the US Defense Medal, the citation for which notes: "For meritorious achievement while participating in aerial flights in North Africa between 17th November 1942 and 14th December, 1942. The manner in which this officer performed these missions reflects great credit upon the military services of the United Nations." These dates coincide with Operation Torch – the Allied invasion of North Africa. From enlistment in the RCAF in January 1941 to his death a little more than two years later, Daniel Murray McKenzie of Stellarton had eagerly embraced aviation. The BCATP had taught him well but, sad to say, this could not save him from some other eager and well-taught young fellows on the delivery end of a flak barrage.

Instructor and Warrior

Born in Halifax on February 26, 1919, John Ernest McLurg was raised in Montreal. He studied at Westmount High School, then spent 1937-38 taking science courses at McGill University. He held some clerical and sales jobs locally, before enlisting in the RCAF in September 1940. AC2 McLurg spent September at 1 MD in Toronto, then was sent to Dartmouth early in October for about a month, likely on guard duty or what the students used to call "useless duties". He returned to Toronto to attend 1 ITS beginning November 14. Here, he placed 23rd in a class of 154, receiving this comment from his assessor: "Very good pilot material. Sincere and 'on the bit'. Above average."

After five weeks at 1 ITS, Johnny McLurg was promoted from AC1 to LAC and joined the course at 13 EFTS at St. Eugene. He finished here on February 9 with a fine assessment from the CFI: "Above average, very keen, officer material, good conduct, first class fighter pilot". His ground school instructor, F/L M.E. Ferguson, added: "Conduct excellent, very capable student, shows good judgment;, superior type, but not a snob." LAC McLurg finished 4th in his class, then proceeded next day to 9 SFTS at Summerside, PEI. Here, he did well on the Harvard, logging 92 hours dual/solo, day/night. In ground school he scored: Airmanship and Maintenance (157/200), Armament Written (75/100), Armament Practical (87/100), Navigation and Meteorology (141/200), Signals Written (86/100), Signals-Practical (50/50). He finished SFTS on May 4, placing second in a class of 23. Not surprisingly, he received a commission, then was posted to instruct at Trenton. This would have been a disappointment, as every pilot leaving SFTS was anxious to get on operations.

From June 16 to July 25, 1941 P/O McLurg took the instructor's course at Trenton, flying on single- and twin-engine types. On June 21, 1941 his student, AC2 C.W. Hunt, practicing a forced landing with McLurg aboard, hit a fence post and damaged Finch 4723. Then, on July 1 he was on an exercise with F/O Brian A. Casey, who landed with the brakes on. Result? No injuries, but Finch 1013 ended on its back. (F/L Brian A. Casey, MiD, age 25 from Sandwich West, Ontario, would die with his 5 (BR) Squadron crew on May 5, 1943. Shortly after taking off on an anti-submarine patrol from Gander in Canso 9807, they crashed inexplicably.) At the end of his course P/O McLurg was favourably assessed by F/L Russ Bannock: "This student showed above average ability throughout his advanced course. Aerobatics on Harvard are average and instrument flying was above average."

P/O McLurg now began his teaching days. From August to November 1941 he instructed on Tiger Moths at 31 EFTS at DeWinton, near Calgary, then came postings to 13 SFTS at St. Hubert and Central Flying School at Trenton. In an incident at St. Hubert, he made an error in judgment. This took place on March 30, 1942 during a low-level exercise in Harvard 3768 with student pilot LAC L.G.R. Blair. McLurg brushed some tree limbs, slightly damaging a wing, but he was in the designated low-flying area. He received only a minor reprimand for this. When assessed by W/C A.W. Watts of 13 SFTS, McLurg was highly recommended: "Has done a good job of instructing on this station. Very young but with further experience will make a very good all round officer." He now was posted on staff to 1 Flying Instructor's School at Trenton.

Johnny McLurg was promoted to flying officer in July 1942. His assessment for upgrade to A-2 instructor category was completed on October 10 by S/L Ingram and W/C F.C. Carling-Kelly of CFS. It noted that McLurg had flown 892:25 hours single-engine solo, 108:50 single-engine dual, 203:10 twin-engine solo and 9:35 twin-engine dual. His instructional times totalled: 31 EFTS – 393.20 hours, 13 SFTS – 213.55 and 1 FIS – 373.20. He was assessed under the standard headings: Sequence – "Sound knowledge", Voice – "Clear", Manner – "Pleasant and Interesting", Ability to Impart Knowledge – "Above average", Ability as a Pilot – "Careful pilot, accurate and smooth", Remarks – "Instrument flying very good." McLurg was promoted to fight lieutenant in December 1942. On March 26, 1943 he ground-looped and wrecked a Kittyhawk at Trenton. In another case he reportedly landed his Harvard atop another airplane, so McLurg was gaining a reputation for bending airplanes, but getting away with it.

Like many a long-serving instructor, F/L McLurg pined to escape the BCATP. In an assessment of August 13, 1943 W/C J.G. "Pat" Twist of 1 FIS, an old-time bush pilot, made this reference to McLurg: "This officer is carrying out his work in a worth-while manner, but is reaching the state where an overseas posting is needed to boost morale ... An above average officer in all respects." Commenting further on October 9, Twist wrote how McLurg's efficiency was waning due to "the urge to get on operations overseas". Twist emphasized that McLurg would become "a splendid operational pilot." Likely thanks to these memos "up the line", in October 1943 McLurg was posted to 36 OTU, a BCATP school at Greenwood, Nova Scotia, where pilots and navigators converted to the Mosquito.

The flying side of Mosquito OTU was brief for F/L McLurg: 4.20 hours – day dual, 31:30 – day solo, 1:10 – night dual and 13:00 – night solo. He also spent 12:30 hours in the Link. At all this he was assessed as "Above Average". His ground school scores were: Airmanship – 95%, Navigation – 90%, Signals – 96%, Armament – 87%, Aircraft Recognition – 95%, Meteorology – 76%, Intelligence – 96%, Technical – 90%, Electrical – 92%. Ground school instructor S/L W.J. Henney described McLurg as "Keen, excellent, all round. Good type,"

On January 20, 1944 McLurg embarked at Halifax for the UK, arriving 11 days later. Following his stint at 3 PRC in Bournemouth, on February 15, 1944 he went on course at 13 OTU (Mosquitos) at Bicester in Oxfordshire. Following one dual sortie of 1:25 hours, he flew the rest of his course on solo exercises: 37:30 hours day, 2:55 night. Ground courses included: Airmanship (243/300), Armament (158/300), Meteorology (65/100), Navigation (162/200) and Signals (67/100). Flying-wise he scored: General Flying (250/400), Applied Flying (150/200), Instrument Flying (180/200), Night Flying (70/100) and Link (35/50). On March 28, 1944 F/L McLurg joined 107 Squadron at Swanton Morley about 15 miles west of Norwich.

On April 9, 1944 F/L McLurg and P/O H.W. Parkinson were airborne near Chivenor in Mosquito HJ824 when they faced an emergency. McLurg's report notes: "Flying low level formation on training flight, a loss of power was noticed on starboard engine. Smoke also was observed. Throttle was closed and gas turned off to that engine... Airspeed being very low (150) and being at very low altitude, I didn't feather prop right away, but used power available to clear a hill. Then carried out normal fire drill, feathering prop and switching off gas and switches and pressing Graviner button as fire was still burning." McLurg then made a normal single-engine landing. His experience as a cool-headed instructor would have been an asset in any such dicey situation. But it did not help on another occasion – one day over the English Channel, McLurg inadvertently shot down a Mitchell, killing its Dutch crew. Even though he was exonerated, he would have carried this cross for the rest of his days. His tour on 107 otherwise was auspicious, as partially described in this recommendation of October 24, 1944 (perhaps from his CO, DFC awarded December 18, 1944):

Flight Lieutenant McLurg has carried out 50 sorties during his present tour of operations, including four daylight sorties. He has always shown the greatest keenness ... when his navigator had to be screened after 43 sorties on medical grounds, he flew the remainder of his tour with a new navigator who had not done any operations previously.

Flight Lieutenant McLurg has had some excellent results from his night sorties. On one occasion he attacked an oil train which exploded and a column of smoke approximately 1,500 feet high occurred after the attack. ... He could always be relied upon to find something to attack during his sorties, often despite very unfavourable weather conditions and ground opposition.

He has taken part in many successful daylight sorties including those on the chateau near Chatelleraut, when he led the last box of five aircraft, the attack on the marshalling yards at Chalons-sur-Soane, where he acted as No.2 to the leader and, despite the fact that there was very accurate light flak from the marshalling yards, he pressed home his attack and caused several explosions

F/Ls John E. McLurg of Montreal and Eric G. Smith of Navan, Ontario during their tour flying Mosquitos on 107 Squadron. (E.G. Smith Col.)

amongst the railway trucks with his cannon strikes. He also led a box of four aircraft on the barracks at Arnhem on the 17th September 1944 in support of the airborne landings ... Flight Lieutenant McLurg possesses the offensive spirit to a high degree and in view of his excellent record during his operational tour I strongly recommend him for the award of the Distinguished Flying Cross.

F/L McLurg flew his last combat mission on September 10, by then having logged 138:25 hours "on ops". Tour expired in November 1944, he had a total of 302:40 hours on various marks of the Mosquito. In January 1945 he joined No.1 Aircraft Delivery Flight, initially at Middle Wallop. Here he kept busy ferrying many aircraft. Three times he had to file incident reports, including on January 3, 1945 when he taxied Spitfire MJ441 into a van at Epinoy, France. The final report about this noted, "Blame was shared between pilot and driver." On May 10, while taking off at Colerne in Spitfire NH607, he immediately had to land when his engine overheated – a case of a

coolant hose breaking. But, when he bent the propeller of Spitfire MJ783 four days later, 11 Group HQ took a dim view, the investigator noting McLurg was "sufficiently experienced to avoid an accident of this type." A red log book endorsement was recommended, but McLurg evaded this – by good fortune his log book already had been despatched to Canada (Spitfire MJ783 survives in the Belgian Air Force Museum in Brussels).

By war's end McLurg's log book showed entries for many types, most of which he flew with No.1 ADF: Anson, Auster, Beaufighter, Boston, Dominie, Finch, Harvard, Hurricane, Master, Martinet, Mitchell, Mosquito, Mustang, Oxford, Proctor, Spitfire, Tempest, Tiger Moth, Typhoon, Walrus, Warwick and Wellington. Samples of his times on types included: Spitfire – 43:50 hours, Tempest – 24:35 and Walrus – 23:00. McLurg returned to Canada in August 1945. He applied at Trans-Canada Air Lines, but was not hired (although TCA was expanding at war's end, hundreds of pilots were applying there for a few dozen jobs).

Eager to remain in aviation, McLurg re-joined the RCAF on September 30, 1946. His background got him a posting to Trenton. In October 1947 W/C F.R. Sharp of CFS described McLurg: "An officer with a strong personality. Sometimes extreme in his views. More suitable for a Headquarters Staff position than an Adjutant position." From June to December 1948 he was on the prestigious instructors' course at the RAF Empire Flying School at Hullavington. There, his instructor, S/L H.R. Studer, described his ability and experience as warranting "the highest category." His wing commander also was impressed: "With a natural ability well above the average and a wide flying experience, work in the air has been of a high standard and, though classed as

The front page headline reporting the McLurg-Keillor crash. (Canada's Heritage from 1844 – The Globe and Mail)

The Globe and Mail

Very Warm and Humid

Detailed Weather Report on Page 4.

Final Edition   TORONTO, WEDNESDAY, MAY 18, 1949.   5 Cents Per Copy   38 PAGES

2 War Aces Die at Trenton As Trainer Plunges Into Pond

an above average pilot, he is always eager to receive further instruction." However, the EFS commandant, Air Commodore E.D. Barnes, was more reserved: "McLurg is a very experienced officer, quick and intelligent, with a strong personality and a very self-assured manner – possibly he is a little too self-assured..."

McLurg was promoted to squadron leader in January 1949. On May 17, 1949, sad to say, he and S/L H.G. "Cub" Keillor, DSO, DFC, formerly of Coastal Command, died when Auster 16657 crashed near Trenton. The Toronto *Daily Star* reported next day: "A low-flying light training plane crashed into three feet of water in a pond about a mile northeast of the R.C.A.F. station here yesterday, carrying two veteran R.C.A.F. pilots to their death... McLurg, who had more than 3,000 flying hours, flew with a Mosquito squadron during the war. About five months ago, he returned from England, where he was taking a course at the Empire Flying School. A native of Montreal, he was qualified on some 60 types of aircraft and was considered one of the most experienced pilots in the R.C.A.F." The RCAF concluded of this accident: "The investigation of the subject accident has revealed that the cause was a defect in the aircraft and it has been established that neither of the occupants were in any way to blame for the crash." Thus did a random accident take the lives of two superb RCAF officers, each of whom had spent his war excelling at his trade and being a flying ambassador for the BCATP.

F/L Alf Barton Aylmer Album

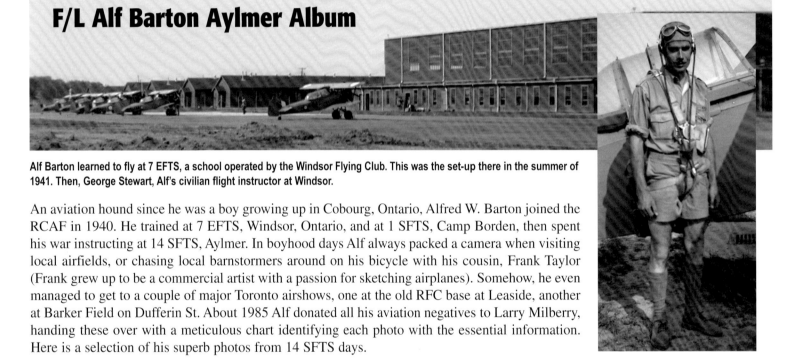

Alf Barton learned to fly at 7 EFTS, a school operated by the Windsor Flying Club. This was the set-up there in the summer of 1941. Then, George Stewart, Alf's civilian flight instructor at Windsor.

An aviation hound since he was a boy growing up in Cobourg, Ontario, Alfred W. Barton joined the RCAF in 1940. He trained at 7 EFTS, Windsor, Ontario, and at 1 SFTS, Camp Borden, then spent his war instructing at 14 SFTS, Aylmer. In boyhood days Alf always packed a camera when visiting local airfields, or chasing local barnstormers around on his bicycle with his cousin, Frank Taylor (Frank grew up to be a commercial artist with a passion for sketching airplanes). Somehow, he even managed to get to a couple of major Toronto airshows, one at the old RFC base at Leaside, another at Barker Field on Dufferin St. About 1985 Alf donated all his aviation negatives to Larry Milberry, handing these over with a meticulous chart identifying each photo with the essential information. Here is a selection of his superb photos from 14 SFTS days.

"D" Flight instructors at 14 SFTS: Keith Black, Alf Barton, Steve Sanderson, P.P. Pearson, Elmer McLeod, Mike Kobierski, Red Cockburn, Fred Ward and Ron Knewstub. Great stories surround each of these outstanding characters. Mike Kobierski, for example, was raised in Sioux Lookout.

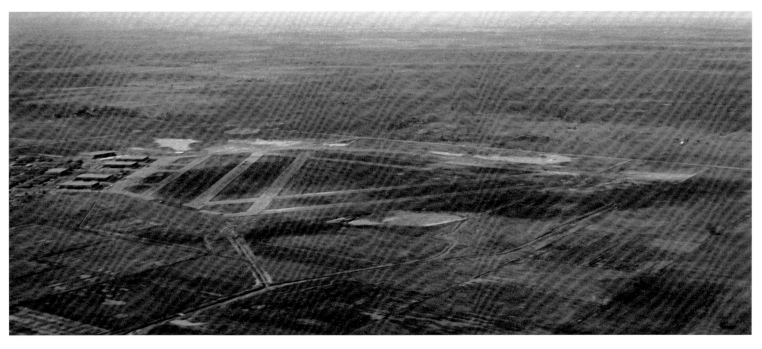

Aerial views of Aylmer, one high, one low (looking north). These give "the lay of the land" to anyone interested in the big picture.

Fellows from the same flight in a more relaxed snapshot – little to do while their students were on solo cross-countries: (behind) Keith Stringer, Bob Brown, Don Lamont, (in front) Gord McLean, Keith Black and Harry Plewes, (right) unknown. Then, 14 SFTS students Kellond (RCAF), Green (RAF), Freeman (RCAF), Gibson (RCAF) and Andrews (RAF).

Bolingbroke target tug 9970 appeared one day at Aylmer.

A nice pair of "first cousins": Yale 3443 and Harvard II 3070. After the war 3070 served the RCN, then was sold, becoming CF-MSZ with Skyway Air Service of Langley, BC.

Lysander 2322, in from 4 (B&G) School at nearby Fingal, draws a mob of curiosity seekers. Then, a flock of visiting "Lizzies".

Harvards on the tarmac at 14 SFTS. On January 4, 1944, No.3209 collided in flight with Harvard FE662, which crashed, killing a Fleet Air Arm student. The other three airmen involved survived with injuries: P/O A.R. Sceviour of Kirkland Lake, Ontario; P/O John Sweet of Aylmer and LAC K.G.R. Child (RAF). No.3093 was lost in a crash on March 28, 1942, while 3125 survived the war and last was heard of being donated by Canada to the Italian Air Force in 1957.

Another bombing and gunnery type that visited Aylmer was the Fairey Battle. Here is L5184, perhaps from 1 (B&G) School at nearby Jarvis.

This snappy-looking Kittyhawk was an eye-catching transient.

A rare visitor was this Brewster Bermuda naval attack plane, of which the RCAF acquired three in 1943 for R&D projects.

When Visiting Flight or some VIPs winged into Aylmer, they often used one of the RCAF's speedy Lockheeds. Here is Lockheed 212 7642, which was on RCAF strength 1940 – 46. Sold back into the US, it flew for years as N60755 with the great Hollywood stunt pilot, Paul Mantz. Sold and re-registered as N16020 (previously the registration used by Amelia Earhart), it was lost in a California crash on December 16, 1961. In the second view, Lockheed 12A 7653 had dropped by. Postwar it was back in the US as N17342 with such companies as Gulf Oil. Harvard FE647 later became another casualty, being lost on October 4, 1944.

Tiger Moth to Mosquito

While Canada supplied most of the instructors for its 100+ air training stations, a few BCATP graduates upon reaching the UK were fingered to instruct in the BCATP on that side of "the pond". One of these was Hugh Bartley. Raised in Headingly, Manitoba, where his father was with the CNR, Hugh was finishing high school at United College in Winnipeg when war began, so had to wait until March 1941 to enlist in the RCAF. He passed through 2 MD in Brandon, attended 4 ITS in Edmonton, then was posted to 8 EFTS at Sea Island. There he flew first in Tiger Moth 4067 on August 22 with Mr. D. Colthurst. He soloed on September 7, finished his course on October 4, then advanced to 3 SFTS at Calgary, flying initially there with F/L Cardell in Anson AW449. He soloed on November 15, progressed through the usual myriad of exercises, completed the course on December 28 and was posted overseas.

Having crossed the Atlantic aboard the troop ship *Volendam*, Sgt Bartley passed through 3 PRC at Bournemouth, from where he was posted to 6 (P) AFU at RAF Little Rissington. There he commenced flying on the Oxford on April 17, 1942. Beam approach training was included, then Bartley proceeded to 5 FIS at Perth, Scotland to qualify as a flying instructor – so the mystery of what posting awaited him was solved. He flew first at FIS with Sgt Cooper in Tiger Moth 5815 on June 26 and completed his course on August 16.

By this time Sgt Bartley's log book showed 308:15 flying hours on all types. He commenced instructing on August 20, 1942 at 4 EFTS at RAF Brough, near Hull. Henceforth, he was busy in the fast-paced EFTS world where, on a typical day, an instructor would fly several exercises with two or three students (e.g. six trips on August 26, 1942). For October 1942, alone, he flew 95 times for 74:00 flying hours. Many months would exceed 80 hours (so his situation was similar to instructors in Canada such as Ernie Weeks).

Sgt Bartley was not the only Canadian instructing at Brough – Rod Clement, Chick Fyfe and Rocky Tremlitt also were there. A few others had been WWI pilots or served in combat early in WWII, so there was a mix of experience. In this period, Brough airfield was occasionally bombed, not so much to disrupt 4 EFTS, as to knock out the adjacent Blackburn aircraft factory (which suffered an occasional hit).

While attending a dance in Hull, Sgt Bartley met Barbara Hobson, and they quickly became a pair. Too bad, but Hugh, by now a pilot officer, was posted about a hundred miles away to 28 EFTS at

Hugh and Barbara Bartley enjoying a typical RCAF social function in post-WWII days. (Bartley Col.)

RAF Wolverhampton, near Birmingham. Here it was more of the same – endless Tiger Moth exercises. There was, however, something different – besides Commonwealth students, 28 EFTS also trained Turks. Thus do such names as Barut, Ozalp and Yurdakol appear in Bartley's log. This was even stranger, since the neutral Turks had officers training with the Luftwaffe in Germany. Bartley's Turks proved to be capable students.

P/O Bartley was re-posted to Brough in September 1943, where his instructing days ended with an exercise on April 4, 1944 in Tiger Moth N9385. On this day his log read 1251:00 hours, so he now had more than 800 hours instructing. He now was destined for operations. First, he went to 11 (P) AFU for an Oxford refresher course, flying initially on April 24. Some leave followed, after which he commenced flying on July 8 at 1655 Mosquito Training Unit at RAF Warboys. There he crewed with Sgt John L. Hartley (RAF). They later joined 128 Squadron (8 Group, Pathfinder Force) at RAF Wyton, Bartley having but 35:45 hours on Mosquitos.

Bartley and Hartley flew initially at 128 on September 12 in Canadian-built Mosquito KB210, then departed that night in the same aircraft carrying 4 x 500-lb bombs to Frankfurt, a 4-hour mission. Their second operation was to Brunswick on September 16/17. While outbound to target, however, KB210 flew into weather so severe at 25,000 feet that it broke up. Pilot and navigator were thrown from the aircraft. Somehow, Bartley got his 'chute open and landed in Belgium with injuries, but Hartley did not make it. This was 128 Squadron's first loss since forming on Mosquitos on September 5.

Sheltered initially by a Belgian farm family, Bartley soon was in a US Army field hospital near the front, then was moved to the rear and evacuated by C-47 to England to recuperate in a US Army hospital near Hereford. Initially, his whereabouts were unknown to the RAF, so he was listed as missing. His flight commander, S/L Ivor Broom, inscribed his log book for September 16/17: "Ops ... Failed to return", an ominous note. However, word filtered back that Bartley was safe. Barbara visited, finding Hugh in a ward packed with American casualties. He soon was transferred to a Canadian convalescent unit, run under the auspices of the Hon. Vincent Massey. Next stop was a Canadian "repat" depot, from where he was given leave for his upcoming marriage. In this period he became F/L Bartley. The wedding took place in Hull on December 9, 1944. Hugh and best man Rod Clement went down the aisle each with a cane, Hugh with a limp and Rod with his head bandaged due to a recent Lancaster prang.

Intruder Navigator's Training Route

Alistair Donald McLaren was born in the UK on December 6, 1922. The family emigrated to Canada in 1927, so Don grew up in Toronto. He was attending Northern Secondary School in Toronto when war broke out. He enlisted in the RCAF on his 18th birthday, but the recruiting officer encouraged him to finish Grade 13 before putting on his uniform. He did this, then began the step-by-step RCAF training process at 1 Manning Depot in May 1941. Next, he joined a draft of recruits awaiting its next course at RCAF Station Jarvis. This worked out for AC2 McLaren, who got up there on his first flight. Finally, he went on to 5 ITS in Belleville. Here the training schedule included plenty of sports, which suited McLaren, who had excelled at basketball, football, etc.

Done at 5 ITS, McLaren was selected to train as an observer. This was a let-down, for he had his hopes of being a pilot. His instructor explained how his excellent marks in mathematics made him a natural for the observer trade. Unimpressed, McLaren soon found himself on course at 9 AOS at St. John's,

south of Montreal. He flew initially with Mr. Parham in an Anson on December 17. The course proceeded to March 11, 1942, by which time LAC McLaren had logged 70:55 hours. Succeeding on this course, he returned to Jarvis for bombing and gunnery training, flying initially with F/O Olmstead on March 26. Exercises henceforth included high- and low-level practice bombing, plus camera gun and live firing at drogues and at targets floating in Lake Erie. The course, which ended with an April 24 exercise, entailed 32 flights/31:25 flying hours in the Fairey Battle. McLaren left Jarvis wearing his observer's wing and sergeant stripes.

Next on the agenda was a course in astral navigation. This took McLaren to 2 ANS at Pennfield Ridge, New Brunswick where his first air exercise was on April 30, 1942. The course was short but intense – many hours in the classroom plus eight air exercises. Sgt McLaren now was posted to Ferry Command at Dorval. This was more of an interlude and involved little flying. In the spring, he finally was posted overseas.

At Bournemouth, Sgt McLaren accepted the offer of Mosquitos, contingent upon taking a signals course at No.1 Radio School at RAF Cranwell.

This he accepted and in this period was promoted to pilot officer. From Cranwell, he and course mates F/L Lawrence B. "Duke" Abelson of Ottawa, and F/L Al Eckert of Seaforth, Ontario were sent in early June to 3 (P) AFU to teach radio on airborne exercises, while awaiting the next opening at OTU. Abelson and Eckert then were posted on course to 60 OTU (Mosquitos) at High Ercall.

McLaren felt left out and wondered what was in the cards for him. In July, however, he was posted directly to 418 Squadron without attending OTU. The explanation was that 418 suddenly needed a replacement navigator. Instead of getting on ops, however, McLaren ended in a non-flying job – duty navigator. Finally, in September 1943 he was posted to 60 OTU. Here he crewed with F/O Dennis E. Roberts, an artist from Saskatoon. They flew initially on September 13, then gained steady experience on the Mosquito. Meanwhile, McLaren flew several exercises on the Anson, getting familiarized with the "Gee box" navigation aid. This course ended late in November. He and Roberts now looked forward to a tour at 418 Squadron, so were not too pleased to hear that they were posted to a Mosquito squadron in India.

A log book spread from Don McLaren's log book showing bombing and gunnery exercises on the Battle while at Jarvis. Then, Don McLaren (observer) and Dennis Roberts (pilot) crewed up at 60 OTU. and flew their operations with 418 Squadron. (McLaren Col.)

Willing Warrior, Reluctant Instructor

Having fought in the Battle of France and the Battle of Britain, P/O Noel K. Stansfeld, DFC, was sent home to Canada late in 1940. His record in combat was a score of 5½-2-0. On December 27 he was promoted to flying officer, and a year later was F/L Stansfeld. Until the end of the war he would have several BCATP postings, starting at 34 SFTS in Medicine Hat from January 1941 to October 1942. Little yet is known of his service in the training system, nor why he was home in the first place. In some cases, men grew battle weary, were even "on the edge". A good CO would recognize when a pilot was faltering and try to arrange leave or a less stressful posting for him. Eventually, many such pilots would return to operations.

In February 1941, 34 SFTS had formed in the UK as an RAF school to operate in Canada. Its "demographics" were unique, since it mainly trained Brits on Harvards and Oxfords, but there also were other Commonwealth, Americans, Czechs, Free French, Poles, etc. The school's ORB for month's end May 1941 noted that it had on strength: Harvards 25, Oxfords 14, officers RCAF 1, officers not RCAF 40, other ranks RCAF 27, other ranks trainees 135, additional other ranks not RCAF 605, civilians 1. The course in progress had been reduced with the deaths in flying accidents of two students and the injury of two others. Another pupil had been "CT'd" (ceased training), i.e. failed due to poor progress; and a sixth had been CT'd for health reasons. (In this period young Thomas Dobney earned his wings at 34 SFTS. Dobney had lied his way into the RAF at age 14, earned his wings in Medicine Hat and ended as a 15-year old bomber pilot. He flew on operations, but soon was exposed and sent home. He eventually re-entered the RAF where, postwar, he was a pilot in the RAF's prestigious King's Flight.)

Towards the end of his tour at 34 SFTS, F/L Stansfeld was commended by the OC 34 SFTS, G/C A. ap Ellis, a BEF and RFC veteran: "An extremely loyal officer. Is a Canadian serving in the RAF. Splendid spirit and a good example to others". Stansfeld next served at Patricia Bay with 32 OTU, were he flew such aircraft as the Beaufort and Hampden. G/C E.S. Weston, OC 32 OTU, commented about Stansfeld on September 22, 1943: "a loyal officer; suited to instructional duties". Two days later, however, S/L Lloyd (perhaps his flight or squadron commander) described him as, "A good average training officer – not likely to provide good leadership on operations".

Some time in this period Stansfeld, perhaps hoping to get back on operations, got overseas again. But in the UK he remained, perhaps reluctantly, in the training system. From January to March 1944 he was at 2 FIS at Montrose in Scotland, then moved to 20 (P) OTU at Kidlington, before returning to Montrose. At Kidlington he received a glowing report from his CAN-RAF OC, G/C Nels W. Timmerman, DSO, DFC, MiD: "An above average officer who is a useful flying instructor and has done a good job as assistant to the Wing Commander Training." In February 1945, Stansfeld transferred to the RCAF. He then served with 426 and 436 squadrons in the UK, returned to Canada and finally left air force life in December 1948.

Dicey Start, Smooth Ending

John T. "Jack" McCreight was born in Toronto on February 6, 1924. With his older brother Victor, he grew up in the west end on McRoberts Ave. As they were for so many Canadian families through the Great Depression, times were tough for the McCreights, but they got by. Jack had a busy childhood, which included getting a solid musical foundation. He still was at Western Technical and Commercial School when the war began, but was keen to get into the RCAF. This he did on August 6, 1942 at the recruiting office at Bay and Wellington streets.

Initially, McCreight was with a cadre of RCAF "hopefuls" for three months of academic upgrading at Central Technical School on Bathurst St. This scheme, known as the "War Emergency Training Plan" bought the air force some time to deal with the flood of recruits, and smarten them up a bit at the same time. From "WET Pee", as the class dubbed their course, they went up one day to 1 ITS at the Hunt Club on Avenue Rd. to be fitted for uniforms, then joined their course at 1 Manning Depot at the

Jack McCreight at home in Unionville, Ontario on January 9, 2010. On display are models of each of the types on which he trained: Bolingbroke, Anson, Wellington, Tiger Moth and Lancaster. (Larry Milberry)

As boys, brothers Jack and Victor McCreight were keen on photography. With a camera, a roll of film and a jerry-rigged darkroom, a fellow had one of the best hobbies going. This is the exciting scene caught by Jack along St. Clair Ave. near Christie St. as Torontonians filled the streets in honour of the Royal Visit in May 1939. Both boys soon would be involved in photography for other purposes. Then, another of Jack's prewar photos: his militia regiment – the Royal Regiment of Canada – embarked on the famous Toronto steamer *Cayuga*. The contingent was bound for Niagara-on-the-Lake for summer training. (All, J.T. McCreight Col.)

An RCAF parade marches north on Spadina Avenue from No.1 Manning Depot in the CNE grounds.

On a stroll one day in Souris, some RCAF recruits came across this worn-out Pietenpol Air Camper, which locals Kitchen and Suddaby had built in 1935. Due to wartime restrictions (non-availability of fuel, etc.) the plane was grounded. Here, Jack McCreight and Ernie Ivey of Toronto take their first "flight" of the war in the tiny Pietenpol.

Jack McCreight (left) and pals on the famous Souris swinging bridge. Then, the visitors from the east inspect some improvised Manitoba winter transportation.

One of the entertainment troupes regularly cross-crossing Canada entertaining the soldiers, sailors and airmen was "The Combines". Jack photographed them on the station platform at Brandon.

Shenanigans at 7 ITS, Jack McCreight on the left in the mock parade, then in front as the guys play around on the obstacle course.

Canadian National Exhibition. From here some had an extra surprise – in January 1943 they boarded the train for Souris, a small Manitoba farm town near Brandon. Souris was being established that winter and the following March would open as 17 SFTS. The recruits shipped from Toronto were given some classroom instruction and physical training, and did odd jobs around the station. In March they packed up and headed east on various assignments. AC2 McCreight ended back in Ontario at 16 SFTS Hagersville, where he and his mates kept busy for a month on such tasks as cleaning the airmen's mess.

At long last AC2 McCreight escaped manning depot duties. He returned west, this time to 7 ITS in Saskatoon, from where he graduated in May 1943. Things were finally starting to happen and he was pleased when selected for pilot training and posted to 15 EFTS at Regina. On June 28, 1942 he flew initially with Sgt Elvin in Tiger Moth 5045, then got into the swing of things. He soloed in 5013 on July 7 (his 11th flight), but his hopes came to a shattering end the next day: while flying solo he lost control of Tiger Moth 5827 and ploughed into the ground. He was rushed to Regina General Hospital, but his injuries proved too severe to be treated there. Accompanied by a nurse, he and

another injured student pilot were sent by train to Toronto. There they recuperated in Christie Street Hospital, an institution established in 1919 to treat WWI veterans.

By October 1943 McCreight was considered fit again. He was offered the chance to return to pilot training, but his parents, understandably, objected.

15 EFTS Tiger Moth crash survivors Jack McCreight (left) and Al Bettridge with one of their nurses at the Christie Street Hospital in Toronto. In 2010 Jack recalled: "We both spun in on July 8, 1943. Al got into a flat spin at 5000 feet. I went down nose first from 400 feet, while turning in to land." Statistically, Canada had a higher accident rate compared to the BCATP in Rhodesia and the UK.

Instead, he remustered to air navigator/bomb aimer (Navigator "B" category). This began with a course at 6 (Bombing and Gunnery) School at Mountain View, near Trenton. His first post-crash exercise was on November 15th in Anson 8416 with P/O Leishman. McCreight soon was flying bombing and gunnery exercises over Prince Edward Country and Lake Ontario.

The Bolingbroke was the chief gunnery trainer at Mountain View, McCreight flying first in aircraft 10003 on November 26. This was a camera gun exercise with F/O Duncan on which McCreight "fired" 50 feet of film. His first air firing from the Boly was from 10014 two days later. High level bombing exercises, where a student's chief instrument was the bomb sight, were done in the Anson. LAC McCreight last flew at Mountain View on an exercise in Boly 9855 with FSgt Grainger of December 22. His flying time on course totalled: Day bombing 13:55 hours, night bombing 5:35, gunnery time 14:00.

LAC McCreight's class did not leave Mountain View without losses: LAC Lawrence Collins (age 20 from Halifax), LAC Nelson Galloway (age 21 from Vancouver) and LAC Raymond Jolly (age 23 from Weyburn, Saskatchewan) died on December 14, 1943 along with

their pilot P/O Allan M. Curry (age 26 from Orangeville, Ontario). Curry had been landing Bolingbroke 10014 after a gunnery exercise, when something went afoul. LAC Galloway had trained originally at the RCAF trades school at St. Thomas, Ontario. He had been overseas on some such duties, but had remustered to aircrew.

Having passed bombing and gunnery, LAC McCreight and his class became Course 92 doing the navigation part of the "Nav B" syllabus at 10 AOS Chatham. Their flying exercises were done on Ansons flown by civilian pilots. LAC McCreight first flew on March 21 – a 3:05-hour exercise with Mr. Biron. Flying proceeded to May 9, by when McCreight had logged 119:45 hours day and night. He finished 11th in his class of

Bolingbroke Mk.IVTs ("T" for trainer) were used at 6 (B&G) School for gunnery training, while Ansons flew the bombing exercises. This model used the 920-hp Bristol Mercury engine. Basic specs were: length 42' 9", wing span 56' 10", empty weight 8963 lb, all-up weight 14,500 lb, top speed 214 mph. Some 407 Mk.IVTs were on RCAF strength.

RCAF Form R.96D noting course results at 6 (B&G) School for LAC McCreight: final result 84.4%.

26, passing on with a grade of 74%. The class now was posted to Y Depot, but not at its busy Halifax operation. Instead, they went to the Y Depot satellite at Maitland, Nova Scotia. Several weeks passed there, perhaps since the air war in Europe was winding down and the rush to ship aircrew across had passed.

Neat and informative log book entries in LAC McCreight's log book from 10 AOS days. Then, the official form showing his course assessment.

R.C.A.F. R.96D
(Revised)
15m—11-42 (2944)
H.Q. 885 R.96D

RESULTS OF AB INITIO BOMBING COURSE

Unit: #6 B.&G. School, Mt. View, Ont.

Duration of Course .... from 1-11-43 to 27-12-43

Exercise	Bombs Dropped	Average Error in Yards (radius)	Type of Aircraft
H.L. Grouping (Day)	42	Cumulative Average	Anson
H.L. Grouping (Night)	18	100	
H.L. Moving Target	------	------	
Low Level (Day)	20	67	"
H.E.			

Pupil's Flying Time 19:30

Examination Results: % 84.4

REMARKS:—Pass/Fail   C.J. Bullock F/O C.I.

Nº 10 A.O.S.

TIME CARRIED FORWARD:— 27:55 | 5:35

DATE 1944	HOUR 1430	AIRCRAFT TYPE AND No.	PILOT	DUTY	REMARKS (Including results of bombing, gunnery, exercises, etc.)		FLYING TIMES DAY	NIGHT
JAN 8	1430	ANSON 11793	MR. HUTCHISON-1	NO AIR NAVIGATOR 1/3 1ST, 2/3 2ND	PINPOINTING NO1		1:25	
JAN 9	0845	ANSON 9X254	MR. McENTYRE	AIR NAVIGATOR 1/3 1ST, 2/3 2ND	PINPOINTING NO2		1:55	
JAN 13	0845	ANSON 6653	MR. JACKSON	AIR NAVIGATOR 1/3 1ST, 1/2 2ND	PINPOINTING NO3		2:05	
JAN 23	0855	ANSON 6887	MR. BEATTY	AIR NAVIGATION	PINPOINTING & TRY G/S W/V'S NO4		2:40	
JAN 24	1430	ANSON 138	MR. REESOR	AIR NAV. (FIRST)	DR. AHEAD BY TRY G/S PINPOINTING NO5		3:00	
JAN 26	1430	ANSON 35	MR. BURNS	AIR NAV. (SECOND)	TR X G/S W/V'S - PINPOINTS - 1 BOMB NO6		3:05	
FEB 2	1430	ANSON NOSE 77	MR. WILSTON	AIR NAV. (FIRST)	AIRPLOT - NO7 - AIRPLOT W/V'S NO7		2:50	
FEB 3	0900	ANSON NOSE 132	MR. LAUZON	AIR NAV. (SECOND)	PINPOINTING - TRY G/S W/V'S - 1 BOMB NO8		3:10	
FEB 9	1430	ANSON NOSE NS	MR. BORIBES	AIR NAV. (SECOND)	PINPOINTING - TRACK PLOT - 1 BOMB NO10		2:40	
FEB 13	2100	ANSON NOSE 59	MR. CRAPP	AIR NAV. (FIRST)	AIRPLOT - CHECK POSN. PINPTS - AIRPLOT W/V NN1			3:25
FEB 14	1430	ANSON NOSE 69	MR. TOMLINSON	AIR NAV. (FIRST)	AIRPLOT - MULTI DRIFT W/V'S NO12		3:10	
FEB 16	0900	ANSON NOSE 64	MR. WALLACE	AIR NAV. (SECOND)	DF + AS. CO FIXES - TRACK PLOT CAMO6 NO9		3:00	
FEB 17	1500	ANSON NOSE 91	MR. TITIAN	AIR NAV. (FIRST)	AIRPLOT - DF + ALCO FIXES - AIRPLOT W/V NO10		2:50	
FEB 26	1500	ANSON NOSE 44	MR. BURNS	AIR NAV. (FIRST)	AIRPLOT - DF + ASCO FIXES - CLIMB TR NO11		3:30	
MAR 3	2100	ANSON NOSE	MR. McKWAN	AIR NAV. (SECOND)	TR PLOT - STAR SHOTS NN2			3:25
MAR 4	1400	ANSON NOSE 91	MR. SOUTHAM	AIR NAV. (FIRST)	AIRPLOT - CLIMB DESCEND TR NO13		3:10	
MAR 5	2100	ANSON NOSE 135	MR. McCLURE	AIR NAV. (SECOND)	TR PLOT - STAR SHOTS NN3			3:15
MAR 8	1400	ANSON NOSE F3	MR. SUTTON	AIR NAV. (SECOND)	TR PLOT - STAR SHOTS NO14		3:30	
MAR 10	0845	ANSON NOSE A9	MR. HUGHSON	AIR NAV. (SECOND)	TR PLOT - STAR SHOTS NO14 FIRST		3:10 1:25	
MAR 11	1400	ANSON NOSE 135	MR. HUGHSON	AIR NAV. (COMBINED)	LOW LEVEL - PINPOINTING & SECOND NO16		1:30	
MAR 14	1400	ANSON NOSE F4	MR. BOWEN	AIR NAV. (FIRST)	SEA CRAWL - 3 CO W/V'S G/C FROM QR NO16		3:25	
MAR 15	1400	ANSON NOSE 135	MR. VEIKLE	AIR NAV. (FIRST)	SEA CRAWL - 3 CO W/V'S G/C FROM QR NO16		3:00	

TOTAL TIME.... 82:25 | 15:40

R.C.A.F. R.96A (Revised)
30M—6-43 (3326)
H.Q. 885 R-96A

NAVIGATION COURSE

FOR

NAVIGATORS OR AIR BOMBERS

Held at # 10 A.O.S. Chatham, N.B.

From Jan. 3/44. To May. 19/44.

GROUND WORK			AIR WORK		
Subject	Marks Allotted	Marks Obtained	Subject	Marks Allotted	Marks Obtained
Air Nav.—Elements	200	163	Air Nav.—Day	350	282
Air Nav.—Theory	200	162	Air Nav.—Night	200	145
Air Nav.—Exercises	200	146	Log Keeping	150	120
Meteorology	100	78	Reconnaissance	100	78
Signals—Written	A.V. 50	45	Photography	50	42
Signals—Practical	V.A. 50	47	Met. Observations	50	48
Aircraft Recognition	100	94	Bombing	100	55
Reconnaissance	50	40	Signals—Air Operating		
Photography	50	48	TOTAL	1000	740
Armament			%		74.0

TOTAL	1000	823
%		82.3

FLYING TIMES ON COURSE

Type	Day	Night
Anson	79.50	39.55
TOTAL		

Passed ✓   Failed

REMARKS:
Standing in Class
11/26

A.M. Christie S/L
Chief Instructor

Jack McCreight – A Chatham Gallery

Always a photography fan, Jack McCreight kept his camera ready for action, even though unapproved photography on any air station was strictly forbidden by the RCAF. Happily, there were such keen fellows who were ready to face the consequences if caught taking pictures. Without them, much about life in wartime Canada would have been lost. Jack shot this winter scene above Chatham showing the triangular runway design standard for all BCATP air stations.

When Hurricane 5636 dropped by Chatham one day, the students were keen to have a look. Jack McCreight shot this decent view for the record. While with 126 Squadron at Dartmouth, this Hurricane was lost in a crash on October 24, 1944.

"Nose 11" – an ordinary yellow Anson V nav trainer at 10 AOS.

The student observer's view through the nose of a 10 AOS Anson. His bomb sight is in the foreground.

One of the civilian Anson pilots with whom Jack McCreight flew from Chatham. On a typical exercise a staff pilot would have along two student observers and a wireless operator (RCAF). Before going flying, they all would have been briefed by an academic instructor, so the pilot had an idea of what sort of exercise he had ahead. En route, the student would advise the pilot of course changes/corrections, so they all usually got home in one piece. Then, some of Jack McCreight's Course 92 pals at Chatham. Accommodations were bare bones for airmen at all wartime training stations. Sitting on the bunk are three RAF lads: W.D. "Dave" Crail from Liverpool, W.H. "Dasher" Davies from Crewe in Cheshire, and J.H. "Jock" Cranston from Glasgow.

The course at AOS always included aerial photography assignments. On one flight, LAC McCreight framed up this view of Chatham sitting along the Miramichi River.

Sgt Jack McCreight receives his observer's wing in May 1944. For graduation the class turned out a commemorative booklet: "Course 92, The Course with Characters – All 28 of them". They dedicated this to their three course mates killed in Mountain View Days. The editor's note about McCreight reads, "Any idea where we are," said Jack, gaily handing the pilot a reciprocal course. This he had obtained by taking bearings on the port navigation light." Then, Course 92 upon graduation at 10 AOS. The instructors in front are J.M. "Monty" Jones of Vancouver and George S. Dundas of Markdale, Ontario. Jack McCreight is the man in the middle in the back row.

Homecoming... on returning from overseas many a young veteran found his front porch decked out for the occasion. So it was when the McCreight brothers got home to McRoberts Ave in Toronto. Then, F/O Victor McCreight with his parents. While overseas as a navigator on 424 Squadron, he was shot down and evaded for several weeks. His parents would have been delighted to see his name in the RCAF Casualty List of September 22, 1944 under the heading "Reported Missing on Active Service, Now Reported Safe in United Kingdom". Earlier, Victor had another exciting day. While thumbing a ride in England, he was picked up by a shiny limousine. In the back was Queen Mary who was on her way to inspect the troops at Victor's station!

A musician since boyhood, Jack McCreight was still enjoying his hobby in 2010.

Finally, Course 92 sailed on Canadian Pacific's *Empress of Scotland*, which previously had been the *Empress of Japan* (things all around the ship still were labelled in Japanese). The ship docked at Gourock from where P/O McCreight passed through Bournemouth, from where he was posted to 8 (O) AFU in remote Anglesey, Wales. There he first flew on an Anson exercise ("climb on track") on October 7, 1944. Various "land", "sea", "land and sea", "bombing", etc., exercises ensued until the final one of January 4, 1945. The course entailed 79:50 hours day and night flying.

Two more training phases awaited before McCreight could be operational. Next he attended 22 OTU at Wellesborne Mountford, which had been training bomber crews on the Wellington for much of the war. Hundreds of RCAF men passed through here, and many others, having finished operational tours, returned to instruct. F/O McCreight first flew at 22 OTU on March 12 in Wellington LN561 with F/L Brochu. He soon crewed up with an American, F/L Rosson, who previously had instructed in the BCATP. They finished OTU on April 30, McCreight having logged 77:00 hours on 28 flying exercises. The Rosson crew now killed time at Dalton awaiting HCU, then proceeded to Lancaster training at 1659 HCU, an RCAF unit at Topcliffe. There they flew initially in Lancaster "RV-L" on July 5, but their course was cut short on July 25 after McCreight had flown only 17 times for 36:45 hours.

Not all parents were so fortunate as to see their sons coming up the walk at war's end – the whole ordeal had cost the RCAF more than 16,000 airmen overseas, and more than a thousand others at home. Here, the McCreights' neighbour on McRoberts Ave., Mrs. McHale, holds a portrait of her beloved son, Thomas Patrick, killed at age 24 on November 27, 1944. A navigator on 138 Squadron, his crew had been dropping supplies and agents over Denmark when shot down. The Toronto *Daily Star* of January 2, 1945 mentioned McHale as a graduate of St. Michael's College. He had worked at Swift Canadian Co., a meat packer in his part of Toronto. In a rare case of specific details being reported under wartime censorship, the *Star* also revealed that McHale had been in a Stirling doing secret operations.

The future of all new aircrew in the UK now was uncertain. VE-Day had been celebrated and the war was winding down in the Pacific. There was some talk that crews such as Rosson's would convert to the Lincoln and join "Tiger

The Rosson crew flew only one trip over Germany. The war was over so, on July 24, 1945, they took a low-level look at Cologne, by then a symbol of Hitler's glorious "Thousand Year Reich". P/O McCreight recorded this dreadful scene as they roared over. One can see what the German emergency measures people meant when, having suffered a visit from Bomber Command, they sometimes described a city as "ploughed over".

Force" to help finish off Japan. This was settled early in August when America brought Japan to its knees with the atomic bomb. Millions of soldiers, sailors and airmen now could go home, instead on facing another year of horrors in the Pacific.

F/O McCreight came home aboard another famous liner of the era – the *Duchess of Richmond*, which carried him from Liverpool to Halifax. Back in Toronto, he was "de-mobbed" at the RCAF reception centre in the CNE. On Civvie Street, he returned to his pre-war job at Salada Tea and married his fiancée, Marg McKeown. They soon settled in Winnipeg, where Jack's job took them. He later spent many years with General Bakeries, from where he retired in 1988. Jack McCreight's had been an unusual war, starting at EFTS, surviving a serious accident, then switching to "Nav B", only to be sent home at war's end, his only trip over Germany being to see the sights.

10 AOS Staff Pilot

The AOS training system primarily involved dedicated classroom instructors teaching their students the basics of air navigation, then sending their students on carefully planned air exercises in Anson trainers. The third part of this equation was the staff pilot – a civilian who flew the Anson according to the particular student exercise, whether over land, sea or both. One of these AOS pilots was George Neal. Born on the family farm in North Toronto, George learned to fly at the Toronto Flying Club, earning his pilot's licence in 1936. While working first as an auto mechanic, he enjoyed many an aviation adventure, especially with his pals Fred Hotson and Don Murray. One project was helping Fred build a tiny Heath Parasol. In 1937

10 AOS Anson V 11884 doing a snappy departure at Chatham. While the RCAF's supply of original Anson Is and IVs was dwindling, Canada developed the ultimate Anson – the Mk.V. This version had a molded plywood fuselage based on technology developed by Aircraft Research Corp. in New York. The prototype first flew in January 1943 and soon was replacing older BCATP types. Anson V production totalled 1048. Then, a photo of staff pilot George Neal at the controls of a 10 AOS Anson. (All, George Neal Col.)

The civilian-run BCATP schools were managed by experienced men from Canada's flying clubs and pioneer bush flying companies. Typical was R.H. "Dick" Bibby, an old hand from Canadian Airways. Here, Bibby accompanies Princess Alice, Countess of Athlone, Honourary Air Commandant of the RCAF Women's Division, during a 10 AOS inspection tour. On parade are the school's civilian women, whose tasks included everything from running the canteens to fuelling Ansons, packing parachutes and driving any type of vehicle on the station.

10 AOS pilots George Neal and John Habasinski circa 1990. John passed on in September 1997. While George pursued a life-long aviation career, John gave up flying after the war for a career in heavy equipment. (Larry Milberry)

George was hired by de Havilland of Canada, where he worked assembling Tiger Moths, then Avro Ansons, including the first example shipped from the UK early in 1940.

As did Fred Hotson and Don Murray, George got into the AOS as a staff pilot. Don, who also checked out Fred Hotson, took George on his initial flight, a 3:10-hour cross-country from 1 AOS Malton in Anson 6042 on June 23, 1941. He soloed in 6054 on July 9, then built up time at Malton until posted to 10 AOS in Chatham. The school was run by the Northumberland Air Observer School Ltd. An old-time Canadian Airways bush pilot, R.H. "Dick" Bibby, managed the operation with Harry Bruton as his operations man and C.J. Ferguson, formerly of Canadian Vickers, heading maintenance.

George Neal first flew at Chatham in Anson I W2446 with Hugh Clarke on August 14, 1941. He now slipped straight into the daily routines enjoyed by Chatham's cadre of civilian pilots. Daily duties normally entailed two student trips, whether two in daylight, two at night, or one of each. George would happily take whatever the scheduler decreed, but he sometimes preferred night flying, since the summer air usually was smoother and what few lights there were below were easily identified after a fellow had made a few night trips. Pilot pay varied between day and night flying, the rate per month (day) being $375 and (night) $400. For the

students, exercises included navigation, bombing, aerial reconnaissance and photography.

The staff at 10 AOS mainly were Canadians, but there were a few Americans and even a Brit – Charles W.A. Scott, the renowned racing pilot who, with partner Campbell Black, had won the 1934 MacRobertson Air Race between London and Melbourne. Among the Canadians with whom George Neal flew were Harry Bruton, formerly instructing at the Kingston Flying Club;

Charlie Campbell, a bush pilot from North Bay; Hugh Clarke and John Habasinski of Toronto; and Glenn White of the Hamilton Flying Club. Few, except the odd fellow like Campbell, had come to Chatham with much flying experience. John Habasinski, for example, was hired by the AOS with 125 flying hours on light planes.

Naturally, there was some turn-over among AOS pilots, especially when opportunities began appearing at Ferry Command. Before long, George had heard that his buddies Hotson and Murray of 9 AOS had opted for Ferry Command, where the pay was better and the aircraft types more exotic than an Anson. From 10 AOS, Charlie Scott made the move. So did Murray Martin, another Toronto boy. Sad to say, but Martin, fellow Canadian pilot Ted Talbot and crew all died on February 6, 1945, when they had an engine fail on takeoff from Bermuda in Liberator B.VI KL386.

Life at Chatham was always interesting for George Neal. Besides daily student trips, sometimes there was a special transportation flight or a weather check to make, so by November 1942 George easily passed his 1000th hour on Ansons. Then, when the Anson Vs started coming off the line at Federal Aircraft at Amherst, Nova Scotia, he was busy ferrying old Anson Is to Amherst for scrapping, then bringing new Anson Vs back to Chatham. His first Anson V fight was with 11726 on September 11, 1943. The Mk.V was a gem compared to a Mk.I, which was drafty and more prone to engine failure. George also did instrument check rides for RCAF Anson pilots. He eventually became the school test pilot, which kept him hopping. On a typical day test flying (January 19, 1944) he flew Mk.Vs 11778, '785, '787 and '793, and took Mk.I 6587 up three times.

The civilian pilots were subject to the same strict check rides that RCAF pilots faced on the home front. This work was done by Visiting Flight – part of CFS at Trenton. AOS pilots dreaded their check rides, knowing how demanding Visiting

Murray Martin, who left 10 AOS for the lure of Ferry Command, only to lose his life in a Liberator crash.

Flight always was. On February 26, 1943 F/L Don MacFadyen gave George a check ride. He criticized George for caging his gyro while taxiing out. George explained how taxiing was very bumpy and could throw off the gyro, but MacFadyen didn't agree. George feared a poor assessment, but MacFadyen, who knew his job well, gave George a glowing report (MacFadyen ended overseas, where he excelled as a Mosquito intruder pilot).

Ansons were lost at Chatham as at any BCATP station. George Neal's log book shows a search for a missing Anson on November 11, 1941. Beginning on April 6, 1942 he was part of a big search for one of Chatham's American pilots, Larry Berriman who, along with the students on board, had disappeared (forever) out to sea in Anson 6631. The last heard from Berriman was that they were between Summerside and Chatham on the final leg of their exercise. Eight days later a press release stated: "Two New Zealanders and a civilian pilot were aboard a bomber missing in the vicinity of Chatham, N.B., since the night of April 6... The student New Zealanders were Leading Aircraftman E.R. McFarlane and Acting Cpl. H.S. McKinnon. The civilian pilot was L. Berriman, whose home town was not known..."

One of the many Anson Is flown by George Neal on student exercises and test flights. Formerly RAF W1626, 6300 served until disposed of for scrap in February 1945.

With air exercises and other flights pretty well every day at 10 AOS, accidents were inevitable. End result? Plenty of work salvaging and repairing Ansons. On May 8, 1942 "Nose 28" (6689, ex-RAF W2416) ditched in Chaleur Bay near Bathurst, New Brunswick, after the weather closed in around Chatham. Deemed to be beyond repair, 6689 was written off.

A bent Anson with the work gang waiting ready to pitch in.

Anson 11879 after what likely was assessed as a "Cat C" prang at 10 AOS on a blustery February 11, 1944. (Below) Anson I W2621 caught fire and burned to a skeleton at Chatham after a tire failed on August 27, 1943.

In an astounding case, one night an Anson staggered into Chatham in weather unfit for flying. The crew was from 31 GRS, the RAF nav school at Charlottetown. They had been looking for Moncton. By some total fluke of good luck, instead of crashing en route they ended in Chatham with no idea of where they were. Oddly, when advised of their location, they refused to believe this, insisting that they must be in Moncton. Even though denied permission to take off, they did so and were never seen again. On February 28, 1943 George Neal was on a search for a missing Hudson, which someone else later spotted crashed in the New Brunswick bush.

Spare time at Chatham offered plenty of worthwhile activity. In summer there was sailing in the beautiful coastal waters. There were plenty of social get togethers with friends and when things were quiet, George could build a model airplane or do some photography. He also had Christmas leave and a week in summer at home. George last flew at 10 AOS on April 24, 1945. That day he and C.J. Ferguson had a pleasant final flight together in Anson 12067. George now returned to Ontario, knocked around a bit doing some interesting flying then, on January 6, 1946 started work at De Havilland of Canada at Downsview, where he would remain until retiring in 1983. The other AOS pilots soon also found their slots in the postwar world. Some such as Fred Hotson and Don Murray were lucky to find nice jobs in aviation, where they stayed until retirement. Others went elsewhere. John Habasinski, for example, became a heavy equipment operator in the construction industry and rarely flew again. Hugh Clarke returned to his pre-war job in display at the T. Eaton Co. in Toronto.

We Fly Ansons

Many a drinking song was created during RCAF days. There usually was some creative type around who could spin up a few lyrics, put it to a tune that everyone knew, and ... let the fun begin. On average, these songs are X-rated, but Jim Bales and Maurice Pateman of 8 AOS, Ancienne Lorette, put their ditty together – "We Fly Ansons" – that's cleared for a general audience. The recommended tune is not given. For better or worse, quite a few of the pilots at 8 AOS get remembered in "We Fly Ansons", some of the 21 nutty verses of which are included here.

We're pilots for the aircrew
At an Observer School.
We fly those airplanes
Like the boys from Manning Pool.
We fly and fly, and fly and fly.
Morning, noon and night
And anyone seeing us fly those crates
Would think that we were tight.

(Chorus)

We fly Ansons, Anson
The best aeroplanes they'll ever be.
We pour on all the coal,
But we never reach our goal:
We're flying Ansons on to Victory

The navigator says to me:
"I think we're off our track,
And if we don't soon alter course,
I don't think we'll get back."
I look at my old compass
And it seems to be OK.
But, confidentially, fellows,
We're going the other way...

One night Sergeant Texas
Called up all his crew,
Says, "My engines are failing
And I don't know what to do."
The navigator says, "Jumping is
The only thing I can see."
OK, says Sergeant Texas,
"We'll jump, you follow me"...

And then there's Captain Grattan -
We all know his worth.
Used to fly those Junkers crates
Way up in the North.
Now he's flying Ansons
And waiting for the day
When Canadian Pacific Airlines
Will give him a raise in pay...

When we think that we are lost.
We call out to the WAG:
"Give me a DF bearing."
He says, "It's in the bag."
We fly his courses hours,
And lose about six pounds.
And dream of owning airlines,
And staying on the ground...

Captain Mews came back one night,
The ceiling it was low.

Looking for the airport,
Where, he didn't know.
He overshot the field six times
And finally staggered down.
Jumped out of his Anson,
And stooped to kiss the ground...

Captain Hayes one dirty night
Got lost near Thetford Mines.
Let down on a main street
To read the local signs.
He curses all the blackouts,
Turns on his landing light,
Says, "Open up your arms, Lord,
I'm coming home tonight."

Sergeant Pilot Harvey
Coming in to land,
Listening to sweet strains
Of Glenn Miller's band.
Forgets to call the Tower,
Then we hear an awful smack.
He piled up his old Anson
Upon another's back...

Two pilots back from USA
Were flying the Burma Road,
Dodging Japs and income tax
And carrying quite a load.
They soon got tired of Zeros
Shooting off their ears –
So back they came to AOS
To spend their aging years...

And then there's Wilf Stevenson.
He likes to have his fun.
Steps up to our bar and says:
"Boys, have another one."
He says, "Don't worry, lads, drink up,
As I am going to pay."
We look at him dumbfounded
And say, "That will be the day" ...

Our manager is Mr. Beck,
He flew them years ago.
But sitting at a desk so long,
Has made his middle grow.
He's really quite a good sort,
He'll give you the glad hand,
And almost anything you want,
Except the Ferry Command.

There's a guy who ain't no student,
'Cause he's not on any course.
Got a military figure
And he's going to the wars.
He's aiming for Group Captain –
Air Commodore to be –
But actually, fellows ... he's just our W/C.

George Neal's Chatham Album

10 AOS in an oblique photo showing the details of a standard BCATP air station. (Inset) This old crow toting a map in its beak and a bomb in its claws became the emblem of 10 AOS. (Below) A fine summer's day, so pop out the windows and enjoy it all: Anson I 6892 (ex-RAF AW460) cruises lazily along out of Chatham.

Survival equipment – a life raft and parachute – gets inspected at 10 AOS. Pilots and crew expected all such equipment to work as advertised, especially as they often were far out to sea or over very unfriendly countryside.

Anson V 12059 with the 10 AOS control tower beyond.

Activity seen any day of the week in the 10 AOS shops, including Anson "B5" in for a maintenance check.

A 10 AOS flight sergeant instructs student navs. He's using one of the visual aids of the day – an epidiascope, which projected an opaque image onto a screen. Note the slide projector on the desk behind, and the standard aircraft recce aids. Then, students in radio class, maybe honing their Morse Code skills.

It was always fun when some interesting aircraft dropped in. Keen types like George Neal would be sure to sneak a photo before the transient disappeared. In this case, he caught a handsome RAF Mitchell passing through on its long ferry to Prestwick.

Life in the mess: an RCAF and a civvie pilot wind down in the mess with their gals. Then, three of the fellows pretty well into it, and a friendly game of dice in full flight. Finally, some of the New Zealanders letting off steam less boisterously – their mothers would be pleased.

For any young airman far from home, the mail was like manna from heaven. These New Zealanders on course at Chatham couldn't have been farther away from home, so are eagerly checking out their packages from family and friends. This was a PR set-up photo, of course, and is dated November 10, 1942. Sports was vital in RCAF life, especially for younger fellows in training. Here's the cup-winning 10 AOS soccer team for 1942.

George Neal not only enjoyed photographing an idyllic New Brunswick scene such as this, but took up sailing himself while stationed in Chatham. Then, the Governor General, the Earl of Athlone and the great Air Marshall W.A. "Billy" Bishop, VC, in the mess during a vice-regal inspection tour. They are flanked by S/L A.D. Blackmore and school manager Dick Bibby.

A motley-looking bunch when not in uniform – the civilian pilots at 10 AOS: Fred "Pappy" Bryant, Murray Martin, Larry Berriman, Ozzi Lauzon, George Sheard, Harry Bruton, Arnold Cowitz, Charles Hurley, Pappy Ryan, Charles Wiese, George Neal, Wally Willardson and Harry Wilson. The two "pappys" and Berriman were Americans.

Wings Parade at 10 AOS on May 4, 1944. From the parade square at Chatham, the new pilot officer and sergeant navigators were on their way to the operational world.

Air Gunner's Course

Born on May 4, 1922, George R. "Joe" Davis grew up in Toronto's east end, where he attended Riverdale Collegiate. On leaving high school, he worked at the booming Dunlop Rubber plant on Queen Street East, his first job being mixing latex at 31 ½ cents an hour. He switched into the tape department, all along putting up with the horrible conditions of a wartime factory. Joe stayed at this until deciding to enlist in the RCAF, which he did in December 1942. Meanwhile, he had met Marg Toner at a local dance – they married in July 1942.

Joe Davis began his air force days at 1 Manning Depot, an experience that in 2010 he still preferred to forget. The thought of it brought back memories about such things as the inoculations that gave everyone a sore arm. Then a sadistic drill instructor would get the recruits on the parade square, making them swing their arms extra vigorously. Finished here, AC2 Davis was sent to Camp Borden on guard duty with the routine being to man a guard post with an empty Enfield rifle. The best part about this brief assignment was a flight that Davis scrounged. His pilot wrung out the Harvard, but Davis kept his breakfast down, so was duly confident that he would make a good airman. Next came several weeks attending "smartening up" academic refresher courses at Beal Secondary School in London, a 2-hour train ride west of Toronto.

From London, where he finally heard that he was destined for air gunner training, AC2 Davis entrained with his draft at Toronto for Quebec City. However, against the rules he met his wife for a brief visit and missed his departure. He quickly enquired about other trains, boarded the next one without a ticket, got away with that and, luckily, reconnected with his draft in Montreal. Eventually arrived in Quebec City, he became part of a guard of honour on duty during the Churchill-Roosevelt-King summit then in progress. At long last he and his mates reached RCAF Station Mont Joli, home of 9 (Bombing and Gunnery) School.

AC1 Davis first flew at 9 (B&S) School on September 9, 1943, going up in Fairey Battle No.106 on a 1:15 hour "famil" flight with WO2 Scott. His course progressed smoothly, each of his

December 28, 2009 and veteran RCAF air gunner Joe Davis looks over his log book and photos from days long past. Then, Joe and his wife Marg. They married in 1942, the summer before Joe enlisted. (Larry Milberry, Joe Davis Col.)

AC1 G.R. "Joe" Davis was part of this Quebec City guard of honour during the King-Churchill-Roosevelt summit of August 17-24, 1943. (Joe Davis Col.)

27 flights entailing either a cine camera exercise or firing at a towed drogue. Normally, 100-200 rounds were fired during a gunnery trip. Scores were never stellar. On his exercise with WO2 Wood of September 22, for example, Davis scored 8 hits for his 200 rounds. His final exercise was with Sgt Warren on October 12, when he scored 8 hits for 100 rounds. On the whole, he logged 14:30 hours in the Battle turret – the rest of his 23:25 hours aloft he was waiting in the

A Fairey Battle – the type on which Joe Davis trained at 9 (B&G) School – in a gunnery student's sight during a typical exercise. (CANAV Col.)

Members of Joe Davis' course at 9 (B&G) School in a picture dated September 25, 1943. Behind are LACs Brown, Ison, Slevar, Davis, McBain, Patterson, Lussier and Folds. In front are LACs Waddell, Hergott, Seath, Adamson, Harkness, McNally, Harrison and James. As always, much history is involved with these names. There were three wartime casualties among these fellows. P/O Gerald A. Hergott (age 20 from Waterloo, Ontario) was posted to 427 Squadron. On March 31, 1944, while on their first operation (Halifax LW618), he and his crew were lost over Nuremberg. On August 31, 1944 FSgt Norman T. James (age 23 from New Liskeard, Ontario) died along with his 103 Squadron crew when shot down in Lancaster LM243 on operations over France. On November 25 P/O John Richard Patterson (age 21 from North Bay, Ontario) was killed along with his 12 Squadron crew when shot down in Lancaster ND342 on operations to Duisberg. Patterson had survived an earlier crash while at 28 OTU. Kenneth E. Lussier went on the Bomber Command. Shot down on ops with 408 Squadron, he evaded for several weeks, returning to the UK to finish his tour. He survived the war as F/O Lussier, DFC, MiD, then remustered to pilot. On April 25, 1952 he had Lancaster KB893 on a test flight. When KB893 bounced on landing, Lussier decided to go around, but crashed. All four aboard were killed. In 2010 Joe Davis reported that of 123 men with whom he trained during the war, 30 were killed in action, 4 were POWs and 1 evaded. (Joe Davis Col.)

cramped Battle cockpit as a second student tried his luck in the turret. Davis passed out of 9 (B&G) School with an overall average of 76.6%, was posted to "Y" Depot in Halifax, then sailed aboard the troopship *Mauretania* for the UK on October 31.

A week later LAC Davis disembarked at Liverpool and made his way to 3 PRC in Bournemouth. Everyone was glad to be ashore – most had been seasick on the

crossing. Davis had survived this ugly experience, but the sight, sound and smell of so many airmen being ill all day long kept him from eating most meals. Instead, he subsisted on candies. (Sea sickness was simply another of the endless realities experienced by RCAF personnel travelling to and from postings. D.J. "Dave" Davies, a fitter who serviced Typhoons on 143 Wing, once told of his sea crossing: "It was really first class. We

had six meals every day – three down and three up!") LAC Davis had about a 6-week stay in Bournemouth before finally getting his posting to 82 OTU at Ossington. There he would begin the next stage of his air gunner training, this time on Wellingtons.

Bombing and Gunnery OC

BCATP station officers OCs (officers commanding) usually were group captain in rank and had pre-war service. They had distinguished themselves enough to be considered leadership material, but were too old for the fighting part of the war. In practice, station commanders varied greatly. Some proved to be eminently suited for the job, others were barely competent. A few even failed as station commanders, the bottle sometimes being their downfall. One OC who was almost a superman was G/C Roy H. Foss.

Born in Sherbrooke, Quebec in 1894, Foss served in the artillery in the First World War, transferred to the RFC in 1918, then flew Camels with 28 Squadron. Back home, he operated a construction company, but returned to flying in the late 1920s. He took refresher courses at Camp Borden and instructed at the Montreal Light Aeroplane Club. In 1934 he joined the RCAF, where he flew Moths with 15 Squadron (later re-numbered 115 Squadron and equipped with Battles and Harvards). Foss was commanding 115 when war was declared. His men then were absorbed into 1 (F) Squadron and were sent overseas in June 1940.

In the UK, S/L Foss' duties did not take him into the fray during the Battle of Britain, although he kept current on the Hurricane. On September 7, 1940 he flew what likely was his sole combat sortie. He then worked in RCAF Overseas HQ, where he was highly regarded. W/C Foss returned to Canada in the summer of 1941. He was posted to EAC in Gander and promoted to group captain that October. In Newfoundland he became legendary as a search and rescue pilot, unusual alone considering his high rank. In November 1942 G/C Foss was given command of 9 (Bombing and Gunnery) School at Mont Joli. He served well here until June 1943 and resulted in A/V/M J.L.E.A. de Niverville (OC 3 Training Command, Montreal) putting Foss up for

A spread from LAC Joe Davis' log book showing typical bombing and gunnery exercises at Mont Joli.

1943		BATTLE	#9 B&G			TIME CARRIED FORWARD:—		
DATE	HOUR	AIRCRAFT TYPE AND No.	PILOT	DUTY	REMARKS (Including results of bombing, gunnery, exercises, etc.)		FLYING TIME	
							DAY	NIGHT
SEPT 9	1300	106	SCOTT W/02	FAM.	COMPLETE	H FILM.	1·15	
10	1425	128	DESKIN	FAM	COMPLETE		1·25	
11	1535	50	McLEAN FLT SGT	CG 1	COMPLETE	½ FILM	1·25	
12	1300	102	WEINMEISTER FLT SGT	CG 2	COMPLETE	½ FILM	1·25	
12	1525	45	ANSLEY SGT.	CG 2	COMPLETE	½ FILM	1·00	
14	0705	99	CHAMBERLAIN	G 7	COMPLETE	100 ROUNDS	·50	
16	1350	102	GREEN SGT.	G 7	COMPLETE	100 ROUNDS	·35	
17	1455	128	EVANS	G 7	COMPLETE	100 ROUNDS	·35	
17	1640	92	ROBERTSON	G 7	COMPLETE	100 ROUNDS	·30	
22	1250	130	WALTER HOUSE SGT.	G 2	INCOMPLETE	—	1·00	
22	1400	97	WALTER HOUSE SGT.	G 2	COMPLETE	9 HITS 175 ROUNDS	·35	
22	1500	99	McLEOD W/02	G 2	COMPLETE	8 HITS 200 ROUNDS	·40	
22	1615	129	O'SULLIVAN P/0	G 2	INCOMPLETE	—	1·15	
26	0825	123	WHYTE SGT.	G 3	COMPLETE	15 HITS 200 ROUNDS	·55	
26	0940	110	WHYTE SGT.	G 3	COMPLETE	5 HITS 200 ROUNDS	·45	
26	1155	97	STOCKWELL FLT/SGT	G 3	COMPLETE	6 HITS 200 ROUNDS	·40	
26	0745	111	WHYTE SGT.	G 3	INCOMPLETE	—	·30	
28	1120	111	RUSSELL	G 3	COMPLETE	16 HITS 200 ROUNDS	1·00	
28	1535	117	ST. JOHN P/0	G 3	COMPLETE	6 HITS 200 ROUNDS	·45	
29	0745	101	SCOTT WO/2	G 3	COMPLETE	3 HITS 200 ROUNDS	·40	
29	0915	129	DEAN FLT/SGT	G 4	COMPLETE	2 HITS 200 ROUNDS	·55	
OCT 5	0945	132	PROVENCHER SGT.	G 4	COMPLETE	14 HITS 200 ROUNDS	·55	
						TOTAL TIME...	19·35	

CBE (Order of the British Empire). de Niverville already had observed about him: "... it is with regret that I see him leave the Command of No.9 BGS." He noted in his recommendation how G/C Foss had "raised the standard of training and efficiency of his unit to a marked degree", and spoke of his "ability far above the average and his fearless leadership and sense of duty". Nonetheless, de Niverville's nomination failed to reach the priority list and no CBE was awarded to Foss.

Other BCATP postings for G/C Foss included: 5 OTU, Boundary Bay; 8 (B&G) School, Lethbridge; 2 Wireless School, Calgary; and 10 Repair Depot, Calgary. Foss left the RCAF in September 1945 to return to his construction company. In June 1946 he finally was formally recognized when awarded the Order of the British Empire, the citation for which summed up this great Canadian's contributions:

The experience and knowledge gained by this officer during his service with the Auxiliary Active Air Force have been invaluable to the Royal Canadian Air Force since the outbreak of hostilities. His outstanding ability, hard work and zeal have been largely responsible for his success as a station commander. Through his leadership qualities he has been instrumental in building up a high state of morale and efficiency in all with whom he has served.

In 1966 Roy Foss was appointed Honourary CO of 401 Squadron (whose antecedent had been 1 (F) Squadron). Foss passed away in 1977.

Wireless Air Gunner Training

Born on January 26, 1924 and raised in Toronto, Colin Clark attended Danforth Technical School before joining the RCAF in 1942. At ITS he was

disappointed at not getting into pilot training, instead being pegged to be a wireless operator. Posted to 2 Wireless School in Calgary, he had his initial flight with P/O Nelson in Cessna Crane 8132 on May 5, 1942. For some reason

Fleet Fort 3590 taxies for an exercise at 2 Wireless School. Then, a pencil sketch made by Colin Clark while on course. "Accident at Shepard, morning July 6/43. 3645 my kite", he noted of this botched effort. (All, Colin Clark Col.)

A fine view at 5 (B&G) School, Dafoe, Saskatchewan as Anson II 8467 taxies by a line of Bolingbrokes. The chief difference between the Anson I and II was engines: 350 hp Cheetah vs 330 hp Jacobs. Being an American product, the Jacobs promised a more secure supply, and also proved to be more reliable. All-up weight for the Anson I was 8000 lb, for the Anson II 7650.

At the end of their gruelling and seemingly endless training, those who persevered got an operational squadron or were assigned some useful duties on the home front. Colin Clark's training odyssey led him to membership in a very exclusive club: a Halifax heavy bomber crew at 433 Squadron at Skipton upon Swale in Yorkshire. Standing in this crew photo are George Leppan (MuG), Colin Clark (WOpAG), Orv L. Orendorff (skipper) and Ron Dent (BA). In front are Ken Smith (FE), Don Draper (RG) and Chuck Wuori (Nav).

his course did not commence until July 2, his first air exercise being in Norseman 2457 with F/O Gieg. Fifteen further exercises followed in Norsemans 2457, 2459, 2492 and 3526 and Fleet Forts 3588, 3590, 3595, 3600, 3645 and 3655. He finished his course on July 13 having logged 33:45 flying hours.

LAC Clark now was posted to 5 (Bombing and Gunnery) School at Dafoe, Saskatchewan, where he flew initially with WO1 McKay in Bolingbroke 9993 on August 2, 1943. This course entailed 18 exercises, 15 in Bolingbrokes, 3 in Ansons for 15:00 flying hours (3:35 at night). Clark's training here included small arms training (85 rounds Enfield rifle and revolver), Browning .303 machine gun on the range (1125 rounds), air-to-air (3900 rounds .303) and 54 feet of film exposed with the cine camera. He flew his final exercise in Anson "914" and on September 6 qualified as a wireless operator/air gunner.

In October 1943 WAG Sgt Colin Clark went overseas where, following Bournemouth, he joined a course at 9 (O) AFU at Llandwrog, North Wales. Here, between October 11 and December 12, he completed 10 air navigation exercises in the Anson Mk.I. These totalled 23:15 hours (day) and 6:20 (night). While airborne, Sgt Clark logged 23:35 hours on the radio set. He also spent 59 hours in the classroom studying general electronics (radios, beacons, intercom, etc.); 40 hours on such topics as Harwell boxes and Marconi T1154 radios as used by Bomber Command; and 26 hours on Morse code. He now was posted to 24 OTU at Honeybourne, where he joined P/O Orendorff's crew. They flew initially on Whitley T4326 on December 31, then proceeded through the course until February 20, 1944, by which time Clark had flown 38 times day and night on the Whitley, and Anson for 72:45 hours. One Whitley sortie was a Nickel raid to Paris

– 5:40 hours on the night of February 8.

The crew now progressed to 1659 HCU at Topcliffe. For his first flight in the Halifax (April 15), Orendorff had an instructor pilot, then (with 40 minutes of 4-engine time – the training system was not for pansies, most of whom had been weeded out by this time) he soloed the same day with his crew. Many of the crew's earlier flights were for pilot proficiency, then bombing and gunnery exercises were added. The course, which wrapped up on April 30, had entailed 22 flights for 28:10 hours (day) and 24:00 (night). The crew now joined 433 Squadron at Skipton-on-Swale, where it flew initially on the Halifax III on May 7. There were three more training flights before their first operation – bombing railway yards at Ghent on May 10. Clark's tour included several gardening trips and 2 or 3 encounters with night fighters, but with no fire exchanged.

F/O Colin Clark following his tour at 433 Squadron. Note his Operations Wing pinned on the breast pocket (the "Ops Wing" was awarded at the successful end of a tour).

Home after the war, many veterans kept their aviation ties alive. Colin Clark revelled in the world of art, sports cars and vintage planes. Here is his Tiger Moth at Maple Airport near Toronto (CF-CLB had been RCAF 3939 of 9 EFTS, St. Catharines). Colin often had a commission to build a model for a movie production or advertising project. Here he is *circa* 1984 in his studio/garage in Toronto's Yorkville Village, showing off a GeeBee model that he was tailoring for a client.

Colin (2ⁿᵈ from left) with his helpers while assembling the full-scale "Visa" Silver Dart. The replica could taxi using a small electric motor. It survives today with the Canadian Bushplane Heritage Centre in Sault Ste. Marie.

He completed his tour with his 32ⁿᵈ op – bombing Castrop Rauxel on November 21. His RCAF time totalled 424:55 hours, including 159:50 on ops (137:40 being at night). Dénouement: postwar, Colin Clark (who passed away in January 1985) was a photographer, retoucher and illustrator in Toronto. He obtained a private pilot's licence and through the years owned several exotic sports cars, a Tiger Moth and a Harvard. In 1983-84 he produced several paintings for *Sixty Years: The Royal Canadian Air Force 1924-1984*. His most interesting venture, however, was constructing a full-size Silver Dart replica. In 2010 long-time aviation history aficionado Peter Allen recalled this astounding project:

In the late 1970s, Colin built a Silver Dart replica to be used in a VISA card commercial. It even had a small engine, so it could taxi and appear in motion. After the filming, which was part of a series about famous moments in Canadian history, Colin convinced Visa to donate the replica to the Canadian Aviation Historical Society. CAHS stalwart, Charlie Catalano, then pulled out all the stops and had it hung in the hobby building at the CNE, where it remained for several years. In 1983 Charlie was advised by the CNE to remove the airplane. Desperate to keep it from the wreckers, I called Ray Lank, President of the Great War Flying Museum in Brampton, to see if they would take it. They would not, but Ray arranged for them to store it while he hatched his scheme for the 75th anniversary of the first Silver Dart flight. Ray convinced a number of companies, including Air Canada and Alcan, to sponsor a 1984 cross-Canada tour of the replica.

Colin helped restore the Silver Dart to display condition and helped Ray and I learn how to assemble, disassemble and maintain it. It appeared from Halifax to Montreal, Toronto and Vancouver. I took it to Vancouver (shipped by truck) and assembled it at Expo, where it hung in the Air Canada pavilion at Expo 86. It also travelled by C-130 Hercules to the Shearwater airshow so, in a way, I was the only one to fly it, since the crew let me fly the Herc. After the 75th anniversary, Ray sold the Silver Dart three times – once to a Toronto entrepreneur, once to the Collingwood museum and, finally, to the bushplane museum in the Soo. In this way, he raised over $100,000 for the CAHS, ensuring its survival. In this way the Silver Dart truly fits in as the logo of the CAHS.

Oddball Station Commander

Normally commanding each BCATP air station was an experienced group captain, as was each training school. Next to the school OC was a wing commander in charge of flying, squadron leaders over each training squadron and flight lieutenants heading the training flights. There also were non-flying "middle management" officers in charge of other basic station functions. Many of these officers were pre-war RCAF, but there were some CAF and WWI veterans, old timers who came "out of the woodwork" to volunteer in time of great need. One who served was William I. Riddell. Born in 1899, he had trained as a pilot in the RFC (Canada), then served overseas. In 1921 he took some refresher training at Camp Borden, joined the RCAF in January 1925, then received his Permanent Commission with the rank of flying officer in October 1926.

In 1928 F/O Riddell was on an advanced instructor's course at the RAF Central Flying School at Wittering. He flew such types as the Avro 504, Gamecock, Grebe and Siskin, but ended with a slightly ambiguous assessment: "A sound pilot who has had previous experience in instructing. Knows the system ... but imparts his knowledge in an uninteresting manner." Later that year, however, he was assessed by W/C Croil, station commander at Camp Borden: "Flying Officer Riddell is a very good pilot and a capable instructor... He is keen and energetic. He is smart in appearance, conscientious and has shown considerable keenness in the administration of the flight which he has commanded for the past month." Croil, however, had a less complimentary notation for 1929: "Does not control his habits regarding alcoholic beverages."

Riddell was promoted to flight lieutenant in April 1931. In May he took command of the Siskin flight at Camp Borden, then led it across Canada on the spectacular Trans-Canada Air Pageant. When the Siskin flight moved to Trenton, Riddell continued as CO. By 1933 he was known as an "abstainer" and received an excellent annual review: "Flight Lieutenant Riddell is an exceptionally keen and able single seater fighter pilot. During the past summer he led a formation which gave aerobatic displays at Montreal and Toronto. These ... reflected great credit to the RCAF... exceptional in his department during the past year... careful and smart in his appearance both on and off parade." (In the July 1935 issue of *Canadian Aviation* magazine, pilot/journalist Sandy MacDonald described Riddell as possessing "all the attributes of a forceful personality ... an inexorable taskmaster." These were apt traits for a fighter pilot keeping an aerobatic team on its toes, but not so useful in running day-to-day air force operations.)

Following his high profile Siskin years, F/L Riddell's reputation again slipped. A note while he was at Trenton in 1937 states (without elaboration): "It has been necessary to parade him to the Commanding Officer on two occasions during the past 4 months on matters connected with his work and conduct." Even so, Riddell was promoted to squadron leader in April 1938. Promoted to wing commander in May 1940, he took command of Rockcliffe. G/C Francis Vernon Heakes assessed him on December 17, 1940: "Keen, energetic CO who takes interest in every phase of Station activities ... Personal conduct entirely satisfactory." On June 15, however, Heakes felt obliged to add how Riddell could also be "over-aggressive and somewhat non-co-operative with Unit Commanders."

In May 1941 W/C Riddell was posted to command 7 (Bombing and Gunnery) School at Paulson, Manitoba. The station opened in June and soon had a flightline crowded with Ansons, Battles, Bolingbrokes and Lysanders. Hundreds of bomb aimers and air gunners soon were being graduated. Smooth and steady management was vital and a station commander set the tone for success. By this stage, however, RCAF HQ was worried about the sometimes oddball W/C Riddell. On October 9, 1941 Air Commodore A.B. Shearer, wrote without elaboration: "This officer has shown lack of tact and good judgement during the short time he has been at No.7 BGS." RCAF HQ would not tolerate any such behaviour in wartime, so in December it relieved Riddell, passing command to W/C W.E. Dipple (RAF). Riddell went on sick leave with instructions to take retirement. He objected, claiming that the medical board reviewing his case had operated irregularly. Meanwhile, two junior officers at 7 (B&G) School took the rash measure of sending a telegram to Air Marshal Breadner, pleading that Riddell be retained, referring to him as the "finest commanding officer in the air force" (their careers likely suffered for this indiscretion). W/C Riddell soon faded from air force life. He died in Ottawa on December 18, 1969.

Technical Training

While thousands of aircrew were being turned out by the BCATP, far more were graduating from technical courses. These were the airframe and engine specialists, then everyone from radio, instrument and electrical technicians to drivers and fire fighters. In 1939-40 these mainly trained at Camp Borden, Trenton and such civilian centres as the Galt Aircraft School and Central Technical School in Toronto. In this February 1943 scene, student tradesmen practice sheet metal at No.1 Technical Training School in St. Thomas, the RCAF's most important such centre once the war took hold. In the background are two Battle training aids. (DND PL14880)

The RCAF's obsolete Northrop Deltas were front line service aircraft in 1939, but soon were retired for technical training. As such they received new serial numbers, Delta 667 becoming A143, 669 – A145. Historian John A. Griffin explains this re-numbering using "A", "B" and "C" prefixes: "'A' [indicates] an airframe where engine running could be practiced... 'B' ... was used where the aircraft was suitable for stripping ... 'C' was used to indicate sectioned aircraft to be used solely as visual aids." (Al Martin)

Avro 626 Tutor 267/A95 is man-handled at St. Thomas in a scene from July 1940, perhaps so the students can do a practice run-up. Such aircraft were obsolete for flight; others had been damaged in accidents, but they remained useful in trades training. (DND PL1044)

Students at the Galt Aircraft School were posed by a real master to create this scene of intense activity in the engine shop. Then, a class of student techs at Toronto's Central Technical School. Every graduate was assured a job on graduation, whether in the RCAF or in the country's burgeoning aircraft industry.

St. Thomas had many airframes and engines on which tradesmen learned their skills. Included were the only Halifax bombers in Canada. Many courses had their group photos taken with one of these. This group of mainly pilots is unknown, but includes a number of older looking officers, who likely were instructors. Then, a more detailed view of one of the Canadian-based Halifaxes. (via Janet Stubbs, Alf Barton Col.)

BCATP: The Accident Scene

From Day 1, the BCATP was ready for the down side of training – accidents. There was no avoiding them and they would happen non-stop until thousands of students and instructors had been killed and injured. Every participant in the war in the air since 1914 accepted such a cost. Canada had its own first hand experience: in 1917-18 the RFC (Canada) training plan, while turning out more than 3200 pilots and observers, suffered some 125 fatalities, many grave injuries in crashes, and lost hundreds of JN-4s.

The causes of BCATP accidents were many, but inexperience headed the list. Some students crashed on their solo flights, sometimes fatally. Sprog pilots were often spooked by the slightest surprise, e.g. a cross wind on landing, which could lead to a prang. There were mid-air collisions, aircraft took fire, engines failed, and there were countless cases of them panicking, getting lost, running out of fuel or getting entangled in weather. Occasionally, a student simply froze up at his controls, sometimes with fatal results.

On December 8, 1940 AC2 John Henry McNally (age 20, wireless air gunner student from Minaki, Ontario), F/O Leon A. Hood (pilot, age 33 from Adrian, Michigan) and AC2 Ernest W. Bourne (age 25, wireless air gunner student from Oshawa, Ontario) died when Fairey Battle 1650 of 4 (B&G) School at RCAF Station Fingal crashed into Lake Erie. A story in the press told how McNally and his fiancée, Muriel McGrath, had agreed not to wed until after the war, as John had not wished to leave behind a widow. They had met at a YMCA dance while John was at 1 Manning Depot in Toronto.

On December 16, 1940 the newspapers still were reporting on the Lake Erie search for Battle 1650, but there was no sign of it. At the same time a search was underway over Muskoka where Nomad trainers 3512 and 3521 from 1 SFTS Camp Borden had been missing since the 13th. "Fifty Planes Seek Fliers, Cover 10,000 Square Miles" shouted a headline. Missing were F/L Peter Campbell (RAF) and FSgt L. Francis (RAF) and their student pilots LACs Theodore S. Bates (age 27 from Guelph, Ontario) and William J.P. Gosling (age 22 from Edmonton).

BCATP accidents injured and killed hundreds of instructors and students. Such losses were calculated – there was a built-in allowance ensuring that the air force overseas would not be short of men. This Anson crash wrecked an airplane, but the four men aboard reportedly survived. Anson II 6821 of 5 SFTS, Brantford, Ontario went down on March 2, 1942. This is possibly the crash reported next day in the Toronto *Star*. The story tells of men working on a radio tower near Hornby, about 40 miles northeast of Brantford. From their high perch they watched an Anson, both engines stopped, crash land. (Robert Finlayson Col.)

Reports told of local Indians reporting a plane coming down, of tracks found in the snow made by RAF-type flying boots and of an oil slick in a lake, but all this was disproved and no sign ever was found of the lost crews. Meanwhile, on December 14 LAC James D. Bilkey (age 24 of Montreal) had died in the crash of Yale 3351 at Dunnville.

Such stories of BCATP disasters filled the newspaper pages until the last day of the war. Another such came on September 23, 1942, the day that P/O James I. McIntyre (age 24 from Guelph, Ontario) was on an exercise from 6 SFTS at

Buried in Lake-of-the-Woods Cemetery in Kenora, Ontario is AC2 John H. McNally, killed with his crewmates on December 8, 1940. John's epitaph reads "Born 28th Jan. 1920. He counted not his life dead unto himself." (Larry Milberry)

Dunnville with fellow instructor, WO2 Norman E. Kirk (age 22 from Hamilton, Ontario). Although they were experienced, soon after takeoff in Harvard 3180, they pitched up very steeply and crashed fatally straight into the Grand River. Adding to the dreadful suffering of the McIntyre family, on April 21, 1944 they lost a second son – F/O Archibald B. McIntyre, age 27. While low-flying that day from 14 SFTS at Aylmer with student J.P. Boning of the Fleet Air Arm, he crashed fatally in Harvard 3025.

One of the RCAF's most disastrous training accidents involved B-24 Liberators KH107 and KG880 at 5 OTU, Abbotsford on the night of July 4, 1945. Nine RCAF airmen were killed or badly injured. A press release describes the ugly scene:

Eleven men were aboard one of the Liberators which ... was taking off on the wrong runway when it collided with the other aircraft carrying a crew of four, which was taxiing in... Gasoline exploded, enveloping the two planes in roaring flames. Practice bombs went off and machine gun ammunition flew in all directions.

There is a "list too long" of 5 OTU Liberator losses. Some of these aircraft are missing to this day. Several crashed in the mountains in bad weather, others went down at sea. Losing so many 4-engine bombers in training seems unbelievable, but such was price to be paid (5 OTU Liberator losses were aircraft EW127, EW130, EW134, EW210, KG880, KH107, KH108, KH110, KH173, KH175 and KK241).

All across Canada at the 105 BCATP air stations there were almost daily accidents. A crash that destroyed an airplane was designated "Category A". If the damage could be repaired at the factory or an RCAF repair depot, it was listed as "Category B". If repairs could be made at home base, it was a "Category C" accident. Here is Finch 4702 following a "Cat B" mishap at 12 EFTS, Goderich on May 14, 1941. A student responsible for an accident could be "washed out" of pilot training. (Bruce Best Col.)

Tiger Moth 4087 with front-end damage after a "Cat C" prang in a mucky field near 31 EFTS, De Winton, Alberta. Then, 4164 (14 EFTS, Portage la Prairie) turned turtle on March 25, 1942 and deemed "Cat A". (Bruce Best, Robert Finlayson Cols.)

The sight of a training plane up on its nose was a daily occurrence. Here is the case of 2 WS Fort 3604 at Shepard, Alberta. (S. Mouncey Col.)

A horrible ending to what began on September 21, 1941 at 16 EFTS, Edmonton as a normal Tiger Moth exercise. When things went bad, the instructor baled out. Sadly, his student froze in fear and went down with the plane. (W.P. "Bill" Dunphy Col.)

With some extra momentum a plane could pass the point of no return after a bad landing, ending on its back. Yellow-and-black drogue-towing Lysander 2328 from 6 (B&G) School, Mountain View went over hard on September 18, 1944. (Art Walker)

Harvards 3335 and 2969 of 6 SFTS Dunnville collided disastrously on June 30, 1942. They fell together, neither pilot surviving. (Ken Smith)

Each air station had a salvage team that got more efficient as the war progressed. Here is Cornell 10525 nicely packed for haulage out of the boonies. Fresh from the factory at Fort Erie, it had been en route to some western school on December 23, 1942, when it ran into trouble around Hearst in Northern Ontario. The accident occurred before the plane had been taken on strength – that wasn't done until January 14. The engineering people deemed 10525 not worth repairing. It was cannibalized and SOS on February 20. (Robert Finlayson Col.)

Cornell FH818 (23 EFTS, Davidson, Saskatchewan) in what turned out to be a "Cat C" incident on February 15, 1943. (CANAV Col.)

The pilot might have mused about the gremlin on the cowling of Harvard 2632 having something to do with this incident at Aylmer. (Robert Finlayson Col.)

A mid-air collision was an ever-present danger in any busy BCATP training circuit. The result often was deadly, but in this case of one Anson landing atop another at 7 SFTS, Fort Macleod, Alberta the crews survived. In his book *Flights into the Night*, Tony Leiscester describes his own such terrifying experience in December 1941, while landing solo in an Anson at 33 SFTS, Carberry, Manitoba. (Robert Halford Col.)

Salvaging an Anson after some winter misfortune. (Robert Finlayson Col.)

Views of 16 SFTS Anson 7184 – a total loss after a forced landing in a field of stumps near Hagersville in April 1943. (J.T. McCreight Col.)

Norseman 679 on its back at 1 Wireless School, Mount Hope; then being righted. 679 was resurrected, flew to war's end, then was CF-SAH with the Saskatchewan Government Air Service 1946 - 55. Later, with Carter Air Service of Hay River, NWT it was badly damaged in 1962. In 2010 its bones were in storage at the Reynolds-Alberta Museum. (Harry Pattinson Col.)

BCATP: Airmen at Peace

Hundreds of airmen, killed one way or the other in BCATP days, lie at rest in cemeteries across Canada. In nearly all cases, when a Canadian or American airman or airwoman died, the remains were shipped to the home town for a funeral in a local burial ground. If an airman was from overseas, however, regulations decreed that he be interred locally.

Most RCAF WWII graves are marked by a simple gray granite stone provided by the Department of National Defence. Sometimes, however, a family preferred its own headstone, and this was allowed. Over the decades, all such stones have weathered elements fairly well. This gallery honours some of those who gave their lives for freedom, even though they missed their chance to get directly into the fray.

Airmen's official grave markers bear the same basic information – name, rank and serial number. The symbol of the RCAF – an albatross with the motto "Per Ardua ad Astra" – dominates each DND stone. Sometimes there is a brief epitaph inscribed at the base.

LAC Robert Haig Guthrie lies in St. John's Norway Cemetery, Toronto. On the night of November 19, 1941 he was on an exercise in Harvard 3110 when fog enshrouded 13 SFTS, St. Hubert. While floundering around looking for the 'drome, Guthrie crashed fatally into a barn.

On July 2, 1942 Sgt Harry K. Cox (age 19 from Union Point, Manitoba) was airborne on a night exercise from 19 EFTS, Virden. Somehow his flight plans fell apart – Cox crashed fatally in Tiger Moth 3878. Here is the Union Point United Church pioneer cemetery along Hwy 75 south of Winnipeg – not quite such a peaceful venue any more. Then, a detail of the Cox stone. (All, Larry Milberry)

On June 24, 1942 Sgt Francis C. Frigerio was flying solo in Tiger Moth 7564 near 32 EFTS at Bowden, Alberta, when he crashed. A graduate of Danforth Technical School in east Toronto, Frigerio had worked as a chemist before enlisting. He trained at 1 MD, 5 ITS, 1 EFTS and 5 SFTS, where he earned his wings in March 1942. He then was posted to instruct at 32 EFTS but, reported the press at the time of his death, had his sights set on getting overseas. Frigerio lies in Our Lady of Victory Cemetery in Toronto.

SGT.-PILOT FRIGERIO GETS LAST TRIBUTES

Full Military Honors Will Be Given to Victim of Crash

Military honors will be paid at the funeral Tuesday morning of Sergeant Pilot Francis C. Frigerio, 21, son of Mr. and Mrs. Francis Frigerio, Beachview Cres., who died in a plane crash last Wednesday near Innisfail, Alta. Officials of the R.C.A.F., Manning Depot, where he received part of his training, will attend. It will be held from his par-

Francis Frigerio

Another of the RCAF's many fatal Harvard crashes. (Jack McNulty Col.)

A family headstone: on June 14, 1943 LAC Herbert J. Lee was making a single-engine approach at 16 SFTS in Hagersville, when he crashed fatally in Anson 6191. He lies here with his parents in St. John's Norway Cemetery in Toronto.

Many airmen lie in St. George's Cemetery on the western edge of Trenton, Ontario. One is RAF air gunnery student, LAC Denis W.P.G. Showell. On June 13, 1942 he and LAC R.D. Young (age 24 from Ogdensburg, NY) were aboard Nomad 3494 on a cine gun exercise from 6 (B&G) School, Mountain View, a few miles south of Trenton. Somehow the pilot, P/O Jack A. McGregor (age 20 from Regina) lost control and crashed into the Bay of Quinte, killing everyone aboard.

Canadian-built Mosquito KB119 lies badly broken after an emergency landing on March 9, 1944. (CANAV Col.)

The de Havilland family of Toronto placed this stone in St. John's Norway Cemetery to honour their beloved Victor, killed while serving at 9 AOS. "Till We Meet Again" was their simple parting comment. He died when his Anson (6554) crashed in the St. Lawrence River east of Cornwall, Ontario on September 15, 1942. Also lost were wireless operator Sgt T.P. Fraser (RAAF), and student navigator LAC W.H. Smale (RAF). The press reported that a Sgt S.D.R. Cook was pulled alive from the river. This terrible event boiled down to one stupid decision. Spotting a ship in the river, Sgt de Havilland decided on a bit of razzel-dazzel. He dove at the ship, but hit a mast and plunged into the river.

"We have love him in life. Let us not forget him in death." The grave in Kingston, Nova Scotia of F/O J.D. Walsh, RNZAF, killed on January 18, 1944 when 36 OTU Oxford EB506 crashed taking of from Greenwood. Also lost were F/L Lawrence J. O'Connell, DFC (age 25 from Halifax), F/L Harold W. Church (age 26 from Prince Alberta, Saskatchewan) and RNZAF F/O R.J. Walls. O'Connell had a DFC for his good efforts in 1942 flying Hudsons on 407 Squadron.

On September 16, 1944 P/O de Waerbeek lost his life during a training flight in Mosquito KB289 from 8 OTU, Greenwood. Along with his RAF navigator, Sgt Claude V. Groensteen, de Waerbeek lies in the cemetery in Kingston, Nova Scotia.

Not all lost BCATP airmen and airwomen were victims of flying accidents. A study of *They Shall Grow Not Old: A Book of Remembrance* reveals a myriad of causes. Many died in automobile accidents, others drowned, died in fires, one man fell from a window, and many others died of natural causes. One airman's death is listed as "died of a gunshot wound while absent without leave" – a possible suicide. LAC Marcel R. Bridgeman, buried in Toronto's St. John's Norway Cemetery, lost his life in a bus accident in Calgary. For his epitaph the family selected a verse from Laurence Binyon's 1914 poem 'For the Fallen': "They shall grow not old, as we that are left grow old. Age shall not weary them, nor the years condemn. At the going down of the sun and in the morning we will remember them."

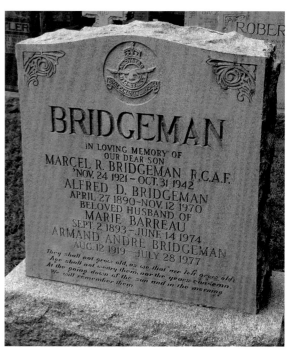

BCATP Honours and Awards: George Cross and George Medal

Many in the BCATP were recognized for their service as flying instructors, administrators, aircraft maintenance staff, armourers, etc. Some also were honoured for heroic deeds. Sometimes, such awards were sniggered at by those who had been overseas under fire, but this was shabby treatment for brave men toiling diligently on the home front – on the long, painful road to victory.

The indispensible role played by those on the training scene is covered in such valuable books as Dr. John Blatherwick's *Royal Canadian Air Force: Honours, Decorations, Medals 1920-1968*. The most prestigious of their honours was the George Cross, awarded twice to BCATP personnel (five Canadian airmen received the "GC" in 1939-45). A posthumous George Cross was awarded on June 11, 1942 to an 18-year old Canadian of Swedish blood, LAC Karl Mander Gravell. Having enlisted in Vancouver in 1941, he established a dubious reputation, several times being on charge for foolishness. Once he even made off from the barracks where he was "CQ'd" – confined to quarters. Another time he was caught asleep while on guard duty.

None of this mattered much on November 10, 1941, when Gravell was aloft on an exercise from 2 Wireless School in Menasco Moth 4833. Somehow, the Moth crashed. Gravell was severely injured, his clothes were ablaze, yet he struggled to save his pilot, F/O James Robinson (age 44 of Jasper, Alberta). Mrs. Frances Walsh, a local teacher, rushed to pull Gravell from the inferno. Neither airman survived. The citation to this George Cross explains about Gravell: "Had he not considered his pilot before his own safety and had he immediately proceeded to extinguish the flames on his own clothing, he probably would not have lost his life." Mrs. Walsh, herself burned in the struggle, was awarded the George Medal.

The second BCATP George Cross, also awarded posthumously, went to student navigator LAC Kenneth G. Spooner, age 20 of Smiths Falls, Ontario. Aloft on a student navigation exercise from 4 AOS at London, Ontario, Sgt Dana A. Nelson suffered some sort of

LAC Gravell of Vancouver, George Cross recipient. (RCAF)

medical episode while piloting Anson 7064. The plane went out of control, but LAC Spooner, who so far had been scoring exceedingly well in his course, took charge. This enabled LAC R.H. Bailey and LAC J.A. Curtis to bale out. Spooner kept control for about an hour, but the Anson eventually crashed, killing him, Sgt Nelson, and Sgt William J. Brown. The citation to Spooner's George Cross finishes: "This airman, with complete disregard for his personal safety and in conformity with the highest

LAC K.C. Spooner of Smiths Falls, Ontario. (RCAF)

tradition of the Service, sacrificed his life in order to save the lives of his comrades."

FSgt Floyd B. Lummis of Frankfurt, Ontario received a George Medal in June 1942 for having acted swiftly when a pail of gasoline ignited in a hangar at Trenton on December 22, 1939. Lummis carried the flaming pail outside, suffering grave burns in the process. The citation to this GM notes how Lummis "thereby saved 12 aircraft which, at this date, were invaluable to Canada's air training plan."

British Empire Medal

Among those in the RCAF receiving the British Empire Medal during the Second World War was FSgt James A. Nicholson. Born in Moose Jaw in 1917, he was raised in Calgary and Vancouver. He served in the pre-war Canadian Army, then enlisted in the RCAF in June 1938. He qualified initially as a fitter (airframe technician) at the Technical Training School at Camp Borden. He was promoted to AC1 in April 1939 and to LAC in October. His RCAF career evolved impressively. Nicholson was posted to CFS at Trenton in January 1940, promoted to corporal the following month, then to sergeant in October.

Through the war Nicholson had a string of challenging postings, on each of which he shone. In December 1941 he commenced duties at 3 Repair Depot in Vancouver, then was successively at 2 FIS, Vulcan, Alberta; 17 SFTS, Souris, Manitoba; the Composite Training School, Toronto; and 6 Repair Depot, Trenton, where he finished the war. While at 2 FIS, in July 1944 Sgt Nicholson was put up for the BEM, S/L W.E. Jamison noting in his recommendation:

This non-commissioned officer is in charge of the Repair Squadron at this unit and it is very largely owing to his keenness and qualities of leadership that this section has operated so efficiently and smoothly during the past fourteen months. He has at all times been a source of inspiration and an excellent example to junior airmen, always assisting them in every possible manner to become more efficient and capable in their trade.

The school OC, G/C J.B. Harvey, agreed: "He stands out unmistakably both as an NCO and in personal qualities." Even with the backing of A/V/M G.R. Howsam, AOC 4 Training Command, however, the recommendation was not approved in time for Ottawa's 1945 New Year's honours list. Nicholson finally was awarded the BEM on January 1, 1946.

At war's end FSgt Nicholson reverted to corporal's rank. He continued in his technical trade with such postings as 8 Field Technical Training Unit at RCAF Station MacDonald, a key training base equipped with T-33s. In 1957 he was commissioned from the ranks. In a 1961 personnel assessment he was described by a superior as "a quiet, conscientious officer who applied himself diligently to all tasks". F/L Nicholson, BEM, died of natural causes in 1962.

The Air Force Cross

Many who served in the BCATP received the Air Force Cross for excellent service, one of these being flying instructor F/L Carlyle Clare Agar. Born in Ontario in 1901, Agar learned to fly in the late 1920s in Edmonton. He farmed through the 1930s, then joined the RCAF as "an old man" in January 1941. Through the war he instructed at various BCATP schools,

and was awarded the AFC in November 1944. AFC citations usually were brief, as was Agar's: "For the past four years this officer has made an excellent record in elementary flying training. He has displayed at all times flying skill and devotion to duty which have set a very high example for other instructors to follow." In 1947 Agar introduced the commercial helicopter to British Columbia. His company, Okanagan Helicopters, rose to be global in scale (in 2010 its legacy continued under the Canadian Helicopters banner).

The AFC often was awarded to BCATP personnel primarily for long service and hours flown. F/L Alfred W. Barton of Cobourg, Ontario, received the AFC in June 1945 for persistently excellent service at 14 SFTS at Aylmer. His personal contribution to the war effort is summed up by the citation: "This officer's steady and progressive spirit has done a great deal to further the efforts of the training organization. ... He has at all times been an example to his fellow officers and instructors ..." An aviation fan since his boyhood, Barton had built models, followed local barnstormers from field to field on his bicycle and avidly photographed

airplanes (some of Alf's photos appear in these pages). Postwar, his enthusiasm continued, and he was an early supporter of the Canadian Aviation Historical Society.

In the case of AFC recipient F/O Gordon J. Anderson of Edmonton, he instructed at the EFTS level for five years, during which he filled several log books with 3200 flying hours, or well over 5000 instructional flights. Ian Sommerville of Trail, BC, also received an AFC. Having earned his commercial pilot's licence in 1930, he was a bush pilot and air engineer until enlisting early in 1940. After completing FIS at Trenton, he instructed at several schools, finishing as CFI at 15 EFTS in Regina. He received the AFC in April 1943. His "keen interest" and "enthusiasm and devotion to duty" were cited. He later instructed in the UK, then was an early graduate from the Empire Test Pilots School. His ETPS assessor singled out Somerville for "keenness and enthusiasm", adding how "his flying ability is beyond reproach." Somerville next served on the RAF Foreign Aircraft Flight, where he ferried and tested such diverse types as the Fw.200, He.219, Ju.388 and Me.110.

Many BCATP flying instructors were awarded decorations for their service on the home front, while many former BCATP instructors received gallantry awards for later overseas service. Shown are "D" Flight instructors at 14 SFTS, Aylmer (one name is unknown). These men worked tirelessly instructing on the Harvard, turning out top-grade pilots. Shown are Alf Barton, Don Lamont, Ron Knewstub, Fred Green, Fred Ward, Ross Perrin and Elmer McLeod. In June 1945 Barton, who logged more than 2000 instructional hours, was awarded the Air Force Cross. His AFC citation notes, "This officer's steady and progressive spirit has done a great deal to further the efforts of the training organization." Another "D" Flight instructor, Leslie R. Naftel, also received the AFC. Elmer McLeod received the AFC, but for his good services later with 145 Squadron in Eastern Air Command. Don Lamont later got overseas. Posted to 428 Squadron on Lancasters, he ended with a DFC. His DFC citation notes: "As Flight Commander he has shown exceptional leadership and great initiative and has contributed to a major degree in the operational success of the unit." Lamont's success on operations certainly had much to do with his solid grounding as a flying instructor. (Alf Barton Col.)

Some AFC recipients who began as BCATP students, served overseas in combat, then came home tour expired to BCATP postings. F/O George D. Aiken of Edmonton was one such case. Having enlisted in December 1940, he did flying training at 5 EFTS Lethbridge and 10 SFTS Dauphin, where he earned his wings in August 1941. Overseas, he flew Spitfires on 416, then 403 squadrons. Shot down by an Me.109 on June 2, 1942, he parachuted into the channel, but soon was back on ops. Home in 1943, he was posted to 2 Wireless School in Calgary, where he was promoted to flight lieutenant and became OC of flying training. He flew the three types of wireless trainers in service – Harvard, Yale and Norseman, logging some 1300 hours by war's end. His final duty was to "ferry" the school's station wagon to Calgary for disposal, then he took his release on May 24, 1945. Postwar, George enjoyed a long career in administration with the provincial government. His AFC was presented in February 1949. In recommending him for this award, his station commander had noted:

This officer, since being returned from Overseas, has planned, organized and carried out his duties in an exceptionally efficient manner. His devotion to duty has been most commendable and the very efficient way in which his section now functions is the result of untiring efforts on his behalf and long, tedious continuous hours of concentrated work. He has displayed exceptional devotion to duty as operations officer of the flying squadron.

Commended for Valuable Services

Born in St. Thomas, Ontario in February 1910 Stanley Yendle Broadbent developed into an exceptional athlete. He played professional football, graduated from St. Thomas Vocational School in 1930 and enlisted in the RCAF that June. Trained as a rigger at Camp Borden, he was posted to Jericho Beach in Vancouver. In July 1931 he was promoted to AC1 and qualified as a coppersmith later that year. In August 1932 he was in Trenton with 2 Army Cooperation Squadron, then equipped with the Atlas. The following year he qualified in sheet metal and was

promoted to LAC in May 1934. Broadbent attended the Air Gunnery and Bombing Course at Camp Borden from October 1933 to March 1934, qualifying "Above the average" as an Air Gunner, his marks being: Photography (83%), Map Reading (80%), Airmanship (75&), Signals (90%), Gunnery (79%), Engines (64%), Bombing (70%), Airframes (79%), Air Pilotage (85%), Meteorology (89%), Semaphore Sending (98%), Semaphore Reading (100%), Telegraphy Sending (100%) and Telegraphy Reading (99%). While on course he flew as passenger in the Fairchild (22:55 hours), Avro Tutor (8:25) and Courier (2:50). In trapshooting he scored 53 percent on his last three sessions, 50% in bombing within 100 yards of target, and air gunnery 6.4%. S/L A.A. Leitch observed of Broadbent on this course: "This airman has worked hard during his course, with good results. He is neat in appearance and would make a good instructor." Being a tradesmen made it awkward for Broadbent to apply for the Airman Pilots Course. Nonetheless, he was accepted.

On December 14, 1938 W/C R.S. Grandy, CO of the Flying Training School at Trenton, described Broadbent as, "A keen ab initio pupil making satisfactory progress." By that time he had 29:15 hours of dual instruction time, and 15:10 hours solo. He had begun his flying training on the Fleet in October 1938, then progressed to the Moth, then designated as a "service" type aircraft. In this period one assessment for Broadbent noted: "This NCO is keen, reliable and capable of undertaking responsibility. Inclined to be too familiar with junior officers." By end of course he had scored: Air Pilotage/Navigation (147/200), Meteorology (36/40), Airmanship (119/170), Engines, Written (142/200), Engines, Practical (248/300), Rigging, Written (94/100), Rigging, Practical (191/200), Administration (70/100), Organization (36/50), Law (81/100), History (16/25), Theory of Flight (27/50), Armament, Written (53/65), Armament, Practical (178/200), Signals, Written, (100/100), Signals, Practical (72/100). Flying tests were completed on the Fairchild, Fleet and Wapiti. Broadbent was promoted to sergeant in April 1939, then qualified as a Sergeant Pilot in June 1939. He attended the Flying Instructor School at Camp Borden in September –

October 1939, was commissioned on November 15, 1939 and posted to Trenton.

Broadbent joined 1 SFTS at Camp Borden in April 1940, then instructed on Harvards at 2 SFTS in Ottawa when it began operations in July. He was promoted to flight lieutenant in March 1941, then was posted to 16 SFTS at Hagersville that August. He was promoted to squadron leader in July 1942 and posted in December to 6 SFTS at Dunnville in December. In January 1943 Broadbent was Commended for Valuable Services, the accompanying citation noting:

This officer worked his way up from an aero-engine mechanic in the ranks of the permanent RCAF. As a Sergeant Pilot he was instructing at Camp Borden at the commencement of the war. For the past fourteen months he has commanded a Training Squadron at No.16 SFTS where he has shown a keen devotion to duty and set an excellent example both as an officer and flying instructor to those under him. He has carried out 1,500 hours flying, mostly instructing, without a single accident. His record as an instructor, devotion to the service, and keen interest in the airmen's welfare and training has been of inestimable value to the war effort.

This award had its history as a recommendation for the Air Force Cross, but Air Marshal L.S. Breadner saw fit to downgrade this to a Commendation. Various postings ensued, including Trenton, beginning in February 1943, then AFHQ in May. From June to September S/L Broadbent was on an advanced instructor's course at the Empire Central Flying School at Hullavington, England. Home in Canada, he had postings to RCAF HQ, 14 SFTS in Aylmer, Ontario, then took the Liberator course with 5 OTU at Boundary Bay. In December 1943 Broadbent, then at 16 SFTS Hagersville, again was put up for the AFC, the text reading in part:

Squadron Leader Broadbent has by conscientious effort gradually risen from an aero engine mechanic to Chief Instructor. Because of his outstanding ability, his vast experience and good judgement, he was selected to assist in supervising the opening of new flying stations. Except for a few weeks while on temporary duty, this officer has been on

A typical service flying school graduating class. These 19 students finished at 10 SFTS, Dauphin, Manitoba in late June 1942. (W.H.D. Meaden Col.)

the strength of this station since it opened. For approximately fourteen months Squadron Leader Broadbent commanded a training squadron ... where the excellent results obtained by the students ... indicated not only the high regard in which he is held by all his pupils, but also indicate that he has earned the respect of the instructors under him. He has set an excellent example both as an officer and as a flying instructor. All told, Squadron Leader Broadbent has carried out some 1,600 hours of flying, which record has not been marred by any flying mishap.

While instructing at 14 SFTS, Broadbent was sited for a heroic event, when the controls of Harvard 2672 failed. For this good show, in August 1944 Broadbent was put up by W/C G.L. Ingram for the George Cross. Again, the recommendation was down-graded, Broadbent instead being Commended for Valuable Services, the citation noting: "By the use of elevator trim, the nose was brought up, but control was difficult to maintain. He ordered the crewman to abandon aircraft ..." Broadbent then kept enough control to effect a forced landing.

The citation concluded: "Not only was loss of life averted and a valuable aircraft saved but the preservation of the aircraft intact disclosed evidence of the cause of the accident." May to October 1945 S/L Broadbent served in Eastern Air Command, including on 11 (BR) Squadron. In October 1946 he reverted to flight lieutenant rank and joined the Flying Instructor School at Trenton. In June 1948, while serving at CFS, he again was promoted to squadron leader. Tragically, however, on June 1 Broadbent died when his Vampire crashed into Lake Ontario.

Order of the British Empire and British Empire Medal

The Order of the British Empire and British Empire Medal were other awards available to airmen. Receiving the Order of the British Empire was F/L Wishart Campbell of Barrie, Ontario, whose field was entertainment, while posted with No.3 Training Command HQ in Montreal. Pre-war, Campbell had worked in motion pictures. The citation for his gong notes: "This officer, an

outstanding concert singer, has given unstintingly of his talent in the entertainment and welfare field in the Royal Canadian Air Force ... He has repeatedly given performances under the most trying conditions ..." Another case was G/C Ernest C. Tennant, station commander at Mountain View, a key BCATP base. Tennant was recognized, in part, for being "a tower of strength with all with whom he has served during the war". G/C David A. Harding, station commander 16 SFTS Hagersville also received the Order of the British Empire. An RFC pilot and original member of the RCAF, he was lauded in the medal's citation: "The splendid state of morale and efficiency of the station which he commands reflects the leadership and ability displayed by this officer."

S/L Arthur M. Ward received the Order of the British Empire for stalwart duties as engineering officer at 23 EFTS Yorkton, Saskatchewan. His maintenance wing was credited as being "responsible to a marked degree for the success of the training program". Also receiving this prestigious award was F/L Frederick J.S. Garratt, the Works and

Building Engineer at 39 SFTS, an RAF school at Swift Current, Saskatchewan: "He has displayed outstanding ingenuity and efficiency in the maintenance of the buildings and aerodrome, often under very adverse conditions ..." Stationed at 6 SFTS Dunnville, WO1 Leonard H. Perry received the Order of the British Empire for his efforts in running the station Motor Transport Section.

Receiving the BEM was Cpl Lewis G. Adair, who toiled in aircraft maintenance at the Air Armament School at Mountain View, Ontario. He was described in the citation (awarded in June 1946) as performing duties "involving work of a highly trying nature in maintenance of aircraft". Sgt Julius Cappel of 13 SFTS St. Hubert was honoured regarding his instructional skills and for "the maintenance of an efficient technical store section". FSgt Harold C. Daw received a BEM for his efforts at maintaining the 3 SFTS Calgary station electrical system without a breakdown in four years. This citation to his award notes: "Night flying has never been held up on account of a failure in aerodrome lighting." Another BEM recipient was LAC Lloyd A. Scrimshaw of 2 SFTS Ottawa, whose specialty was aircraft control: "By his constant vigilance, he has prevented at least six crashes ..." A BEM was awarded to FSgt Thomas Stewart of 13 EFTS St. Eugene on account of his being "one of the outstanding disciplinarians of the RCAF". The BEM also was awarded for acts of bravery. Student air gunner LAC John E. Gelineau received a BEM for rescuing a fellow student when their Bolingbroke crashed. Badly injured himself, Gelineau also persevered fruitlessly in rescuing the trapped pilot. The citation to his award noted: "Leading Aircraftman Gelineau showed courage and coolness of the highest order."

AFROs and DROs

Air Force Routine Orders and Daily Routine Orders were published by RCAF HQ and by individual units, and often were in reference to BCATP matters. Those of December 4, 1942 record how P/O Robert Joseph Garvin of RCAF Station Hagersville had flown "in a foolhardy and dangerous manner". He was severely reprimanded and fined $200 but, happily, not sent home to his mother.

He later served on 427 Squadron, where he ended with a DFC. The citation to this award removed any fear that Garvin might be a danger to anyone but the enemy, noting how he "has set a very fine example of skill, keenness and devotion to duty".

In AFROs of December 30, 1942 Sgt Raymond Philip Willison of Moose Jaw, then at 12 SFTS, Brandon was on the carpet for low flying and damaging one of His Majesty's aircraft. Suddenly, he again was LAC Willison and hurting still further from a $35 fine. On November 9, 1944, F/O Willison, by then age 22, died in the crash of an 82 OTU Wellington at RAF Rednal.

Other Dumb Stunts

"Absenting himself without leave" was a common infraction in the RCAF. But, according to AFROs, AC2 Francis L. O'Connor complicated his life by being apprehended wearing sergeant stripes and an air gunner's badge. He was found guilty of these offences on July 21, 1943, sentenced to 45 days detention and obliged to repay $7.71 to the Crown. That, someone in accounting had calculated, was the cost of apprehending O'Connor and returning him to his unit in Toronto. Examples from DRO HQ200-5-14 of June 2, 1944 describe other cases of RCAF home front shenanigans:

A flying instructor took over control from a student and proceeded to fly at a height of 50 to 100 feet above ground level. The aircraft struck power lines and was damaged. The pilot was sentenced to be dismissed from His Majesty's service.

Four flying instructors ... flew in unauthorized formation and carried out ... low flying over the surface of a lake. The officers were sentenced to be dismissed from His Majesty's service, and the airman to be reduced to the ranks and to 60 days detention.

A flight sergeant staff pilot at a bombing and gunnery school attempted to take up position along side a drogue aircraft ... This jockeying ... resulted in a

Air Marshall W.A. Bishop, VC, congratulates Edgar Leroy Clary on receiving his pilot wings at 2 SFTS, Ottawa. From Chippewa Falls, Wisconsin, Clary went on to flying Beaufighters with 47 Squadron. While on operations on November 13, 1943 near Leros, Greece, Clary and his navigator, FSgt W.E. Finbow, were lost. (DND PL9635)

collision, two aircraft crashing and four members of the crews being killed and one seriously injured. The pilot was found guilty of negligence ... sentenced to be reduced to the ranks and to 120 days detention.

A student pilot about to graduate and expecting to go overseas flew low about 20 feet above the roof of a school he had previously attended. He had received his commission before the offence was reported, was tried by general court-martial, found guilty of unauthorized low flying ... sentenced to be dismissed from His Majesty's service... Three students on their last solo flight before graduation shot up a town ... each found guilty ... sentenced to 35 days detention.

BCATP in Retrospect

In a paper prepared for the Canadian Aviation Historical Society 1979 annual convention, DND historian F.J. "Fred" Hatch, author of the seminal book, *The Aerodrome of Democracy*, summed up the BCATP:

Unidentified civilian flying instructors at 12 EFTS, Goderich in March 1941. (Bruce Best Col.)

If any criticism is to be made of the BCATP it is simply that it was too successful. By the end of 1943 it was running like a well-oiled machine and turning out pilots faster than they could be absorbed into operational squadrons. In February 1944, after consulting with British authorities, Air Minister Power decided that the scheme must be slowed down. When the brakes were applied, there were still thousands of recruits in various stages of training, and they were jolted and jarred like passengers in a railway express that suddenly grinds to a halt. To their dismay and discouragement, those anxiously waiting to begin flying training were told that they were no longer needed as pilots.

Courses just begun were cancelled and the trainees given the choice of transferring to another category of aircrew, or joining the army or navy, or taking their discharge. Student pilots who were well advanced in their training were allowed to continue, but understood that they had little chance of being sent overseas, and might be released at any time. Only the instructors, freed from their training duties and given priority in overseas postings, found reason for rejoice.

Training continued until March 31, 1945 when the BCATP came to an end. The total number of graduates was 131,553 ... As proclaimed by President Roosevelt, Canada, indeed, had become "the aerodrome of democracy".

Unidentified Australian student pilots at 2 SFTS, Ottawa. (Australian War Museum)

Harvard Mk.II 3181 in a classic setting. This fine looking trainer was lost in a crash on August 2, 1943 while at 14 SFTS. (Alf Barton Col.)

Another view showing the standard layout of a BCATP flying station. This is one of the RAF schools – 32 SFTS, Moose Jaw. Construction is still in progress in this October 1940 photo. Flying commenced in December using Harvards. The first draft of RAF students was relieved to arrive at 32 SFTS, since several ships in their convoy had been sunk by the German battleship *Admiral Scheer*. (DND PL1686)

During WWII, Kittyhawks and Hurricanes equipped numerous RCAF Home War Establishment squadrons from Torbay to Alaska. These dapper-looking RCAF Kittyhawks were photographed in 1942 at Annette Island, a US Army post near Ketchikan. (Murray Castator)

Home War Establishment

From the outbreak of hostilities in September 1939, Canada rushed to prepare for war on the home front and overseas. Its air force as yet was a tiny, almost rag-tag, operation under Chief of the Air Staff, Air Marshal Breadner. It had 4153 men and 270 aircraft on strength. Of 28 aircraft types, except for 19 Hurricanes, 10 Fairey Battles and 9 Stranraer, most were obsolete. Among relics still in front-line service were 13 Atlas army co-operation planes, 5 Siskin fighters and 22 Wapiti bombers. It was a discouraging picture, but RCAF HQ was determined to make a quick transition. Air operations in Canada were placed under a new umbrella organization – the Home War Establishment, comprising Eastern Air Command and Western Air Command.

RCAF war plans were implemented in the weeks preceding Canada's declaration of war. Recruiting offices already were being swamped by applicants. Some modern aircraft were on order, so re-equipment and the formation of new squadrons were in the works. Ottawa soon adopted a British proposal to turn Canada into a vast air training ground, and decided to send some token squadrons to the UK. These soon had embarked: 110 (Aux) Squadron with Lysanders in February 1940; 1 Squadron with Hurricanes, and 112 (Aux) Squadron with Lysanders in June. No.1 quickly distinguished itself in the Battle of Britain.

RCAF expansion in 1940 was unprecedented. This would continue late into

As Canada prepared for war in 1939 most of the RCAF's 270 aircraft were obsolete general purpose types. Fairchild 71s 640 and 643, seen at Calgary early in the war, were typical. Taken on strength in 1930, they remained in good condition, but were in need of replacement. They were sold in October 1941 to Wings Ltd. of Winnipeg. Such bush operators were happy to add equipment, obsolete or not, to use in urgent wartime business – mining, etc. (Chas. Hayes)

1943, when it was clear that the Allies were prevailing. Certain factors seemed to justify a strong Home War Establishment. There was a nation-wide fear of direct Japanese action on the West Coast, especially following Pearl Harbor and Japan's occupation of the Aleutians. There also was near-panic at the success of the German U-boat campaign in the western Atlantic Ocean – there even were U-boats in the St. Lawrence River. Some argued, however, that the HWE was becoming a bloated monster, when resources were so desperately needed overseas.

Facing the original threat of U-boats, even of a possible German aircraft carrier, the Home War Establishment put its meagre Eastern Air Command resources straight to work. Obsolete Atlases, Deltas, Goblins and Wapitis flew some of the earliest patrols, but soon began giving way to Bolingbrokes, Cansos/Catalinas, Digbys, Hudsons and Hurricanes. Into 1943 the U-boats still dominated, roaming the western Atlantic almost at will. Only when the RCN received new corvettes and destroyers with modern sonar, radar and weapons; and EAC re-equipped with long range Cansos and Liberators did the tide begin to turn. In *RCAF Squadrons and Aircraft*, Griffin and Kostenuk summarize EAC's role: "Carefully searching the gray expanse of water, aircraft forced enemy

submarines to crash-dive or remain submerged, and thus kept them away from convoys. It was wearisome and unglamorous work, but its importance cannot be too much stressed."

On the West Coast, Bolingbrokes, Cansos/Catalinas, Stranraers and Venturas patrolled incessantly, while Hurricanes and Kittyhawks provided air support from Tofino to Annette Island and out into the Aleutians. Once Japan withdrew from the Aleutians, the RCAF left Alaska. A new air station was opened at Terrace, from where RCAF Venturas continued covering the strategic port of Prince Rupert. By war's end there had been 19 EAC and 18 WAC squadrons. Their efforts were heroic, considering the remoteness of many air stations, the complicated logistics, dearth of communications and often impossible weather.

Eastern Air Command Pioneer

The Home War Establishment did not lack for talented aircrew volunteers, even if many who served were considered too old for "the young man's war" overseas. These men would lead the way on the home front from Tofino to Torbay. Norville E. "Molly" Small was already 31 when war broke out. Born in 1908, he was

The 1920s Atlas, Siskin and Wapiti remained in frontline RCAF use in September 1939. Atlases equipped 2 (AC) Squadron at St. John, New Brunswick, and flew that unit's first wartime operation on September 7. No.2 AC re-equipped with Lysanders in November. Wapiti 508 is seen nosed-up at Uplands on January 14, 1938. 10 (B) Squadron was flying Wapitis at Halifax when war broke out. Happily, these were replaced by Digbys in April 1940. (DND, C.L. Annis Col.)

When war began the RCAF had a handful of Siskin and Hurricane fighters – it was a pitiful situation, but no other modern types were available on a moment's notice. As a stop-gap measure, Ottawa purchased 15 Grumman Goblins from CanCar at Fort William. These had been lying in the snow when Ottawa stepped in with the buy. The Goblins were delivered to 118 Squadron at Rockcliffe in December 1940. No.118 relocated to Dartmouth in July 1941 and the Goblins were replaced that November with new Curtiss Kittyhawks. (DND PL5954)

Beginning in September 1937 the RCAF acquired 20 Northrop Deltas. Badly out-moded though it was, the Delta did good work in these desperate times, serving several home front units into 1942, then continuing as ground school training aids. Operating from Sydney, Nova Scotia on September 9, 1939 Delta 674 flew 8 (GR) Squadron's first wartime operation. Here is 676/MX-C of 120 (BR) Squadron, Patricia Bay, BC (on June 30, 1940, Delta 675 flew 120 BR's first wartime operation). It had begun the war at 1 (Fighter) Squadron, St. Hubert, where it was a stepping-stone trainer for pilots advancing to the Hurricane. (CANAV Col.)

Delta 676 of 8 (GP) Squadron on wartime duty at Sydney, where it served alongside the squadron's Bolingbrokes. (LAC PA63532)

In September 1939 two obsolete Canadian Vickers types remained in RCAF service. The small, wooden-hull Vedette was the RCAF's basic flying boat trainer; the large, metal-hull Vancouver still was on general coastal duties. First flown in 1924 and 1929, these provided useful service regardless of vintage. Vedette 803 is seen at Jericho Beach over the summer of 1935. A Vancouver rests at its buoy in the distance. On November 4, 1935 Sgt N.E. Small had a serious accident with 803, after which it was struck off charge. Then, Vedette 108 on operations on the BC coast in pre-WWII times. The Vedette served 4 BR into May 1940, and 13 (OT) Squadron into May 1941. (Gordon S. Williams, CANAV Col.)

Vancouvers tied down at Jericho Beach in a scene dated March 11, 1938. As war clouds brewed, the RCAF modified these dowagers to carry machine guns and bombs. On September 12, 1939, FSgt J.W. McNee and crew flew 4 BR's first wartime mission in Vancouver 906 – mercifully, the enemy was not met. (LAC PA133578)

Vancouver 906 with a machine gun mount fitted in the nose turret. This type served 4 BR into July 1939, when it was replaced by the Stranraer. The Vancouver remained with 13 (OT) Squadron into November 1940. (Gordon S. Williams)

One of the Blackburn Sharks that served well in BC with 4, 6 and 7 (BR) squadrons between November 1938 and May 1943. Sharks (26 were on RCAF strength) also served on 111 and 122 squadrons at Patricia Bay, BC, and 118 Squadron at Saint John, NB. Built in Vancouver by Boeing of Canada, Shark 514 crashed and sank at Jericho Beach on September 5, 1939. (Vancouver Public Library 45060)

Shark 503 newly assembled at Ottawa, having arrived crated from Blackburn in the UK. This photo was taken on the occasion of its first flight in Canada, November 7, 1936. No.503 joined newly-formed 6 (TB) Squadron at Trenton, and later served 4 BR, 7 BR and 111 CAC squadrons in BC. It was scrapped in April 1944. No example of this classic RCAF aircraft was saved for posterity. (LAC PA63191)

The Supermarine Stranraer was enthusiastically welcomed when it reached the West Coast in July 1939. Built by Canadian Vickers in Montreal, 40 "Strannies" served the RCAF, beginning with 5 BR at Dartmouth in November 1938. Quickly replaced on the East Coast by the Catalina and Canso, the Stranny found happy homes with several West Coast units. They served into 1944 by which time there was not a mile of the coast from the Oregon border to Alaska with which their crews were not familiar. Here, 915/FY-B of 4 BR is seen on the ramp at Jericho Beach. Formed initially as 4 (FB) Squadron in 1933, this unit was redesignated 4 (GR) Squadron in 1939 then became 4 BR on September 10, 1939. (RCAF via J.W. Jones Col.)

Stranraer 957 in a classic West Coast setting. Taken on strength in November 1941, this aircraft served to war's end (LAC PA115764)

raised in Hamilton. He enlisted in the RCAF in 1928, beginning at Camp Borden as a labourer. He later trained in aero engines, was accepted for pilot training and earned his wings in June 1931. That summer he qualified on flying boats, then served on the Vancouver and Vedette on the British Columbia coast. On November 4, 1935 he was badly injured in the crash of Vedette 803 and, on another occasion, was hurt when smacked in the face by a duck as he flew along in Vancouver 906.

All along, Small was receiving excellent assessments. On September 8, 1937, for example, W/C A.A.L. Cuffe, his CO at 4 Squadron (Vancouver), described him as "A good reliable pilot. Keen on flying and anxious to improve his flying ability". About this time Small left the RCAF for Canadian Airways, then was briefly with Imperial Airways and TCA in 1939. In November he rejoined the RCAF and was posted immediately to 10 (BR) Squadron at Halifax to fly Wapitis.

In April 1940 Small delivered one of 10 BR Squadron's new Douglas Digbys from Winnipeg. He now had several challenging taskings, including a circumnavigation of Labrador and northern Quebec. This part of Canada had not yet been surveyed to assess the condition of harbours that might be needed on short notice. There also was fear that the enemy might set up clandestine installations on the Labrador, Hudson Strait or Hudson Bay shores. Small's expedition was to advise on potential flying boat harbours and report on any shipping sighted. Small was briefed about fuel caches at such places as Hopedale, Labrador; and Lake Harbour, Baffin Island, but had no weather data to go by.

On August 27, 1941 the expedition left Dartmouth in Catalina Z2138. Small's crew included F/L R.H. Hoodspith (pilot), P/O R. Jones (nav), 1063 Sgt J.F. Langan (WOp), LAC J.G.E. Laflamme (fitter), AC1 R.E. Brown (fitter) and LAC F.A. Lamourne (rigger). Z2138 got airborne at 32,700 lb, about 1000 lb over normal gross weight. Its equipment included two machine guns and an F.24 aerial camera. Full fuel was some 1460 Imp. gallons. First stop was Northwest River, Labrador after a flight of about seven hours. Engine trouble had to be rectified, so the mission did not continue until the afternoon of August 30. The crew over-nighted next at

F/L N.E. "Molly" Small in a portrait *circa* 1940. (DND PL6880)

Hopedale, then left on the 31st at 1320 GMT for Hebron. They refuelled, pushed on to a landing at 50° 47' N, 65° 23' W to inspect a site, then continued to Fort Chimo, anchoring at 2227 hours. In poor weather they proceeded on September 1, patrolling and photographing the south shore of Hudson Strait until landing after 6½ hours at Sugluk on Quebec's northwest extremity. Nothing was found here but an old shack, so they continued in menacing weather to a landing at 60° 50' N, 77° 05' W near Povungnituk on the east coast of Hudson Bay. Next day they continued south about 150 miles to Port Harrison where they had to battle the elements:

In order to refuel it was necessary to anchor exposed to heavy sea and wind, which was now near gale force. Refuelling was completed with considerable difficulty and a decision was made to find a more sheltered anchorage. At 1645 hours GMT aircraft proceeded to the south end of Harrison Island, where a small cove provided shelter from the high wind which blew till early morning.

On September 3, 1941, Z2138 took off at 1045 GMT, passed scenic Richmond Gulf, landed for fuel at 1315 at Great

Whale River, continued over the Belcher Islands, landed at Rupert House at 1830, then proceeded to Moosonee. But the weather there was so grim that they flew on to Gravenhurst, Ontario, arriving at 0010 hours on September 4. Later they reached Ottawa, then Montreal. On the 5th they completed their final leg to Dartmouth. Flying time en route since August 27 totalled 48:30 hours.

In his final report about the expedition, F/L Small recommended several sites as potential seaplane harbours, Great Whale and Richmond Gulf included. The old Hudson Strait Expedition base at Wakeham Bay was not recommended, due to its exposure to open water. The report also described radio reception and existing radio facilities along the way, e.g. an abandoned wireless station at Hopes Advance Bay with the building still in good condition. At their various stops, Small and crew had enquired as to any sign of unusual activity. Of this Small reported:

Nothing was determined to indicate enemy activity. Quite often lone Eskimo kayaks were seen miles from the nearest post. That these Eskimos would immediately bring news to the nearest post of any strange aircraft or ships was demonstrated in many ways. At one or two places Eskimos armed themselves on our approach and were quieted only after assurances from the Hudson Bay Company managers that we were friendly aircraft. That the various trading posts were alert was proven by the fact that our arrival was anticipated at several points, the post being forewarned through the Hudson's Bay Company radio network or the Department of Transport Stations.

In these times, similar flights covered other parts of Canada, enabling Ottawa to improve its general overview of the *status quo* in preparing home defences. In June 1942 F/L Small was awarded the AFC, the recommendation for which noted: "Flight Lieutenant Small is an outstanding pilot who has been utilized as an advanced instructor and ferry pilot most of the time since the start of the war." Reference was made to his northern expedition and to five trans-Atlantic trips ferrying aircraft from Bermuda (perhaps while he was listed as "special duties aircrew" at 3 Training Command, Montreal early in 1941).

The versatile Hudson was based on the pre-war Lockheed 14 airliner. Some 3000 Hudsons were delivered by war's end. Hudsons made the first RCAF EAC U-boat kill and the first three for the US Army Air Corps and US Navy. The first Hudson reached the RCAF in September 1939, days after the outbreak of war. Three years later 246 had been delivered to Canada. Shown first is Hudson I (1000-hp Wright R-1820s) N7360. On June 10, 1940, by then re-numbered 770, it crashed en route from Ottawa to Toronto. Killed were the Minister of National Defence, Norman Roger, F/O John J. Cotter (skipper, age 26 from Halifax), AC1 Oscar D. Brownfield (WOp, age 27 from Big River, Saskatchewan) and AC1 James E. Nesbitt(fitter, age 33 from Saskatoon). (CANAV Col.)

(Above) Another early Hudson, RCAF N7382 later was 777. First flown in 1937 the speedy Hudson cruised at 200 mph. All-up weight was 18,000 lb. A Hudson could carry a 1600-lb bomb load and had a pair of forward-firing .303 machine guns. Some also had a 2-gun dorsal turret, although that feature was usually deleted to lighten and speed the plane. This Hudson, by then re-numbered 777, was lost in an accident at Dartmouth on October 15, 1941. (Lou Wise)

(Left) Hudson N7350/765 also was in the RCAF's original 1939 batch. On July 6, 1942, while on 13 (OT) Squadron at Patricia Bay, it crashed while the pilots were practicing at Bellingham, Washington. Three aboard died: P/O Robert B. MacLachlan (pilot, age 21 from Regina), P/O Ernest R. Brooks (age 28 from Belleville, Ontario) and Sgt Victor A. Utting (age 20 from Woodstock, Ontario). Injured were P/O J.C. Olsen of Regina, Sgt D.P. McLean of Smithers, BC, LAC L.A. Beatty of Oshawa, Ontario and LAC C.R. Merredew of Sidney, BC. (RCAF HC8987)

Hudson 772 was TOS in February 1940. It flew with 11 (BR) at Dartmouth until made surplus (11 BR converted to Liberators beginning in July 1943). 772 ended its days as ground training aid A-420, then went for scrap in July 1945. Here it is on a barge at Toronto Island Airport, details unknown. This aircraft had been delivered as N7371 via Pembina, North Dakota. Many aircraft destined for the RCAF landed at this border town, then were towed about 2 miles by road into Canada. This was done in order to meet a US neutrality regulation that forbade flying combat planes into a friendly nation which was at war. (CANAV Col.)

Hudson V AM752 was destined for the RAF, but diverted by the British Air Ministry to the RCAF. TOS on June 26, 1941, it was assigned to 4 AOS at London, where it had this accident shortly afterwards on July 22 (the Hudson was infamous for ground looping on landing and for vicious stalls). AM752's career ended with a more serious crash on September 21, 1944. The "2834" on the nose is the manufacturer's serial number. (L.B. Best Col.)

S/L Small Sinks U-754

Canada's role in the U-boat war is covered in dozens of books from *Far Distant Ships* (Schull) to *The Battle of the Atlantic* (Milner), *U-Boats against Canada* (Hadley), *Canadian Squadrons in Coastal Command* (Hendrie), *Search, Find and Kill* (Franks) and *The Creation of a National Air Force* (Douglas). Such sources must be consulted for the big picture. S/L N.E. "Molly" Small was the first in Eastern Air Command to sink a U-boat. Having joined 113 (BR) Squadron at Yarmouth on June 18, 1942, on July 31 he was patrolling in Hudson BW625 with the crew of P/O G.R. Francis (nav), Sgt R.A. Coulter (WAG) and Sgt D.P. Rogers (WAG). From 3000 feet and three miles they spotted a U-boat at position 43°00'N, 64°39'W (off

S/L Small while commanding 113 Squadron at Yarmouth from June 1942 to January 1943. (DND PMR77-177)

the southwest tip of Nova Scotia). Small attacked instantly, dropping four depth charges from 50 feet, spaced at 60 feet. The U-boat appeared to sink, but soon resurfaced. Two machine gun passes were made, then the U-boat again disappeared. Small remained in the area then, after 55 minutes on station, the crew noted an eruption in the water. HMS *Veteran* arrived to report much oil on the surface, so a kill seemed likely. It later was confirmed that Small and crew had sunk *U-754* with the loss of its 43 crew. *U-754* was a prize, considering that it had sunk 13 vessels for some 56,000 tons. This was Eastern Air Command's first U-boat kill. One assessment of S/L Small's interesting character is dated in the period – August 3, 1942: "An outstanding leader who radiates enthusiasm. Tireless worker

A 113 BR Lockheed Hudson III (1050-hp P&W R-1830s), the type flown by S/L Small and crew when they sank *U-754* on July 31, 1942. The side letters had a simple message: "LM" was 113's identifier, while "S" was the particular Hudson on squadron. (via Rob Schweyer)

whose only hobby is his work." In January 1943 S/L Small received the DFC, the citation noting:

This officer has displayed outstanding airmanship, courage and devotion to duty on operational flying in the face of the enemy over the sea off the coast of Nova Scotia... In the course of 335 hours operational flying during the last four months, this officer has on several occasions distinguished himself by his initiative and by the completion of difficult tasks under adverse weather conditions; in particular he has been of prime assistance in effecting more than one sea rescue of survivors of sunken or damaged vessels.

At the beginning of 1943 the innovative S/L Small was discussing with his 5 BR crews how to extend Canso range. Small suggested 250-lb instead of

450-lb depth charges, and removing the bow and tunnel machine guns plus 1000 rounds of ammunition from each of the blister guns. This would allow an extra 1269 pounds (181 Imp. gallons) of fuel. On January 7, 1943 S/L Small and crew had just departed Gander at 0630 local time in Canso 9737 when they crashed. Small died along with P/O Donald L. Hudson (age 29 from Saskatoon), F/O Aubrey M. Tingle (age 28 from Chilliwack, BC), FSgt J.T. Mangan (age 23 from North Bay, Ontario) and Sgt Harold E. White (age 29 from Saint John, New Brunswick). Sgt J.E.V. Banning and Sgt W. Wilson survived. (The Tingle family would be in deep mourning by war's end. Aubrey's brother, S/L Cyril N. Tingle, killed in a traffic accident in Brussels on November 27, 1944; while his brother P/O Leicester J. Tingle was lost in a Ferry Command Dakota crash in Iceland on March 5, 1944.)

Prey for the U-boats ... a typical North Atlantic convoy. RCAF sprog pilot, Stafford Marlatt of Oakville, Ontario broke the rules in photographing this scene while sailing overseas from Halifax aboard the SS *Ausonia* in June 1941.

One of the U-boats that hounded shipping and naval surface craft in Canada's Atlantic region. Under Capt Friedrich Brauecker, *U-889* had sailed on March 15, 1945 on its first operational patrol, but the European war ended on May 8. On the 14th *U-889* was spotted by an RCAF Liberator, then soon surrendered to the RCN off Cape Race, Newfoundland. Here the war prize waits at Shelburne, Nova Scotia. (DND PL36512)

Coming up Empty

Born in Ottawa in 1919, Maurice John Belanger grew up in British Columbia. As a young man he worked in the north, then enlisted in the RCAF in June 1940. By December he had earned his wings at 1 SFTS, Camp Borden, then became a flying instructor. After an advanced navigation course at Central Navigation School, Rivers, Manitoba, in June 1942 he joined 113 (BR) Squadron at Yarmouth, Nova Scotia. On September 25 he was flying Hudson 624 from 113's detachment at Mont Joli, Quebec. His crew comprised P/O J.H. Houser (navigator), FSgt D.C. Bullock (WAG) and Cpl F.N. LeMarre (Radio Mechanic). From 2000 feet in clear weather a submarine was sighted at about a mile (map location 49°37'N, 64°48'W). Belanger manoeuvred to get the target into the moon path. As soon as the target was confirmed (0153 GMT), he attacked. Four 250-lb depth charges, set for a depth of 25 feet, were released from 40 feet with a 40-foot spacing. As the Hudson passed, it machine-gunned the U-boat. The depth charges straddled the target, but clouds now obscured the moon, so results could not be observed. "No damage" is how the attack had to be assessed.

Belanger's second U-boat attack (same Hudson) occurred at 1959 GMT the same day northwest of the Magdalen Islands (47°34'N, 62°36'W). His crew comprised P/O J.H. Houser (navigator), FSgt D.C. Bullock (WAG) and Sgt R. Cameron (WAG). Conditions were similar as they quickly dropped four DCs. One landed within 10 feet of the hull, but the others overshot at 40-foot stages. Nothing suggested any serious damage being done to the U-boat. On September 29 at 1723 hours GMT, while he was returning from patrol to Chatham, New Brunswick, F/L Belanger attacked a target at 48°42'N, 63°55'W (crew of Houser, Bullock and Cameron). Visibility was good when the U-boat was spotted from 5000 feet. Four DCs landed well, the combat report later concluding:

The depth charges were seen to explode straddling the hull slightly ahead of the conning tower while the conning tower was still visible. The U-Boat's bow then came up out of the water; all forward motion seemed to have ceased, and it then settled out of view. With the depth charges set 40 feet apart and with an individual lethal radius of 16 feet, the submarine's pressure hull should be damaged by three depth charges.

Unfortunately no evidence of damage was noted. Three flame floats and four sea markers were dropped to mark the position, but during the one hour and 55 minutes that the aircraft stayed in the vicinity, no air or oil bubbles were noted. The sea was very rough, so minor disturbances would not have been seen. The depth of water is about 150 fathoms. The relieving aircraft also patrolled this section but no reports were received of any further evidence at any time after the attack.

Belanger's attacks were on one or more of five U-boats that had penetrated the Gulf of St. Lawrence and St. Lawrence River in the summer of 1942. These sank 17 merchant ships, the US troopship *Chatham*, RCN vessels *Raccoon* and *Charlottetown*, and the Newfoundland ferry *Caribou*. This huge U-boat victory caused the Gulf of St. Lawrence to be closed to merchant shipping. In *U-Boats against Canada*, Michael L. Hadley concludes that all three of Belanger's attacks had been against *U-517* commanded by U-boat ace Paul Hartwig, who later praised RCAF tactics. Following the attack of the 29th, Hartwig reported that his crew found an unexploded depth charge lodged against a deck gun.

For his efforts on 113 Squadron, in January 1943 F/L Belanger received the DFC. The citation credited him with "inflicting damage on one, probably sinking a second and possibly sinking a third" U-boat. In fact, the most that seems to have occurred was the rattling of nerves aboard *U-517*, which finally was sunk in the Bay of Biscay on November 21, 1942. F/L Belanger was posted to the UK in January 1944. He joined 425 Squadron, flew many a harrowing bombing raid, was repatriated in February 1945 and in May was awarded a Bar to his DFC.

The End of U-658

Raised in Vancouver, F/O Edward Lepage Robinson worked pre-war with the Bank of Montreal, then enlisted in the RCAF in April 1941. Beginning with elementary training at 8 EFTS, Vancouver, he earned his wings at 3 SFTS, Calgary in December, when he was commissioned. He was taken on strength by Eastern Air Command in March 1942, initially at 11 (BR) Squadron, but in May joined 145 at Torbay. On October 30, 1942 Robinson was one of two Hudsons on patrol. With him in Hudson 784 were Sgt K.U. Lunny (nav), Sgt P.A. Corbett (WAG) and Sgt E.F. Williams (WAG). At 1205 GMT they encountered *U-658* at 50°32'N, 46°32'W, or some 300 miles east of St. John's, Newfoundland. Their later report described the target and setting: "The submarine had one large gun forward of the conning tower; wire cutters were noticed at the bow. The colour was dark greenish-grey... The weather was hazy with a visibility of five miles. The sea was rough, with a 30-knot wind on a bearing of 290 T. Solid strato-cumulus clouds were above 2,000 feet." The U-boat was still surfacing when Robinson rained down four DCs: "The first depth charge landed 15 feet off the port stern; the second 15 feet off the port beam just back of the conning tower; the third appeared to hit the submarine and roll off and explode; and the fourth exploded six feet off the starboard bow... One-third of the submarine then lifted out of the water ... the screws were clearly seen ... It then settled straight down out of sight."

The Hudsons patrolled the area for about an hour, observed a huge oil slick, then flew home to report this action as likely having "seriously damaged" a U-boat. It later was confirmed that their victim had been *U-658*. It had been on its second patrol and had a record of three ships sunk for 12,000+ tons. Capt Hans Senkel and his 48 crew all were lost. On August 31, 1943 Robinson was recommended for an AFC (not awarded). By that time he had 466:50 hours on operations (111 sorties). On October 2, 1943 he, S/L Richard L. Lee (age 23 from Centreville, New Brunswick) and F/O Acton F. Daunt (age 25 from New Westminster, BC) were taking off at Torbay in Ventura 2160 when they crashed fatally. They lie today in Gander Cemetery. On November 26, 1943 F/O Robinson was awarded a posthumous DFC, the citation for which noted how, during his U-boat attack, he had "manoeuvred into position and was able to carry out a perfect attack which, it is believed, destroyed the submarine."

U-520 Sent to the Bottom

Eastern Air Command celebrated twice on October 30, 1942, since it also sank *U-520*. This occurred when 10 BR Digby 747, flown from Torbay by F/O Daniel F. Raymes, AFC, caught its prey on the surface at 47°47'N, 49°50'W. Captain Volkmar Schwartzkopff and his 52-man crew all went to the bottom. They had been on their first war patrol and had no victories. Raymes crewmates in this action were P/O J. Leigh of Toronto (pilot), F/O R.B. Martin of Toronto (navigator), P/O J.S. Johnson (WOpAG) of Ottawa, Sgt J.J. Gilfillan (WOpAG) and Sgt F.H. Bebee (WOpAG). Under a banner headline "RCAF Planes Skim Waves To Shatter Hun Subs Along Coast", the Toronto *Evening Telegram* of December 2, 1942 quoted Martin about the attack:

We had been out on patrol since early morning, when we bumped into that baby... Diving down, we dropped right on his tail... When the alarm sounded I immediately took up position in the front gun turret. It is remarkable how the mind functions. Everything is so well rehearsed there is no need for commands and perhaps it is a good thing, for it sure

An exceptional view of an RCAF Digby. In its hour of dire need, Canada was fortunate in latching onto 20 of these sturdy planes to use against the U-boats. (Lialla Raymes Col.)

takes your breath away when, after spending hundreds of hours on patrol, you run smack into a sub... I could see the first depth charge hit... I called up to Danny, 'That was a lovely stick'".

Prairie Farm Boy in the U-Boat War

Born on March 28, 1918, Daniel Francis Raymes spent his boyhood in Saskatoon. He attended Bedford Road Collegiate, where he did well in sports, but was not such a star at his studies. After graduation, he worked for the CNR, where his father was a conductor. At age 22 he enlisted and on April 15, 1940 began his indoctrination course at 1 Manning Depot in Toronto. But the place was barely functioning at this early date, so AC2 Raymes' sojourn was brief. On April 25 he already was at No.1 Initial Training School as part of the first course there. His log book shows this as "Eglington Initial" (the school occupied the former Toronto Hunt Club located at Avenue Rd. and Eglinton Ave.). Schools were only beginning to appear. Staffing and equipping them, and getting

F/O D.F. Raymes in Digby days. This dedicated young Canadian had a solid war against the U-boat, then switched to flying transports. (DND PL12613)

curricula organized and students flowing through made this a hectic period.

From ITS, Danny Raymes backtracked to begin flight training in more familiar country at the Moose Jaw Flying Club (the RCAF had not opened its first EFTS). Barely six weeks after joining the RCAF, Raymes was in the air, going up initially with Mr. M. Knox in Tiger Moth

Sgt Danny Raymes took these candid snapshots from the cockpit of his Digby during a typical convoy escort patrol. Of note in the left photo is the closest vessel – a CAM ship (Catapult Armed Merchantman) which carried a single Sea Hurricane on a rocket catapult on the bow for convoy defence. (Lialla Raymes Col.)

On his first day of flying, Danny Raymes flew this Gipsy Moth at Moose Jaw, but on wheels. Registered in Canada in May 1929, CF-ADI served such operators as Northwest Aero Marine and Prairie Airways until joining the Moose Jaw Flying Club in July 1937. Superseded by newer trainers, it faded from the scene some time in 1941. (William J. Wheeler Col.)

CF-CBR on May 26 – a 15 minute familiarization flight. On the same day he had a 30-minute lesson in Gipsy Moth CF-ADI. Knox now kept his student flying twice a day, usually, until trusting him to go solo on June 5 in CF-CBR. That day Raymes endorsed his own log book: "I hereby certify that I understand the ignition, petrol and lubrication systems of the Tiger Moth aircraft."

Through June, LAC Raymes flew intensively with Mr. Knox, but also with civilian instructors A. Snyder and R. Love. On June 28 he passed his 20-hour flight test in Tiger Moth CF-CHD, receiving a "Satisfactory" from F/O Gordon. On July

5 Knox took him up for the first time in the Fleet 7 – 15 minutes in CF-CGJ. His last trip at Moose Jaw was in Tiger Moth

CF-CBR. This was his 50-hour test, also with F/O Gordon. He now was posted to 1 SFTS, Camp Borden, where his familiarization flight was made on July 24 with F/O H.M. Hallatt in Harvard 1350.

Not four months since he enlisted, LAC Raymes arrived at Camp Borden with a total of 52:15 hours on light biplane trainers. Here, his next training plane was not a larger single-engine type. Instead, he began the "intermediate" phase of his training on July 31, 1940 by flying three times with Sgt J. Harper in a big, twin-engine Anson – tail number 6029. On August 12 Harper sent Raymes solo on his eighth Anson trip. On the 17th and 18th he flew on the Oxford on four exercises, but had no further time on this type. He logged his first dual night training exercise and first night solo on

The first type flown by LAC Raymes at Camp Borden was the Anson I. This excellent view of 6056 was found among his memorabilia in 2010. (all, Lialla Raymes Col.)

Having mastered the Anson, students on the first class of BCATP pilots were handed the Yale. These three are seen at Camp Borden with an Oxford beyond. (Lialla Raymes Col.)

Although the Fairey Battle was in use at Camp Borden in 1940 as an advanced trainer, Danny Raymes did not fly it. He was, however, interested enough to photograph this pair. A Harvard I is in the distance.

Labels on cockpit image: FUEL GAUGE SELECTOR, BOOST GAUGES FUEL GAUGE, OIL PRESSURE, OIL TEMP, FLAP INDICATOR, ENGINE CUTOUT, U/C INDICATOR, MIXTURE, THROTTLE CLAMP, U/C WARNING LIGHT, R.P.M., BRAKE PRESSURE, FLAP CONTROL, BRAKE, CB 592 9-4-40. AVRO ANSON COCKPIT CAMP BORDEN.

RCAF teaching aids were straight-forward at Camp Borden, e.g. student were given simple labelled photographs to help them memorize cockpit details.

August 22. Next day he made his first cross-country flight.

On August 29 LAC Raymes graduated from the Anson to the Yale, Harper taking him up for 1:10 hours in Yale 3372. For August alone he flew 41 times on what were, on average, 1-hour exercises. So this was how an RCAF recruit progressed at the time: Tiger Moth to Anson to Yale. For the rest of his course, LAC Raymes flew the Yale, on which he soloed on his fifth flight on September 2. He flew his last exercise on September 17, going up in 3367 with F/O Vincent. On September 29, 1940 he passed his course, receiving an "Average" rating from S/L W.E. Kennedy, the OC 1 Training Squadron, Camp Borden. He finished with 28:35 hours day/night on the Anson and Oxford, 36:55 hours on the Yale.

Next day the BCATP held its first pilots' wings parade. Presiding over the event, Air Commodore G.O. Johnson told the sprogs, "When you go overseas you will be carrying a personal message ... that it is not against Hitler [you are] making war, but the British Commonwealth of Nations." He reminded the class that each man represented a financial investment and that "It is your responsibility to preserve that investment," and added a warning against the dangers of alcohol and reckless flying. Also present on the parade square this day was the Minister of Defence, Hon. J.L. Ralston, G/C A.T.N. Cowley (outgoing station commander) and G/C R.S. Grandy (incoming station commander). Graduates on the parade square included (mention is made for those later killed):

P/O A.L. Pendergast
    (Norwood, Manitoba)
P/O J.T. Reed (Ottawa)
P/O D.E.T. Wood (Ottawa)
LAC D.A. Angus (Montreal,
    KIFA 27-5-41, 6 SFTS)
LAC D.H. Armstrong
    (Gananoque, Ontario)
LAC T.A. Barr (Edmonton,
    KIFA 6-10-40, 1SFTS)
LAC J.R.C. Bishop
    (Fort Garry, Manitoba)
LAC T. Burke (Regina)
LAC C.H. Carscadden (Red Deer,
    Alberta, KIFA 4-2-45, 5 OTU)

LAC Raymes ready for a solo exercise in one of Camp Borden's Harvard Is.

The first wings parade in BCATP history – Camp Borden, September 30, 1940. (Lillia Raymes Col.)

LAC F.C. Colbourne (Calgary)

LAC. R. Condie (Crystal City, Manitoba, KIFA 2-4-41, 7 SFTS)

LAC R.H. Cousins (New Westminster, BC)

LAC J.T. Davis (Westmount, Quebec)

LAC J.K. Dawson (Chicoutimi, Quebec)

LAC R.J. De Beaupré (Hawarden, Saskatchewan)

LAC A.L. De La Haye (Vancouver)

LAC W.N. Douglas (Haileybury, Ontario, died 14-5-45, 416 Sqn)

LAC N.R. Farnham (Aroostook, New Brunswick)

LAC H. Freeman (St. James, Manitoba, KIA 24-5-44, 198 Sqn)

LAC J.E.J. Hutchinson (USA)

LAC K.A. Jones (Buffalo, NY)

LAC J.D. Laydon (Montreal)

LAC L.M. Linnell (Morse, Saskatchewan, KIA 21-9-44 434 Sqn)

LAC N.N. Lougheed (Calgary)

LAC J.E.R. Martin (Winnipeg)

LAC W.G. McElrea (Winnipeg)

LAC J.W. McIntosh (Winnipeg, KIFA 2-4-41, 7 SFTS)

LAC T.C. Mears (Port Arthur, Ontario)

LAC R.J. Mullin (Kenora, Ontario)

LAC J.D. Orr (Elm Creek, Manitoba)

LAC R.F. Patterson (Richmond, Virginia, KIA 121 Sqn 7-12-41)

LAC C.A. Rawson (Brandon, Manitoba)

LAC D.F. Raymes (Bounty, Saskatchewan)

LAC A.M. Regimbal (Transcona, Manitoba)

LAC G.F. Ryan (Winnipeg,

KIFA 2WS Calgary 11-12-41)

LAC J.H. Simpson (Kingston, Ontario)

LAC J.H. Thomson (Winnipeg)

LAC A.B. Whiteford (Saskatoon)

LAC E.C. Williams (Bermuda)

The class now did further advanced training at 1 SFTS. For Raymes this began on September 27 with two Northrop Nomad flights. He flew the Harvard (aircraft 2511) for the first time

The formal photo taken of the graduating pilots and some staff at 1 SFTS. (Lialla Raymes Col.)

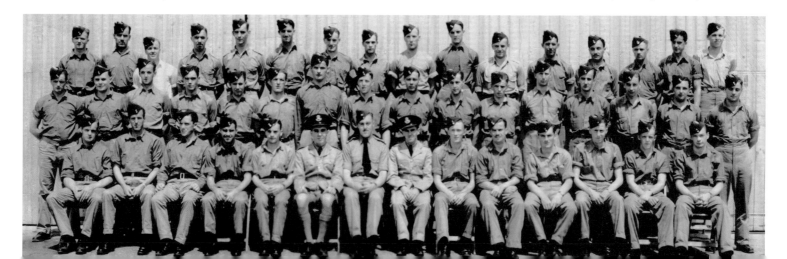

Air Commodore G.O. Johnson pins on LAC Raymes' wings. Then, newly winged pilots from the graduating class of September 30, 1940. In front are P/Os F.C. Colbourne, J.E.R. Martin and D.E.T. Wood. The sergeants are R.H. Cousins, D.F. Raymes, N.N. Lougheed and J.K. Dawson. (Lialla Raymes Col.)

on the 10th, then was busy until finishing on November 4. Meanwhile, classmate LAC Thomas A. Barr (age 22 from Edmonton) had lost his life. On his 22nd birthday, October 6, he was aloft in Harvard I 1334 with AC2 E.A. Frymark (age 19 from Milwaukee). He got into a fatal spin, crashing on David Dunn's farm near Alliston (the Harvard I was prone to violent spinning).

On this course there was much practice with formation flying, cross-country navigation, air-to-air combat and practice bombing. For Raymes the course totalled 42:05 hours. He graduated with another "Average" rating. The class officially graduated on November 5, 1940. In *The Aerodrome of Democracy*, Fred Hatch mentions that the class at the end totalled 34 new pilots, 27 of whom immediately were fingered to be flying instructors, the others going to home defence squadrons. This would be the picture until the BCATP had all the instructors and staff pilots needed to function smoothly.

Finished at Camp Borden, Sgt Raymes was sent cross-country by train to Patricia Bay for an advanced course at 13 (Operational Training) Squadron, commanded by S/L R.G. Briese. Here he soon met a number of legendary pilots – Briese himself, F/L C.C. "Chuck" Austin

of Austin Airways fame, F/L Z.L. "Lewie" Leigh, one of the pioneers of flight down the MacKenzie River Valley and the first pilot hired by Trans-Canada Air Lines in 1937, and F/L Harry Winny, another pioneer bush pilot. Raymes first flew on November 11, going up with F/L Leigh in Norseman 695. On the 18th he flew first in Vedette 816 for 1:15 hours with F/L Winny. He flew 816 again on the 19th and 21st, both times with F/L Austin, then soloed on the 19th after 3:40 hours of instruction. He flew 816 seven more times. His final Vedette flight was in 817 on June 12, his total time on type being 12:45.

On the 21st Raymes was introduced to the Goose, going up with the CO in 917. November 18, 22 and 26 he was on four nav exercises in Lockheed Electra 7634 with F/Ls Leigh and Winny; then he finished his course on the 18th and 21st with exercises in Hudson 7373 with F/L Leigh. Having pioneered with Canadian Airways and TCA on the Lockheed 10 and 14, Leigh at this time was Canada's top Lockheed pilot. Raymes finished his course with an "Above Average" as a pilot and an "Average" in "B.R. Knowledge". His time on course was 76:50 hours and he left Patricia Bay with his log book showing a total of 221:55

The RCAF accepted the first of its 44 Canadian Vickers Vedettes in July 1925. At 13 (OT) Squadron LAC Raymes qualified as a flying boat pilot on this ancient type. His Postwar photo collection revealed this rare view of Vedette V 816. Taken on strength as G-CYZD in June 1929, it was finally scrapped in May 1941 – the taxpayers had gotten their money's worth. Note how 816 was flying this day with the rudder of 809.

A standard US Army Air Corps Douglas B-18 of the 7th Bomb Group, 8th Bomb Squadron, Hamilton Field, California. In FYs 1936-38, 350 B-18s were ordered. By USAAC standards, these were obsolete for serious warfare, but they did useful service otherwise in home-front coastal patrol, training bomber crews and in transport. As the Digby, this type performed brilliantly during Canada's anti-submarine efforts in the darkest early days of WWII. (Peter M. Bowers)

hours. Now ready to fight the war, he was posted to 10 (BR) Squadron Dartmouth – on the opposite side of the country.

By this time 10 BR had exchanged its "What-A-Pity" Wapitis for relatively modern Douglas Digbys (the squadron still was using Shark 526 as a target tug). The Digby was a version of the Douglas DB-1 (USAAC B-18 Bolo) first flown in 1935. Powered by two 960-hp Wright R-1820s, the DB-1 was based on the DC-2. In this version it could carry a 2260-lb bomb load 1100 miles and had a top speed of 170 mph. On the eve of war Ottawa placed a rush order for 20 DB-1s each at about $65,000. These were taken

on strength in December 1939 – months before they were delivered. They entered service with 10 BR the following April (first operational patrol under S/L Carscallen on June 17, 1940). By the time Sgt Raymes arrived on 10 BR, he was in the midst of a team of top coastal patrol men, who already had made several U-boat attacks.

Sgt Raymes first flew at 10 BR with the CO, W/C R.C. Gordon, in Digby 752 on February 6, 1941, then began an intensive training program mostly under F/L W.C Van Camp. On February 14 he accompanied F/L A.G. Kenyon and crew on an anti-submarine patrol. His first

such operation, this was a 7-hour mission in Digby 754. On the 19th he was part of W/C Gordon's crew on what he logged as "Outer Anti-Sub Patrol ... 8:50". Sgt Raymes, therefore, was an operational pilot a little more than six months after his first Tiger Moth flight at Moose Jaw.

The urgency of anti-submarine warfare gave little time for rest if one was on an EAC squadron. In April 1941, for example, Sgt Raymes flew 26 times. This was mainly on training, since he remained a junior pilot on a big, sophisticated airplane. His first sortie of the month was a test flight with F/L Kenyon on Digby 757. On the 6th he flew as co-pilot with F/L Ralph A. Ashman on what was logged as "Patrol I". This was an inner patrol, skimming the coast line, doing harbour recces, etc. For April, Raymes flew seven of these, each at about three hours duration. On April 15, 1941 W/C H.M. Carscallen took command at 10 BR from W/C Gordon.

On May 14, 1941 Sgt Raymes flew his first patrol as a captain, having F/O Horne as co-pilot in 755. This was an interesting case of the skipper being a sergeant, the co-pilot an officer – the skipper was in command. On May 19 Raymes flew with F/L Rand's crew in

Views of Digby 755, which caused such a buzz in Millinocket, Maine. Sgt Raymes was fortunate to find an airport "in the middle of nowhere" – 200 miles west of Fredericton. This remote town owed the existence of its airport to the Civilian Conservation Corps, a Depression era relief organization established under President Roosevelt. The "CCC" was similar to MacKenzie King's relief scheme which built the trans-Canada airway in the same era.

Big Army Plane Forced Down At Millinocket

Is Largest Ever At Local Port; May Stay Awhile

Digby 740 on Atlantic patrol. This aircraft survived the war. Then, an angle showing bomb bay doors open – the Digby normally carried 6 x 250-lb depth charges. (Lialla Raymes Col.)

757 – six hours on a "Patrol III". Then, on the 22ⁿᵈ he crewed with F/L Laut in 757 on a patrol of 10:30, this showing what great range the Digby had with a war load. On May 24 he somehow got onto an American B-24 doing an 18-hour search for the German battleship *Bismarck*. On the 27ᵗʰ and 28ᵗʰ he was on long Digby "special" patrols – 9:45 and 9:00. These may also have been on *Bismarck* recces. June 3 saw 10 BR, Raymes included, searching for a missing Bolingbroke (9:40 hours in 740).

On July 13, 1941 Raymes was out in 755 doing an ice recce, likely mapping icebergs. This marathon mission ended at Dorval after 11:25 hours. On the 16ᵗʰ they headed home, but engine trouble forced them into Millinocket, Maine. Here, the curious locals swarmed out to see what was going on. The Bangor Daily News knew they had a good story in this and milked it all to the limit, lathering on the verbiage while, in typical newspaper style, saying little of substance:

A huge Canadian army plane, containing five airmen commanded by a sergeant, was forced down by engine trouble at Millinocket airport late this afternoon.

The plane, a Douglas Digby, largest ever to land at the local airport, was on a flight from Montreal to Newfoundland. It was heard coasting in shortly before 4 o'clock and it barely missed the trees at the port's entrance. But it landed safely – a beautiful job by the pilot, for both motors were almost dead...

Mechanics are on their way from

Montreal, but many think that more than repairs and mechanical skill will be needed for a successful take-off. The plane's vast bulk seems too great for the 3,000 foot runway ... Members of the crew ... are cheerful about their adventure and glad its ending was no worse.

Next day they continued home, but weather forced them into Moncton, from where they did not depart for base until the 21ˢᵗ. In this period 10 BR moved to Gander. On July 23 Raymes departed Dartmouth for Gander in 755, getting there via Sydney in 3:30 hours. Next day he patrolled in 740 for 8:00 hours. A mission of August 25 in Digby 750 resulted in Raymes' comment "Searching

for crash. Smith crash found."

October 1941 was a normal month for Sgt Raymes, who flew 20 times for 76:45 hours. Included were one "sweep", five anti-submarine/convoy patrols and one photo recce mission for a total of 54:15 hours on operations. By month's end his log book showed 757:30 total flying hours. By this time life at 10 BR, now known far and wide at "The North Atlantic Squadron", was one of routine. There no longer was any shortage of well-trained crews, and the Digby long-since had proven itself to be a reliable plane. Naturally, there would be mishaps, including the ditching of 752 on June 21, 1941. While far out to sea on patrol, F/L Ashman ran into impossible weather,

The Raymes memorabilia includes several aerial snapshots of the "Smith" crash site. Smith put his Hudson down very nicely following some urgent need.

Digby 751 in a rare in-flight view. Sgt Raymes had his personal history with 751. He first flew it on February 2, 1942 on a local sweep with P/O Padden as co-pilot (1:45 hours). On March 2 he had it on a transport trip with P/O Sanderson (8:10). Next he took it on a 1-hour test flight on May 9 then, on May 30, flew with P/O Ingrams on a training sortie dropping DCs. On July 7 he was out with P/O Cheater in 751 practicing low level bombing (1:10). On September 9 he flew it on a lengthy sweep (8:10) with P/O Leigh. The same duo took it on a 5:20-hour convoy patrol on October 16. On November 8 Raymes was with P/O Haggman in 751 on a convoy patrol (9:30). On January 17, 1943 he and F/O McLean had it on a sweep of 6:45. He last flew 751 on February 12, going out with McLean on an unspecified trip (7:30).

Danny Raymes at the controls of a Digby. (Lialla Raymes Col.)

training flight in 753, Sgt Raymes crashed on the airfield at Gander. The Digby was destroyed, but the crew was safe. A sweep four days later in 747 had his crew out for 11:40 hours.

A patrol in 741 of April 1, 1942 was typically long – 8:15 hours. This ends, however, with a startling log book annotation, "Shot up, returned base". One of Raymes' crew was hurt in this incident, the report for which stated, "Gunshot wound in right hand from small arms fire, believed from merchant vessel in convoy being escorted." For some reason, Raymes did not fly again until April 24. Towards the end of the month he logged his 1000th flying hour. Beginning in May, he was mainly crewed up with co-pilot P/O Leigh. They flew together for the first 15 trips that month, then usually

were a team. The rest of the crew likely also were the same bunch. May proved busy with 103:05 flying hours in Raymes' log book. July was even busier at 117:25 hours on sweeps, convoy patrols and anti-submarine patrols. July 25 to August 18, Raymes, Leigh and crew had 755 on a mission to Ottawa, about which there are no details.

October 1942 began with a convoy patrol in 747. Eight convoy patrols, some dual training and bombing practice brought Raymes to month's end. On the 30th he, Ingram and crew took off on a convoy patrol of 11:30 hours. While returning to Torbay they encountered *U-520*, which they promptly sank. All Raymes had to say about this in his log book was "Convoy, sub attacked, sank". Life continued normally, Raymes flying

The oil slick marking the spot in the Atlantic where U-520 disappeared forever. (Lialla Raymes Col.)

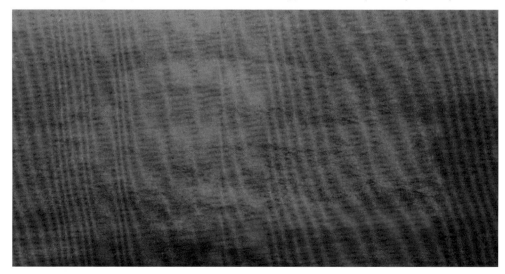

eventually running out of fuel. He ditched near the Newfoundland schooner *Chesley R*, which quickly rescued all the crew.

January 1942 was a busy month for Raymes. Although he flew only 13 times, every trip was operational – either a patrol or a search. Total time was 63:40 hours. While on a 12:00 hour patrol in 741 on February 16, 1942, Raymes ran into dreadful weather. So much ice was accumulated on the Digby that he unloaded his depth charges (a usual load was 6 x 250-lb DCs for a total of 1500 lb). On March 26, 1942 while on a local

On March 26, 1942 Sgt Raymes and F/L Williams had been practicing in the circuit with Digby 753 when "situational awareness" in the cockpit somehow broke down. Result? One mangled Digby. Of the RCAF's 20 Digbys, 10 were lost in disastrous "Cat A" incidents; two others were severely damaged in "Cat B" crashes. This horrendous loss rate mainly indicates the intensive use of these EAC aircraft, and likely also hints at the severity of Atlantic Canada weather. The postwar fate of surviving RCAF Digbys has not yet been uncovered. Some are said to have been sold "south of the border". (Lialla Raymes Col.)

an 8:30-hour patrol two days later in 757. On November 11 he took the chance for a 3:00-hour familiarization flight in a Canso under command of F/L Colbourne, perhaps the same Colbourne with whom he had trained at Camp Borden. All of Raymes' flying in December 1942 was on transportation with 741 – trips to Dartmouth, Moncton, Montreal, etc. for a total of 25:10 hours. At month's end he noted: "Total operational trips to date 156. Total operational time 1106:35." In January 1943 Raymes was awarded the

Air Force Cross, the ceremony taking place at Government House in Ottawa on April 16, 1943, the AFC citation noting: "Pilot Officer Raymes' exceptional ability as a pilot coupled with his devotion to duty and the cheerful manner in which he performs any task, makes him an outstanding example to those with whom he works."

In April 1943, 10 BR began re-equipping with the B-24 Liberator. At Gander on May 1, 1943 F/L Raymes checked out on the B-25. Then, from

May 2 he started training on the B-24. This period included several missions with a legendary Liberator man – the great Lindy Rood of TCA and Ferry Command. On April 24 Raymes was with a P/O Dale on Liberator 729. This was his first operational Liberator mission, a sweep from Gander that ended 12 hours later at Sydney. For May he logged 78:40 hours, all on Liberators other than 13:00 on the Digby and 4:30 on the B-25. June was F/L Raymes' last month on his beloved 10 BR – he flew his final

10 BR flight crew in a grand set-up photo. The fellows have all their kit ready for a mission. Once 10 BR converted to the Liberator, its Digbys found further employment. RCAF records show, for example, that 741, 751, 754 and 756 continued in the U-boat war with 161 Squadron at Dartmouth from May 1943 to January 1944 (working alongside the squadron's Cansos); while 740, 747, 748 and 755 flew in the transport role with 167 Squadron, also at Dartmouth. (Lialla Raymes Col.)

The first USAAC bombers stationed in Newfoundland were six anti-submarine B-18s of the 21ˢᵗ Reconnaissance Squadron, which arrived in May 1941. The B-18s soon were replaced by B-17Cs of the 41ˢᵗ Reconnaissance Squadron. In July 1941 US Ferry Command made its first flight through Gander. Shown are three B-17Cs with Digby 740 of 10 BR. (LAC PA501329)

Gander scenes – the famous hangar and administration building with Liberators on the ramp. Then, two photos of a rare bird passing through: Danny Raymes snapped the massive, one-and-only Boeing XB-15. First flown in October 1937, by this time it had been converted to the XC-105 cargo plane with an all-up weight of 92,000 lb. (Lialla Raymes Col.)

operational trip on the 5ᵗʰ in Liberator 729. The following day he logged his 2000ᵗʰ flying hour during an instrument training flight in 739 with Capt Rood.

F/L Raymes now left 10 BR but, according to his log book, seems to have been around Gander for a few months. He flew two familiarization trips in a Catalina and finished his Gander days with four PV-1 flights, the last on November 6. He now transferred to 168 (T) Squadron at Rockcliffe, where he first flew on January 14, 1944. By this time, his mother, then a widow, had moved to Toronto. Raymes last wartime trip began at Rockcliffe on June 27, 1945 in B-17 9202 and ended back there on July 9. In February 1946 he was awarded a DFC, the citation noting how, "Under his leadership an attack was made and brilliantly executed."

Ever the "photo bug", Danny Raymes kept his camera ready to shoot any interesting airplane. This Handley Page Harrow was one of a pair on RCAF strength from October 1940. These had been used in 1939 doing experimental in-flight refuelling of Short Empire flying boats. With the war the Harrows were impressed by the RCAF. One was cannibalized, while 794 was sent to Gander on general duties. It was withdrawn from service in November 1941. (Lialla Raymes Col.)

10 BR's CO from March to July 1942, and April to August 1943 was W/C Clare L. Annis. From Highland Creek near Toronto, he had joined the RCAF in 1936. He flew all the 10 BR types – Wapiti, Digby and Liberator. Later postings included station commander Gander and Linton-on-Ouse. In January 1943 W/C Annis was warded the OBE and in January 1945 a Mention in Dispatches. Post-WWII he commanded Air Materiel Command, retired as Air Marshal Annis in 1967 and died in Ottawa in 1994. Here he is (seated, lighting cigarette) at a 10 BR drinking and bull-shooting session. Danny Raymes is second from the left. Two to the left of Annis and sporting the

"CANADA USA" shoulder flash is Bertrand Hutchinson, a soldier of fortune type who had been awarded a Croix de Guerre and, rumour had it, had been in Spain pre-war. On New Year's Day 1944 the RCAF awarded Hutchinson a Mention in Dispatches, which noted: "He was one of the first captains who bore the load of mid-ocean operations during exceedingly bad weather conditions, when the performance, endurance and range of aircraft and the employment of communication and search equipment were still experimental. Flight Lieutenant Hutchinson has displayed courage and ability as an operational captain." (Lialla Raymes Col.)

Annis (left) once the evening had gotten going a bit and the dress code had gone down the drain. Then, the fellows well into it, but no sign of the CO. (Lialla Raymes Col.)

Wherever he was, even in Timbuktu, nearly every airman kept close by mail with his parents, especially his mother. Here is a typical press release of the times from the Saskatoon *Star Phoenix*: Mrs. H.L. Raymes and her treasured flyboy son, Danny. (Lialla Raymes Col.)

5, 1943.   **The Star-Phoenix Goes Home.**

Saskatonian Honored

Singled out for special mention after attacks on enemy submarines, Flying Officer D. F. "Danny" Raymes of Saskatoon is awarded the Air Force Cross. He is shown with his mother, Mrs. H. L. Raymes, now living in Toronto. He is with the Eastern Command R.C.A.F.

Canso at Work: 5 BR Victory

On May 4, 1943 the 5 (BR) Squadron Canso crew of S/L Barry H. Moffit, AFC (skipper), F/O John D. Hooper (pilot), FSgt Lyndon A. Hunt (nav), WO Charles E. Spence (WAG), FSgt Phillips A. Corbett (WAG), Sgt William Bedwell (FE) and Cpl Harry Knelson (FE) was patrolling between Greenland and Labrador. Using ASV radar, at 1758 hours GMT a U-boat was encountered at 56°38'N, 42°32'W. The initial range was seven miles, the weather was iffy – ceiling 2000 feet, 10/10 cloud, high winds. Cpl Knelson sighted the target at 2½ miles. Moffit immediately charged in at 150 knots, 75 feet over the waves. He dropped 4 x 250-lb depth charges set to explode at 22 feet, spaced at 35 feet. All DCs landed close to target, two within 12 feet. Moffit's combat report later stated: "Coming in straight we let our depth charges go, and as the aircraft passed over the sub I could see two of the Jerries still on the conning tower platform ... The explosion ... blew the submarine, which had crash-dived, back into a fully-surfaced position for about ten seconds before it finally sank." Debris and a large oil slick covered the sea.

Moffit remained in the area for a half-hour, then returned to base, where a claim of "probably damaged" was made. Intelligence identified his victim as *U-630*. But *U-630* eventually was confirmed sunk nearby about the same time by the WWI destroyer HMS *Vidette*. It now seems that Moffit's U-boat may have been *U-209*, but it did not sink immediately. On May 6 it reported having been severely damaged, then disappeared forever with its crew of 46. Moffit and

Canada's WWII war artists produced hundreds of original works at home and overseas. This national treasure resides in Ottawa in such locations as the Canada War Museum, but bits of it sometimes are "on the road". Here is RCAF war artist Paul Goranson's 1942 watercolour rendition depicting the EAC Canso era. In "East Coast Sentry" he details the blister gunners. One is on his RT, while his mate reaches for a drum of .303 ammunition. An under-wing depth charge is just visible. Cansos usually patrolled as lone wolves, so the nearby presence of a second one is fanciful – but the war artist had his privileges. Born in 1911, Goranson had been the oldest surviving member of the Emily Carr Institute of Art. His obituary (August 3, 2002) notes that he "... served with distinction as an RCAF War Artist in Canada, the United Kingdom, North Africa, Sicily, Italy, France, Belgium, Holland and Germany. His interest in portraying air force life was paramount and to attain his ends he had on many occasions gone far beyond the ordinary requirements of duty." (DND PL47542)

crew were honoured for their good work in this action: Moffit - DFC, Hooper - MiD, Hunt - MiD, Spence - DFC, Corbett - MiD, Bedwell - MiD, Knelson - DFM. The citation for Moffit's gong notes, "This officer has been flying on anti-submarine patrol duty for approximately thirty-two months and has at all times displayed excellent leadership and skilful flying in the performance of his duties." Spence was singled out for his diligent use of ASV equipment (radar) in locating the target. Knelson was lauded for being first to eyeball the target: "His sighting and quick action in drawing attention to the target made possible the success of the attack." FSgt Corbett had been on the 145 crew that sank *U-658* on October 30, 1942. Moffit served in the postwar RCAF, where his duties included command of 404 (Maritime Reconnaissance) Squadron and an RAF exchange tour.

The Consolidated PBY-5/PBY-5A Catalina (flying boat and amphibian versions) was a key weapon in the U-boat war. In RCAF service the PBY-5A, known in Canada as the Canso, equipped EAC and WAC RCAF squadrons and was far more numerous than was the Catalina (224 *vs* 30 aircraft on strength). Armed with depth charges and machine guns, EAC Cansos scored well against the U-boat. However, there were no WAC Catalina/Canso engagements with the Japanese. Shown is Catalina Z2138 of 116 (BR) Squadron. Formed in June 1941, 116 BR flew both PBYs side-by-side, until the Catalina was withdrawn in August 1943. The squadron also served at Botwood, Gander, Shelburne and Sydney. 116 BR finished its war having made three U-boats attacks, but claimed no victories. (DND PL5951)

A Gallery of HWE Coast Defence Aircraft

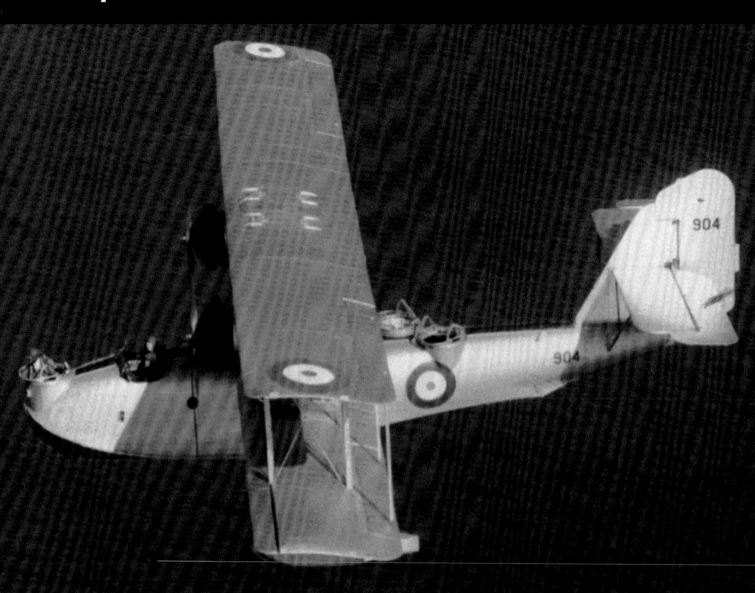

One of 4 (GR) Squadron's "combat ready" Canadian Vickers Vancouvers, the type with which the squadron carried out its first operation of WWII on September 12, 1939. The nose and rear positions of 904 are fitted with machine gun mounts, and a small bomb load could be carried underwing. Happily, the Vancouvers soon were replaced by Stranraers. (LAC PA133577)

Another obsolete type that kept on paying dividends into the early war years was the Northrop Delta. Here is 672/YO-C of 8 (BR) Squadron during its sojourn at North Sydney, Nova Scotia. Delta 672 served from February 1937 to November 1941, working alongside 8 BR's Bolingbrokes on coastal patrol duties. (Robert Finlayson Col.)

Much solid work was done by the RCAF's Blackburn Sharks. They flew many early war missions on the West Coast, then were kept busy with such duties as towing targets for naval vessels. Shark 514 of 6 (BR) Squadron is shown during torpedo training at Sea Island in August 1939. On September 5, it crashed while taking off on floats, while carry a heavy war load. Happily, the crew escaped. (LAC PA100023)

One of the RCAF's solid if obsolete types early in the war was the Supermarine Stranraer flying boat, 40 of which were on strength beginning in November 1938. In the first view, taken on December 18, 1937, a good dozen men of 4 (GR) Squadron are struggling to secure Stranraer 908 for beaching – a chilly and risky business by the looks of it. Then, four "Strannies" at their moorings in Dartmouth on May 21, 1939. (LAC PA133570, PA133572)

Stranraer 907 of 5 GR at Dartmouth with its floats and hull well iced-up. Then, 937 patrolling. Nose and tail machine guns are evident, as are underwing depth charges. (LAC PA133571, DND PL9601)

Besides the Stranraer, the RCAF was fortunate to have the Lockheed Hudson to counter the U-boat on the East Coast early in the war. Hudson 786 was taken on strength in March 1940 and issued to 11 (BR) Squadron. (DND RE20601-1)

An unknown RCAF Hudson in a maritime setting. Then, a common sight at war's end – a scrap yard jammed with surplus aircraft. Nearest is Hudson AM884, while BW643 is side-on beyond. BW643 had been a trainer at 7 OTU, Debert, but AM884? It apparently never was on RCAF strength, but is known to have served in the UK on several units. How it ended in a Canadian scrap yard is unknown. (CANAV Col.)

The Bolingbroke was another stop-gap anti-submarine resource at the beginning of WWII. Quickly replaced by Hudsons, Venturas, etc. on the East Coast, it served longer on the West Coast. Shown is 9055/SZ-R of 147 (BR) Squadron. Formed in November 1942 at Tofino, 147 flew 560 operations before disbanding in March 1944. Along the way it lost four Bolingbrokes and 11 crew. (Ventura Memorial Flight Association)

Just before splash-down – 4 BR Canso 9771 in BC waters. On the nose is painted a stork slinging a bomb (instead of a baby). This Canso, built by Boeing in Vancouver, also served on 160 Squadron. Since it was SOS in December 1944, it may have suffered some accident or been retired due to corrosion or other technical issue. (DND PL21933)

RCAF Canso 9706, which joined the RCAF in November 1941, served on 117 Squadron at North Sydney. The RCAF had three basic versions of the PBY-5: the "Catalina" flying boat (30 received via the British government), 7 other "Canso" flying boats paid for by Ottawa, and something like 217 amphibians known as the "Canso A". (Ross Lennox Col.)

Farmer George Ventress of Brighton, Ontario purchased dozens of war surplus aircraft from locations all across the southern part of the province. Included were B-24s at $40.00 per aircraft. He also had several Cansos, including "Sad Sack" (Canso 9829, wartime service with 116 Sqn), which he converted into a house boat and sailed from Brighton harbour on Lake Ontario. "Sad Sack" eventually was acquired by Ray Cox in Washington state. There, parts of it were used to restore a former US Navy PBY-5A N84857, which had had its nose section damaged in a fatal accident. Hugh A. Halliday photographed "Sad Sack" in May 1964. In April 1964 he also photographed this derelict PBY-5A location not certain, but thought to be on the George Ventress farm.

Atlantic Canada weather conditions often impeded normal operations. Here some sturdy 10 BR ground crew battle to get Liberator 590/G ready for some flying. 590/G met an untimely end – it was one of five Liberators destroyed in a hangar fire at Gander on June 4, 1944. (DND NA-A88)

Liberator BZ734 of 10 (BR) Squadron (later re-numbered 599) taxies at Gander. This aircraft served from June 1943, when 10 BR was converting from the Digby. It flew 10 BR's final mission of the war, escorting a convoy on May 26, 1945. It was sold for scrap in August 1946. The intense involvement of 10 BR in the war effort is seen by its accomplishments – 3 U-boats sunk, by the number of hours flown – 38,307 of which just 7976 were non-operational, and by its honours and awards: DFC – 24, AFC – 6, GM – 1, BEM – 3, MiD – 33. (CANAV Col.)

In July 1943, 11 BR converted from Hudsons to Liberators. Although 11 BR recorded 10 U-boat sightings and 8 attacks, no victories resulted. One dramatic 11 BR incident involved Liberator 3728/J skippered by F/L Allan A. Early on February 28, 1945. While on convoy duty, Early had trouble with No.2 engine. He turned for base (Dartmouth) but, after passing Sable Island, found that he could not maintain altitude once No.1 engine failed. He returned to Sable Island to make a flawless landing on a beach, ending in shallow water. The local people assisted and next day a Canso flew the crew home. In July 1945, F/L Early received an MiD, the citation for which mentions his good show on Sable Island. (Canada's Wings Col.)

One of the most dramatic photos showing the death of a U-boat at the hands of the RCAF. (RCAF)

U-190 at the jetty in St. John's, Newfoundland after its surrender on May 8, 1945. A Type IXC launched in June 1942, *U-190* sank one freighter (MV *Empire Lakeland*) , then one naval vessel (the minesweeper HMCS *Esquimalt* on April 16, 1945). *U-190* was used for target practice and sunk by the RCN on October 21, 1947. (DND PL117120)

Lockheed PV-1 Venturas on the flightline at 34 OTU, Pennfield Ridge, New Brunswick. This is where RCAF and other Commonwealth crews were trained before going to overseas Ventura squadrons, or Home War Establishment units. Ventura FN974 is nearest. (via Kenneth I. Swartz)

A flight of 115 Squadron Venturas off the BC coast. 115 disbanded at Tofino in August 23, 1944 – part of the general downsizing of Western Air Command, as Japan's offensive might waned in the Pacific. (via Kenneth I. Swartz)

Ventura 2207 was aircraft "Q" of 145 Squadron, Torbay. (RCAF)

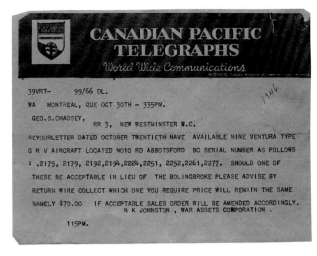

After the war many WAC Venturas ended their days at Vulcan, Alberta. Seven can be seen in this view. Then, the telegram sent by War Assets Disposal Corporation to George S. Chadsey of Montreal, offering him 9 Venturas for sale at $70.00 each. (Ventura Memorial Flight Association)

Ventura 2195 was taken on RCAF strength on June 14, 1943. During the war it served 149 Squadron. Postwar, 2195 served briefly as an RCAF bombing and gunnery trainer, then was SOS in March 1951. Next, it was sold to Spartan Air Services, becoming CF-FAV. On August 14, 1953 it crash landed in the bush near Yellowknife, NWT. In 1987 Northwest Territorial Airlines pilot Tony Jarvis began organizing to recover CF-FAV. To support this sophisticated project, he established the Ventura Memorial Flight Association. Using a 447 Squadron Chinook helicopter from Namao, on June 18, 1988 the aircraft was slung out to Yellowknife. While the wings and other components reached Edmonton aboard an NWT Air Hercules, the fuselage was barged and trucked south. Since then, Ventura 2195/CF-FAV has had a safe home in the Edmonton Aviation Heritage hangar, where restoration to flying status continued in the 2000s. (Ventura Memorial Flight Association)

Hurricanes and Kittyhawks served on coastal duties from Torbay to Tofino. These of 135 Squadron are seen at Terrace, BC. 135 had formed under S/L E.M. "Ed" Reyno at Mossbank, Saskatchewan in June 1942, but soon moved across the mountains to Patricia Bay. It was part of RCAF "Y" Wing at Annette Island in the second half of 1943, then operated at Terrace through the winter of 1943-44 defending Prince Rupert and escorting 149 Squadron's Venturas. In March 1944, 135 returned to "Pat Bay" and converted to Kittyhawks. Its war record included 3542 operational sorties. In training and "on ops" it lost 9 aircraft and 7 pilots. Hurricane 5406 (nearest) was not SOS until June 1947. In its brief RCAF career it flew a mere 311:20 hours. (Ventura Memorial Flight Association)

Canso 9750 served on 116 and 161 BR squadrons, then had a long career as CF-DIL, working on the DEW Line in the 1950s and as a fire bomber in Canada and Spain. It later was N314CT in California and in 2008 reportedly was N206M with Black Cat Aviation in Indiana. (CANAV Col.)

EAC Canso WAG

Born in 1913 in Cobalt, Ontario, James E. Victor Banning grew up in Timmins, where he worked for Hollinger Gold Mines. Having enlisted in January 1941, he completed his indoctrination at 1 Manning Depot satellite at Picton, east of Toronto, and at 4 MD in Quebec City. He then attended wireless school (Guelph) and did bombing and gunnery training (Jarvis). Placing 15th in a class of 29 at Jarvis, he was assessed as "An attentive, hard-working student with an average sense of responsibility." From Jarvis, Sgt Banning was posted in December 1941 to 10 (BR) Squadron as a WAG on anti-submarine Digbys. In the spring of 1942 he transferred to Cansos at 162 Squadron in Yarmouth, his first patrol (May 1) being 17.3 hours. For May he crewed on 15 missions for 99:30 hours. On January 7, 1943 P/O Banning was badly injured when Canso 9737 (S/L N.E. Small, skipper) crashed near Gander. Recovered from this, he returned to 162 to fly many more gruelling Canso missions. On January 1, 1944 P/O Banning was awarded an MiD for his solid performance – 900 hours flown on 65 sorties. The MiD noted: "This officer ... has been outstanding in his devotion to duty, and the efficient manner in which he has carried out all duties assigned to him has been an inspiration to all ranks."

In February 1944 Banning was in Iceland with 162, flying his first patrol from there on February 10 (13:50 hours). Sadly, on April 6 he died along with F/O J.R. Rankine (age 22 from Winnipeg) and FSgt Richard B. Bamford (age 20 from St. John, New Brunswick) when Canso 9809 crashed at sea (F/L C. Cunningham survived). On June 27, 1944 Banning

was posthumously awarded the DFC. The citation mentioned his tigerish spirit in returning to operations "with undiminished enthusiasm" as soon as he had recovered from the Gander crash, then how: "During a recent attack on an enemy submarine this officer, who was manning the front guns of his aircraft, by his accurate firing, stopped the return fire from the U-boat. He has at all times displayed skill, courage and great devotion to duty."

"We Will Hunt Them Even Through the Lowest Deeps"

The fighting record of 162 Squadron is noteworthy: 5 U-boats sunk, one shared, one damaged. Included in its honours is a posthumous Victoria Cross awarded to F/L David E. Hornell, lost after a daring attack on *U-1225*. This story, along with other 162 victories, is covered in *The*

Royal Canadian Air Force at War 1939-1945 and *Canada's Air Force at War and Peace*, Vol.2. The squadron lived up to its motto "We Will Hunt Them Even Through the Lowest Deeps", but suffered much in the process, operational losses being 6 Cansos and 34 crew, with a further 3 Cansos lost with 8 killed non-operationally. Honours and awards at war's end were: VC – 1, DSO – 2, MBE – 2, DFC – 16, AFC – 3, DFM – 4, BEM – 1, MiD – 21. On June 25, 1944 Air Chief Marshal Sir Sholto Douglas, AOC-in-Chief, Coastal Command, commended 162 Squadron in a letter to Air Marshal Leckie:

I would like to express to you my appreciation of the fine work that 162 Squadron have been doing ... In 750 flying hours they have attacked and sunk no less than 4 U-boats ... I am also much impressed by the spirit of the aircrews,

Captured in this highly-retouched photo is the final rescue of David Hornell's crew by HSL 2507. (DND PL-25505)

who appear to be quite undaunted by the odds they are facing. These are considerable, as evidenced by the loss of three aircraft in the process. I am glad to say the I have just heard that the crew which was shot down in yesterday's attack [Hornell] has been taken aboard a HSL.

F/L Robert E. MacBride typifies the outstanding airmen of 162 Squadron. Born in 1919 and raised in Woodstock, New Brunswick, he completed his education at the University of New Brunswick. In pre-war years he worked in forestry until enlisting in January 1941. Following the usual preliminaries (MacBride placed 2nd in his class of 159 at ITS), he passed through 3 EFTS at London, placing 6th among 36 student pilots. Here he was favourably assessed with reservation: "A capable pilot. Slight inferiority complex. Very steady and conscientious. Aerobatics fair, instrument flying good." MacBride won his wings at 6 SFTS, Dunnville in December 1941. This was typical of the times for the BCATP – taking in a raw recruit, then pinning on his wings in less than a year.

From Dunnville, MacBride trained for coastal operations at 1 (GR) School, Summerside. This was demanding, but MacBride excelled, his classroom marks

U-342 under attack by F/O Tommy Cooke and crew in Canso 9767. A few minutes later the U-boat sank with all 51 crew. (RCAF)

being: DR Navigation (84/100 and 261/300), Astro Navigation (85/100), Compasses and Instruments (114/200), Meteorology (104/200), Signals (80/100), Reconnaissance (180/200), Coding

(83/100), Ship Recognition (148/200), Photography (83/100), Visual Signals (Pass). His chief ground school instructor noted: "This pupil has worked hard throughout the course and has acquired a sound knowledge of G.R. subjects." Most 1 (GR) School graduates ended in RAF Coastal Command, but MacBride went to EAC in March 1942 – first to 10 (BR) Squadron, then to 162, where he first flew on October 8 from Yarmouth. (The transition from Anson to Canso was done on squadron – EAC pilots at this time did not have the luxury of a flying boat OTU.)

On June 3, 1944 F/L MacBride and his seven crewmates were patrolling from Wick, Scotland in Canso 9816 when they encountered a U-boat at 63°59'N, 01°37'W. MacBride attacked with four DCs. These exploded perfectly, raising the submarine momentarily from the water. The vessel sank, leaving a few survivors in the water. MacBride was awarded the DFC for this effort, the citation noting: "Despite intense ... anti-aircraft fire [MacBride] pressed home an excellent attack and the U-boat was probably destroyed." This vessel later was identified as *U-477*, a Type VIIC

A 162 (BR) Squadron Canso sets off on an anti-submarine patrol from its base at Reykjavik, Iceland. It carries the standard offensive load of 4 x 250-lb depth charges. (DND PL33839)

schnorkel boat. Commanded by Karl-Joachim Jenssen, it had been on its first patrol and had no victories. All 51 aboard were lost.

On June 30 MacBride and crew again were on the prowl. This time they encountered a U-boat at 63°28'N, 00°43'W. MacBride attacked, his DCs hung up, and his Canso suffered considerable damage from defensive fire. His wireless operator, however, contacted an 86 Squadron Liberator under F/O E.M. Smith, who homed on the U-boat, by then at 63°27'N, 00°50'W. Smith attacked with six DCs, which immediately destroyed the target, later confirmed as *U-478*. Commanded by Rudolf Rademarcher, it had been on its first patrol and had no victories. All 52 crew were lost. Of this incident, a Coastal Command document later noted of MacBride's effort: "Aircraft came down to attack and met violent flak from target... fire was returned and strikes seen on conning tower. At 300 yards aircraft was hit on port wing. Attack was made at 45 degrees from starboard beam to port bow, but depth charges failed to release. Aircraft then circled and homed Liberator E/86 ..."

F/L MacBride last flew with 162 on September 2, 1944. His EAC record totalled 148 sorties for 1505:15 flying hours. In October he was promoted to squadron leader. He was released from the service in September 1945, but re-entered the RCAF in 1946 and by 1951 was W/C MacBride. From June to September 1956 he converted to the CF-100 at North Bay. Even though he was an old Canso pilot used to flying at 150 mph, he excelled on jets, one assessment describing him as, "An extremely capable pilot who carries out all instrument requirements with ease and confidence. CF-100 conversion presented no difficulties. Aircraft handling and airmanship were of top-notch calibre... a well above average all-weather pilot with no apparent weakness." MacBride took command of 419 Squadron at North Bay in September 1956, then led his squadron to its NATO home at RCAF Station Baden-Soellingen, West Germany. Leaving here in December 1958, he was promoted to group captain. He served in NORAD at North Bay until taking command of 2 (F) Wing at Grostenquin, France in August 1961. On July 29, 1963 G/C MacBride died of natural causes.

F/O James M. McRae and *U-715*

On June 13, 1944 F/O James M. McRae and crew of 162 Squadron sank *U-715*, but were themselves shot down in the U-boat's dying moments. In 2010 Jim McRae looked back on the most dramatic day of his tour.

There was a feeling of anticipation aboard Canso 9816 as it taxied out at Wick in northern Scotland on the morning of June 13, 1944. Today our CO, W/C Bill Chapman, was in the left seat so it was different, somehow, since that was usually my seat as skipper –

today I was in the co-pilot's seat. By this time, our crew had been together since leaving Yarmouth in January 1944 – we had over 500 hours under our belts. Today we felt confident as we set out to search an area some 200 miles north of the Shetland Islands, but there was added anticipation, for just two days earlier F/O Larry Sherman had sunk U-980. On patrol again today, Larry had sent out another sighting report, but hadn't not been heard from since.

This Canso for this operation had earned its baptism of fire ten days earlier, when F/L MacBride attacked and sank U-477. Intense flack had been

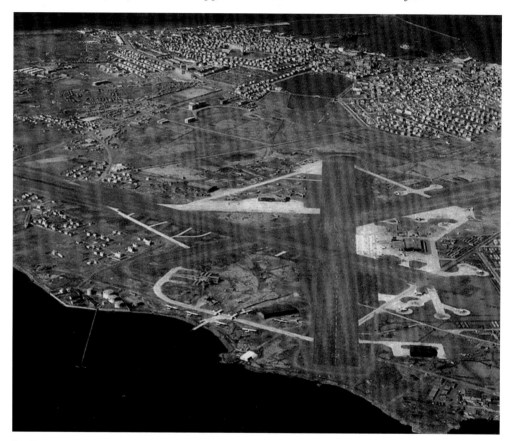

Reykjavik airfield in 1945 during 162 Squadron's era. The squadron hangar is at the lower right. (Below) The hangar close up. (all, J.M. McRae Col.)

Jim McRae's first crew with whom he flew to Reykjavik when 162 moved there in January 1944 (at that time operational control changed from Eastern Air Command to RAF Coastal Command). Standing are Paul Presidente (pilot), Harry Leatherdale (FE), Jim McRae (skipper), Frank Reed (WAG), Dave Waterbury (nav). In front are Joe Bergevin (WAG), Bob Cromarty (FE) and Gerry Staples (WAG). Leatherdale, Reed and Staples did not survive the action with *U-715*.

Crew of Canso 9813 June 13, 1944

W/C Cecil G.W. "Bill" Chapman (pilot),	DSO awarded
F/O James M. McRae (pilot),	DFC awarded
F/O Dave J. Waterbury (navigator),	DFC awarded
WO2 Joseph J.C. Bergevin (WOP),	DFC awarded
WO2 Frank K. Reed (WAG),	KIA
FSgt Harry C. Leatherdale (FE),	KIA
FSgt Gerald F. Staples (WAG),	KIA
Sgt Robert F. Cromarty (FE),	DFM awarded

encountered, but 9816 had not been hit. Leaving Wick, we skirted the Orkney Islands and the British Naval base at Scapa Flow, flew along the west side of the Shetlands and set course from the RAF seaplane base at Sullom Voe. The crew took up positions. FSgt Gerry Staples manned the twin .303 Browning machine guns in the nose. Sgt Bob Cromarty was in the flight engineer's position and WO2 Joseph Bergevin was at the radio. FSgt Harry Leatherdale and WO2 Frank Reed took up lookout positions in the blisters each armed with a pair of twin machine guns. F/O Dave Waterbury was our navigator.

Flying at 1000 feet over a relatively calm sea, we had not yet reached the search area when I spotted something off the starboard bow several miles away. Maybe it was just a patch of seaweed, a school of porpoises, or a wave. A closer look using binoculars put us straight – it was a schnorkel and periscope leaving a feathery wake. Action stations was sounded. Chapman turned in the direction indicated, Waterbury plotted a position and Bergevin sent out a sighting report. I turned to confirm the settings on the bomb control panel on the bulkhead behind Bergevin. Chapman had not yet spotted the periscope and I feared that the U-boat may have submerged. The Winco picked up the binoculars again and there it was, a little more to starboard. We started descending to drop our depth charges from 50 feet. I picked up the hand held K20 camera and started taking pictures.

The Winco continued the run in from a few degrees off the submarine's port bow and dropped our four depth charges in a perfect straddle. Holding course for several seconds, he activated the rear facing camera to get a series of pictures our attack. Waterbury had proceeded to the blisters to use the second K20. As we passed over the U-boat, the conning tower railings could be seen just breaking the surface at the bottom of the swell.

Climbing back to 1000 feet, Chapman turned to port and circled at a safe distance. From the plumes of the exploding depth charges, the U-boat surfaced and started a slow turn to starboard. From its original westerly heading, it was facing north, then slowly stopped and started to go down by the bow. The conning tower disappeared and the stern emerged at a steep angle with screws and rudder visible. Now was the time to get pictures to confirm our attack. Closing in from the north, we dove in on a run similar to the original attack, passing directly over the sub at high speed to get more pictures with the rear-facing camera. Some of the U-boat crew could be seen in the water.

We turned, climbed again to about 1000 feet and circled to make another run from the same direction. The option to fly alongside at low level, thereby giving us the best possible view of what was happening while using the K20, was not taken. At some time in the excitement the intercom had become u/s as though one of the microphones had stuck on. Communication among us became next to impossible. Chapman was very intent on what he was doing and there was little opportunity to confer on tactics.

The survivors from the *U-715* action (except for the CO): Bob Cromarty, Jim McRae, Dave Waterbury and Joe Bergevin.

The stern of the U-boat was getting lower in the water and finally disappeared – it appeared that the vessel had gone down for the last time. We continued our run-in, not realizing that there might still be some danger. Then the guns on the conning tower resurfaced. At the very last moment Chapman saw the puffs of the antiaircraft fire and pulled quickly up. Still using the K20, I suddenly found the camera down in my lap. I had just breathed a sigh of relief, thinking the danger had passed, when we were hit. Flying directly over the sub, 9816 was a point-blank target. Our port engine began pouring black smoke. Attempts to feather the propeller failed and it was windmilling. Chapman had enough speed to reach 1000 feet then, realizing that we could not hold altitude very long, he set course for the Shetlands. 9816 was gradually losing altitude, even with full power on the good engine.

Cromarty lowered the wing tip floats for landing, then we struck the top of a wave and bounced into the air. Another mile or two was made before we hit again – a heavy jolt and flying speed was lost. Chapman and I held the control column back as 9816 settled, this time more gently, just at the top of the swell. We were safe on the water and no one was injured, but the aircraft was flooding from a hole in the hull. The crew launched our two 5-man dinghies from the port and starboard blisters and we began loading them. Included were our two metal cases of survival gear and a Gibson Girl emergency radio, the two K20s, the magazine from the rear facing camera, a very pistol and some cartridges. There was time for us to don our ditching suits. Bergevin remained at the radio as long as possible, ensuring that our emergency message got out. The sea remained relatively calm with a long, gentle swell.

All seemed to be going very well when the port dinghy exploded. Everything in it was lost. Almost immediately the starboard dinghy was holed somehow and rapidly deflated. It was not possible to keep enough air in it to hold more than two people, so we had to jettison all other equipment. The dinghies had unfortunately been fitted with extra large CO2 bottles, and as the cold gas warmed up, the pressure was too great. The aircraft was by now so low in the water that just the top of the wing and the tail

Canso 11090 "X" of 162 Squadron runs up before a patrol. Note that standard war load of four depth charges underwing. Postwar, former 162 Sqn Canso 11090 became CF-OBK with the OPAS. In 1946-47 it sprayed budworm-infested forests in Ontario, then went to Brazil where it operated as PP-PCW. Some time in the 1960s, it reportedly met with a fatal accident. (J.M. McRae, CANAV Cols.)

were visible. Soon the wing submerged and we watched as the tail slowly disappeared. We were alone except for one sea gull which appeared from nowhere and seemed to welcome the company as it swam a few feet away.

From then on our difficulties came one after another. Our rubberized emersion suits were not as waterproof as expected. Frigid water began seeping in, rising inside the legs. Our plan to keep changing positions in the dinghy became next to impossible, due to the weight of the water trapped in our suits and the flabbiness of the damaged dinghy. Hypothermia began taking effect on some of us. Then a Sunderland appeared and we were heartened when a message was flashed that help was on the way. Shortly, an ASR Warwick carrying an airborne lifeboat arrived. After a run to drop smoke floats to determine wind, the lifeboat was released. For a moment it appeared that it would drop right onto our dinghy, but it drifted downwind about 175 feet away. Normally, the dinghy would have drifted toward us but, with most of us in the water hanging on to the dinghy, the lifeboat was drifting away. F/O Waterbury then decided to swim for it. He removed his heavy clothing, put on his mae west and began. Unfortunately, he discovered the lifeboat holed – its deck was awash and only the two inflated portions at bow and stern were above water. The oar locks

proved useless, so he had to paddle the heavy boat from the stern.

By this time, Leatherdale, who had been hit by fire from U-715, had weakened – there was nothing we could do and we lost him. Meanwhile, we could only see Waterbury when both he and our dinghy were at the top of a swell. Progress was slow, but he finally reached us, but was by then exhausted. Now began the difficult process of getting everyone out of the water and into the lifeboat. Staples and Reed were in very bad shape and it was with great difficulty that they were brought aboard. The legs of their immersion suits were cut off to release the water and they were kept as much as possible above the surface. A second Warwick dropped a 10-man dinghy, but it fell too far away, so another was dropped. This one was retrieved and, although damaged, was of help in keeping us out of the water. We were also able to mount the lifeboat mast, which gave us something to hang on to. From then it was just a matter of doing everything possible for Reed and Staples and await rescue.

At last the Warwick began approaching at low level from the south and it became evident that it was directing a rescue launch. That was very a welcome sight and soon was alongside. Taken aboard after eight hours at sea, we were given dry clothing, but efforts to *revive Staples and Reed failed. The trip to Lerwick in the Shetlands was uneventful. We were hospitalized for a couple of days and debriefed while there. We learned that our attack had been successful and that some of the U-boat crew had also been rescued. We later were flown back to Wick in a Ventura and on return to Reykjavik had some leave. U-715 was the fourth German submarine sunk by 162 Squadron. Unfortunately, the desire for pictures to confirm the results of the attack led to the loss of Canso 9816, and the unserviceability of the dinghies due to over-inflation, to the tragic loss of three of our crew.*

June 13, 1944 proved doubly tragic for 162 Squadron. Also on patrol that day, F/O Larry Sherman (age 22 from Yarmouth, Nova Scotia) and crew in Canso 9842 encountered a U-boat off Norway at about 64°10'N 00°. The submariners shot the Canso into the sea. Three crew died in the initial moments and four others eventually perished in the liferafts. FSgt J.E. Roberts (WOp) of Toronto was picked up by a Norwegian fishing boat. Hospitalized, he spent the rest of the war as a POW. Those lost besides Sherman were F/O Gordon W. Besley (pilot, age 21 from Toronto), F/O John L. Harrison (nav, age 22 from Winnipeg), F/O Francis W. Lawrence (WAG, age 25 from Falmouth, Nova Scotia), F/O Ralph R. Ward (WAG, age 20 from Victoria Vale, Nova Scotia), WO2 Frederick R. Dreger (FE, age 27 from Woodley, Saskatchewan) and FSgt Magnus A. Gislason (WAG, age 21 from Winnipeg). On July 11, F/O Sherman was awarded a posthumous DFC for his action against *U-980*.

The funeral December 24, 1944 in Reykjavik of the crew of 162 Canso 11061. Returning in poor weather from a patrol, it flew into a ridge a few miles from base. Lost were WO2 Earl R. Attree (FE, age 27 from Prince Albert, Saskatchewan), FSgt Donald G. Bewley (FE, age 20 from Winnipegosis, Manitoba), F/L Edward P. Oakford (skipper, age 23 from Hythe, Alberta), F/L Thomas J. Pettigrew (WAG from Jacquet River, New Brunswick), F/O Frank W. Latham (WAG from Moose Jaw), WO1 Joseph N. MacDonald (nav, age 26 from Montreal), F/L Gerald P. McKenna (pilot, age 22 from Milford, Ontario), P/O Hymie Steinberg (WAG from Winnipeg). Then, the fellows' well-tended graves today – a bleak, wintry scene replaced by a summery one. (all, J.M. McRae Col.)

U-Boat Record: 162 Squadron

Date	Skipper	U-Boat	Results
17-04-44	F/O T.C. Cooke	U-342	sunk
03-06-44	F/L MacBride	U-477	sunk
11-06-44	F/L Sherman	U-980	sunk
13-06-44	W/C Chapman	U-715	sunk*
24-06-44	F/L Hornell	U-1225	sunk*
30-06-44	F/L MacBride	U-478	sunk‡
04-08-44	F/O Marshall	U-300	damaged

* Canso shot down
‡ shared with 86 Sqn

On September 12, 2009 Canso CF-PQL (11084 of 162 Squadron) visited Yarmouth for a Centennial of Flight airshow. Jim McRae was on hand to enjoy a flight. Here he looks over the cockpit he once knew like the back of his hand.

While RCAF Cansos, Hudson, Liberators, etc. covered the seas from Tofino to Terrace and from Yarmouth to Reykjavik, the USAAC and US Navy were involved in the same war, sometimes over the same waves. American B-17s, Catalinas, Mariners, Venturas, etc. operated from the Aleutians to Newfoundland and Iceland, while the eastern Atlantic was largely covered as far as Iceland (even Greenland) by RAF Coastal Command with PBYs, Liberators and Sunderlands. These US Navy Catalinas were seen in 1942 while on a stop-over at Annette Island, Alaska. (Murray Castator Col.)

Grubby-looking Canso 9769 in a summer setting, location unknown. This was aircraft "N" during 162 Squadron's bloody yet victorious Iceland era – January 1944 to June 1945. In those few months 9754, 9767, 9816 and 9842 of 162 all were involved in decisive U-boat actions. (CANAV Col.)

An unknown HWE Canso at an RCAF Station Edmonton open house at war's end. Note the underwing radar antennae. (Leslie Corness/ CANAV Col.)

Their U-boat hunting days over, many war weary Cansos continued postwar. The last in the RCAF retired in 1962, but civil Cansos continued in northern transportation and fire fighting. Here is postwar RCAF SAR Canso 11084 at Trenton on May 28, 1960. Later it served for years as Quebec government fire bomber CF-PQL. (Left) In 2010 it was CF-VIG with the Canadian Warplane Heritage and dedicated to F/L David Hornell, VC. (Larry Milberry, J.W. Jones)

The Cansos of 162 (BR) Squadron*

Formed at Yarmouth, Nova Scotia on May 19, 1942, 162 (BR) Squadron served at Yarmouth, then at Reykjavik, Iceland. It disbanded at Sydney, Nova Scotia on August 7, 1945. This list is of the individual PBY-5A Cansos on 162 BR strength. A few notes tell of U-boat action and losses. Some of these Cansos served in the postwar RCAF, but many were sold after the war by the War Assets Disposal Corporation, the federal institution tasked with getting rid of all military war surplus equipment and supplies. Usually, such Cansos were purchased by war surplus specialists such as the Babb Corporation of New York, which then re-marketed their spoils to local scrap dealers or air operators, or to overseas military and commercial entities. The best

source covering the histories of former 162 BR Cansos is David Legge's superb book *Consolidated PBY Catalina: The Peacetime Record*.

Original aircraft of 162 BR: 9746, 9748, 9749 (later to France as F-BBCC) and 9750 (later CF-DIL) were delivered in May 1942; 9739 and 9740 (later to Colombia as HK-134) were loaned by 5 BR and operated only in June and July 1942.

On April 17, 1944 Canso 9767 sank *U-342* on a mission from Iceland. Postwar, 9767 was sold by the War Assets Disposal Corp. to Canadian Pacific Airlines, where it became CF-CRR. Here it is at Red Deer, Alberta on August 19, 1976, by which time it was a fire bomber with Avalon Aviation. In October 1998 CF-CRR flew the South Atlantic from Dakar to Natal, commemorating the French trans-Atlantic air mail of the 1930s. In 2010 it was in a museum at Orly Airport, Paris. (Larry Milberry)

Cansos originally operated by 162 Sqn from Reykjavik, Iceland:

9754	(aircraft P, sank *U-1225*, Hornell's aircraft, lost in this action)
9755	(R, later CF-CRV)
9759	(W, later Argentine Navy 0276)
9765	(J)
9766	(K, later to Indonesia as PK-CTC)
9767	(S, sank *U-342* 17-4-44, later CF-CRR)
9768	(M, later Argentine Navy 0239)
9769	(N, later to Colombia as HK-133)
9770	(Q, later to Colombia as C-34)
9772	(later 116 BR, damaged, became A510 instructional airframe)
9779	(D, later to Sweden as 47003)
9808	(O, later 116 BR)
9809	(V, later 116 BR, sank at sea 3-5-44)
9810	(V, later 116 BR, later to Sweden as 47001)
9841	(A, later Argentine Navy 0238)
9842	(B, sank *U-980* 11-6-44, aircraft shot down and lost in this action)

Canso replacement aircraft during 162 Squadron's Reykjavik period:

9763	(P, from 5 BR, later Argentine Navy 0263)
9777	(C, from 5 BR, later 161 BR, later to Brazil as PP-PCY)
9791	(Z, from 160 BR, later to France as F-BBCD)
9796	(G, from 160 BR, later 161 BR, later to Indonesia as PK-CTA)
9812	(E, from 160 BR, later to Indonesia as PK-CTB)
9816	(T, from 161, sank *U-477* 13-6-44, aircraft lost in this action)
9837	(B, from 161 BR, later CF-CRP)
9840	(U, from 161 BR, later to Danish Air Force as FM51)
11023	(E, from 160 BR, lost 23-7-45)

11033	(R, postwar RCAF, later CF-OFJ)
11034	(from 116 BR, later to Danish Air Force as FM53)
11039	(F, later to Danish Air Force as FM54)
11056	(Z, postwar RCAF, later CF-PQI)
11057	(H, from 116 BR)
11060	(L, postwar RCAF, later CF-NDJ)
11061	(L, from 116 BR, lost 19-12-44)
11062	(L, lost Foula Island, Shetlands 29-7-44)
11065	(Y, lost 20-1-45)
11066	(O, lost 3-4-45)
11067	(B, from 116 BR, postwar RCAF, later CF-NTL)
11074	(A, postwar RCAF, later CF-OWE)
11075	(L, from 116 BR, postwar RCAF)
11076	(lost 20-4-45, 11077 (J)
11081	(V)
11089	(C, postwar RCAF, later CF-PQO)
11090	(X, later CF-OBK)
11091	(G, postwar RCAF)
11092	(Q), 11093 (D, postwar RCAF, later CF-NJL)
11094	(U, postwar RCAF, later CF-NJE)
11095	(W, lost at Sea Island 19-7-55)
11096	(K, later CF-IHN)
11097	(M, later to Danish Air Force as FM55)
11098	(N, later CF-DIK)

*(chief sources: John Griffin, Sam Kostenuk, David Legg, Ragnar J. Ragnarsson)

Ex-162 BR Canso 11095 following a disastrous accident at Sea Island that killed both pilots and gravely injured another crewman. (Leslie Corness)

Former 162 BR Cansos that served in the postwar era. RCAF 11033 of 103 Rescue flight at Greenwood, Nova Scotia, was photographed at Trenton on July 1, 1961. It later was Newfoundland water bomber CF-OFJ. (Larry Milberry)

Another view of the famous CF-CRR, this time at Parry Sound, Ontario in October 1982. (Larry Milberry)

Canso CF-CRP in its postwar days with Canadian Pacific Airlines. Later with Eastern Provincial Airlines, then a water bomber with the Newfoundland government, it now resides in Gander with the North Atlantic Aviation Museum. (Robert Finlayson Col.)

In Postwar years, Canso 11098 of 162 Squadron became CF-DIK with Hollinger Ungava Transport, plying the airways and waters between Mont Joli and Knob Lake, Quebec. It was sunk (without injury) after a bad landing in the summer of 1953. (Harry Mochulsky)

RCAF Station Torbay

One of the first new RCAF coastal patrol bases of the war was near the tiny Newfoundland hamlet of Tor Bay, a few miles north of St. John's. A site of about 1350 acres was selected in November 1940 and immediately surveyed. McNamara Construction Co. from Ontario was contracted to build the station and soon had 450 men and much heavy equipment at work. Around the clock ground was levelled, bogs drained and rock blasted. As soon as the site was ready, hangars, barracks, runways, etc. began appearing. On October 18, 1941 the first aircraft touched down – three USAAC B-17s and an RCAF Digby destined elsewhere, but forced into Torbay by harsh weather.

The first RCAF personnel reached Torbay in November 1941. They faced a rough-and-ready situation, but each day brought improvements. The first aircraft officially to land were four Hudsons of 11 (BR) Squadron on detachment from Dartmouth. Conditions remained basic, toilets being outhouses, showers available only in St. John's, and sick bay comprising three cots. For aircraft maintenance, the only relief from the weather were some nose hangars and shacks. Yet, men made do and airplanes came and went on operations. Even in these early days Torbay was being watched. When a hangar collapsed under a load of snow, Germany's infamous propagandist, "Lord Haw Haw", reported this on Nazi radio. Tragedy struck on May 6, 1942 when, moments after takeoff, an 11 (BR) Squadron Hudson piloted by FSgt William F. Colville (age 25 of Bowmanville, Ontario) crashed, killing all eight aboard.

In June 1942 Torbay welcomed its first resident flying unit – 125 (F) Squadron equipped with Hurricanes. A Lysander also arrived on Army co-operation duties. F/O Pettam was the full complement for the Lysander unit. Also in June, the first Americans arrived. Meanwhile, barrack blocks, the main administration building, drill hall, theatre, messes and other facilities steadily were opening and life was becoming normal. The first draft of some 30 RCAF WDs arrived in the summer of 1942.

Two ordinary 1943 snapshots showing historic Newfoundland centres: Tor Bay from an overlooking pasture, and St. John's in a low-level aerial looking across the harbour and out into the Atlantic, where the U-boats lurked. (Gordon Webster Col.)

Torbay Resident Units 1941 - 1945

Squadron	Aircraft	Period
5 (BR) Squadron	Canso	April 1943 - August 1944
10 (BR) Squadron	Liberator	June - August 1945
11 (BR) Squadron	Hudson	November 1941 - May 1942
		October 1943 - June 1944
113 (BR) Squadron	Ventura	June - August 1944
125 (F) Squadron	Hurricane	June 1942 - June 1943
128 (F) Squadron	Hurricane	June 1943 - March 1944
160 (BR) Squadron	Canso	August 1944 - June 1945

Liberator BZ725 589/B (formerly USAAF 42-40447) of 10BR in full Eastern Air Command configuration. Its ASV (anti-surface vessel) radar was housed in the chin radome. 589/B was lost with all aboard in Gander Lake during weapons training on September 4, 1943. Killed were the CO, W/C John M. Young (pilot, age 31 from Oakville, Ontario), S/L John G. MacKenzie (pilot, age 34 from Lucknow, Ontario), F/O Victor E. Bill (pilot, age 22 from Winnipeg) and LAC Gordon Ward (fitter, age 19 from Toronto). (RCAF)

Torbay Honour Role

For a small outpost on the western edge of the Atlantic, Torbay suffered badly. The worst event took place in St. John's on December 12, 1942. At about 11:00 PM the Knight's of Columbus Hall, where a dance was underway, suddenly exploded in flames. Within minutes there was such a conflagration that fire fighters were helpless. Panic ensued and 110 of some 600 attending the dance lost their lives, 16 from Torbay: LAC Gomer C. Bellerive, age 22 of Montreal; AC1 Frank E. Burton, airframe mechanic, age 19 from Eden, Manitoba; AC2 Vincent Callery, age 26 from Deloro, Ontario; AC2 Roy B. Chapman, age 25 from Hamilton, Ontario; Cpl Roy H. Corner, aero engine mechanic, age 21 from Lac Vert, Saskatchewan; AC2 Joseph E. Cusak, age 19 from Saint John, New Brunswick; LAC Lester E. Hoggard, aero engine mechanic, age 22 from Redwing, Ontario; Sgt Wallace L. Ibbotson, age 26 from Sudbury, Ontario; AC1 Frederick A. Langley, airframe mechanic, age 23 from Oshawa, Ontario; LAC James A. Lawrence, age 19 from Glace Bay, Nova Scotia; LAC Joseph A.I.R. Legris, age 24 from Montreal; AC1 Joseph G.A. Lepine, age 29 from St. Boniface, Manitoba; AC2 Stuart C. Murray, wireless operator, age 22 from Verdun, Quebec; LAC Joseph F.R.A. Ouellet, age 25 from Ste. Anne de la Pocatière, Quebec; AC1 Frank J. Sawanda, age 21 from Niagara Falls, Ontario; and AC2 Ralph R. Sturgeon, airframe mechanic, age 21 from Bruce Mines, Ontario

Sgt George F.W. Lyon of Ottawa receives the George Medal in a May 26, 1944 ceremony at Gander. Sgt Lyon acted heroically during the Knights of Columbus fire in St. John. The citation to his decoration reads in part: "This airman ... realizing the possibility of jamming at exits, immediately ran to the building, smashed a window and climbed to the opening ... from where he shouted to people to come to the window... After being thrown to the ground ... and severely burned, he returned to another window and continued to aid others to safety until just before the collapse of the building... this airman, although badly burned and bleeding profusely from numerous cuts caused by broken glass, undoubtedly was responsible for the saving of at least ten lives." (DND C42456)

Loss Details: 11 (BR) Sqn Hudson 761

On May 6, 1942 Hudson 761 of 11 (BR) Squadron had just departed Torbay on a passenger run, when it crashed disastrously. Lost were: Sgt Monty H. Brothers, passenger, age 33 from Wroxeter, Ontario; FSgt William F. Colville, pilot, age 25 of Bowmanville, Ontario; LAC Smith E. Crymes, passenger, armourer, age 34 from Lonoke, Arkansas; F/L Rudolph I. Eherlichman, passenger, pilot, age 45 from Seattle, Washington; Cpl C.F. Else, passenger, airframe mechanic, age 24 from St. Thomas, Ontario; LAC N.C. Fleischman, passenger, age 21 from Hespeler, Ontario; F/L Joseph H.U. Leblanc, passenger, administration officer, age 25 from St. Joseph, New Brunswick and FSgt Harold F. Taylor, WAG, age 23.

125 Sqn Hurricane 1360

On August 27, 1942 Sgt Douglas B. Ruggles, age 21 from Kenora, Ontario, crashed while on a low-flying exercise.

145 (BR) Sqn Hudson BW449

On November 1, 1942 Hudson BW449 of 145 (BR) Squadron disappeared without a trace while on patrol. Lost were: Sgt Harry C. Beattie, wireless air gunner, age 22 from Montreal; P/O John R. Davies, pilot, age 25 from Victoria; FSgt Leonard Feldman, observer, age 19 from Windsor, Ontario and FSgt Lewis G. Robinson, WAG from Edmonton.

Some of the original officers on 125 Squadron at Torbay. In front are F/O MacDonald (Adj), S/L Norris (CO), F/L Harry Pattinson and F/O Lamont Parsons. Standing are P/Os Ivens, Guy Mott, John Gilmartin, Jack Boyle, Bud Young and Trujillo. Then, five 125 old timers at a 1980 Ottawa get-together: Bob Hayes, Guy Mott, Jack Boyle, Harry Pattinson and Sten Lundberg. (Pattinson Col.)

One of the RCAF's earliest Hudsons, 760 joined 11 BR Squadron at Dartmouth in September 1939. It later came to grief with 145 Squadron. (George Webster Collection)

145 (BR) Sqn Hudson 760

On January 28, 1943 Hudson 760 of 145 (BR) Squadron was on convoy patrol from Torbay. Lost were: P/O Roland R. Barnes, wireless operator air gunner, age 22 from Mattagami Heights, Ontario; FSgt Jack S. Boyer, navigator, age 22 from North Bay; FSgt Joseph E. Ouellette, air gunner, age 21 of Grand Falls, New Brunswick and F/O William F.C. Snow, pilot, age 28 from Vancouver.

145 (BR) Sqn Hudson 771

On February 14, 1943 Hudson 771 of 145 (BR) Squadron crashed near Dartmouth while on a navigation exercise. Lost were: F/L John T. Hook, passenger, signals officer, age 34 from Bridgeport, Connecticut; FSgt Robert C. Rolfe, WAG, age 30 from Huntingdon, Quebec; WO2 James R. Stick, WAG, age 24 from St. John's, Newfoundland; Lt Snell, passenger, US Army; F/O W.H. Thompson, passenger, signals officer, age 46 from Ottawa and P/O Thomas A.K. Watterson, pilot, age 30 from Manotick, Ontario.

145 (BR) Sqn Hudson 762

On July 9, 1943 145 (BR) Squadron Hudson 762 crashed while landing on one engine at Charlottetown. One crewman died – F/L Jack R. Hastie, pilot, age 24 from Webb, Saskatchewan.

In June 1942 the RCAF acquired its first of 286 Lockheed PV-1 Venturas for coastal operations. Two EAC squadrons (113 and 145), previously with Hudsons, re-equipped with Venturas in the spring of 1943. EAC Hurricane pilot George Webster photographed these unidentified Venturas at Dartmouth.

Torbay Aircraft Losses

Unit	Aircraft	Date	Fatalities
11 (BR) Sqn	Hudson 761	May 6, 1942	8
125 (F) Sqn	Hurricane 1320	August 27, 1942	1
145 (BR) Sqn	Hudson BW449	November 1, 1942	4
145 (BR) Sqn	Hudson 760	January 28, 1943	4
145 (BR) Sqn	Hudson 771	February 14, 1943	6
145 (BR) Sqn	Hudson 762	July 9, 1943	1
145 (BR) Sqn	Ventura 2169	August 5, 1943	4
145 (BR) Sqn	Ventura 2160	October 3, 1943	3
11 (BR) Sqn	Hudson BW719	December 18, 1943	5
11 (BR) Sqn	Hudson BW646	May 19, 1944	3
5 (BR) Sqn	Canso 9773	May 20, 1944	11

145 (BR) Sqn Ventura 2169

On August 5, 1943 Ventura 2169 of 145 (BR) Squadron crashed while taking off at Torbay. Lost were: WO2 Gerald C. Drynan, WAG, age 22 from London, Ontario; P/O Milton E. Griff, navigator, age 27 from Stratford, Ontario; WO2 Wilbur M. Lee, WAG, age 24 of Donalda, Alberta and P/O William R.G. Richardson, pilot, age 27 from Waterloo, Ontario.

145 (BR) Sqn Ventura 2160

On October 2, 1943 Ventura 2160 of 145 (BR) Squadron crashed while taking off at Torbay. Lost were: F/O Acton F. Daunt, pilot, age 25 from New Westminster, BC; S/L Richard L. Lee, pilot, age 33 from Centreville, New Brunswick; F/L Edward L. Robinson, DFC, pilot, age 33 from Vancouver. On October 30, 1942 Robinson and crew had sunk *U-658*.

11 (BR) Sqn Hudson BW719

On December 18, 1943 Hudson BW719 of 11 (BR) Squadron was on a night navigation exercise from Torbay. It failed to return to base, having crashed in a remote area in west central Newfoundland. Lost were: FSgt Clifford W. Bennett, navigator, age 27 from Saskatoon; F/O Clarence W. Mannett, navigator, age 23 from Halifax; F/O Stuart W. Morton, WOpAG, age 26 from Ailsa Craig, Ontario; F/O Hugh D. Pawson, pilot, age 24 from Sudbury,

Home War Establishment U-Boat Kills

Squadron	Date	Aircraft	Skipper	U-boat
113 (BR) Sqn	31-07-42	Hudson BW625	S/L N.E. Small	*U-754*
10 (BR) Sqn	30-10-42	Digby 757 "PB-K"	F/L D.F. Raymes	*U-520*
145 (BR) Sqn	30-10-42	Hudson 784	F/O E.L. Robinson	*U-658*
5 (BR) Sqn	04-05-43	Canso 9747 "W"	S/L B.H. Moffit	*U-209**
10 (BR) Sqn	19-09-43	Liberator 596 "A"	F/L R.F. Fisher	*U-341*
10 (BR) Sqn	26-10-43	Liberator 586 "A"	F/L R.M. Aldwinkle	*U-420*
162 (BR) Sqn	17-04-44	Canso 9767 "S"	F/O T.C. Cooke	*U-342*
162 (BR) Sqn	03-06-44	Canso 9816 "T"	F/L R.E. MacBride	*U-477*
162 (BR) Sqn	11-06-44	Canso 9842 "B"	W/C C.G.W. Chapman	*U-715*
162 (BR) Sqn	13-06-44	Canso 9842 "B"	F/O L. Sherman	*U-980*
162 (BR) Sqn	24-06-44	Canso 9754 "P"	F/L D.E. Hornell	*U-1225*

*Previously noted as U-630

Ontario and F/O Glenn E. Weir, pilot, age 22 from Victoria.

11 (BR) Sqn Hudson BW646

On May 19, 1944 Hudson BW646 of 11 (BR) Squadron disappeared on a training exercise off Newfoundland. Lost were: WO1 John H. Cowan, WAG, age 28 from Alexandria, Ontario; F/L Douglas J. Jones, pilot, age 26 from Toronto and WO Lawrence G. Martin, navigator, age 25 from Winnipeg.

5 (BR) Sqn Canso 9773

On May 20, 1944 Canso 9773 of 5 (BR) Squadron crashed on a weapons exercise over Conception Bay. Aboard, likely on a lark, were three non-RCAF passengers.

Lost were: F/L Alan G. Byers, pilot, age 28 from Montreal; FSgt Archibald B. Campbell, WAG, age 21 from Medicine Hat, Saskatchewan; WO1 Charles E.B. Clow, FE, age 29 from Emerald, PEI; Lt G. Garand, passenger; Capt P.E. Gauthier, passenger; FSgt Donald L. Herman, armourer, age 32 from Gimli, Manitoba; FSgt Bruce R. McGimsie, FE, age 23 from Guelph, Ontario; F/O Leo J. Murray, pilot, age 24 from Winnipeg; FSgt Walter F. Nolan, WAG, age 19 from Saint John, New Brunswick; F/O Joseph B. Poole, navigator, age 34 from Arnprior, Ontario and Leading Seaman H.A. Williams, passenger

Fighters in the HWE

Many RCAF fighter squadrons were formed to defend Canada – on the East Coast from the Germans and on the West Coast from the Japanese. Of these squadrons little has yet been written, although there is some history in print about RCAF Kittyhawk operations from Annette Island, near Ketchikan, Alaska and in the Aleutian Islands.

Hurricane OTU

Combat-seasoned aircrew often were posted at tour's end to instruct at training establishments. These were so-called "rest tours". A rest tour had various interpretations. Authorities occasionally posted someone off a squadron to some relatively quiet place as a form of discipline, should the man involved have put up some black. Sometimes a fellow who had cracked under pressure or was "on the edge" might be sent to some quiet place to calm his nerves for a bit. One of the worst such "rest tours" was for a gung-ho airman to be posted on public relations duties. This often meant being toured around Canada to pep rallies and war bond events to say encouraging things to the citizens, and be photographed with politicians and movie stars. When Buzz Beurling had such a tour foisted upon him, he did not try to

HWE Kittyhawk AK860/TM-A of 111 Squadron at Rockcliffe just before 111 moved west to Sea Island in December 1941. Under S/L K.A. Boomer, from July to October 1942 the squadron had a 12-plane detachment at Umnak Island in the Aleutians helping the Americans dislodge the Japanese in that god forsaken region. In action over Kiska on September 25, S/L Boomer shot down a Japanese fighter. (Lou Wise)

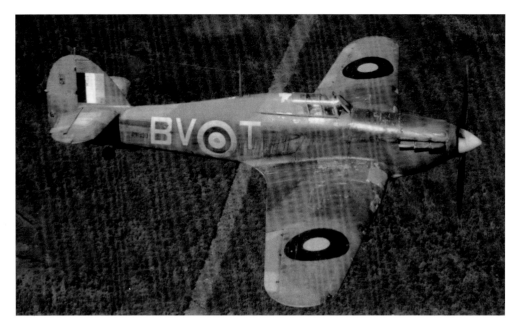

HWE Sea Hurricane Ib BW850/BV-T of 126 Squadron. Formerly assigned to the Royal Navy, BW850 was originally assigned to 118 (F) Squadron and stored at Dartmouth as a reserve aircraft for the RAF's Merchant Ship Fighter Unit (MSFU). Following a 'Cat D' crash in late 1942, it was reconstructed as a Mk. XIIA (retaining it's 8-gun wing) by CanCar and returned to 126 (F) of EAC. Formed at Dartmouth in April 1942 under Battle of Britain veteran, F/L A.M. "Art" Yuile, 126 had a prominent role in Eastern Air Command. It amassed nearly 15,000 flying hours by the time it disbanded in May 1945. Along the way it lost 9 aircraft and 7 personnel in flying accidents. (DND REA253-48)

conceal his disgust. Hugh Halliday describes this in his book *The Tumbling Sky*: "For him, to be non-operational was purgatory, but the tasteless idolatry showered upon him was hell itself." In the Montreal Forum Beurling was presented with a bouquet of roses for each of his many victories. This cheesed him off to no end and he soon arranged to return overseas.

Many experienced fighter pilots "got joed" with an instructional tour at 1 OTU, Bagotville. Established on July 20, 1942, this OTU provided instruction on the Hurricane to pilots fresh from service flying training schools. Having such a school within the BCATP, it was reasoned, took pressure off RAF AFUs and OTUs by getting sprog pilots into the RAF training system with some fighter savvy. Instructors on rest tours from overseas brought a bit of glamour to 1 OTU, sharing valuable experience with their students in the sky and over beers in the mess. Instructors who hadn't yet been overseas normally had solid instructional experience or may have been on one of the home-based fighter units.

One seasoned instructor at Bagotville was F/O Harry E. "Junior" Fenwick. Having spent his boyhood in Winnipeg and Sioux Lookout, he had enlisted late in 1940, trained on the Finch and

Sea Hurricanes and the Merchant Ship Fighter Unit

Established in May 1941 to counter the threat of long-range enemy aircraft to convoys, the RAF's Merchant Ship Fighter Unit put RAF pilots aboard rocket-catapult armed freighters. Seen in early June 1942, the two lower photos illustrate the process of unloading a Sea Hurricane Ia from CAM-Ship M/V *Eastern City* in Halifax harbour – in the words of W/C "Tim" Elkington, "an expensive way of doing it ... 13 rockets on launch make an awful racket!". These aircraft were then transported by scow to RCAF Stn Dartmouth while the CAM-Ship remained in port. These Sea Hurricanes would occasionally be flown for practice by RCAF stationed at Dartmouth. Distinguishable from later Sea Hurricanes by the absence of the tail-hook, the Sea Hurricane Ia was essentially a standard Mk.1 Hurricane equipped with catapult spools. The use of CAM-Ships was superseded by small "Jeep" carriers in July 1943. (All, W/C (Ret'd) J.F.D. (Tim) Elkington

A high level wartime aerial view of RCAF Station Bagotville in Quebec north of the rugged Laurentide mountains. Little wonder that few staff or students were thrilled at hearing that they were off to 1 OTU! (Bagotville Air Defence Museum via Richard Girouard)

Harvard, then went overseas. After his fighter course at 52 OTU, in February 1942 he joined 81 Squadron in North Africa. Here, his record on the Spitfire Mk.Vc was stellar: 4 e/a destroyed, 1 probable, 6 damaged (4-1-6). In February 1943 Fenwick was awarded a DFC. He tallied his final kill on April 23, 1943, then came his Bagotville tour. Like most such pilots, however, he would have been itching for more operations. So it happened that in May 1944 F/O Fenwick joined 401 Squadron at Tangmere, just in time for the Normandy campaign. On June 18 his squadron moved to the beachhead at B.4 Bény-sur-Mer. On the 21st Fenwick flew his final sortie – he was shot down fatally in Spitfire NH207 near B.6 Coulombs. Conflicting explanations for what happened include: "shot down by enemy ground fire", "shot down by our own anti-aircraft fire" and "shot down by a Thunderbolt". F/O Fenwick is buried in the Canadian cemetery at Bény-sur-Mer.

Also at Bagotville was F/L H.W. "Wally" McLeod, whose earlier Malta tour was legendary. Born in 1915 and raised in Regina, McLeod had been managing a movie theatre when he joined the RCAF in September 1940. Posted to 603 Squadron in Malta in June 1942, he tallied a score of 11-1-8 before being repatriated in October and posted to Bagotville. From March 1943 to January 1944 he made the most of a job he did not relish, to the point that he ran afoul of his superiors and jeopardized his chances of returning to operations. McLeod finally escaped Bagotville. Back overseas he commanded 443 Squadron, where he added eight more kills. On September 27, however, he was shot down and killed near Wesel, Germany, while on a sortie led by W/C J.E. Johnson. (McLeod's biography is well-covered in Hugh Halliday's *The Tumbling Sky*.)

Commanding OTU in 1944 was G/C Vaughan B. Corbett, DFC, of Toronto. A 1932 RMC graduate, he had earned his wings at Camp Borden. He fought with 1 Squadron (RCAF) in the Battle of Britain, shooting down an Me.109, sharing in another and damaging a Do.217. On August 31, 1940 he was shot down and wounded. He commanded 402 Squadron in 1941, leading it on some of the early hit-and-run "Hurri Bomber" raids over France. The citation to his DFC notes: " This officer ... has always displayed the greatest keenness." On February 20, 1945 the great Corbett, having recently changed his command to Debert, died in the crash of Bolingbroke 9179 near Bagotville.

Staff and students of Course 24 at 1 OTU in Bagotville. In front (staff) are P/O Skudder, F/L M.E. "Milt" Jowsey, DFC, F/O Omand, F/O Edgar A. "Bud" Ker, DFC, S/L Woledge, S/L Semple, DFC, G/C Vaughan B. Corbett, DFC, W/C Foster, P/O Appleby, F/L Noel A. Ogilvie, DFC, F/L John McClure, DFC, F/L Payne and F/O Kelman. In the middle row are students P/O Warhurst, P/O Wingate, P/O Scott, P/O Goodson, P/O Raynor, P/O Forbes, P/O Borch, WO2 Hart, P/O King, P/O Gray and Sgt Crittenden. Behind are Sgt Nelson, P/O Gildner, P/O Lilleyman, P/O Newell, F/O Cheyney, P/O Bruce, P/O Wilding, P/O McClelland, P/O Day, P/O Armour, P/O Dunne, P/O Keating, P/O Riel, P/O Milne, P/O Havill and P/O Graham. Any such wartime staff would have oozed leadership and experience. (John McClure Col)

Home War Establishment Hurricane Squadrons

Squadron	Formed	Disbanded/Renumbered
1 (F) Squadron	Sept. 21, 1937 Trenton	March 1, 1941 UK (became 401 Squadron)
123 (ACT) Squadron	Jan. 15, 1942 Rockcliffe	January 1, 1944 Germany (became 439 Squadron)
125 (F) Squadron	April 20, 1942 Sydney	November 1943 UK (became 441 Squadron)
126 (F) Squadron	April 27, 1942 Dartmouth	May 31, 1945 Dartmouth
127 (F) Squadron	July 1, 1942 Dartmouth	December 1943 UK (became 443 Squadron)
128 (F) Squadron	June 7, 1942 Sydney	March 15, 1944 Torbay
129 (F) Squadron	August 28, 1942 Dartmouth	September 30, 1944 Gander
130 (F) Squadron	May 1, 1942 Mont Joli	March 15, 1944* Goose Bay
133 (F) Squadron	June 3, 1942 Lethbridge	September 10, 1945† Patricia Bay
135 (F) Squadron	June 15, 1942 Mossbank	September 10, 1945§ Patricia Bay
163 AC) Squadron	March 1, 1943 Sea Island	March 15, 1944• Patricia Bay

* Originally had Kittyhawks   † Later had Kittyhawks, then Mosquitos   § Later had Kittyhawks   • Had misc. other types

Home War Establishment Kittyhawk Squadrons

Squadron	Formed	Disbanded
14 (F) Squadron	January 2, 1942 Rockcliffe	February 8, 1944 UK (became 442 Squadron)
111 (F) Squadron	November 3, 1941 Rockcliffe	February 8, 1944 Germany (became 440 Squadron)
118 (F) Squadron	December 13, 1940 Rockcliffe	November 18, 1943 Germany (became 438 Squadron)
132 (F) Squadron	April 14, 1942 Rockcliffe	September 10, 1945* Sea Island
163 (F) Squadron	October 14, 1943 Sea Island	March 15, 1944 Patricia Bay

*Later had Mosquitos

F/L M.E. "Milt" Jowsey of Ottawa enlisted in October 1940. His first operational posting was flying Spitfires with 234 Squadron in England. From August 1942 through September 1943 he was in North Africa on Hurricanes with 33 Squadron, then Spitfires with 92 Squadron. He was awarded the DFC in September 1943, the citation describing him as, "A cool and capable leader, his courage and determination to engage the enemy have set a fine example to his fellow pilots and have contributed in no small measure to the successes achieved by his squadron." Jowsey next fought in Malta and Sicily, then was posted to Canada in November on a rest tour. He flew Kittyhawks with 135 Squadron, then at Terrace, BC, and was at 1 OTU from April to August, 1944. In September, Jowsey again sailed for the UK, this time for a tour on 442 Squadron. On February 21, 1945 he baled out of his Spitfire, then successfully evaded for 40 days. He finished the war with a score of 5-2-3.

F/O Edgar A. "Bud" Ker enlisted at Niagara Falls, Ontario in December 1940. 1943 found him in North Africa flying Spitfires on 145 Squadron. Here he claimed two MC.202s and one Me.109 destroyed. His DFC, awarded in September 1943, notes: "In May 1943, when on patrol off Cap Bon Peninsula, he sighted a force of more than eighteen Messerschmitt 109s. He succeeded in breaking up the formation and destroyed one of the enemy aircraft." F/O Noel J. "Buzz" Ogilvie served at Bagotville from December 1943 to June 1944. He also had fought at Malta, where he shared in two kills. Next, he instructed at 56 OTU

Lloyd G. Schwab while instructing at 1 OTU over the winter of 1942-43. (Bagotville Air Defence Museum via Richard Girouard)

in the UK, and flew briefly on 401 and 403 squadrons, before being posted home. He commenced his tour at Bagotville on December 7, 1943. S/L Gordon C. Semple, DFC, was instructing at Bagotville at the same time. A few months earlier he had been CO of 411 Squadron flying Spitfires in England.

A famous Beaufighter night fighter pilot, R.C. "Moose" Fumerton, instructed at 1 OTU from January to May 1943. He next returned to the UK to command 406 Squadron, finishing with the outstanding score of 14-0-1. Other combat-seasoned instructors at Bagotville in 1943 were F/Ls Colin Grey (RNZAF) and Ian Ormston, DFC. After his Bagotville tour (August 1942 - May 1943) Ormston fought in England with 401 Squadron. Back there in May 1943, he commanded 411, but was injured in a Spitfire crash. Sent home yet again, from June 1944 to January 1945 he commanded 133 Squadron (Kittyhawks) on the West Coast.

From Niagara Falls, Ontario, Lloyd Gilbert Schwab joined the RAF in 1936 at age 21. After earning his wings, he was posted to the Middle East. When war broke out, he was flying Gloster Gladiator biplanes in North Africa with

112 Squadron. On August 17, 1940 he shot down an SM.79 bomber, then added two more e/a on October 31. On February 20 Schwab fought in a furious dogfight over Greece which ended in 12 e/a shot down, one by him. On April 4 Schwab took command of 112, but a few days later British forces were driven from Greece. They sought haven on Crete, then had to retreat to Egypt. Nonetheless, 112 with its rugged little Gladiators had destroyed some 75 enemy aircraft.

F/L John McClure during his Whirlwind days. John was one of many veterans who got joed into an instructional tour at Bagotville. Another was desert ace F/L Bert Houle, DFC. Here is Bert during an inspection by A/V/M Harry Broadhurst, AOC of the RAF desert airforce. (McClure Col., DND PL18493)

Schwab, whose final tally was 6-1-0, later received the DFC and the Greek Flying Cross. Such instructors were held in awe by the students at 1 OTU. Many lively war stories were related by them in the Bagotville messes. These stories inspired the sprogs, but likely also scared a few. Postwar, Schwab remained in the RAF, retiring in 1958 as W/C Schwab.

When Whirlwind pilot F/L John

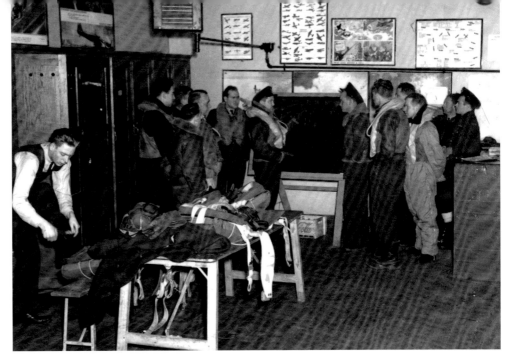

The pilot's ops room at 1 OTU during a briefing. Notice all the paraphernalia from flying kit to the blackboard and the aircraft ID profiles. (DND PL29488)

McClure, DFC, was posted to 1 OTU in January 1944, his assignment was to help establish an air firing flight, where students could practice strafing and rocket-firing. McClure flew first at 1 OTU in Hurricane 5478 on January 21, 1944. The job proved interesting, with much work on the air-to-ground range at nearby St. Honoré. Also included were some cross-country trips, including in the Maritimes doing rocket firing demonstrations. The flight had several Bolingbroke target tugs. These sometimes were used on swans to such places as Montreal and Toronto. On staff at the AFF were other experienced men. The boss

was S/L A.U. "Bert" Houle, DFC, who had made his name flying Kittyhawks in the desert and had a score of 11-1-7. A flying mate of McClure's in this period was F/L Stafford D. Marlatt, home after a tour on Hurricanes and Typhoons at 247 Squadron. An excerpt from *Canada's Air Force at War and Peace*, Vol.1, describes some "extra curricular activities" enjoyed by the Bagotville instructors:

There was a lot of fun in this part of northern Quebec. One break was delivering Hurricanes for overhaul to Scoudouc, New Brunswick. Marlatt and his buddies would ferry via Mont Joli

While on course F/O Johnny Buzza took this photo of 1 OTU Hurricane 5670. Having survived a tour as a wireless operator on 106 Squadron, Buzza remustered to pilot. He first flew the Hurricane at Bagotville on September 25, then went on to Typhoons overseas. Then, a cheerful-looking gang of RCAF armourers getting rockets ready for a 1 OTU armament exercise. (John Buzza)

and Chatham ... One day instructors De Nancrede, McClure, Marlatt and Westcott were routing via the US base at Presqu'Ile, Maine. They envisioned a night or two of cutting loose but, following McClure (leading in a Bolingbroke – none of the planes had radios), they got lost... They back-tracked, hoping to reach the St. Lawrence River and Mont Joli. They barely made it. De Nancrede ran out of gas after touchdown. That evening the drinks were courtesy of McClure.

The Tale of an HWE Fighter Squadron

Established under F/L C.C. Moran at Sydney in July 1942, 128 "Dragon" Squadron originally comprised 6 Hurricanes and some Harvards. Flying commenced on July 14, when 13:25 hours were logged, the squadron diary noting: "Practice low level section attack on anti-aircraft guns carried out." Two days later the station held its first dance, organized by the YMCA in the station recreation hall. Due to the blackout, curfew was early – 2200. All such details, whether exciting or mundane, are recorded in 128's operational record book, an important document normally kept up on a daily basis by the adjutant or one of his clerks. In hind sight, most RCAF ORBs are adequate in coverage, a few are superb, but some are poor. Not only does a good ORB cover the day's flying – who flew which machine at what time for how long – but also mentions the weather, various exercises, postings, promotions, comings and goings on courses, people's health, VIP visits, social and sporting events from skeet shooting to baseball and hockey, matters of equipment, and more. The 128 Squadron diarist did his job well.

On July 18 the squadron suffered its first loss. When Hurricane 1364 caught fire in flight, the pilot baled out, but soon was back at the station. When the wreck of 1364 was being surveyed, someone counted the machine guns, which should have numbered 12. Only 10 were found, so the matter was put in the hands of the RCMP. Also on the 18th, Harvard 2902 flown by Sgt D.B. Dack tangled with a flock of gulls, suffered considerable damage, but landed OK. On the 20th the diary observed that the RCMP had returned to Sydney two machine guns from Hurricane 1364. Enterprising

children had made off with these before anyone else had reached the crash.

July 22 being a bad weather day, the pilots spent their time at lectures and "flying" the Link Trainer. For everyone's edification, "Sections 4 to 44 inclusive of the Air Force Act were read on parade." Air force routines continued in this way at least until August 1. That day P/O Veenis was aloft in Harvard 2965 with LAC Hickey, when he dug in a wingtip while flying over Bras d'Or Lake. The Harvard crashed and sank, but the crew got out: "They inflated their Mae Wests, which kept them afloat 'till rescued by a local resident in a boat." Next day the diarist reported, "Pilot Officer Veenis discharged from Station hospital and placed under open arrest by OC 128 (F) Squadron. Charges to be laid in connection with loss of Harvard 2965." (On October 3 Veenis was found guilty of negligence, but remained with 128.). The squadron's bad luck continued on August 6 when P/O Fairfield had to bale out of Hurricane 1368 when his engine caught fire. He descended with minor injuries.

September 10 offered good weather, but only one serviceable Hurricane. Eventually there were four and the day finished with 29:35 flying hours ("25 air firing exercises, visits to range, cross country & instrument flying."). Also on the 10th, F/L Napier and Sgt Fowler ferried Hurricanes 1371 and '78 to 127 Squadron at Gander, then returned on the 119 Squadron Hudson that had shepherded them to Newfoundland. In a training exercise this day, 128 armourers loaded eight guns on a Hurricane in the good time of 6 minutes, 4 seconds. Next day the station crash boat crew went to the aid of a deer floundering in the bay. The animal was brought ashore, but succumbed. Seeing an opportunity, the crew delivered the carcass to the station kitchen. A diary entry for September 14, 1942 refers to Harvard 2965 damaged by P/O R.M. Veenis, but recovered for repair: "value of damage ... $27,230.00". This Harvard served to November 1957 when it was donated to Turkey under a NATO plan.

An ORB entry of January 13, 1943 noted: "Flying Officer Maclean, D.B., appointed to Court of Inquiry regarding missing revolvers on this station." Flying for this day was up to par: " Total flying time 28:05 hrs. Weather checks, test flights, formation and attacks, low flying, instrument, bombing, section

formation, aerobatics. Hurricane IIB 5623 & 5641 ferried here from Dartmouth." Later in February, Disney in Hollywood agreed that 128 could paint one of its cartoon characters on its Hurricanes. The name "Dragon" was forsaken for "Fox" and a crest showing a pugilistic red fox was introduced.

On January 17 there was a flap that saw 128 Squadron on an air-sea rescue operation. A Liberator was overdue, but everyone was stood down when it landed at Moncton. Next day Sgt L.C. Saunders cracked up on takeoff. Hurricane 1375 was badly damaged, but Saunders was safe. On January 30 F/O G.O. Frostad in Hurricane 5688 and P/O R.A. Johnstone in 1372 had a close call landing on an icy runway at Sydney. Trying to overshoot, Johnstone had engine trouble, touched down, then ran into Frostad. "Both pilots log books are being endorsed", advised the diarist, meaning that their CO, S/L E.C. Briese, would be getting out his red ink to make comments in their logs about sloppy airmanship.

On February 16-17 the squadron was busy searching for a missing Hurricane and a bomber. Unaccounted from 128 was FSgt D.B. Dack in Hurricane 5465. Having taken off at 1030 hours, he failed to return as expected. Happily, at 1430 came news that Dack had crash-landed, been rescued by two local boys and taken to their home. On February 19 S/L T.M. Bullock, DSC, DFC, RAF, gave an informal talk to 128 aircrew. On April 6, 1943 A/V/M J.A. Sully, AFC, visited. For this occasion the squadron put up a welcoming escort of nine Hurricanes. Next day F/O M.W. Rowley set off in Harvard FE626 to collect some target tow gear at Moncton. At noon he telephoned from Ecum Secum, Nova Scotia reporting that, having become lost, he had force-landed short of fuel. He and passenger LAC L.P. Hammel were safe, but Rowley likely was in for a grilling by the CO. On May 17, 1943 the squadron suffered its darkest day. P/O Jean Baptiste Normand Roy, age 29 of Point-Vertu, NB, and FSgt John Edward Whelan, age 24 of Hearst, Ontario, were flying in Harvard 2891. Something went awry and they were never seen again, likely having crashed at sea.

In June 1943 the squadron relocated to Torbay. A new type of operation here was patrolling out to sea with Hurricanes armed two 250-lb depth charges. On July

13 there were reports of two U-boats near Flat Point. S/L A.E.L. Cannon and FSgt H.F. Ulmer scrambled to investigate, but returned with no news. On the same day, Cannon was appointed to a board of enquiry looking into the crash of 145 Squadron Hudson 762 at Charlottetown in which F/L J.R. Hastie died. On July 30 WO2 Dack and Sgt Clouthier were on a bush survival course: "It is intended to continue this until all aircrew have had a day's instruction." At month's end the diarist noted squadron strength: officers 11, other ranks 98, attached other ranks 4. Aircraft: Hurricane XII 9, Harvard 4. Total flying time 508:20 hrs (incl. 81:20 on operations).

A major exercise on August 8, 1943 saw three Hurricanes opposing an "invading" force of RCN landing craft. Then three Harvards "bombed" the vessels, while Hurricanes flew top cover. Later, the Hurricanes switched to supporting the landing force by shooting up beach defensive positions with live ammunition, while Harvards dropped 11.5-lb practice bombs. This same day A/V/M Sully spoke to the senior NCOs and officers about discipline, physical fitness and morale. On August 4, 12 Hurricanes overflew St. John's to celebrate the defeat of Italy. Later in the month 128 Squadron had a training exercise with US Navy forces at Argentia.

On September 27, 1943 A/V/M A.E. Godfrey conducted a base inspection and next day had the station complement on the parade square, congratulating everyone on their sharpness. On October 7 the diarist reported that new telecom equipment recently installed to link 128 Squadron and 1 Group HQ in Torbay was operational. On October 16 six Hurricanes were scrambled when unknown aircraft were reported, but no bogies were found. In a major exercise of November 21, six Hurricanes intercepted 10 RN Swordfish of FAA 816 Squadron escorted by five Seafires.

Noteworthy entries for January 1944 included four shows on the 27th put on by an RCAF entertainment troupe. There was a base defence night exercise on the 28th, with the "invading" force being US Army infantry. On February 6 flying was curtailed after a Liberator crashed on the runway. On the 9th the two readiness Hurricanes scrambled after a reported U-boat off St. John's. They arrived just as a freighter exploded about seven miles off

St. John's harbour, but the Hurricanes saw no trace of a U-boat. On February 22 F/O Joseph Ronald Beasley and P/O D.G. Cleghorn scrambled after an unknown bogey – they intercepted a Canso.

"Secret Organization Order No.176" was issued on March 6, 1944 stating that effective on March 15, "It is the intention to disband No.128 Squadron". The squadron flew its last mission on March 13 – two Hurricanes on dawn patrol. In all, 128 had flown 760 sorties for 6647 training hours plus 927 on operations. Seven aircraft and two pilots had been lost. Like most of the hastily-formed Home War Establishment squadrons, 128 quickly faded from memory.

The casualty list did not quite end for 128 on March 15, 1944. Several squadron pilots soon received overseas postings, including F/O Beasley of Ottawa. From 128 he joined 416 Squadron on Spitfire Mk.IXs. On December 24, 1944 he was in action in the infamous Malmedy area of Belgium. That day German flak gunners got Beasley (age 24) in their sights and killed him. P/O William Robert Gibbs from Peterborough later found himself on 440 Squadron. All his good flying experience on 128 Squadron could not help him when, on February 28, 1945, the flak experts got onto him as he attacked a train near Goch.

Newfie Tours: Hurricanes to Hudsons

Born on October 1, 1924, George Ramsay Webster was raised in Port Credit, near Toronto. At age 16 he joined the 30th Battery, a local militia unit, but soon decided to get into the RCAF. Initially, he was on an RCAF pre-enlistment course at Central Technical School in Toronto, from where he officially was on RCAF strength on his 18th birthday in 1942. After ITS at Belleville, he was posted to flight training at 10 EFTS at RCAF Station Pendleton in eastern Ontario. There he flew first on March 9, 1943, going up with P/O Grant in Tiger Moth 8941.

Webster soloed in the same plane on March 29, then moved through the system until his final flight in 8663 with P/O White on May 1. Upon graduating, Webster's log book showed 30:10 hours dual and 23:5 solo on the Tiger Moth about which he took pride.

The system now moved LAC Webster into advanced training, sending him to 1 SFTS at Camp Borden. On May 5 he flew with F/O Reeves in Harvard 2905, then

The unique patch worn by staff and students of 1 Armament Training Unit at 1 SFTS, Camp Borden.

LAC George Webster in EFTS days. Then, one of the Harvards at Camp Borden during his course. (all, George Webster Col.)

The snapshot that P/O Webster got of F/L Fenwick's 1 OTU Hurricane. Moments later, he brushed Fenwick's wingtip and the formation split up.

began going up regularly with P/O Clayton, one of the RCAF's many "Yanks". He soloed in Harvard 3004 on May 12, progressed as expected, then had his wings check with F/L Stevenson in Harvard 3312 on July 2. His course went

Classmates at 1 OTU: P/Os George Webster and Bob MacDonald.

into a brief holding pattern, when he was sent on a preliminary armament course at Camp Borden's relief field, Elmvale. During a night exercise of August 15, Webster's friend, LAC Hugh R. Warren of Niagara Falls, somehow got into trouble, crashing fatally in Harvard 3084 and bringing the course to a somber end.

LAC Webster finished with 89:45 hours dual and 68:15 solo on the Harvard. He was promoted to sergeant's rank, had a few days of leave, unexpectedly was promoted to pilot officer, then was posted to the Hurricane conversion course at Bagotville. He flew here for the first time with F/L Bishop in Harvard FE385 on August 31, 1943. On September 2 he went up in Hurricane "21" – each OTU Hurricane carried such numbers in large numerals on the nose. Otherwise, Webster saw that the OTU Hurricanes were a grimy-looking lot in their faded, chipped paint. Nonetheless, to an 18 year old sprog, a 1250-hp fighter was the loveliest plane in the sky. Sad to say, but Bagotville in this period was cursed with accidents, which the sprog pilots would ruefully note in their log

Hurricane "D-Dog" of 129 Squadron at readiness in a revetment at Dartmouth. Inset, a close-up of the squadron mascot crest – a pugilistic coyote.

books. In Webster's first few days, four RAF student pilots died. Then, on September 9, P/O Gordon K. Teal of Ridgeway, Ontario, a pilot on 130 Squadron, died near Bagotville in the crash of Hurricane 5686.

September proved busy for P/O Webster with 22:40 hours on Hurricanes, 17:30 on Harvards. October 1 through 24 saw him on various sorties (as listed in his log book): "formation & tail chase", "formation & cross-over turns", "low flying", "aerobatics", "attacks at 25,000", "cine gun", "attacks on drogue", "interception at 10,000" and "air to air live". October 24 saw the OTU airborne for a fly-by welcoming a new course.

P/O Webster was flying on the wing of F/L Harry E. "Junior" Fenwick, DFC, as the formation took shape. Always a keen photographer, here was a chance Webster didn't want to miss, so he pulled out his little Brownie box camera to line up a shot of Fenwick. Getting a bit too focused on his viewfinder, sad to say, he bumped Fenwick's wingtip. Suddenly, all hell broke loose and the formation broke up. Happily, with no harm done, other than to Webster's pride.

Pilots of 129 Squadron in a murky snapshot at Dartmouth early in 1944. On the wing are Anderson and McCrae. Standing are Osborne, Postcavage, unknown, Torrance, MacDonald, Craig, McDermott and Christie. In front are Webster, James, Fiander, Davey and Keyes.

P/O Webster flew last at Bagotville on October 26 – a 1-hour sortie in Hurricane "41" logged as "Cine gun & air combat". He had flown 58:30 hours on Hurricanes, 24:05 on Harvards, and had a log book now bulging with 297:05 hours. He had some leave, then joined his first squadron – 129 "Husky" Squadron at Bagot-ville. Equipped with Hurricanes and Harvards, 129 had formed at Dartmouth in August 1942 under F/L C.C. Moran. It moved to Goose Bay in November under S/L Lipton, then to Bagotville in October the following year under S/L W.F. Napier. S/L Paul A. Gilbertson took over in January 1944 (of these COs, Moran later received a DFC flying Bostons on 418 Squadron).

Webster first flew on 129 on November 20, 1943, going up in Harvard "648" on a local flight with P/O Postcavage (a "Yank" who later died on USAAF fighter operations). Unlike overseas, life on a Home War Establishment outfit was fairly tame. Daily routines consisted of dawn and dusk patrols where almost nothing unexpected occurred, the worst danger being a change in the weather. The atmosphere was a bit like that around the local flying club, but people had to do these jobs, as long as there was the slightest possibility of enemy incursions.

Late in 1943, 129 Squadron relocated to Dartmouth, where P/O Webster began flying on January 4, 1944. May 14 through 16 he was on a search for a missing aircraft that sent him on six patrols of 1:20, 1:10, 1:25, 1:25, 2:25, and 1:40 hours (he would fly on other searches, as there frequently were missing aircraft in Atlantic Canada). He was on a 1:25-hour cross-country exercise of May 21, logged as "Annapolis Royal-Wolfville-Base". He

had a dicey experience on May 24 when his cockpit filled with smoke at 15,000 feet. A squadron mate reported that he was streaming smoke. In 2009 Webster recalled: "I went through the parachute drill, shut down the engine and turned back toward Dartmouth. I trimmed the aircraft at its best gliding speed – about 100 mph – then, after jettisoning the panel on the right side of the aircraft, I stepped onto the wing." On looking down, however, he re-appraised his situation - the Hurricane did not seem to be burning and it looked like a long way down. Webster climbed back into the cockpit and flew his Hurricane to a smooth dead-stick landing at Dartmouth.

In June 1944 the squadron was again on the move, this time to Gander, where Webster first flew on June 8. Here, each pilot was assigned a personal Hurricane, Webster's being 5665 "M". All the usual flying ensued – daily patrols, cross-country trips, dog fighting, gunnery, radio range training, searches, etc. On July 3

The end of P/O Webster's "M-Mary" in a Newfie bog. Then, other 129 prangs: 5486 "P-Peter", which survived the war to be SOS in July 1947; and 5700 neatly deposited in a farmer's field on September 11, 1943.

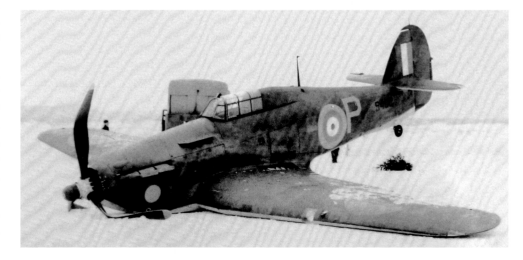

Another of George Webster's "no-no" snapshots – dozens of USAAF bombers awaiting delivery overseas. The distant hangar at far centre left was the home of 129 Squadron.

Webster and some mates flew in a Digby to Argentia, where several Fleet Air Arm Avengers awaited ferrying to Gander. After three familiarization flights, Webster delivered Avenger "279" to Gander. On August 9 he had another dicey do. While on a training sortie at about 5000 feet, a cam shaft broke in his Merlin. He sized up a stretch of muskeg and force-landed. Next morning a dozen men appeared from nearby Carmanville, an outport north of Gander (to attract their attention, Webster periodically had fired his machine guns into the bog). Gander sent a Norseman to Carmanville and Webster soon was back on squadron. Of all this he noted in his log book: "Combat and tail chase. Spent night in the bush, not a scratch. Claim 1 Hurri Mk.IIB 5665 M".

In September 1944 President Franklin D. Roosevelt, Prime Minister Winston Churchill and their host, Prime Minister W. L. Mackenzie King, met in Quebec City to discuss postwar plans regarding Germany. Much as Ottawa later would put CF-18s on readiness for such events as G-8 meetings or Olympic games, 129 would help with security at Quebec City. But getting it positioned from Gander became a bind. On September 2 the squadron departed with 10 Hurricanes escorted by a Hudson, P/O Webster flying 5717 "S". They made it into Stephenville for a first refuelling stop. Here, for reasons unknown, on departure on the 4th F/L Christie performed some unauthorized low flying, including beat-ups of the control tower. The Hurricanes then continued to Sydney. Fog, however, engulfed their loose formation and everyone was forced back to Stephenville. There the base commander made certain to chew out F/L Christie. The weather improved, 129 making it to Sydney that day.

On September 5 the squadron flew to Moncton in 1:30 hours, then pushed on to Chatham in 0:30. Next day the object was Mont Joli, but Webster had to return with engine problems. On the 7th it was weather

129 Squadron lined up at Chatham en route to the Quebec Conference. The Hudson was their shepherd along the way. Then, Hurricane "X" seen from the Hudson en route to Quebec.

that forced them back again to Chatham, so it was the 8th before they reached Mont Joli. The squadron finally was together at Quebec on the 9th, when local recce sorties commenced. P/O Webster's log book

shows that he was scrambled on Quebec Conference duties on September 11, 12, 13 and 16, when the conference ended. 129 now sojourned in Quebec for a few days, then flew its final operational flights

The big names at the Quebec Conference: Prime Minister King is standing second from the left with Governor General The Earl of Athlone on his right. President Roosevelt is between Anthony Eden and Princess Alice (Athlone's wife) and Prime Minister Churchill is seated right. (John McClure Col.)

Aircraft of 1 (Comm) Flight: Norseman 491 which, postwar, became CF-FDP with Air Gagnon of Chicoutimi. On June 6, 1947 it was lost in an accident at Mistassini Post, Quebec. Then, Goose 385 with the crew of Stew Mawhinney, George Webster and George Langlais. Postwar, 385 became CF-EXA with the Quebec government.

The 1 (Comm) Flight patch showed the unit as both a communications and composite unit. Officially, however, it was 1 (Communications) Flight.

on the 18th. On the 23rd the Hurricanes ferried to St. John's, Quebec for disposal; 129 disbanded a week later.

The squadron's personnel were shuttled back to Newfoundland, Webster travelling in Dakotas 660 and 662 via Moncton to Torbay. For a few days there was gossip about what would come next – the pilots heard that they might be going to the Far East. But rumours faded and people dispersed here and there. P/O Webster remained at Torbay, posted to No.1 Composite Squadron, mainly to fly the Hudson, Goose and Norseman on general duties (his log book now showed 650 flying hours). Here the OC was F/L Phil Sauvé, a renowned pre-war bush pilot.

As far as Webster was concerned, things now took a 90 degree turn, compared to the cushy life on the Hurricane "flying club" scene. His new squadron carried passengers and freight, towed targets for the coast artillery, did army co-operation and air-sea rescue, and trained ceaselessly. No one was ever going to be shooting back, but this in no way lessened the importance of the work. For F/O Webster (promoted in June 1944) the work was challenging and always fun. He first flew on November 11 in Hudson FK550 with WO Gregory, and the same day flew Norseman 491 with F/O Osborne. On December 2 he flew Goose 385 with F/O Bowser. The squadron also

had Harvards FE624, FE631 and FE935, and Tiger Moth 9695 for swanning around. This was ideal for any young pilot who lived to fly. A typical month for Webster was March 1944: Hudson – 78:35 hours, Goose – 7:20, Harvard – 0:45 and Tiger Moth – 1:45. His favourite passenger was Torbay's station commander, the revered G/C Roy Grandy. It was not always so rosy at 1 CS, however, as with the loss of FSgt John J. Kervin, age 21 of Callander, Ontario. While on an April 5, 1945 army co-op sortie in Harvard FE624, he crashed fatally.

On July 6, 1945 F/O Webster ferried Hudson FK562 from Torbay to Mount Pleasant, PEI for storage. Aboard were several aircrew en route to Moncton to be demobilized. The flight was normal until Webster neared Mount Pleasant, then found that his undercarriage would not cycle. The left gear came down, the other stayed up (he learned later that FK562 had leaked most of its hydraulic fluid):

After trying many dives with abrupt pull-ups, the right wheel finally came down and locked, so I went ahead with a normal approach, keeping in mind the conditions and that Mount Pleasant had short runways. When I selected 40% flaps, however, nothing happened. Since we weren't set up for a flapless landing, I had to apply full power for an overshoot.

At that critical moment, those huge Fowler flaps came down 100%, as the surge in power pushed the remaining hydraulic fluid through the lines. This was dire: flaps and undercarriage down, a hot day, no wind, nine men on board, and having to do a circuit in a plane prone to stalling violently.

I nursed the Hudson to 300 feet, did gentle, flat turns all the way around, and landed. The WAG then let me know that the bomb doors had fallen open and that we were trailing fluid. He added that he had noticed reddish fluid draining over the wing all the way across the Gulf of St. Lawrence, and hadn't bothered saying

One of EAC's lifeboat-carrying Hudsons.

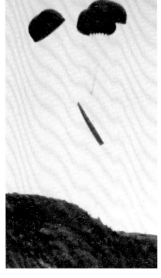

In his March 1944 HWE "Monthly Review", the Chief of the Air Staff reported on a new ASR resource – a Hudson equipped with a life boat. The self-righting 23.5' x 5.5' mahogany boat came with a sail, 4 oars and 2 small engines along with such essentials as food, clothing, transmitter, flare pistol and fuel. This sequence shows a lifeboat training session conducted by 1 (Comm) Flight.

anything! Guess who paid for the drinks in the mess that night!

On July 20 F/O Webster passed 1000 hours while flying the Tiger Moth. Over Bay Bulls Pond on July 25 and 26 he made three trial drops of a lifeboat especially developed for the ASR Hudson. On August 9, when Webster was busy in Harvard FE631 escorting the Tiger Moth from Gander to Torbay, F/O George Cameron was flying Hudson FK495. This was not Cameron's lucky day. Barely checked out on type, he lost an engine, but ditched successfully in Gull Pond. On September 17, 1945 F/O Webster ferried FK466 to Summerside. On the 30th he took one of the groundcrew on a local flight in the same Hudson. He made his last wartime flight when he took Anson 11987 to Moncton on November 14. Three days later he was demobbed, by which date his log book showed 1077:05 hours.

Webster returned to Port Credit, where he and his ex-RCAF friend Jim "Jesse" James got into trucking. This was a flop, so Webster tried the wholesale food business. In 1947 he married Joan Rickaby then, in 1952, returned to air force life. Following a refresher course on Harvards at Calgary, he did the instructors' course at Trenton, flying some tired old USAF T-6 Texans. His course remained here from June to September, training some *ab initio* students from the University Reserve Training Plan. He then was posted to 1 FTS at Centralia to instruct on Harvards and Chipmunks. Here, he earned the coveted "A-1" instructor's category. In the fall of 1955 he joined a group of top instructors in Trenton to re-write the RCAF *ab initio* flight training syllabus. About this time he was offered a Permanent Commission, but turned this down for civilian life. His last flight in the RCAF was in Chipmunk '028 on November 6, 1956. At this point his log

book showed 2860:55 hours. He and Joan then took over the Rickaby family gift and book shop in Bowmanville, east of Toronto, running the business until 1992, when they retired.

In the summer of 1993 George was visiting Nova Scotia when he spotted the hulk of a Lockheed Hudson in the countryside near Halifax. He pulled in and took some pictures. On closer inspection he found that this was FK466. It had been converted to target tug duties in 1945, then was struck off strength in December 1947. Sold for scrap, it somehow survived until rescued from a junk yard by the Atlantic Canada Aviation Museum. In 2010 FK466 was a long-term restoration project at the museum.

Lifeboat Hudson FK466 in RCAF service, then as George Webster saw it at the Atlantic Canada Aviation Museum.

Security Issues

Unauthorized use of cameras was a daily topic among military personnel and civilians alike. According to AFRO1536 of December 19, 1941, taking photographs on air stations was forbidden. Among civilians most photography was forbidden when the subject matter, even the distant background, included such features as factories, transportation or military activity. When he took a Victoria-Vancouver flight on a Canadian Airways de Havilland Rapide during the war, Hugh Curtis, then a boy, recalled in 2009 how the curtains were drawn while the plane taxied out and took off, so that no one could see, let alone photograph, activity at either port. Yet, in spite of regulations, service personnel such as P/O Webster regularly took photographs – everyone wanted to have a record of service days and some souvenir photos to mail home. Airmen routinely swapped their photos. But RCAF security frowned upon all this and to tighten up on such infractions AFROs of July 24, 1942 re-addressed the issue:

To eliminate this practice, which is most dangerous to general security, commanding officers are to instruct all ranks that interception of photographs – however harmless the subject matter – which indicates unlawful possession of a camera, will result in the offender becoming liable to disciplinary action, prosecution, and confiscation of camera under the Defence of Canada Regulations.

In the end it seemed like a losing battle on the part of security. Thousands of airmen kept breaking the rules, but were discrete about who saw their pictures. This later proved a boon to researchers and writers, for millions of forbidden photos gradually emerged after the war. These continue to reveal new facets of RCAF history and fill endless gaps – subject matter that was not covered by RCAF photographers. AFROs of October 11, 1940 reminded RCAF members of another security issue: "Instances have recently occurred where personnel warned of posting overseas have communicated with their families and friends and advised them of such postings. They have also disclosed such vital information as date of sailing and numbers proceeding. The importance of secrecy in these matters cannot be stressed too strongly, and any future incidents of this nature which may be discovered will result in severe disciplinary action being taken against the personnel involved." AFROs of January 8, 1943 covered the same topic, complaining how "Personnel have been indiscreet in passing information when sending telegrams and cables … offenders are to be dealt with severely."

West Coast "BR" Days

The West Coast also was home to several busy bomber reconnaissance squadrons. By far the best source book covering these units and their bases is Chris Weicht's *Jericho Beach and the West Coast Flying Boat Squadrons*. Doing its part in West Coast operations was 4 (BR) Squadron, which had formed as 4 (Flying Boat) Squadron in Jericho Beach in 1933. The squadron had a proud heritage in civil government air operation on fisheries, forestry, smuggling and immigration duties. Now it had to go to war, but in September 1939 was not ready. After all, it still was flying 1920s Vedettes, although it had begun re-equipping with "modern" Sharks and Stranraers. In May 1940 "4 BR" moved from Jericho Beach to Ucluelet to take over from a detachment of two 6 BR Sharks. Five Sharks, two Stranraers, one Fairchild 71 and about 250 men comprised the squadron, whose chief task was to protect Barkley Sound and the Alberni Canal at the head of which lay Port Alberni. This was a challenge, as conditions at the base were topsy-turvy, mainly because of on-going construction.

Early in the war, 4 BR still had many pre-war men – some even dated to the 1920s RCAF. Included in 1941 was J.P. "Jay" Culliton, a renowned Northern Ontario bush pilot, who had volunteered to help out in the RCAF as soon has he could get leave from the Ontario Provincial Air Service. These were dicey times, when the RCAF was almost panicking to get onto a war footing. It was fortunate to have a cadre of such skilled old timers as Culliton eager to help.

Having completed a rush indoctrination at 1 Manning Depot, Camp Borden and Picton, Culliton received his RCAF wings, was posted to Test and Development Flight at Rockcliffe, then quickly was sent in May 1941 to 4 BR to qualify on flying boats. This was essential, as his job at "T&D" would entail test flying Stranraers and Cansos. En route to 4 BR, Culliton had to report first to Western Air Command in Victoria. Much to his surprise and pleasure, there he found that the senior administration officer to whom he reported was his former OPAS boss, S/L W. Roy Maxwell, a WWI pilot and the man who had set up the OPAS in 1924. At 4 BR F/O Culliton readily adapted and soon was flying operational patrols. One of his instructors was Tom "Barnacle Bill The Sailor" McMahon, another OPAS man whom Culliton first had met in Sioux Lookout about 1928. As a former HS-2L pilot, McMahon was "a natural" on the Stranraer. In his unpublished memoir Jay Culliton recalls a bit about his 4 BR interlude:

Stranraer 915 of 4 (BR) Squadron at Sea Island, Vancouver in 1940. Although overshadowed by the PBY, the "Stranny" did solid work on both coasts from September 1939. Postwar, 915 became CF-BYJ, serving the BC coast with Queen Charlotte Airlines until an accident in January 1948. Other ex-RCAF Strannies operated postwar from Labrador to the Caribbean. (Gordon S. Williams)

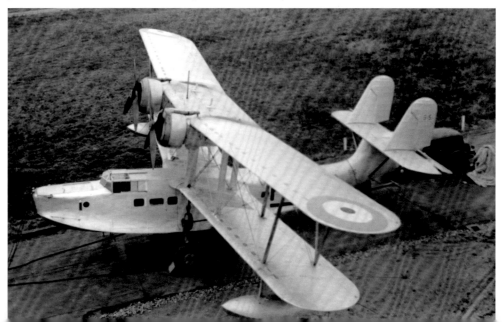

Stranraer 937 of 9 (BR) Squadron at Bella Bella, BC on July 7, 1942. This aircraft had begun on the East Coast with 117 BR in 1941, but the EAC Stranraers were the first replaced by Cansos, due to pressing needs in the U-boat war. That freed them for West Coast use. Deployed to Bella Bella two days after Pearl Harbor, 9 BR remained there until disbanding in September 1944. Although it later added Cansos and Catalinas, it kept its reliable "Strannies" for most of the war. (DND PL9598)

Tom McMahon took me out on my first sea patrol. After that, we would take turns, one time as captain, the next as navigator. When we were flying the big triangular courses at sea, and he was navigator, I was always a bit dubious of the course changes he would send up to me – Tom was always full of "the old Nick". I'd do my own navigating, keeping my calculations on a sheet under my seat. This gave me a rough check on Tom.

On one patrol, when I was captain, we checked on a vessel heading towards Alaska. We were supposed to take the ship's profile, and get as much identifying information as possible for debriefing back at base. I circled and circled, giving Tom and the crew every angle to get as much detail as possible. The crew called up that they still couldn't read the name of the ship, so I went down quite low and cut across the bow. The ship promptly heeled over and almost turned on its side in changing course. Then, from the mast came a couple of lines of multi-coloured flags, some of different shapes. I interphoned back to Tom, asking him what the signals meant. After many calls, he finally came up front to report, "I forgot the

bloody book". This was the code book required to decipher messages, flags, etc. When we landed back at Ucluelet, I had to remain out in the bay until a boat came out. Tom went in, picked up the book and came back out. While I was taxiing up to the anchoring barge, he figured out the message of the flags: "We have noted your protest". Maybe they had thought we were steering them away from a mine field.

Ucluelet was still under construction when I arrived. In front of our hangars we had a big concrete platform that terminated at the sea where, at high tide, ships docked with supplies. At low tide there was a drop of almost 14 feet to the water. The only dry area we had for drill was this strip of concrete. S/L C.M.G. "Con" Farrell, DFC ("The Moaner" of early air mail days), was the Commanding Officer of No. 4 Squadron. Prior to the war he had been with Western Canada Airways and before that had flown in WWI. Con wasn't very keen on drill – perhaps he had forgotten what he once knew. Regulations, however, demanded that he report on squadron inspections and drills. There were small

entrances set in the large main hangar doors, so a person could go in or out of the hangar without opening the main doors. When Con started drilling us, he would stand in front of one of the small doors, with the drill manual, barking out the commands.

The squadron had three drill flights. Tom Mahon had one, I had one and John McNee had the third. Our parade ground was the concrete strip, about one hundred yards long. Con marched us up and down. As the last flight would pass, he would pop into the hangar, through a small door, glance at his manual, then pop out to give another command in time to reverse the parade and keep us on the strip. Tom was leading No.1 Flight and was on a reverse, where he had to go around his flight and lead in a new direction, now heading towards the end of the pier. Con apparently lost his place in the drill manual, but Tom was nearing the end of the pier and the big drop. His knees were going higher and higher, and his steps were getting shorter and shorter. In desperation he looked back and called out, "Con, for God's sake, say something, even if it's only goodbye."

Our Officer's Mess at Ucluelet was primitive, but adequate for a small establishment. We were visited one day by some senior officers on an inspection. At a Mess meeting, the senior officer asked if there were any complaints. Tom rose and said, "The food is not too good. The airmen eat better than we do. In fact, all the mice have left the Officer's Mess, and gone over to the Airmen's Mess."

4 BR Canso Days: A Navigator's Career

Born and raised in Toronto, James G. "Jim" McGuffin attended Eastern High School of Commerce. On his 18th birthday in 1942 he enlisted in the RCAF. His first assignment was a 2-month stint at the University of Toronto Schools. There he and his fellow RCAF "hopefuls" took some academic courses sponsored by the Canadian Legion. At UTS, McGuffin chummed with Colin Clark, a pal from boys' choir days in 1936 at St. Paul's Anglican Church on Bloor St. In 2010 McGuffin recalled the UTS experience as vital to those

"Acie Ducie" Jim McGuffin at the start of his RCAF career. (all, McGuffin Col.)

involved who were hoping for a pilot or observer slot once the real training began.

AC2 McGuffin was sworn in on June 4, 1942 and immediately was absorbed into the RCAF basic training program, commencing at 1 Manning Depot, Toronto. This began with two weeks

"confined to barracks" in Reception Wing. Here, recruits learned such essentials as how to wear, clean and press their new uniforms, and how to shine buttons and shoes to perfection. They were taught how and when to salute, and how generally to conduct themselves in uniform. Next came a month in Training Wing, where the essentials of foot drill were pounded into the recruits until, as McGuffin recalled in 2010, "We could respond automatically to any command given by our drill instructor". There was a final drill test, then the class graduated and commenced two weeks of rifle drill and PT. After this, noted McGuffin, "We felt we were truly eligible candidates for precision drill squad selection."

Next stop for AC2 McGuffin was 4 Manning Depot in Quebec City on a pre-ITS course. This entailed a further six weeks of academic upgrading, after which he was posted to 6 ITS at the old Normal School in downtown Toronto. From here he was selected for training as an observer, so next found himself on the bombing and gunnery course (Crs.73) at

Jim McGuffin's class while on their "smartening up" course in Quebec City. Behind are Bill Haire, F.E. Welsh, Bill Kay, F.M. Brown, C. Sproat, Hal Tracy, Norm Gillen and W.J. Hutchinson. In the middle are Clare Strong, Dave Leishman, Dave Barrett, Ernie Bobzener, Bill Bonter, Jim Mitchell, Lorne Farley, J. Ross Robertson and G.O. Dawson. In front are Tex Bennett, Dave Sproule, Jim Schwerdfager, Ross Smith, FSgt Vinish (course NCO), George Peterson, T.E. Flanagan, Albert J. Smith and Jim McGuffin. Not all these men would survive the war (casualty rates for such classes at this time in the war were 30% - 40%). One of those lost was James E. Schwerdfager (bomb aimer, age 20 from Ottawa). On October 25, 1944 he was with his 431 Squadron crew on a training flight over England in Lancaster KB813. The plane caught fire and crashed, killing everyone aboard. Albert J. Smith (pilot, age 22 from Port Burwell, Ontario) died flying his 47 Squadron Beaufighter in Ceylon. On May 28, 1944 Thomas E. Flanagan (nav, age 20 from Ottawa) died with his 550 Squadron Lancaster crew while on operations to Aachen. David L. Sproule (pilot, age 24 from Westmount, Quebec) was lost with his crew when Catalina AH551 of 131 OTU crash in Ireland. Gerald O. Dawson (pilot, age 30 of Peterborough) was killed in an AFU Oxford in England on December 29, 1943; while George F. Peterson (age 22 from Toronto) was shot down by flak while flying his 402 Squadron Spitfire near Arnhem on April 11, 1945.

6 (B&G) School, Mountain View. He flew initially on February 22, 1943 with F/O Ellson in Bolingbroke 10005. The "Boly" flight at Mountain View was dedicated to gunnery, but McGuffin also had to take bombing, which was done on Ansons, once the students got out of the classroom. LAC McGuffin's first such exercise was in Anson 7379 on March 8 with Sgt Holt. For the course he completed 38 air exercises, his flying times being: Anson 26:30 hours (day), 8:30 (night) and Bolingbroke 13:05 (day).

McGuffin last flew at Mountain View on March 31, then his class progressed to 8 AOS at Ancienne Lorette (Quebec City airport). Here, he first flew in the Anson with Mr. Elie on April 12, 1943. The course was busy with a host of flying exercises from point-to-point navigation to reconnaissance to aerial photography. McGuffin's last flight was on August 18, after which came the course wings parade. Presenting each graduate this day with his wing was W/C Guy Gibson, VC, who was in Canada with Prime Minister Churchill's Quebec Conference party.

Next in his training, Sgt McGuffin spent September and October at 1 (GR) School at Summerside, another Anson operation. This was a special course in tactical and coastal navigation, learning how to intercept a moving convoy, etc. This totalled 10 flights for 32:10 hours, then McGuffin joined his operational unit – 4 (Bomber Reconnaissance) Squadron. "4 BR" was a Canso squadron stationed at Ucluelet on the west coast of

A 4 BR Canso in local waters near Tofino.

The casual look at 8 AOS: air observer trainees Jim McGuffin of Toronto, Ian Rutherford of Sarnia and Eric Goring of Vancouver.

Vancouver Island (Ucluelet was a water-base operation). McGuffin's first day's work came on November 5, 1943 when he flew as "2ⁿᵈ Nav" on an 8-hour sortie in Canso 9804 with the crew of F/L George Seldon. He logged this as "Sea Patrol, Drifts, 8:00 hours" (taking drifts was done from the rear of the Canso, looking down through a drift meter to get a bearing from wind and wave direction). The 4 BR ORB for the end of November shows 4 BR's manning as: officers – 41, NCOs – 87, airmen – 109.

A typical 4 BR mission usually would be briefed before dawn, with the Canso airborne by first light. A standard crew comprised 2 pilots, 1 navigator, 2 FEs and 3 WOpAGs. Standard Canso armament was 4 x 250-lb depth charges plus .303 cal. machines guns in the rear

blisters and nose (the squadron's Catalinas carried .50 cal. machine guns). Sgt McGuffin enjoyed 4 BR from the start, especially since the personnel were such a solid, bunch of good fellows. The station commander was an especially fine fellow. W/C Harold J. "Harry" Winny had been a pre-war bush pilot with Canadian Airways and the Hudson's Bay Company. Having joined the RCAF early in the war, he was a flight commander at 13 (OT) Squadron at Sea Island, then under S/L Z.L. Leigh, then was at Alliford Bay flying boat station before taking command at Ucluelet. Winny routinely called a weekly inspection parade, for which he would turn up wearing his bush pilot's outfit! 4 BR's CO in Jim McGuffin's time was another revered type, S/L Romney H. Lowry.

A crowd of 4 BR personnel with Canso 11044 at Tofino on October 27, 1944. Note the standard under-wing war load – 4 x 250-lb depth charges.

4 BR usually had on strength nine Cansos, three Catalinas and 1 Stranraer. These always were busy, weather permitting. In February 1944 alone Sgt McGuffin logged 16 sorties, the longest being 10:50 hours. For the month he flew 80:30 hours (day) and 3:20 (night). Most operations were general recces watching for possible Japanese submarines (which no one ever saw), friendly naval and commercial shipping, or searches for vessels or aircraft in distress.

All ships sailed under strict radio silence, so communications between

Canso and ship were by Aldis lamp and ship's flags. Each US or Canadian vessel ran with a 4-letter code, e.g. the US troopship *David W. Branch* was KKRX. The last two letters had code value that was related to other numbers and letters of the day, which would be sent by Aldis lamp or flags to confirm that the ship being interrogated was friendly. Other sorties by 4 BR ranged from practice bombing and gunnery training to photography and air-sea rescue. Bomb practice usually was done using bombs and depth charges that were old stock. 4

BR sometimes responded to a possible enemy submarine when alerted by a CPR coastal vessel. No sub was ever found (whales or large deadheads sometimes were mistaken for submarines), so such sorties were sometimes logged as "CPR" alerts. There also was the "CLA" entry – creeping line ahead. On such a patrol a Canso would zig-zag back and forth up a predetermined line looking for anything.

Sgt McGuffin's first Stranraer flight was in 907, a local flight on March 14, 1944. The "Stranny" was used for odd jobs, such as grocery runs to Port Alberni when something like the fresh milk supply was getting low at Ucluelet. That month was a high for McGuffin in flying time – 114:30 hours (day), 7:45 (night). On May 6 he was on F/O Jim Gillies' crew in 9801 towing a drogue for a coastal ack-ack battery. A mission of May 16 in Canso 11017 with F/O Buchanan was a marathon effort – 12:10 hours. On May 19 he was with P/O Dawson on a climb-to-height effort. This was a short flight of 2:35, but Dawson nudged his kite up to 16,000 feet. On the 21st he again was with Dawson, this time on a training exercise dropping 2 x 500- and 2 x 250-lb bombs. For May 29 the mission was more serious – a Mitchell was missing. McGuffin and his mates searched in Catalina FP291 and other 4 BR crews also likely were doing the same. On June 6 he logged a 9-hour "Night Search", again with Dawson. A search on July 17 in FP291 was for another Mitchell. McGuffin was never on a search that came up with anything, but 4 BR did have some successes, as on February 7, 1944 when it had picked up the pilot of a Tofino-based Hurricane who had ditched.

4 BR Canso men take a lunch break on patrol. The work space was spartan and everything functional, but ergonomics had not been a big consideration in their design. Patrols often exceeded 10 hours, but crews somehow got by. (McGuffin Col.)

The RCAF marine section supported operations on both coast, the Great Lakes, Lake Winnipeg, etc. Vessels of many classes were used. *B160 Takuli* (radio call sign "Irium H") was one of the powerful 70-foot RCAF West Coast Marine Section rescue boats. Then, the 38-foot ASR vessel *M.266 Teal* that was stationed at Bella Bella during WWII. (McGuffin Col., DND PL9593)

On August 27, 1944 the squadron relocated to Tofino, where it became land-based. By this time FSgt McGuffin had been promoted to pilot officer. On September 21 he was with P/O Hawkins when the nose wheel collapsed on landing, putting 11018 temporarily out of service. On October 3 he flew in Dakota 954 to Vancouver to start a month's leave. Back on operations, he soon was involved in more ASR sorties, there being two such with F/O Les Murdock on November 10 and 13 looking for a missing Liberator. On the 14th, 4 BR began searching for one of its own – 11017 had gone missing. McGuffin went out that day with the crew of 9802 on a search of 8:20 and was with the many other search aircraft and vessels involved on the 15th and 17th, but nothing was found of 11017.

The 84-foot tug *M.205 Sekani* serviced such air stations as Ucluelet and Tofino. Then, the 72-foot, 70-ton RCAF supply vessel *B.C. Star/M.427* of Patricia Bay. It was lost with all hands en route to Cape St. James in the Queen Charlotte Islands on or after July 23, 1943. The converted fishing boat was carrying construction material to a new radar site, but its movements were so secret that no one at the receiving end knew it was coming (*B.C. Star* was prohibited from transmitting other than in code). It was 10 days before the boat was missed. The bodies of 3 of the 12 POB were all that ever was found. (McGuffin Col., LAC PA176034)

In this period P/O McGuffin was on F/O Murdock's crew. Then Murdock, one of "Canada's Yanks", decided on a transfer home to the US forces. He wanted something new, so would have been a bit browned off when the Americans found the perfect spot for him in Biloxi, Mississippi – instructing on the PBY, a.k.a Canso. McGuffin now was flying mainly with F/O Grieve. About this time he was also looking for a change, so was able to secure a slot at the Dakota OTU at Comox. He last flew on 4 BR in 11013 with F/O Grieve on March 26, 1945. He began at 6 OTU with a flight in Expeditor 101 on April 21, 1945. Next stop was to be one of the RCAF Dakota squadrons in the UK. OTU progressed routinely, McGuffin flying last at Comox on June 9. By this time his log book

Jim McGuffin's log book entries for September 1944.

4 BR Canso 9802 and crew back at Tofino in the rain after a long patrol. Then, Jim McGuffin with Canso pilot Herb Hawkins of Hamilton, Ontario.

showed 1195:55 hours (day), 149:50 (night), mostly on the Canso. He now was posted to "Y" Depot at Moncton to await transport overseas. However, the war in Europe had ended, so McGuffin's next posting was back to Toronto to be demobbed at 4 Personnel Reception Centre at the Canadian National Exhibition.

On October 6, 1945 Jim McGuffin again was a civilian. He returned to his pre-war employment at the Toronto Transit Commission. There he did a number of jobs, including a few years as a streetcar operator. He gradually worked up to a senior slot in the TTC's traffic department. All along he enjoyed the company at the TTC of other ex-RCAF veterans including Bill Tarling, who had been at Tofino in radar; Norm Dawber, DFC, who had flown Typhoons; Don Elliot, who had been an observer on bombers and a POW; and Charlie Konvalinka, a Spitfire pilot.

Jim McGuffin often heard about how other 4 BR veterans were doing. Most found useful careers as did S/L Lowry. He became a medical doctor, eventually headed the Institute of Aviation Medicine in Toronto, and was a consultant to NASA. There his brilliance shone, as can be seen in this quote from one of his academic papers: "People by nature are competitive. At best, this characteristic takes the form of an individual competing with himself to achieve technical, artistic or moral excellence ... Today we may hope that the so-called space race will provide a noble and peaceful outlet for the competitive spirit of the great powers."

During Jim McGuffin's days on 4 (BR) Squadron, Cansos on strength were 9752, 9753, 9771, 9788, 9801, 9802, 9804, 11006, 11016, 11017, 11018, 11019 and 11044; Catalinas on strength were JX211, FP291 and FP294. At war's end most of these were sold. Their final fates are usually not known, but they mainly went to local scrap dealers and eventually were melted down. Two, however, had interesting postwar flying careers. Built by Boeing of Canada in Vancouver, Canso 9752 "Shady Lady" was sold in 1946 to become FAB6527 with the Brazilian Air Force. There it served to 1980 with 1 Transport Squadron, mainly on the Amazon. FAB6527 may be seen today in the Aerospace Museum in Rio de Janiero.

Built by Canadian Vickers at Cartierville, 11016 was struck off strength in 1946 and sold to The Babb Company, a huge US-based war surplus operator. This Canso seems to have been dormant for several years, then was acquired in 1955 by Austin Airways of Toronto. On July 2, 1959 it crashed at Povungnituk, far up the east coast of Hudson Bay. That day 'IHB suffered an engine failure shortly after a water takeoff. Capt Jack Humphries, co-pilot Colin Grant and flight engineer Eric Hazeldine struggle with the situation. Humphries saved the day by putting the Canso down in shallow water, breaking its back. The crew and nine passengers all were rescued. The DOT accident report pegs fuel contamination as the cause of the engine failure. 11016/CF-IHB finished its flying days with some 4000 flying hours. Other ex-4 BR Cansos may have operated postwar, but the records of many such aircraft have disappeared with the passing decades. Stranraer 907, on which Jim McGuffin crewed several times, also was a survivor. It became CF-BYI with Queen Charlotte Airlines, but on January 25, 1948 it caught fire in flight. The captain set down near Rock Bay, BC, where 'BYI burned and sank.

This December 1970 photo at Base Aérea dos Afonsos (Rio de Janeiro) illustrates former 4 BR Canso 9752 "Shady Lady" in her post-war service with Brazilian Air Force. (FAB/Museu Aeroespacial - MUSAL)

West Coast BR Pilot: A Brief Profile

Born in Toronto in 1917, James G. Easson received a degree in mechanical engineering from the University of Toronto before enlisting in the RCAF in May 1940. Having begun his flying days at 4 EFTS, Windsor Mills, he advanced to 2 SFTS, Uplands, receiving his wings there from Air Marshall Billy Bishop in December. Sgt Easson then instructed at 6 SFTS, Dunnville, where he had a routine tour with only one known "black". This was put up on September 18, 1940. when he taxied Yale 3427 into a sentry hut, while instructing a New Zealand student. Easson was assessed as "careless" over this minor incident. In May 1942 he attended the navigation course at 1 ANS, Rivers, Manitoba from where he was posted to flying boats on the West Coast. At this time he was commissioned.

P/O Easson completed the flying boat course at Patricia Bay from July into October 1942. Included were about 75 flying hours on the Stranraer, 26 on the Link Trainer. On armament exercises he dropped 42 bombs on fixed targets, 32 on moving targets, scoring well in both cases. He also qualified in gunnery on the ground, air-to-ground and air-to-air. He was assessed as having shown "keen and intelligent interest" through his course. Easson now joined 6 (BR) Squadron, Alliford Bay, as a Stranraer pilot, flying initially on a 6:30-hour patrol on July 16. Here, he seemed to fit in normally, even though F/L V.A. Margetts once assessed him as "not temperamentally" suited for flying boat operations, suggesting that he be sent back to the single-engine world. However, Easson remained on squadron until his final mission on July 20 the following year.

In December 1943 Easson transferred to 7 BR at Prince Rupert. Commencing on December 11 he flew the Catalina and Canso, his longest mission being that of June 23, 1944 – 20:40 hours. On April 13, 1944 his CO, S/L R. Dobson, noted confidentially of Easson: "He is a fully qualified Canso pilot. He has developed a high spirit of esprit de corps in his crew." To October 13, the date of his final flight at 7 BG, F/O Easson had logged 806:10 hours on 113 sorties. On leaving 7 BR, he joined 9 Transport Group at Rockcliffe. In January 1945 he was awarded the DFC with the comment: "This officer, since completing a successful non-operational tour as a flying instructor, has completed an operational tour in which he has proven himself to be an equally capable and energetic pilot on operations. His keenness and devotion to duty have been a splendid example to all ranks in his squadron." Easson, home on leave when word came of the DFC, was quoted in the local press as being dumbfounded: "I haven't the slightest idea what it would be for. If it's true, they must have picked my name out of a hat." So it was with many RCAF types, and sometimes it almost was true about the hat — awards sometimes were "doled out" on a quota system.

October 2-6, 1945 F/L Easson was the co-pilot under S/L Jack Scott on a pioneer Arctic flight led by S/L David S. Florence, DFC, chief navigation officer at 9 (T) Group. F/O N.M. Roberts (WAG) and LAC Lloyd Raymond completed the crew. The mission was organized after the HBC supply vessel *Nascopie* reported that typhoid had taken 45 lives at Cape Dorset. Half a ton of medicine was urgently needed to treat victims and vaccinate others. The Canso parachuted supplies at Cape Dorset on the southwest shore of Baffin Island, and at Pangnirtung far up Cumberland Sound. Such Arctic flights still being rare and hazardous, on October 27 the Canso crew was honoured by Air Marshall Leckie, Chief of the Air Staff. Easson subsequently had postings in the UK, AFHQ and 1 Air Division HQ in France. On March 2, 1957 a VIP B-25 Mitchell was returning from Churchill, Manitoba to Ottawa with A/V/M R.C. Ripley and some of his staff. While on approach to land, it suddenly crashed in flames, killing all eight aboard, W/C James G. Easson, DFC, included.

122 (Composite) Squadron: "The Flying Joes"

On January 10, 1942, 122 (Composite) Squadron formed under S/L Gordon G. Diamond at Patricia Bay near Victoria, its chief duties being transport, coast artillery co-operation and air-sea rescue. The squadron began as a a rag-tag outfit, by late summer 1942 having at least one each of the Bolingbroke, Goose, Lockheed 10, Lysander, Norseman and Shark (the Anson, Crane, Harvard, Hudson and Ventura came later). Initially, 122 had four flights: communications, CAC, target towing (land – Lysander) and target towing (sea – Shark). In May 1944 a radar calibration flight was added and there was a target towing detachment at Terrace.

July 21, 1942 brought the sort of excitement that no squadron wanted. That day Goose 917, skippered by P/O P.H. Gault, was operating in Alaska from Yakutat to Anchorage. With nine aboard

PBY-5 Catalina FP293 served 9 (BR) Squadron at Bella Bella in 1944. Although an RCAF PBY-5 Catalina had a better payload (e.g. more fuel) than the PBY-5A Canso, the latter was more versatile. A Canso was easier to service and maintain, not dependent on sea conditions and usually had more recovery options when arriving from a patrol. If seas were rough, any airfield would do. (CANAV Col.)

On 122 Squadron the Lysander flew search and rescue, towed targets for ground and air gunnery training, did artillery spotting, flew low-level Army co-operation missions and did general transportation. Pilots who liked a hot-performing, single-engine plane invariably praised the Lysander. (Ventura Memorial Flight Association)

Ill-fated Grumman Goose 917 of 122 Squadron had been in the RCAF inventory since July 1938. (Lilla Raymes Col.)

On July 31 Preston, Pepper, Baily and three civilians took off to find the crash site. They landed nearby in a glacial lake close to the Bagley Icefield. Gault and the other survivors were flown out next day, but the weather deteriorated and Preston had to back-track to his glacial lake. On August 2 he finally got everyone out to the coast at Yakataga. He then returned returned with a work party. They buried Cpl Donald on site. On the 3rd Preston flew two trips to Yakutat with survivors. There they were weathered in until the 7th, when Preston flew them all to Pat Bay via Annette Island.

For his fine efforts Sgt Baily received the George Medal, one of only 20 awarded in WWII to RCAF members. The citation to his GM notes: "After several hazardous days of travel which involved the suffering of considerable hardships, he was instrumental in securing aid. He later guided the rescue party to the scene of the crash and assisted them with their work. His initial rescue work and subsequent care of the injured undoubtedly saved the lives of the other four survivors of the crash." Preston received the AFC, which noted: "His courage and judgement in carrying out this operation under adverse weather conditions, landing on a glacial lake covered with floating blocks of ice, and the part he subsequently played in rescue operations were most praise-worthy achievements, to which those rescued owe their lives." Preston later commanded 166 (Comm) Squadron at Sea Island, and No.1 Winter Experimental and Training Flight at Kapuskasing, Ontario. He left the RCAF in December 1944. Baily served in the postwar RCAF.

plus plenty of kit, the Goose was loaded to the max. The weather was duff and Gault eventually became hopelessly lost and, ultimately, clipped the treetops and crashed. The scene immediately was one of disaster, but Sgt Francis M. Baily (a passenger) quickly took charge, assisting the worst-off. Gault was found unconscious and Cpl Tom B. Donald (122 Squadron, age 36 from New Westminster, BC) was dead.

As soon as some order was attained, AC1s John McIntosh and Silberman set out for the coast for help; next day Sgt Baily and AC1 Maylor followed. They met up with Silberman, who reported that McIntosh (122 Squadron, age 24 from Penticton, BC) had drowned at a crossing. July 24-26 the party struggled with dangerous rivers and dense forest. On the 26th they came across a cabin with a small stash of rice and flour. On the 28th they were spotted from the air and, later in the day, a USAAC Hudson dropped supplies. Next day Baily and Silberman made it to the coast. Baily's diary for the 30th states: "Silberman's head and nerves in bad shape ... walked along beach by ocean for approximately 10 miles. Met old miner with dog cart who rode us into a construction camp." There they found 122 Squadron Goose 940 under F/L George de Long Preston. Along with him, Preston had a medical officer, F/L Pepper.

RCAF 695 of 122 Squadron was Norseman No.2, originally CF-AZA, first flown in 1936 and in service that year with Mackenzie Air Service. It was impressed by the RCAF in February 1940 and scrapped in 1944. 697 was Norseman No.8, taken on RCAF strength in February 1940. It spent the war on the West Coast, then became CF-CRU with CPA. Many owners later, on November 22, 1968 it was lost in a crash in Northwest Ontario. (CANAV and Lilla Raymes Col.)

The Handley Page Hampden equipped 32 OTU at Patricia Bay, where the syllabus focused on torpedo tactics. The Hampden was one of the first modern aircraft manufactured in Canada, 160 having been built by the Canadian Associated Aircraft consortium. Components were assembled by Fairchild at St. Hubert and National Steel Car at Malton, then most of the 160 aircraft were shipped to the UK for the offensive against Germany. Some returned to serve at 32 OTU. Several were the object of West Coast air-sea rescue, when they failed to get back to base. (CANAV Col.)

The squadron ORB for June 1, 1943 lists some typical 122 activities. Visibility was good for much of the day. Bolingbroke 9094 made some test flights. Aircraft were sent to spot for the artillery at Macauley Point, target towing was done for a battery at Harrison Point, and army co-operation work was conducted at Point Grey. Norseman 695 went to Jericho Beach and back, while Norseman 2470 flew a photo route from Estevan Point to Prince Rupert. Goose 940 operated Terrace-Prince Rupert, Goose 942 carried G/C Luke to Princeton and back from "Pat Bay", while Goose 798 "returned from Annette Island and way stations". Events next day included: army co-op with two Lysanders at Christopher Point, artillery spotting, "Shark 545 target towing at Macauley Point for 2nd Bty", Norseman 695 to Ucluelet with passengers, "W/C Main deplaned from Beaufort 9968 from Sea Island" and "Goose 942 to Penticton to emplane party for Oliver". Next day was as busy and included a visit by three P-38s from Olympia, Washington.

On June 6 the daily diarist, who in this period was doing an excellent job, noted such happenings as: "One Lysander is standing by for air sea rescue work during daylight hours. At 1500 hrs. the plane despatched to sea in search of a missing Hampden. No results were obtained. Photo survey of Estevan continued with [Norseman] 2470 and later to Bella Bella and returned to Pat Bay... Goose 942 to Vernon and Revelstoke. Electra arrived with W/C Chalk ... Air cadets visited the squadron hangar." The missing Hampden was AJ992, which was never seen again. Some of the excitement next day saw Bolingbroke 9090 doing fighter affiliation and Shark 545 returning to base in a panic when a wing began separating. When the ASR Lysander was scrambled next day, it was airborne 65 seconds after the call.

On June 20, 1943 four Lysanders were on a training sortie to Port Angeles, Washington (122 often flew down the US west coast). Next day two Lysanders made a surprise attack on a gun emplacement at Alberta Head, and Norseman 3539 returned from a timber cruising job in the Queen Charlottes with a civilian forestry crew, probably gathering information as to forestry stocks. On the 22nd a Bolingbroke visited McChord Field, Washington with some WAC staff interested in studying USAAC

target towing equipment. The CO in this period was S/L George Preston, AFC.

Operations at 122 changed little as the war progressed. The ORB for March 1944 notes interesting goings-on. Once the ceiling had lifted by mid-afternoon on March 12, there was a target towing sortie to Point Grey for a 40-mm ack-ack unit. A Norseman had a transportation flight down to Boeing Field and, wrote the squadron diarist, "One aircraft carried out photography around Comox and Campbell River area." Next day there was target towing for the aircraft carrier HMS *Ruler* and a Lysander did photo work over Hornsby Island. On the 14th three Lysanders and a Norseman were on an army co-operation exercise, doing simulated gas- and smoke-laying attacks for advancing infantry, low-level strafing (blank ammunition), and simulated bombing and photography. Three army men were along to let them experience the air side of operations.

On March 15, 1944 Cessna Crane 8686 was acquired from 163 Squadron for proficiency training. The weather next day being duff, two feature movies were shown. On the 17th two Lysanders made a surprise attack on the Point Grey and Burnaby ack-ack sites. The Chief of the Air Staff visited briefly, before leaving on a tour of north coastal bases. On the 19th a Harvard, a Lysander and

two Bolingbrokes flew simulated attacks on the aircraft carrier HMS *Arbiter*. WO2 Folkerson was noted as having soloed in the Harvard, and a Ventura flew a radar calibration mission at No.7 RDF (radar) station. While a Lysander towed a target for the 40-mm unit at Point Grey, Hurricanes did beat-ups of the same emplacement. Next day Anson Vs 12385 and 12386 were taken on strength. Numerous flights were made in this period carrying Army officers on camouflage observation duties. An ORB entry for March 24, 1944 reads: "Ceiling 3-5000, became unlimited by 0130 hrs. Lowered to 3-4000 from 1530-1830 and unlimited for rest of day... Detachment at Comox carried out attacks on troops on Denman Island, also strafed troops, barges and motor convoys with flour bombs, blank machine gun fire. 17 sorties flown ... Pat Bay Gremlins defeated Vancouver Combines in first two basketball games at Vancouver. Ventura aircraft carried out calibration for #7 R.D.F. at 11,000 ft."

On March 27, 1944 Anson 12384 was taken on strength, while Harvard 3195 was returned to "Command Reserve". F/O Yates soloed on the Bolingbroke, and low-level simulated attacks were made on the escort carrier HMS *Queen*. In this period the squadron's dedicated ASR aircraft were Lysanders 483 and 484.

Lifeboat Hudson BW628 served 122 Squadron. Here it is along the BC coast in early postwar days while with 123 (S&R) Flight. (Neil A. MacDougall)

Flying hours for March totalled: target towing – 149:50, line flying 118:50, communications – 52:30, test – 40:20, calibration – 27:20, Army co-operation – 27:15, photo – 23:50, navy co-operation – 14:05, air sea rescue – 0:50, range – 0:30, other 1:30, total 462:30. The aircraft establishment at 122 included: Anson – 3, Bolingbroke – 11, Crane – 1, Norseman – 1, Ventura – 2. From May to August 1945, 122 Squadron operated at Port Hardy, due to overcrowding at Patricia Bay. At war's end most RCAF squadrons ceased operations within weeks. In the case of 122 Squadron, by then returned to Patricia Bay, it heard of its demise by means of "Secret Organization Order 299" of September 8 authorized by A/V/M F.S. McGill for the CAS:

As a result of the successful conclusion of the war in Europe and of the war against Japan, the continued operation of this unit is no longer required... This unit is to cease the performance of its function effective 5 Sept 45 and is to disband effective 15 Sept 45... The posting of staff personnel is to be arranged by AFHQ and the AOC, WAC... Equipment, supplies, forms, stationary and publications are to be disposed of in accordance with existing instructions... A Board of Officers is to be appointed by the AOC, WAC, for the purpose of disposing of documents.

Griffin and Kostenuk note in *RCAF Squadrons and Aircraft* that 122 Squadron logged 23,778 flying hours from beginning to end. It lost three aircraft and six personnel. On September 16, 1945 No.3 (Composite) Flight at Sea Island formed to take over 122's former roles in transport, target towing, air-sea rescue, etc.

Annette Island during RCAF days in 1942-43. A summer's scene with 14 Squadron's Kittyhawks lined up on their way to Unmak Island in the Aleutians, where they would fly some 200 combat missions. A 115 Bolingbroke is in the distance. Nearest are two P-39s and Marauder 40-1457 of the 73rd Bombardment Group, then fighting in the Aleutians. This production batch of Marauders ended far and wide – 1442 was shot down by flak in the Torbriand Islands, 1443 crashed in Texas, 1451, 1459 and 1464 crash-landed in northern British Columbia on January 16, 1942 and 1468 was lost in New Guinea in a collision with an enemy Zero. In 2010, 1464 was the world's only flyable B-26, having been recovered from the BC boonies. Then, in a wintry scene a 115 Squadron Bolingbroke sits among a pair of B-26 Marauders likely involved in the Aleutian campaign, a C-47 and a Pan Am Lodestar. In the distance and tarped-over against the elements are three USAAC Bell P-39 Airacobras and six 115 "Bolies" with ground crews getting ready for some activity. (Murray Castator Col.)

Annette Island

The RCAF's role at the USAAC post on Annette Island, Alaska is well covered in such books as *Creation of a National Air Force*, *Royal Canadian Air Force at War 1939-1945* and *Canada's Air Force at War and Peace, Vol.1*. Annette Island had its beginnings when the first 500 men of the US Army 28th Engineers landed in August 1940 to begin construction of a major airfield. The first operational unit (a small meteorological detachment) commenced duties in July 1941, followed by the vanguard of a communications detachment, which arrived in August on a Dolphin amphibian. The first transient arrivals seem to have been Douglas B-18 No.7536 and a Beech AT-7, which landed on November 18 in bad weather. By then two runways of 6000- and 7500-feet were ready. Annette Island initially was an air defence installation covering southeast Alaska and BC. With the defeat of Japan in the Aleutians, however, this role ended. The official USAAF Annette Island history notes of this:

... 1 November 1943 to 31 May 1944 was the period of reduction of Annette Island Air Base from its status as a tactical and patrol base ... to an air transport refuelling base ... Except as a stepping stone for tactical aircraft proceeding to the Aleutians, Annette bowed out of the war, sending its excess men and its bomber and fighter squadrons to the more urgent areas. The first signs of reduction of the base were the moving out of the two Canadian squadrons [the] 135th ... and the 149th ... on the 9th of November 1943... They had left behind them many of their buddies lost in hazardous patrols over South Eastern Alaska's mountains, and in training flights...

RCAF units at Annette Island included 115 Squadron (Bolingbrokes – April 1942 to August 1943), 118 Squadron (Kittyhawks – June 1942 to August 1943), 135 Squadron (Hurricanes – August to November 1943) and 149 Squadron (Venturas – August to November 1943). 115 Squadron had formed in August 1941 at Rockcliffe as a fighter squadron flying Bolingbrokes. It served at Patricia Bay from October 15, 1941 to April 25, 1942, when it moved north to Annette Island. To date its Bolingbrokes had been configured

A fine Annette Island scene taken by Murray Castator showing a 115 Squadron Bolingbroke.

as long-range fighters with 4x.303 machine guns in a belly pack and a single gun in the rear turret. For Alaska, however, the fighter role was considered inappropriate, as mentioned by a memo on June 18, 1942 from the Chief of the Air Staff's office:

There is an urgent need for squadrons on the West Coast which can be used as a striking force. No.115 Squadron is temporarily stationed at Annette Island, Alaska, and is equipped with Bolingbroke fighter aircraft. These ... are better suited for bomber reconnaissance ... than for fighter operations, and can be converted at this base from fighter to bomber reconnaissance aircraft... No.115 Squadron is to be converted to a Bomber Reconnaissance Squadron effective June 23, 1942.

From Annette Island 115 specialized in shipping and anti-submarine patrols into August 1943. That year it suffered a painful loss – the March 26, 1943 crash of 122 Squadron's Norseman 2481, while returning to base from Ketchikan with several passengers. All nine aboard died: S/L Fred B. Curry (115 Squadron, age 25 from Ottawa), F/L I.M. Dowling (age 35 from Brantford, Ontario), F/L Ernest B. Stapleford (115 Squadron, age 34 from Moose Jaw), LAC Edward K. McMichael (115 Squadron, age 27 from Goderich) and three young women from a USO entertainment troupe – M. Gloeckner, A.J. Kaiser and C. Street. From August 14-18 the squadron was re-equipping with Venturas and ferrying its Bolingbrokes to Boundary Bay near Vancouver.

The 115 ORBs for March 1944, by which time the squadron was at Tofino, describe some of the standard goings-on with a WAC squadron. On March 17, for example, the Chief of the Air Staff, Air Marshal Robert Leckie, arrived by Lodestar for a quick base tour. With him were the AOC of WAC, A/V/M L.F. Stevenson and Air Commodore K.M. Guthrie. They met with S/L T.H. Christie of 115, and S/L J.A. Thompson of 132, the local Kittyhawk squadron. At 0400 next morning the station was alerted to a Dakota being missing. But the weather closed in and no flying was done all day. The search began in earnest on the 19th, but with no sign of the Dakota. Next morning eight Venturas set out to search again, but there was landing gear trouble with aircraft 2222. After burning off fuel, jettisoning his underwing tanks, etc., F/O MacLeod landed 2222 on a partially extended gear.

Poor weather often hampered operations but, when the sun shone, 115 got in maximum flying, as on August 4, 1944: "A welcome break in the weather and a total of 38 hrs. was put in ... No.8 patrol took off at 0930 hrs. and the pm patrols got away at 1400 hrs. Five high level bombing exercises were carried out and two at low level." The next three days also were fine, the diarist noting of the 7th: "Weather C.A.V.U. All patrols were cancelled and low and high level bombing, instruments and radio range exercises were carried out." On August 18 the squadron suddenly heard that it would be disbanding – effective immediately. Next day the Venturas ferried to Port Hardy for storage. Many squadron members were posted to

A hard landing on February 11, 1943 spelled the end for 8 BR Bolingbroke 9044.

8 Squadron, Patricia Bay (Venturas) and flew out next day on Dakotas. Others soon were on their way to Pennfield Ridge, New Brunswick, home of 34 OTU (Venturas, Dakotas). On the 20th there was a bit of merriment – a party thrown by G/C Lister, station CO. Everyone later continued at the King's Own Rifles Mess into the wee hours. The diarist noted: "The splendid friendship which existed between the Army and the Airforce at Tofino has resulted in many pleasant evenings being enjoyed in the 'bush'." The Pennfield Ridge draft left by boat on August 21 and the admin staff rapidly completed all the paperwork. Meanwhile, 132 Squadron received orders to proceed to Sea Island. Other WAC squadrons also were winding down, a clear sign that RCAF HQ realized that such vast resources no longer were needed on the West Coast. The war in the Pacific now was centred far to the south, where the Allies were closing in on Japan.

149 (BR) Squadron

October 26, 1942 saw the formation at Patricia Bay of 149 (Torpedo Bomber) Squadron. Equipped with Bristol Beauforts (the only RCAF squadron with this type), "149 BR" was established to support the US fighting the Japanese in the Aleutians. The Japanese were defeated in that theatre in the summer of 1943, so 149's *raison d'être* evaporated. In July the squadron exchanged its obsolete Beauforts for Venturas, but still did not have a particular role. WAC HQ suggested that it also might support the Americans in Alaska. Commanding the region was Admiral Frank Jack Fletcher, USN, whose war record included command in the 1942 battles of the Coral Sea and Midway. When consulted about 149 Squadron, he pointed to problems with his own Venturas – an inadequate war load, insufficient range, imperfect performance in the anti-submarine attack mode, etc. In a memo of July 28, 1943

While the Beaufort, Bolingbroke, Digby, Hudson and Stranraer did good early work on RCAF HWE coastal operations, they were stop-gap types urgently needing replacement. The Canso, Liberator and Ventura ultimately resolved this. A natural development in Lockheed's family of twins, the first Ventura (also known as the PV-1 and B-34) flew in July 1941. Shown is prototype AE658. Venturas quickly entered RAF service as tactical bombers over France and Holland, but fared badly against the Luftwaffe. The Ventura found its best use on coastal operations and equipped several RCAF home squadrons. After its test flying duties were completed in California, AE658 served at 34 OTU, the RAF Ventura training school at Pennfield Ridge, New Brunswick. There it ended its days after an accident on July 25, 1943. The RCAF had 286 Venturas during the war. A few continued postwar as air armament trainers, then some surplus Venturas found work with Spartan Air Services of Ottawa. The sole Ventura remaining in Canada is being restored in Edmonton by the Ventura Memorial Flight Association headed by airline pilot A.T. "Tony" Jarvis. (Lockheed)

Air Marshal L.S. Breadner, RCAF Chief of the Air Staff, commented: "Due to these factors, the Admiral is considering the withdrawal of Ventura squadrons from Alaska ... The AOC Western Air Command has therefore been advised that if the U.S.N. does not want an R.C.A.F. Ventura squadron for operations in the Aleutians, the subject is to be dropped." In the end, 149 BR was assigned to the defence of the strategic port of Prince Rupert.

Following delivery of its Venturas, 149 BR served under W/C R.R. Dennis at Annette Island from August to November 1943 – a temporary arrangement pending construction of a permanent home at Terrace. The ORB describes this period in excellent detail. Except for crews ferrying Venturas from Sea Island to Annette Island, 149 travelled by sea to Prince Rupert August 15-17. Next day they continued by sea north to Annette Island. Training began in earnest on September 1 – 23 flights were made for 27:45 hours. Ventura 2195 landed from Sea Island, bringing 149's strength to 15 aircraft.

The ORB is rich in all the details of life at Annette Island. Commanding the RCAF detachments was W/C Gordon G.

Diamond, a revered pre-war officer. Everything from requests from prairie airmen for "harvest leave" to the painting of the officers' mess is mentioned. On September 7 a Canso arrived with the Governor General and Princess Alice on a station inspection. When the regal party sailed for points north three days later, their vessel was escorted by 149 Venturas. That day S/L Bolduc of 149 checked out W/C Diamond on the Ventura. For the month 149 statistics included 33 officers and 420 other ranks on strength. The 15 Venturas flew 415:40 hours, 339:30 being on training – instrument flying, air firing, dropping depth charges, bombing and navigation, cross-country flying, etc. Only 31:25 hours were flown "on ops". Due to poor weather, these often were not completed. Otherwise, the usual comment in the files for any operational patrol reads ""Nothing sighted", or something like "Diverted to Smithers due to weather."

October 26, 1943 brought bad news when Ventura 2193 piloted by WO2 George C. Marshall (age 21 from St. Walburg, Saskatchewan) did not return from a patrol in duff weather. The ORB commented next day, "Next of kin have not yet been notified as there is still hope

Typical Venturas of 149 Squadron. (Ventura Memorial Flight Association)

they may be safe ... and have not been able to contact us." Bad weather continued so that even by the 28th few ASR missions had been flown: "Crews standing by for any lift in weather for this purpose." Thirteen ASR flights were made on the 29th. Next day the diarist noted: "No clues to the whereabouts of #2193 were located owing to poor visibility ..." Weather permitting, ASR missions were flown into November, when the squadron was packing for Terrace. On November 6 the diarist reported, "The Committee of Adjustment have almost completed the collecting and listing of the personal belongings of the missing personnel." That night a farewell dinner was held to honour the departing Canadians, US Army LCol Gibson officiating. Also noted was that 149 BR had met its $54,000 5th Victory Loan drive goal.

On November 9, 1943 ten Venturas ferried to Terrace to join 135 Squadron (Kittyhawks). Most of the week was dogged by bad weather in the area where 2193 was missing. Postings this week included S/L Bolduc, who was going overseas to Bomber Command. Squadron personnel were awaiting clear weather, so the transport planes could get in to move everyone to Terrace (equipment, etc. went on the steamer *Catala* to Prince Rupert, a sail of 8 1/2 hours). On November 17 W/C Dennis led 135 Squadron into Terrace. Meanwhile, four Venturas continued the search for 2193. Bad weather again moved in, but on November 24 three Venturas were out. Training commenced in earnest at Terrace, the pilots getting used to the local geography. The search intensified on the 30th, when a 7 BR Canso arrived from Ketchikan with a party of US Coast Guard ground search specialists. Squadron strength at month's end was 270 personnel and 15 Venturas. Due to much bad weather and the time needed in the base move, only 185:25 hours were flown.

Weather remained a problem for most of December. Mud was a nightmare and quarters, the hangar and other infrastructure still were not outfitted. Due to weather, aircraft often were having to recover at such places as Juneau, Smithers, Masset and Prince George. On December 17 the diarist noted: "Weather entirely unsatisfactory ... aircrew rounded out the day listening to lectures. One

The 149 Ventura crew of Holton, Ross, Scharff and Tommy Causy seen at Annettte Island. Post war, Causy became the RCAF's first helicopter pilot. (Ventura Memorial Flight Association)

good one concerned the woodcraft or bush knowledge accumulated by F/O Mills which was delivered in the hope that it might benefit future lost crews... The radar mechanics are taking a large share of night guard duties around the aircraft."

On December 18 the squadron supported a local mountain warfare course by para-dropping supplies and equipment, and doing aerial photography. Next day was noted as CAVU but, with no mention of 2193 search missions, it seems that 149 no longer was involved. In the end, Marshall and crew were declared dead. Besides Marshall, these were F/O Alfred J. Chandler (age 22 from Edmonton), WO2 Vernon C. Arnold (age 24 from Regina) and FSgt Henry Chambers (age 20 from Winnipeg).

On the 19th, the weather closed in at night. A Ventura returning from Prince George failed with its approach, so diverted to Smithers. On December 21 two Venturas flew to Woodcock, about

60 miles northwest of Terrace to support those cleaning up at the site of a fatal Hurricane crash. Christmas was nigh, so partying and leave-taking took precedent. The diarist heaved a sigh of relief on Christmas Day: "Nobody complained when the low ceiling and fog left no doubt about flying being washed out." Still, there had to be a 149 crew on standby throughout the day. Wash-out weather continued, so only 218:30 hours were flown for the month.

A concert was the highlight for New Year's Eve: "The senior N.C.O.s were guests of the Officers at their Mess from 1100 to 1200 hours ... New Year's dinner was enjoyed immensely by all... Ventura 2197 returned to base after several unsuccessful attempts to reach here because of poor weather ... No local flying or patrols." No serious flying took place until January 10. On the 12th there was so much ice on the station that flying again was scrubbed: "Lectures were given today on Signals and Armament."

These small stones mark the communal grave of the four men lost on Ventura 2193. The wreck and some remains were found long after the crash by an Indian trapper. (Ventura Memorial Flight Association)

Like all RCAF aircraft types, nearly all the Venturas were disposed of soon after war's end. AJ194 was bought for scrap by farmer George Ventress of Brighton, Ontario. Prices were as low as $70 for a Ventura "as is where is".

Since the weather got worse, lectures were the order of the day until the 20th, when conditions brightened somewhat.

There never was a shortage of ideas for lectures. On January 23, for example, there was a one about war games, then films covering air sea rescue and gas mask drill. With duff weather on the 27th, aircraft and ship recognition were reviewed and there was dinghy drill. Next day there was a CO's parade and this comment from the

diarist: "There was no route march owing to the heavy rain and the balance ... was spent in rifle exercise in the hangar." Flying for all of January totalled 265:30 hours, so 149's 15 Venturas were still barely broken in. In February, alone, there were 14 spare Venturas stored under guard at Smithers.

Rotten weather persisted into early February. The diarist noted on the 7th, "Word was received this afternoon of the ditching of two Venturas near Campbell

River ... The captains are considered to be capable and reliable pilots." Periodically, a 165 Squadron Lodestar visited Terrace with passengers, freight and mail, but often could not land due to weather. Several good flying days this month resulted in some operational patrols. These, however, never had anything much to report, other than friendly shipping. On February 25 WO2 T.A. "Tommy" Causey landed 2192 while doing night training, then had his undercarriage collapse. Meanwhile, sports, movies and the occasional dance helped add some balance to squadron life. For February 1944 the squadron logged 573:30 hours, mainly due to improved flying conditions.

The squadron now received its notice of disbandment. Secret Organization Order No.89 stated: "No.149 squadron is to become operationally inactive effective 1st March, 1944... the establishment is to be cancelled effective 15th March ..." On March 1 the diarist noted, "Orders were received to discontinue patrols and gradually prepare aircraft for long term storage." The station technical people began inhibiting the engines on several Venturas and personnel began disappearing on new postings, a few for overseas. Aircraft were grounded on March 8 other than for ferrying or special transportation flights. Two days later 135 Squadron departed by train for Patricia Bay. On March 13, 149's diarist lamented, "There is a feeling of sadness which seems to permeate the hangar." Next day he reported all Venturas "bedded down for long term storage". Next day he waxed poetic: "Zero, zero with rain ... It would seem that mother nature and Jupiter Pluvius were aware of the disbandment and commiserating with 149 on this the last day of its existence ... A short life although nothing drab about it." On the last day 149 BR's talented diarist added:

Numerous ex-RCAF Venturas migrated to the US. Dee Howard of Texas purchased many to convert into speedy, luxurious corporate planes. Here is his Super Ventura conversion N5034F at Toronto in April 1966. Formerly RCAF 2244, it began its "life of luxury" with the Fruehauf Trailer Co. of Detroit in 1954. In 1961 it joined the Firestone Tire and Rubber of Akron and later served many other companies. It last was heard of dormant in Bogotá in the early 1990s. (Al Martin)

Other ex-RCAF Venturas operated in their original configuration with Spartan Air Services of Ottawa. Spartan owned 19 although only a few were flown, the rest being spares. Spartan's Venturas roamed the continents for several years in the 1950s doing high-level aerial photography. Here is CF-HBW (ex-RCAF 2174) at Santa Lucia in the Caribbean. This aircraft later went to Dee Howard. As a Super Ventura it served numerous companies, but eventually fell into disrepute. Being speedy and commodious, the Ventura gained particular favour with drug smugglers. In 1984 this Ventura was apprehended in Nassau with drugs, impounded, then was left to rot. (Harry Mochulsky)

There is little rejoicing, only the feeling of thwarted ambition ... The rain continues to fall heavily ... The magnificent Venturas, which have been the pride of the squadron. have been cared for by loving hand, but are now stripped of all offensive weapons and prepared for a long sleep... So ends the life of a gallant squadron – Ready, Aye Ready!

Annette Island during 118 Squadron Days

Murray E. Castator grew up in the 1920s-30s in Long Branch on the western edge of Toronto. As a boy he earned his spending money as a golf caddy and eventually became very good at the game himself. When finished high school, Murray took up printing with the Bryant Press, one of Toronto's oldest book manufacturers. He enlisted in the RCAF early in the war, training as a mechanic at 1 TTS at St. Thomas. He then joined 118 Squadron at Dartmouth, with whom he travelled by rail across Canada to Vancouver, thence north to Prince Rupert and on to Annette Island aboard the RCAF vessel *Sekani*. Everyone was happy to reach destination, one of those on board recalling: "Many meals were contributed to the fishes from the rail of the 'Sick Annie'."

Murray Castator had always been a "photo bug" – he took pictures of everything that caught his eye. Being an aviation hound, no airplane could pass that he didn't "shoot", regardless of the rules against photography. These pages are a tribute to this great Canadian, who passed away on May 30, 2000. Some of these photos also appear in *Canada's Air Force at War and Peace*, Vol.1, but here they are accompanied by fresh data.

The meticulously-kept maintenance board at 118 Squadron. The board notes each airplane by tail number and squadron letter, the name of the last pilot to fly whichever Kittyhawk or Harvard, who were the mechanics signing it out, the airframe and engine hours and inspections due. In other words, the board is a microcosmic eye on the squadron. Then, the pilot's briefing room, the other focus of 118 operations.

An RCAF Kittyhawk in one of 118 Squadron's improvised nose hangars. If the weather was fine, however, work was done in the open air.

Unidentified 118 ground crew at Annette Island 1942-43. Many of these men later were overseas. Murray Castator ended on Typhoons at 143 Wing, where there was much more of tent life plus the dust of Normandy and the mud of Eindhoven. But anyone toughened up by Annette Island could handle whatever 143 Wing asked of him.

Murray Castator's photo files included many candid photos of squadron personnel including W/C A.D. Nesbitt, DFC., who commanded the Canadian operation at Annette Island from June to October 1942. Earlier, he had fought in the Battle of Britain and commanded 401 Squadron. Subsequently, he was overseas again, commanding 144 Wing, then 143 Wing. On September 15, 1940 Nesbitt had shot down an Me.109, then himself had been lucky to escape his burning Hurricane by parachute. (Right) Murray posing in gear appropriate for the weather. The sign points the passer-by towards the Canadian encampment. Then, Murray in work apparel with one of his 6-gun Kittyhawks.

F/Os Bill Stowe and Jack Biernes learned the basics of the fighter game at Annette Island. Bill ended overseas flying Spitfires on 41 and 130 squadrons, where he scored several victories. Jack flew Typhoons on 438 – the overseas version of 118. The Typhoon business was hazardous, but Jack made it to war's end. Then, while leading his squadron in a victory flypast over Copenhagen on June 1, 1945, something went wrong – S/L Jack Beirnes, DFC and Bar, crashed fatally. Bill Stowe also had a DFC by war's end, the citation for which notes: "This officer has destroyed at least three enemy aircraft and in addition destroyed and damaged more than 180 enemy transport vehicles including trains, barges, tugs and mechanical transport. He has served with outstanding success as a flight commander."

After his Alaska tour, Arthur C. Brooker stayed with 118 once it re-formed as 438. On November 30, 1944 Art and his 438 sidekick Bill Beatty were returning from leave in the UK when the Dakota they were aboard was shot down by German flak. Happily, the pilot did a good job of crash-landing.

Herb Ivens went to the Far East following Alaska. He flew Hurricanes and Thunderbolts on 261 Squadron, but ended as a Japanese POW. Somehow, Herb survived his brutal captors' efforts to destroy him mentally and physically.

Pete Wilson of North Vancouver was another hardcore 118/438 pilot. Pete came to a grim end on January 1, 1945 when the Luftwaffe pounced on Eindhoven. He was scrambling in response to the raid when his Typhoon was clobbered by a Hun fighter – he died within a few minutes.

George Baxter, who hailed from Victoria, BC, was one of 118 Squadron's "originals" at Dartmouth. On October 12, 1942 he met with a freakish death – somehow his dinghy inflated in flight. George could not control his Kittyhawk (AL210) and crashed fatally into the sea.

Allan E. Studholme of Toronto left 118 for 401 Squadron. Over Holland one day his Spitfire conked out. He crash landed OK, but for the rest of his war was a guest of the Third Reich.

Frank G. Grant commanded 118 from February to July 1943, then was 438's first CO. He finished the war as W/C Frank G. Grant, DSO, DFC, and also had the Croix de Guerre with Silver Star (France) and Netherlands Flying Cross. The citation to his DSO sums up this superb RCAF officer: "The great success achieved by his wing has been directly attributable to Wing Commander Grant's exceptional skill and outstanding leadership."

A highlight in the air force always was pay day. Here 18 lines up to receive its just desserts. The paymaster always had his armed guard – note the flight sergeant keeping an eye on things. Then, break time for a few minutes on the flightline.

Maintaining a squadron of fighter planes kept dozens of ground crew busy day and night. There was no shortage at Annette Island of heavy lifting.

Everyone at Annette Island had to be combat ready, lest the place be attacked. Every Canadian was familiar with the standard Enfield rifle and his basic kit included such items as a tin hat and gas mask. Here the Canadians take time out from air force duties to train in base defence. One airman poses in his basic soldier's kit.

Recreation at Annette Island offered the usual baseball, fun in the messes, etc., and the fishing, hiking and camping were there for the taking. These 118 fellows (Murray Castator on the right) were not missing out.

The RCAF got involved in all sorts of interesting activities. Here 118 parades on the main street in Ketchikan, helping its American cousins celebrate Memorial Day on May 30, 1942. Then, some of the participants on the boat that ferried them to and from the mainland.

Photos and pin-ups from home and elsewhere boosted a fellow's morale when the wind, dust, rain, sleet or snow of Annette Island were getting everyone down. So did the USO and other such entertainment troupes, which regularly showed up with a live show.

Bob Hope made his first overseas tour with the USO in September 1942. In this candid Annette Island scene he and sidekick Jerry Colonna are surrounded by Canucks. To make such a trip, any civilian required a special travel permit issued by Western Defence Command and Fourth Army, Alaska Travel Control.

When the dust settled at the end of a shift, sometimes a fellow wanted to join his buddies in the canteen or ... maybe felt more like stretching out in his bunk, as Murray Castator is doing here.

Ketchikan (where the girls were) was off limits most of the time to the RCAF, and fraternizing with the locals was a strict no-no. So ... what did a bunch of fellows do in wartime on an isolated island with no women? Their mothers would not want to know! Here, 118 whoops it up on a Saturday night.

Something a bit more "traditional" – Coke, Schlitz and Ritz crackers in 118s NCOs' mess.

Fighters of many types passed through Annette Island on the Northwest Staging Route from (if upbound) Montana to Edmonton and on to Alaska. Bell P-39 41-7038 is seen on a refuelling stop. The records show little about this beautiful fighter, other than that it was "condemned" on June 17, 1942.

Lockheed P-38E Lightning 41-2069 "Itsy Bitsy" taxis away at Annette Island. This fighter had a brief career – records show it as "salvaged" in May 1942 – it had crashed at Casco Cove on Attu Island in the outer reaches of the Aleutians. Then, a pair of P-38s – on the left, '2069 '76' and 41-1984 '73' – draws a crowd, including some Canucks.

Kittyhawk woes at 118 Squadron. Unfriendly weather, rough airfield conditions and who knows what other factors contributed to many Kittyhawk prangs at Annette Island as shown in these well-taken Murray Castator photos.

VW-K being hauled back to servicing after a prang.

Canso 9752 of 4 (BR) Squadron at Annette Island while escorting 14 (F) Squadron north to Kiska in the Aleutians in March 1943. A 115 Squadron Bolingbroke and a Kittyhawk of 14 or 118 squadron are in the background.

A US Navy Catalina likely on an Aleutians assignment sits at Annette Island. Note the bomb under the starboard wing, and how the plane is anchored with concrete-filled 45-gallon drums.

This Douglas B-18 Bolo was staying long enough that the crew chief got out his wing covers – a simple solution that meant they could get moving when needed without having to spend an hour sweeping snow.

USAAC Lockheed A-29 41-23399 taxiing at Annette Island. This version of the RAF Hudson had an open-air dorsal gun position rather than a turret. Then another Lockheed beauty – a US Navy PV-1 Ventura.

North American B-25 41-29987 was modified to the F-10 photo reconnaissance version. The crew dubbed it "All Your'n".

Folks at Annette Island tended to gather around and watch when something like a B-24 rolled up the taxiway.

In May 1943 C-47 14-38717 was assigned from the factory to the Alaska Wing of USAAF Air Transport Command. It was here for a sad event – transporting the body of F/L Arthur Jarred, one of Canada's Yanks. On March 28, 1943 this 27-year old from Lansing, Michigan had died after getting into a spin. This happened after he had rolled Kittyhawk AK821 while carrying a large bomb. Kittyhawk pilots were aware that aerobatics with a war load were dangerous. Notice the guard of honour sending off Jarred to his broken hearted family.

06999 was a US Navy R4D-3 (USAAC equivalent: C-53C). Later in the war it joined Pan American, then had a long list of operators until ending badly. Icing and poor airmanship caused it to crash, while approaching O'Hare Airport in Chicago on March 9, 1964. Of 30 aboard, 29 survived.

This US Navy Douglas C-54A was ordered as USAAC 41-37285, but began its service days in April 1943 as US Navy 39139. Here it awaits at Annette Island while on some Alaskan mission. As in so many of these photos, RCAF Kittyhawks are evident (note the dust rising from 118's dispersal across the runway). In 1946 this C-54 joined Transocean Airlines as N79998. On August 15, 1949 it departed Rome westbound for Shannon with a crew of nine and 49 Italian immigrants heading for Venezuela via New York. Due to navigation errors, the plane overflew Shannon, where it had been due at 00:23 hours. Far out to sea, the crew realized its error and turned back at about 00:50. At 01:06 the flight contacted Shannon while still about 100 miles west. At 02:40 N79998 was out of fuel and ditched 7 miles off Lurga Point. Eight of those aboard had died by the time ships came to the rescue.

Two beautiful Lockheed Lodestars. NC33664 began with Pan Am's Alaska Division in March 1941. It later transferred to the US Navy and was stricken from USN records *circa* 1948.

A US Navy Grumman Widgeon refuels at Annette Island. Then, visiting US Civil Aeronautics Administration Douglas Dolphin NC26 (originally and latterly NC14205). Once Bill Boeing's private plane, the last owner of this rare piece of Americana was the great Renaissance Man and antique airplane buff, Cole Darden. NC14205 last flew on October 30, 1998, then joined the US National Naval Aviation Museum in Pensacola, Florida.

HWE – Further Losses

The story of the first RCAF aircraft lost on WWII operations is well documented. A few days before war broke out, 8 (GR) Squadron had left Rockcliffe on a wartime footing for Sydney, Nova Scotia. One aircraft – Delta 673 crewed by FSgt J.E. Doan and LAC D.A. Rennie – landed en route in Maine with technical problems. After an engine change, it proceeded on September 14, failed to reach destination and could not be located. Doan and Rennie eventually were declared dead. In July 1958 the wreckage of 673 was discovered north of Fredericton and shipped to the National Aviation Museum in Ottawa.

Three days after Delta 673 disappeared, Stranraer 911 of 5 (BR) Squadron departed base at 0520 hours to intercept a convoy and conduct an "Outer Anti-Submarine Patrol". Aboard were S/L R.C. Mair (skipper), F/O W.H. Stapley, Cpl T.A. Calow, AC1 S.J. Pomes, S.J., LAC J.A. Daniels, AC1 J.W. Hornick, AC1 R.C. Magnus, AC2 R.L. Alexander and AC2 W.F. Phillips. Due to unfavourable winds and poor visibility, accurate drift readings could not be made and the convoy was not met. At 0932 S/L Mair set course for Sable Island off Halifax, but this also was missed, so he turned for the mainland. Attempts to jettison the depth charges failed, as did wireless operator Cpl Calow's efforts to contact any station (electrical storms were raging).

At 1225 Mair alighted. The armourers released the depth charges and an SOS was sent via pigeon. A sleeping bag saturated in oil was streamed from the nose, in the hope that its oil slick might be spotted from the air, and the life raft was inflated and secured atop the fuselage. A watch was set up and Cpl Calow kept sending SOS. His efforts finally succeeded – Dartmouth replied at 2330 hours. It was 0705 before a search plane appeared – an 8 (GP) Squadron float-equipped Delta, but it missed 911 in spite of Aldis signals being made. At 1000 the Swedish tanker *Pollux* appeared at about five miles. The Stranraer sent up flares and the WOp kept sending to Dartmouth, which was in touch with the tanker. Two Deltas were circling and contact finally was made. The *Pollux* drew near and sent out a lifeboat, while the crew of 911 sank all its secret

One of the first RCAF home front losses involved 5 (BR) Squadron Stranraer 911. A combination of good fortune, training and experience saw the crew safely home after 911 sank far out to sea. Shown is another 5 BR "Stranny" – 914 which, in its own right, would have survived many a hazardous mission. (DND PL2731)

documents. They then swam for the lifeboat and all were safe by about 1045 hours on the 18th.

With seas of 25-35 feet Capt Adolf Olsen of the *Pollux* could not save the Stranraer, but stood by awaiting the salvage tug *Cruiser*. By that time the seas were too heavy to get a line onto the aircraft. The RCAF crew now transferred to the *Cruiser*, which took them into Louisburg at 2200 hours. Word later arrived that 911 had sunk while under tow on the 19th. An official report of this incident signed by A/V/M N.R. Anderson, AOC Eastern Air Command later noted:

It is pointed out that the Pollux was kept from her normal work for a considerable period of time, and that her lifeboat was severely damaged, due to the roughness of the sea ... It is strongly recommended that official recognition be given to Captain Adolf Olsen, and to Chief Officer Fred Lundgren, coxswain of the lifeboat, in view of the efficient rescue work under difficult circumstances, and the most excellent treatment accorded to the rescued crew.

For his efforts, Cpl Calow was put up for the Air Force Medal. S/L Mair was

cleared of blame, the official report noting: "Two other Stranraers experienced the same difficulty in accurate navigation on that date, owing to poor visibility and change in wind direction and velocity, and they were very fortunate in being able to make a landfall, although they did not return to their base until the next day." The report lauded the Stranraer for being such a durable aircraft. On June 11, 1942 Cpl Calow was awarded the British Empire Medal, the citation for which noted:

On 17th September, 1939, this NCO was wireless operator on a Stranraer which made a forced landing in the sea. During 22 hours, suffering from exposure, sickness and cold, Corporal Calow stuck to his post through this long period and was unceasing in his efforts to reach the base and the various DF stations in the area. His devotion to duty is of the highest order.

Another early HWE Stranraer emergency did not end so well. On December 15, 1941 Stranraer 927 of 13 (OT) Squadron, Patricia Bay was forced to land in heavy swells at Nanoose Bay, Vancouver Island. All aboard died: F/L Donald C. MacDougall (pilot, from

Winnipeg), P/O R. Wood (WOpAG, age 29 from Winnipeg), Sgt George H. Andrews (pilot, age 24 from Abbotsford, BC), Sgt John C. Gunn (WAG, age 35 from Roland, Manitoba), Sgt Russell T. Mitchell (pilot, age 20 from Strasbourg, Saskatchewan), LAC William D. Riley (fitter, age 20 from Regina), AC1 Robert W. Adams (rigger, age 20 from Edmonton) and AC Robert A. Blakely (age 20 of Kamsack, Saskatchewan).

Even into 1941 the RCAF was flying its 1930s airplanes on operations. One of these – Delta 682 of 8 (BR) Squadron – crashed disastrously on August 16. Piloted by F/O Peter C.E. Lay (age 25 from Regina), 682 went down at sea near its home base – Sydney. Also killed were LAC Gerald R. Raymond (WOp, age 29 from Norton Station, New Brunswick) and LAC Andrew J. Hurley (WAG, age 22 from Montreal). Even though 8 BR began re-equipping with the Bolingbroke in December 1940, it flew the antiquated Delta as late as November 1941.

On October 1941 RAF Coastal Command 32 OTU relocated from England to Patricia Bay, near Victoria, BC. The aircrew output originally was intended for 415 (RCAF), 144 (RAF) and 455 (RAAF) squadrons overseas. Beauforts and Hampdens were operated and the syllabus concentrated on torpedo tactics. Numerous accidents plagued 32 OTU, one of which occurred at 1135 hours on November 15, 1942. Hampden P5436, piloted by a Sgt Brown, had been doing dummy torpedo runs when, according to Brown's later testimony, his controls jammed and he had to ditch. He, WAG Sgt Smith and air gunners Sgt Fink and Sgt Blood, got into the sea where they struggled in churning waters.

Meanwhile, S/L Emerson W. Cowan, a pre-war RCAF pilot, was nearby in Stranraer 947. Observing the Hampden ditching, he landed within 40 seconds. His crew hauled the Hampden men aboard, then Cowan put Sgt Brown in charge of 947, while he resuscitated one of the survivors, who was in distress. Cowan then flew back to base, where the rescued crew was hospitalized. In the meantime, RCAF crash boats *M12* and *M200* also were on the scene, but were not needed due to Cowan's quick action. For this good show, Cowan was Commended for Valuable Services in the Air, for which the citation notes: "His skilful and courageous action carried out

under hazardous conditions was undoubtedly responsible for the saving of the lives of the four crew members."

Cowan had grown up in Atlantic City, NJ, joined the RCAF in July 1938 and earned his wings the following June at age 24. Posted to Ferry Command in July 1941, on September 20-22 he delivered Hudson AE580 from Dorval to Prestwick. Following his Patricia Bay tour, he made at least one more ferry flight, delivering Hudson FK805 from Dorval via Goose Bay and Reykjavik on July 1-11, 1943. Next in his career S/L Cowan joined 415 "Swordfish" Squadron to fly Albacores in Coastal Command. On the night of January 20 he and his navigator, F/O D.T. Wood, RAF, were part of a sortie along the English Channel. Two German destroyers were attacked near Le Touquet, the crew of F/Os D.C. Thompson and A.H. Bartlett successfully dropping 250-lb bombs on one ship. Some heavy flak then was thrown at the Albacores. When the 415 crews returned to base at RAF Manston, Cowan and Wood were missing. Nothing was ever found of them.

Sydney Disaster

Sunday afternoon was a time for airmen, friends and family to gather at RCAF Station Sydney for some good times, sometimes even a bit of fun flying. On October 3, 1943 this was the picture as Ventura 2148 of 113 "Wolverine" Squadron made a snappy fly-by, before setting course for Montreal. But this salute to those watching went badly wrong – the big patrol plane crashed before everyone's eyes, killing the six men aboard. Lost were the CO, W/C Albin Laut (pilot, age 27 of Crossfield, Alberta), F/L Robert B. Duncan (medical officer, age 29 from Montreal), F/O George D. Isaacs (pilot, age 24 from Port Arthur), WO2 William R. Drake (WAG, age 25 from Dublin, Ontario), WO2 Frederick P. O'Donnell (WOp, age 26 of Toronto) and WO2 Francis L. Tyo (Nav, age 23 from Calgary).

Nearly three generations after this accident one normally would have little idea who these six fine Canadians were, other than their names and bare data. In 2010, however, Lialla Raymes, the widow of Daniel Raymes, then on 113 Squadron, provided the author with a copy of October 1943 edition of the

station newspaper The Sydney *Patrol*. Here one gets a human connection with the lost crew. First, the CO is eulogized:

Wing Commander Laut was one of the outstanding pilots of the Eastern Air Command. Born in Crossfield, Alberta in 1915, he was educated at the University of Alberta and University of Saskatchewan. Joining the RCAF in 1938, he won early recognition as a keen flyer, and at the age of 26 was named leader of a bomber squadron. Coming to the Wolverines last January, he proved a worthy successor to S/L "Molly" Small, whose brilliant record was cut short by a similar accident.

An efficient flyer, "Al" Laut was remarkable above all by his gift of leadership. Despite his youth, he enjoyed the complete respect and loyalty of his men. He never set them a task that he would not share with them, and he frequently took his turn on patrols along with the rest. Fitting recognition of his courage and ability came last February when he was mentioned in dispatches for anti-submarine action.

F/L Duncan is mentioned as being on a visit to Sydney from Gander. The son of a Montreal medical specialist, he was following in his father's footsteps. This day he was being flown back to Montreal to visit his family. F/O "Dal" Isaacs had enlisted in July 1940 and earned his wings at McLeod, Alberta and had been at Trenton, Paulson and Patricia Bay before joining 113 BR in April 1942. The station newspaper noted: "Blessed with a sense of humour, happy-go-lucky, generous to a fault, he was deservedly popular with all ranks. With his going we have lost a real friend."

WO2 Bill Drake had trained at wireless school in Calgary and in bombing and gunnery at MacDonald: "Bill held a great admiration for ground crew personnel and was highly respected by them." Trained at Jarvis, "Freddie" O'Donnell was another treasured member of 113 BR: "He was keenly interested in good music and good literature. His soft voice, sparkling smile, devotion to home and sound judgment were a part of the Wolves and the memories will long remain. WO2 Tyo had earned his observer's wing at Rivers, then joined 113 BR: "As one of the oldest members of the Wolverines, 'Fran' completed over a hundred sorties over the sea. He was a

The RCAF West Coast high speed rescue boat *B.160 Takuli* picking up the crew of a ditched Anson at 47° 58'N, 126° 05W on August 23, 1943. This incident is thought to have involved Anson 6869 piloted by Sgt A.G. Jagger, who had four others aboard on an exercise from 32 OTU. 47 minutes after takeoff, one engine quit on the Anson, obliging Jagger to set down at 1525. Ucluelet-based *B.160* picked up the crew at 1850. In this period *Takuli* carried the RCN recognition number *B.160* (its RCAF number was *M.232*). Postwar, *Takuli* sailed from Vancouver on September 2, 1947 via the Panama Canal, arriving in Halifax on October 14 after covering some 7000 miles. *Takuli* was one of four Montreal-built HSLs, three of which survived as civilian BC vessels in 2010. (DND CX83-2022)

keen amateur photographer... Fran also was a student with a deep thirst for knowledge. His quick wit, ready smile and deep religious faith were well known and are truly missed by his team-mates... "This terrible crash was bad enough on all the families, but worse so for the Laut's, a farm family in Alberta, whose son F/O Ross K. Laut also never came home. A pilot with 427 Squadron, he died with his crew on February 21, 1944 – their Halifax crashed moments after take-off.

Ventura Ditching

Another of the hundreds of WAC wartime mishaps involved a pair of new Lockheed PV-1 Venturas. On February 7, 1944 three Venturas of 149 (BR) Squadron had departed Sea Island at 0950 local time. Destination: Terrace far to the north. Each carried a pilot, navigator and wireless operator. While setting course soon after takeoff, Ventura 2275 suddenly lost power in its starboard engine. Aboard were P/O R.D. "Don" Hall (pilot), P/O D. Swiffen (nav) and WO MacCullough (WOp). From 1000 feet Hall turned towards Comox, then his other engine quit. He attempted to restart by switching from one fuel tank to another, but was unsuccessful. From 500 feet the WOp transmitted an SOS and someone opened the rear door. P/O Hall set up to ditch at 100 knots, rounded out and gently landed in the water at about 85 knots. The time was 1035. No one was hurt and all quickly evacuated by the rear door.

The "Vent" sank in less than a minute. The crew then was in a pickle, as their life raft would not inflate, so they had to trust their Mae Wests. By this time Ventura 2274 (WOs J.E. Thompson, W. Spence Littlejohn and C.B. MacDonald) was overhead. 2210 was reporting the emergency to Comox, and trying to alert vessels about eight miles from the survivors. 2274 dropped survival kit, but this landed too far away. About 90 minutes after the ditching, the scene suddenly went from bad to worse. While 2274 was at only 200 feet, both of its engines quit. WO Thompson quickly feathered his props and safely ditched. As with 2275, this aircraft went straight to the bottom in seconds. The crew had scurried out via the cockpit overhead hatch, but their dinghy also proved useless.

By this time, Larry Salter, the pilot of a CPA Rapide, was involved. From a distance he had observed what looked like a whale blowing. He swung off his course to have a look, only to find that his whale had been 2274 splashing down. Salter quickly landed and picked up that trio, then flew over to collect 2275's crew, one of whom (Swiffen) seemed to have drowned (this trio had been more than an hour in the water). Thompson recalled this years later: "Salter, MacDonald and I hauled Swiffen onto a float, then onto the wing ... Hall and MacCullough felt it was no use, but I went to work on him anyway. In a few minutes Salter said he thought there was a good chance Swiffen would survive and we got him inside the cabin ... Hall and MacCullough were in bad shape from the cold water." Even though his Rapide was grossly overloaded, Salter got it airborne and soon reached Campbell River. By then, Swiffen was

breathing on his own and was rushed to hospital. The rest of the airmen got dry clothes and were driven the 50 miles down to Comox. Ventura 2210 soon had them back at Sea Island.

The investigation into this double ditching made several recommendations, i.e. that dinghies be serviceable upon takeoff, but also that "Knowledge of their dinghy and topping-up pump would have allowed the crew of 2274 to inflate their dinghy by hand." However, these dinghies were designed to automatically inflate in the water. Thompson noted: "A manual inflation was supposed to be possible if the automatic system failed, by pulling another smaller cable. This failed to operate on both dinghies." A summary of this incident in "R.C.A.F. Sea Rescue Bulletin #71" makes no mention of what caused the calamity. In his memoir, however, Thompson explains that two newly-delivered Venturas 2274 and 2275 had a modified fuel system (2210 had the system familiar to 149 BR pilots). Hall and Thompson had noticed something different – a new gadget on their instrument panels. No one knew what this was, nor to what the placards "OFF", "MAN" (manual) and "AUTO" referred. None of the techs had a clue (they thought the switches had to do with the radios) and the CTechO refused to help. The pilots test flew their planes, had no issues, so decided to head for Terrace.

F/O Joe Thompson who ditched Ventura 2274. Then, a crewman wearing the immersion/sea survival kit of the day. A shortcoming with this suit was that it leaked. A survivor in the water eventually would suffer hypothermia due to this. (Ventura Memorial Flight Association)

Hall and Thompson eventually realized what had happened. They had been used to Venturas that fed fuel straight to the engines from any tank selected. Thompson explained how 2274 and 2275 had a fuel pump which transferred fuel to the front main tanks from any other tank as selected: "The engines only drew fuel from the front mains." Without knowing this, a serious snafu was inevitable. Ventura 2274 was salvaged and barged to Jericho Beach. Investigators found that the main tanks each contained about 40 gallons of fuel and that the fuel valve system was different from what 149 BR pilots understood. The RCAF, however, had its own way of dealing with an embarrassing predicament. The two pilots faced a court martial, but were told that this would be dropped if each accepted a severe reprimand. They agreed to this, but each then was posted to a new Ventura squadron. The irresponsible CTechO glided safely away from any responsibility for the loss of two expensive airplanes.

Labrador Rescue

From Riverside, Ontario, Garnet R. Harland joined the RCAF in February 1941. After training at 1 MD, 3 ITS, 9 AOS, 6 (B&G) School and 2 ANS, he joined 10 (BR) Squadron in December 1941. Except for the period May 1942 to April 1945, he remained with "10 BR" until war's end. On February 19, 1944 Harland was on the crew of Liberator 586 which iced up over Labrador, then crashed while preparing to land at Goose Bay after a flight from Iceland. Five crew survived, but F/O David Griffin (age 39 from Hamilton), an RCAF PR officer, was lost. Alive with injuries were: S/L A.A.T. Imrie, DFC, (skipper), F/L Harland (nav), F/O J.D.L. Campbell (co-pilot), P/O M.J. Gilmour (WAG) and WO1 A.C. Johns (WAG). After four days

The versatile Grumman Goose amphibian was another fine search and rescue plane when a crew was missing at sea. Through WWII there were no dedicated RCAF rescue squadrons. ASR duties were provided on an ad hoc basis by operational squadrons and training schools, but also by communications/liaison units such as 13 Squadron at Sea Island or 1 (Comm) Flight at Torbay, both of which flew the Goose. (Lialla Raymes Col.)

stranded 13 miles from Goose Bay, the party was rescued by a US Army team. The story of this harrowing event is detailed in a lengthy RCAF press release. According to this, soon after crashing the crew found Griffin's body thrown from the wreck, then:

They spread a red-and-white parachute beside the wreck to attract search planes, then built a fire. Under an up-tilted wing they tramped out a sleeping place and laid a layer of balsam boughs, a half-dozen spare suits of flying clothing, three layers of silk parachutes, and greatcoats. They covered Gilmour and Johns, the two casualties, and huddled about them. Afraid the flames might ignite the fuel tanks, still laden with 800 gallons of high-octane gasoline, they let the fire go out the first night ... all were too cold and miserable to sleep.

They spent the next day improving their shelter by carpeting it with flight maps and small sheepskin rugs they were bringing as souvenirs from Iceland. F/O Campbell chopped wood and salvaged necessities from the aircraft. From metal covers of life raft canisters they made cooking tins to melt snow water and to heat food. From twisted metal bomb doors they made a base for the wood fire.

All took turns searching for the "Gibson Girl" portable radio ... but it was never found ... They rationed their meagre supplies sparingly, for three of the six emergency ration kits had been lost in the wreck. Each man was allotted three-quarters of a tin of corned beef, three squares of chocolate, and three or four hardtack biscuits daily.

On February 21 the party was found by trapper Joe Goudie while he was inspecting his line. He trekked out with the news. Meanwhile, a USAAF C-47 spotted the wreck and dropped a rescue kit. G/C Hanchett-Taylor and a medical officer, S/L Ross Robertson, then landed in a Norseman, but became bogged down in snow. A US Army Piper Cub arrived next and got away with the injured men, Gilmour and Johnson. Imrie, Campbell and Harland made it out on foot to Goose Bay on February 25. In May 1944 F/L Harland, then Navigation Leader at 10 BR, was awarded the DFC. By this time his log book showed nearly 1200 flying hours, 752 on operations.

Liberators Down in the Atlantic

The last week of July 1945 was a tragic one for Liberators. On July 4 two of them collided disastrously at Abbotsford. Then came word the same day that Ferry Command's Liberator JT982 en route from Dorval to Northolt with 15 crew and VIPs was missing. The nine passengers were a party under Sir William Malkin of the British Foreign Office; they had been attending a pioneer session of the United Nations in San Francisco. The press reported: "It was the first time that women passengers of the R.A.F. Transport Command had been reported missing on a transatlantic flight." A huge search effort began immediately for JT982, but one of the search planes, Liberator 595 of 10 BR, then also was reported missing in the same area.

Ill-fated Liberator 595-X of 10 BR. (RCAF)

This is the sight the survivors of 595-X would have seen as the 1 (Comm) Flight Hudson dropped its lifeboat to them. (Bill Ford Col.)

Some hours later word came via a DND press release that, "Life rafts believed to be those of a Liberator ..." had been spotted and that rescue measures were being rushed. A further report stated that the RCAF "believed Sir William's party had been sighted in the Atlantic in rubber boats". This, however, soon was rescinded, when those people were found (at 51°47'N 47°41'W) to be the missing 10 BR crew. These men soon

were rescued, but nothing ever was found of the Ferry Command Liberator.

Concentrating on the 10 BR story, RCAF announced: "The rescue of the men marked the first successful operational dropping of an air-sea rescue lifeboat in North American Atlantic waters." This was effected by a Hudson of 1 (Comm) Flight at Torbay. The 10 BR diarist later noted: "A most commendable and practically perfect job was done, the

lifeboat landing very close to the dinghies, and the survivors were seen to enter the lifeboat." Meanwhile, several other 10 BR Liberators and an RCAF rescue vessel had been involved, the aircraft dropping Lindholme survival gear and marking the rafts with coloured smoke.

Completing the final rescue was an RAF Canso from Dorval on detachment at Gander and skippered by F/O Jack R. Revill, RAF (later Commended for Valuable Services in the Air). Revill landed to pick up six survivors, but the skipper of 595, F/O Francis D. Gillis (age 28 from Sydney, Nova Scotia), was not recovered. Those rescued included F/L Arthur Fitzroy (pilot, Exeter, Ontario), F/L Duncan S. McNab (nav, Abbotsford, BC), F/O James G. MacArthur (WAG, Windsor, Ontario), P/O R.B. Lundy (FE).

Fires, Sinkings and Other Losses

Home War Establishment members died in a great many ways. Some went from natural causes, or in such terrible things as the Knights of Columbus fire in St. John's, traffic accidents, by drowning, etc. The RCAF suffered a fierce blow on October 13, 1942, when the Port-aux-Basques to North Sydney ferry SS *Caribou*, in service since 1925, was torpedoed by *U-69*. Of 237 souls aboard *Caribou*, only 101 survived. Among the dead were 25 RCAF personnel. Another multiple disaster occurred on February 15, 1945, when Sgt William J.A. Dunning (age 29 from Hazel Hill, Nova Scotia and LACs Herbert F. Hicks (age 20 from Buckingham, Quebec), Roy R. Whiteside (age 24 from London, Ontario) and Herbert W. Collins (age 23 from Belleville, Ontario), all of 116 (BR) Squadron at Sydney, lost their lives when an aircraft exploded in the hangar. AC1 David Smith (WOp, age 25 from Winnipeg came to a gruesome end. Then with EAC HQ in Halifax, he died in hospital on March 15, 1941 after being stabbed by an assailant. AC1 Franklin H. Smith (armourer, age 23 from Cobalt, Ontario) died on March 24, 1944 at Bella Bella, BC after being shot while on guard duty.

On May 10, 1945 three 10 BR personnel drowned when their small boat capsized in fierce weather on the squadron's bombing range Suleys Pond,

The RAF Canso which flew in from Dorval to aid in the search and which ended up rescuing the survivors. (RCAF)

Newfoundland. Lost were FSgt Dennis A. Cooke (age 28 from St. Thomas, Ontario, FSgt Shannon S.J.H. Smith, age 24 from St. Thomas and LAC Wilford B. Farrow (armourer, age 19 from Red Deer, Alberta). The dangers of fighter affiliation were emphasized on November 1, 1944. That day F/O John E. Thomson (age 24 of Nanaimo, BC) was piloting Kittyhawk 839 doing "fighter affil" with a 5 OTU Liberator. Such exercises normally involved a fighter making realistic passes on a bomber from various angles, giving each gunner a chance to practice his tactics. In this case, F/O Thomson pressed in so close that he collided with the bomber, then crashed fatally near White Rock, BC. The Liberator landed safely.

RCAF Test and Development Flight

Having worked as a youth for the Hudson's Bay Company, in 1928-29 J.P. "Jay" Culliton learned to fly in Winnipeg with Northern Aerial Mineral Exploration. He flew for NAME until it folded, then joined the Ontario Provincial Air Service, flying mainly from Sioux Lookout. As "an old timer" (age 36), in 1941 he joined the RCAF. He completed the necessary preliminaries at 1 MD in Toronto, then did a special flying course at Camp Borden and Picton on the Battle, Harvard and Yale. He received his RCAF wings and his commission at Picton, then was posted as a test pilot to Test and Development Flight at Rockcliffe. In May 1941 he was sent to 4 BR at Ucluelet to get some flying boat time, and was back at Rockcliffe at the end of June.

Every day at "T&D" seemed to bring a new experience. Dozens of test programs using many aircraft types were steadily under way, so a pilot had to be adaptable. Culliton had an interesting experience on August 1, 1941. That day he took off in Battle 1315 with Cpl Arnold, who was conducting some sort of sound analysis. Just after takeoff, however, the engine quit, so Culliton had to act quickly. He picked a cornfield and crash-landed. Back injuries put Culliton in hospital, but his crewman walked away unscathed.

In September 1941 the Canso replaced the Stranraer at 5 BR. Plans then were made to get the remaining EAC Stranraers to the West Coast. These

RCAF Test and Development Flight pilots F/L Fred King (Toronto), S/L H.R. McLaughlin (Winnipeg), F/L J.P. "Jay" Culliton (Sioux Lookout), F/L James C. Snyder (Waterloo) and F/L R.L. "Bobby" Davis (Vancouver). "T&D" had its beginnings at Rockcliffe in the 1920s under such great men as W/Cs E.W. Stedman and Alan Ferrier. Much of the test and evaluation flying done was *ad hoc*, as with the Imperial Gift aircraft. A dedicated RCAF test flight eventually arose, but this story in its entirety is yet to be told. T&D Flight of WWII did much-needed work in a time before the trained test pilot or experimental air engineer existed. "Freddy" King was one of several T&D personnel honoured for exceptional service. In November 1944 he was awarded the Air Force Cross, the citation for which praised him for his "readiness and desire to undertake any flying duty, however hazardous, tedious or exacting", and his "energy, co-operation and good performance". Receiving the AFC for aircraft anti-icing research flying efforts at T&D Flight (June 1945) was F/L Snyder: "As the research entailed requires the deliberate accretion of ice on the aircraft in various ice-forming weather conditions, this flying has been of the most hazardous nature, requiring great flying skill." At war's end T&D Flight became RCAF Experimental and Proving Establishment. EPE became the Central Experimental and Proving Establishment. Today's offspring of CEPE is AETE – the Aerospace Engineering Test Establishment at Cold Lake. (DND PL21996)

came first to Rockcliffe for some upgrades, e.g. fitting controllable pitch propellers. Supervising that work and test flying each Stranraer was F/O Culliton. As aircraft were ready, crews ferried them across Canada. But winter inevitably set in, freezing all the lakes and rivers en route.

Once the Fairey Battle had shown its Achilles Heel in early combat over France and Holland, the RAF withdrew it from operations. It then was available for the RCAF, which eventually listed 740. Although most were assigned to BCATP duties, the Battle was one of nearly 100 types flown in WWII by T&D Flight. Here is T&D Battle 1315 after Jay Culliton's forced landing. 1315 was from the first batch of 20 RCAF Fairey Battles delivered in the weeks before war broke out. (Ellis Culliton Col.)

Stranraer 912 at Jericho Beach. This is said to show 912 on arrival after its trans-continental ferry flight of December 1941. (Vancouver Public Library 45061)

Plans now were made to deliver the remaining aircraft by a southern route. F/O Culliton crewed on 956 – one of three Stranraers that left Ottawa on December 6, 1941 under F/L Bob Thomas, a pre-war RCAF type. First stop was Norfolk, Virginia, a flight of 5:40 hours. Here they over-nighted at the US Navy base. Next morning, as they flew farther south, they got word of Pearl Harbor. The news was so shocking that they wondered if the broadcast might be another "War of the Worlds" radio hoax. As they neared the US Navy base at Charleston, South Carolina, Culliton's airman in the nose position reported ack-ack fire. Culliton landed at the naval station after 3:40 hours, where the explanation for the ack-ack was given as "Pearl Harbor" – the local air defence battery could not identify the strange-looking flying boat, so had decided it must be Japanese!

Next day, Culliton and crew continued to Naval Air Station Pensacola (5:45). On landing there, Culliton feared that he had set down among rocks in shallow water, then realized that the "rocks" flashing by were dolphins. Next's day's destination was Fort Worth (5:50), where they were delayed with some enquiry about the Charleston incident. With this resolved, they continued on December 10 to Elephant Butte, New Mexico (6:55), thence on the 12th to Roosevelt Lake near Phoenix (3:35). Culliton describes what ensued on December 13-16:

Flying west from there, we covered a lot of desert country. We had planned to only go as far as San Diego, but the weather was so good, we headed for Los Angeles, landing there at San Pedro [4:35]. The U.S. Navy provided us with a car and driver and we had a full day seeing the city. That evening Bob Thomas and I took in a Jack Benny show. We were put on radio silence here, and were obliged to maintain that for the remainder of the trip. From Los Angeles, we flew to San Francisco, landing there at the Alameda Naval Air Station [4:25].

Although it was foggy next morning (August 19), F/L Thomas decided to push north. The met report promised improving visibility, but that did not pan out. The Canadians had to turn back and were fortunate to get in to Bodega Bay to over-night, after floundering around for five hours. "That night", recalled Culliton, "the U.S.O. brought us fruit and candy bars. We had just become allies."

Next morning 956 continued to Astoria, Oregon (4:25). As had become his style after Charleston, Culliton landed straight in. In the Officers' Club that night they were told by some US Navy fellows that they certainly would have been fired at by Astoria, had they dillydallied about their arrival. Other than that, Culliton recalled how "Everyone we met had been most helpful. Nothing was too much trouble for them." On August 21 he and crew pressed on to Vancouver in murky weather:

We flew well off shore where it was a bit better, but as we got farther north, we had to turn closer to the shoreline. This was to ensure the proper track to Vancouver. As we neared the coastline, we ran into fog, very close to the water and were forced to climb. We cut across at Aberdeen, flew east to Tacoma, then up to Seattle. Above Seattle there was a big hole in the cloud, and we spiralled down, close to the water again. We followed the water from then on, avoiding islands that might have had hills on them. It was tiring flying... We delivered our aircraft to Vancouver, then rushed to get tickets for the train trip back to Ottawa. I reached home at nine o'clock, Christmas morning.

In early 1942 F/O Culliton was busy with Fleet Fort ski trials. He was promoted to acting flight lieutenant in April (rank confirmed in August). Sadly, in April T&D's OC Flying, S/L F. E. R. Briggs, died when the wings came off a Cessna Crane during dive tests. "Shortly after this", recalled Culliton, "the Crane had its permissible gross weight reduced and a restriction imposed on its top speed... Briggs was a good pilot. He had done all the acceptance tests on the first Harvard off the line at Noorduyn." On August 29, 1942 F/O Culliton and F/O Fred King (another vintage bush pilot) flew some VIPs in Stranraer 933 to the luxurious International Paper Co. fishing lodge on Lac Oriskany, about 150 miles north of Ottawa. Their VIPs included Air Marshal L. S. Breadner (Chief of the Air Staff), Air Marshal Gus Edwards (AOC RCAF Overseas) Air Vice Marshal W. A. "Billy" Bishop, VC, Air Commodore K.G. Nairn and G/C R.R. Collard. Culliton and his men had a thoroughly fine time eating, drinking and fishing to their hearts' content, until flying their passengers back to Ottawa on September 2. One day Culliton fished with Air Marshal Edwards:

We got our tackle and a small case of beer, then went down to the lake. Air Marshal Edwards gave me some lessons on fly casting. He had just come from overseas, and was due to go back in a couple of days. It must have been greatly relaxing for him, getting away from the burden of running the Air Force. A/V/M Bishop proved to be game for anything and was a lot of fun. We were impressed at how these men all were so down to earth.

F/L Jay Culliton's duties at RCAF Test and Development Flight demanded total professionalism. Every day came new challenges – a range of aircraft to fly and new and often dangerous assignments. These log book excerpts from Culliton's T&D days illustrate the scope of the test pilot's job at T&D.

For the drop trials, a Norseman was modified to drop-test 'chutes from either side. Sgt Bennett, with more than 1000 jumps to his credit, did the live jumps. Then, in March 1943 Culliton was assigned to ski trials with a Lockheed PV-1 Ventura. An ice strip near Port Arthur was prepared for the program. On this project F/L Culliton met two old cronies from bush flying days. The first was W.J. "Jack" McDonough, who had

Sample test flights from Jay Culliton's wartime log book.

Date	Aircraft	T&D Crew	Sortie
2-2-42	Oxford AT601	F/L Holman	partial climbs
3-2-42	Oxford AT601	F/L Gerhardt	service ceiling
10-2-42	Oxford AT601	F/L Gerhardt LAC St. Jean	cabin temp tests
11-2-42	Lysander 459	LAC Davidson	drogue towing test
13-2-42	Oxford AT601	F/L Gerhardt	flaps down climb
18-2-42	Anson I 6195	F/O Bowerman	service ceiling climb
10-4-42	Fort 3573	Cpl Paton	ski trials
22-4-42	Stearman FD975	F/L McLaughlin	A&E test
27-4-42	Anson II 7150	S/L Gordon	Hoover air screws
1-5-42	Anson I 6195	F/O Bridgeland	A&E test
6-5-42	Hampden AN118	F/L Cline F/O Bowerman	carb temp
8-5-42	Oxford AT601	F/L Holman	single engine performance
11-5-42	Hudson BW638	3 crew	carb & cyl head
13-5-42	Norseman 3527	F/L Holman F/L McNaughton F/O Travers	compass tests
19-5-42	Harvard 3277	F/O Bridgeland	test - spinning tires
16-6-42	Stearman FD975	one crew	bombing observation
17-6-42	Harvard 3277	one crew	prop governor tests
7-7-42	Cornell FH652	F/L McNaughton	check on type
8-7-42	Finch 4580	one crew	tail wheel tests
10-7-42	Hampden AN118	two crew	oil heater tests
4-1-43	Bolingbroke 9074	F/L Bowerman	test u/c hydraulics
6-1-43	Bolingbroke 9075	Cpl Jennings	NRC - RDF
7-1-43	Norseman 3523	S/L Holman	simultaneous chute drops
7-1-43	Bolingbroke 9075	S/L Gordon	drogue target towing
22-1-43	Lysander 2425		ski tests
30-1-43	Anson II 7069	F/O Finlayson Mr. Gorman NRC	brake temp tests
2-12-43	Anson I R9696	F/O Youngman	supply 'chute drops
3-12-43	Anson II/V 8450	F/O Youngman	low level bombing
7-12-43	Anson VI 13881	F/L Brown	air sickness tests - NRC
10-12-43	Bermuda 732		local flying
13-12-43	Lysander IIITT	F/L Bowerman	engine temps

Ventura AE860 as it arrived on wheels at Port Arthur for ski trials in March 1943. (William J. McDonough Col.)

The "Ski Ventura" project included several participants. The streamlined skis were developed by the National Research Council of Ottawa. Test and Development Flight had been involved on an on-going basis testing NRC ski designs for such types as the Hart, Harvard and Hurricane. Central Aircraft of London manufactured the skis and had the contract to do the installation and flying; the RCAF provided two Venturas and H.A. "Doc" Oaks of Port Arthur had the contract to build and maintain ice strips needed at the Lakehead and Orient Bay. Here, Ventura AE860 sits along the Port Arthur shore of Lake Superior, where its skis were fitted. Anson 8450 was the project support plane. This was an odd-ball aircraft – an Anson II with P&W R-985 engines, the only such conversion. (all, William J. McDonough Col.)

One of four ice strips built by Doc Oaks' company at Port Arthur. Two were 5000 x 200 feet, two were 6000 x 300 feet. At the left is the grooming rig used to level and roll the strip. Here, AE860 is without skis. Comments on the back of this old photo include: "Wheel runways were made by dragging, bulldozing and scarifying down to glare ice, which was an average of 24" in thickness, and then re-laying approximately 1" of snow by drags and spreaders and re-rolling. Ski runways were made by ploughing and dozing down to 6" of snow above the ice, followed by rolling ... All runways were marked out by large spruce boughs at 100' intervals." These views were taken by Toronto photographer Allan W. Gifford.

The chronology of this project was unknown at publication time. However, AE860 was involved in the spring of 1943. AJ430 seems to have been used the following spring, when the base was at Orient Bay at the southeast corner of Lake Nipigon. AJ430 is shown at the ski installation stage, then in flight. It still wears its USAAF markings.

With Mike deBlicquy at the controls, AE860 gets ready to taxi on the ice for its first ski flight. Next – moments after lift-off, then touching down after a successful mission.

Other aircraft tested on NRC streamlined skis were a Hawker Hart, and Hurricanes 1362 and 5624. The Hurricane skis were manufactured by Noorduyn. Hurricane 1362 is seen at Canadian Car and Foundry in Fort William on May 12, 1942. In trials at Rockcliffe, the top speed for 5624 on skis was 280 mph, considerably slower than a standard Hurricane. None of the WWII ski trials done with RCAF fighters or bombers resulted in any practical applications. (CANAV Col.)

The Hawker Hart on skis at Rockcliffe. (LAC PA63345)

taught him how to fly and now headed Central Aircraft in London, which had the ski contract. Along with S/L Don Holman, senior aeronautical engineer at T&D, Culliton flew McDonough to Port Arthur via Anson. The second old friend was the great H.A. "Doc" Oaks, Culliton's former boss at Northern Aerial Mineral Exploration – Oaks had the contract to build the ice strip. Harry Umphrey of TCA would fly the Ventura: "We were on the ice when he landed. He stepped out of the aircraft and chatted with us for a few minutes. That was all the time it took for his warm boots to freeze into the ice. Suddenly, as he turned, there was a snap and Umphrey had a broken leg." Oaks then called on Mike deBlicquy, another bush flying crony, to fly the ski trials.

One evening after hours a de Havilland Mosquito was delivered to T&D. No one knew who the pilot had been and he didn't leave any paperwork ... not even the Mosquito operating instructions. This airplane was for trials to determine why several Mosquitos had exploded on operations overseas. W/C Tom Louden, OC Test and Development Flight, decided to bring in an experienced Mosquito pilot. This turned out to be F/L "Rosie" Miscampbell, who would check out F/L Culliton. First, however, Miscampbell and his tech took off for a quick test flight. As Miscampbell approached to land, however, the "Mossie" rolled and plunged to the ground, killing both crew. That was the end of the Mosquito project. T&D later heard a possible explanation for the exploding Mosquitos. Gas fumes could accumulate in the bomb bay (fuel lines ran through that area). When the electrically-operated bomb bay doors opened, a spark could be set off that might ignite the lingering fumes.

A log book with extra notes, let alone photos or illustrations, suggests an airman in love with his trade. Jay Culliton was one such fellow. This spread shows a month's worth of flying that he did early in his T&D days. That April of 1942 he had plenty of fun flying the Anson, Fort, Norseman, Oxford and Stearman. (Ellis Culliton Col.)

In January 1943 Jay Culliton was flying a slightly different list of planes: Anson, Bolingbroke, Lysander and Norseman. (Ellis Culliton Col.)

In June 1944 F/L Culliton was on the instructor pilot course at CFS, Trenton. Later that year W/C John Angus MacLean, DFC, recommended Culliton for the Empire Test Pilots School course at Boscombe Down. AFHQ turned this down, considering Culliton "over the hill". Another T&D pilot got this slot – F/L Roger Mace, who was killed on

At war's end J.P. Culliton returned to flying with the OPAS in Sioux Lookout. He was District Supervisor there into 1959, then held a civil service job in Toronto until retirement. (Ellis Culliton Col.)

course flying a Mustang. Another T&D story involved Prince Bernhardt of the Netherlands. He often would show up to fly a Cornell, which T&D kept ready for his pleasure (the Dutch royal family was spending the war in Ottawa). The Prince was an avid pilot, but wasn't allowed to fly solo. F/L Andy McNaughton, the son of renowned General A.G.L. McNaughton, always accompanied him.

By the end of 1944 the war was winding down – the RCAF was letting men out, starting with older pilots. F/L Jay Culliton last flew in the RCAF on December 20, 1944 – a 6-hour test flight evaluating a Janitrol cabin heater in a Canso. His total RCAF flying time was 1108:40 hours, his grand total by then – 3669:15 hours. On February 25, 1945 he was transferred to the Special Reserve "E" Active Pilots list, effectively ending his RCAF career. Soon after, at a ceremony at Rideau Hall in Ottawa, Governor General, The Earl of Athlone, presented Culliton with a Commended for Valuable Services in the Air, the citation to which stated:

For the past three and one-half years this officer has been a test pilot at Test and Development Establishment. He has flown on many hazardous flights with skill and determination. As officer in charge of writing pilots' notes and then as officer in charge of flying, he has displayed energy and ability of a high order. By his constant good work he has made an outstanding contribution to the prosecution of the war.

Technical Issues

From earliest days the RCAF was involved in aeronautical projects studying all its designs, and potential ways of improving safety and performance. This work expanded greatly with WWII, T&D being the centre of RCAF activity. One of F/L Culliton's test flying projects was the Cessna Crane, which suffered a serious design problem. According to AFROs of September 4, 1942 Crane wing leading edges had separated in flight. AFROs warned that the Crane was not to be flown above 180 mph indicated air speed, and that students were not to fly the Crane in cloud. The aircraft was not to exceed 5100 lb gross weight, and sudden manoeuvres were to be avoided. Meanwhile, the USAAF was doing structural tests on the wings of its equivalent, the T-50 Bobcat. AFROs of December 30, 1942 reported: "A modified, stronger aircraft wing is being manufactured by the Cessna Aircraft Company which is to be incorporated in production in later series of the Crane IA aircraft and which is also to be supplied as spares for the Crane I and IA."

Another type causing big worries was the Airspeed Oxford, many of which crashed in the UK and Canada with deadly results. F/L Culliton's involvement with the Oxford was intense as he flew many performance-evaluating sorties. This was two years before the case described here: On April 25, 1944 F/O William N. Wiegand (age 24 from Toronto), FSgt R.R. Skipsey and LAC A. Paton were on a training exercise (practicing stalls) in Oxford LX322. Wiegand was an instructor at 20 (P) AFU at Kidlington, Skipsey was his student and Paton was a flight engineer under training. Wiegand was highly experienced, having 1252 hours on type, 1340 hours total time. Yet he lost control of the situation this day, allowing LX322 to enter a flat spin. The official RAF report describes the outcome:

The aircraft took off from Kidlington at 14:55 hours in excellent weather and some 15 minutes later was seen in a flat spin at a height of about 2000 feet. The aircraft crashed shortly afterwards without recovering from the spin. No one had attempted to bale out and all three occupants were killed instantly.

The RAF concluded that the accident resulted when a stall manoeuvre went wrong: "The only contributing factor is considered to be the Oxford's inherent design fault in spin recovery." The station commander at Kidlington was especially perturbed by this accident, which claimed one of his best instructors. He made it clear that this was not an isolated case and that such Oxford exercises must be explained more carefully in the training

The Cessna Crane gave the RCAF ulcers when structural problems arose. Crane I 7862 was on RCAF strength from August 1941 to March 1945. In September 1948 it was sold by WADC, becoming CF-FGF with Matane Air Services, where it served into 1965. It then spent several years based in Ottawa doing aero survey work, until acquired by the Canadian Warplane Heritage. Here it is at Hamilton in 1993. 7862/CF-FGF appears to be the most long-lived of RCAF Cranes, even though it no longer was airworthy in the 2000s. (Larry Milberry)

Airspeed Oxford 1503 in 1940 in front of one of the WWI hangars at Camp Borden. Of the RCAF's initial batch of 25 Oxfords taken on strength between May and November 1939, 18 are known to have been in serious accidents (Cat. A, B or C). However, 13 of the planes remained on strength into 1945 and there were only 4 Cat.A crashes among the 25. (Lialla Raymes Col.)

syllabus. "Demonstration of stalling", he proclaimed, "should only be given on aircraft which will recover to normal flight from any attitude."

Air Marshal P. Babbington, AOC-in-Chief RAF Flying Training Command concurred with reservation and requested that the Handling Squadron at Empire Central Flying School amend the training syllabus. However, he favoured keeping stall training in the syllabus, allowing students to fly the Oxford to the edge of stalling, thus maintaining "the principle of teaching pilots to fly their aircraft to the limit". A/V/M C.E.W. Lockyer put it this way: "Deliberate spinning is not permitted ... particular care is to be taken to avoid circumstances leading to a spin and to check any tendency to spin as promptly

as possible." He then carefully reviewed the prescribed spin recovery process, concluding with the emphasis on abandoning any aircraft still spinning when below 5000 feet. Lockyer also urged that spin recovery be practiced and discussed well beyond the training system, i.e. by operational squadrons. The court of enquiry in the case of LX322 was dismayed that none of those aboard had attempted to use their parachutes. The final conclusion regarding the accident was "an error in judgment on the pilot's part".

The Airspeed Oxford was no peach of an airplane, but quite the opposite. It had poor flying traits that killed many airmen in the UK and Canada. The RCAF had 819 Oxfords on strength, including 188 that were "Canadianized" as Oxford Vs using P&W R-985 engines and metal propellers. Oxford II (Cheetah X engines, wooden propellers) 1510 is seen at Trenton in the late summer of 1939. It served from June 1942 to February 1945. No RCAF Oxford survived into the postwar years. Since they were designated as bombers, regulations decreed that all (fortunately) had to be axed. (DND RE19873-3)

In 1943-45 a branch of T&D – No.1 Winter Experimental and Training Flight – was busy with cold weather trials. This work was done using various aircraft at Kapuskasing, Ontario and Gimli, Manitoba. Lancaster EE182 is shown at "Kap". The engine tents likely were on the list of cold-weather equipment being tested. In this period WE&TF was commanded by S/L G.D. Preston, AFC, whose involvement in the search for Goose 917 appears earlier in this chapter. (LAC PA196937)

A close-in view of 10 Repair Depot at Calgary as an Anson flies low over the busy tarmac. Other repair depots were at such centres as Edmonton, Winnipeg and Debert. Much test flying was involved at these bases, as aircraft were constantly being repaired, overhauled and modified. (Charles E. Hayes Col.)

Leadership Profiles: Robert Leckie

At the outbreak of WWII the RCAF was blessed with solid leadership. Those at the top in AFHQ in Ottawa still included many WWI veterans. These had estab-lished the original Canadian Air Force (England) in February 1920 and the RCAF in April 1924. From these beginnings arose a solid leadership cadre, many being graduates of Royal Military College in Kingston, Ontario – the likes of Hugh Campbell and C.R. Slemon. One of the wartime veterans was Robert Leckie, DSO, DSC, DFC. Born in Glasgow in 1890, he had emigrated to Toronto in 1906 to work in his uncle's ship chandler business.

In 1915 Leckie began a life-long involvement in aviation, when he began training at the Curtiss school in Long Branch, Ontario. He trained further with the RNAS in England. Posted thence to large flying boats, F/S/L Leckie excelled. He was involved in several anti-submarine actions and, with seven interceptions and two kills, established the best anti-Zeppelin record in the British air services. He also was renowned for an episode of September 5-8, 1917: having pursued two Zeppelins, he landed in rough seas to save a D.H.4 crew, then spent three days at sea awaiting rescue. In 1918 he took command of 228 Squadron (Curtiss flying boats) at Great Yarmouth.

In 1919 LCol Leckie commanded No.1 Squadron in the short-lived Canadian Air Force in England, then joined the Air Board in Ottawa. There he was an early proponent of airmail. In 1920 he flew the Halifax-to-Winnipeg legs of the first trans-Canada flight.

Air Marshal Robert Leckie. He emigrated from Glasgow to Toronto as a boy, fought in WWI, then rose to command the RCAF. For his service in the Second World War he received honours from Belgium, Canada, Czechoslovakia, France, Mexico, Norway, Poland and the United States. (DND PL117262)

He also assisted the Air Board in developing specifications for new aircraft, which would be needed as Canada's war surplus types aged. Through the efforts of such key figures as Leckie, Ernest Stedman and J.A. Wilson, an order was placed in 1923 for eight Vickers Vikings, mainly to be manufactured in Montreal by Canadian Vickers.

In 1922 Leckie returned to the RAF where, on one project, he was involved in aircraft carrier trials. In August 1924, however, he wrote to J.A. Wilson about his lack of interest in developing military air power, and how he longed for the more interesting Canadian-type operations. "Canada," he told Wilson, "is too fine a country to stay away from indefinitely, and sooner or later I must return there."

When the RAF was discussing a new Commonwealth recruiting and training plan in 1936, G/C Leckie was superintendent of the RAF air reserves. He recommended Canada as the ideal place for the RAF to train, and Air Commodore Tedder, head of RAF air training, agreed. The British cabinet, however, did not, and this plan was shelved. In 1940 Air Commodore Leckie, then in command of RAF forces in the Mediterranean, was posted to the BCATP in Ottawa. In January 1944 he became RCAF Chief of the Air Staff, where one of his goals was to reduce the RCAF's bloated Home War Establishment. Orders for new HWE aircraft from B-26s to P-39s and Liberators were cancelled, and several EAC and WAC squadrons were

276

disbanded. An important spin-off was that hundreds of HWE aircrew became available to help in the final drive to crush Germany. Also, morale was boosted, since a majority of HWE aircrew had been pining to get overseas into "the real war".

Being a hands-on type, Air Marshal Leckie also had a personal interest in operations. When a 10 (BR) Squadron Liberator failed to prosecute a U-boat attack due in part to crew unfamiliarity with some equipment, Leckie fired a rocket at the AOC of Eastern Air Command, urging that any known U-boat be hounded mercilessly around the clock and not be allowed to slip away for any reason. Leckie remained at the head of the RCAF until retiring in 1947. He retired in Ottawa and passed away on March 31, 1975.

Lloyd Breadner

Another great RCAF leader was Lloyd Samuel Breadner. Born in Carleton Place, Ontario in 1894, he trained as a young man in the jewelry trade. With WWI he learned to fly at the Wright school in Dayton, Ohio and, in mid-January 1916, was aboard the SS *Adriatic* sailing for England. In February and March he was training at Redcar and Cranwell, then joined 5 (Naval) Wing at Dover on May 29, 1916. Flying Moranes, Nieuports and Camels, Breadner excelled and eventually commanded 3 (Naval) Squadron. His DFC was gazetted on May 23, 1917, the citation noting: "For conspicuous gallantry and skill in leading his patrol against hostile formations … On the 6th

April 1917 he drove down a hostile machine, which was wrecked while attempting to land in a ploughed field. On the morning of the 11th April 1917 he destroyed a hostile machine which fell in flames, brought down another in a spinning nose dive with one wing folded up, and forced a third to land." In the period April 8 to June 12, 1917 Breadner was credited with five e/a "driven down", four destroyed and a Gotha bomber forced down in British territory. According to *The Brave Young Wings*, Maj Breadner finished the war with eight confirmed kills. He had been shot down twice over France and crashed twice.

Soon after the war Breadner joined the Canadian Air Board. As an Air Certificate Examiner, his salary in September 1920 was $2940 per annum. An early assignment was in January 1921 – inspecting the Imperial Oil "air harbour" at Peace River, to qualify it for operations. In June 1921 he passed the Air Engineer's Theoretical and Practical Examinations covering all aspects of airframe and engines. On June 22 he was awarded Air Board Private Pilot's Certificate No.3 and Air Engineer's Certificate No.155. Early in 1922 he was doing refresher flying at Camp Borden. From March 2 to March 25 he made 28 flights in the Avro 504 and JN-4C. He took his instruction from F/L Roy S. Grandy, while S/L A. Cuffe was his examiner. Returning to inspection duties, on June 26, 1923 he and C.M. McEwen met at Canadian Vickers to test fly a new RCAF Viking. Later, he was on

a western swing then, in October, was in Haileybury inspecting the Laurentide Air Services fleet. That winter he visited Laurentide in Montreal to look over their overhaul operation.

In January 1924 S/L Breadner was promoted to acting wing commander and became station commander at Camp Borden. There he was reprimanded by G/C J.S. Scott for having arranged a visit by an engineering officer to Camp Borden to discuss tail skid problems with the Avro Lynx. Scott expressed his annoyance: "I would like you to bear in mind that the Technical Branch was fully occupied, and I do not contemplate using their time on minor obvious difficulties like repairing tail skids." Scott also grumbled about how little the Lynx was being used at Camp Borden and threatened to transfer them away, unless this changed. Breadner countered with a detailed justification of his actions.

In September 1925 Breadner was assigned to studies at the Royal Military College. He impressed the colonel in charge, who noted that "his work here has been very much to his credit". Especially mentioned was how well he had done at "equitation", in spite of what the colonel described as "being at a disadvantage on account of his build". Following this "prep" course, S/L Breadner was posted in 1926-27 to RAF College, Andover. At course end in July 1927, his superior officer, Air Commodore Ludlow-Hewitt, praised him for his "unfailing cheerfulness". He described him as "the simple, direct and rather forceful type without subtlety", having "great common sense and some originality" and having natural abilities that "fit him particularly for command".

For his 1927 flying at Camp Borden, Breadner included a familiarization flight in Siskin J7759, the hottest machine he had flown. He must have revelled at this opportunity and been reminded of earlier days flying Camels. In January 1929 W/C Breadner was appointed Assistant Director of the RCAF under W/C J.L. Gordon. In 1932 MGen A.G.L. McNaughton described Breadner's tenure: "His advice and opinions are inevitably based on careful investigation … I expect to see him rise to the highest positions in the service in due course." McNaughton also mentioned that Breadner had "lost no opportunity to keep up his flying". In 1934 he was in

Breadner was always a hands-on type. In 1922 he tested the CAF's first new production plane – the Vickers Viking. He also thought that the Wapiti was a good deal for the RCAF, so lobbied to acquire the first of these in 1930. (DND, Jack McNulty Col.)

charge of the relief project that saw the rise of RCAF Station Trenton from fields and woods along the Bay of Quinte. That July, McNaughton centred out Breadner, who had been in charge: "This project has been well administered. The men have been well cared for … and the costs have been strictly maintained within approved estimates."

In 1935 W/C Breadner attended the Imperial Defence College in England. He visited several air stations, getting a first-hand look at how the RAF was expanding. Before Breadner returned to Canada at year's end, Air Commodore Croil suggested that he familiarize himself with the latest developments in coastal reconnaissance, about flying boats and torpedo bomber developments, and learn what he could about a new all-metal bomber being developed by Bristol. Several visits to special establishments were arranged, then Breadner returned to Ottawa.

Likely due to Breadner's recommendations, in 1936 the RCAF, as yet with few service aircraft, oversaw the purchase of some ex-RAF Wapiti bombers and four new Blackburn Shark torpedo planes. Years later, J.C. Charleson recalled seeing the Wapitis uncrated at Ottawa Car early in 1936. He claimed that desert sands from earlier campaigns had to be swept out of them. The "What-a-Pity", as some called this plane, was nothing more than an improved version of the WWI D.H.4. Its acquisition was not one of Breadner's greatest moments.

Breadner was promoted to group captain in February 1936, then to air commodore in August 1938. From May 1940 to December 1943 Air Marshal Breadner was Chief of the Air Staff. In this period his two great responsibilities were instituting and overseeing the BCATP and the Home War Establishment. Both tasks were well accomplished, but this work was demanding and stressful, e.g. from August 18, 1940 to September 16, 1941 Breadner travelled by air on 62 days. He also was involved in the effort beginning in 1940 to "Canadianize" the RCAF abroad, which led to a number of RCAF establishments overseas, 6 Group, Bomber Command, being paramount. In this drive he had the support of Minister of National Defence, Col J.L. Ralston and Ralston's successor, C.G. Power.

A/M Breadner seemed to have *carte blanche* in building up a large home defence air force, so large that the Americans balked at equipping it fully. As the war progressed and Japan pulled back,

The famously affable Breadner was always happy to get into the field. Here he is greeted by G/C G.R. McGregor, OC 126 Wing at Beny-sur-Mer in Normandy over the summer of 1944. (DND PL31000)

it was evident that the HWE was over-supplied with everything from Hurricanes to Venturas and Cansos. In his book *And I Shall Fly*, G/C Z.L. Leigh credits Breadner with clearing the way so that Leigh could establish a long-range RCAF air transport operation. Whenever Leigh needed some roadblock cleared, he counted on his old friend from Camp Borden days. For his accomplishments in this period, in 1943 Breadner was awarded the Commander, Order of the Bath, the citation for which noted, "Air Marshall Breadner, more than any other individual, symbolizes the objectives of the Royal Canadian Air Force." Breadner surely had the human touch and, as he prepared to go overseas to assume duties in London, he wrote to everyone in the RCAF:

I know full well that many a man and woman among you would give a great deal for the opportunity … of getting nearer to the great drama being enacted overseas… I can tell you that your Air Force is going to pound the enemy ceaselessly, relentlessly and with ever-increasing force, until he is down on his knees … It is my cherished hope that when I next return to Canada peace will again have come to the world.

From January 1944 to March 1945 Air Marshal Breadner was AOC RCAF Overseas HQ in London. There his secretary was his eldest daughter, Doris, also in the air force. Tragically, on November 30, 1944 he lost his son, P/O Donald Lloyd Breadner (age 19). That day Donald and navigator F/O K.B. Bennett were on an exercise from Debert, Nova Scotia in Mosquito KB278, when they crashed on a hill near Westchester. The reality of the times prevented Air Marshal Breadner from attending his son's funeral at Beechwood Cemetery in Ottawa. In 1945 Breadner became Air Chief Marshal Breadner, the only one to attain this rank in the RCAF. In 1948 he was instrumental in establishing the Royal Canadian Air Force Association. However, he did not seem much interested in other productive efforts once the war ended, and took to drinking. Ill health dogged him but, having fallen in with Christian Science, he did not seek medical help. In 1952 he visited the cult's centre in Boston, and he died there on March 14.

Interwar Men: Leading by Example

The interwar years produced top-notch permanent and non-permanent force RCAF officers and airmen nearly all of whom were eager to serve come September 1939. Among these great Canadians was Henry Myles Carscallen. Born in Hamilton in 1908, he attended Royal Military College 1926-30. A dedicated scholar, he then studied law in Toronto and engineering at Queen's

The great RCAF's renowned "Cars" Carscallen (DND PL104080)

University in Kingston. He earned his wings at Camp Borden in May 1933 and was promoted to flying officer. While on course he was favourably assessed, perhaps by the OC Flying Training, S/L R.S. Grandy: "A bold pilot who flies with vigour and confidence. Good in most sequences but lacks finish in turns. In forced landings he glides too close to the field and turns too steeply. He instils confidence and is a good type of pilot. " After Carscallen had taken some advanced flying, S/L C.M. McEwen, MC, DFC, of Camp Borden added: "This officer flies the Fairchild 51 very well considering the amount of time flown on the type... Has maintained a good average standard throughout the course. Deportment exemplary."

In the spring of 1934 Carscallen qualified in Ottawa on flying boats. The syllabus illustrates the skills required for a pilot to master this course: handling of floatplanes and flying boats, particular attention being paid to taking off and landing in rough and glassy water, use and handling of motor boats, launching and bringing in seaplanes, picking up and slipping from buoys, towing disabled aircraft, refuelling at sea, etc. For the practical part of the course Carscallen began on a Moth seaplane, progressed to the much larger Fairchild 71 seaplane, then to the Vedette flying boat. He flew 25:45 hours on course, leaving his instructor pleased: "This officer showed good judgement both in the air and on the water. He absorbs instruction readily. Should make a good operational pilot."

For the 1935 season, when he logged 132:10 hours in the field, Carscallen did a decent job. His superior officer, W/C A.E. Godfrey, MC, AFC, noted: "This officer has been in command of the Indian Treaty Flight during 1935 and carried out his duties in an efficient and praiseworthy manner. He has shown keenness, initiative and sound judgement ... takes keen interest in all sports and is manager of the RCAF hockey team. He is a desirable type of officer to have in the service." Various flying and staff postings ensued, including command in 1937 of a West Coast photo detachment with two Deltas. In December one of his superiors at 8 (GP) Squadron, S/L C.R. Slemon, commented:

Flight Lieutenant Carscallen has served as Officer in Charge of No.6 (G.P.) Detachment of No.8 (G.P.) Squadron throughout the 1937 operational season. He has executed his duties with entire satisfaction. His Detachment was required to carry out photographic operations on the B.C. coast in mountainous country which presents great difficulty in photographic navigation and where adverse photographic weather normally exists. The Detachment was equipped with new and comparatively untried type of aircraft... Through the keenness and effort of Flight Lieutenant Carscallen and his exercise of sound judgment, the Detachment's photographic work was improved consistently throughout the season ...

F/L Carscallen joined 5 (FB) Squadron at Dartmouth in January 1938. In April 1939 he was promoted to squadron leader, then commanded the first EAC unit in Newfoundland – a 10 BR Digby detachment. He commanded 5 BR from November 1940 to April 1941, 10 BR from April to September 1941, then 5 BR from September 1941 to July 1942. In this period he was being assessed by some iconic figures from W/C Basil D. Hobbs, DSO, DFC and Bar, MiD, to G/C M. Costello and G/C A.L. Morfee. In December 1941 Hobbs put Carscallen up for the AFC, his nomination noting: "This officer has rendered outstanding service not only on

war flights but in testing and ferrying aircraft. He has taken part in the organisation and training of No.10 (BR) and No.5 (BR) Squadrons and through his efforts has brought them to a high standard of efficiency." No AFC was awarded, however, and Carscallen by now was agitating for an overseas posting (Hobbs and Morfee observed of him in July 1942: "Has been a little discontented lately due to not being posted overseas before this date.")

In July 1942 W/C Carscallen ferried a Liberator from Dorval to the UK, then trained on Wellingtons at 22 OTU. While on this course, he put up a serious black. Returning after his final air exercise of the course, he landed at the wrong airfield, severely damaging his aircraft. This might have spelled the end to his Bomber Command ambitions, but the OC at 22 OTU, G/C R.B. Jordan, intervened. He pointed out how the weather had been duff, how Carscallen was a good pilot, if more of a flying boat man, how he was "hard working, keen and efficient", etc. Jordan concluded, "In this instance I do not consider that the pilot's Log Book should be endorsed 'Carelessness'".

Some may have assessed this as "nice to have friends in high places", but W/C Carscallen was off the hook. In October 1942 he took over 424 Squadron, part of newly-formed 6 RCAF Group. On November 8 he was skipper on the first flight of a 424 Wellington. Intensive training ensued until the night of January 14-15, 1943 when 424 received its "baptism by fire". With Carscallen leading, 424 had three Wellingtons in a force of 122 bombers attacking the French U-boat port of Lorient. The effort proved ineffective, 424 got its aircraft home (not so 426, which lost a Wellington and crew – 6 Group's first operational casualties of the war). Next night Carscallen led five Wellingtons back to Lorient, where results proved more impressive. The CO's next operation was on January 21 – 424's first "gardening" (mine laying) operation. On January 26, 424 lost its first Wellington while on another Lorient raid. It seems that in giving his crew the time needed to bale out, Sgt V.F. McNargh (skipper), sacrificed his own life. The war gradually heated up for 424, but W/C Carscallen was tour-expired in April 1943. In July 1943 he received a DFC with this citation:

Wing Commander Carscallen has been continuously employed on operations since the outbreak of the war. He has displayed outstanding fortitude and skill during numerous operational sorties. Many of these were anti-submarine patrols involving long distance flights of a hazardous nature. He has also participated in a number of bombing attacks. Throughout all his missions he has displayed exceptional qualities of resourcefulness and devotion to duty. As Commanding Officer of his squadron he has built up a fine record of achievement setting an example to all who serve under him.

On leaving 424, Carscallen was promoted to group captain and took command of RCAF Station Leeming into June 1943. He moved to Station East Moor until February 1944, then was repatriated. In June 1944 G/C Carscallen received an MiD with another glowing citation:

This officer was posted overseas, eventually assuming command of No.424 (RCAF) Squadron. He led his squadron on many operations, establishing an enviable record. After a short period as Acting Station Commander at Leeming, he was posted to command RCAF Station East Moor in May 1943, on its being raised from sub-station status. He perfected a smooth-running organization in record time, and under his leadership and direction No.429 (RCAF) Squadron became a first-line squadron. He successfully supervised the establishment of No.1679 Heavy Conversion Flight and the conversion of No.432 (RCAF) Squadron from twin to four engine bombers. Group Captain Carscallen has shown excellent administrative ability, leadership and devotion to duty of a very high order.

Various postings followed, including to Washington, DC from November 1944 to April 1945. From June into September 1945 He was attached to the USAAF 20th Air Force in the South Pacific and Australia to observe long-range B-29 operations on Japan (a unit of 20th Air Force – the 509th – ended the war by A-bombing Hiroshima and Nagasaki in August 1945). In a letter of September 10, 1947 to Air Commodore R.C. Gordon at the Canadian Joint Staff Mission in Washington, BGen George W. Mundy recalled serving in the Pacific with Carscallen: "... he didn't limit his observations to ground activities alone, but voluntarily flew operational missions in order to gain first hand information on the tactics of long range bombardment... his personality and integrity gained for him the respect and liking of the entire organisation."

Back from the Pacific, Carscallen was Canada's Air Attaché in Washington. In 1948 he was promoted to Air Commodore. Later postings included Northwest Air Command, National Defence College, 4 ATAF in NATO (chief of staff to MGen E.J. Timberlake, USAF), Air Materiel Command and Training Command, from where he left the RCAF in August 1963. Air Commodore Carscallen was revered by his boss at 4 ATAF. In May 1958 MGen Timberlake was prompted to pen these words to Air Marshall Hugh Campbell: "As my Chief of Staff, Air Commodore Carscallen has uniformly manifested all of the exacting characteristics that his assignment required ... [he] has been of immeasurable assistance to me and the members of my staff ... he is eminently fitted to discharge the duties of Air Vice Marshal and I would, if so empowered, recommend accordingly."

At the end of his RCAF career, A/V/M Carscallen had log books brimming with aviation history. He had piloted everything from the tiny D.H.60 Moth (122:45 hours) to the Vedette (36:40), Delta (174:10), Digby (414:25), Stranraer (465:30), Canso (174:35 and Wellington (119:45). He even crossed into the jet age with a few hours on T-33s. His flying time as of January 31, 1957 totalled 2463 hours. A/V/M Carscallen died in Ottawa in 1986.

Founded in Kingston, Ontario since 1876, Royal Military College produced many officers who later fought in the First World War. Postwar, RMC continued to graduate elite young men, many of whom served in the peacetime RCAF. With the Second World War these, along with some of the 1914-18 veterans, led the RCAF through its greatest era. This aerial view of RMC (*circa* 1920) looks northeasterly. In the foreground is Fort Frederick (1846) with its defensive Martello tower. The historic RMC buildings are grouped around the parade square. Across Navy Bay is Fort Henry, beyond which are lands now occupied by CFB Kingston. Inset, four RMC graduates who excelled during WWII: W.A. "Billy" Bishop, Leonard J. Birchall, Paul Y. Davoud and Hartland deM Molson. Having received the Victoria Cross in WWI, Bishop was a leading morale-booster for all Canadians during WWII. He attended countless public events, especially parades, where he pinned the wings on hundreds of graduating airmen. Birchall commanded 413 Squadron in Ceylon, where he was involved in the reconnaissance that located a Japanese fleet. In that action his Catalina was shot down. "Birch" spent the rest of the war as a POW. Davoud became a heroic figure in the early days of night fighters defending the UK, then commanded the RCAF Typhoon Wing after D-Day. Molson led 1 Squadron (RCAF) during the Battle of Britain and commanded 118 (F) Squadron at Dartmouth. (Royal Military College)

Broken Hearts on the Home Front

Canadians suffered immeasurable sadness on hearing of lost loved ones (some 16,000 RCAF members would die 1939-45). First to suffer were immediate families, especially parents. By the time brothers and sisters, grandparents, cousins, schoolmates, workmates and neighbours were counted, millions of Canadians were in mourning by war's end. Worst by far was the anguish of mothers, many of whom lost two or more sons. Several had raised fine twin boys, only to lose them both. Imagine the grief caused when the 10,000-ton freighter *Amerika* was torpedoed off Greenland on April 22, 1943. Of 53 RCAF airmen aboard, only 16 were rescued. Among the dead were twins Andrew James and Robert William Mosser of Preston, Ontario, recently graduated as air navigators and heading for the UK.

The Colville Brothers

During WWII Annie and Alexander Colville of Bowmanville, Ontario lost three sons: Alexander at age 28, William at 25 and John at 24. When she laid a wreath at the National Cenotaph in Ottawa on Remembrance Day 1945, Mrs. Colville represented the mothers of Canada who had lost children to the war. In 1994 the Clarington, Ontario town council passed a resolution that the Bowmanville clock tower in Rotary Park be named in honour of the Colvilles: FSgt William Freeborne Colville died on May 6, 1942, while a navigator with 11 (BR) Squadron. On takeoff from Torbay for Dartmouth, something went awry with Hudson No.761, piloted by F/L J.H.U. LeBlanc. The plane crashed, killing all three crew and five passengers. F/O Alexander Colborne Colville was lost with his 408 Squadron crew on March 16, 1944. They had been on night ops to Stuttgart in Lancaster LL718. No trace was ever found of them. John Spencer "Sandy" Colville of 440 Squadron was killed when his Typhoon was brought down by friendly fire on August 18, 1944. He inadvertently had been shooting up a Canadian convoy which, naturally, fired back. On July 17, 1946 the Toronto *Daily Star* reported on the Colville family, but did not refer once to the dreadful heartache that would have

MRS A. J. COLVILLE is shown here with the three sons she lost in the war, left to right, John, William and Alex. Special mention was made of Mrs. Colville by the Earl of Athlone when her youngest son received his wings

On July 17, 1949 this newspaper clipping appeared in the press honouring the Colville family, which lost three RCAF sons. (Lialla Raymes Col.)

been weighing on Mrs. Colville. The paper's tone is typical of the time, as if a mother was just delighted to have sacrificed her family. (Not only had Mrs. Colville lost her three flying sons, but had been widowed in 1942 and lost a

Alexander C. Colville. While doing elementary pilot training at the Moose Jaw Flying Club in the spring of 1940, he struck up a friendship with Danny Raymes of Moose Jaw. Later he mailed Danny this photo with the scribble on the back, "A.C. Colville, 43 Carlisle Ave. Bowmanville Ont – Phone 267". (Lialla Raymes Col.)

On June 2, 1996 Bowmanville, Ontario dedicated a park, clock tower and plaques in honour of the Colvilles. Attending were several RCAF Typhoon pilots who had known Sandy Colville on 143 Wing in Normandy days. (Larry Milberry)

fourth boy at home. Only her daughter Katherine remained.):

Believed to be the only mother in Canada to lose three officer sons in the war, Mrs. A.J. Colville wears the proudest decoration any mother could wear, three silver crosses on a silver chain. The living room of her home on Church street here is adorned with countless pictures of her three gallant RCAF sons ... Sandy had just received his senior matriculation when he joined the air force, "to avenge the death of his brothers", as Mrs. Colville put it.

In his last letter to a friend back home Sandy said, "Every time I press the gun button, I think of my brothers, Alex and Bill. I just sit in the cockpit and grin like a maniac and watch the vermin squirm.

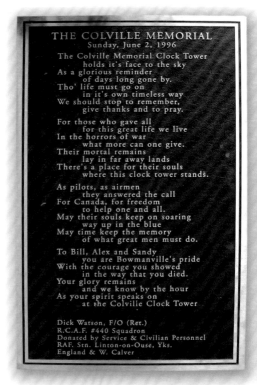

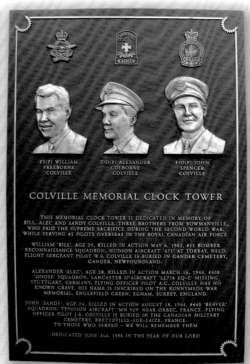

Here is the plaque honouring the brothers, and the poem composed for the occasion by Typhoon pilot Dick Watson of Wawa, Ontario. (Larry Milberry)

My second cannon burst is for Mom."... One of Mrs. Colville's most treasured possessions is a book, "The RCAF Overseas", presented to her by Air Marshall Robert Leckie, chief of the air staff, Ottawa, June 1946.

R212772 FSgt G.S. Breckels

Official word of an airman being killed, wounded or missing reached a man's family by telegram. Other official telegrams and letters would follow, sometimes after the war had ended. Besides the important information being shared, these communications show the overall (if not always perfect) attention to detail and compassion at the bureaucratic end, even to "the system" providing families with photos of their sons' final resting places.

The worst thing that a mother could experience was to open her door to the boy from the Canadian Pacific telegraph office. Thus would Mrs. Mary Breckels of 367 Eglinton Ave. in Toronto nearly have collapsed when she received the curt telegram announcing that her boy (age 19) – air gunner George Stanley, was missing: "From RCAF Message Cypher : REGRET TO ADVISE YOU THAT YOUR SON R TWO ONE TWO SEVEN SEVEN TWO FLIGHT SERGEANT GEORGE STANLEY BRECKELS IS REPORTED MISSING AFTER AIR OPERATIONS OVER-

SEAS SEPTEMBER NINETEENTH STOP LETTER FOLLOWS" A few days later, Mrs. Breckels would have despaired further on receiving a letter of September 20, 1944 from her son's CO at 190 Squadron (RAF Fairford), S/L D.S. Gibb. Although the CO's letter suggested some hope, its tone was grave. Gibb knew the score. He had written such letters before and tried not to mince his words:

Dear Mrs. Breckels,

It is with the deepest regret that I am writing to you with confirmation of the telegram which has already been sent to you regarding your son (R.212772) F/Sgt G.S. Breckels, who is missing from Air Operations on the 19th September, 1944.

The aircraft in which your son was flying took off at approximately 1:00 PM on the 19th September, 1944, for operations over Holland and, from the time of take-off, no signals were received from the aircraft.

There is a possibility that the crew were able to bale out over enemy territory, and are now prisoners of war. If this is the case we should know in due course through the International Red Cross Society, but it is sometimes quite a period before such news does eventually get through. I assure you that you will be informed immediately any information is received.

I think you will like to know that during the time your son was with us at this Squadron, he had become well liked by everyone, and his loss is felt keenly. The crew were carrying out a most successful tour of operations and had formed themselves in an excellent team. Their loss has been a sad blow to the Squadron, quite apart from the personal grief which all are feeling. I can only say that we are hoping sincerely that we may receive good tidings of him in due course.

His personal effects have been collected and forwarded to the R.A.F. Central Depository and in due course you will receive a further communication concerning these from the Administrator of Estates, Ottawa.

May I again express on behalf of the entire Squadron and myself, the heartfelt sympathy which we all feel with you in your anxiety. I appreciate to the full your dreadful suspense and wish there was more that I could do than merely saying how sorry I am. We are all hopeful that news will be received that your son is safe, but if in the meanwhile, I can be of any assistance to you in any way, please do not hesitate to write me. Yours sincerely, D.B. Gibb S/Ldr

A letter of September 26, 1944 from the RCAF Casualty Office in Ottawa added a few details: "… your son and the entire crew of his aircraft failed to return to their base after taking off at 1:13 P.M. on September 19th, 1944, on para-trooping and glider towing operations over Holland." This letter then advised: "Your son's name will not appear on the official casualty list for five weeks. You may, however, release to the Press or Radio the fact that he is reported missing, but not disclosing the date, place or his unit."

On April 16, 1945 a letter from the RCAF Casualty Office in Ottawa to Stanley's father delivered more bad news: "I greatly regret that since my letter of September 26th, no further information has been received regarding your son…" Meanwhile, the Allies had moved from France and Holland into Germany, so new information was being gathered about missing airmen. Except when the news was good, however, specifics were relayed to a family. In Breckels' case, it was known as early as April 12, 1945 that human remains had been found among the wreckage of his aircraft. According to one report these were "buried in the same grave at St. Michel Gestel Cemetery" and were thought to belong to RAF airmen FSgt S.H. Coeshott (skipper) and FSgt J.F. Jeffrey.

On July 4, 1945 came a final blow – Casualty Officer S/O W.M. Wismer in Ottawa advised Mr. Breckels: "It is with deep regret that, in view of the lapse of time and the absence of any further information concerning your son … the Air Ministry Overseas now proposes to take action to presume his death for official purposes." Then, on July 6 Stanley's brother, F/O Albert L. Breckels, replied that the family had heard from the widow of Stanley's pilot in the UK, "that her husband and the bombardier were buried by a Dutch padre in or near a village approx. 30 miles from Arnhem (the target area) … There was no mention of the other four members of the crew. This might suggest that the four missing members had time to get out of the plane, bearing in mind that the two members buried were in condition to be identified." The brother then requested the names of the RCAF padre who had passed this news to the pilot's widow, and the name of the Dutch padre. On July 21 G/C T.K. McDougall from Ottawa wrote to the Canadian Casualty Branch in London enquiring: "May the name of the R.C.A.F. Chaplain be obtained …"

On July 28 George Stanley Breckel's name appeared on the "Presumption of Death Lapse of Time List 88C". W/C J.S. Harris, RCAF Overseas then reported on August 3, 1945 that the Canadian padre was Capt R.F. Filer and the Dutch padre, Rev. W. Van Hessel of St. Michel Gestel. Filer later reported that many body parts had been collected and buried in the Coeshott/Jeffrey grave and that "there was no doubt that the remains of all the crew were buried" and that he had "fixed up" the grave and placed a cross for Sgts Coeshott and Jeffrey.

On August 14 Air Marshal Robert Leckie wrote to Mr. Breckels that his son "is now for official purposes presumed to have died on Active Service Overseas". However, public notice of FSgt Breckels' death already had appeared in the press on August 25 under the headline "Toronto Air-Gunner Now Presumed

Dead". Mentioned was how he had been on a Stirling para-dropping supplies at Arnhem when shot down, and that he and his crew "were buried by a Dutch padre in a little village in Holland". The fateful trip had been Breckels' 25th operation. On August 27 Ottawa reported to the family the names of the padres sought by F/O Breckels, and how "you may rest assured that immediately any word of your brother is received you will be at once advised."

On October 6, 1945 F/L F.A. Willson of the RAF Missing Research and Enquiry Service at The Hague reported to Air Ministry: "I have visited the scene of the crash at St. Michel Gestel (Map reference E.34) and found the aircraft to be completely buried. For this reason I visited the Mayor and asked if it were possible for it to be dug out, as there are almost certainly bodies underneath it. The Mayor was willing to give any help he could…" Willson interviewed Van Hessel and reported that photos had been taken of the graves, but noted: "There are local rumours that three airmen may have jumped, but nothing definite can be obtained at this point as opinion is divided and nobody will commit himself in this connection." Arrangements were made to have 151 Recovery Unit salvage the site and for war graves men to dig up the grave to see how many men may be in it. 151 RU reported on November 19, 1945: "Wreckage certified now clear of human remains. It is possible that any other bodies would have been totally burnt by intense fire" (all this was reported to F/O Albert Breckels on December 14).

On October 15, 1945 a Canadian Casualty Office had received a translation of an eye witness report from the burgomaster of St. Michel Gestel: "On the 19th of Sept. 1944 at about 1730 hrs, a two motored transporting aeroplane hit by German Flaktroops, crashed down on the grounds DE Bleeke south east of the Rurvenberg, St. Michelgestel N. Brabant." He added how 2000 French francs, 3 pounds, 10 shillings, a 25 Guilder bank note, a wrist watch, 30 Belgium francs, 1000 French francs, a ring of keys, some photos, etc. had been recovered and that, "The mortal remains were buried on the Twentieth of September 1944 at 1600 hrs. in the cemetery of the Dutch Reformed Church at St. Michelgsestel after a funeral

service was held in the church by the pastor W. Van Hessel". This translation was forwarded to Stanley's brother, the casualty office in Ottawa explaining, "note an error in the first paragraph … twin motored instead of four motored."

Much further correspondence fills the Breckels file, including a letter of January 22, 1945 from Mrs. Janet M. Wood of Surrey, enquiring of a Mr. Williams (RAF casualty branch?) regarding a set of keys carried by her son, George, of the Breckels crew. On February 6, 1946 the RCAF Casualty Liaison Office in London wrote to the RCAF Estates Office in Ottawa reporting that a Rolex watch with "George" inscribed had been catalogued, but two crew had been named George. It seems that the watch first was sent for identification to Mrs. Wood, who did not recognize it. On March 19 Mr. Breckels heard that the Rolex was being sent to her from Ottawa by registered mail. As this watch had been found in the common grave, it was assumed that Breckels remains were there.

There is correspondence about Stanley's $1000 life insurance policy; about his personal effects being forwarded to Ottawa in November 1945, e.g. clothing, shaving kit, photos, wallet, keys, pen knife; and of Mrs. Breckels receiving the $320.02 War Service Gratuity that was due to her son. An October 5, 1946 report from 2 Missing Research and Enquiry Unit noted that the town of St. Michel Gestel had erected crosses to Coeshott, Jeffreys, Breckels and Moss.

As were most families who lost sons, the Breckels were anxious to receive all of their son's effects. Not all, however, even knew that each aircrew kept a log book – the record of their training and operational flying. If they knew about log books, any family would have wanted this memento. It is not surprising to see that Mrs. Breckels had been enquiring about Stanley's log book. On December 27, 1946, she wrote Ottawa with a tone of relief: "We understand the log books have arrived. Would you kindly send my son's to me." This was done on January 10. Later she requested an Operations Wing and this was sent with the certificate "in recognition of the gallant services rendered by your son". On October 27, 1947 the family received confirmation from Ottawa of Stanley being buried at St. Michel Gestel: "These graves will be registered collectively for these four airmen." On September 14, 1948 a photo of the grave was mailed to Stanley's mother along with words of assurance that the Imperial War Graves Commission would be minding the graves perpetually.

One of the final details in tidying up FSgt Breckel's estate concerned his campaign stars medals – he was entitled to the Defence Medal, 1939-45 Star, France Germany Medal, Canadian Volunteer Service Medal, and the War Medal 1939-45. The family received these soon after the war, although some snafu had them mailed inadvertently to the Bremner family in Bralorne, BC, whose son John had been lost on operations with 419 Squadron. To honour their lost son and brother, on the 2-year anniversary of his death, the Breckels placed this memorial notice in the Toronto *Star* of September 19, 1946:

Somewhere back in the sunset,
Where loveliness never dies,
He lives in a land of glory
Midst the gold and blue of the skies.
And we, who love him dearly,
Whose passing has brought many tears,
Will cherish his memory always
To brighten the drifting years.

RCAF Publications

Members of the RCAF encountered many publications throughout their careers. The basic rules of service were King's Regulations for the Royal Canadian Air Force – best known as "K.R. (Air)". These were loved by generations of barrack room lawyers, none more famous than Sergeant Shatterproof, a fictional character who appeared for years in the RCAF journal *The Roundel*. Sergeant Shatterproof faded with the death of his creator, Warrant Officer Ray Tracey.

"K.R. (Air)" laid out the general rules of the service, from oaths on enlistment to court martial procedures to military funeral entitlements. A step down from "K.R. (Air)" was a series of special publications dealing with Pay, Flying Orders, etc. There were documents known as AFAOs (Air Force Administrative Orders), AFROs (Air Force General and Routine Orders) and DROs (Daily Routine Orders). AFAOs

were expanded upon "K.R. (Air)", spelling out the details of how and when things were to be done. While "K.R. (Air)" generally fit into a single volume, AFAOs ran to 10 or 12 tomes, stuffed into ring binders. They were frequently amended and many a clerk or officer cadet was "joed" into removing redundant orders from the various volumes and replacing them with the latest amendments.

AFROs dealt with more mundane matters. If "K.R. (Air)" decreed what constituted a serious court martial offence, and AFAOs laid down the rules of evidence for courts martial, AFROs handled changing details, e.g. expenses that could be paid for travel by witnesses, and reported the outcome of the most serious courts martial. Some dealt with surprising subjects. One such Order published on January 8, 1943 spelled out the approved hair styles for members of the Women's Division, adding that it was the duty of WD officers and NCOs to "check airwomen with unruly hair and to order them to conform with the instructions promulgated on hair styles." An interesting appendage to AFROs was the weekly "Supplements", also known as "green sheets. These briefly reported the commissioning, promotion, retirement or passing of officers, casualties (regardless of cause or rank) and decorations (regardless of rank).

Most important to personnel were the DROs produced at every "self-accounting base" (i.e. a base that was administratively self-contained) and went into such matters as personnel being "taken on strength" (posted in) and "struck off strength" (posted out), appointment of

Orderly Officers and Deputy Orderly Officers (which rotated) and fire marshals, special local and short-term regulations such as extra precautions during forest fire season, temporary suspension of bus runs and special events ranging from Victory Bond drives to winter carnivals. Because of the mundane content and volume (generated by hundreds of units), DROs generally were removed from bulletin boards and destroyed within a month. Consequently, few DROs survive for the modern historian to study. Those that can be found, constitute a rich source of history as to how the RCAF operated day by day.

AFROs of October 16, 1942 reminded all members of the existence of the Aircraft Detection Corps, a civilian volunteer organization responsible for reporting "aircraft movements, submarines, strange vessels, and/or other possible enemy activity". Any such reports received top priority and were relayed to operations centres for verification. Few ADC reports resulted in serious action being taken, although they might lead to pinpointing crash, sinking or ditching. AFROs of May 7, 1943 covered the conservation of scarce resources in wartime:

It is suggested that gardening committees be set up at all stations, that a survey of available land be made, and that suitable plots be allocated to the various flights or sections. The interest of personnel may be stimulated by arranging competitions … It is further suggested that implements, seeds, and plants be purchased from canteen funds, and the resultant produce be distributed to the various messes … The Dominion

From Day One of their training, RCAF recruits had regulations and routines drummed into their skulls. These students at 19 EFTS, Virden already were well indoctrinated, but some still would run afoul of the rules. The great CPR photographer Nicholas Morant took this photo in October 1944. (LAC PA176329)

Department of Agriculture ... will give advice and assistance in the establishment of R.C.A.F. gardens ... describing the most suitable times for sowing seed and setting plants ..."

AFROs of April 2, 1943 addressed fuel conservation. One AFHQ study suggested that, using conservation methods, a single service flying training station could save 250,000 gallons of fuel annually:

Aviation gasoline must be conserved! On every flight, the pilot of a ... training aircraft is to operate the engine(s) of his aircraft to obtain the most economical results. The practice of running engines at their most economical speed will not only reduce consumption of gasoline in Canada with its attendant saving of railway and shipping space, but will also result in excellent training for pilots. Economy in fuel consumption can be practiced ... by reducing manifold pressure (boost pressure) and r.p.m. below the figures currently employed, and by maintaining the mixture strength at all times at the recommended minimum ... An engine should never ... be left running on the ground between flights, unless it is absolutely certain that the period for which the aircraft is to be left will not exceed two minutes...

This AFRO noted ideal fuel consumption (gallons per hour) for various types, e.g. Anson I (Cheetah IX engines), Anson II & III (Jacobs L6) as 24-30 gallons per hour; Oxford (Cheetah X) 20-22 gph; Crane (Jacobs 4) 23-25 gph; Harvard (Wasp S3H1) 14-18 gph; Bolingbroke (Mercury XV) 40-45 gph.

Home Front Infractions in AFROs

Every day at home or abroad RCAF members overstepped the bounds of authority. For their pains, miscreants could suffer grave consequences. Those abusing King's Regulations might have been lowly AC1s, but not necessarily. W/C Harry Neville Compton of 4 Training Command HQ in Calgary was noted in AFROs of September 25, 1942, as "cashiered" and "imprisoned for six months" for an infraction relating to trust. Born in Winnipeg in 1899, Compton had been a bank clerk before

Hundreds of aircraft accidents on the home front were the result of some sort of infringement of RCAF regulations. The worst cases involved unauthorized low flying or reckless formation antics. The end result often was death and destruction. Anson 8547, crashed for whichever reason, was a write-off. In most such cases, officialdom blamed the pilot for poor airmanship, i.e. a breach of regulations. (CANAV Col.)

enlisting in the Canadian Army. Transferred to the RFC, he had flown Dolphins on 23 Squadron. He had five victories and a DFC "in recognition of distinguished services rendered during the war". Between the wars Compton worked in accounting. A certain AC2 is mentioned in the same AFROs as charged on September 2, 1942 for "improperly" taking the place of another man at a mathematics exam. In AFROs of November 13, 1942 Cpl William F. MacDonald was noted as found guilty by court-martial, reduced in rank and sentenced to 56 days incarceration for having cheated in a dice game.

Not all low flying was forbidden but, according to AFROs of December 10, 1943, could be authorized at EFTS, SFTS or OTU by a flight commander or flying instructor. However, unauthorized low flying was almost a daily occurrence. This was severely punished and for good reason – aircraft were being damaged or destroyed and men injured and killed by reckless flying. So serious was this that RCAF HQ set stringent rules. This issue was often addressed in AFROs, as on June 2, 1944 :

Illegally performing aerobatics below the minimum height prescribed or in an aircraft not authorized for the performance of aerobatics is a serious breach of flying regulations ... This order is to be read out once a month to all aircrew personnel including trainees at all flying units. A record that this has been done is to be kept by the unit... This order applies to all RCAF and RAF personnel in Canada ... This order is to be reproduced quarterly in unit AFROs.

AFROs of October 29, 1942 mention F/O William Evans Thomas being reduced in rank for flying his aircraft between the masts of a steamship, "carrying away a portion of the aerial and causing danger of bodily injury to his crew." (On August 12, 1945 Thomas died of natural causes in the Canadian General Hospital in England.) AFROs of December 4, 1942 record how P/O Robert Joseph Garvin of RCAF Station Hagersville flew "in a foolhardy and dangerous manner". He was severely reprimanded and fined $200 but, happily, not sent home to his mother. He later served on 427 Squadron, where he ended with a DFC. The citation to this award removed any fear that Garvin might be a danger to anyone but the enemy, noting how he "has set a very fine example of skill, keenness and devotion to duty".

In the court martial of F/O John Thomas Reed, it also was good that he was not dismissed for beating up 3 SFTS Calgary on July 30, 1941. Instead, Reed was reduced in rank. A bank clerk in Ottawa before enlisting in January 1940, he had been instructing on Ansons at the time of his lapse in judgment. Posted overseas in May 1942, he flew Sunderlands on 422 Squadron, did important work with the RAF Marine Experimental Establishment, then flew Dakotas on 512 and 437 squadrons. On June 8, 1945 he was awarded a DFC for his good work during such operations as Arnhem and the Rhine crossing. In 1949-51 S/L Reed was on exchange with the USAF 314th Troop Carrier Wing, flying C-54s, C-82s and C-119s. This earned him the US Bronze Star, the citation for which notes: "By virtue of such distinguished service he brought great credit upon himself, the United States Air Force and the Royal Canadian Air Force."

P/O Charles E. Cussion faced a serious charge at his court-martial of April 2, 1943: "Being guilty of neglect in flying which caused loss of life". While instructing, Cussion allowed his pupil to fly too close to another Harvard. A collision ensued and the other aircraft crashed fatally. Cussion was cashiered. But a dismissed pilot was not necessarily out of the RCAF for good. RCAF HQ realized that it had an investment in each pilot, so there was a process for self-redemption, although this did not apply to cashiered pilots. This is described in AFROs of August 20, 1943 explaining that pilots "who have been or are dismissed from the Service by sentence of court-martial for flying offences, may make application to enlist as airmen pilots in the Special Reserve". At the time of dismissal, a pilot received papers explaining how he could get back in. "He is to be handed a notice", said AFROs, "duly completed by his commanding officer, notifying him of such opportunity." A pilot now could visit an RCAF recruiting office, present his paperwork, then fill out all the usual enlistment forms. If accepted, he would be made a temporary sergeant "special group", and might return to flying.

Arctic Pioneering

Manned flight in the polar regions commenced with a Danish balloon expedition led by Salomon August Andrée. With his two companions, on July 11, 1897 he drifted away from Dane's Island, Spitsbergen in the Svalbard Archipelago, hoping to reach the geographic North Pole. Their great hydrogen-filled balloon *Eagle* followed an erratic course for 65 hours, finally crashing on the ice about 300 miles from base. The aeronauts spent months seeking salvation, reached land, but eventually died. Their remains, including diaries and photographs, were discovered in 1930.

The next known Arctic flight was by Lt Jan Nagorski (1888-1976) – a Polish pilot in the Russian Imperial Navy. On August 21, 1914 he flew a 4:20-hour mission from Novaya Zemlya in a Farman seaplane, searching over land and the Barents Sea for the lost Sedov polar expedition. Four other flights ensued, the last on September 13. About 10 hours were logged, but nothing was found. Nagorski made several useful recommendations about polar aviation, including painting aircraft red for visibility. Next came various failed attempts to reach the North Pole by air. In 1925, for example, Roald Amundsen (discoverer of the South Pole) and

Lincoln Ellsworth launched a 6-man expedition with two ski-equipped Dornier Wal flying boats. They departed Dane's Island on May 21, but soon were ice-bound at about 88°N after one Wal had engine trouble. To save themselves, the men cleared a 1000-foot ice runway but, reduced to meagre rations, gradually wore out, and two of them nearly drowned in a mishap. On the morning of June 15 everyone crowded into one overloaded Wal. Pilot Riiser Larsen then safely made the 525-mile hop back to Spitzbergen. Many other such Arctic and North Atlantic attempts followed (books, journal articles, internet sites, etc. about these abound).

From April 6 to September 28, 1924 a US Army expedition using Douglas Air Cruiser seaplanes circumnavigated the globe, routing up the west coast of North America from Seattle to Alaska, then west to Siberia, Japan, India, on to Britain, then home using the previously unconquered route through Iceland and Greenland. On August 31 they were at Icy Tickle, Labrador, then continued two days later through Hawkes Bay, Newfoundland; Pictou, Nova Scotia; Maine and on to home base in Seattle. Two of the expedition's four planes were lost, but all eight crew got home after covering 26,345 miles and piling up 363 flying hours.

Maj R.A. Logan displaying the CAF flag at Craig Harbour, NWT in 1922 during the expedition aboard the research vessel *Arctic*. Frank Ellis notes of this great Canadian: "He was a qualified surveyor, and his job was to investigate flying conditions and stake out possible sites, particularly on the northern tip of Baffin Island, and on Devon and Ellesmere islands." Logan was the first Canadian air force officer in the Arctic. One of the sites he surveyed was Pond Inlet. When one lands there today, it is on the very ground that Logan paced off. (A comment in the *Canada Flight Supplement* of 2010 notes of this 'drome: "Possible presence of large animals within airport perimeter.") (DND RE13996)

MacMillan Expedition

In 1925 the National Geographic Society sponsored the MacMillan Expedition to Ellesmere Island. Two ships and three US Navy Loening Amphibians were used, the aircraft commanded by LCMDR Richard E. Byrd (who had consulted with Nagorski prior to that undertaking). From Etah, Greenland (78°19'N, 72°28'W) flights were made, including to Ellesmere Island, over which Byrd and his men first flew in the Loenings on August 8. On the 12th they made the first ever landings on Ellesmere, touching down in Hayes Fiord at 79°03'N, 76°75'W.

In another case, on April 15, 1928 G.H. Wilkins and Carl Ben Eilson flew a Lockheed Vega 2200 miles from Point Barrow, Alaska, to Spitsbergen. On May 9, 1926 Richard Byrd and Floyd Bennett crewed a Fokker trimotor on a return non-stop Spitsbergen-North Pole flight. This was hailed as one of the world's greatest air ventures, but decades later was shown conclusively to have missed the pole completely. Two days after Byrd-Bennett, the Italian navigator Umberto Nobile, Roald Amundsen, Lincoln Ellsworth and crew flew the airship *Norge* from Spitsbergen to the North Pole and on to Teller, Alaska. In 72 hours they covered 3400 miles.

On May 23, 1928 Nobile set out from Spitsbergen in a new airship, the *Italia*. The North Pole was attained but, returning on May 25, *Italia* crashed. Men were thrown from the gondola and injured, then the ship was swept away with seven still aboard. The first major Arctic air-sea rescue effort ensued, during which Amundsen and five companions on a search plane disappeared forever. A Swedish air force Fokker found Nobile and his companions, flew Nobile to safety, but crashed upon its return. On the 48th day of their ordeal, five remaining survivors were picked up by the Russian icebreaker *Krasin*. Some 23 aircraft and 20 vessels from several nations had taken part in this effort.

Another daring Arctic flight was made in August 1928 by R.J. "Bert" Hassell and Parker Cramer. Hassell's dream was to prove the practicality of a high latitude air route between North America and Europe. He would demonstrate his idea by flying from Rockford, Illinois to Stockholm via the Greenland icecap. About half way en

The doomed trans-Greenland fliers Pacquette and Cramer shortly before they were swallowed up by the North Sea. (CANAV Col.)

route, he would refuel at the University of Michigan observatory at Mount Evan near Söndre Strömfjord on Greenland's west coast – opposite Padloping Island and almost on the Arctic Circle. Flying the Stinson Detroiter *Greater Rockford*, Hassell and Cramer set out on August 16. They made Cochrane, Ontario, then departed two days later for Greenland. The Mount Evan staff was standing by at an improvised runway, but no plane arrived. Two weeks later Hassell and Cramer were spotted by Greenlanders not far from their destination. Having lost their bearings on crossing Davis Strait, they had landed about 70 miles from Mount Evan. They quickly secured their plane and struck off with little food and scant equipment. They were rescued hours before the main university party was due to sail south, so their luck had held.

The following year Cramer flew north again, but his plane was wrecked by a storm on Hudson Strait. Undeterred, he tried again in 1931, setting off on July 28 from Detroit in a diesel-powered Bellanca floatplane with his crewman, Oliver Pacquette of Cochrane, Ontario. They stopped in Cochrane, then Rupert House, Great Whale River, Wakeham Island and, on August 1, Holsteinborg, Greenland. That day they flew up the Greenland Ice Cap, which took them to about 10,000 feet. They could climb no higher, so made their flight barely above the ice surface, jettisoning equipment and supplies in order to stay airborne. They landed at Angmagssalik, then flew on the 7th to the

Faeroes. Two days later they reached the Shetlands in stormy weather, then rushed to get off for final destination, Copenhagen. Sadly, Cramer and Pacquette flew into the raging North Sea storm and never again were seen.

Following the 1927 Hudson Strait Expedition, the RCAF rarely ventured "North of 60". Soviet Arctic flying, however, was very busy supporting a host of scientific expeditions. Canada was aware of this, but did nothing to challenge or emulate the USSR. However, with the advent of WWII Britain, the US and Canada began reconsidering the Arctic, as plans were developing to ferry thousands of warplanes overseas from US factories.

The ferry agencies would be needing more than one route, in view of the volume of airplanes and the ever-changing Atlantic weather systems. A route to the UK via Baffin Island, Greenland and Iceland seemed like a solution. At first Britain pressed Ottawa to send a military force to take over Greenland, which was along the planned ferry route. But Prime Minister King and his chief deputy, C.D. Howe, were cagey about getting involved in such overt action. Instead, the US, as yet still neutral, assumed the defence of Greenland (in co-operation with Danish officials in exile). This action was essential – the Allies could not let Greenland fall under German control (Greenland was a source of strategic minerals, and potential haven for U-boats).

On April 22, 1941 an ATFERO (Atlantic Ferry Organization) Liberator, captained by the renowned D.C.T. Bennett, made the first photo reconnaissance flight along the Greenland coast, looking for potential airfield sites, much as S/L Small would do on the Labrador coast the following August). Having departed Gander, Bennett and crew finished this mission with a landing at Dorval about 15 hours later. A site was chosen in July for the first airfield in what would become a chain of such installations leading north and east around the North Atlantic. Located on Hamilton Inlet, Labrador, the first site developed was Goose Bay.

Worried about the cost, Ottawa at first vacillated about building Goose Bay. London and Washington, however, were determined to have this done, so forced Ottawa's hand. Canadian teams surveyed the site in August, and the first ships with men and supplies soon reached Hamilton Inlet. By freeze-up in early December runways and some buildings were serviceable. The overall authority for this monumental project was Canada's Department of Transport. Meanwhile, the Americans began building similar airports on the Greenland coast: Bluie West 1 (Narsarssuak), Bluie West 8 (Söndre Strömfjord) and Bluie East 1 (Angmagssalik); and at Keflavik, Iceland. Other bases arose: Crystal 1 (Fort Chimo on Ungava Bay), Crystal II (Frobisher Bay) and Crystal III (Padloping Island on the Baffin Island coast opposite Greenland). Each was a combined airport and weather station. Aircraft would flow along this route from staging bases at Dorval (RAF Ferry Command) and Presque Isle and Houlton in Maine (USAAF Ferrying Command).

In February and March 1942 two RCAF Norsemans and an RAF Hudson conducted the first survey of the Crystal sites. The Norsemans were piloted by bush pilot Louis Bisson and Ferry Command's Don McVicar. George Evans, an American on contract to Ferry Command, captained the Hudson. This hazardous mission was completed in the face of challenging Arctic weather. One Norseman was lost, but everyone got safely back to Dorval. One lesson learned was that single-engine aircraft could safely follow a northern route to the UK. With Ottawa's approval, similar routes were developed by the Americans

RCAF Station Goose Bay soon after becoming operational early in 1942. The first Ferry Command mission from here (two Cansos and a Liberator) departed for the UK on April 6. On the 17th pilots Bisson, Evans and McVicar left to deliver three Hudsons non-stop. Not all departures from "Goose" had happy endings. On September 14, 1944, for example, a US Navy PB4Y-1 (B-24) departed eastbound, but ran out of fuel and ditched off Donegal Bay, Ireland, after overshooting its destination – Iceland. Of 10 aboard, 5 were lost. (Ernie Weeks Col.)

Crystal II (Frobisher Bay, now Iqaluit) soon after completion by the US military in the spring of 1943. The main N-S gravel runway was 6000 x 200 feet (now 8600 x 200). (Ernie Weeks Col.)

through central Canada: via Detroit, North Bay, Kapuskasing, Moosonee and Richmond Gulf; and via Regina, The Pas, Fort Churchill and Southampton Island. These would merge at Fort Chimo, then continue via Baffin Island, Greenland and Iceland. The whole network was code-named "Crimson". Except for Goose Bay and The Pas, the new installations were built by the Americans.

The first three aircraft delivered on the Crimson route were two Cansos and a Liberator piloted by the intrepid trio of Bisson, Evans and McVicar. On April 5, 1942 they flew from Dorval to Goose Bay, from where they continued via BW-8. Their leg to Iceland proved hazardous, but they reached Prestwick and were back in Dorval (travelling in the bomb bay of a Liberator) after nine days. Being so anxious to prove the viability of the Crimson route, A/C G.J. "Taffy" Powell, commanding ATFERO, was pleased with this successful outcome. Soon the Arctic route was busy with aircraft on delivery, the first, it seems, being a USAAF B-24 commanded by Col Milton W. Arnold. Commencing at Presque Isle, he set down at BW-1 on April 12, 1942, then continued to the UK. Through the rest of the year the USAAF ferried some 650 aircraft via Goose Bay, mainly B-17s, C-47s and P-38s. Meanwhile, ATFERO despatched 123 aircraft on the same route. Most crews made it across, but there was a price to pay. ATFERO losses were 11 Hudsons, 4 Bostons, 4 Venturas, 1 Liberator and 1 Mitchell. (Of one early wave of USAAF aircraft despatched via Goose Bay, 5 P-38s and 2 B-17s force-landed on the Greenland Icecap. All 25 crew were rescued within days. (Over the summer of 1992 P-38 41-7630, part of the Greenland "ghost squadron", was salvaged from under 250 feet of ice. Shipped in pieces to Middlesboro, Kentucky, it was painstakingly restored. Phoenix-like and christened "Glacier Girl", 41-7630 took to the air again in October 2002.) Canada's early reluctance to join in the Crimson project partially concerned the fact that the construction fervor was overblown. In the end, the central routes were rarely used operationally. Meanwhile, as Carl Christie points out in his seminal book, *Ocean Bridge,* the successful war waged against the U-boats meant that thousands of airplanes could safely get overseas by sealift. He sums up the Crimson story:

Three other key airports built in 1942-43 by the US military for the Crimson Route were The Pas and Churchill in Manitoba, and Southampton Island, NWT. These all were used postwar by the RCAF and today are busy modern airports. (Ernie Weeks Col.)

On 1 August 1944 Prime Minister King tabled an exchange of letters between Canada and the United States, and announced in the House of Commons that provision had been made for the northern bases to be transferred to Canadian control. The Americans were reimbursed more than $13 million for the cost of those facilities that were of a permanent nature, and the books were closed on the North East Staging Route.

Don McVicar

One of Canada's great wartime ferry pilots was Donald Moore McVicar. Born in 1915 in Oxbow, Saskatchewan, Don grew up in Edmonton where he developed a passion for ham radio, but he also "got the flying bug". He earned his private pilot's licence in 1936 at the Edmonton and Northern Alberta Aero Club. He honed his radio skills in the RCNVR and early in WWII was working in the control tower at Winnipeg airport. From there he took a staff job flying Ansons at 2 AOS in Edmonton, then progressed to Ferry Command at Dorval in November 1941.

McVicar completed many trans-Atlantic ferry flights on the northern or southern routes. Included were some "reverse" ferry flights, including of Hampden P1230 on the Crimson Route from August 18-23, 1942. The trip with navigator Johnson began routinely, although their Hampden was a well-worn crate and little things kept happening that a pilot didn't much enjoy. In his 1983 book *North Atlantic Cat*, McVicar describes events as he was over Greenland in P1230:

Far below I spotted BE-2, Angmassalik, which was a gravel strip far up a narrow fjord. It didn't look too inviting. So when Johnson announced our direction-finding receiver had just quit, it was time for another decision. It was improbable any American base would have the spares to repair the old set. But to go back meant more delay, and a chance the RAF there couldn't fix it either. And the last weather we'd had showed Reyk on its way down. Ahead was clear air. I thought of the chances the old-time explorers had taken. What I was doing was, in comparison, like walking a baby carriage. Or so I convinced myself.

When we came to the west side of the icecap the visibility was good. But where was BW-8 ... That unserviceable radio would have come in handy now with its two wavery needles pointing towards Bluie's beacon. I stayed high and, more on instinct than anything else, turned north about 50 miles from the Davis Strait. My eyes were bugging with strain before I saw the narrow brown strip which marked my destination runway.

As McVicar suspected, there was nothing to be done to fix the radio at

The great Don McVicar of Ferry Command and World Wide Airways fame. This photo dates to about 1985. (Larry Milberry)

BW-8. Next morning he and Johnson set off and made Crystal II in 3:45 hours. After a 5-hour break, during which they had lunch with the famous Arctic explorer, Vilhjalmur Stefanson, McVicar and Johnson flew to Coral Harbour on Southampton Island, landing there after 0225 hours. After over-nighting, they faced their greatest challenge – a 1200-mile leg to Edmonton.

I looked at the weather folder in the morning. If [the met man's] crystal ball was working on at least three cylinders, I was in for a lousy flight... For the first hour we flew over Hudson Bay and I

got a pin-point on Chesterfield Inlet. It looked then like my optimistic outlook was the right one. But once we crossed the rugged coastline and over the tundra, featureless and unmapped, I wondered if I should turn back. Ahead were threatening banks of cloud and below – nothing... Now my magnetic compass was swirling around. At each little bump it would spin away, unhappy with the close proximity of the magnetic North Pole, reputed to be under King William Island just 500 miles away. Before we went into the clouds I got a sun shot and set my directional gyro, which made me decide to keep going. No doubt the clouds would open up at some time along the route and I'd get another sun shot. Of course.

But they didn't, and a couple of hours later I became worried enough about the wind to descend closer to the bleak tundra and fire my Verey pistol into the bog to see which way the wind on the ground was blowing. A drift sight was another feature lacking on the Hampden. The forecast wind was from the west, but now I saw a smoke trail from the southwest, so I altered course southwards by 13 degrees. Then back into the cloud to pick up some airspeed. Radio kaput, of course, so there was one ground feature I could not afford to miss ... the Athabasca River ...

What I finally found was the southern shore of a big lake which I identified as Lake Athabasca. I thanked the RCAF for its efforts in getting good photographs of the area as far back as the early thirties. But I realized I was damn near 120 miles northwest of track. As I turned almost due south, the weather started to clear up and it was now downhill all the way. When I finally landed at Edmonton, I'd been in the air 7 hours and 20 minutes [which] made my ground speed a respectable 164 mph.

On August 22 Don McVicar delivered P1230 to RCAF Station Patricia Bay, then resumed his busy Ferry Command career. Postwar, he operated World Wide Airways, a major DEW Line cargo carrier. Ultimately, World Wide was carrying tourists on the Atlantic in Super Constellations, until folding in hard times in 1965. Don McVicar passed away in Dorval in 1997. Happily, he left a legacy in print with a series of excellent books, several about Arctic aviation.

The volume of traffic on the Northwest Staging Route was intense. Aircraft moved up in the thousands, mainly to combat the Japanese invasion in the Aleutians, and to supply military installations along the route. Then came thousands of Lend Lease aircraft on their way to the USSR – P-39s, B-25s, C-47s, etc. This scene at Edmonton shows the tarmac on June 19, 1942. A US Army Douglas UC-67 Dragon and Beech C-45 are on the left, but most of the transients are C-47s and P-39s with some RCAF Kittyhawks in the distance. In the foreground is P-39F 41-7281, which would survive the war to be disposed of for scrap by Reconstruction Finance Corporation at Ontario, California in February 1945. (Provincial Archives of Alberta)

North by Northwest

As the Crimson Route was taking shape, the Northwest Staging Route was being rushed into service. This urgent project had been spurred by Germany's June 1941 invasion of its former ally – the USSR. With that, America extended Lend-Lease to the Soviets, so urgently needed a string of airports to ferry warplanes from a main base at Great Falls, Montana, north to Edmonton and on to Alaska, from where they could be handed over to Soviet crews. When America joined the war in December 1941, an added panic became the defence of Alaska and Aleutians against Japan, which had sizeable land, sea and air forces in that theatre.

In conjunction with development of the east-west trans-Canada airway, in 1935 Ottawa had made a preliminary survey for an Edmonton-Whitehorse airway via Grande Prairie, Fort St. John, Fort Nelson and Watson Lake. But no measures were taken as to engineering or construction. Nonetheless, civil aviation thrived along the route, with floatplanes in summer and ski planes in winter; and United Air Transport of Edmonton pioneered with some ground-breaking, pre-war services (Edmonton and Vancouver to Whitehorse) mainly using a Ford Trimotor.

Canada and the US quickly agreed to rush the Northwest Staging Route. The first contracts (for airports at Fort Nelson and Watson Lake) were awarded by Ottawa in February 1941. Canada financed these projects, with the US supplying most of the equipment, materiel, and brute force labour. Canadian bases would be operated by the Department of Transport (the RCAF took over in 1944). By year's end 1941 the initial airports were functioning with the support of weather stations, radio communications, navigation aids (radio ranges), runway lighting for night flying, etc. The airway soon was busy with mass flights of Siberia-bound A-20s, B-25s, C-47s, P-39s, etc. The system was strengthened through 1942-43 and tied in to the newly-opened Alaska Highway.

Meanwhile, USAAC, USN and RCAF aircraft involved in the defence of Alaska were plying the airway. The RCAF had Alaska-based squadrons and detachments flying Kittyhawks, Bolingbrokes, Venturas, etc. These were spread from Annette Island near Ketchikan to remote Umnak Island in the Aleutians. Also, RCAF Western Air Command HQ in Edmonton, was doing northern airlift, liaison and search and rescue. One NWAC unit was 6 (Communications) Flight in Edmonton with a Lockheed 12 and a few Norsemans. These were steadily involved on liaison, freight, air mail and search and rescue duties along the staging route. In July 1943 the flight was supplemented by a detachment of 165 Squadron Dakotas and Lodestars.

Typical at 165 Squadron was F/L W.H. "Wess" McIntosh. A Winnipeg boy, he served pre-war in the RCNVR, specializing in telegraphy. He mined in northern Manitoba, learned to fly, then joined the RCAF in 1939. Among 165's original cadre, he put in his first day's work on July 22, he and co-pilot F/O Ritzel taking Dakota 654 from Edmonton to Whitehorse via Fort Nelson in 7:05 flying hours. Aircrew soon found that working on the staging route was not for a slacker. In August alone F/L McIntosh covered 48 legs, logging 154:10 hours. From August 22-26 he flew 11 return trips on the 200-mile Whitehorse-Snag route.

At the same time, commercial carriers were working up and down the line. Northwest and Pan American connected the "Lower 48" with Alaska via Edmonton with Lodestars and DC-3s, while Edmonton-based Yukon Southern Air Transport and Mackenzie Air Services were flying skeds and charters. Fully aware of the contributions being made to the war effort by Yukon Southern, in 1942 Washington and Ottawa arranged for two ex-Pacific Alaska Airways Lodestars to be loaned to the company. When CPA formed in 1942 (absorbing YSAT), it was allotted several Lodestars. In all of this activity there was solid Canada-US co-operation as to the construction, improvement and use of airfields; dissemination of flight plans and weather information; standardizing radio communications; and providing search and rescue.

RCAF Arctic Survey

It has been said that a sudden interest in Ottawa in an Arctic geodetic expedition was spurred by Russian activity. This had continued in the far North into mid-1941, when Germany invaded Russia. Ottawa was concerned that Russia, ultimately, might have land claims that would challenge Canada's Arctic boundaries. Although Great Britain and the United States were told about a possible survey, Russia was kept out of the picture. A very modest geodetic expedition was planned for 1943: a few geodetic men and three RCAF aircraft. F/O F.E. "Ernie" Weeks was one of the pilots. His profile (Ch.4) typifies the solid citizens who had rushed

Norseman 791 in an in-flight view from the collection of S/L Rae Reid, a pilot on Arctic survey operations in 1945. Then, a typical summer camp scene at one of the sites. In this case, some of the always-sociable tundra people have dropped by. Besides poor weather, black flies were the bane of such camp life, as mentioned by Norseman pilot Bill McRae: "One day I emerged from a tent believing it had started to rain, only to find that it was hordes of black flies bouncing off the tent." (Ernie Weeks Col.)

forward at the beginning of the war as RCAF volunteers. Having instructed diligently in the BCATP, Weeks was selected for the Eastern Arctic Survey Detachment, formed especially for the survey (administratively, the EASD was an adjunct of 124 Ferry Squadron based at Rockcliffe). F/O Weeks joined F/Ls Crossley and Glover, and F/O Norris, all pilots. A Canso and two Norsemans were assigned to the unit. The initial word was that Canada was to survey its Arctic regions photographically, but preliminary

Ernie Weeks looking over some old Arctic maps at his home in Hamilton, Ontario in 2009. (Larry Milberry)

geodetic work had to be done, i.e. taking permanent position fixes to establish ground control points for aerial mapping that would come in later years. In June 1943 the expedition set off. F/O Ernie Weeks had crewman LAC Tony Gelinas and geodetic surveyor John Carrol in Norseman 790. These personnel are known to have been on the expedition:

Officer Commanding and Canso captain: S/L Jack Hone
Canso co-pilot: P/O Frank Seaman
Canso flight engineer: F/O Dick Skuce
Norseman pilots: F/L Carl Crossley, F/L B.M. Glover, F/O E.M. Norris, F/O F.E. Weeks
Norseman technical personnel: FSgt G. Deland, FSgt J.W. McNealy, Sgt R.V. Hawke, Cpl F.J. Kontzie, Cpl E.A. Rankin, LAC Tony Gelinas, LAC L.J. Hughes
Radio operator: FSgt R. Morgan
Cook: Cpl J.E. Vaughan
Photographer: WO2 R.G. Sweeney
Geodetic surveyors: John Carrol, Collin Duncan, Hal Leitch, Douglas Roy

This project was at a high level of secrecy, a topic addressed by Ernie Weeks in 2009:

At first only the pilots were told what our job entailed. It was only when we landed on our way north at the HBC at Mistassini that we learned where we were going and what we would be doing – we were on a secret mission. Our address was a New York City box number and our mail would be censored, so we would have to be careful what we wrote. On returning to base one day, we heard the we had been on the radio. The Nazis somehow knew of our activity. This was reported by their "Germany Calling" propagandist broadcaster, Lord Haw Haw.

The main support plane for the Eastern Arctic Survey Detachment on 1943-44 was Canso 9815 "Nugluk" skippered by S/L Jack Hone. (via Rae Reid)

June 22 to July 24, 1943 Norseman 790 was at Fort McKenzie in northern Quebec, from where it spent several days surveying at a lake at 68°18'43"N, 55°04'43"W. John Carrol later named this "Weeks' Lake". On July 24 Weeks and crew traversed the Ungava region, then crossed Hudson Strait to Baffin Island. After 6:40 flying hours that day, they alighted at their summer base – Amadjuak Lake (known to the surveyors as Stn. 27). This was about an hour's flight west of Crystal II, the secret US military airstrip being built at the head of Frobisher Bay.

The surveyors soon were busy at their various stations, pinpointing the grid reference positions that would be needed for the eventual high-level, aero-photo phase, e.g. setting up stone geodetic markers and doing their detailed record keeping. The team was supported by the occasional visit by Canso 9815 *Nugluk*, (meaning "big white goose"). *Nugluk* was captained by the renowned pre-war civil-ian bush pilot S/L Jack Hone. In the 1930s he had flown for Sherritt-Gordon in Northern Manitoba, ran Arrow Airways, and had his own mining and trading interests. Early in the war he used his bush flying expertise to salvage several RCAF aircraft. In one case, from March 10 to 16, 1940 he salvaged a damaged Battle 1306 from Georgian Bay. He supervised a crew making patch-up repairs, then flew the Battle off the ice and back to Camp Borden. For such good work he was awarded the AFC in June 1942.

Hone's crew on *Nugluk* were co-pilot P/O Frank Seaman and flight engineer F/O Dick Skuce. On August

17, 1943 Weeks flew with Hone to Crystal II, as yet still a rough gravel strip. That summer Weeks and crew mainly worked the western half of lower Baffin Island – the Foxe Basin side. Such names as Bowman Bay, Hantzsch River, Kommanik River, Kungovik (Bluegoose) River, Mingo Lake, Nettling Lake, Shugba Bay and Travener Bay, along with many references to this or that station, appear in Weeks' log. There also was a trip to Lake Harbour on the southeast coast. Issues handled through the season included unfamil-iarity with tide patterns, poor beaching areas, locating gas caches and coping with some ferocious weather. In one case the surveyors heard of a mountain range between Pangnirtung and the north coast of the Cumberland

Peninsula. Word was that these were hills of 1000 feet, but were found to have peaks to 7000.

Sample Entries
F/O Weeks' 1943 Diary

F/O Ernie Weeks kept a diary of the summer's highlights, beginning on June 22 when he noted about the expedition pulling out of Rockcliffe:

June 22: *Left Rockcliffe at 1700 hrs. Flew formation with Canso 9815 and Norseman 789 ... To Lake Mistassini, arrived 2130 hrs.* They slept on the floor of the Hudson's Bay Co. post. Next morning they refuelled from the Canso, then departed at 1200 hrs. for Fort McKenzie post, landing at 1845.

June 24: *Re-fueled 789 from Canso. S/L Hone flew Canso to Ft. Chimo to pick up surveyors and their equipment, also more fuel for Norsemen. Went across river to H.B. Co. for empty fuel drums. Stinson arrived at Post, Jimmy Bell (Sudbury) pilot.* Ernie wrote a letter home, which Bell took out with the mail. June 25 was a quiet day of hiking and shooting grouse.

June 26: *Aircraft too heavily loaded, couldn't get off. Flew Mr. Carrol with part of his equipment to Station 3. Helped him set up camp and returned to Ft. McKenzie.*

June 27: *Flew Hal Leitch to Station 3 with equipment. Moored aircraft and set up camp. Inflated rubber dinghy and helped Mr. Carrol paddle down the lake to set survey mark on an island. Sky overcast,*

Typical EASD Norseman flying as per Ernie Weeks' log book during his first season.

YEAR 1943		AIRCRAFT		PILOT, OR 1ST PILOT	2ND PILOT, PUPIL OR PASSENGER	DUTY (INCLUDING RESULTS AND REMARKS)
MONTH	DATE	Type	No.			TOTALS BROUGHT FORWARD
JUNE	12	Lockheed 10	1526	F/L McLEAN	SELF	ROCKCLIFFE → MALTON ST. MARGRET'S LAKE
"	15	Norseman	787	F/L CROSSLEY	SELF	BASE - DOMAINE D'ESTREL
"	16	"	787	SELF	F/O NORRIS	ROCKCLIFFE - KINGSTON
"	16	"	787	SELF	F/O NORRIS	KINGSTON - ROCKCLIFFE
"	18	"	790	SELF	F/L MacNAMARA	BASE - ROUND LAKE - RADIO RANGE
"	18	"	790	SELF	F/O MacNAMARA	ROUND LAKE - BASE - RADIO RANGE FORCED LANDING - BROKEN OIL LINE
"	19	"	790	SELF	F/L GLOVER	BEAM PRACTICE - TRENTON
"	22	"	790	SELF	F/O SKUCE	ROCKCLIFFE → LAKE MISTASSINI
"	23	"	790	SELF	F/O SKUCE	LAKE MISTASSINI → FT. McKENZIE
"	26	"	790	SELF	LAC. GELINAS	FT. McKENZIE → WEEKS' LAKE
"	26	"	790	SELF	LAC GELINAS	WEEKS' LAKE → FT. McKENZIE
"	27	"	790	SELF	LAC. (H. LEITCH) GELINAS	FT. McKENZIE → WEEKS' LAKE
JULY	1	"	790	SELF	LAC. GELINAS	WEEKS' LAKE → FT. McKENZIE
"	1	"	790	SELF	J. CARROL	PHOTOGRAPHY, WEEKS' LAKE
"	2	"	790	SELF	LAC. GELINAS J. CARROL	FT. McKENZIE → WEEKS' LAKE
"	2	"	790	SELF	LAC. GELINAS J. CARROL	WEEKS' LAKE → FT. McKENZIE
"	3	"	790	S/L HONE	SELF	LOCAL (FT. McKENZIE)
"	24	"	790	SELF	S/L HONE	LOCAL (FT. McKENZIE)
"	24	"	790	SELF	LAC. GELINAS	FT. McKENZIE → AMADJUAK LAKE (BAFFIN ISLAND)
"	25	"	790	SELF	LAC. GELINAS DUNCAN REY	AMADJUAK L. → BOWMAN BAY (FOXE BASIN)
"	25	"	790	SELF	LAC. GELINAS	BOWMAN BAY → AMADJUAK L.
"	28	"	790	SELF	LAC. GELINAS	AMADJUAK L. → BOWMAN BAY VIA KUNGOVIK (BLUEGOOSE) RIVER
"	28	"	790	SELF	LAC. GELINAS DUNCAN REY	BOWMAN BAY → AMADJUAK L. RAIN - FOG - NIGHT LANDING
					GRAND TOTAL [Cols. (1) to (10)] 2373 Hrs. 00 Mins.	TOTALS CARRIED FORWARD

unable to take shots... About this time Station 3 was officially named Weeks' Lake. One task next day was to chop down several tall spruce trees, so that surveyor Carrol could make observations.

June 29: *Caught quite a number of fish ... Mr. Carrol having trouble with his chronometer tabulator. Found fault and helped him fix it...*

June 30: *Astronomical observations complete. Accompanied Mr. Carrol across lake in dinghy (50 minute paddle). Climbed to crest of what appeared to be highest hill (450 feet above lake). On return found remains of 3 Indian wigwams...* This effort was to allow Carrol to take wide photographic views of the lake. Next day the party left Weeks' Lake for Fort McKenzie. On July 2 they returned to take aerial photos. Three bad-weather days followed during which the Norseman gang read books borrowed from the HBC, cut firewood, evaded the black flies, did target practice, played poker and waited for the Canso, so the move north could get done. The Canso arrived on July 8.

July 9: *Weather good. Canso left for Frobisher with load of supplies and Mr. Fry with his outfit. Tony painted floats. Found much oil on bottom of a/c. Tightened up and checked oil lines.* The Canso was back next day reporting all water in that area ice-covered, so the rest would be sitting tight for a few more days. Meanwhile, 790 was found with a cracked oil tank. On the 11th a loud explosion was heard. This caused much speculation, but next day the mystery was solved when some of the fellows paddling by the Canso noticed that its starboard tire had exploded. Since the Canso had to return to Goose Bay for servicing on the 12th, the oil tank was sent for welding. Meanwhile, for some unknown reason the lake level was falling a bit each day, so an empty fuel drum was used to mark a newly-revealed rock.

July 20: *Canso did not arrive till evening. Still no oil tank. Looks like Tony & I are bushed with a u/s aircraft. The skipper found good spot for camp site on Amadjuak Lake.* Next day 9815 and 789 departed for Baffin Island. The Canso delivered 790's oil tank on the 23rd.

July 24: *Tony up at 3 A.M. and installed oil tank alone. S/L Hone and myself went up for a test flight. A/c OK ... Loaded up both a/c. "Nugluk's" water line 2" under. 790 all 5 tanks full and extra load. Got off OK. Flew via Ft. Chimo and Ungava across Hudson Strait to Big Island. Straits full of* floating ice and partly closed in by fog. Found campsite on S.E. corner of lake. Next day Weeks flew out his first party, going to Bowman Island. "Mighty desolate part of the world", is mainly what he had to say about the place. July 26 was spent exploring around base camp, fishing, and shooting snipe, which later ended in a stew. A trip two days later to Bluegoose River to drop off some surveyors put the fear of God into F/O Weeks. They got into some duff weather and felt lucky to have survived. Poor weather continued for several days with winds to 50 mph.

August 4: *Canso left about 21:30 hrs. to get ... badly needed supplies at Frobisher. We are out of gas at base.*

August 5: *Canso arrived during night with gas, mail, etc. Fueled up 790 and left to pick up Hal at Stn.33. Couldn't find him, went over to move Duncan and Roy (Stn.30). Unable to land due to low tide and bay full of ice. Returned via Stn.33, still no Hal! Returned to base after 6 hours in the air. Turned 790 over to Bill [Glover] to go get Hal.* August 7 was a busy day's flying, moving surveyors around to stations. F/O Weeks got away on his first leg at 0430.

August 7: *Another fine day! Bill and I loaded 2 drums of gas on 790 and set out to establish a gas cache on Nettling Lake. Freddie Kontzie came along to help us. After lunch we made another run ... Sgt Reggie Hawke came along to lend a hand. Dropped in to see how Mr. Carrol and Hal were getting on. We had not heard from them on the air for a few days. Brought Hal out. Left Mr. Carrol till he can get an observation. Returned to base and enjoyed a late supper. The boys have been catching quite a few Arctic char.* Next day Bill Glover flew Hal to Stn.23 – Hantzsch River. Ernie Weeks went out in *Nugluk* on a photo trip, after which they scouted for caribou at low level.

August 9: *With Cpl Rankin in 789. Picked up J. Carrol at Stn.27 and left for Stn.23. Weather good with increasing cumulus and alto stratus on trip north. Ceiling 1500. Near coast right on deck! Engine running rough and considerable carburetor icing. Carb heat not working. Had to backfire engine ... scared John Carrol pretty badly. Couldn't land at Stn.23 due to fog off ice and action of engine. Went back to Stn.25 where we found an excellent sand beach. The trip from 23 to 25 was quite eventful and we kept as close to lakes as possible in case the engine might give up, which it didn't. Typical of Wasps. Left Caribou Pt. for Magnetic Pt. where Doug Roy and Collin Duncan prepared a light meal for*

A page from Ernie Week's daily diary as kept during the first season's work with the EASD.

us... Put on drum of gas, then Alex made shelter with engine cover and we made some hot chocolate. Slept in aircraft.

August 11 *Up at 7 o'clock. The nicest day we have had since arriving on "Censored" [Baffin] Island. Left about 8:30 to pick up John Carrol ... John required a few pictures from 3000 ft... Landed in bay [Stn.23] at 12:45 and had to anchor out for about 1 1/2 hrs. for tide ... Hal had lunch for us ... while eating, an Eskimo walked in on us. After shaking hands with everyone he unslung his rifle and mariner's telescope and accepted some food.* For the next few days the fliers were weathered out.

August 15: *Weather unfit for humanity in general. Cold and damp. Heard from Canso at Pang.* Next day they learned that the Canso had been weather-bound in the Pangnirtung fjord, with no anchorage, so had been unable to fly due to weather. They made it to Amadjuak base on the 16th, all very tired.

August 17: F/O Weeks was Canso co-pilot on a trip to Frobisher. There he was happy to have a hot shower, but passed on lunch, as word was that the meat served was horse. They proceeded south to Lake Harbour to collect Mr. Fry and his equipment from the schooner *Nannuk*, then got back to Amadjuak in weather. Next day a re-supply trip to Stn.23 was scrubbed due to a low battery on 789, and a bit of damage sustained when 789 drifted into the Canso. F/O Weeks spent the 19th moving the geodetic camp from Stn.23 to Stn.24. On the 21st they moved to Stn.25. John Carrol was taken to Stn.31 Cape Dorchester on the 24th. Next day the Canso went to Cape Dorset with Hal Leitch and equipment.

August 27: *Up to check the weather at 0400 ... Fog! Back to bed till 6:30 ... Canso left for Frobisher and east coast about 9:00 hrs. We took off about 10:00, but forced to return – visibility zero on west side of Amadjuak Lake. Landed about 11:30 hrs. Weather improving steadily and at 13:20 we took off again for Nabukjuak Bay. Encountered much low and medium cloud near Kommatik River, but found it fairly clear and 1000 foot ceiling near Cape Dorchester. Landed at what appeared to be best beach at 16:00 hrs. Tide almost right*

out, no difficulty tying up to rocks and unloading. Found this to be an Eskimo camp site. Many articles lying around such as old kayaks, paddles, bits of ivory, etc. Found cairn above camp site of J. Carrol containing notes of both Sopher and Putnam [George P. Putnam Arctic expeditions 1926 - 27]. Just as we were leaving, Hal Leitch arrived by boat with his party of Eskimos... Left about 19:00 hrs and, after passing through layers of strato-cumulus clouds near Kommatik Lake, found CAVU

Occasionally over the 1943-44 seasons, the EASD would encounter some of the local people. In these Ernie Weeks photos two hunters get a close-up view of the countryside using his telescope. Then, three fellows travelling somewhat precariously by kayak. Finally, a long-lost burial site on the tundra that included the bones of the occupant's beautifully-crafted kayak, and what would have been another prized possession – his old steamer trunk.

weather ... landed about 21:30 hours. Next day was spent in camp, the fellows doing a 150-hour check on 790, working on a trap to catch foxes that were raiding their fish, experimenting with radio antennas on 790, and painting on it the name *Metik II* (*Metik I* was 789). Radio reception was nil, so there was no word from the 9815 or 789. Several days in camp ensued, since the Canso was out of touch and the weather on and off. By September 4 food was getting low, so fishing became

more serious. As conditions worsened, F/O Weeks noted in his diary, "Beastly rotten weather ... In my opinion the camping season was over about the 1st of September on Baffin Island!"

On September 6 the Canso finally was heard to be safe at Crystal II: "Ate our meals with our parkas on. Out of fuel oil for stove in big tent. Also out of white gas for cook stove and heaters," wrote F/O Weeks. *Nugluk* and *Metik I* returned late next day and everyone got busy breaking camp, just as the first

snow came down. On the 12th all three planes flew to Frobisher, where the fellows enjoyed the luxury of comfy beds. On the 14th they headed south, skimming across Hudson Strait at 300 feet due to cloud, then pressing on to Fort McKenzie, the day's flying totalling 5:30 hours. On the 16th they made Roberval in 6:30, then continued to Rockcliffe next day in 2:45 hours. The first RCAF geodetic season in the Arctic was over. For his summer's work, F/O Weeks had logged 177:05 hours.

Eastern Arctic Survey Detachment Gallery

Norsemans 2496, 371 and 372 somewhere below the tree line. Then, 372 and 2496 in a tundra setting at one of the geodetic camps. The Norseman was the best available bushplane in the Canadian northland in these days. It carried a half-ton of cargo at about 130 mph, and could suffer a good beating. Nonetheless, it was not every pilot's dream. Bill McRae recalled, "The Norseman was, and still is, a great aircraft with many good qualities, but short takeoff was not one of them. When fully (or over) loaded, its rate of climb was not impressive – to put it kindly." Norseman 371 was on RCAF strength into 1956, then returned to Noorduyn for a rebuild. Next, it was CF-ILR to Gold Belt Air Service of Rouyn. In October 1960 it joined Lamb Airways of The Pas. On August 9, 1961 it was on a lake at 65° 18'N/73° 8'W when it sank in a storm. Meanwhile, 372 went to the Royal Norwegian Air Force, where it flew as R-AR/372. It later served Wideroe's as LN-BDT, but was lost in Bodø harbour after colliding with a fishing boat on October 25, 1955. (Ernie Weeks, W.K. Carr Cols.)

A pair of RCAF Norsemans visiting one of the geodetic surveyor's Baffin Island camps. The main job of these aircraft was to put the surveyors out into field, keep them supplied, then move them on to the next site. (Ernie Weeks Col.)

Norseman 372 refuels at some habitation along the way. (Ernie Weeks Col.)

A Norseman comes in on what the bush pilots called (and respected as) glassy water. (W.K. Carr Col.)

Norseman 372 "Betsy" gets some daily engine maintenance. Then 371 on a surveyor's beach between hops. (Ernie Weeks Col.)

Ernie Weeks with one of the survey teams (Stilwell on the right) and a newly-erected cairn at one of their astro-observation sites. (Ernie Weeks Col.)

The HBC post at Lake Harbour on southeast Baffin Island, which occasionally was visited by EASD aircraft. This was one of the few permanent settlements on all of Baffin Island. (Ernie Weeks Col.)

Ernie Weeks busy on wash day out in the boonies. Then, one of the fellows showing off supper. (Ernie Weeks Col.)

Canso 11079 puts a field party ashore. Then, another view of 9815 and a great action shot of the Canso doing a beat-up as the whole camp watches in amazement. (Ernie Weeks, W.K. Carr Cols.)

The patch worn by Ernie Weeks during the Eastern Arctic Survey Detachment.

Geodetic Survey: Year Two

Back at Rockcliffe in September 1943, F/O Ernie Weeks did a Dakota and Lodestar conversion course at 164 Squadron at Moncton, then flew some Dakota trips as co-pilot, usually Moncton to Goose Bay. In the spring of 1944 he was back at Rockcliffe getting ready for another Arctic expedition. His unit now was 13 (Photo) Squadron, commanded by S/L J.A. "Squirt" Wiseman and he was flying such aircraft as Ansons 11895, 1898 and 12418, Goose 390, and Norsemans 371, 372 and 792. Early June was spent on an Army exercise in Algonquin Park. Then, on June 14 F/O Weeks and LAC Gelinas departed in 371 for Lac Mouchalagan about 100 miles north of Chicoutimi. There they added surveyors Walter Stilwell and M. Narroway. After working at a few local sites, they moved into the Great Whale River area on June 24. On July 4 the Norseman blew an exhaust stack, so they were grounded until the Canso brought parts. They were back in action on July 8 in and around Clearwater Lake near Richmond Gulf. Port Harrison was the next base, beginning on July 14. Norseman 791, missing on July 27, was found by 371 out of fuel at the east end of Minto Lake, 100 miles north of Clearwater Lake. F/Os Weeks and Seaman with LAC Gelinas flew to a gas cache, returning with fuel for 791.

Early August found F/O Weeks and crew were operating with surveyors Narroway and Stilwell between Moose Factory and Fort Albany-Attawapiskat. August 15 to September 8 they were working from Winisk, far down the Hudson Bay coast, then the season ended. On the 10th they flew to Remi Lake near Kapuskasing in 3:45, and next day made it home to Rockcliffe in 4:30. Ernie Weeks' flying time for the summer of 1944 (June 1 to September 11) was 160:15 hours. By now his log book showed a total of 3194:25 hours. Over the winter of 1944-45 he participated in Ex. Eskimo. Centred at Prince Albert, Saskatchewan, this was an Army co-operation exercise mainly evaluating winter equipment and tactics. Everything from clothing to tents, aircraft skis,

cameras and radios were being tested. F/O Weeks mainly flew support missions in Anson 12285 and Norsemans 2469, 2472 and 3538. He returned to Rockcliffe in March 1945. Over the summer of 1945 he was again on survey duties, beginning with some training in Northern Ontario flying Norseman 371. Next they moved into Northern Manitoba at Brochet and Nueltin Lake. With Weeks for the 1945 season were F/Ls W.R. "Bill" McRae and W.K. "Bill" Carr, both recently home from combat tours. McRrae had been with 401 Squadron flying Spitfires over Normandy in the D-Day period; Carr had been on PR Spitfires in Malta. In July 1944, McRae had downed two Me.109s. Now he was on 13 (P) Squadron flying anything from vintage Spitfires to the Norseman and Anson. In 1999 he described how Ernie Weeks qualified him and Bill Carr on the Norseman:

Neither Carr nor I had flown off water so, late in April 1945 we were checked out on Norseman 371, dodging the many logs and deadheads in the Ottawa River beside Rockcliffe airfield. This was done Beaufighter style, with Ernie Weeks standing behind us, Carr in one seat and I in the other, swinging the control column from one to the other as we each took a turn. Later on we practiced glassy water procedures on Britannia Bay. By mid-May we had been assigned our aircraft for the summer, mine being 372, Weeks 371 and Carr 2496. On the 17th we went on a 4-day training trip which took us through Sudbury and in to beautiful, unspoiled lakes north of what is now Elliot Lake. This gave us experience at just about every technique required by a float pilot – proper loading, glassy water and rough water takeoff and landing, turning on the step, lifting one float out first, sailing, docking, beaching, reading the bottom for rocks and shallows, and so on. Something it did not give us was experience at doing all these things in an overloaded condition, which was yet to come. When I took off on 1 June for the summer's job, accompanied by crewmen Bob Souder and Stan Biggars, I had acquired 30 hours of float time, a very long way from considering myself a bush pilot.

In *Air Force Magazine* (Spring 2001) Bill McRae reviewed some of the work done in the summer of 1945.

Early in the spring of 1945 Detachment No.2 of No.13 Photo Flight was formed with the objective of establishing a grid of astro survey (ground control) points over a roughly 150,000 square mile area, from Reindeer Lake in northern Manitoba in the south, to Baker Lake, NWT in the north, and from Lake Athabasca on the west to Hudson Bay on the east. Detachment leader was Rae Reid, an experienced veteran ... Flying the Canso, he would keep the detachment supplied with fuel in drums, food and other camp supplies. Three float-equipped Mk.VI Norseman aircraft, flown by F/L Bill Carr (later LGen), Ernie Weeks and myself, would provide transport for four two-man survey parties ...

The Norseman pilots worked their areas independently, spending most of the time in the field with the surveyors and returning to base only for fuel and routine maintenance, and to replenish provisions. A fairly powerful communications radio was set up at the base camp, maintaining daily radio contact with the surveyors.

Although the maps ... were of no use for map reading, they did include lines of latitude and longitude, and the lines of magnetic variation. Together, these references were used, along with wind speed and direction estimated from the surface of the water, to calculate dead reckoning headings to fly between planned point locations.

On reaching ETA it was often necessary to search in an area for a suitable body of water that could satisfy both the requirements of the aircraft and those of the surveyor, i.e., distinguishing features which could be easily located on the photo mosaic, yet small enough to be completely captured by the hand-held Fairchild camera. When the cartographers eventually got around to this area, these photos would be used to accurately locate this specific spot on the high level photos. Each control point was also marked by a brass marker cemented into the rock. It was gratifying to realize the unqualified trust the surveyors placed in us. They never seemed concerned about being left on their own, two people in a vast area of barren rock, or hundreds of small lakes, their location known only to the pilot ... By the end of

August the four parties had surveyed 60 locations, five more than originally planned ...

By August they were in far northern Baker Lake. At month's end Weeks ferried back to Rockcliffe via Flin Flon, The Pas, Kenora and Remi Lake. He now left the RCAF to return to civilian life. In a letter to him of June 10, 1946, Walt Stilwell of the Geodetic Service of Canada (which came under the Department of Mines and Resources, Surveys and Engineering Branch), described what would be going on that summer:

We're going to miss you and 371 this year. Your plane was out on Muskox and that detachment is keeping it out. I expect we'll have four Norsemen this year, but six parties. Norsemen 372 & 2496 will be out, also 2495, which was on Muskox, and one other. Canso 11079 will supply us with possible assistance of another Canso. We go into Ungava first, then across Southampton Is. to Wager Bay. Barney is in charge again. Manning, Corcoran and Dave, Al Rae and myself will be observers. Our assistants are all new except Mrs. M. Mine is an ex-air force navigator, Don Gillbie. John Woodruff is going out with Dave, Chas. Blancher with Corcoran, Don Coates with Al Rae, and Don Coombes & Len Stock with Barney. Stock will take over Barney's party after a couple of stations & leave Barney back at base camp. Bill Carr, Lloyd Sinclair, Bob Merlin and King Game are to be Norseman pilots. Sinclair and Merlin hope to get a Norseman in partnership after they get out of the air force and want this summer's experience. Jake Drake is in charge of the expedition. Joe Ledbetter won't be along at all, I don't think. Jerry Delande will be out, though it looked for a while like he wouldn't. Stan Biggar is the only other experienced man. He'll be on the Canso.

Stilwell's letter names many a geodetic and air force character. From PR Spitfire days, Bill Carr had a DFC which noted that his many sorties had produced "results of the greatest accuracy and materially contributing to the success of the 8th Army". Bob Merlin had a DFC from Bomber Command operations with 77 Squadron. J.F. "Jake" Drake would receive an AFC for later Arctic efforts

and command 405 Squadron in Argus days. With a log book showing some 2918:35 flying hours, Ernie Weeks returned to Waterdown to run the family hardware store. He was little tempted to return to flying, other than going up on occasion with his son, Vince, who flew a homebuilt. Ernie eventually retired in Hamilton.

AC2 to General

William K. "Bill" Carr was born in Grand Bank, Newfoundland on March 17, 1923. Early in WWII he was attending Mount Allison University in Sackville, New Brunswick, then enlisted in the RCAF in August 1941. He flew initially in Finch 4501 at 22 EFTS at Quebec on February 2, 1942, then soloed on the 24th after 6:45 hours of flight instruction. Posted to 2 SFTS at Uplands, he trained on the Harvard to July 24, then received his wings from Air Marshal W.A. "Billy" Bishop, VC.

Bill Carr as a young Spitfire pilot in Malta days. (W.K. Carr Col.)

P/O Carr next found himself, reluctantly, at 1 General Reconnaissance School in Summerside on a course for pilots and navigators. This usually led to a posting to Coastal Command, but when he reached the UK, Carr volunteered to do some high-altitude tests in a decompression chamber at Farnborough. As a reward he was offered the option to train on the Spitfire. He accepted this and began training at 17 AFU near Watton. AFU was followed by the course at PR OTU at Dyce, near Aberdeen. There, on April 10, 1943 P/O Carr flew a Spitfire for the first time, then finished OTU on May 20.

With 366:30 hours total time (54:25 on Spitfires), Carr joined 543 (PR) Squadron at Benson. This posting was brief – the RAF needed PR Spitfires in Malta. Bill Carr was given EN674 to work up on, then deliver to Luqa, Malta, where he joined 683 Squadron. His first operation came on August 21, a sortie to Naples. Flights of more than six hours were possible, since PR Spitfires carried extra fuel instead of armament. P/O Carr would fly 142 PR operations for 300:20 hours, about double what a Spitfire pilot on a fighter squadron normally would log. He last flew the PR Spitfire on September 26, 1944. The detailed story of Carr's PR tour appears in the Winter 2001 edition of the *Canadian Aviation Historical Society Journal*.

On returning to Canada in December 1944, F/O Carr was posted to Rockcliffe, flying first with 13 (P) Squadron, then EP&E, primarily on air photo work with the Norseman, Mitchell and Lancaster. Much of his duties were on Arctic photo survey, spending summers flying a Norseman on floats. This is described in the CAHS *Journal* (Winter 1999 and Spring 2000). His most interesting event in this period was photographing the Ungava Crater and being the first pilot to land in it. In December 1954, at the suggestion of Dr. Peter M. Millman of the Dominion Observatory in Ottawa, he recorded this story:

I first saw the Ungava Crater about the 28th of June 1946, while flying a float-equipped Norseman in the Ungava district of Northern Quebec. At that time I was in charge of a flight of Norseman aircraft engaged in the transportation of personnel from the Geodetic Service of the Department of Mines and Technical Surveys of Canada. The Geodetic

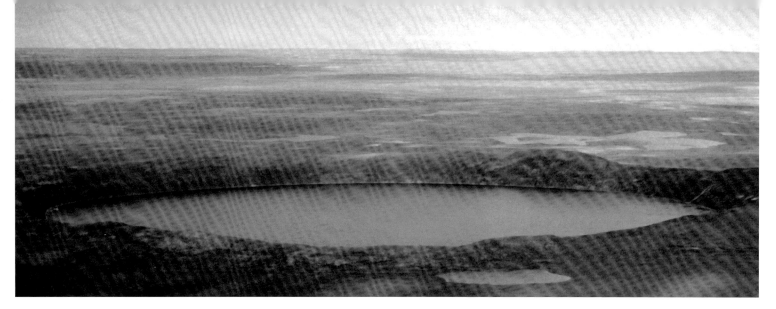

The spectacular Ungava Crater (aka Chubb Crater) in one of the first photos of it. This RCAF photo is listed as "REA470-14 Crater in Ungava Region 20 July 48". Then (below) a higher level view. (W.K. Carr Col.)

personnel were in the area to obtain astronomic fixes, which were later used in the positioning and scaling of aerial photographs. This was a small but essential part, at that time, of possibly the largest aerial mapping program ever undertaken by any country.

Until now, vast areas of Northern Canada (approx. 2,500,000 million sq. mi.) had never been adequately mapped. (I use "adequately" from the airman's point of view, i.e. accurate 8 mile to 1 inch coverage.) Of this 2,500,000 sq. mi. approximately 1,750,000 had never been mapped at all. Numerous 8 mile to 1 inch map sheets had been published with nothing but parallels of latitude and longitude, and in bold type "Unmapped" printed across them. Being fairly familiar with much of Canada's North, I would say, taken as an area, the Ungava District was the poorest mapped area on the mainland.

The Ungava Crater first appeared as a bit of detail on a very inaccurate 16 mile to 1 inch chart issued in 1942. The information for this map was obtained from a tri-camera photographic run done by the USAAC during the winter of 1941-42 along the west coast of Ungava Bay. The limit of plotable data in the photographs was along a line which just included the crater. When the map was drawn up, a small round lake on it was identified with the word "crater".

Flying in unmapped country, where there are no aids to navigation (not even a navigator), a pilot quickly finds ways to keep from getting lost. Remembering features of the ground over which he flies, and good air sense are paramount. In the northern latitudes of Canada, compasses are not reliable and often don't work. Therefore, the pilot quickly develops this facility and, in flight, is always mentally recording outstanding features of the terrain. The Ungava Crater was one of these outstanding features.

The crater is located near the edge of a Greenstone area in the great Precambrian shield. The surrounding country is mostly barren flat country, with scattered rocks deposited by the receding ice cap. Along the edges of the thousands of shallow lakes and numerous streams and rivers grew the many species of Arctic flora.

Having flown back and forth across the area several times, on one occasion I was returning to base camp from delivering a geodetic party to a lake approximately 300 miles north, when I ran into what appeared to be a line squall. I decided that the best thing to do was to land in some lake, and wait for the squall to pass by. I happened to be a few miles from the crater, so altered course and did a "dummy run" over it, after which I landed and tied up to the northeast shore. I stayed on the lake about two hours.

From the inside, the lake appeared to be 200 feet above the surrounding terrain, particularly along the south and southwest side, and the lake appeared about two miles in diameter. The walls were very steep yet, in places, a mass of tumbled rocks. The lake was obviously fairly deep. It definitely did not appear volcanic in origin, nor was it similar to any of the other lakes in the region.

After I returned to base camp, we quite often discussed the crater and its origins (see Arctic Unfoldings p.198 by Nicholas Palnin, published by Hutchison & Co., London, 1949). Throughout the summer we pilots continued to use the crater as a landmark. It was particularly good as such during conditions of low ceilings, because the rim could be seen from a distance of 20 to 30 miles. As a result of the foregoing, the personnel who were in the area in 1946 were greatly amused when the crater officially was "discovered" in 1950, and named the Chubb Crater after the discoverer.

In 1947 Bill Carr was sent on 2-year course to the Institute of Technology in Rochester, New York to study physics and chemistry, and the latest in photographic equipment. Returning to Rockcliffe, he was placed in charge of RCAF aerial photographic R&D. During a trip of July 20, 1948 between Fort Chimo and Coral Harbour in a Lancaster captained by S/L C.L. Olssen, Carr suggested that the Ungava Crater be photographed. Several excellent exposures were made by FSgt M.L. Konick. In May 1952, Carr joined 426 Squadron at Lachine (Dorval) during Operation Hawk – the Korean airlift. This enabled Carr to see the Far East for the first time. In 1953 he attended RCAF Staff College in Toronto, then was promoted to squadron leader and posted to a personnel slot at AFHQ. Next, he was CO of 412 Squadron, the RCAF's largest squadron with some 800 personnel and 31 aircraft. At 412 W/C Carr flew the North Star, C-5 and Comet, his first flight in the latter being Ottawa-Marville in 5301 on May 13, 1958.

In August 1960 W/C Carr left 412, was promoted to group captain and spent six months heading the 15-nation United Nations Air Force in the Congo. Once home, he was station commander at Namao, the home of 418 (Expeditor) and 435 (C-119 and C-130B) squadrons. Namao also temporarily hosted such

G/C Bill Carr as Station Commander, Namao. He is flanked by two of his COs – W/C R.D. "Joe" Schultz (425 Sqn, left) and W/C K.C. Lett (6 (ST) OTU). Then, MGen Carr at Winnipeg in 1975 accepting the official documentation for newly-formed Air Command from the Chief of Defence Staff, General Jacques Dextraze.

Bill Carr escorts HRH Queen Elizabeth during the 2nd Arctic and Northern Boy Scout Jamboree, held at Churchill, Manitoba in May 1970.

other flying units in Carr's period as 425 Squadron (Voodoos), 6 ST/R OTU (CF-104), CEPE, and the USAF Strategic Air Command's 3955th air refuelling squadron (KC-97). The Cuban Missile Crisis of October 1962 brought some added excitement with the presence for a few days of SAC B-47s and B-52s. As station commander G/C Carr often flew and logged more than 1000 hours on the C-130B.

From Namao, Carr spent a year in Kingston at the National Defence College. In 1965-66 Air Commodore Carr served at Mobile Command HQ in St. Hubert, then was Director General Air Forces at NDHQ. Promoted in 1968 to major general, he commanded Training Command and, in 1971, was Deputy Chief of Staff with NORAD in Colorado Springs. In 1973 he returned to NDHQ as Chief of Air Doctrine and in 1974 was promoted to lieutenant general and became Deputy Chief of the Defence Staff. Finally, he was in a slot where he could do something to rejuvenate Canada's air forces. This led to the formation of Air Command on September 2, 1975. Air Command was headquartered in Winnipeg and LGen Carr was its first commander. LGen Carr retired from the Canadian military in 1978. He next spent several years with Canadair/Bombardier marketing the Challenger business jet. In 2001 he was inducted into Canada's Aviation Hall of Fame.

Honours for Jack Hone

Few of those on the 1943-46 Arctic survey expeditions received any honours – it was "all in a day's work" as far as RCAF HQ was concerned. S/L Jack Hone, however, was singled out on January 1, 1945 for the Air Force Cross (citation below). On the following January 1, Hone was awarded a Bar to his AFC for subsequent geodetic expeditions.

This officer, for two successive seasons, has organized, equipped and taken survey parties into unmapped territory surrounding Hudson Bay and extending far to the east and the west. Due to his vast knowledge of flying in Canadian bush and unexplored territories, triangulation stations have been so well established that subsequent mapping by air surveys can proceed without loss of time. Of the party who accompanied this officer on the first season's operations, all volunteered to accompany him the following year despite the fact that such an expedition is far removed from civilization and depends for its food to a large extent upon the natural resources of the territory. During the last season this officer undertook a search for a lost United States aircraft, last heard from near Churchill on Hudson Bay. He found the aircraft on the second day of the search, although the occupants had perished. The outstanding success of the two years of exploration work can only be attributed to Squadron Leader Hone's outstanding leadership, initiative and ability under the most trying circumstances. This officer's skill, resourcefulness and devotion to duty are outstanding.

EAC Marine Squadron: Labrador Cruise

Since the 1920s the RCAF operated small boats and vessels at its seaplane and flying boat stations, then gradually added larger marine equipment to tug boat size. Through WWII it also had a fleet of high speed rescue launches. Over the summer of 1941 the RCAF operated a marine mission to refuelling bases in Newfoundland and Labrador. This was repeated in 1942 to such places as Canada Bay, far up the east coast of Newfoundland's

Petit Nord Peninsula; and Cartwright, Labrador, well-known in the 1920s and '30s as a haven for pioneer airmen braving the North Atlantic. The 1942 mission commenced on June 22 when RCAF Marine Craft *M361* (formerly the *OK Service* of 150 tons, impressed into RCAF use) sailed from Dartmouth with a crew of 15 and 12 passengers. *M361* was commanded by F/L J. Howell.

After a fuel stop at Imperial Oil, at 1645 hours *M361* sailed through Harbour Gap, Halifax, into the Atlantic. Next day its log showed 233.3 miles covered by midnight. Having averaged 9.3 knots, it

Previously a civilian mariner in charge of one of the Nova Scotia-based *OK Service* work boats, F/L John Howell was well-known in pre-war days as one of the most daring and colourful East Coast rum-runners. (DND PL24425)

had reached 46°54'10"N and 59°21'30"W. On the 24th it passed Fox Head, northeast of Cape St. George, where it was engulfed in fog, but eventually got into Corner Brook, which *M361's* diarist described as "a thriving centre of the wood pulping industry". His entry for Friday the 26th is colourful and incisive:

Along the coastline now we see black hills of Labrador. The dense and gloomy blue-green of the southern coast of Newfoundland vanishes. In its stead we make way alongside hills whose slopes are tinged in a dull brown – an indication, probably, of iron ore, which may account for the abnormal variations of our compass. We sight and photo-

graph our first icebergs ... the larger ones are no serious danger to our navigation in clear weather; but smaller growlers are, especially in fog, for they are not readily seen and could easily be run down ... We head for St. Anthony, tying up there at 1900 hours...

On June 27 *M361* anchored in Canada Bay. All hands set to work unloading cargo – food, timber, coal, etc. Before nightfall, the crew also had helped lay the foundation for a new generator house. Swarms of mosquitoes made life miserable, but some relief was found by lathering on lard mixed with chemical cleaner. Work continued steadily until day's end on June 30. This included inspection and servicing of several aircraft moorings. On departing Canada Bay in fog at 0300 on July 1, *M361* missed by seconds colliding with an iceberg. Fog drove it into St. Anthony later that day. Here, the captain agreed to carry some cargo to the Grenfell mission in Cartwright. First stop next day was Battle Harbour on the Labrador shore, about 80 miles from St. Anthony.

An aircraft mooring had to be checked at Battle Harbour. The mission proceeded on July 4, but again had close encounters with ice, then had to seek haven in Gready's Island Harbour, when fog swept in. Sunday morning, July 5, they sailed to Cartwright, docking at 1045: "Crew and detachment worked till 2100, unloading equipment and supplies, and erecting forms for the generator house." On July 7 the crew was busy making a new aircraft mooring and dragging for an older one that had sunk. On July 8 the diarist noted: "This morning we were unloading sand, gravel and coal for the detachment. In the afternoon we hoisted the old aircraft mooring that was found the day before." Other old moorings were unsuccessfully dragged for on the 10th. Another project bore some fruit:

After dinner two of our crew stay with the Ranger to search for the moorings, while the rest of us leave to inspect the Ventura aircraft that had crashed last winter. We find that it will be possible to salvage it ... we rigged sheers, hoisted one of the motors on to the H.B.C. scow, and towed it to M361, hoisted it aboard and stowed it in the hold.

RAF Ventura AE721 pranged on Belle Isle at the head of the Strait of Belle Isle on June 7, 1942. The hardy salvage crew got it stripped of engines and other useful parts and equipment. It is not known whether or not the airframe was salvaged, but this often was not the case. Some such wrecks sit to this day where they came down. (via Hugh Halliday)

At dinner that night, some local citizens were entertained aboard ship, including HBC factor Howell and his wife; Grenfell Mission nurse – Miss Compton; and Newfoundland Ranger – Sgt Summers. Next day work continued on the Ventura: "The wings and upper part of the fuselage seem in fair condition." However, there was some concern about possible damage from salt corrosion. *M361* sailed from Mary Harbour at 1355 on July 13, arriving back at St. Anthony at 2130. A 6-hour sail next day brought them to Canada Bay, then they made Botwood, a 12-hour sail. At each stop, the crew usually had some duties servicing moorings. Having departed Botwood on July 17, *M361* came across the brig *Hazel Blackwood* which appeared out of trim. Some of F/L Howell's men rowed to the vessel to find its crew repairing their engine. That night *M361* anchored in Bonavista Cove above Trinity Bay and next night were in Bay Bulls, about 30 miles below St. John's. July 22 is described in *M361*'s ORB as quite routine:

On the last day of our cruise the fog begins to lift at 0420. We are able to go full ahead. At 1540 we sighted – too far away to identify the number – a PBY. We replied to the challenge of a Navy corvette that we met at 1705 and at 1810 received permission to enter the Gate. Passing through at 1826, we arrived at Base and made fast to the wharf at 1850.

Capt Howell later was promoted to squadron leader and commanded the RCAF marine section at Dartmouth. In January 1944 he received a Mention in Dispatches, after having braved harrowing seas supporting the move of 162 Squadron from Yarmouth to Reykjavik and, in general, for leading "several expeditions resulting in the establishment of several 'out' stations in the far North in the face of most difficult circumstances".

Ferry Command

The story of Ferry Command is covered in innumerable sources, prominent being Carl Christie's 1995 book, *Ocean Bridge: The History of RAF Ferry Command*. The organization's task had been simply defined by the summer of 1940: in the coming 2-3 years to deliver to the UK thousands of aircraft manufactured in US factories. Great figures such as William Maxwell Aitken (Lord Beaverbrook), A/V/M D.C.T. "Don" Bennett, Sir Frederick Bowhill, Winston Churchill, C.H. "Punch" Dickins, C.D. Howe, William Lyon MacKenzie King, Patrick McTaggert-Cowan, Air Commodore G.J. "Taffy" Powell, C.G. "Chubby" Powers were involved in the plan. The initial operation was established by the Canadian Pacific Railway Air Services Department. Led by Bennett, the first ferry flight (six Hudson bombers), crewed mainly by Canadians and Americans, flew safely from Gander to Ireland on November 10/11, 1940.

The CPR organization soon evolved into the Atlantic Ferry Organization (ATFERO), a branch of the British Ministry of Aircraft Production, itself headed by Canada's Lord Beaverbrook. Ferrying soon became routine, but ATFERO soon was overwhelmed by the pace. To keep the system rolling, in July 1941 RAF Ferry Command under Air Chief Marshal Sir Frederick Bowhill took over the whole operation (ironically, Bowhill earlier had pooh-poohed the idea of trans-Atlantic ferrying). Ultimately, some 10,000 aircraft were safely delivered by Ferry Command and its predecessors (at the same time, the US was operating its own vast system, ferrying thousands of warplanes over the oceans).

One of the iconic RAF Ferry Command aircraft was Liberator AL504 "Commando". (IWM CH14142)

Delivered from Consolidated in August 1941, "Commando" joined RAF 45 Group at Dorval as a standard Liberator II. In 1944 it was converted to RY-3 configuration with a single-fin and faired-over cargo nose. "Commando" was lost over the Atlantic while heading for Ottawa on March 26, 1945. (CANAV Books Col.)

One of the grandest views of Gander during its booming RAF and USAAF trans-Atlantic ferry days. The photo was taken from 3000' on May 27, 1943. More than 100 aircraft (mainly B-17s) can be seen. (CANAV Col.)

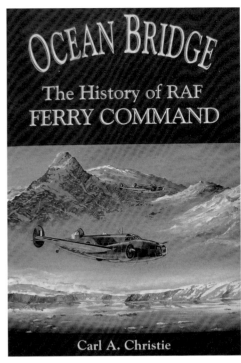

The risk of shipping aircraft by sea was made all too clear in the first three years of the war – hundreds of ships were torpedoed by U-boats. Here is Martin Baltimore AG859 during a visit to Rockcliffe. It later went by sea in a consignment of aircraft aboard the merchantmen *Thursobank* (unescorted, sunk March 22, 1942 by *U-373*) and *Loch Don* (unescorted, sunk April 1, 1942 by *U-202*). The cost of these torpedoings was 33 sailors and 31 Baltimores. The aircraft ferrying plan reduced such losses dramatically. (DND PL8166)

Published in 1995, Carl Christie's history of Ferry Command should be on every aviation reader's bookshelf.

Ferry Command Liberator AL578 "Marco Polo" at Dorval, where it was delivered from the Consolidated plant in San Diego in April 1941. Used initially for pilot training, it was damaged, then sat derelict for months. Once restored, it entered Dorval-Prestwick service in April 1943. In October of that year it carried Lord Louis Mountbatten to India and China, so was the first aircraft to originate in Canada and land in China (it was dubbed "Marco Polo" while at New Delhi). AL578 completed many Atlantic crossings, including a 19:46-hour, 3653-mile trip of July 20, 1944 from Northolt (London) to Washington, DC. Carrying Lord Beaverbrook and other VIPs, this was the first non-stop London-to-Washington flight. The 6-man crew that day included Capt George P. Evans of Brooklyn, NY, flight engineer Alex Wright of Toronto and radio officer Cyril P. Meagher of Halifax. Evans, a legendary Ferry Command pilot, Meagher and 14 others were lost in Liberator JT984 on July 4, 1945 while crossing from Dorval to Northolt. (CANAV Col.)

At the receiving end of the North Atlantic ferry route: a view at Prestwick jammed with aircraft -- Lancasters, Liberators, Dakotas, B-17s, Mitchells, a C-54, a Mosquito, etc. (IWM CH17840)

Ferry Command Radio Operator

Hundreds of Canadians became involved in ferrying. There were well-paid civilian pilots, navigators and radio operators, and RCAF men earning a few dollars a day. One of the civilians was Glenn Scott. Born in Saint John, New Brunswick in 1923, Glenn had a special interest in aviation and radio by the time he had finished high school in 1940. In

Ferry Command radio operator Glenn Scott during leave in Saint John. (all, Scott Col.)

1942 he moved to Toronto to take some courses at the Radio College of Canada. Having passed his exams, he visited Ferry Command at Dorval looking for work, was hired on the spot in ground radio and, after a short posting at Dorval, served in Gander over the winter of 1942-43. He then returned to Dorval, where he found some digs with a number of young Ferry Command fellows in a house on the Lakeshore.

Glenn Scott now got to combine his two big interests. Better still, the pay was excellent – radio operators and navigators earned about $400 monthly ($1000 for pilots). Training commenced on June 12, 1943 with a 2:36-hour flight from Dorval in Mitchell II FV917. His first experience on the Liberator was in KN748 on July 10, then Scott flew on Ventura AE948 on the 19th. In this period

PV-1 Ventura FP553 being serviced somewhere on the southern route in the summer of 1943.

he became used to flying (two trips a day was typical), to his equipment and to the radio operator's routines – keeping all his en route records, making hourly station reports, etc. After logging some 44 training hours, he was assigned to his first Ferry Command delivery. Under an American skipper named Garrigan, on July 25, 1943 they departed Dorval in Ventura GR.V FP553 on the following route:

Date	Destination	Time (hrs)
July		
25	West Palm Beach	8:09
28	Borinquen, Puerto Rico	7:45
29	San Juan, Puerto Rico (test flight)	0:30
30	Piarco, Trinidad	3:50
31	Zandery, Dutch Guiana	3:25
August		
1	Belem, Brazil	3:55
1	Sao Luis, Brazil	1:43
2	Natal, Brazil	3:48
5	Ascension Island	7:28
7	Takoradi	7:13

Weather permitting and the airplane working satisfactorily, the routine in Ferry Command was to keep the show moving. One extended stop-over, however, always was Natal, where each plane had to be carefully inspected by technical staff in preparation for the 1200+ mile leg to Ascension Island, and about the same distance on to Accra or Takoradi, West Africa. As careful as Ferry Command was, however, aircraft would be lost on these daunting legs.

The weather was always an issue on any ferry flight but, if a crew flight-planned diligently, i.e., watching for line squalls in the inter-tropical convergence zone off West Africa, they would get through. (Crews still must respect conditions in this region. In June 2009 Air France A330 G-GZCP was brought down by storms off Brazil.) Other hazards would dog Ferry Command. Once, as they taxied for take-off at Zandery (Dutch Guiana), Scott watched a B-26 take off ahead. Just as it started to climb, it lost an engine and dove straight into the ground. Otherwise, there were bound to be surprises along the way.

No matter how run-of-the-mill Ferry Command assignments might have seemed, danger was ever-present. Crews often were inexperienced on their aircraft, were operating in unfamiliar country and often were fatigued. In this tragic scene, Martin A-30 Baltimores FA114 and FW377 came to grief at Belem on September 17, 1943 – FW377 lost an engine on take-off, then crashed into FA114. (CANAV Col.)

During the delivery of B-26 HD744, Capt Pickup had an attack of appendicitis while en route Natal-Ascension. So great was his pain that he lay on the floor for some hours, while P/O Norm Flavin flew the plane. As they approached destination, Pickup returned to his seat for the landing. He ended in hospital with an appendectomy. His mates returned to Nassau, while another crew took over HD744. With an airplane finally delivered, a ferry crew would return to Dorval or Nassau, usually on USAAF aircraft. Glenn Scott didn't log these return trips, but recalls flying back to base on such types as the C-46. In the end he would crew on 20 Ferry Command deliveries.

Trip 11 with B-26 Marauder HD554 took Scott's crew beyond the usual destination of Accra. From Accra they set course in another B-26 (HD457) across sub-Saharan Africa to Cairo, then flew west across North Africa to Castel Benito, near Tripoli in Libya, then to Blida, near Algiers. There, HD457 was turned over to the RAF Desert Air Force, for which the B-26 was a key tactical bomber.

Trip 14 also continued from West Africa to Cairo, thence to Habbaniyah in Iraq, Bahrain on the Persian Gulf, and Karachi in West Pakistan, where Dakota KJ857 was delivered on September 24, 1944. For Trip 15 they delivered Dakota KJ926 beyond Karachi to Allahabad about half way to Calcutta. They did the same on Trip 18 with Dakota KN227. In this period, the British South East Asia

A typical mixed civilian – RCAF Ferry Command crew. The fellows had just landed in B-26 HD457 at Khartoum in 114ºF weather: Glenn Scott, P/O Bob Clouthier, Capt Pickup and P/O Wally Johnson. Then, Scott and Pickup "playing tourist" in the Valley of the Kings at Luxor, Egypt.

Ferry Command Deliveries crewed by Glenn Scott

	Date	Aircraft	Capt/Crew	Route
1	25/7-7/8 '43	Ventura GR.V FP553	Garrigan	Dorval-Takoradi
2	13/9-17/9	Ventura FP619	Richards	Dorval-Accra
3	31/10-9/11	B-26 FB489	Martin	Nassau-Accra
4	10/12-15/12	Ventura JS909	Martin, P/O Walker	Nassau-Takoradi
5	19/12-20/12	Baltimore FW576	Weiben	Natal-Accra
6	10/1-16/1 '44	Ventura JS944	Quick	Nassau-Takoradi
7	13/2-27/2	Baltimore FW668	Church, F/O Roadhouse	Natal-Accra
8	15/2-20/3	Dakota KG413	Martin, P/O Walker	Nassau-Accra
9	5/4-11/4	Baltimore FW796	Bob Pickup, P/O Johnson	Nassau-Accra
10	24/4-2/5	B-26 HD461	Pickup, P/O Clouthier, P/O Johnson	Nassau-Accra
11	13/5-26/5	B-26 HD554/HD457	Pickup, P/O Clouthier, P/O Johnson	Nassau-Accra-Blida (Algeria)
12	7/6-13/6	B-26 HD557	Pickup, P/O Clouthier, P/O Johnson	Nassau-Accra
13	21/8-29/8	C-47 KJ825	Pickup, P/O Coughlin	Nassau-Takoradi
14	7/9-24/9	C-47 KJ857*	ditto	Nassau-Karachi
15	9/10-24/10	C-47 KJ926	ditto	Nassau-Allahabad
16	18/11-6/12	C-47 KK110	ditto	Nassau-Allahabad
17	19/1-27/1 '45	B-26 HD744	Pickup, P/O Flavin, P/O Clouthier	Nassau-Ascension
18	12/2-28/2	C-47 KN227	P/O Latta, F/O Atkins	Nassau-Allahabad
19	14/3-29/3	B-26 HD739	P/O Latta, F/O Saywell, F/O Northcott	Nassau-Cairo
20	8/4-12/4	C-47 KN474	ditto	Dorval-Cairo

*later missing in action on November 27, 1943

air force was expanding in order to supply China and Allied forces up and down the Bay of Bengal. Out of Accra, the trail of KN227 took it to Khartoum, Aden, Salalah on the Saudi Arabian coast, Masirah Island, then across the Arabian Sea to Karachi and Allahabad.

Glenn Scott's final trip was abroad Dakota KN474. They departed Dorval on April 8, 1945 on a 4:55-hour leg to Gander. Next day they made the Azores (7:49). On the 11th they flew to Rabat, Morocco (6:16) next day made Castel Benito (6:10) and Cairo (5:54). Scott now returned to Dorval, his tour done. He was asked to do one more delivery, but turned down the offer. His log book at the end showed 962 Ferry Command hours. Now he spent a leisurely summer in Saint John, before commencing engineering studies at the University of New Brunswick. He would work in this field until retiring in 1984.

People may wonder what became of all the aircraft delivered by Ferry Command. Five of Glenn Scott's Dakotas have interesting stories. KJ857 joined 435 Squadron (RCAF) and was shot down by Japanese fighters at Schwebo, Burma on January 12, 1945. KJ926, taken on strength by 357 Squadron in India/Burma in October 1944, later carried Yugoslav Air Force markings. KN227, which flew with 48 Squadron in India/Burma, went for scrap in 1948 following an accident in the UK. KG413 went to 117 and 194 squadrons. On June 23, 1944 it crashed while landing at Sylhet, northeast of Dacca. Beginning in September 1944, KJ825 had a long career in the South African Air Force. On September 21, 1987, however, it caught fire in flight then was wrecked on crash landing.

Ferry Command B-26 "Hellzapoppin" at Dorval. CGTAS Lancaster CF-CMS is on the runway beyond. (CANAV Col.) Then a view Glenn Scott snapped of a B-26 instrument panel along its ferry route. Speed 200 mph, altitude 9000'.

An RAF Dakota on delivery from Nassau. Then, a big R-1830 engine piggybacking on a ferry flight – whenever possible supplies and equipment were forwarded aboard aircraft heading for war zones.

One day off the US east coast Scott's pilot formated with this PBY Catalina starting out on the long-haul to Russia.

Ferry Command's 10 Consolidated PB2Y Coronados plied the Atlantic from such bases as Montreal, Botwood and Bermuda. Their passengers often were ferry crews returning from overseas deliveries. First flown in 1937, the Coronado had four R-1830s. The inner engines had reversible 4-blade propellers to ease the tricky business of manoeuvring on the water. Shown in Iceland is Coronado "Brisbane" getting some maintenance. (LAC PA202899)

The RAF Coronados belonged to 231 Squadron, headquartered at Dorval, but using moorings at Boucherville, across the St. Lawence River from Montreal. RCAF Hurricane pilot George Webster photographed this Coronado on Gander Lake, Newfoundland. Coronado all-up weight was about 68,000 pounds. Its range was limited to about 1200 miles with any sort of a useful load.

Ferry Command pilots sometimes also travelled between assignments aboard Pan American Boeing flying boats. This example is seen on Gander Lake. (George Webster Col.)

F/L Daniel, DFM, DFC

Tour-expired aircrew who were keen to continue flying sometimes found postings in Ferry Command. Born in India in 1921, A/F/L Dennis Leith Daniel served two operational tours in Bomber Command. While flying Lancasters on 207 Squadron, he was awarded the DFC in July 1943, the citation for which describes the man's character: "He has always shown the utmost determination, skill and courage in the execution of his tasks … On all occasions Flight Lieutenant Daniel's personal example has been worthy of the highest praise."

F/L Daniel was attached to Ferry Command at Dorval in July 1943. Likely on account of his experience on type, he primarily delivered Lancasters built by Victory Aircraft at Malton, near Toronto. Records show that he began his first trip on November 13. That day he set off in KB705, which he delivered next day to Prestwick. In a very short time, Daniel had ferried 15 Lancasters, 2 Liberators.

A new Canadian-built Lancaster runs up at Victory Aircraft. F/L Dennis L. Daniel (RAF) ferried 15 such aircraft away from Malton to the UK. (CANAV Col.)

F/L Daniel's First 15 Ferry Command Deliveries

Lancaster	Departing Dorval	Aircraft Fate	Date
KB705	November 13, 1943	428 Sqn, 1666 HCU	SOC 4/45
KB708	November 30	419 Sqn, crashed	25-26/8/44
KB710	January 11, 1944	419 Sqn, lost	12-13/5/45
KB721	January 24	419 Sqn, Canada 6/45	SOC11/48
KB723	February 23	419 Sqn, lost	4-5/7/44
KB744	April 16	428 Sqn, Canada 5/45	SOC 5/47
KB752	May 5	419 Sqn, lost	7-8/4/45
KB755	May 16	419 Sqn, lost	7-8/8/44
KB764	June 1	428 Sqn, ditched Azores	4/6/45
KB768	June 10	428, 426 Sqns, lost	5-6/12/44
KB775	July 4	419 Sqn, lost	25-26/8/44
KB787	August 1	419 Sqn, lost	4-5/2/45
KB802	August 20	419, 431 Sqns, Canada 6/45	SOC 1/47
KB811	September 1	419 Sqn, Canada 6/45	SOC 8/50
KB835	October 1	431, 434 sqns, lost	15-16/3/45
Liberator			
KH338	November 8	86 Sqn, lost	26/4/45
KK272	November 28	104 Sqn	SOC 3/46

The cornerstone of the Air Transport organization has been 164 Squadron, which commenced operations in January of this year with four Digbys borrowed from E.A.C. supplemented by two new C-60As (Lodestars). Almost from the first, insurmountable obstacles presented themselves on every hand. Selecting Moncton as the most suitable ... base for service to Goose Bay, the squadron commenced operations in mid-winter lacking hangar space and the most elementary necessities ... on January 23rd of this year, the first aircraft took off for Goose Bay. Undaunted by difficulties and staffed by highly trained and enthusiastic pilots from No.12 Communications flight at Rockcliffe, the first aircraft with its 3,000 lbs. has today grown to a full-fledged operation with a capacity ten times that amount daily, and has successfully transported approximately 3,000,000 pounds of freight and passengers to date... the Squadron now operates regular scheduled services three times weekly to Goose Bay, Gander and Torbay.

More of Air Transport

The RCAF had several transport flights and squadrons across Canada through WWII. In August 1943 these were formalized under the Directorate of Air Transport Command, which (February 1945) became 9 (Transport) Group under G/C Z.L. "Lewie" Leigh. The urgency of having an organization was made clear in 1942, when U-boat attacks sank vessels carrying supplies to the site of a new Goose Bay airport on Hamilton Inlet, Labrador. A hastily-organized airlift led by two converted Digbys was able to re-supply Goose Bay. The secret *Monthly Report of R.C.A.F. Operations North America* for August 1943 gives the first detailed description of DATC:

The RCAF operated six Boeing B-17 Flying Fortresses on its overseas airmail services. Here, airmen unload mail from 168 Squadron Flying Fortress 9204 at Prestwick on December 23, 1943. (DND PL22544)

An off-beat mission for 164 occurred in November when a Dakota flew 200 crated pigs from PEI to Gander on behalf of what was referred to as "the new R.C.A.F. piggery" there. A typical month's flying for 164 was April 1944. By then flying Dakotas and Lodestars, that month it carried 348 tons of cargo, 20 tons of mail and 1527 passengers on the Moncton-Goose Bay route alone. Meanwhile, DATC had a parallel western counterpart – 165 Squadron, operating from Sea Island throughout BC, and from Edmonton on the Northwest Staging Route. The *Monthly Review* for December 1943 reported on 165 also supported parachute training at Camp Shilo, Manitoba. Through the year some 340 hours were flown and 2110 jumps were made by Canadian troops in training. DATC also had a ferry unit – 124 Squadron at Rockcliffe primarily delivered aircraft from

Two versions of the 168 Squadron wartime patch. (CANAV Col.)

factories to flying stations, and also to and from maintenance and repair depots. The *Monthly Review* noted of 124 for November 1943: "A total of 555 ferry trips were carried out ... During the first eleven months of this year

5,038 aircraft were ferried ..." For April 1944 the squadron ferried 891 aircraft deliveries, logging hours 4479. Larger types ferried included the Bermuda, Canso, Dakota, Mosquito and Ventura.

Ferry Command Prangs

AM920 was one of the early RAF Liberators converted to Mk.C.1 standards to carry passengers and cargo mainly on the Dorval-Prestwick run. Operated by a BOAC crew, on June 3, 1943 AM920 had trouble landing at Dorval. Repaired, and re-registered G-AHYB, it remained in postwar use. Under Capt D. Anderson, on February 10, 1946 it completed BOAC's 2000th Atlantic crossing. It later was F-VNNP – the personal aircraft of emperor Bao Dai of French Indochina. (CANAV Col.)

Ferry Command Liberator AL591 crashed while approaching Gander on February 9, 1943. Of 21 aboard, 19 died, including BOAC, RAF Ferry Command and USAAF Ferry Command personnel. A Norseman and Fox Moth rushed to the scene and flew the survivors to Gander. Casualties included two RCAF passengers: F/O Robert I. Scott (nav, age 32 from Govan, Saskatchewan) and FSgt Wilton H. Kyle (air gunner, age 22 from Winnipeg). Ferry Command Canadian civilians lost were flight engineer Ernest G. Longley of Winnipeg, radio operator Frederick Scrafton of Toronto and flight engineer Wilmot I. Wilson of Vancouver. One survivor was Capt A.E. "King" Parker listed as a Montrealer, but actually a renowned American ferry pilot. (CANAV Col.)

Boston IV BW404 crash-landed at BW1 while en route from Canada to the UK on March 24, 1944. (CANAV Col.)

Hudson AM844 "Chinook" had this wheels-up landing while en route from Canada with Ferry Command. It later served 53 Squadron. (CANAV Col.)

Initially assigned to a conversion unit in Miami from June 1942, about a year later Hudson EW898 was passed on to 45 Group at Dorval. While being delivered on August 6, 1943, it crashed fatally near Martintown, Ontario, about 50 miles west of Dorval. Lost were two American pilots – John M. Smithers and Leland C. Lloyd, and RCAF radio operator, Sgt George S.B. Newman, age 20 from Victoria, BC. (CANAV Col.)

In June 1942 Hudson FK393 joined Ferry Command. It came to grief in an ugly accident near Maple, Ontario at about midnight on November 10, 1942. Farmer Wesley Wall was amazed to answer his door to the sight of four banged-up airmen – three RAF and one RCAF. On a training mission from Dorval to Malton, they flew into the ground on descent. (CANAV Col.)

Hudson FK792 swung on takeoff from Goose Bay on June 15, 1943. The crew got out, but this was one Hudson that would not be reaching the RAF. (CANAV Col.)

On approaching Ascension Island on August 22, 1944, B-26 Marauder HD605 landed short, ending in this messy scene. The crew escaped. Those aboard FB454 (3 RAF, 1 RCAF) had no such luck. While training from Windsor Field, Nassau on October 13, 1943 their Marauder caught fire and dove into the sea near Lyford Cay. Included among the dead was P/O Douglas W. Cormack (pilot), age 21 from Winnipeg. (CANAV Col.)

Long-Range Transport Pilot

DATC had one trans-oceanic operation – 168 (Heavy Transport) Squadron. Much has been written of 168 in such books as *Air Transport in Canada*, *And I Shall Fly*, *Permission Granted*, *RCAF Squadrons and Aircraft*, *The Consolidated Liberator and Boeing Fortress* and *The Royal Canadian Air Force at War 1939-1945*. This additional sampling of 168 activities is based on the log book of F/L D.F. Raymes, AFC, DFC.

Formed at Rockcliffe in October 1943, 168 (HT) Squadron carried Canada's vital trans-Atlantic mail and freight in support of the country's fighting forces overseas. The squadron began with some Lodestars flying domestic services, then took delivery of the first of several B-17 Flying Fortresses in December. The first oceanic operation saw B-17 9202 lifting off at Rockcliffe on December 15, 1943 with 5500-lb of mail. Captained by the CO, W/C R.B. Middleton, it routed via Dorval and Gander to Prestwick. From that point, Fortress 9203 carried on with the load to Cairo via several mail and refuelling stops. 9203 returned to Prestwick on January 11, 1944. By the time 168 disbanded on April 21, 1946 it had completed 636 Atlantic crossings:

Along with the Flying Fortress, the Liberator toiled on 168 Squadron long-range operations. Here is a fine view of Liberator 576. After 168 disbanded, 576 was stored to Debert, Nova Scotia, then sold for scrap in July 1947. Scrap prices were as low as $40 per Liberator. (Lialla Raymes Col.)

Liberator 332, Fortress – 240, Dakota 64. Flying time totalled 26,417 hours. By war's end 168 had lost five aircraft and 18 men. Having served an exhausting war in Eastern Air Command and sunk *U-520*, F/L D.F. "Danny" Raymes arrived at 168 Squadron in January 1944. He had more than 2000 hours showing in his log book, mainly on the Digby, and recently had converted to the Liberator at 10 BR. W/C Z/L Leigh, when forming up the RCAF's new transport operation, had heard of Raymes, and wanted him. On November 8, 1943 he wrote to Raymes' former CO, G/C Clare Annis, then station commander at Linton-on-Ouse, an RCAF bomber base in the UK:

We can certainly use a few good pilots due to our recent expansion. I have had Flight Lieutenant Raymes, AFC, name placed on our pilots list, and will make a determined effort to get hold of him in time for the next Transport Course, which should start approximately December 1st. I imagine that in his case, taking the course would be a mere formality ... Will let you know as soon as we require more pilots, navigators, etc., as your chaps are certainly the type we require.

G/C Annis sent a copy of this letter to F/L Raymes with a note in the margin: "The above letter will speak for itself, Danny. Best of luck." Raymes first flew at Rockcliffe on January 14 – a check ride in Dakota 662 with F/O Cy Torontow. Next day he checked out on Lodestar 559 with F/O Bennett. He trained steadily on these types through February, then flew the line into March. Meanwhile, F/L "Wess" McIntosh had checked him out on B-17 9202 on February 3.

F/L Raymes' first oceanic trip began on March 3, 1944, when he departed Rockcliffe as captain of Dakota 658 (co-pilot – F/O George Potter). They flew first to Moncton in 3:20 hours, then continued to Gander on the 5th in 3:45. Next day they made the Azores in 8:20 hours, then pushed on on the 7th in 8:30 hours to Gibraltar, where they rested a few days. On March 13 Raymes flew with F/L B.G. Smith on a test flight on Fortress 9207 (this aircraft crashed on April 2 at Prestwick, killing the crew of five). March 15-16 Raymes took Dakota 653 on a typical 168 Mediterranean milkrun: Gibraltar to Algiers, Bari, Naples, Algiers and back to Gibraltar for

F/L Danny Raymes and F/O Van Rassel at the controls of a 168 Squadron Flying Fortress. (Lialla Raymes Col.)

19:40 flying hours. Such trips not only carried the mail, but all sorts of priority cargo and passengers, including the sick and wounded. For March, F/L Raymes logged 79:10 flying hours.

June 1-5, 1944 F/L Raymes had Dakota 962 on the Gibraltar - Cairo run (28:40 flying hours). On the 9th and 10th he returned in Fortress 9205 from Gibraltar via the Azores and Moncton to Rockcliffe, adding a further 21:05 hours. This kind of flying was not for the faint of heart. On July 5 Raymes set out again with F/O Potter – back they went to "Gib" in a Fortress. This involved two Gibraltar-Prestwick return trips. They set off again from Gibraltar for Rockcliffe on July 18 routing via the Azores and Gander, landing home on the 19th. In August and September, Raymes was mainly at Northolt near London from where he and Potter flew 12 medevac trips to B.14 in Normandy. On September 16 they set off on 9203 from Lyneham going to Prestwick (2:00 hours), Gibraltar (8:40), Azores (6:40), Gander (9:00) and Rockcliffe (6:30), landing there on the 21st. He then had a week off, likely to spend at home with his wife Lialla and baby. Back to work on the 30th, he and Potter took Dakota 975 to Toronto Island, Camp Borden and home for an easy day of 3:35 hours.

Early in October, F/Ls Raymes and Van Rassel did some training on Liberator 576, then took 576 on a Gibraltar rotation from October 20-26. This trip operated Rockcliffe-Gander-Azores-Gibraltar-Prestwick-Gibraltar-Azores-Gander-Rockcliffe. Raymes never was one to elaborate on any such work – it was all just ordinary work. This, after all, was the same pilot who, having sunk a U-boat, noted the event in his log book simply as "Sub attacked and sank". However, not everything always was rosy with such intensive flying, as with the following trip in Fortress 9202: December 14, 1944 Rockcliffe-Gander (4:40 hours), 16th Lagens in the Azores at night (6:15), 17th Rabat (5:30), 19th Lagens (6:50), 19th Summerside (12:25 including 10:00 at night), 20th Presque Isle, Maine (3:05), 22nd Uplands (2:35, Rockcliffe weathered in).

F/L Raymes' WAG on this rotation was WO1 Anthony Cinquina. Having grown up in Montreal and Cornwall, Ontario, he had determined to get into aviation after watching the airship *R-100* cruising over Montreal during its 1930 visit. In 1940 Cinquina joined the RCAF at age 18, completed wireless training at 3 WS, Winnipeg, then did his gunnery course at 2 (B&G) School at Mossbank, Saskatchewan. He served on 164 Squadron from

Moncton, then joined 168, where he delighted in crewing with F/L Raymes. Cinquina later described how the trip nearly ended in disaster:

On December 14, 1944 Fortress 9202 with the crew of Danny Raymes, Van Rassel, Jimmy Hewson, me and a crewman departed Ottawa for Gibraltar with stops at Gander and Lagens in the Azores. The trip went smoothly, except for returning, for a cold front was predicted en route. According to Ops, at 22,000 feet we would only have the leading edge to deal with.

We departed Rabat Sale on December 19 for Lagens, where we refuelled for Gander. I kept in contact with a TCA Lancaster and a BOAC Avro York. As the front increased, Danny realized that we were in for a rough trip. At the "point of no return", the ice build-up was so severe that we lost our DF loop antenna and fixed aerial, and our de-icing system malfunctioned.

The aircraft stalled twice, but Danny and Van Rassel kept control. We were down to 7000 feet and could not have survived another stall. I sent my W/T messages using the trailing aerial. Bermuda relayed my SOS to the east coast stations and confirmed this for me.

Danny, meanwhile, was scraping ice off a small corner of the windshield in order to have any sort of view ahead. Suddenly there was a break in the clouds and he picked up the lights of a runway ahead, made a straight-in approach and landed. As we taxied to a stop, one tire blew on account of the weight of the ice covering the airframe. We now learned that we were in Summerside. From here we were dispatched for repairs to Presque Isle, Maine, headquarters of the USAAF ferry service.

In February 1945 Raymes flew a number of Goose Bay-Reykjavik trips in Liberator 572. These mainly were with mail, spare parts, etc. for 162 Squadron based in Iceland with Cansos. February 4 to 6, 1945 he operated Reykjavik-BW1 return, averaging 4:30 per leg. Raymes flew his final trip with 168 from June 27, 1945 to July 9. This was in Fortress 9202: Rockcliffe - Goose Bay - Prestwick - Reykjavik - Goose Bay - Rockcliffe.

F/O Tony Cinquina of 168 Squadron. Then, 50 years later at a 1992 squadron reunion with Wesley H. "Wess" McIntosh, who had been a flight commander on 168. (Lialla Raymes Col.)

That final leg to Rockcliffe was his last in the RCAF. At the end of it all, on July 9, 1945 his log book showed 3220:50 hours.

Danny Raymes and Lialla Henderson of Bounty, Saskatchewan had married in 1943. Now, Lialla was waiting at her parents' place in Bounty, and Danny was in Saskatoon, working again with the CNR and looking to buy a house. At this point he was fed up with flying, but

A shiny 168 Squadron Liberator ready for a mail mission on a winter's day. (DND PL35413)

While Ferry Command and 168 Squadron plied the Atlantic, so did the speedy Lancasters of the Canadian Government Trans-Atlantic Air Service. CGTAS service began in October 1943, high priority passengers, freight and mail being carried. These Lancasters reverted to TCA at war's end, then continued on the North Atlantic until replaced by North Stars in 1947. (Ralph Clint Col.)

worrying about his future. Then, Lialla reminded him how George Lothian and Lindy Rood of TCA had urged him back in Gander days to be sure to let them know if he ever needed a flying job. Lialla had to twist Danny's arm to try this – she even wrote the letter to TCA when Danny reluctantly agreed. He quickly was hired and the Raymes were connected with TCA and Air Canada for years to come. In January 1969 Danny accepted an offer to move to Jamaica, where a cadre of TCA people was helping fledgling Air Jamaica get established. This was a 7-year tour, after which the Raymes spent a few years retired in Florida, before returning to Saskatchewan. Danny Raymes passed away on October 31, 1993.

Several 168 Squadron personnel received gallantry and non-gallantry awards: 1 DFC, 8 AFC, 1 AFM, 1 BEM and 1 Croix de Guerre (France). F/O Horace B. Hillcoat of Amherst, Nova Scotia, already had the AFM in January 1943 for good service as an instructor at 19 EFTS, when he was awarded the AFC. Having later served on 165 Squadron, he joined 168. In this May 1944 photo he is receiving the AFC from the Earl of Athlone. This was awarded for his superb airmanship of the previous January 23. While piloting Fortress 9205 that night from Prestwick to Gibraltar, his aircraft collided head-on with a Wellington. The Wellington went into the sea, but Hillcoat and crew, now flying with two engines out and other damage, were able to return to the UK coast and land at Predannack (all five crew were "gonged" for this good show). On December 15, 1944 F/L Hillcoat was aboard Fortress 9203 when it disappeared between French Morocco and the Azores. (DND PL25145)

F/L Daniel Francis Raymes receives the AFC at Government House in Ottawa on April 16, 1943. Presenting the medal is Governor General, The Earl of Athlone. Then, Raymes with his beaming admirers – sister Georgina and wife Lialla at the same affair. (DND PL16035, PL16008)

Other RCAF Transport Aircraft on the Home Front

During WWII the RCAF used a host of aircraft types for domestic transport needs. Many of these odd-ball aircraft were impressed into service or hastily purchased in the US. The superb family of Lockheed twin-engine transports was widely used. Early on, the RCAF acquired 26 commercial Lockheed 10s, 12s and a 212. Several Hudsons were diverted from coastal duties to serve as general transports then, beginning in January 1943, a fleet of 18 Lockheed 18 Lodestars was established. Shown is Lockheed 10B 7648, which served from July 1940 into 1945. Postwar it flew with various US operators until wrecked in Alaska in 1960. (Jack McNulty Col.)

Two Lockheeds which brought the Duke of Kent and his party to 5 AOS, Brantford on August 15, 1941. These likely belonged to 12 (Comm) Squadron of Ottawa, which specialized in VIP services. Nearest is L.12A 7654 which had served Humble Oil and Refining Co. from January 1937. Beside it is L.12A 1531, another former US corporate plane. (DND RE18554-3)

In a photo provided by Steve Mouncey, Lockheed 12A 7837 is seen with Anson I 6170. Inscribed finely on the Lockheed's nose is "Central Flying School Trenton". CFS usually had one or two Lockheeds for general transportation and multi-engine pilot training. 7837 had been an airliner in the United States before joining the RCAF in October 1940. It had a long postwar career back in the US, then Dr. Peter Ramm of St. Catharines, Ontario acquired it for restoration. Ken Swartz photographed it at St. Catharines in 2008.

Hudson BW456 is believed to have served initially (March 1943) at 7 OTU, Debert, then moved to Test and Development Flight at Rockcliffe on general duties. (CANAV Col.)

Grumman Goose 943 in a VIP-type paint job. Having joined the RCAF in August 1941, it served 12 (Comm) Squadron into November 1944. As late as 1980, this Goose was N13CS with Air Catalina of San Pedro, California. (Robert Brachen Col.)

Urgently in need early in WWII of any sort of transport aircraft, the RCAF acquired eight Boeing 247Ds beginning in June 1940. This "247" had begun in 1934 as NC2666 with Phillips Petroleum of Oklahoma. Once the HWE had modernized with Dakotas and Lodestars, such older types were released for other purposes. In May 1942, this example was loaned to Quebec Airways, where it flew as CF-BVZ. In April 1945 it was sold to war surplus kingpin Charles Babb, and returned to the US. (DND REA412-73)

By war's end the RCAF had taken about 100 Norseman utility transports on strength. These served everywhere on the home front on a myriad of valuable tasks. Here 3528 sits at Watson Lake, Yukon in June 1944. On October 18, 1945 it was wrecked at Fort Simpson, NWT. (DND PL25434)

Norseman 365 after being salvaged from a Northern Ontario lake in July 1945. Following repairs, it served the RCAF into 1953, then was sold in Australia as VH-GSF. It was lost in a crash at sea off New South Wales on January 18, 1970. (Art Walker Col.)

Several types of light planes were useful on general transport duties. Included was this Fairchild 24, which served 12 (Comm) Squadron, usually as a "flying taxicab" for senior officers and government flunkies. (DND PL1953)

Selected Glossary

AAHS — American Aviation Historical Society

ab initio — elementary training

AC — air commodore or aircraftsman or army co-operation

AFC — Air Force Cross

AFHQ — Air Force Head Quarters

AFROs — Air Force Routine Orders

AFU — Advanced Flying Unit

AG — air gunner

ANS — Air Navigation School

AOC — Air Officer Commanding

AOS — Air Observer School

ASR — air-sea rescue

ASV — anti-surface vessel radar

ATAF — Allied Tactical Air Force

ATFERO — Atlantic Ferry Organization

Aux — auxiliary

A/V/M — air vice marshal

B — bomber

B&GS — Bombing and Gunnery School

BC — British Columbia

BCATP — British Commonwealth Air Training Plan

BEF — British Expeditionary Force

BEM — British Empire Medal

BOAC — British Overseas Airways Corporation

BR — bomber reconnaissance

BW — Bluie West airstrips

C — composite

CAC — coast artillery co-operation

CAF — Canadian Air Force

CAHS — Canadian Aviation Historical Society

CanCar — Canadian Car and Foundry

Capt — captain

CAS — Chief of the Air Staff

Cat "A" — category "A" accident (airframe destroyed)

CAVU — ceiling and visibility unlimited

CBE — Commander of the Most Excellent Order of the British Empire

CCA — Controller of Civil Aviation

CCGS — Canadian Coast Guard Ship

CEF — Canadian Expeditionary Force

CF- — Canadian registered civil airplane

CFI — chief flying instructor

CFS — Central Flying School

CGAO — Civil Government Air Operations

circa — about

CNE — Canadian National Exhibition

CNR — Canadian National Railway

CO — commanding officer

Col — colonel

Comm — communications

Cpl — corporal

CPR — Canadian Pacific Railway

CTechO — chief technical officer

cu.ft — cubic feet

DC — depth charge

DFC — Distinguished Flying Cross

DFM — Distinguished Flying Medal

D.H. — de Havilland

DHC — de Havilland Canada

DLS — Dominion Land Surveyor

DND — Department of National Defence

DOT — Department of Transport

DROs — Daily Routine Orders

DSC — Distinguished Service Cross

DSO — Distinguished Service Order

EAC — Eastern Air Command

EFTS — Elementary Flying Training School

ETA — estimated time of arrival

F — fighter

FAA — Fleet Air Arm

FB — flying boat

FE — flight engineer

FIS — Flying Instructor School

F/L — flight lieutenant

F/O — flying officer

F/Sgt — flight sergeant

ft. — feet

FTS — Flying Training School

FY — fiscal year

G-CA — Canadian registered civil airplane 1920-28

G-CY — Canadian registered government airplane 1920-28

GC — George Cross

G/C — group captain

GM — George Medal

GP — general purpose

GR — general reconnaissance

GTR — Grand Trunk Railway

HBC — Hudson's Bay Co.

HMCS — His Majesty's Canadian Ship

HMS — His Majesty's Ship

hp — horse power

HQ — headquarters

HSL — high speed launch

HT — heavy transport

HWE — Home War Establishment

ID — identification

Imp. — Imperial (measure)

ITS — Initial Training School

IWM — Imperial War Museum

Ju. — Junkers

KIA — killed in action

KIFA — killed in flying accident

LAC — leading aircraftsman

LAC — Library and Archives Canada

Lat. — latitude

LCMDR — lieutenant commander

Long. — longitude

Lt — lieutenant

Maj — major

MC — Military Cross

MD — Manning Depot

m/g or mg — machine gun

MGen — major general

MiD — Mention in Dispatches

Mk. — mark (version of an aircraft type)

MND — Minister of National Defence

mph — miles per hour

NATO — North Atlantic Treaty Organization

NCO — non-commissioned officer

NDHQ — National Defence Head Quarters

Many RCAF aircraft have had amazing careers, Lockheed Lodestar 559 included. The Lodestar first flew in September 1939. It then was a military and civil air transport mainstay for more than three decades. Built as a military C-60A, 559 was delivered from Lockheed in Burbank, California in June 1943. It served 165 Squadron on the Northwest Staging Route but, no doubt, its duties took it all over Canada and the US. SOS in March 1947, it became a corporate plane with such US firms as Michigan Tool and Ex-Cell-O-Corp. In 1965 it was converted in Texas to Howard H-250 standards with a tricycle undercarriage. Inevitably, its flying days ended and in 2010 it was rusting out at Watsonville, California. It's shown in original RCAF form, then during tri-gear days with Everett I. Brown Co. Larry Smalley photographed N6711 at San Francisco in November 1970. (Leslie Corness/CANAV Books, Walt Redmond Cols.)

NPAAF	non-permanent active air force	RCAF	Royal Canadian Air Force	T&D	Test and Development Flight
NRC	National Research Council	RCMP	Royal Canadian Mounted Police	TB	torpedo bomber
NS	Nova Scotia	RCN	Royal Canadian Navy	TCA	Trans-Canada Air Lines
NWT	Northwest Territories	R&D	research and development	TOC/TOS	taken on charge/taken on strength
O	observer	RDF	radio direction finding		
OBE	Officer of the Most Excellent Order of the British Empire	RFC	Royal Flying Corps	TTS	Technical Training School
		RG	record group, e.g. RG24 in LAC	UK	United Kingdom
				USAAC	United States Army Air Corps
OC	officer commanding	RMC	Royal Military College	USAAF	United States Army Air Force
OPAS	Ontario Provincial Air Service	RN	Royal Navy		
		RCNAS	Royal Canadian Naval Air Service	USAF	United States Air Force
ORB	operations record book			USO	United Service Organizations
OTU	Operational Training Unit	RCNVR	Royal Canadian Navy Volunteer Reserve		
P	pilot or photographic			USN	United States Navy
PAAF	permanent active air force	RNAS	Royal Naval Air Service	VC	Victoria Cross
P&W	Pratt & Whitney	SFTS	Service Flying Training School	VIP	very important person
PEI	Prince Edward Island			WAC	Western Air Command
P/O	pilot officer	Sgt	sergeant	WAG	wireless air gunner
POW	prisoner of war	skipper	NCO or officer in charge of an aircraft and crew	W/C	wing commander
P/P/O	provisional pilot officer			WO	warrant officer
PR	photo reconnaissance or public relations	S/L	squadron leader	WOpAG	wireless operator air gunner
		SOC/SOS	struck off charge/struck off strength	WS	Wireless School
PRC	Personnel Reception Centre				
PT	physical training	specs	specifications		
RAF	Royal Air Force	stn	station		

Selected Bibliography

Allison, Les and Hayward, Harry, *They Shall Grow Not Old: A Book of Remembrance*, Brandon, Manitoba, Commonwealth Air Training Plan Museum, Inc., 1991.

Avery, Norm, *North American Aircraft 1934-1998, Vol. 1*, Santa Ana, California, Narkiewicz/Thompson.

CAHS Journal, Canadian Aviation Historical Society, Toronto.

Canadian Civil Aircraft Register, Ottawa, Department of Transport, various editions from 1955.

Carter, David J., *Prairie Wings: RAF 34 Service Flying Training School*, Medicine Hat 1941-1944, Elkwater, Alberta, Eagle Butte Press Ltd., 2001.

Christie, Carl, *Ocean Bridge: The History of RAF Ferry Command*, Toronto, University of Toronto Press, 1995.

Creed, Roscoe, *PBY: The Catalina Flying Boat*, Annapolis, Maryland, Naval Institute Press, 1985

David, Donald and Lake, Jon, *Encyclopedia of World Military Aircraft, Vols.1 and 2*, London, Aerospace Publishing, 1994.

Douglas, W.A.B., *The Creation of a National Air Force: The History of the Royal Canadian Air Force, Volume II*, Toronto, University of Toronto Press, 1986.

Eastwood, A.B. and Roach, J.R., *Piston Engine Airliner Production List*, West Drayton, England, The Aviation Hobby Shop, 2002.

Ellis, Frank H., *Canada's Flying Heritage*, Toronto, University of Toronto Press, 1954.

Ellis, John R., *Canadian Civil Aircraft Register G-CAAA to G-CAXP 1920 to 1928*, Toronto, Canadian Aviation Historical Society.

Ellis, John R., *Canadian Civil Aircraft Register 1929-45*, Toronto, Canadian Aviation Historical Society.

Fahey, James C., *US Army Aircraft 1908-1946, Ships and Aircraft*, New York, 1946.

Fletcher, David C. and McPhail, Doug, *Harvard: The North American Trainers in Canada*, San Josef, BC, DCF Flying Books, 1990.

Franks, Norman, *Search, Find and Kill: The RAF's U-Boat Successes in World War Two*, London, England, Grub Street, 1995.

Fuller, G.A., Griffin, J.A. and Molson, K.M., *125 Years of Canadian Aeronautics: A Chronology 1840-1965*, Willowdale, Ontario, Canadian Aviation Historical Society, 1983.

Gradidge, J.M.G., *et al, The Douglas DC-1/DC-2/DC-3: The First Seventy Years*, Tonbridge, England, Air-Britain (Historians) Ltd., 2006.

Green, William, *The Observer's World Aircraft Directory*, Frederick Warne & Co., London, 1961.

Griffin, J.A., *Canadian Military Aircraft Serials and Photographs*, Ottawa, Canadian War Museum, 1969.

Hadley, Michael L., *U-Boats against Canada: German Submarines in Canadian Waters*, Montreal, McGill-Queen's University Press, 1985.

Halliday, Hugh A., *Not in the Face of the Enemy: Canadians Awarded the Air Force Cross and Air Force Medal 1918-1966*, Toronto, Robin Brass Studio, 2000.

Hatch, F.J., *Aerodrome of Democracy: Canada and the British Commonwealth Air Training Plan 1939-1945*, Ottawa, Department of National Defence, Directorate of History, 1983.

Hendrey, Andrew, *Canadian Squadrons in Coastal Command*, St. Catharines, Ontario, Vanwell Publishing Ltd., 1997.

Hitchins, W/C F.H., *Air Board: Canadian Air Force and Royal Canadian Air Force*, Ottawa, Canadian War Museum, Paper No.2, Mercury Series, 1972.

Hotson, Fred H., *The De Havilland Canada Story*, Toronto, CANAV Books, 1983.

Jackson, A.J., *British Civil Aircraft 1919-59 Vol.1*, Putnam, London, 1959.

Jackson, A.J., *British Civil Aircraft 1919-59 Vol.2*, Putnam, London, 1960.

Jefford, W/C C.G., MBE, *RAF Squadrons: A Comprehensive Record of the Movement and Equipment of All RAF Squadrons and Their Antecedents Since 1912*, Shrewsbury, England, Airlife, 1988.

Juptner, Joseph P., U.S. *Civil Aircraft Series, (Vols. 1-9)*, Blue Ridge Summit, Pennsylvania, TAB Aero, 1981.

Knott, Captain Richard C., USN, *The American Flying Boat: An Illustrated History*, Annapolis, Maryland, Naval Institute Press 1979.

Kostenuk, S. and Griffin, J.A., *RCAF Squadrons and Aircraft*, Toronto, Samuel Stevens Hakkert & Co., 1977.

Legg, David, *Consolidated PBY Catalina: The Peacetime Record*, Annapolis, Naval Institute Press, 2002.

Leigh, Z.L., *And I Shall Fly, The Flying Memoirs of Z. Lewis Leigh*, Toronto, CANAV Books, 1985.

Lewis, Peter, *The British Bomber Since 1914: Fifty Years of Design and Development*, London, England, Putnam, 1967.

Lewis, Peter, *The British Fighter Since 1912: Fifty Years of Design and Development*, London, England, Putnam, 1965.

MacDonald, Capt Grant and Strocel, Capt Terry, *442 Squadron History*, 1987.

Marion, Normand, *Camp Borden: Birthplace of the RCAF, RCAF 80th Anniversary Edition*, Borden, Ontario, 2004.

Marson, Peter, *The Lockheed Twins*, Tonbridge, England, Air-Britain (Historians) Inc., 2001.

McGrath, T.M., *A History of Canadian Airports*, Toronto, Lugus Publications, 1992.

McVicar, Donald M., *North Atlantic Cat*, Shrewsbury, England, Airlife Publishing Ltd.. 1983.

One of the RCAF's outstanding *ab initio* trainers of the pre-and early-WWII years was the Fleet Fawn, 482 of which were on strength. (Gordon S. Williams)

Milberry, Larry *Air Transport in Canada*, Toronto, CANAV Books, 1997.

Milberry, Larry, *Aviation in Canada*, Toronto, McGraw-Hill Ryerson, 1979.

Milberry, Larry, *Aviation in Canada: The Pioneer Decades*, Toronto, CANAV Books, 2008.

Milberry, Larry, *Aviation in Canada: The Formative Years*, Toronto, CANAV Books, 2008.

Milberry, Larry *Canada's Air Force at War and Peace, Vols. 1, 2, 3*, Toronto, CANAV Books, 2000-01.

Milberry, Larry, *Fighter Squadron: 441 Squadron from Hurricanes to Hornets*, Toronto, CANAV Books, 2003.

Milner, Mark, *Battle of the Atlantic*, St. Catharines, Ontario, Vanwell Publishing Ltd., 2003.

Mingos, Howard, *The Aircraft Year Book for 1946*, New York, NY, Lanciar Publishers, 1946.

Mitchell, Kent A., *Fairchild Aircraft 1926-1987*, Santa Ana, California, Narkiewicz/Thompson, 1997.

Molson, K.M., *Canada's National Aviation Museum: Its History and Collections*, Ottawa, National Aviation Museum, 1988.

Molson, K.M and Taylor, H.A., *Canadian Aircraft since 1909*, Stittsville, Ontario, Canada's Wings, 1982.

Molson, K.M. and A.J. Shortt, A.J., *The Curtiss HS Flying Boats*, Ottawa, National Aviation Museum, 1995.

Moyes, Philip, *Bomber Squadrons of the RAF and Their Aircraft*, London, MacDonald & Co., 1964.

Schweyer, Robert, *Sights on Jarvis: No.1 Bombing and Gunnery School, 1940-1945*, Nanticoke, Ontario, Heronwood Enterprises, 2004.

Sutherland, Alice Gibson, *Canada's Aviation Pioneers: 50 Years of McKee Trophy Winners*, Toronto, McGraw-Hill Ryerson, 1978.

Swanborough, Gordon, *Civil Aircraft of the World*, New York, Charles Scribner's Sons, 1980.

Swanborough, F.G. and Bowers, Peter M., *United States Military Aircraft since 1909*, London, England, Putnam, 1963.

Thetford, Owen, *Aircraft of the Royal Air Force since 1918*, London, England, Putnam, 1962.

Thetford, Owen, *British Naval Aircraft since 1912*, London, England, Putnam, 1962.

Thompson, Kevin, *North American Aircraft 1934-1999, Vol. 2*, Santa Ana, California, Narkiewicz/Thompson.

Vincent, Carl, *The Blackburn Shark*, Stittsville, Ontario, Canada's Wings, 1974.

Vincent, Carl, *Consolidated Liberator and Boeing Fortress*, Stittsville, Ontario, Canada's Wings, 1975.

Wagner, Ray, *American Combat Planes: A History of Military Aircraft in the USA*, London, England, MacDonald & Co., 1960.

Weicht, Chris, *Jericho Beach and the West Coast Flying Boat Stations*, Chemainus, BC, MCW Enterprises, 1997.

Wise, S.F., *Canadian Airmen and the First World War: The Official History of the Royal Canadian Air Force, Volume I*, Toronto, University of Toronto Press, 1980.

Who's Who in World Aviation, Washington, DC, American Aviation Publications, Inc. 1955

Index

Abelson, F/L Lawrence B. 143
Abraham, J.B. 108
accident categories 166, 168
accidents: 13, 18, 23, 24, 49, 51, 64, 65, 68, 69,
    84, 95, 97, 98, 103, 104, 107, 117, 118, 126,
    134, 136-138, 146, 153-155, 168-175, 178,
    186, 189, 190, 191, 196, 200, 205, 219, 222,
    223, 232-235, 247, 257, 260, 262-267, 269,
    273, 278, 281, 285, 304, 306, 307, 312-315,
    318, 320
Adair, Cpl Lewis G. 179
Adams, AC1 Robert W. 263
Adams, L.S. 127
Adamson, LAC 161
aerial photography 33-36, 43, 45, 51, 59, 74, 89,
    95, 98, 101
Aerial/Aviation League of Canada 77, 83
Aero Club of British Columbia 83
Aeronca 127
AETE 267
AFROs 178-180, 236, 274, 284-286
Agar, F/L Carlyle C. 176
Aiken, F/O George D. 177
Air Board Act 13, 14, 47, 51
*Air Board, Canadian Air Force and Royal
    Canadian Air Force* 14
Air Cadets 102
Air Canada 318
Air Catalina 320
Air Command 302
Air Force Cross 114, 176, 177, 200, 244,
    267, 279, 293, 303
Air Force Magazine 299, 300
Air Force Medal 262
Air Force Routine Orders 178-180, 236,
    274, 284-286
Air France 307
Air Gagnon 234
air mail 49, 77, 78, 125, 201, 311, 312, 315-318
Air Transport in Canada 315
Aircraft Manufacturers Ltd. 13
Aircraft Repair Ltd. 116
Aircraft Research Corp. 150
airship 50
Airspeed Oxford 113, 117-119, 142, 193,
    274, 275
Aitken, William Maxwell 304
Alachasse 76
Alaska 224, 243-245-261, 291
Aleutians 224, 246-248, 257, 291
Alexander, AC2 R.L. 262
Allen, Peter 165
Alliston, Ontario 196
Amadjuak Lake, NWT 293, 295
Amerika 281
Amherst, Nova Scotia 152

Amundsen, Roald 286
And I Shall Fly 278, 315
Anderson, A/V/M N.R. 25, 50, 64, 262
Anderson, AC1 H.F.84
Anderson, Capt D. 312
Anderson, Cpl A. 46, 47, 50
Anderson, F/O Gordon J. 176
Anderson, P/O C.M. 21, 22, 66
Andrée, Salomon August 286
Andrews, LAC 139
Andrews, Sgt George H. 263
Angus, LAC D.A. 194
Annette Island 110, 182, 218, 244, 246-261, 291
Annis, W/C Clare L. 202, 315
ap Ellis, G/C A. 144
Appleby, P/O 226
Apps, F/L Gordon 94
Archdeacon, Cpl 47
Arctic 38
Arctic exploration 38-42, 286-303
Arctic Gold Exploration Co. 41
Argentia, Newfoundland 230, 233
Armour, P/O 226
Armstrong Siddeley engines:
    Cheetah 117, 162, 275, 285
    Lynx 23
Armstrong Whitworth:
    Atlas 66, 69, 70, 74, 91, 101, 184
    Siskin 49, 66-68, 71, 72, 74, 80, 84,
    85, 91, 165
    Whitley 163
Armstrong, LAC D.H. 194
Arnold, Col Milton W. 289
Arnold, Cpl 267
Arnold, WO2 Vernon C. 249
Ascension Island 307, 308, 314
Ashman, F/L Ralph A. 197, 198
Ashton, F/O A.J. 51
ATFERO 288-290, 304
Atlantic Canada Aviation Museum 235
Atlantic Ferry Organization 288-290, 304
ATR-42 39
Attewell, Sgt W.G. 84
Attree, WO2 Earl R. 217
Attwood, AC1 W.T.C. 84
Ault, Cpl J.G. 84
Austin Airways 93, 242
Austin, F/L C.C. 93, 196
Avalon Aviation 218
Avro:
    504 4, 15-17, 21, 23, 24, 26, 27, 33, 34,
    37, 47, 58
    552 35, 46, 49
    Anson 4, 117-119, 126, 134, 146-159, 162,
    163, 168, 171, 174, 179, 193-195, 239, 245,
    246, 264, 270, 276, 285

Avian 82, 98
Lancaster 275, 306, 310, 311, 317
Tutor 102, 166
Aylmer Lake, NWT 62, 95
Ayres, F/L 129

B.C. Star (M.427) 241
Babb Corporation 218
Babb, Charles 320
Babbington, A/M P. 275
Baffin Island 38-42, 286-298
Baggs, William 128
Bailey, LAC R.H. 175
Baily, Sgt Francis M. 244
Bales, Jim 155
Balfour, Capt H.H.108
Balfour, F/L R. 134
Bamford, FSgt Richard B. 212
Banghart, F.I. 99
Banning, F/O James E.V. 190, 212
Bannock, F/L Russ 136
Barker Field 138
Barker, Col W.G. 25, 71, 97
Barkley-Grow T8P-1 100
Barlow, Keith 115, 130
Barlow, Shirley 130
Barnes, Air Commodore E.D. 138
Barnes, P O Roland R. 223
Barr, LAC Thomas 194, 196
Barrett, Dave 238
Barrow, T.A. 108
Bartlett, F/O A.H. 263
Bartley, Barbara 142
Bartley, W/C Hugh 142
Barton, F/L Alfred W. 114, 138-141, 176
Bates, LAC Theodore S. 168
Battle Harbour, Newfoundland 303
Battle of Britain 183, 225, 226, 252
Baxter, George 253
Beamish, F/L F.V. 71
Beasley, F/O Joseph R. 230
Beattie, Sgt Harry C. 222
Beattie, WO 103
Beatty, Bill 253
Beatty, LAC L.A. 189
Bebee, Sgt F.H. 192
Bedford Road Collegiate 192
Bedwell, Sgt William 203
Beech 18 99, 100
Beechwood Cemetery 278
Belanger, F/L Maurice J. 191
Belem, Brazil 307
Bell P-39 246, 257, 291
Bell-Irving, S/L A.D. 83
Bell, Jimmy 293
Bell, Ralph 121

Bella Bella, BC 95
Bellanca: CH-300 62, 73, 74, 76, 89
Belle Island, Newfoundland 304
Bellerive, LAC Gomer C. 222
Bennett, A/V/M D.C.T. 288, 304
Bennett, F/O 315
Bennett, F/O K.B. 278
Bennett, Floyd 287
Bennett, Prime Minister R.B. 78
Bennett, Sgt 269
Bennett, Tex 238
Bennetts, LAC R.W.N. 106
Bergevin, WO2 Joseph J.C. 214-217
Berriman, Larry 153, 159
Berry, Matt
Besley, F/O Gordon W. 217
Bessoneau hangar 19, 35
Best, Bruce 110
Bettridge, LAC 146
Bewley, FSgt Donald G. 217
Bibby, R.H. 151, 152, 159
Biernes, F/O Jack 252
Biggar, Col. O.M. 13
Biggars, Stan 299, 300
Bilkey, LAC James D. 168
Bill, F/O Victor E. 221
Binyon, Laurence 174
Birchall, S/L Leonard J. 280
Biron, Mr. 147
Bishop-Barker Aeroplanes 16
Bishop, A/M W.A. 11, 121, 159, 179, 243,
   269, 280, 300
Bishop, F/L 231
Bishop, LAC J.R.C. 194
Bismarck 198
Bisson, Louis 288, 289
Black Cat Aviation 212
Black, Campbell 152
Black, F/L Keith 138, 139
Blackburn Shark 91, 97, 103, 186, 205,
   236, 245
Blackmore, S/L. A.D. 159
Blair, LAC L.G.R. 136
Blakely, AC Robert A. 263
Blatchford Field 66
Blatherwick, Dr. John 175
Blood, Sgt 263
Bloor Collegiate Institute 134
Blythe, Richard R. 126
BOAC 312, 313, 316
Bobby Anakatok 53-55
Bobzener, Ernie 238
Bodnoff, FSgt Israel I.J. 213
Boeing of Canada 91, 97, 186
Boeing, Bill 261
Boeing:
   247 320
   B-17 201, 221, 306, 311, 315-318
   BB-1 13
   PT-26 85
   XB-15/XC-105 201
Bolduc, F/L R.L. 248, 249
Boning, J.P. 168
Bonshor, LAC F.A. 84
Bonter, Bill 238
Boomer, S/L K.A. 224
Borch, P/O 226
Borden, Prime Minister Robert 13
Border Cities Aero Club 61
Bourassa, Henri 50
Bourne, AC2 Ernest W. 168
Bowerman, F/O 269

Bowhill, A/C/M Sir Frederick 304
Bowling, G/C V.S. 135
Bowmanville, Ontario 235, 281, 282
Bowser, F/O 234
Boy Scouts 302
Boyer, FSgt Jack S. 223
Boyle, P/O Jack 222
Bradfield. Frank M. 22
Brantford, Ontario 85
Bras d'Or Lake 229
Brauecker, Capt Friedrich 190
Brazilian Air Force 242
Breadner, Doris 278
Breadner, F/O Donald L. 278
Breadner, W/C Lloyd 32, 64, 90, 97, 165, 177,
   183, 248, 269, 277, 278
Breckels family 282-284
Breckels, F/O Albert L. 283
Breckels, FSgt George S. 282-284
Bremner, FSgt John D. 284
Brenton, H.B. 13
Brewster Bermuda 141
Bridgeland, F/O Ed 269
Bridgeman, LAC Marcel R. 174
Briese, S/L E.C. 229
Briese, S/L R.G. 196
Briggs, S/L F.E.R. 269
Brighton, Ontario 250
Brintnell, Leigh 125
Bristol:
   Beaufort 248
   Beaver 86
   Bolingbroke 97, 110, 140, 146-147, 162,
   163, 178, 207, 226, 239, 245-247
   F.2b Fighter 15, 17, 30, 33
   Mercury 147
   Pegasus 91
British Commonwealth Air Training Plan
   106-181, 276; units: 1 ANS (Rivers) 243;
   1 AOS (Malton) 4, 122, 125, 126, 152; 1
   EFTS (Malton) 122; 1 FIS (Trenton) 112,
   119, 136; 1 GRS (Summerside) 213, 239,
   300; 1 IFS (Deseronto) 134; 1 ITS (Toronto)
   109, 129, 134, 136, 192, 265; 1 MD
   (Toronto) 129, 134-136, 143, 145, 160, 172,
   192, 212, 236, 238, 265, 267; 1 NAGS
   (Yarmouth) 128; 1 OTU (Bagotville) 119,
   224-229; 1 SFTS (Camp Borden) 138, 168,
   177, 191, 193-196, 230, 231; 1 Visiting
   Flight (Trenton) 134, 141, 152; 1 WS
   (Mount Hope) 171; 2 ANS (Pennfield
   Ridge) 143, 265; 2 AOS (Edmonton) 122,
   290; 2 EFTS (Fort William) 107, 122; 2 FIS
   (Vulcan) 122, 123, 175; 2 MD (Brandon)
   142; 2 SFTS (Ottawa) 114, 177-180, 243,
   300; 2 WS (Calgary, Shepard) 115, 162, 169,
   175, 177; 3 B&GS (MacDonald) 116; 3
   EFTS (London) 122, 213; 3 RD (Vancouver)
   175; 3 SFTS (Calgary) 8, 118, 142, 178,
   191, 285; 3 TC (Montreal) 161, 178, 188; 3
   WS (Winnipeg) 316; 4 AOS (London) 175;
   4 B&GS (Fingal) 116, 168; 4 EFTS
   (Windsor Mills) 122, 243; 4 ITS (Edmonton)
   142; 4 MD (Quebec City) 212, 238;
   4 SFTS (Saskatoon) 118; 4 TC (Regina)
   176, 285; 5 AOS (Brantford) 319; 5 BGS
   (Dafoe) 162; 5 EFTS (Lethbridge) 177;
   5 ITS 143, 172; 5 OTU (Abbotsford,
   Boundary Bay) 162, 168, 177, 266;
   5 SFTS (Brantford) 168; 6 B&GS (Mountain
   View) 146, 147, 170, 239, 265; 6 ITS
   (Toronto) 238; 6 OTU (Comox) 123, 241;

6 RD (Trenton) 175; 6 SFTS (Dunnville)
   128, 168, 170, 177, 178, 213, 243; 7 BGS
   (Paulson) 165; 7 EFTS (Windsor) 138; 7 ITS
   (Saskatoon) 146; 7 OTU (Debert) 207, 320;
   7 SFTS (Macleod) 122; 8 AOS (Ancienne
   Lorette) 155, 239; 8 BGS (Lethbridge) 162;
   8 EFTS (Sea Island) 142, 191; 8 OTU
   (Greenwood) 174; 8 SFTS (Moncton) 135;
   9 SFTS (Summerside) 114 136; 9 AOS
   (St. John's) 125, 143, 155, 265; 9 B&GS
   (Mont Joli) 160-162; 9 EFTS (St. Catharines)
   164; 10 AOS (Chatham) 118, 147-159; 10
   EFTS (Mount Hope, Pendleton) 127, 128,
   230; 10 RD (Calgary) 162, 276; 10 SFTS
   (Dauphin) 118, 126, 177, 178; 12 EFTS
   (Goderich) 110, 124, 168, 180; 12 SFTS
   (Brandon) 123, 179, 285; 13 EFTS (St.
   Eugene) 134, 136, 178; 13 SFTS (St.
   Hubert) 136, 172, 178; 14 EFTS (Portage
   la Prairie) 169; 14 SFTS (Aylmer) 114, 134,
   138-141, 168, 176-178, 181; 15 EFTS
   (Regina) 111, 146, 176; 15 SFTS
   (Claresholm) 9, 125; 16 EFTS (Edmonton)
   169; 16 SFTS (Hagersville) 129, 146, 177,
   178, 285; 17 EFTS (Stanley) 135; 17 SFTS
   (Souris) 146, 175, 179, 286; 19 EFTS
   (Virden) 120, 125, 126, 284; 20 EFTS
   (Oshawa) 127, 129, 134; 22 EFTS
   (Ancienne Lorette) 110, 300; 23 EFTS
   (Davidson, Yorkton) 170; 31 EFTS
   (DeWinton) 136, 169; 32 EFTS (Bowden)
   172; 32 OTU (Patricia Bay) 119, 144, 245,
   263, 264; 32 SFTS (Moose Jaw) 181; 33
   ANS (Mount Hope) 117; 34 OTU (Pennfield
   Ridge) 210, 248; 34 SFTS (Medicine Hat)
   144; 36 OTU (Greenwood) 119, 123, 136;
   39 EFTS (Swift Current) 178; Central Flying
   School 119, 125, 127, 136, 319; "Y" Depot
   (Halifax) 122, 147
British Empire Medal 175, 176, 178, 179
Broadbent, S/L Stanley Y. 177, 178
Broadhurst, A/V/M Harry 228
Brochu, F/L 150
Brooke-Popham, A/C/M Sir Robert 108
Brooker, P/O Arthur C. 252
Brookes, S/L George E. 27, 31, 32, 90, 103
Brooks, P/O Ernest R. 189
Broom, S/L Ivor 142
Brothers, Sgt Monty H. 222
Brown, F.M. 238
Brown, F/L 269
Brown, F/L Bob 139
Brown, LAC 161
Brown, P/P/O R.B. 64
Brown, Sgt 263
Brown, William H. 22
Brownfield, AC1 Oscar D. 189
Brownlee, AC1 R.S. 84
Bruce, P/O 226
Bruton, Harry 152, 159
Bryant Press 251
Bryant, Fred 159
Bryusziewicz, Stanley 51
Buchanan, F/O 240
Buhl CA-6 50
Bullock, FSgt D.C. 191
Bullock, S/L T.M. 229
Burke, LAC T. 194
Burton, AC1 Frank E. 222
BW-1 (Greenland) 313, 317
Byers, F/L Alan G. 224
Byrd, Adm. Richard E. 126, 287

Cairns, P/O J.R. 33, 43
Caldwell, C.S. 30
Callery, AC2 Vincent 222
Calow, Cpl T.A. 262
CAM-Ship 192, 225
Cameron, Cpl 46, 47
Cameron, F/O George 235
Cameron, Sgt R. 191
Camp Petawawa 70
Camp Shilo, Manitoba 83, 312
Campbell River, BC 250
Campbell, A/M Hugh L. 65, 276, 280
Campbell, Charlie 152
Campbell, F/L Peter 168
Campbell, F/L Wishart 178
Campbell, F/O Graham 213
Campbell, F/O J.D.L. 265
Campbell, FSgt Archibald B. 224
Campbell, Sir Gerald 108
Canada's Air Force at War and Peace 212, 228,
    247, 251
Canada's Aviation Hall of Fame 302
Canadair Ltd. 302
Canadian Aero Film Co. 13
Canadian Air Board 10, 13, 15, 16, 32, 33,
    276, 277
Canadian Air Force (England) 11, 276
Canadian Air Force 10, 13-47
Canadian Air Force Association 23
Canadian Air Force stations:
    Camp Borden 12-32, 46, Dartmouth 45, 49,
    High River 18, 35, 36, 43, 46,
    Jericho Beach 4, 19, 34, 36, 44, 46,
    Morley 19, 35,
    Norway House 33, 34,
    Ottawa 19,
    Roberval 19, 36,
    Sioux Lookout 35, 36, 103,
    Victoria Beach 14, 18, 33, 35, 36, 45,
    Winnipeg 33
Canadian Aircraft since 1909 59
Canadian Airways 99, 100, 122, 152, 188
Canadian Associated Aircraft 245
Canadian Aviation Historical Society 14, 165,
    176, 300, 301
Canadian Aviation magazine 65, 71, 83, 84,
    90, 165
Canadian Bushplane Heritage Centre 164
Canadian Car and Foundry 272
Canadian Flying Clubs Association 78
Canadian Government Trans-Atlantic Air
    Service 317
Canadian Helicopters 176
*Canadian Military Aircraft Serials and
    Photographs* 14
Canadian National Exhibition/CNE 71
Canadian National Exhibition/CNE 71, 165
Canadian National Railway 192
Canadian Pacific Airlines 100, 116, 218, 220,
    244, 264, 292
Canadian Pacific Railway 284, 304
Canadian Pacific vessels:
    Empress of France, 51,
Canadian Pratt & Whitney 84
Canadian Squadrons in Coastal Command 190
Canadian Vickers Ltd. 23, 49, 50, 73, 89, 97,
    152, 187
Canadian Vickers:
    Vancouver 65, 73, 76, 95, 101, 103, 185,
    186, 204
    Vanessa 50
    Varuna 46, 49, 59, 73, 95

    Vedette 45, 49, 62, 64, 73, 74, 95, 185,
    188, 196
Canadian War Museum Paper No.2 18
Canadian Warplane Heritage 115, 218, 274
Canadian Wright 73
Cannon, S/L A.E.L. 230
Cape Dorset, NWT 243
Cappel, Sgt Julius 179
Cardell, F/L 142
Carew, F/O H.W. 65
Caribou 191, 266
Carling-Kelly, W/C F.C. 136
Carr-Harris, Brian G. 25, 51, 53, 54
Carr-Harris, P/O R.M. 49
Carr, LGen W.K. 299-302
Carrol, John 292-295
Carscadden, LAC C.H. 194
Carscallen, W/C Henry M. 95, 197, 279, 280
Carter Air Service 171
Carter, F/L A.W. 36, 50, 103, 104
Carter, F/O Albert 46, 47
Carter, F/O F.M. 84
Cartierville, Quebec 61, 101
cartography 90
Cartwright, Newfoundland 303
Casey, F/L Brian A. 136
Castator, Murray 247, 251-261
Catala 249
Catapult Armed Merchantman 192, 225
Causey, WO2 T.A. 249
Cayuga 144
cemeteries:
    Beechwood Cemetery 278,
    Lake-of-the-Woods Cemetery 168,
    Our Lady of Victory Cemetery 172,
    St. George's Cemetery 173,
    St. John's Norway Cemetery 172-174
Central Aircraft Ltd. 120, 269-272
Central Technical School 144, 166, 167
Cessna T-50 Crane/Bobcat 118, 120, 245,
    269, 274
Ceylon 280
CGTAS 317
Chambers, FSgt Henry 249
Chandler, F/O Alfred J. 249
Chanute Field, Illinois 47, 104
Chapman, AC2 Roy B. 222
Chapman, W/C Cecil G.W. 214-217
Charity, George 93
Charleson, J.C. 129
Charlottetown, PEI 73
Charron, F/O L.R. 33
Chasse, Cpl R.E. 84
Chatham 191
Chatham, New Brunswick 149, 233
Cheater, P/O 199
Chesley R 199
Cheyney, F/O 226
Christie Street Hospital 146
Christie, Carl 289, 304
Christie, F/L 233
Chubb Crater 301
Church, F/L Harold W. 174
Churchill, Manitoba 289, 302
Churchill, Prime Minister Winston 233, 239,
    304
Cinquina, WO1 Anthony 316, 317
Civil Aeronautics Administration 261
Civil Government Air Operations 43, 74-76
Civil Operations Branch 13, 17
Clark, Colin 162-165, 238
Clark, Dr. W.C. 108

Clarke, Hugh 151, 152, 155
Clary, LAC Edgar L. 179
Clayton Knight Committee 126
Cleghorn, P/O D.G. 230
Clement, Rod 142
Clerget engine 4, 32
Cline, F/L 269
Clouthier, Sgt 230
Cloutier, P/O Bob 308
Clow, WO1 Charles E.B. 224
CNE/Canadian National Exhibition 71
Cockburn, F/L Red 138
Coeshott, FSgt S.H. 283
Coghill, F/L F.S. 51
Colbourne, P/O F.C. 195, 196, 200
Coleman, F/L Sheldon W. 95
Collard, G/C R.R. 269
Collins, Cpl 97
Collins, LAC Herbert W. 266
Collins, LAC Lawrence 146
Collis, F/O A.R. 84
Cologne, Germany 150
Colonna, Jerry 255
Colthurst, Mr. 142
Colville, Annie and Alexander 281, 282
Colville, F/O Alexander C. 281, 282
Colville, F/O John S. 281, 282
Colville, FSgt William F. 221, 222, 281, 282
Commended for Valuable Services in the Air
    178, 263, 266, 274
Compton, W/C Harry N. 285
Condie, LAC R. 195
Congo 302
*Consolidated PBY Catalina: The Peacetime
    Record* 218
Consolidated:
    Courier 82
    Liberator 4, 168, 190, 200, 201, 208, 209,
    214, 221, 259, 264-267, 289, 304-306,
    311-313, 315, 317
    PB2Y Coronado 310
    PBY-5 3, 188, 203, 207, 208, 212-220, 238-
    243, 246, 258, 266, 292-295, 298-300, 310
Controller of Civil Aviation 31, 50, 76
convoys 190, 192
Cook, "Bud" 47
Cook, Sgt S.D.R, 174
Cooke, F/O T.C. 213, 217
Cooke, FSgt Dennis A. 267
Cooper, Sgt 142
Copeland, J.F. 127
Copp, F/O E.A. 84
Corbett, FSgt Phillips A. 203
Corbett, G/C Vaughan B. 226
Corbett, Sgt P.A. 191
Cormack, P/O Douglas W. 314
Corner, Cpl Roy H. 222
Corness, Leslie 4
Costello, G/C M. 279
Cotter, F/O John J. 189
Coughlin, P/O 308
Coulter, Sgt R.A. 190
Courtney, A/M Sir Christopher 108
Cousins, Sgt R.H. 195
Cowan, S/L Emerson W. 263
Cowan, WO1 John H. 224
Cowitz, Arnold 159
Cowley, G/C A.T.N. 36, 194
Cox, P.B. 20, 47
Cox, Ray 208
Cox, Sgt Harry K. 172
Crabb, F/L H.P. 83

Craggie, Sgt 55
Craig Harbour, NWT 41, 286
Crail, LAC W.D. 148
Cramer, Parker 287
Cranston, LAC J.H. 148
Creation of a National Air Force 247
Crimson Routes 289
Crittenden, Sgt 226
Croil, A/V/M George M. 17, 27, 31, 36, 43, 97, 101, 103, 104, 109, 165
Cromarty, Sgt Robert F. 214-217
Cross, Lt Ronald H. 24
Crossley, F/L Carl 292
Crosswell, William J. 85
Cruiser 262
Crymes, LAC Smith E. 222
Crystal II 288, 290, 293
Crystal Routes 288
Cub Aircraft 126
Cuban Missile Crisis 302
Cuffe, Albert A.L. 22, 23, 45, 75, 188, 277
Culliton, J.P. 236, 267-274
Cunningham, F/L C. 212
Curry, P/O Allan M. 146
Curry, S/L Fred B. 247
Curtis, Hugh 236
Curtis, LAC J.A. 175
Curtiss-Reid Rambler 61
Curtiss:
    America 10
    H-16 10, 11, 15, 16
    HS-2L 4, 15, 17-19, 32-34, 36, 37, 45, 46
    JN-4 12, 13, 16, 25, 51, 72, 104
    Hawk 71, 72, 85
    Kittyhawk 4, 5, 141, 182, 246, 250-258, 260, 290
Cusak, AC2 Joseph E. 222
Cussion, P/O Charles E. 286

Dack, Sgt D.B. 229, 230
Dagenais, AC1 J.E. 84
Daily Routine Orders 178, 284-286
Dale, P/O 200
Dandurand, Senator R. 108
Danforth Technical School 162, 172
Daniel, A/F/L Dennis L. 310, 311
Daniels, LAC J.A. 262
Darden, Cole 261
Dart trainer 121
Daunt, F/O Acton F. 191, 223
David W. Branch 240
Davidson, LAC 269
Davidson, R.D. 43
Davies, David J. 161
Davies, LAC W.H. 148
Davies, P/O John R. 222
Davis, F/L R.L. 267
Davis, George R. "Joe" 160, 161
Davis, LAC J.T. 195
Davis, Marg 160
Davoud, G/C Paul Y. 122, 280
Daw, FSgt Harold C. 179
Dawber, Norm 242
Dawson, Gerald O. 238, 240
Dawson, Sgt J.K. 195
Day, P/O 226
De Beaupré. LAC R.J. 195
de Havilland Canada:
    D.H.82C 4, 95, 107, 109, 111, 127, 128, 164, 169, 172, 235
    DHC-6 Twin Otter 41
de Havilland, Sgt Victor D. 174

de Havilland:
    D.H.4 15, 17, 18, 21, 33, 36, 45, 58, 103
    D.H.9 15, 16, 86
    D.H.60 Gipsy Moth 52, 53, 58, 60, 72, 81, 83, 96, 193
    D.H.80 Puss Moth 127
    D.H.82 Tiger Moth 142, 192, 193
    D.H.89 Rapide 264
    D.H.90 Dragon Rapide 98
    D.H.98 Mosquito 119, 136, 137, 142, 143, 174, 278, 306
De La Haye. LAC A.L. 195
de Lesseps Field 84
De Nancrede, F/L 229
de Niverville, A/V/M J.L.E.A. 161, 162
de Waerbeek, P/O 174
deBlicquy, Mike 272, 273
Defence of Canada Regulations 236
Delahaye, S/L Roger A. 90
Deland, FSgt G. 292
Dennis, W/C R.R. 248, 249
Dent, Ron 163
Department of Fisheries and Marine 51, 52
Department of Indian Affairs 32
Department of Marine 91
Department of Mines and Technical Surveys 300
Department of Munitions and Supply 121
Department of National Defence 172
Department of Railways and Canals 50, 51, 52, 91
Department of the Interior 33, 36, 90
Department of Transport 91, 99, 188, 288, 291
DePew, Richard 126
Devon Island, NWT 286
Diamond, S/L Gordon G. 243, 248
Dickins, C.H. 304
Dipple, W/C W.E. 165
Distinguished Flying Cross 135, 137, 174, 176, 178, 191, 201, 223, 226-229, 237, 243, 252, 253, 265, 279, 280, 285, 310
Distinguished Service Cross 253
Doan, FSgt J.E. 262
Dobney, Thomas 144
Dobson, S/L R. 243
Dodds, Robert 30
Dominion Observatory 300
Dominion Skyways 122,
Donald, Col Tom B. 244
Doran, LAC E.G. 95
Dorval 305-309, 312, 313
Douglas, LAC W.N. 195
Douglas:
    Air Cruiser 286
    B-18 Digby 192, 197-200, 221, 247, 258
    Boston 313
    C-47 (Dakota) 260, 291, 306, 308, 309
    C-53 260
    C-54 260
    Dolphin 261
    R4D-1 260
Drake, J.F. 300
Drake, WO2 William R. 263
Draper, Don 163
Dreger, WO2 Frederick R. 217
DROs 284-286
Drynan, WO2 Gerald C. 223
Duchess of Richmond 151
Duke of Kent 128, 319
Duncan, Collin 292, 294
Duncan, F/L Robert B. 263
Duncan, F/O 146
Duncan, John R. 37

Dundas Harbour, NWT 41
Dundas, George S. 149
Dunlop Rubber 160
Dunlop, F/L C.R. 90
Dunn, David 196
Dunne, P/O 226
Dunning, Charles A. 51, 52
Dunning, Sgt William J.A. 266
Durnin, E.J. 21, 22
Durnin, H.M. 21
dusting 51, 61, 64

Eardley, AC1 J.T. 44
Earhart, Amelia 141
Earl of Athlone 233, 248, 274, 318
Early, F/L Allan A. 209
Easson, W/C James G. 243
Eastern Air Command 64, 183-226
Eastern Arctic Survey Detachment 128, 292-303
Eastern City 225
Eastern High School of Commerce 238
Eastern Provincial Airlines 22
Eckert, F/L Al 143
eclipse (1925) 32
Eden, Anthony 233
Edmonton 66, 122, 291
Edmonton Aero Club 125
Edmonton Technical Institute 125
Edwards, A/M Gus 269
Egypt 308
Eherlichman, F/L Rudolph I. 222
Eilson, Cal Ben 287
Elford, R.E. 108
Elkington, W/C J.F.D. 225
Ellesmere Island 39, 42, 286
Elliot, Don 242
Ellis, Frank 286
Ellson, F/O 239
Ellsworth, Lincoln 286
Else, Cpl C.F. 222
Elvin, Sgt 146
Emily Carr Institute of Art 203
Empire Air Training Plan 108, 125
Empire Lakeland 210
Empress of Japan 150,
Empress of Scotland 150
English Bay, BC 37
ERCO 121
Ercoupe 121
Eric Cove, Quebec 52, 53
Ericson, F.G. 13, 25
Eskimos 41, 42, 53, 54, 295
Essa, Ontario 29
Evans, George P. 288, 289, 306
Everett I. Brown Co. 323
Ex-Cell-O Corp. 323
Expo 86 165

F.E.2D 40
F/L I.M. Dowling, F/L I.M. 247
Fairburn, J.V. 108
Fairchild (Canada) 59, 97, 110, 245
Fairchild:
    24 321
    51 59, 92
    71 59, 73, 75, 88, 91, 92-95, 103, 183
    FC-2 series 4, 59, 60, 64, 65
    KR-34 97
    Cornell 112, 120, 170
Fairey:
    Battle 4, 109, 116, 119, 140, 143, 160, 166, 168, 193, 267

C.3 15, 16
    IIIF 80, 94
    Swordfish 262
Far Distant Ships 190
Farley, Lorne 238
Farnham, LAC N.R. 195
Farrell, S/L C.M.G. 237
Farrow, Wilford B. 267
Federal Aircraft 117, 152
Feldman, FSgt Leonard 22
Felixstowe F.3 10, 14, 15, 18, 33
Fenwick, F/O Harry E. 225, 226, 231
Ferguson, C.J. 152, 155
Ferguson, J.H. 47
Ferrier, G/C 121
Ferry Command 125, 143, 152, 200, 263, 265,
    266, 288-290, 304-311
Filer, Capt R.F. 283
Finbow, FSgt W.E. 179
Fink, Sgt 263
Finlayson, F/O 269
Firestone Tire and Rubber 250
First Air 38, 39
fisheries patrol 19
Fitzroy, F/L Arthur 266
Flanagan, Thomas E. 238
Flavin, P/O Norm 308
Fleet Air Arm 91, 230, 233
Fleet Aircraft Co. 88
Fleet:
    2 Fawn 124
    7 Fawn 61, 74, 90, 96, 119; 21 96
    Finch 109, 110, 126, 134, 168
    Fort 115, 162, 169, 269
Fleischman, LAC N.C. 222
Fleming, Sgt Arthur 47, 97
Fletcher FBT-2 121
Fletcher, Wendell F. 121
Florence, S/L David S. 243
Fokker:
    D.VII 29, 71
    Universal 49, 50-57
Folds, LAC 161
For the Fallen 174
Forbes, P/O 226
Ford Trimotor 63
forestry 49, 51, 59, 95
Forestry Island, Manitoba 34
Forst, LAC John N. 134
Fort Churchill, Manitoba 49
Fort Erie, Ontario 115, 170
Fort Fitzgerald, NWT 73
Fort McKenzie, Quebec 293-295
Fort Simpson, NWT 320
Fortey, LAC J.E. 84, 95
Foss G/C Roy H. 161, 162
Foster, W/C 226
Fowler, Sgt 229
Fowler, Walter W. 84
France 113, 116
Francis, FSgt L. 168
Francis, P/O G.R. 190
Fraser, Sgt T.P. 174
Freeman, LAC H. 195
friendly fire 137
Frigerio, Sgt Francis C. 172
Frobisher Bay, NWT 288, 293
Frostad, F/O G.O. 229
Fruehauf Trailer Co. 250
Fry, Eric 34
Fry, Mr. 294, 295
Frymark, AC2 E.A. 196

Fullerton, G/C Elmer G. 85
Fumerton, S/L R.C. 227
Fyfe, Chick 142

Galbraith, Capt Murray B. 23
Galloway, LAC Nelson 146, 147
Galt Aircraft School 166, 167
Gananoque, Ontario 129
Gander Lake 310
Gander, Newfoundland 220, 305
Garand, Lt G. 224
Garratt, F/L Frederick J.S. 178, 179
Garvin, P/O Robert J. 179
Gaspé, Quebec 76
Gault, P/O P.H. 243, 244
Gauthier, Capt P.E. 224
Gear, Cpl W. 84
Gelinas, LAC Tony 292, 294, 299
Gelineau, LAC John E. 179
General Aeronautics Corp 121
George Cross 175, 178
George Medal 222
Gerhard, F/L 269
Gibb, FSgt 91
Gibb, S/L D.S. 282
Gibbs, P/O William R. 230
Gibraltar 315-318
Gibson, LAC 139
Gibson, W/C Guy 239
Gieg, F/O 163
Gifford, Allan W. 270
Gilbertson, S/L Paul A. 232
Gildner, P/O 226
Gilfillan, Sgt J.J. 192
Gillen, Norm 238
Gillespie, Sgt George 94
Gillies, F/O Jim 240
Gillis, F/O Francis D. 266
Gilmartin, P/O John 222
Gilmour, P/O M.J. 265
Gimli, Manitoba 275
Gislason, FSgt Magnus A. 217
Glen, Maj J.A. 15
Gloeckner, M. 247
Glover, F/L B.M. 292, 294
Glynn, B.C.C. 21
Gobeil, F/O Fowler M. 71, 83
Godfrey, S/L A.E. 31, 44, 45, 49, 64, 75, 77,
    97, 230, 279
Gold Belt Air Service 296
Goodson, F/O 226
Goodwin, Edward 32
Goodyear blimps 71
Gordon, A/C R.C. 197, 280
Gordon, F/O 193
Gordon, W/C Lindsay 50, 64, 277
Goring, Eric 239
Gosling, LAC William P. 168
Goudie, Joe 265
Governor General, Earl of Athlone 233, 248,
    274, 318
Graham, P/O 226
Graham, WO2 Martin 64, 84
Grand Rapids, Manitoba 95
Grande Prairie, Alberta 60
Grandy, Capt Roy S. 31, 32, 65, 84, 90, 103,
    177, 234, 277, 279
Grant, Colin 242
Grant, Frank G. 253
Grant, P/O 230
Gravell, LAC Karl M. 175
Gray, G/C A. 108

Gray, P/O 226
Great Depression 78
Greater Rockford 287
Green, Dr. J.J. 65
Green, F/L Fred 176
Green, LAC 139
Greenland 38, 287, 289, 290
Gregory, WO 234
Grenfell Mission 304
Grey, F/L Colin 227
Grieve, F/O 241
Griff, P/O Milton E. 223
Griffin, F/O David 265
Griffin, Fred G. 32
Griffin, John 14, 166, 183, 246
Groensteen, Sgt Claude V. 174
Ground Instruction School 21, 31
Grumman:
    Avenger 233
    Goblin 184
    Goose 103, 234, 243-245, 264, 320
    Widgeon 261
Guigan, J. 84
Gunn, Sgt John C. 263
Guthrie, A/C K.M 247
Guthrie, LAC Robert H. 172

Habasinski, John 151
Hadley, Michael L. 191
Haire, Bill 238
Hale, Ed 126, 127
Halifax *Morning Chronicle* 24
Hall, P/O R.D. 264, 265
Hall, Ted 127
Hallatt, F/O H.M. 193
Halliday, Hugh A. 14, 15, 208, 225
Hamilton Aero Club 127
Hamilton, John G. 22
Hamilton, Lt J.G. 25
Hamilton, Ontario 96, 126-128
Hammell, LAC L.P. 229
Hanchett-Taylor, G/C 265
Hand, Sgt John 94
Handley Page:
    Halifax 167
    Hampden 119, 245, 263, 290
    Harrow 201
Hanna, F/O W.F. 83
Harding, G/C D.A. 25, 30, 32, 71, 178
Harding, George 24
Harkness, LAC 161
Harland, F/L Garnet R. 265
Harris, W/C J.S. 283
Harrison, F/O John L. 217
Harrison, LAC 161
Hart, WO2 226
Hartley, Sgt John 142
Hartwick, Fred 51
Hartwig, Capt Paul 191
Harvey, G/C J.B. 175, 176
Hassell, R.J. 287
Hastie, F/L J.R. 230
Hatch, Fred J. 108, 180
Havill, P/O 226
Havre-Saint-Pierre 76
Hawke, Sgt R.V. 292, 294
Hawker:
    Audax 80
    Fury 84, 85
    Hart 81, 272, 273
    Hurricane 95, 103, 104, 119, 148, 211,
    225-233, 272

Osprey 81
  Sea Hurricane 192, 225
  Tomtit 82
  Typhoon 228
Hawkins, P/O Herb 241, 242
Hawman, R.A. 104
Hawtrey, R. Court 47, 71
Hayes Fiord, NWT 287
Hayes, Bob 222
Hazel Blackwood 304
Hazeldine, Eric 242
Headingly, Manitoba 142
Heakes, G/C Francis V. 165
Hearst, Ontario 170
Heath Parasol 125, 151
Heeney, A.D.P. 108
Henderson, Lialla 317
Henning, F/O J.L. 97
Hergott, P/O 161
Herman, FSgt Donald L. 224
Heslop ("Hislop"), F/L Hubert W. 68
Hewson, F/L Henry W. 71
Hewson. Jimmy 316
Hickey, LAC 229
Hicks, LAC Herbert F. 266
Hillcoat, F/O Horace B. 318
Hiltz, F/O 124
Hiroshima 280
Hitchins, F.H. 14, 18, 36, 45, 74, 95
HMCS: *Charlottetown* 191, *Esquimalt* 210,
  Raccoon 191
HMS: *Apollo* 81, *Arbiter* 245, *Queen* 245,
  Ruler 245, *Veteran* 190, *Vidette* 203
Hobbs, S/L Basil D. 13, 33, 36, 43, 279
Hobbs, W.H. 99
Hobson, Sgt G.L. 84
Hoggard, LAC Lester E. 222
Holden, John 112
Holland, S/L Hubert L. 18, 24, 35-37
Hollinger Gold Mines 212
Hollinger Ungava Transport 220
Hollinghurst, G/C L.N. 108
Holman, S/L Don 269, 273
Holt, Sgt 239
Home War Establishment 105, 182-321
Home-Hay, Capt J.B. 18
Hone, S/L Jack 292, 293, 303
Hood, F/O Leon A. 168
Hoodspith, F/L R.H. 188
Hook, F/L John T. 223
Hooper, F/O John D. 203
Hope, Bob 255
Horne, F/O 197
Hornell, F/L David E. 212, 213, 217, 218
Horner, A.J. 50
Horner, FSgt 95
Hornick, AC1 J.W. 262
Hotson, Fred 125, 126, 151, 152, 155
Houle, F/L A.U. "Bert" 228
Houser, P/O J.H. 191
Howard Aircraft Corp 121
Howard Super Ventura 250
Howard, Dee 250
Howard, F.R. 108
Howe, Hon C.D. 99, 108, 287, 304
Howell, F/L J. 303, 304
Howsam, F/O George R. 25, 51, 71, 176
HRH Princess Alice 151, 233, 248
HRH Queen Elizabeth 302
Huck's Starter 66
Hudson Bay Railway 48, 49, 64
Hudson Strait Expedition 50-57

Hudson, Ontario 100
Hudson, P/O Donald L. 190
Hudson's Bay Co. 38, 42, 239, 267, 293, 303, 304
Huggard, F/L J.C. 83
Hughes, Gord 93
Hughes, LAC L.J. 292
Humble Oil and Refining Co. 319
Humphries, Capt Jack 242
Hunt, AC2 C.W. 136
Hunt, FSgt Lyndon A. 203
Hunter, Sgt J.D. 76, 99
Hurley, Charles 159
Hurley, LAC Andrew J. 263
Hutchinson, Bertrand 202
Hutchinson, LAC J.E.J. 195
Hutchinson, W.J. 238

Ibbotson, Sgt Wallace L. 222
Iceland 212-218, 310
Imperial Airways 188
Imperial Conference 76
Imperial Defence College 90
Imperial Gift 10, 14, 15, 58, 95
Imperial Munitions Board 13, 107
Imrie, S/L A.A.T. 265
Ingram, W/C G.L. 178
Ingrams, P/O 199
Institute of Technology 302
International Commission on Aerial
  Navigation 13
International Paper Co. 269
Isaacs, F/O George D. 263
Ison, LAC 161
Italia 287
Ivens, P/O Herb 222, 253
Ivey, Ernie 145

Jackson, LAC C. 106
Jacobi, George 20, 47
Jacobs engine 117, 118, 162, 285
Jagger, Sgt A.G. 264
James, FSgt Norman T. 161
James, Jim 235
Jamison, S/L W.E. 175
Jarred, F/L Arthur 260
Jarvis, A.E. 84
Jarvis, A.T. "Tony" 211, 248
Jeffrey, FSgt J.F. 283
Jennings, Cpl 269
Jenssen, Capt Joachim 214
Jericho Beach and the West Coast Flying Boat
  Squadrons 236
Jewitt, F/O 128
John C. Webster Memorial Trophy 83
Johns, WO1 A.C. 265
Johnson, A/C George O. 15, 194, 196
Johnson, P/O J.S 192
Johnson, P/O Wally 308
Johnson, W/C J.E. 226
Johnstone, P/O R.A. 229
Jolly, LAC Raymond 146
Jones, F/L Douglas J. 224
Jones, J.M. 149
Jones, LAC K.A. 195
Jones, P/O R. 188
Jones, W/C George 108
Jordan, G/C R.B. 279
Jowsey, F/L M.E. 226, 226
Joy, Col Douglas 14, 121
Joy, E. Graham 23
Junkers Ju.52 100
Juptner, Joseph P. 89

Kaiser, A.J. 247
Kananaskis Ranges 33
Kapuskasing, Ontario 275
Kay, Bill 238
Kearney, W.J. 121
Keating, Claude 94
Keating, P/O 226
Keewatin Lumber Co. 17
Kehoe, AC2 B.B. 84
Keillor, S/L H.G. 138
Kellond, LAC 139
Kellway, C.V. 108
Kelman, F/O 226
Kennedy, Marlow 95
Kennedy, W/C W.E. 125, 194
Kenny, A/V/M Walter R. 11, 36
Kenora, Ontario 168
Kenyon, F/L A.G. 197
Ker, Edgar A. 226, 227
Kermode, W/C 123
Kervin, FSgt John J. 234
Ketchikan, Alaska 255
Keystone Puffer 51, 61, 64
Kimball, George F. 20, 47, 64, 98
Kimmurut, Nunavut 41
King, F/L Fred 267, 269
King, P/O 226
King, Prime Minister Mackenzie 9, 107, 108,
  160, 197, 233, 287, 304
King's Regulations 284
Kingston Flying Club 152
Kingston, Nova Scotia 174
Kinner engine 121
Kirk, WO2 Norman E. 168
Kitchener-Waterloo Flying Club 124
Knapman, LAC T.S. 106
Knelson, Cpl Harry 203
Knewstub, F/L Ron 138, 176
Knights of Columbus fire 222
Knowles, R.E. 21
Knox, M. 192, 193
Kobierski, F/L Mike 138
Konick, FSgt M.L. 302
Kontzie, Cpl F.J. 292, 294
Konvalinka, Charlie 242
Kostenuk, Sam 183, 246
Krasin 287
Kyle, FSgt Wilton H. 313

Labrador 188
Lac du Bonnet, Manitoba 64, 74, 95
Laflamme, LAC J.G.E. 188
Lake Harbour, NWT/Nunavut 41, 293, 295, 298
Lake Nipigon 271
Lake-of-the-Woods Cemetery 168
Lamb Airways 296
Lamont, F/L Don 139, 176
Langan, Sgt J.F. 188
Langlais, George 234
Langley, AC1 Frederick A. 222
Lank, Ray 165
Lapointe, Ernest 108
Larch 52
Larock, Cpl W.J. 84
Latham Island, NWT 101
Latham, F/O Frank W. 217
Latta, P/O 308
Laut, F/O Ross K. 264
Laut, W/C Albin 198, 263
Lauzon, Ozzi 159
Lawrence, F/L T.A. 50-54
Lawrence, F/O Francis W. 213, 217

Lawrence, H. 25
Lawrence, LAC James A. 222
Lay, F/O Peter C.E. 263
Laycock, P/O Joseph F. 112
Laydon, LAC J.D. 195
Le Grave, Sgt G.L. 51
Le Royer, Capt Joseph A. 23
Leach, S/L 47
Leaside, Toronto 50, 71, 72, 86, 138
Leatherdale, FSgt Harry 214-217
Leavens Brothers Air Services 127
Leavens, Walt 127
Leblanc, F/L Joseph H.U. 222
Leckie, LCol Robert 15, 44, 107, 109, 129, 243,
    247, 276, 277, 283
Ledbetter, Joe 300
Lee, LAC Herbert J. 173
Lee, S/L Richard L. 191, 223
Lee, WO2 Wilbur M. 223
Legge, David 218
Legris, LAC Joseph A.I.R. 222
Leigh, P/O J. 192, 199
Leigh, W/C Z.L. 128, 196, 239, 278, 311, 315
Leishman, Dave 238
Leishman, P/O 146
Leitch, F/L A.A. 17, 51, 53, 54, 177
Leitch, Hal 292, 293, 295
LeMarre, Cpl F.N. 191
Lend-Lease 291
Lepine, AC1 Joseph G.A. 222
Leppan, George 163
Lett, LAC K.C. 9
Lew Parmenter, Lew 99
Lewis, S/L A. 51, 53, 122
Liberty engine 10
Lilleyman, P/O 226
Link Trainer 8, 98, 120, 122, 126, 129, 134
Link, E.A. 120, 129
Linnell, LAC L.M. 195
Lister, G/C 248
Little, F/L R.H. 83
Littlejohn, WO W. Spence 264
Lloyd, Leland C. 313
Lloyd, S/L 144
Loch Don 306
Lockheed:
    10 99, 100
    12 99, 141, 319
    212 141
    18 Lodestar 246, 261, 292
    Hudson 189-191, 198, 206, 207, 221, 223,
        233-235, 245, 259, 263, 266, 288, 320
    P-38 257, 313, 314
    PV-1 Ventura 210, 211, 223, 247, 248-250,
        259, 264, 265, 269-272, 304, 307
Lockyer, A/V/M C.E.W. 275
Loening Amphibian 287
Logan, S/L R.A. 21, 31, 38-42, 52, 103, 286
Long Branch, Ontario 251
Long, C. Don 50, 85
Longley, Ernest G. 313
Longueuil, Quebec 59, 110
Lord Beaverbrook 304, 306
Lord Riverdale 107, 108
Lothian, George 318
Louden, W/C Tom 273
Lougheed, Sgt N.N. 195
Love, R. 193
Love, Robert C. 22
Lowry, S/L Romney H. 239
Luke, G/C 245
Lummis, FSgt Floyd B. 175

Lundberg, Sten 222
Lundgren, Fred 262
Lundy, P/O R.B. 266
Lunny, Sgt K.U. 191
Lussier, F/O Kenneth E. 161
Lycoming engine 120
Lyon, Sgt George F.W. 222

MacArthur, F/O James G. 266
MacBride, G/C Robert E. 213, 214, 217
MacBrien, James H. 94
MacCallum, F/O 134
MacCullough, WO 264
MacDonald, Cpl William F. 285
MacDonald, F/O 222
MacDonald, P/O Bob 231, 232
MacDonald, P/O D.F. 44
MacDonald, Sandy 71, 165
MacDonald, WO C.B. 264
MacDonald, WO1 Joseph N. 217
MacDougall F/L Donald C. 262
Mace, F/L Roger 274
MacFadyen, F/L Don 153
MacKell, Sgt D.E. 84
Mackenzie Air Service 99, 101, 116, 125,
    244, 292
Mackenzie, Hon I. 108
MacKenzie, S/L John G. 221
MacLachlan, P/O Robert B. 189
MacLaren, Maj Donald R. 15, 99
MacLaren, Sgt W.J.D. 106
MacLaurin, C.C. 13, 18, 36, 37
Maclean, F/O D.B. 229
MacLean, F/O G.A. 84
MacLeod, F/O 247
MacLeod, S/L E.L. 36, 94
MacMillan Expedition 287
Macpherson, F/L 96
Madden, Sgt Humphrey 94
Magnus, AC1 R.C. 262
Main, W/C 245
Mair, S/L R.C. 47, 262
Malkin, Sir William 265, 266
Malta 300
Mangan, FSgt J.T. 190
Manitoba Government Air Service 75
Mannett, F/O Clarence W. 223
Mantz, Paul 141
Maple, Ontario 164, 314
Marconi 163
Margetts, F/L V.A. 243
Markham, Ontario 121
Marlatt, F/L Stafford 190, 228, 229
Marshall, F/O 217
Marshall, Sgt R. 50
Marshall, WO2 George C. 248-250
Martin, F/O 124
Martin, F/O R.B. 192
Martin, Murray 152, 159
Martin, P/O J.E.R. 195
Martin, WO Lawrence G. 224
Martin:
    B-26 246, 307-309
    Baltimore 306-308
Martintown, Ontario 313
Mary River Mine, NWT 39
Matane Air Services 274
Matheson, F/O Sidney E. 213
Mathewson, P/P/O 47
Matthews, P/O T.G.C. 24
Mauretania 161
Mawdesley, Frederick J. 64, 65, 76, 94

Mawhinney, Stew 234
Maxwell, S/L W. Roy 65, 236
Maylor, AC1 244
Maynard, Capt L.F. 68
McBain, LAC 161
McBurney, W/C R.E. 121
McCall Aero Corp. 13
McCall, Fred R. 13
McCauley Cpl W.F. 84
McClelland, P/O 226
McClintock, Donald J. 134, 135
McClure, F/L John 226, 228, 229
McConachie, Grant 84, 95
McConnell, FSgt S. 25
McCoubrey, Jack 13
McCowan, J.R. 55
McCreight, John T. 144-151
McCreight, Victor 144, 150
McDonough, W.J. 269-273
McDougall, G/C T.K. 283
McElrea, LAC W.G. 195
McElwee, Sgt W. 106
McEwen, S/L Clifford M. 27, 37, 277, 279
McFarlane, LAC E.R. 153
McGill University 136
McGill, A/V/M F.S. 246
McGimsie, FSgt Bruce R. 224
McGowan, P/P/O 68
McGrandle, FSgt W.J. 84
McGrath, Muriel 168
McGregor, Gordon R. 83, 278
McGregor, P/O Jack A. 173
McGregor, S/L D.U. 90
McGuffin, F/O James G. 238-242
McGuire, Mr. 134
McHale, F/O Thomas P. 150
McHale, Mrs. 150
McIntosh, AC1 John 244
McIntosh, LAC J.W. 195
McIntosh, Wesley H. 124, 292, 315, 317
McIntyre, F/O Archibald B. 168
McIntyre, P/O James I. 168
McKay, WO1 163
McKee Trans-Canada Trophy 85
McKee, J. Dalzell 31, 49
McKenna, F/L Gerald P. 217
McKenzie, Daniel M. 135, 136
McKeown, Marg 151
McKinnon, H.S. ACpl 153
McLachlan, LCol K.S. 108
McLaren, Alistair Donald 143
McLaughlin, John 64
McLaughlin, S/L H.R. 267
McLean, F/L Gord 139
McLean, F/O 199
McLean, N.B. 52
McLean, Sgt D.P. 189
McLean, W/C John A. 274
McLeod, F/L Elmer 138, 176
McLeod, F/L H.W. 226
McLeod, LAC 84
McLurg, S/L John Ernest 136-138
McMahon, F/L Tom 236, 237
McMichael, LAC Edward K. 247
McNab, F/L Duncan S. 266
McNab, F/O Ernest A. 71, 83
McNally, AC2 John H. 168
McNally, LAC 161
McNamara Construction Co. 221
McNargh, Sgt V.F. 279
McNaughton, Andy 274
McNaughton, MGen A.G.L. 77, 78, 97, 274, 277

McNealy, FSgt J.W. 292
McNee, FSgt J.W. 185
McNulty, J.F. "Jack" 61
McRae, F/L W.R. 296, 299
McRae, F/O James M. 214-217
McTaggert-Cowan, Patrick 304
McVicar, Donald M. 288-290
Meaden, William H.D. 122, 126
Meagher, Cyril P. 306
Mears, LAC T.C. 195
Megantic, Quebec 77
Meicenheimer, Lt H. 12
Memorial Day 255
Merchant Ship Flying Unit 225
Merlin, Bob 300
Merredew, LAC C.R. 189
Michigan Tool 323
Middlemass, W.L. 108
Middleton, W/C R.B. 315
Milberry, Larry 138
Miller, F/L Frank R. 98
Milligan, H.F. 127
Millinocket, Maine 197
Millman, Dr. Peter M. 300
Mills, F/O 249
Milne, Cpl A.J. 43
Milne, P/O 226
Mirabelli, Boy Airman J.C. 84
Miscampbell, F/L "Rosie" 273
Miscou Island, New Brunswick 103
Mitchell, Jim 238
Mitchell, Sgt Russell T. 263
Moffit, S/L Barry 203
Molson, K.M. 59
Molson, S/L Hartland deM. 280
Mont Joli, Quebec 191
Montcalm 55
Monthly Report of R.C.A.F. Operations
    North America 311, 312
Montreal Light Aeroplane/Flying Club 134, 161
Moon, Kris H. 125
Moose Jaw Flying Club 192, 193, 281
Moran, F/L C.C. 232
Morant, Nicholas 284
Morfee, F/O A.L. 24, 32, 279
Morgan, FSgt R. 292
Morrison, Claude W. 20, 47
Morrow, Rev. 65
Morton, F/O Stuart W. Morton 223
Mosser, P/O Andrew J. 281
Mosser, P/O Robert W. 281
Mott, P/O Guy 222
Mouncey, Steve 319
Mount Allison University 300
Mountbatten, Lord Louis 306
Mullin, LAC R.J. 195
Mulock, Col. R.H. 11, 17
Mundy, BGen George W. 280
Murdock, F/O Les 241
Murray, AC2 Stuart C. 222
Murray, Don 126, 151, 152, 155
Murray, F/O Leo J. 224
museums: Atlantic Canada Aviation Museum
    235, Canadian Warplane Heritage
    (Hamilton) 115, 218, 274, National Aviation
    Museum (Ottawa) 262, National Naval
    Aviation Museum (Pensacola) 261, North
    Atlantic Aviation Museum (Gander) 220,
    Reynolds Alberta Museum (Wetaskiwin,
    Alberta) 171, Western Canada Aviation
    Museum (Winnipeg) 88
Myers trainer 121

Nagasaki 280
Nagorski, Lt Jan 286, 287
Nairn, A/C K.G. 269
Nakina, Ontario 77
Nanton, F/O E.A. 102
Napier, S/L W.F. 229, 232
Narroway, M. 299
Nascopie 243
Nassau 308, 309, 314
National Aviation Museum 262
National Cenotaph 281
National Defence Act 32
National Defence College 80, 302
National Naval Aviation Museum
    (Pensacola) 261
National Research Council 65, 80, 269-272
National Steel Car 6, 97, 116, 245
Neal, George 85, 118, 126, 151-159
Nelson, P/O 162
Nelson, Sgt 226
Nelson, Sgt Dana A. 175
Neptune 38
Nesbitt, AC1 James E. 189
Nesbitt, W/C A.D. 252
Newell, P/O 226
Newman, Sgt George S.B. 313
Nicholson, FSgt James A. 175
Nobile, Umberto 287
Nolan, FSgt Walter F. 224
Nolet, Cpl C.H. 84
Noorduyn Norseman 99, 101, 103, 125, 163,
    171, 234, 244, 292-300, 321
Noorduyn, Robert 49
NORAD 302
Norris, F/O E.M. 292
Norris, S/L 222
North American:
    B-25 157, 200, 243, 259, 306, 307
    F-10 259
    Harvard 105, 109, 112-115, 119, 120, 140,
    168, 170, 171, 173, 181, 193, 230, 231, 234,
    235, 320
    Yale 113, 114, 140, 168, 172, 193, 194
North Atlantic Aviation Museum 220
North Atlantic Cat 290
Northcott, F/O 308
Northern Aerial Mineral Exploration 267, 273
Northern Alberta Aero Club 290
Northern Secondary School 143
Northrop Delta 89, 91, 95, 97, 101, 166, 184,
    185, 204, 262, 263, 279, Nomad 116, 168
Northumberland Air Observer School 152
Northwest Aero Marine 193
Northwest Air Command 291, 291
Northwest Staging Route 257, 291, 292, 312, 323
Norway House, Manitoba 34
Nottingham Island, NWT 52, 53, 55
NPAAF 83, 84, 90, 96, 102, 103
numbering/registration systems 15, 47
NWAC 291, 292

O'Brien-Saint, F/O 27
O'Connell, F/L Lawrence J. 174
O'Connor, AC2 Francis L. 179
O'Connor, Sgt 91
O'Grady, A/F/O Augustine 286
O'Hare Airport 260
O'Donnell, Frederick P. 263
Oakford, F/L Edward P. 217
Oaks, H.A. "Doc" 270, 273
Ocean Bridge 289, 304, 306
Ogilvie, F/L Noel A. 226, 227

OK Service fleet 303
Okanagan Helicopters 176
Olmstead, F/O 143
Olsen, Capt Adolf 262
Olsen, P/O J.C. 189
Olsen, S/L C.L. 302
Omand, F/O 226
Ontario Provincial Air Service 65, 236, 267, 274
Op. Hawk 302
Order of the British Empire 161, 178, 202
Orendorff, Orv L. 163
Orient Bay 270, 271
Orillia, Ontario 4
Orly Airport 218
Ormston, F/L Ian 227
Orr, LAC J.D. 195
Ottawa 85, 122
Ottawa Car Co. 69
Ottawa Flying Club 68
Ouellet, LAC Joseph F.R.A. 222
Ouellette, FSgt Joseph E. 223
Our Lady of Victory Cemetery 172
Owen, E.R. 18, 24, 35

Padden, P/O 199
Pafford, F/L Frederick G. 125
Pan American Airways 246, 261, 310
Pangnirtung, NWT 243, 295
parachuting 46, 47, 104
Parham, Mr. 143
Paris Peace Conference 19
Parker, Capt A.E. "King" 313
Parkinson, P/O H.W. 137
Parry Sound, Ontario 220,
Parsons, F/O Lamont 222
Pateman, Maurice 155
Paton, Cpl 269
Patterson and Hill 122
Patterson, F/L A. 134
Patterson, LAC R.F. 195
Patterson, P/O John Richard 161
Pattinson, Harry 127, 222
Paul Presidente, Paul 214-217
Pawson, F/O Hugh D. 223
Payne, F/L 226
Peace of Paris 90
Peace River Airways 55
Pearce, Sgt W.M. 84
Pearce, W/C Francis Henry 122, 123
Pearson, F/L P.P. 138
Pembina, North Dakota 189
Pendergast, P/O A.L. 194
Pepper, F/L 244
Percival, F/O Lloyd S. 112
Permission Granted 124, 314
Perrin, F/L Ross 176
Perry, WO1 Leonard H. 179
Peterborough, Ontario 94, 114
Peters, F.H. 90
Peterson, George F. 238
Pettam, F/O 221
Pettigrew, F/L Thomas J. 217
Phillips Petroleum 320
Phillips, AC2 W.F. 262
Pickup, Capt 308
Pietenpol Air Camper 145
pigeons 44
Pinkerton, Bill 20, 47
Piper Cub 126, 127, 265
Plant, F/L J. 96
Plewes, F/L Harry 139
Poag, S/L William F. 213

Pollux 262
Pomes, AC1 S.J. 262
Pond Inlet, NWT 38-42, 286
Poole, F/O Joseph B. 224
Pooler, P/P/O G.D. 65
Port Arthur, Ontario 269-272
Port Burwell, Quebec 52-55
Porter, F/O C.H. 95
Potter, F/O George 315
Powell, A/C G.J. 289, 304
Power, C.G. 278, 304
Prairie Airways 193
Pratt & Whitney engines 59, 65, 113, 117, 270, 275, 285
Preston, F/L George de Long 244, 245, 275
Pretty, F/L W.P.G. 95
Prince Albert, Saskatchewan 299
Prince Bernhardt 274
Prince Rupert, BC 211
Proctor, Irwin 13
Provisional Pilot Officer 21
Pudney, F/O 28
Putnam, George P. 295

Quebec Airways 320
Quebec City 160, 233, 234
Queen Charlotte Airlines 236, 241, 242
Queen's University 279
Quiet Birdmen 126
Quigley, Capt H.S. 103

R&D 64, 65, 80, 81, 96, 102, 103, 267-276
Rabbit River, Saskatchewan 44
Rabnett, WO1 A.A. 90
Radio College of Canada 307
Ralston, Hon J.L. 108, 194, 278
Ramm, Dr. Peter 319
Ranger engine 120
Rankin, Cpl E.A. 292, 294
Rankine, F/O J.R. 212
Rasmussen, Knud 38
Rassel, F/O Van 316
Rawson, LAC C.A. 195)
Raymes, F/O Daniel F. 192-202, 281, 315-318
Raymes, Georgina 318
Raymes, Lialla 262, 316, 318
Raymes, Mrs. H.L. 202
Raymond, LAC Gerald R. 263
Raymond, LAC Lloyd 243
Raynor, P/O 226
RCAF exercises: Eskimo 299, Muskox 300
RCAF marine vessels: *B.160* (*Takuli*) 241, 264, *M.205* (*Sekani*) 241, *M.266* (*Teal*) 241, *M.427* (*B.C. Star*) 241, *M.12* 263, *M.200* 263, *M.361* 303
RCAF Squadrons and Aircraft 183, 246, 315
RCMP 38, 39, 42, 53, 76, 80, 94, 98, 229
Ready, FSgt J.M. 95
Rearwin 127
Red Deer, Alberta 218
Red Lake, Ontario 100
Redpath, Col R.F. 14
Reed, F/O John T. 285-286
Reed, P/O J.T. 194
Reed, WO2 Frank K. 214-217
Reeves, P/O 230
Regimbal, LAC A.M. 195
Regina, Saskatchewan 65, 90
registration/numbering systems 15, 47
Reindeer Lake Expedition 43
Rennie, LAC D.A. 262
Revill, F/O Jack R. 266
Reykjavik, Iceland 212-218, 304, 317

Reyno, S/L E.M. 211
Reynolds Alberta Museum 171
Reynolds, F/O A.E. 64
RFC (Canada) Air Stations: Camp Borden 12-19, 58, 59 Camp Leaside 12
Richards, Sgt A. 65
Richardson P/O William R.G. 223
Richardson, James A. 99
Richmond Hill, Ontario 24
Rickaby, Joan 235
Riddell, F/L W.I 71, 72
Riddell, G/C William I. 165
Riel, P/O 226
Riley, LAC William D. 263
Rimouski, Quebec 76
Ripley, A/V/M R.C. 243
Ritzel, F/O 292
Riverdale Collegiate 160
Roadhouse, F/O 308
Robb, G/C J.M. 108
Roberge, Sgt H. 84
Roberts, F/O Dennis E. 143
Roberts, F/O N.M. 243
Roberts, FSgt J.E. 217
Roberts, Sgt V.S. 84
Robertson, J. Ross 238
Robertson, S/L Ross 265
Robinson, F/O Edward L. 191, 223
Robinson, F/O James 175
Robinson, FSgt Lewis G. 222
Robson, Charlie 127
Rogers, Don 127
Rogers, Norman M. 108, 189
Rogers, Sgt D.P. 190
Rolfe, FSgt Robert C. 223
Rolls-Royce: Eagle 10, 14, 18, Kestrel 80, Napier 80
Rood, J.L. 84, 318
Rood, Lindy 200, 201
Roosevelt, President Franklin D. 180, 197, 233
Rose, F/O R.K. 84
Ross, A.D. 32
Rosson, F/L 150
Rothesay, New Brunswick 31
Rothwell, Cpl G.P.A. 84
Rowley, F/O M.W. 229
Roy, Douglas 292
Roy, P/O J.B.N. 229
Royal Air Force other units: 1 ADF 137; 1 PRU 135; 1 Radio School 143; 2 FIS 144; 3 (P) AFU 143; 4 EFTS 142; 5 FIS 142; 6 (P) AFU 142; 8 (O) AFU 150; 9 (O) AFU 163, 11 (P) AFU; 13 OTU 136; 17 AFU 300; 20 (P) OTU 144; 22 OTU 150, 279; 28 EFTS 142; 45 Group 305; 52 OTU; 56 OTU; 60 OTU 143; 82 OTU 161, 179, 286; 131 OTU 238; 151 Recovery Unit 283; 1655 Mosquito Training Unit 142; Armament School 90; Central Depository 282, Central Flying School 84, 165; Empire Central Flying School 123, 125, 177; Empire Flying School 137; Empire Test Pilots School 176; Flying Training Command 275; Foreign Aircraft Flight 176; Imperial Defence College 278; Marine Experimental Establishment 285; Missing Research and Enquiry Service 283; PR OTU 300; Staff College 84, 277
Royal Air Force squadrons: *12* 161; *47* 179, 238; *53* 313; *72* 130; *77* 300; *81* 226; *86* 214; *92* 227; *103* 161; *107* 136; *112* 228; *128* 142; *138* 150; *144* 263; *145* 227; *190* 282; *231* 310; *207* 310; *234* 227; *261* 253; *512* 178; *543* 300; *550* 238; *603* 226; *682* 135;

683 300
Royal Air Force stations: Benson 135, Brough 142, Cranwell 143, High Ercall 143, Kidlington 144, 274, Rednal 286, Little Rissington 142, Montrose 144, Northolt 306, Prestwick 306, 311, 315-318, Wittering 165
Royal Australian Air Force 106, 107, 174, 179, 180
Royal Canadian Air Force at War 1939-1945 212, 247
Royal Canadian Air Force other units: 1 Air Armament Training Unit 230, 231; 1 (Comm) Flight 234, 235, 264; 1 (Composite) Squadron 234, 235, 264; 1 Technical Training School 90, 166, 251; 3 (Comp) Flight 246; 3 PRC (Bournemouth) 135, 142, 150, 161, 163; 4 PRC 242; 6 (Comm) Flight 291, 292; 7 RDF 245; 9 Transport Group 243, 311; 123 (S&R) Flight 245; 1659 HCU 150, 163; 1679 HCU 280; Aeronautical Engineering Division 65, 90; Air Armament School 178, Casualty Office (Ottawa) 282, 283; Casualty Liaison Office (London) 283; Eastern Air Command 101; Eastern Arctic Survey Detachment 128, 292-303; Estates Officer 283; Experimental and Proving Establishment 300; Overseas HQ 278, 283, Test and Development Flight 101, 236, 267-276, 320; West Coast Marine Section 241; Winter Experimental and Training Flight 275, Women's Division 8, 151
Royal Canadian Air Force squadrons: *1* 91, 98, 161, 183, 184, 226, 227, 280; *2* 91, 96, 98, 101, 104, 177, 184; *3* 88, 96, 98; *4* 95, 98, 101, 103, 185-188, 205, 236, 237, 239-242, 267; *5* 84, 98, 187, 190, 206, 221, 223, 224, 262, 267, 279; *6* 91, 95, 98, 101, 103, 186, 205, 236, 243; *7* 95, 98, 101, 102, 186, 243, 249; *8* 95, 98, 184, 204, 248, 262, 263, 279; *9* 237, 243; *10* 76, 84, 88, 184, 188, 192-202, 212, 221, 224, 265, 266, 267, 277, 279; *11* 76, 83, 102, 178, 191, 206, 221-223, 281; *12* 76, 83, 319, 320; *13* 185, 186, 189, 196, 239, 262-264, 299, 300; *14* 227, 246; *110* 183; *111* 83, 96, 103, 186, 224, 227; *112* 102, 183; *113* 190, 191, 221, 224, 263; *115* 4, 109, 161, 210, 247; *116* 203, 266; *117* 208, 237; *118* 69, 70, 184, 186, 225, 227, 251-261, 280; *119* 90, 96, 102; *120* 90, 184; *122* 186, 243-245, 247; *123* 227; *124* 292; *125* 221-223, 227; *126* 148, 225; 128 221, 227; *128* 227, 229, 230; *129* 227, 232-234; *130* 227; *132* 227, 248; *133* 227; *135* 211, 227, 247, 249; *145* 176, 191, 210, 222-224; *147* 207; *149* 211, 248-250, 264, 265; *160* 207, 221; *161* 200; *162* 212-220, 224, 304; *163* 227; *164* 299, 316; *165* 292, 318; *167* 200; *168* 125, 201, 311, 312, 315-318; *401* 162, 226, 227, 299; *402* 238; *403* 177, 227; *405* 300; *407* 174; *408* 161; *411* 227; *412* 302; *413* 280. 415 263; *416* 177, 230; *418* 143, 232; *419* 214; *422* 178, 285; *424* 279; *425* 191; *426* 302; *427* 161, 178, 285; *428* 176; *429* 280; *431* 238; *432* 280; *433* 163; *437* 178, 285; *438* 252; *440* 230, 281; *442* 227; *443* 226
Royal Canadian Air Force stations (also see BCATP entries): Alliford Bay 8, 243, Bagotville 225-229, Bella Bella 237, 241, 243, 266, Camp Borden 4, 50, 57, 61, 64-67, 69-71, 74, 75, 80, 84, 86, 90, 92, 94, 96, 103, 104, 113, 124, 125, 165, 177, 188, 193-196, 275, 277, 278, Claresholm 9, Comox 264, Cormorant Lake 48, 49, 60, 65, 73, 75, 95, Dartmouth 75, 84, 223, 225, 232, Debert 278,

East Moor 280, Edmonton 218, Gander 161, 198-202, 232, 233, 305, Gimli 275, Goose Bay 288, 311, 314, Greenwood 220, High River 60, 64, 75, 103, Jericho Beach 89, 95, 97, 185, 186, Leeming 280, Mount Pleasant 234, 235, Namao 302; Norway House 49, Ottawa 75, 84, 90, Patricia Bay 3, 91, 189, 243, 247, 248, 263, 290, Port Hardy 246, 247, Rockcliffe 63, 64, 70, 81, 85, 88, 96, 101, 224, 243, 292, 299, 300, 302, 315-318, Sea Island 224, 236, 246, 248, 264, St. Thomas 167, 251, Skipton-on-Swale 163, 164, Suffield 123, Sydney/North Sydney 208, Terrace 211, 227, 249, 264, Tofino 207, 211, 239, 247, Topcliffe 150, 163, Torbay 210, 211, 221-224, 281, Toronto 76, Trenton 7, 63, 65, 70, 71, 77, 84, 88, 95-97, 122, 138, 165, 175, 218, 220, 278, Ucluelet 236-242, 264, Vancouver 50, 64, 74, 76, Victoria Beach 80, Vulcan 211, Winnipeg 64, 75, 76, Yarmouth 190, 191, 212, 304

Royal Canadian Air Force: Honours, Decorations, Medal 1920-1968 175
Royal Canadian Naval Air Service 11
Royal Flying Corps (Canada) 107
Royal Military College 24, 276, 277, 279, 280
Royal Naval Air Service 10, 18, 276
Royal Navy 225
Royal New Zealand Air Force 106-108, 174
Royal Norwegian Air Force 116, 296
Royal Regiment of Canada 144
Royal Twenty Centers 77, 79
Royal Visit (1939) 103
Royce, LCol Ralph 85
Ruggles, Sgt Douglas B. 222
rum-running 76, 303
Rutherford, Ian 239
Rutland, F.J. 121
Ryan PT-22 121
Ryan, LAC G.F. 195
Ryan, Pappy 159

S.E.5a 11, 15-17, 21, 30
Sabellum Trading Co. 38
Sable Island, Nova Scotia 91, 209
Sad Sack (Canso) 208
Saint John, New Brunswick 307
Salter, Larry 264
Sanderson, F/L Steve 138
San Francisco 323
Saskatchewan Government Air Service 171
Saskatoon *Star Phoenix* 202
Saunders, AC1 L.G. 84
Saunders, Donald W. 99
Saunders, G/C Hugh W.L. 108
Saunders, J.F. 23
Saunders, Sgt L.C. 229
Sauvé, F/L Phil 234
Sawanda, AC1 Frank J. 222
Saywell, F/O 308
Schiller, Lt C.A.
School of Army Co-operation 104
Schwab, F/L Lloyd G. 227, 228
Schwartzkopff, Capt Volkmar 192
Schwerdfager, James E. 238
Scott, Charles W.A. 152
Scott, F/O Robert I. 313
Scott, G/C James S. 31, 45, 46, 277
Scott, G/C Stanley 50
Scott, Glenn 307-310
Scott, P/O 226
Scott, S/L Jack 243
Scott, Sgt Donald 213

Scott, WO2 160
Scrafton, Frederick 313
Scrimshaw, LAC Lloyd A. 179
Seaman, P/O Frank 292, 293
search and rescue/mercy flights 53-55, 65, 91, 234, 235, 240, 241, 243-245, 248-250, 264-267, 286, 287
Search, Find and Kill 190
Seath, LAC 161
Sekani (*M.205*) 241
Seldon, F/L George 239
Selfridge, Michigan 71, 72, 85
Semple, S/L Gordon C. 226, 227
Senkel, Capt Hans 191
Sergeant Shatterproof 284
Shannon, Ireland 260
Sharp, W/C F.R. 137
Shaw, AC1 H.F. 84
Shaw, Cpl R.J. 84
Shaw, D. Campbell 97
Sheard, George 159
Shearer, S/L A.B. 36, 93, 165
Shediac, New Brunswick 75, 93
Shelburne, Nova Scotia 190
Shelfoon, W/C A.J. 123
Sherman, F/O Larry 217
Shoreham-by-Sea 11
Short Skyvan 39
Showell, LAC Denis W.P.G. 173
Silberman, AC1 244
Silsby, Sgt W.O. 84
Silver Dart 164, 165
Simmons, Ernie 114
Simpson, LAC J.H. 195
Simpson, Louis 122
Sixty Years: The Royal Canadian Air Force and CF Air Command 1924-1984 73, 165
Skelton, Dr. O.D. 108
ski development 80, 81, 269-272
Skuce, F/O Dick 292, 293
Skudder, P/O 226
Slemon Lake, NWT 94
Slemon, A/M C.R. 21, 22, 276, 279
Slevar, LAC 161
Smale, LAC W.H. 174
Small, F/L Norville E. 183, 185, 188, 190, 212
Smalley, Larry 323
Smith, AC1 David Smith 266
Smith, AC1 Franklin H. 266
Smith, Albert J. 238
Smith, F/L B.G. 315
Smith, F/L E.G. 137
Smith, F/O E.M. 214
Smith, FSgt Shannon S.J.H. 267
Smith, Gordon 122
Smith, Ken 163
Smith, Ross 238
Smithers, BC 250
Smithers, John M. 313
Smyth, J.R. 108
Snell, Lt 223
Snow, F/O William F.C. 223
Snyder, A. 193
Snyder, F/L James C. 267
Sommerville, S/L Ian 176
Sopwith: Camel 27, Snipe 15, 16
Souder, Bob 299
Souris, Manitoba 145
Southampton Island, NWT 289
Spartan Air Services 211
Spence, WO Charles E, 203
Spooner, LAC Kenneth G. 175
Sproat, C. 238

Sproule, David L. 238
St. George's Cemetery 173
St. Hubert, Quebec 99
St. Jean, LAC 269
St. John's Newfoundland 210
St. John's Norway Cemetery 172-174
St. Laurent, Sgt Fernand 213
St. Michael's College 150
St. Michel Gestel, Holland 282-284
St. Thomas Vocational School 177
Stafford, F/O G.R. 24
Stanley 52
Stanley, F/O Paul G. 64
Stansfeld, F/L Noel K. 144
Stapleford, F/L Ernest B. 247
Staples, Gerald F. 214-217
Stapley, F/O W.H. 262
Starratt Airways 99, 100
Stearman 120
Stedman, W/C E.W. 13, 44, 50, 59, 73, 81, 108, 121, 267, 276
Stefanson, Vilhjalmur 290
Steinberg, P/O Hymie 217
Stevens, W.O. 21
Stevenson, A/V/M L.F. 247
Stevenson, F/L 231
Stevenson, P/O A.W.B. 24
Stewart, FSgt Thomas 179
Stewart, Maj J. Crossley
Stewart, Samuel G. 13
Stick, WO2 James R. 223
Stilwell, Walter 299, 300
Stinson Detroiter 287
Stowe, F/O Bill 252
Strategic Air Command 302
Street , C. 247
Stringer, F/L Keith 139
Strong, Clare 238
Stubbs, Ida 129
Stubbs, P/O Edward M. 129, 134
Studer, S/L H.R. 137
Studholme, Allan E. 253
Sturgeon AC2 Ralph R. 222
Sully, A/V/M J.A. 83, 229, 230
Summit Air 39
Sumner, Bill 127
Sunnucks, F/O S.R. 84
Supermarine:
    Spitfire 135, 137
    Stranraer 95, 97, 103, 105, 187, 205, 206, 236-238, 240, 242, 262-263, 267-269
Sverdrup, Otto 38
Swartz, Ken 319
Sweeney, WO2 R.G. 292
Swiffen, P/O D. 264
Sydney *Patrol* 263
Sydney, Nova Scotia 184, 185
Symington, H.J. 99

Tailyour, Keith 22, 24, 103
Takuli (*B160*) 241, 264
Talbot, Ted 152
Tarling, Bill 242
Taylor, Ernie 126
Taylor, F/L L.F.J. 96
Taylor, FSgt Harold F. 222
Taylorcraft 127
Teal (*M.266*) 241
Teal, P/O Gordon K. 231
Tedder, Air Commodore A.W. 107
Tennant, G/C E.C. 50, 178
Terry, FSgt N.C. 53
The Aerodrome of Democracy 108, 109, 180, 196

The Battle of the Atlantic 190
The Blackburn Shark 91
The Brave Young Wings 277
The Combines 145
The Consolidated Liberator and Boeing Fortress 315
The Creation of a National Air Force 190
The Pas, Manitoba 48, 289
The Roundel 284
The Royal Canadian Air Force at War 1939-1945 315
The Tumbling Sky 225, 226
They Shall Grow Not Old: A Book of Remembrance 174
Thomas Morse Scout 30
Thomas, F/L Bob 268
Thomas, F/O William E. 285
Thompson, Cpl L.S. 97
Thompson, F/O D.C. 263
Thompson, F/O W.H. 223
Thompson, LAC A.B. 126
Thompson, S/L J.A. 247
Thompson, WO J.E. 264, 265
Thomson, F/O John E. 267
Thomson, LAC J.H. 195)
Thursobank 306
Timberlake, MGen 280
Timmerman, G/C Nels 123, 144
Tingle, F/O Aubrey M. 190
Tingle, P/O Leicester J. 190
Tingle, S/L Cyril N. 190
Toner, Marg 160
Toronto Argonauts 25
Toronto Bay 63
Toronto *Daily Star* 12, 15, 17, 21, 22, 25, 32, 54, 138, 150, 168, 281, 284
Toronto *Evening Telegram* 22, 192
Toronto Flying Club 27, 72, 85, 126, 151
Toronto *Globe/Globe and Mail* 23, 24, 71, 73, 94, 129
Toronto Hunt Club 192
Toronto Island Airport 116, 189
Toronto Transit Commission 242
Torontow, F/O Cy 315
Tracy, Hal 238
Trans-Canada Air Lines 99, 137, 188, 196, 200, 318
Trans-Canada Air Pageant 68, 165
Trans-Canada Airway 77-79
Trans-Canada Flight 18
Transocean Airlines 260
Travers, F/O 269
Trecarten, F/L C.L. 95
Tremlitt, Rocky 142
Trenton, Ontario 173
Trethewey, Frank 83
Trim, George K. 25
Tripp, L.J. 51, 127
Trujillo, P/O 222
TTC 242
Tudhope, S/L John H. 45, 51, 85, 99
Turkey 142
Turnbull, Wallace R. 31
Twist, W/C J.G. 84, 136
Tylee, Air Commodore A.K. 15, 17
Tyo, WO2 Francis L. 263

U-Boats against Canada 190, 191
U-boats: *U-69* 266, *U-190* 210, *U-202* 306, *U-209* 203, 224, *U-341* 224, *U-342* 217, 219, 224, *U-373* 306, *U-420* 224, *U-477* 213, 214, 219, 224, *U-478* 214, *U-517* 191, *U-520* 192, 199, 224, 315, *U-630* 203, *U-658* 191, 223, 224, *U-715* 214-217, 224, *U-754* 190, 224, *U-889* 190, *U-980* 214, 217, 219, 224, *U-1225* 212, 219, 224
Ulmer, FSgt H.F. 230
Umnak Island, Alaska 224, 246, 291
Ungava Crater 300-302
Union Point United Church 172
United College 142
United Nations 302
University of Michigan 287
University of New Brunswick 213, 309
University of Toronto 126, 243
University of Toronto Schools 238
University of Western Ontario 129
Upton Airport, PEI 73
US Army 47, 71, 72, 85, 121, 126, 201, 246-261
US Bronze Star 178, 285
US Defense Medal 135
US Legion of Merit 276
Utting, Sgt Victor A. 189

Valiquette, G. 54
Van Camp, F/L W.C. 197
Van Hessel, Rev. W. 283
Van Sickle, Basil 74
Van Vliet, S/L W.D. 25, 104
Vancouver 89, 96
Vaughan, Cpl J.E. 292
Veenis, P/O 229
Ventress, George 208, 250
Ventura Memorial Flight Association 211, 248
Vickers: Viking 25, 33, 34, 43, 44, 46, 276, 278, Vimy 40
Victoria Cross 212
Victoria Island (Ottawa) 75
Victory Aircraft 126, 310
Vincent, Carl 91
Vincent, F/O 194
Vinish, FSgt 238
VISA 164, 165
Volendam 142

Waddell, LAC 161
Wait, F/L George E. 22, 25
Wait, F/O Frank G. 84
Wakeham Bay, Quebec 53, 55-57
Wakeman, George 99
Wall, Wesley 314
Wallace, Tom 25
Walls, F/O R.J. 174
Walsh, F/O J.D. 174
Walsh, Frances 175
War Assets Disposal Corp. 114
War Emergency Training Plan 144
War Service Gratuity 283
Ward, F/L Fred 138, 176
Ward, F/O Ralph R. 217
Ward, LAC Gordon 221
Ward, S/L Arthur M. 178
Warhurst, P/O 226
Warren, LAC Hugh R. 231
Warren, Sgt 160
Warrington, AC2 J.W. 84
Washington, DC 280, 306
Waterbury, F/O Dave J. 214-217
Watson Lake, Yukon 320
Watson, F/O R.A. "Dick" 282
Watson, Lt Kenneth B. 22
Watsonville, Cal. 323
Watterson. P/O Thomas A.K. 223
Watts, W/C A.W. 136
Weaver, P/O W.C. 21, 22, 44
Webster Trophy 83
Webster, AC1 F.C. 84
Webster, F/O George R. 223, 230-235, 310
Weeks, F/O F.E. 126-128, 292-300
Weeks' Lake 293
Weir, F/O Glenn E. 224
Weitch, Chris 236
Welsh, F.E. 238
Wemp, Maj Bert S. 22
Westcott, F/L 229
Western Air Command 236-261
Western Canada Airways 49
Western Canada Aviation Museum 88
Western Technical and Commercial School 129, 144
Westland: Lysander 6, 116, 140, 170, 244, 245, Wapiti 65, 86, 87, 90, 96, 97, 101, 122, 184, 197, 278
Weston, F/L J.W.G. 95
Weston, G/C E.S. 144
Whelan, FSgt John E. 229
White, F/L Joseph 24
White, P/O 230
White, Sgt Harold E. 190
Whiteford, LAC A.B. 195
Whitehorse, Yukon 291, 292
Whiteside, LAC Roy R. 266
Wiese, Charles 159
Wilcox, AC1 A.J. 84
Wilcox, John G. 126
Wilding, P/O 226
Wilkins, G.H. 287
Wilkinson, P/O D. 23
Willardson, Wally 159
William, Leading Seaman H.A. 224
Williams, F/L 200
Williams, Gordon S. 83, 89
Williams, LAC E.C. 195
Williams, LCol J. Scott 15
Williams, Sgt E.F. 191
Willson, F/L F.A. 283
Willson, Sgt Raymond P. 179
Wilson, Harry 159
Wilson, James A. 13, 50, 78, 85, 99, 276
Wilson, Pete 253
Wilson, Sgt W. 190
Wingate, P/O 226
Wings Ltd. 183
Winnipeg Flying Club 83
Winny, W/C Harry 196, 239
Wiseman, S/L J.A. 299
Wismer, S/O W.M. 283
Woledge, S/L 226
Wolseley Viper 46
Wood, Janet M. 283
Wood, P/O D.E.T. 194, 196
Wood, P/O R. 263
Woodsworth, J.S. 50
World Wide Airways 290
Wright engines 52, 56, 59, 62, 64, 65, 73, 76, 95, 113, 189, 197
Wright, Alex 306
Wrong, F.H. 44
Wuori, Chuck 163

Yarmouth, Nova Scotia 217
Yellowknife, NWT 211
YMCA 229
Young, LAC R.D. 173
Young, P/O Bud 222
Young, Sgt L.R. 106
Young, W/C John M. 221
Youngman, F/O 269
Yukon Southern Air Transport 95, 292